Globalization and Poverty

Edited by **Ann Harrison**

The University of Chicago Press

Chicago and London

ANN HARRISON is professor of agricultural and resource economics at the University of California, Berkeley, and a research associate of the National Bureau of Economic Research.

The University of Chicago Press, Chicago 60637
The University of Chicago Press, Ltd., London
© 2007 by the National Bureau of Economic Research
All rights reserved. Published 2007
Printed in the United States of America

16 15 14 13 12 11 10 09 08 07   1 2 3 4 5
ISBN-13: 978-0-226-31794-6 (cloth)
ISBN-10: 0-226-31794-3 (cloth)

Library of Congress Cataloging-in-Publication Data

Globalization and poverty / edited by Ann Harrison.
     p. cm. — (NBER conference report)
   ISBN-13: 978-0-226-31794-6 (cloth)
   ISBN-10: 0-226-31794-3 (cloth : alk. paper)
    1. Poverty. 2. Globalization—Economic aspects. 3. International trade. 4. Capital movements. 5. International economic relations.
I. Harrison, Ann E. II. Series: National Bureau of Economic Research conference report.
   HC79.P6G664 2007
   339.4'6—dc22

                                       2006044594

Relation of the Directors to the
Work and Publications of the
National Bureau of Economic Research

1. The object of the NBER is to ascertain and present to the economics profession, and to the public more generally, important economic facts and their interpretation in a scientific manner without policy recommendations. The Board of Directors is charged with the responsibility of ensuring that the work of the NBER is carried on in strict conformity with this object.

2. The President shall establish an internal review process to ensure that book manuscripts proposed for publication DO NOT contain policy recommendations. This shall apply both to the proceedings of conferences and to manuscripts by a single author or by one or more co-authors but shall not apply to authors of comments at NBER conferences who are not NBER affiliates.

3. No book manuscript reporting research shall be published by the NBER until the President has sent to each member of the Board a notice that a manuscript is recommended for publication and that in the President's opinion it is suitable for publication in accordance with the above principles of the NBER. Such notification will include a table of contents and an abstract or summary of the manuscript's content, a list of contributors if applicable, and a response form for use by Directors who desire a copy of the manuscript for review. Each manuscript shall contain a summary drawing attention to the nature and treatment of the problem studied and the main conclusions reached.

4. No volume shall be published until forty-five days have elapsed from the above notification of intention to publish it. During this period a copy shall be sent to any Director requesting it, and if any Director objects to publication on the grounds that the manuscript contains policy recommendations, the objection will be presented to the author(s) or editor(s). In case of dispute, all members of the Board shall be notified, and the President shall appoint an ad hoc committee of the Board to decide the matter; thirty days additional shall be granted for this purpose.

5. The President shall present annually to the Board a report describing the internal manuscript review process, any objections made by Directors before publication or by anyone after publication, any disputes about such matters, and how they were handled.

6. Publications of the NBER issued for informational purposes concerning the work of the Bureau, or issued to inform the public of the activities at the Bureau, including but not limited to the NBER Digest and Reporter, shall be consistent with the object stated in paragraph 1. They shall contain a specific disclaimer noting that they have not passed through the review procedures required in this resolution. The Executive Committee of the Board is charged with the review of all such publications from time to time.

7. NBER working papers and manuscripts distributed on the Bureau's web site are not deemed to be publications for the purpose of this resolution, but they shall be consistent with the object stated in paragraph 1. Working papers shall contain a specific disclaimer noting that they have not passed through the review procedures required in this resolution. The NBER's web site shall contain a similar disclaimer. The President shall establish an internal review process to ensure that the working papers and the web site do not contain policy recommendations, and shall report annually to the Board on this process and any concerns raised in connection with it.

8. Unless otherwise determined by the Board or exempted by the terms of paragraphs 6 and 7, a copy of this resolution shall be printed in each NBER publication as described in paragraph 2 above.

Contents

Acknowledgments   xi

Globalization and Poverty: An Introduction   1
Ann Harrison

I. GLOBAL (CROSS-COUNTRY) ANALYSES

1. **Why Are the Critics So Convinced That Globalization Is Bad for the Poor?**   33
   Emma Aisbett
   Comment: Xavier Sala-i-Martin

2. **Stolper-Samuelson Is Dead: And Other Crimes of Both Theory and Data**   87
   Donald R. Davis and Prachi Mishra

3. **Globalization, Poverty, and All That: Factor Endowment versus Productivity Views**   109
   William Easterly
   Comment: Aart Kraay

4. **Does Tariff Liberalization Increase Wage Inequality? Some Empirical Evidence**   143
   Branko Milanovic and Lyn Squire
   Comment: Douglas A. Irwin

5. **My Policies or Yours: Does OECD Support for Agriculture Increase Poverty in Developing Countries?** 183
Margaret McMillan, Alix Peterson Zwane, and Nava Ashraf
Comment: Mitali Das

II. COUNTRY CASE STUDIES OF TRADE REFORM AND POVERTY

6. **The Effects of the Colombian Trade Liberalization on Urban Poverty** 241
Pinelopi Koujianou Goldberg and Nina Pavcnik
Comment: Chang-Tai Hsieh

7. **Trade Liberalization, Poverty, and Inequality: Evidence from Indian Districts** 291
Petia Topalova
Comment: Robin Burgess

8. **Trade Protection and Industry Wage Structure in Poland** 337
Chor-ching Goh and Beata S. Javorcik
Comment: Irene Brambilla

9. **Globalization and Complementary Policies: Poverty Impacts in Rural Zambia** 373
Jorge F. Balat and Guido G. Porto
Comment: Matthew J. Slaughter

10. **Globalization, Labor Income, and Poverty in Mexico** 417
Gordon H. Hanson
Comment: Esther Duflo

III. CAPITAL FLOWS AND POVERTY OUTCOMES

11. **Financial Globalization, Growth, and Volatility in Developing Countries** 457
Eswar S. Prasad, Kenneth Rogoff, Shang-Jin Wei, and M. Ayhan Kose
Comment: Susan M. Collins

12. **Household Responses to the Financial Crisis in Indonesia: Longitudinal Evidence on Poverty, Resources, and Well-Being** 517
Duncan Thomas and Elizabeth Frankenberg

13. **Does Food Aid Harm the Poor? Household Evidence from Ethiopia**   561
James Levinsohn and Margaret McMillan
Comment: Rohini Pande

IV. OTHER OUTCOMES ASSOCIATED WITH GLOBALIZATION
(RISK, RETURNS TO SPEAKING ENGLISH)

14. **Risk and the Evolution of Inequality in China in an Era of Globalization**   599
Ethan Ligon
Comment: Shang-Jin Wei

15. **Globalization and the Returns to Speaking English in South Africa**   629
James Levinsohn
Comment: Raquel Fernández

Contributors   647
Author Index   651
Subject Index   657

Acknowledgments

The chapters in this book were first presented at a preconference in October 2003 and later finalized at a conference in Cape Cod, Massachusetts, in September 2004. I would like to thank Brett Maranjian and Rob Shannon of the National Bureau of Economic Research (NBER) for organizing these superb conferences and Helena Fitz-Patrick of the NBER for preparing the manuscript for submission to the University of Chicago Press.

Funding for this project was provided by the Ford Foundation and the NBER. I am especially grateful to Manuel Montes of the Ford Foundation for his support. I would also like to thank Martin Feldstein and Robert Feenstra for suggesting this project and for their thoughtful contributions throughout the development of the book.

Globalization and Poverty
An Introduction

Ann Harrison

1 Overview

More than one billion people live in extreme poverty, which is defined by the World Bank as subsisting on less than one dollar a day.[1] In 2001, fully *half* of the developing world lived on less than two dollars a day. Yet poverty rates are much lower today than twenty years ago. In the last two decades, the percentage of the developing world living in extreme poverty has been cut in half. While poverty rates were falling, developing countries became increasingly integrated into the world trading system. Poor countries have slashed protective tariffs and increased their participation in world trade. If we use the share of exports in gross domestic product (GDP) as a measure of globalization, then developing countries are now more globalized than high-income countries.[2]

Does globalization reduce poverty? Will ongoing efforts to eliminate protection and increase world trade improve the lives of the world's poor? There is surprisingly little evidence on this question.[3] The comprehensive

Ann Harrison is a professor of agricultural and resource economics at the University of California, Berkeley, and a research associate of the National Bureau of Economic Research.

I would like to thank Pranab Bardhan, Ethan Ligon, Margaret McMillan, Branko Milanovic, Guido Porto, Emma Aisbett, Don Davis, Alix Zwane, and two anonymous reviewers for helpful comments and suggestions.

1. The poverty estimates in this paragraph are taken from the World Bank's official poverty web site, at http://iresearch.worldbank.org/PovcalNet/jsp/index.jsp. The $1-a-day poverty line is actually $1.08 in 1993 purchasing power parity dollars.

2. See Harrison and Tang (2005).

3. Although there have been a number of recent studies on globalization and inequality, these volumes focus primarily on distributional consequences of globalization, rather than poverty. There are exceptions, of course; see, for example, Bhagwati (2004). Bardhan's publications on this topic include his Nobel Peace Prize Lecture, published as *Social Justice in a Global Economy* (Bardhan 2000), as well as Bardhan (2003, 2004). See also Hertel and Winters (2005), forthcoming.

studies by Winters, McCulloch, and McKay (2004), Goldberg and Pavcnik (2004), and Ravallion (2004a) all acknowledge that they can review only the *indirect* evidence regarding the linkages between globalization and poverty. There have been almost no studies that test for the *direct* linkages between the two.[4]

Yet one of the biggest concerns of globalization's critics is its impact on the poor. This introduction and the following chapters provide an economist's perspective on how globalization affects poverty in developing countries.[5] By bringing together experts on both international trade and poverty, we hope to bridge the intellectual divide that separates the individuals who study each of these phenomena. The fifteen studies and accompanying discussions that are part of this project ask the following questions: How has global economic integration affected the poor in developing countries? Do trade reforms that cut import protection improve the lives of the poor? Has increasing financial integration led to more or less poverty? How have the poor fared during currency crises? Do agricultural support programs in rich countries hurt the poor in developing countries? Or do such programs in fact provide assistance by reducing the cost of food imports? Finally, does food aid hurt the poor by lowering the price of the goods they sell on local markets?

Although the concept of globalization is quite broad, we focus on two aspects: (1) international trade in goods and (2) international movements of capital—including foreign investment, portfolio flows, and aid. Consequently, most of the chapters measure the impact of increased exposure to trade and international capital flows on poverty. We do not address other aspects of globalization, such as information flows, migration, or trade in services. A number of chapters also address the linkages between our preferred measures of globalization and inequality.

Why is it important to also think about globalization's impact on inequality in a volume devoted to poverty? Most economists expect openness to trade to be associated with higher growth, and growth is good for the poor. Consequently, we would expect that increasing trade should lead to less poverty. Yet if openness to trade is associated with increasing inequal-

4. Winters, McCulloch, and McKay (2004) write in their insightful and comprehensive survey that "there are no direct studies of the poverty effects of trade and trade liberalization." Goldberg and Pavcnik's (2004) excellent review points out that "while the literature on trade and inequality is voluminous, there is virtually no work to date on the relationship between trade liberalization and poverty." The few studies that do examine the links between globalization and poverty typically use computable general equilibrium models to disentangle the linkages between trade reform and poverty. While such research provides an important contribution to our understanding of the channels through which globalization could affect poverty, it is extremely important to be able to look at actual ex post evidence of the impact of trade and investment reforms on the poor. See the studies cited in Winters, McCulloch, and McKay (2004), Ravallion (2004a), Chen and Ravallion (2000), and Hertel and Winters (2005).

5. More information can be found online at http://www.nber.org/books.html.

ity, then the growth gains from trade could be wiped out for those at the bottom of the income distribution. In other words, if the gains from trade are highly unequal, then the poor may not share the benefits. Many of the studies in this volume suggest that globalization has been associated with rising inequality, and that the poor do not always share in the gains from trade.

The new research presented in this volume takes two different approaches: cross-country studies and individual country studies. The cross-country studies use aggregate data to examine the impact of globalization on the number of poor, aggregate growth rates, and inequality. The country case studies typically use microdata for a single country to examine the impact of globalization on the incomes of the poor. Cross-country studies are appealing because they allow authors to generalize beyond one specific case study. Yet many countries have information on aggregate poverty for only two or three points in time, which means that statistical tests using cross-country data may not yield conclusive results. Consequently, most of the studies in this volume rely on the use of microdata. These data sets typically span a number of years, including periods before, during, and after a trade reform.

What are the lessons that emerge from the various chapters? Although the issues are complex, some broad themes emerge.

The poor in countries with an abundance of unskilled labor do not always gain from trade reform. Many economists have used the Heckscher-Ohlin (HO) framework in international trade to argue that trade liberalization should raise the incomes of the unskilled in labor-abundant countries. Most researchers who use this framework to argue that globalization is good for the world's poor make a number of heroic assumptions. These assumptions—such as the necessity that all countries produce all goods— are challenged in this volume. In addition, the country studies show that labor is not nearly as mobile as the HO trade model assumes; for comparative advantage to increase the incomes of the unskilled, they need to be able to move out of contracting sectors and into expanding ones. Another reason why the poor may not gain from trade reforms is that developing countries have historically protected sectors that use unskilled labor, such as textiles and apparel. This pattern of protection, while at odds with simple interpretations of HO models, makes sense if standard assumptions (such as factor price equalization) are relaxed. Trade reforms may result in less protection for unskilled workers, who are most likely to be poor. Finally, penetrating global markets even in sectors that traditionally use unskilled labor requires more skills than the poor in developing countries typically possess.

The poor are more likely to share in the gains from globalization when there are complementary policies in place. The studies on India and Colombia suggest that globalization is more likely to benefit the poor if trade reforms

are implemented in conjunction with reducing impediments to labor mobility. In Zambia, poor farmers are only expected to benefit from greater access to export markets if they also have access to credit, technical know-how, and other complementary inputs. The studies also point to the importance of social safety nets. In Mexico, if poor corn farmers had not received income support from the government, their real incomes would have been halved during the 1990s. In Ethiopia, if food aid had not been well targeted, globalization would have had little impact on the poor. The fact that other policies are needed to ensure that the benefits of trade are shared across the population suggests that relying on trade reforms alone to reduce poverty is likely to be disappointing.

Export growth and incoming foreign investment have reduced poverty. Poverty has fallen in regions where exports or foreign investment is growing. In Mexico, the poor in the most globalized regions have weathered macroeconomic crises better than their more isolated neighbors. In India, opening up to foreign investment has been associated with a decline in poverty. The study on Zambia suggests that poor consumers gain from falling prices for the goods they buy, while poor producers in exporting sectors benefit from trade reform through higher prices for their goods. In Colombia, increasing export activity has been associated with an increase in compliance with labor legislation and a fall in poverty. In Poland, unskilled workers—who are the most likely to be poor—have gained from Poland's accession to the European Union.

Financial crises are costly to the poor. In Indonesia, poverty rates increased by at least 50 percent after the currency crisis in 1997. While recovery in Indonesia has been rapid, the Mexican economy has yet to fully recover from its 1995 peso crisis. Poverty rates in Mexico in the year 2000 were higher than they had been ten years earlier. Cross-country evidence also suggests that financial globalization leads to higher consumption and output volatility in low-income countries. One implication is that low-income countries are more likely to benefit from financial integration if they also create reliable institutions and pursue macroeconomic stabilization policies (including the use of flexible exchange rate regimes). However, foreign investment flows have very different effects from other types of capital flows. While unrestricted capital flows are associated with a higher likelihood of poverty, foreign direct investment inflows are associated with a reduction in poverty. The poverty-reducing effects of foreign direct investment are clearly documented in the chapters on India and Mexico.

Globalization produces both winners and losers among the poor. It should not be surprising that the results defy easy generalization. Even within a single region, two sets of farmers may be affected in opposite ways. In Mexico, while some small and most medium corn farmers saw their incomes fall by half in the 1990s, large corn farmers gained. Across different countries, poor wage earners in exporting sectors or in sectors with incoming foreign

investment gained from trade and investment reforms; conversely, poverty rates increased in previously protected sectors that were exposed to import competition. Within the same country or even the same region, a trade reform may lead to income losses for rural agricultural producers and income gains for rural or urban consumers of those same goods.

The rest of this chapter is organized as follows. Section 2 discusses some issues associated with measuring both poverty and globalization. Section 3 discusses theoretical links between trade and poverty outcomes. Section 4 summarizes the results from the cross-country studies, while section 5 describes the results of the country case studies. The studies that address the impact of capital flows on the poor are summarized in section 6. Although the focus of this volume is on the relationship between poverty and different measures of globalization, a number of authors also address other possible outcomes associated with globalization; these are described in section 7 of this chapter. Since the evidence suggests that globalization creates winners as well as losers among the poor, this chapter moves in section 8 to a discussion of why globalization's critics seem all too aware of the costs of globalization and generally fail to see the benefits. A number of research questions remain unanswered; these are also discussed in section 8. Section 9 concludes.

2 Measuring Globalization and Poverty

There is an enormous literature devoted to trade and poverty measurement. For openness to trade, the authors in this volume use both trade volumes and measures of trade policy. Most contributors favor the use of direct policy measures, such as tariffs or quotas, over trade volumes. Trade volumes are typically measured as shares, such as exports plus imports divided by GDP. Although widely available, trade shares are not ideal because they are determined by trade policies, geography, country size, and macroeconomic policies. Globalization of financial flows is measured either by creating indexes of policy or by using measures of actual flows. Capital controls, which are collected by the International Monetary Fund (IMF), are examples of policy measures; again, actual capital flows are less desirable measures of policy than capital controls since flows are outcomes of many factors.

One important observation that emerges from the various chapters is that different measures of globalization are associated with different poverty outcomes. *How* globalization is measured determines *whether* globalization is good for the poor. Measures of export activity and foreign investment are generally associated with poverty reduction, while removal of protection (an ex ante measure of globalization) or import shares (an ex post measure) are frequently associated with rising poverty. These different effects are consistent with short-run models of international trade (such as

the specific-sector model) where factors of production cannot easily move from contracting or import-competing sectors to expanding or export-oriented ones.

Poverty is typically measured by choosing a poverty line, which reflects the minimum income or consumption necessary to meet basic needs. For low-income countries, the World Bank has calculated poverty lines at $1 and $2 a day.[6] Although these minimum requirements vary across countries and over time, the $1- and $2-a-day measures allow policymakers to compare poverty across countries using the same reference point. The head count measure of poverty identifies the percentage of the population living in households with consumption or income per person below the poverty line. The head count is reported either as a percentage (the incidence of poverty) or as the number of individuals who are poor. Another popular measure is the poverty gap, which measures the mean distance below the poverty line as a proportion of the poverty line.

One area of disagreement in poverty measurement is whether poverty should be measured as the percentage of individuals who are poor (the incidence) or the absolute number of people who are poor. While the incidence of poverty has been falling over the last twenty years, the change in the absolute numbers of poor individuals depends on the poverty line chosen. The number of individuals living on less than one dollar a day declined in the 1980s and 1990s, while the number of individuals living on between one and two dollars a day did not.[7] Critics of globalization frequently use the absolute number of people who are poor as their preferred measure, while globalization's supporters (see the comment by Xavier Sala-i-Martin for chap. 1 in this volume) prefer to use the incidence of poverty. Chapter 1, by Emma Aisbett, shows that this diversity of opinion is one of the reasons that there is so much disagreement about whether world poverty has been falling during the period of globalization.

It is important to emphasize that the poverty line itself is not fixed over time. Eswar S. Prasad, Kenneth Rogoff, Shang-Jin Wei, and M. Ayhan Kose conclude chapter 11 with the following observation:

> One has to acknowledge that poverty is fundamentally a relative measure, which will probably gain an entirely different meaning as the world economy becomes more integrated. . . . For example, if global growth continues at a rapid pace during the next century, it is possible that by the end of the century emerging-market economies, including China and India, could attain income levels exceeding those of Americans today. This implies that Malthusian notions of poverty are likely to become a

6. Actually $1.08 and $2.15 in 1993 purchasing power parity dollars.

7. One possible explanation is that the poor in the world are becoming better off, moving from incomes of less than $1 to less than $2 per day. Yet this possibility has not been adequately explored, in large part because this necessitates being able to follow the same poor household or individual over time.

distant memory in most parts of the world as global income inexorably expands over the next century, and issues of inequality, rather than subsistence, will increasingly take center stage in the poverty debate.

The country case studies show that acceptable poverty lines vary across countries and through time. As discussed by Pinelopi Koujianou Goldberg and Nina Pavcnik in chapter 6, the $1-a-day line is indicative of poverty lines used in very poor countries, but not in middle-income countries such as Colombia. The official poverty line in Colombia is closer to three (purchasing power parity) dollars a day. In the United States, the poverty line in 2004 was closer to thirty dollars a day. As acceptable definitions of poverty shift over time, research on inequality and the overall distribution of income becomes increasingly important. This is one reason why Gordon H. Hanson, Ethan Ligon, and Duncan Thomas and Elizabeth Frankenberg, in their chapters, report the impact of globalization on the entire distribution of income, using nonparametric techniques.

3   Theoretical Linkages between Globalization and Poverty

One of the most famous theorems in international trade is the Stolper-Samuelson theorem, which in its simplest form suggests that the abundant factor should see an increase in its real income when a country opens up to trade. If the abundant factor in developing countries is unskilled labor, then this framework suggests that the poor (unskilled) in developing countries have the most to gain from trade. Anne Krueger (1983) and Jagdish Bhagwati and T. N. Srinivasan (2002) have all used this insight to argue that trade reforms in developing countries should be pro-poor, since these countries are most likely to have a comparative advantage in producing goods made with unskilled labor. From this perspective, expanding trade opportunities should cut poverty and reduce inequality within poor countries.

In chapter 2, which examines the theoretical linkages between trade and poverty, Donald R. Davis and Prachi Mishra argue that "Stolper-Samuelson is dead." They write eloquently that applying trade theory to suggest that liberalization will raise the wages of the unskilled in unskilled-abundant countries is "worse than wrong—it is dangerous." Davis and Mishra show that such arguments are based on a very narrow interpretation of the Stolper-Samuelson (SS) theorem. In particular, SS holds only if all countries produce all goods, if the goods imported from abroad and produced domestically are close substitutes, or if comparative advantage can be fixed vis-à-vis all trading partners. As an illustration, a poor country in a world with many factors and many goods may no longer have a comparative advantage in producing unskilled-intensive goods. This idea is easy to understand in the context of three countries—for example, the

United States, Mexico, and China. Although Mexico might have a comparative advantage in producing low-skill goods in trade with the United States, its comparative advantage switches vis-à-vis trade with China.

Trade reform also affects the poor by changing the prices they face as consumers and producers. Davis and Mishra develop a simple model to show that if imports and domestic goods (produced by the poor) are noncompeting, then the first-order effect of a trade reform would be to raise real incomes of the poor. Clearly, the poor gain from tariff reductions on goods that they buy. If globalization raises the prices of goods produced by the poor—such as agricultural products marketed by farmers—then poverty is also likely to decline.

Many of the authors in this volume do not use the HO model as their framework but adopt a specific-sector framework. In the specific-sector framework, workers or machines may be attached to a specific sector or industry and unable to relocate easily. Consequently, any reduction in protection to sector X will lead to a fall in the incomes of workers who previously produced goods for that sector and are unable to relocate elsewhere. The mechanism is the following: a fall in protection is assumed to put downward pressure on the price of the previously protected good, which in turn shifts labor demand downward. It is important to remember, however, that the reverse is also true: any increase in export activity in sector Y would then be beneficial to workers attached to that sector. The specific-sector model suggests that workers may gain from globalization depending on which sectors (import-competing or exporting) they are attached to; this is very different from the HO framework, which suggests that winners and losers from globalization can be identified by their skill levels, regardless of where they work. If the HO assumption of perfect labor mobility across sectors is violated, then the specific-sector model may be the more appropriate framework, at least in the short run.

In chapter 3, William Easterly also explores the theoretical linkages between globalization and poverty, but in the context of a neoclassical growth model. Easterly shows that globalization could affect the incomes of the poor in two opposite ways. If productivity levels are similar but endowments are different, globalization should raise the incomes of the poor. Globalization, by relaxing constraints on the movement of goods and factors, will allow factor returns to equalize across countries. This is the factor endowment view. If poor countries are more endowed with (unskilled) labor, then relaxing constraints on global trade or factor flows will lead capital to flow to poor countries, and per capita incomes there should rise. A second possibility is the productivity view. Differences in per capita incomes may stem from exogenous productivity differences across countries rather than differences in endowments. This second possibility implies that globalization either will have no impact on poverty or could exacerbate poverty, as capital is drawn away from low-productivity toward high-productivity regions.

Aart Kraay (in the chap. 3 comment), Sala-i-Martin, and Prasad and his coauthors emphasize that globalization could raise the incomes of the poor through a third channel: by increasing long-run growth. To reconcile their perspective with Easterly's framework, this means that increases in trade or capital flows could increase incomes of the poor by raising productivity or through the accumulation of capital. Imports of new goods embody new technology, which in turn raises productivity, while incoming foreign investment provides the possibility for technology transfer. If the income effects are fairly uniform, then the increase in aggregate income resulting from globalization-induced productivity gains should improve the incomes of the poor.

4   Cross-Country Evidence

The cross-country studies present evidence on the relationship between poverty, inequality, and globalization. Easterly finds that increasing trade integration is associated with falling inequality within developed countries and greater inequality within developing countries. His results are consistent with the evidence presented in chapter 4 by Branko Milanovic and Lyn Squire, who construct their own measures of both interindustry and interoccupation wage inequality using detailed information on wages across occupations and industries. Milanovic and Squire find that globalization, measured using average tariffs, leads to rising inequality in poor countries and falling inequality in rich countries.

Both Easterly's and Milanovic and Squire's chapters find that increasing openness to trade is associated with rising inequality in poor countries. Easterly argues that the evidence is consistent with his productivity view, whereby exogenous differences in productivity lead capital to flow from poor to rich countries and exacerbate inequality in poor countries. Milanovic and Squire emphasize the lack of labor mobility and the weak power of unions to explain why increasing openness to trade is associated with rising inequality in poor countries.

In his comment on Easterly's chapter, Kraay reviews the evidence on (1) the linkages between trade and growth, and (2) the relationship between growth and poverty. Although some previous studies on the relationship between trade and growth have been discredited (see Rodriguez and Rodrik 2000 and Harrison and Hanson 1999), Kraay cites several new studies that find that increasing openness to trade is associated with higher growth. Kraay also points to his own work showing that growth is good for the poor, and concludes that since trade enhances growth, which in turn reduces poverty, then globalization is good for the poor.

In chapter 5, Margaret McMillan, Alix Peterson Zwane, and Nava Ashraf use cross-country data to measure the impact of Organization for Economic Cooperation and Development (OECD) support policies for

agriculture on poverty. The vast majority of least developed countries have historically been net importers of food, particularly cereals, which are among the crops most subsidized by the OECD. As net food importers, poor countries may gain from rich-country subsidies (see also Panagariya 2002, 2004; Valdes and McCalla 1999). Even within food-exporting countries, the poorest members of society may be net purchasers of food. However, McMillan and coauthors find no support in the cross-country analysis for the claim that OECD policies worsen poverty in developing countries.

None of these studies directly examine the aggregate relationship between different poverty measures and globalization. Previous research on this topic, including Dollar and Kraay (2001, 2002), combines measures of income distribution derived from household surveys with aggregate national income data to measure the income of the poor. Deaton (2001, 2003) suggests that using aggregate national income data to interpret cross-country correlations between aggregate growth and poverty reduction is likely to be misleading. This is because the observed correlation could be attributable to measurement error as well as biases in national income statistics, which generally suggest a much higher rate of poverty reduction relative to trends in aggregate poverty implied by household surveys.

One solution to this problem is to use measures of poverty based exclusively on household surveys. Yet the limited time series for poverty data from these surveys makes it almost impossible to conclude anything on the aggregate relationship between openness and poverty. I show this in tables 1 and 2, which report regression results on the linkages between openness, GDP growth, and different measures of poverty. I begin by revisiting the evidence on the linkages between trade and growth; these results are presented in table 1. Openness to trade is measured in two different ways, as either (1) the ratio of trade $(X + M)$ to GDP or (2) average tariffs, defined as tariff revenues divided by imports. The results suggest that an increase in openness—using these two measures—is associated with an increase in aggregate income.[8]

The problems of small sample size are illustrated in columns (5) and (10) of table 1. I redo the basic specifications but restrict the sample to the observations for the country-years where poverty rates could be calculated based on household surveys. In the restricted sample the link between

8. To address concerns regarding endogeneity, openness is measured using either its three-year lag or the contemporaneous value instrumented using lagged values. These results are robust to the inclusion of other controls, such as country fixed effects or policy variables likely to be correlated with trade policies. Other extensions, using growth of GDP per capita as the dependent variable instead of income per capita, yield similar results. Although some specifications—notably those that include country fixed effects and instrument for openness using lagged values—are not always significant at the 5 percent level, the evidence is generally consistent with a positive relationship between openness and income or growth. The evidence is also consistent with recent work by Lee, Ricci, and Rigobon (2004), who apply more innovative ways to address the endogeneity of openness and continue to find a positive relationship between openness (measured using trade shares) and growth.

Table 1 Income per capita and trade policy for a panel of developing countries (dependent variable: ln income per capita, in PPP $1993)

	OLS no controls (1)	OLS no controls (2)	OLS includes controls (3)	OLS includes controls (4)	OLS includes controls (5)	IV no controls (6)	IV no controls (7)	IV includes controls (8)	IV includes controls (9)	IV includes controls (10)
A. Income per capita and trade shares										
Three-year lag trade share	0.907 (0.036)	0.514 (0.037)								
Trade share			0.214 (0.038)	0.203 (0.035)	0.081 (0.074)	0.978 (0.037)	0.857 (0.057)	0.426 (0.067)	0.402 (0.064)	0.248 (0.167)
Country fixed effects	No	Yes	Yes	Yes	Yes	No	Yes	Yes	Yes	Yes
Time fixed effects	No	No	Yes	Yes	Yes	No	No	Yes	Yes	Yes
No. of observations	3,294	3,294	1,996	2,657	308	3,288	3,288	1,996	2,657	308
Restricted sample?	No	No	No	No	Yes	No	No	No	No	Yes
B. Income per capita and average import tariffs										
Three-year lag average import tariff	-3.586 (0.377)	-0.721 (0.142)	-0.298 (0.117)	-0.137 (0.119)	-0.250 (0.281)					
Average import tariff						-4.830 (0.441)	-4.830 (0.441)	-0.635 (0.328)	-0.338 (0.379)	-1.831 (1.563)
Country fixed effects	No	Yes	Yes	Yes	Yes	No	Yes	Yes	Yes	Yes
Time fixed effects	No	No	Yes	Yes	Yes	No	No	Yes	Yes	Yes
No. of observations	1,617	1,617	1,261	1,485	212	1,415	1,415	1,125	1,306	189
Restricted sample?	No	No	No	No	Yes	No	No	No	No	Yes

Source: Aisbett, Harrison, and Zwane (2005).

Notes: OLS = ordinary least squares. IV = instrumental variables. Restricted sample is country-year observations for which poverty (head count) data are available. All regressions exclude OECD high-income countries. Columns (3) and (8) include controls for inflation, government expenditure in GDP, currency crises, investment in GDP, and the fraction of the population that is literate. Columns (4), (5), (9), and (10) include controls for inflation, government expenditure, and currency crises. Huber robust standard errors in parentheses. In instrumental variables regressions, trade share is instrumented using three-year lagged value, and import tariff is instrumented using three-year lagged value.

Table 2   Head count poverty and trade policy for a panel of developing countries (dependent variable: ln fraction of households living on less than $1 per day, in PPP $1993)

	OLS no controls (1)	OLS includes controls (2)	OLS includes controls (3)	OLS no controls (4)	OLS includes controls (5)	OLS includes controls (6)	IV includes controls (7)	IV includes controls (8)	IV includes controls (9)	IV includes controls (10)
			A. Head count poverty ($1 per day) and import tariffs							
Three-year lag trade share	-1.921 (0.385)	-1.772 (0.502)	-1.517 (0.484)	0.418 (0.931)	0.685 (1.209)	0.579 (1.086)				
Trade share							-2.164 (0.760)	-1.767 (0.524)	-3.609 (2.240)	2.261 (3.576)
Three-year lag log income per capita		-2.225 (0.252)			-5.154 (1.646)		-6.405 (2.070)		-0.380 (3.926)	
Country fixed effects	No	No	No	Yes	Yes	Yes	No	No	Yes	Yes
Time fixed effects	No	Yes	Yes	No	Yes	Yes	Yes	Yes	Yes	Yes
No. of observations	349	284	325	349	284	325	229	325	229	325
			B. Head count poverty ($1 per day) and average import tariffs							
Three-year lag average import tariff	7.543 (1.229)	0.418 (1.618)	5.606 (1.490)	0.811 (2.167)	0.741 (4.736)	1.018 (4.305)				
Average import tariff							-1.038 (2.266)	6.158 (1.801)	1.549 (22.870)	8.242 (22.706)
Three-year lag log real income per capita		-1.896 (0.263)			-3.662 (1.666)		-2.551 (1.044)		0.843 (6.771)	
Country fixed effects	No	No	No	Yes	Yes	Yes	No	No	Yes	Yes
Time fixed effects	No	Yes	Yes	No	Yes	Yes	Yes	Yes	Yes	Yes
No. of observations	223	202	217	223	202	217	152	194	152	194

Source: Aisbett, Harrison, and Zwane (2005).

Notes: OLS = ordinary least squares. IV = instrumental variables. Huber robust standard errors in parentheses. All regressions exclude OECD high-income countries. Columns (3), (6), (8), and (10) include controls for inflation, government expenditure in GDP, currency crises, investment in GDP, and the fraction of the population that is literate. Columns (2), (5), (7), and (9) include controls for inflation, government expenditure, and currency crises. In instrumental variables regressions, trade share is instrumented using three-year lagged value, and import tariff is instrumented using three-year lagged value.

openness to trade and GDP per capita weakens significantly. The weakness of the association between openness and growth in this small sample suggests that efforts to find any direct relationship between openness and poverty reduction using cross-country data sets are likely to be plagued by limited data availability.

The association between measures of openness, GDP growth, and poverty is presented in table 2. Measures of poverty are derived from household sample surveys made available by the World Bank. While the results are robust to the poverty measure chosen, in table 2 we define poverty as the percentage of households living on less than $1 a day in purchasing power parity (PPP) terms. The evidence in table 2, confirming evidence presented by Besley and Burgess (2003) as well as other researchers, suggests that growth is indeed good for the poor. We use several different measures of income: contemporaneous income, income lagged three periods, and contemporaneous income instrumented using annual average levels of precipitation and temperature. Across all specifications, aggregate income or aggregate income growth (not shown here) is associated with a reduction in the percentage of the population that is poor.[9]

Although the results presented in tables 1 and 2 suggest a strong link from trade integration to aggregate income, and from income growth to poverty reduction, the evidence on direct linkages between trade shares or tariffs and poverty outcomes is quite weak. While the first three columns of table 2 suggest that openness to trade (measured using either trade shares or tariffs) is associated with less poverty, this result disappears when we introduce country fixed effects. I show this graphically in figures 1 and 2. In figure 1, there is a positive relationship between globalization and poverty reduction, but this association disappears in figure 2 with the addition of country effects.[10]

To summarize, there is no evidence in the *aggregate* data that trade reforms are good or bad for the poor.[11] Yet even if we could identify a robust

---

9. The coefficients on real GDP per capita reported in tables 3 and 4 are much larger than those reported by Besley and Burgess (2003). The poverty-reducing effects of growth are larger here because any one of the following changes alone leads to big changes in the coefficient on GDP per capita: the inclusion of time effects, a larger sample with more years of data and more countries, the inclusion of other policy determinants of poverty, or a PPP real GDP per capita measure. The fact that any of these modifications leads to such large changes in the coefficient on GDP per capita suggests that—despite a strong poverty-reducing effect of growth—the exact magnitude of the effect cannot be precisely estimated.

10. Similar results were found when using different poverty measures—such as the percentage of the poor living on less than PPP$2 per day, or the incomes of the poorest quintile or decile.

11. In a comparable exercise using country-level poverty head counts and trade shares, Ravallion (2004b) reaches a similar conclusion; he argues that there is no robust relationship between poverty and globalization in the aggregate data. Possibly the only exception to these general conclusions is Agénor (2004), who finds that there is a nonlinear relationship between measures of poverty and globalization. Agénor finds that at low levels, globalization appears to hurt the poor, but beyond a certain threshold, it seems to reduce poverty. For earlier related studies, see Dollar (2001) and Dollar and Kraay (2001, 2002).

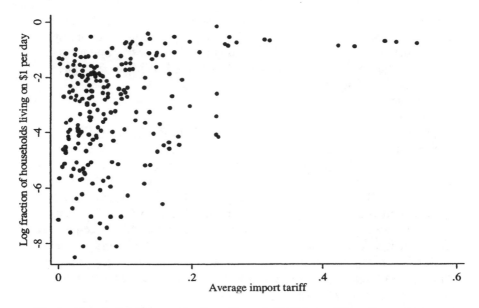

Fig. 1 Correlation between fraction of households living on $1 per day and average import tariff

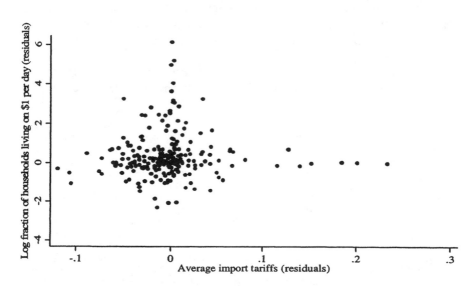

Fig. 2 Correlation between fraction of households living on $1 per day and average import tariff controlling for country fixed effects

relationship between trade reform and poverty reduction in the aggregate data, cross-country work remains problematic for several reasons. First, it is difficult to find appropriate instruments for trade policy at the country level, or to adequately control for other changes that are occurring at the same time. Second, even if cross-country studies point to a positive relationship between globalization and overall growth, such growth may lead to unequal gains across different levels of income. If the growth effects on average are small and there are large distributional consequences, trade-induced growth could be accompanied by a decline in incomes of the poor. The cross-country evidence presented by Easterly and by Milanovic and Squire is consistent with this view: their chapters suggest that globalization has been accompanied by increasing inequality in poor countries. Finally, even if the cross-country evidence presented in tables 1 and 2 overcomes this problem by directly testing for the relationship between poverty and trade reform, there may be significant underlying heterogeneity across different segments of the population (see also Ravallion 2004a). Aggregate poverty could move in one direction or remain unchanged while poverty increases in some parts of a country and declines in others.

For all these reasons, most of the studies in this volume focus on changes in trade policy within a particular country. These studies typically use highly disaggregated data—at the level of the household or the enterprise—to identify the impact of trade policy. Since these studies exploit differences in globalization across sectors or regions within the same country, they are able to overcome the problem that trade reforms are usually introduced concurrently with other countrywide reforms such as exchange rate stabilization or privatization. Due to the availability of detailed household surveys documenting the existence of the poor, these surveys are also able to successfully address the problem of lack of comparable time series data. Finally, the authors of these studies are generally aware of the problem of the endogeneity of trade reform and are usually able to use the panel nature of these data sets to address this issue.[12]

5   Country Case Studies

This section reviews the ten country case studies for the volume. These country studies use household- or firm-level data to measure (1) the impact of globalization on employment and labor incomes of the poor and (2) the

---

12. Even preferred measures of globalization, such as tariffs or capital controls, are likely to be endogenously determined. The possible endogeneity of tariffs, as well as solutions to this problem, is explored in a number of the individual chapters. Since uniformity in tariffs is frequently a goal of trade reform, tariff reductions are often inversely linked to initial tariff levels. To achieve uniformity, policymakers must apply the largest tariff reductions to those sectors with the highest initial protection levels. Consequently, some chapter authors use initial levels of protection as an instrument for changes in tariffs.

impact of globalization on poverty through changes in the prices of goods produced and consumed by the poor.

The Impact of Globalization on Employment
and Labor Incomes of the Poor

Country studies on Colombia, India, Mexico, and Poland examine the relationship between trade reform and labor market outcomes. In chapter 6 Goldberg and Pavcnik investigate the impact of a large reduction in average tariffs in Colombia between 1984 and 1998 on a variety of urban labor market outcomes: the probability of becoming unemployed, minimum wage compliance, informal-sector employment, and the incidence of poverty. Analyzing the relationship between globalization and these different labor market outcomes is useful since poverty is highly correlated with unemployment, informal-sector employment, and noncompliance with the minimum wage.

The Colombian experience suggests that individuals in sectors with increasing import competition are likely to become poorer, while those in sectors where exports are growing are less likely to be poor. Import competition increases the likelihood of unemployment and informality, and is associated with a higher incidence of poverty. Export growth is associated with the opposite: falling informal-sector employment, rising minimum wage compliance, and falling poverty. Goldberg and Pavcnik present evidence suggesting that workers cannot easily relocate away from contracting toward expanding sectors in the context of trade reforms, contradicting the assumption of perfect labor mobility in the HO framework. Consistent with other studies in the volume, this analysis of the Colombian trade reforms suggests the importance of complementary policies for minimizing the adverse effects of trade reform on the poor. When trade reform is accompanied by labor market reforms that make it easier for firms to hire or fire and ease relocation for workers, the adverse impact of tariff reductions on poverty disappears.

This is exactly the conclusion reached in chapter 7 by Petia Topalova, who estimates the impact of trade reform in India on poverty. In the 1990s, India embarked on a remarkable trade reform, reversing decades of protectionist policies that had led to average tariffs in excess of 90 percent. Using household data that span the period before and after the reform period, Topalova relates changes in tariffs to changes in the incidence of poverty. In particular, she uses the interaction between the share of a district's population employed by an industry on the eve of the economic reforms and the reduction in trade barriers in that industry as a measure of a district's exposure to foreign trade. Because industrial composition is predetermined and trade liberalization was unanticipated, she argues that it is appropriate to causally interpret the correlation between the changes in the levels of poverty and trade exposure.

Topalova's chapter on India suggests that the rural poor gained less from the trade reforms than other income groups or the urban poor. A rural district experiencing the mean level of tariff reductions saw a 2 percent increase in poverty, accounting for a setback of about 15 percent of India's progress in poverty reduction over the 1990s. In other words, the progress in poverty reduction experienced in rural India was lower in trade-affected areas, where (rural) poverty may have fallen by an average of 11 instead of 13 percentage points between 1987 and 1999.[13] To identify the net contribution of globalization to poverty reduction in India would require identifying first the contribution of globalization to the overall poverty reduction across all of India during the 1990s, and then netting out the adverse impact on districts with increasing import competition. Topalova also discusses why the rural poor gained less than other groups from liberalization: restrictions on labor mobility in rural areas have impeded adjustment. She finds that the negative impact of trade policy on poverty is reduced or eliminated in regions with flexible labor laws.

While the studies on Colombia and India suggest that the gains from trade reforms were less likely to benefit the poor, the evidence for Mexico and Poland suggests the opposite. In chapter 10 Hanson explores the different outcomes for individuals born in states with high exposure to globalization versus individuals born in states with low exposure to globalization between 1990 and 2000. He finds that the income of individuals in high-exposure states increased relative to the income of individuals in low-exposure states. While labor incomes in the 1990s deteriorated in both regions, due in part to Mexico's peso crisis in 1995, the deterioration was much less severe in states with high exposure to globalization.

While poverty was falling dramatically in India during this period, between 1990 and 2000 poverty in Mexico increased. In the states with low exposure to globalization, poverty increased from 32 to 40 percent; in the states with high exposure, poverty increased only slightly, from 21 to 22 percent. If we take the difference in the increase in poverty within each region over the 1990s, we find that poverty increased by 8 percent in low-exposure states and by only 1 percent in high-exposure states. The difference-in-difference estimator is the differential in these two changes—that is, 8 – 1 equals 7 percentage points—and is the basis for Hanson's conclusions that the incidence of wage poverty in low-exposure states increased relative to poverty in high-exposure states by approximately 7 percent.

How can we reconcile the findings on Mexico and India? As pointed out by Hanson, the peso crisis in Mexico in 1995 is one major reason for the aggregate increase in poverty, in contrast to India, which experienced no ma-

13. These mean poverty rates are taken from the mean poverty rates for the rural areas in the national sample surveys for 1987 and 1999. See appendix tables in Topalova (chap. 7 in the volume). Mean poverty in the urban areas is reported separately. Topalova also reports trends in alternative measures of poverty, including the poverty gap and changes in consumption.

jor adverse macroeconomic shock during this period. In addition, Hanson defines high-globalization states to include those with a high proportion of maquiladoras—production activities designated for exports—and foreign direct investment. Topalova also finds, consistent with Hanson's chapter, that poverty fell more in regions that exported more or received more foreign direct investment. Consequently, both studies suggest that export activity and foreign direct investment are correlated with beneficial outcomes for the poor.

In chapter 8, Chor-ching Goh and Beata S. Javorcik examine the relationship between tariff changes and wages of workers in Poland. Poland embarked on significant trade reforms during the 1990s, when the country moved from a closed to a very open economy, particularly vis-à-vis the European Union. Poland makes an excellent case study in part because changes in its tariffs can be treated as exogenous, as they were stipulated by the Association Agreement between the European community and Poland signed in 1991.

Goh and Javorcik demonstrate that labor mobility is fairly restricted in Poland, placing their analysis also in the context of a specific-sector framework. Their results suggest that workers in sectors that experienced the largest tariff declines experienced the highest increases in wages. They present evidence showing that tariff declines led to wage increases because firms were forced to increase productivity, and productivity increases resulted in higher wages. These micro-level results showing a positive relationship between tariff reductions and productivity increases are consistent with the more aggregate evidence on the positive relationship between openness to trade and aggregate growth. Their results are significantly different, however, from some of the other studies, since they find that workers in sectors with the biggest tariff reductions gained the most.

Impact of Globalization on Poverty via Prices of Production and Consumption Goods

In many developing countries, wages are not the primary source of income for the rural poor. In chapter 9, Jorge F. Balat and Guido G. Porto calculate that in Zambia wages accounted for only 6 percent of income for the rural poor in 1998. Consequently, globalization could affect poverty by affecting the prices of goods consumed by the poor (the consumption channel) and goods produced by the poor (the production channel).

In many cases, the urban poor are net consumers of agricultural products, and the rural poor are net producers of those same products; in this case, an increase in agricultural prices caused (for example) by a removal of export taxes could lead to an increase in urban poverty but a decline in rural poverty. These linkages are explored to various degrees in the studies on Ethiopia, Mexico, and Zambia. In chapter 5, McMillan, Zwane, and Ashraf explore the impact of liberalizing Mexico's corn market on the in-

comes of the poor rural farmers. The evidence suggests that during the 1990s, imports of both white and yellow corn increased, and prices of Mexican corn fell. However, they also find that the majority of the poorest corn farmers are net consumers of corn and hence benefited from the drop in corn prices. The income from corn production among middle-income farmers who are mostly net sellers fell, both as a share of total income and in absolute terms. The decline in income from corn production among those farmers who are net sellers would have translated into an equivalent decline in real income if farmer incomes had not been supplemented with transfers through government programs such as PROCAMPO and PROGRESA.

In their study of Ethiopian rural grain producers in chapter 13, James Levinsohn and Margaret McMillan explore the impact of food aid on both consumption and production of the rural poor. This chapter addresses the concern that food aid further exacerbates poverty by depressing incomes of rural producers. While Levinsohn and McMillan confirm that a more optimal arrangement would be to buy food from local producers and distribute it to poor consumers,[14] they also show that the net impact of food aid on the poor in Ethiopia has been positive. This is because the poor in Ethiopia are primarily net consumers, rather than net producers of food, and consequently food aid has alleviated poverty. As pointed out by Rohini Pande in her excellent discussion of this chapter, these results are contingent on food aid actually reaching the poor. Levinsohn and McMillan argue that this is often the case.

For Zambia, Balat and Porto calculate the impact of liberalizing the market for maize, which was heavily subsidized for both consumers and producers. They find that the resulting price increase led to consumption losses, which were offset by domestic market liberalization. They also measure the potential increase in income due to switching from production for home consumption to production and wage activities associated with production of cash crops. Balat and Porto estimate that rural Zambians would gain substantially from expanding into the production of cash crops, particularly in the production of cotton, tobacco, and maize. However, Balat and Porto also caution that such gains can only be achieved if other complementary policies are in place. These would include extension services, infrastructure, irrigation, access to credit and finance, and education and health services. Balat and Porto also point to the fact that Zambia needs to have access to international agricultural markets in order to realize potential gains.

6   Capital Flows and Poverty

Another avenue through which globalization could affect the welfare of the poor is through financial liberalization, which has increased the scope

14. This assumes that local purchase does not drive prices up for some poor people.

for capital to flow to developing countries. For this volume, Prasad and coauthors document in chapter 11 that both developed and developing countries have become increasingly open to capital flows, measured using either policy instruments such as capital controls or ex post capital flows.

In theory, openness to capital flows could alleviate poverty through several channels. If greater financial integration contributes to higher growth by expanding access to capital, expanding access to new technology, stimulating domestic financial-sector development, reducing the cost of capital, and alleviating domestic credit constraints, then such growth should reduce poverty. Access to international capital markets should also allow countries to smooth consumption shocks, reducing output or consumption volatility. Prasad and coauthors begin by examining the relationship between financial integration and growth. Reviewing over a dozen studies and examining the data themselves, they find that there is no clear relationship between the two. This suggests that the impact of financial integration on poverty—via possible growth effects—is likely to be small. They argue that since there are no clear linkages between financial integration and growth in the aggregate cross-country evidence, direct linkages between financial integration and poverty are also likely to be difficult to find.

They also explore another link: whether financial integration has smoothed or exacerbated output and consumption volatility. They point out that greater macroeconomic volatility probably increases both absolute and relative measures of poverty, particularly when there are financial crises. Since the poor are likely to be hurt in periods of consumption volatility, income smoothing made possible by global financial integration could be beneficial to the poor. However, the authors find that the opposite is true: financial globalization in developing countries is associated with higher consumption volatility. They posit the existence of a threshold effect: beyond a certain level of financial integration (50 percent of GDP), financial integration significantly reduces volatility. However, most developing countries are well below this threshold.

Prasad and coauthors point out that despite the lack of evidence of any association between financial globalization and growth, protectionism is not the answer. They suggest that if financial globalization is approached with the right set of complementary policies, then it is likely to be growth promoting and also less likely to lead to higher consumption volatility. These policies include the use of flexible exchange rates, macroeconomic stabilization policies, and the development of strong institutions. The authors' definition of institutional development and good governance includes transparency in business and government transactions, control of corruption, rule of law, and financial supervisory capacity.

Much of the increases in consumption volatility identified by Prasad and coauthors for less financially integrated countries occurred in the context

of currency crises. How have the poor weathered these currency crises? The justification for addressing the links between currency crises and poverty outcomes in this study is simple: for many developing countries, financial globalization has been accompanied by more frequent currency crises, which in turn have implications for poverty. One study in the volume—chapter 12, by Duncan Thomas and Elizabeth Frankenberg—examines the impact of such a crisis on the poor. Using longitudinal household survey data from the Indonesia Family Life Survey (IFLS), Thomas and Frankenberg examine the immediate and medium-term effects of the East Asian crisis on multiple dimensions of well-being. In IFLS, the same households were interviewed a few months before the onset of the crisis, a year later, and again two years after that, which provides unique opportunities for measuring the magnitude and distribution of the effects of the crisis on the population.

Thomas and Frankenberg demonstrate that in the first year of the crisis, poverty rose by between 50 and 100 percent, real wages declined by around 40 percent, and household per capita consumption fell by around 15 percent. However, focusing exclusively on changes in real resources is complicated by the fact that measurement of prices in an environment of extremely volatile prices is not straightforward. Moreover, it misses important dimensions of response by households. These include changes in leisure (labor supply), changes in living arrangements (household size and thus per capita household resources), changes in assets, and changes in investments in human capital. These responses not only are quantitatively important but also highlight the resilience of families and households in the face of large unanticipated shocks as they draw on a wide array of mechanisms to respond to the changes in opportunities they face.

While the volatility of bank borrowing and portfolio flows may be costly to the poor, many of the authors in this volume emphasize the benefits from another type of inflow: foreign direct investment. Prasad and his coauthors emphasize that the composition of capital flows can have a significant impact on a country's vulnerability to financial crises. They also document that foreign direct investment flows are significantly less volatile than other types of flows. The studies on Mexico, India, Poland, and Colombia all demonstrate that incoming foreign investment is associated with a significant reduction in poverty.

7   Measuring Other Effects of Globalization

While the primary focus of the studies in this volume is on poverty alleviation, several of the studies also examine other outcomes associated with globalization. Three of the country case studies test for the relationship between globalization and inequality, complementing the cross-country

studies by Easterly and by Milanovic and Squire.[15] Past studies that use microdata sets have found that trade and capital flows are frequently associated with an increase in the relative demand for skilled labor.[16] The country case studies on India, Poland, China, and Colombia prepared for this volume, however, suggest that the evidence is mixed. Evidence presented by Topalova on India suggests that despite the increase in inequality in the 1990s, there is no relationship between trade reform and inequality, using the standard deviation of log consumption and the mean logarithmic deviation of consumption as measures of inequality. For Colombia, Goldberg and Pavcnik show that trade reform was associated with increasing inequality, in part because the most protected sectors prior to reform were sectors with a high share of unskilled workers. For Poland, Goh and Javorcik suggest the reverse: trade reforms increased the returns to unskilled workers relative to skilled workers, contributing to a decline in inequality.

A different approach to measuring the impact of globalization on incomes is taken by James Levinsohn in chapter 15. Levinsohn points out that one of the challenges to analyzing the impact of globalization is that increasing openness to trade and investment are typically accompanied by many other changes. In South Africa, the ratio of trade to GDP increased from 44 percent to 70 percent between 1991 and 2002, and there was a 200-fold increase in foreign investment. These changes were accompanied by many other developments, including the end of apartheid, the introduction of democracy, and the HIV/AIDS epidemic. To separate the impact of globalization, he reasons, one approach would be to analyze whether the returns to speaking English increased. The evidence suggests that, controlling for other factors, the returns to speaking English did in fact increase, but only for whites. The fact that the returns to speaking English increased only for whites and not for other races suggests that the impact of globalization has been uneven in South Africa. This pattern of uneven gains is consistent with the other evidence presented in the cross-country studies and several of the individual case studies.

Another consequence of globalization, which is explored by Ligon in his study on China (chap. 14), is its possible impact on household welfare by affecting household risk. Prasad and his coauthors point out in chapter 11

15. As pointed out by Aisbett, Sala-i-Martin, and Milanovic and Squire in their respective chapters, debate continues on the nature and direction of trends in inequality. Within countries, inequality is generally rising. Across countries, inequality is stable or falling if we weight by country size, in large part because of the recent successes of China and India in reducing poverty. As Sala-i-Martin and others have emphasized, the correct measure of global social welfare is to use such country weights when the outcome of interest is the welfare of individuals. This is of course still a very rough proxy, since it disregards income inequality between individuals within countries. Thus, access to most countries' income or expenditure surveys is needed for an accurate picture of individual-level welfare.

16. See chapter 10 for Hanson's review of this literature, which covers microevidence on the relationship between different measures of globalization and inequality for Chile, Mexico, Colombia, and Hong Kong.

that the increase in consumption volatility possibly engendered by financial liberalization among the less developed countries could be harmful to the poor, but they do not explicitly model the impact of increasing risk on household welfare. In China, recent increases in urban income inequality are mirrored in increases in inequality in consumption expenditures. This connection between changes in the distribution of income and consumption expenditures could be entirely attributable to differences in preferences or could be caused by imperfections in the markets for credit and insurance, which ordinarily would serve to equate these intertemporal marginal rates of substitution. Ligon presumes that market imperfections drive changes in the distribution of expenditures, and he uses data on expenditures from repeated cross sections of urban households in China to estimate a Markov transition function for shares of expenditures over the period 1985–2001. He then uses this estimated function to compute the welfare losses attributable to risk over this period and to predict the future trajectory of inequality from 2001 through 2025. Ligon's contribution emphasizes that the amount of risk a household faces depends much more on its position in the consumption distribution than it does on aggregate shocks, whatever their source.[17]

8   Globalization's Critics and Some Remaining Questions

Why does there continue to be so much criticism of globalization? This is the central question of Aisbett's chapter (chap. 1). Aisbett argues that this continued criticism is due to several factors: the use of different methodologies in estimating poverty and inequality, the concerns of globalization's critics about the short-term costs versus the longer-term gains from trade reform, their rejection of a perfectly competitive framework, and different interpretations regarding the evidence. Aisbett argues that people have a natural tendency to weight the information they receive according to their prior beliefs and values. Thus, evidence that is objectively "mixed" is quite likely to be interpreted by one type of person as very positive and by another as very negative. The mere fact that there are some los-

---

17. The contribution of globalization to the decline in poverty within China is clearly a topic that deserves further research. Ravallion (2004a) suggests somewhat provocatively that the significant reduction in poverty in China over the last twenty years is probably not related to its phenomenal increase as a global exporter. He uses as evidence aggregate time series data, in contrast to Shang-Jin Wei (chap. 14 comment), who has access to more disaggregate information. Nevertheless, Ravallion makes the important point that average tariffs and non-tariff barriers barely fell during the period of most rapid poverty reduction in China. It should be evident from this discussion that the choice of aggregation and the measure of globalization are likely to be key in resolving this debate. In addition, Wei in his comment in this volume and in other research employs measures of export activity or foreign investment to show that both are associated with desirable outcomes, while Ravallion looks at overall trade shares.

ers among the poor from globalization will lead people with negative priors to believe globalization is negative.

The second part of Aisbett's answer is to examine what types of beliefs and values lead people to a more negative interpretation of the evidence on globalization and poverty. The values which she identifies include concern over inequality, independent of poverty. In particular, globalization's critics feel differently about the polarization of the income distribution and inequality in the gains that different groups receive from globalization.

As first pointed out by Kanbur (2001), critics of globalization also tend to focus on shorter-term impacts, while globalization's proponents are more concerned about the longer term. Critics of globalization also focus on the losses experienced by subgroups of the poor, even when poverty has declined on aggregate. Aisbett suggests a number of explanations for this value preference, including recent evidence from behavioral experiments.

Aisbett also argues that many people believe that the current form of globalization is based on processes that distill both political and market power upward and away from the poor. In particular, critics of globalization believe that corporate and commercial lobbies have disproportionate access to the international organizations such as the World Trade Organization (WTO) and IMF, and that rich countries exploit their power within these international organizations. This belief about the processes through which globalization occurs is partly what predisposes them to interpret the available evidence negatively.

This volume seeks to address these misunderstandings and also presents comprehensive new evidence on the possible linkages between globalization and poverty amelioration. Nevertheless, a number of research questions remain unanswered, as described below.

1. *What is the relationship between globalization and poverty in the aggregate cross-country data?* Although there are many pitfalls associated with using cross-country data sets, it would nevertheless be useful to have more information on the association between globalization—measured using information on barriers to trade or capital flows—and measures of poverty. Evidence to date suggests that there is generally a positive association between openness and growth, and between growth and poverty reduction. We would have expected that there should consequently be a positive association between openness and poverty reduction; yet the evidence presented in this volume is quite fragile. The question remains: is the evidence fragile because the cross-country data on poverty are too poor to yield meaningful results, or because the costs of trade reforms have fallen disproportionately on the poor? In light of our knowledge that openness to trade is generally associated with growth, and that sectors hit by import competition in regions like India and Colombia have gained less from trade reforms, the possibility exists that the gains from trade in the aggre-

gate have not been big enough to offset some of the adverse distributional consequences for the poor.

2. *Who among the poor are the winners from globalization?* A number of the case studies point to winners among the poor from globalization. These include the poor wage earners in export-competing sectors and in sectors or regions that are recipients of foreign direct investment. Particularly in light of the vocal criticism leveled at globalization, these beneficiaries should be identified and emphasized in any future research agenda on the relationship between globalization and poverty. Of particular interest would be research that could further identify the impact of foreign investment inflows and export growth on poverty in India and China.

3. *How do we integrate the poorest of the poor into the world trading system?* The very poorest individuals are often untouched by globalization. This is evident among the poorest Mexican corn farmers who report that they never sell corn and among the poorest Ethiopian farmers who are net buyers of food. Africa as a continent has seen very little foreign investment and still exports primarily unprocessed agricultural products. More research is needed on how to better integrate the really poor into the global trading system. We need to identify the critical factors, whether these are credit, illness, lack of infrastructure, or land.

4. *Can we identify the dynamic effects of industrial-country trade and aid policies?* Several issues explored in this volume include the role of industrial-country policies in affecting the incidence of poverty in developing countries. Those studies suggest that, at least in the short run, OECD subsidies and food aid have probably helped the poor in other countries. However, further research is needed to identify whether there are longer-term, dynamic effects. For example, even if the poor in Ethiopia are currently net beneficiaries from food aid, there exists the possibility that over the long run food aid has discouraged poor farmers from planting or investing, transforming them from net producers into net consumers.

5. *Can we better identify the complementarities between measures of globalization and other policies?* Many of the country studies identify the importance of complementary policies in determining the benefits or costs of trade reforms for the poor. However, much more work is needed to identify which types of policies should accompany trade reforms. There has been little analysis to show, for example, that financial globalization would be beneficial to developing countries if it was accompanied by flexible exchange rate regimes or better institutions. Additional work is needed to identify whether trade reforms introduced in conjunction with labor market reforms are more likely to reduce poverty, and how to properly design social safety nets to accompany trade reforms. While Mexico has been successful in targeting some of the poorest who were hurt by reforms, these programs are expensive, and additional research could identify whether this approach is realistic for the very poorest countries.

Further research is needed to identify the source of the immobility of labor. While Topalova and Goldberg and Pavcnik show that some of these sources are artificial—stemming from labor market legislation that inhibits hiring and firing—Goh and Javorcik argue that much of the immobility of labor in Poland is due to societal factors that discourage workers from relocating. Further evidence identifying the relationship between gross labor inflows and outflows and trade reforms would be useful in this regard.

The fact that the gains or losses from trade reforms to the poor may hinge on the mobility (or immobility) of labor needs to be more explicitly addressed in existing models of international trade. Some models (e.g., HO) adopt assumptions of perfect factor mobility, while others (e.g., specific-sector) assume no factor mobility. Neither assumption is consistent with reality. In addition, many of globalization's critics perceive the world through the lens of imperfect competition. Yet most trade economists assume perfect competition or zero excess profits, which is not consistent with reality in at least some sectors of developing economies.

9   Conclusion

Many countries have made tremendous strides in reducing not only the percentage of the population living in poverty but also the absolute number of individuals living on less than $1 a day. During the last twenty years, developing countries increased their trade shares and slashed their tariffs. If export shares are one measure of globalization, then developing countries are now more globalized than high-income countries. To what extent is increasing globalization responsible for the fall in the incidence of poverty?

The first theme that emerges across the chapters in this volume is that the relationship between globalization and poverty is complex; in many cases, the outcome depends not just on trade or financial globalization but on the interaction of globalization with the rest of the environment. Key complementary policies include investments in human capital and infrastructure, as well as macroeconomic stability and policies to promote credit and technical assistance to farmers. Financial globalization is more likely to promote growth and poverty reduction if it is accompanied or preceded by the development of good institutions and governance, as well as macroeconomic stability (including the use of flexible exchange rates). The role of complementary policies in ensuring that globalization yields benefits for the poor is emerging as a critical theme for multilateral institutions (see World Bank, forthcoming).

One related issue is that poor workers need to be able to move out of contracting sectors and into expanding ones. The country studies on India and Colombia suggest that trade reforms have been associated with an increase in poverty only in regions with inflexible labor laws. Consequently, any

conclusions that do not take into account the labor market institutions that could undermine labor mobility may be misleading. More research is needed to identify whether labor legislation protects only the rights of the small fraction of workers who typically account for the formal sector in developing economies, or whether such legislation softens short-term adjustment costs and helps the labor force share in the gains from globalization. The role of antisweatshop activists in promoting the right to organize, improving working conditions, and raising wages suggests that selective interventions may be successful (see Harrison and Scorse 2004).

Second, the evidence suggests that globalization leads to clearly identifiable winners. Across several different continents, export expansion has been accompanied by a reduction in poverty. The evidence also points to the beneficial effects of foreign direct investment. While the macroeconomic evidence suggests that foreign direct investment is a less volatile source of capital than other types of inflows, the microeconomic evidence for India, Mexico, Poland, and Colombia indicates that higher inflows of foreign investment are associated with a reduction in poverty.

Third, it is also possible to identify the losers from globalization among the poor. Poor workers in import-competing sectors—who cannot relocate, possibly due to the existence of inflexible labor laws—are likely to be hurt by globalization. Financial crises also affect the poor disproportionately, as indicated by the cross-country evidence and the erosion of real wages following currency crises in Indonesia and Mexico. In Mexico, some poor and most medium-income corn farmers have been negatively affected by increasing import competition.

Fourth, simple interpretations of general equilibrium trade models such as the HO framework are likely to be incorrect. Many economists predicted that developing countries with a comparative advantage in unskilled labor would benefit from globalization through increased demand for their unskilled-intensive goods, which in turn would reduce inequality and poverty. The theoretical and empirical contributions to this volume suggest that this interpretation of trade theory is too simple and frequently not consistent with reality. The cross-country studies document that globalization has been accompanied by increasing inequality within developing countries. One implication is that rising inequality induced by globalization offsets some of the gains in poverty reduction achieved via trade-induced growth.

The conclusions highlighted in these studies have several key implications for the globalization debate. First, impediments to exports from developing countries exacerbate poverty in those countries. Developing countries need access to developed-country markets. The evidence shows a clear link between export activity and poverty reduction in Colombia, Mexico, India, and Poland. This research suggests that efforts to dismantle barriers to developing-country exports through international agree-

ments are likely to lead to further poverty reduction. The evidence for India, Mexico, and Poland also points to a strong link between foreign investment inflows and poverty reduction.

Second, there are losers among the poor from trade reform. In particular, this volume identifies as losers the poor in import-competing sectors following the liberalization of trade. The heterogeneity in outcomes suggests that careful targeting is necessary to help the poor who are likely to be hurt by globalization. This includes the poor in countries hit by financial crises, as well as the smallest farmers who cannot compete with the more efficient larger farmers or with expanding import competition. Mexico's transfer programs played a major role in preventing the smallest corn farmers from experiencing a large decline in income following reforms. In Indonesia, subsidized food was distributed to many communities. Scholarships and free public schooling introduced a year after the Indonesian crisis led to subsequent increases in school enrollments, particularly among the poorest. Extending such subsidies to health care visits and basic drugs might have arrested the decline in the use of health care that occurred after the 1997 crisis.

Finally, the evidence suggests that relying on trade or foreign investment alone is not enough. A critical role for complementary policies is highlighted in the country studies on Zambia, India, Colombia, Indonesia, and Poland. The poor need better education, access to infrastructure, access to credit for investing in technology improvements, and the ability to relocate out of contracting sectors into expanding ones in order to take advantage of trade reforms. Clearly, the concerns of globalization's critics have been heard, but much remains to be done.

References

Agénor, Pierre-Richard. 2004. Does globalization hurt the poor? *International Economics and Economic Policy* 1 (1): 21–51.
Aisbett, Emma, Ann Harrison, and Alix Zwane. 2005. Globalization and poverty: What is the evidence? Paper presented at a conference in honor of Jagdish Bhagwati's 70th birthday. 28–30 January, Gainesville, Florida.
Bardhan, Pranab. 2000. Social justice in a global economy. Geneva: International Labour Organization. Available at http://www.ilo.org/public/english/bureau/inst/papers/sopolecs/bardhan/.
———. 2003. International economic integration and the poor. In *Global governance: An architecture for the world economy,* ed. H. Siebert, 49–61. Berlin: Springer.
———. 2004. The impact of globalization on the poor. In *Brookings trade forum 2004,* ed. Susan Collins and Carol Graham, 271–84. Washington, DC: The Brookings Institution.

Besley, Timothy, and Robin Burgess. 2003. Halving global poverty. *Journal of Economic Perspectives* 17 (3): 3–22.

Bhagwati, Jagdish. 2004. *In defense of globalization.* New York: Oxford University Press.

Bhagwati, Jagdish, and T. N. Srinivasan. 2002. Trade and poverty in the poor countries. *AEA Papers and Proceedings* 92 (2): 180–83.

Chen, Shaohua, and Martin Ravallion. 2000. How did the world's poorest fare in the 1990s? World Bank Development Research Group Working Paper no. W2409. Washington, DC: World Bank. Available at http://econ.worldbank.org/view.php?type=5&id=1164.

Deaton, Angus. 2001. Counting the world's poor: Problems and possible solutions. *World Bank Research Observer* 16 (2): 125–47.

———. 2003. Measuring poverty in a growing world (or measuring growth in a poor world). NBER Working Paper no. 9822. Cambridge, MA: National Bureau of Economic Research.

Dollar, David. 2001. Globalization, inequality and poverty since 1980. Background paper. Washington, DC: World Bank. Available at http://www.worldbank.org/research/global.

Dollar, David, and Aart Kraay. 2001. Trade, growth and poverty. World Bank Development Research Group Working Paper no. 2615. Washington, DC: World Bank.

———. 2002. Spreading the wealth. *Foreign Affairs* 81 (1): 120–33.

Goldberg, Pinelopi, and Nina Pavcnik. 2004. Trade, inequality, and poverty: What do we know? Evidence from recent trade liberalization episodes in developing countries. In *Brookings trade forum 2004,* ed. Susan Collins and Carol Graham, 223–69. Washington, DC: Brookings Institution Press.

Harrison, Ann, and Gordon Hanson. 1999. Who gains from trade reform? Some remaining puzzles. *Journal of Development Economics* 59 (1): 125–54.

Harrison, Ann, and Jason Scorse. 2004. Moving up or moving out? Anti-sweatshop activists and labor market outcomes. University of California, Berkeley, and Monterey Institute of International Studies. Working Paper.

Harrison, Ann, and Helena Tang. 2005. Trade liberalization: Why so much controversy? In *Economic growth in the 1990s: Learning from a decade of reform,* ed. N. Roberto Zagha, 131–56. Washington, DC: World Bank.

Hertel, Thomas W., and L. Alan Winters, eds. 2005. *Poverty and the WTO: Impacts of the Doha development agenda.* New York: Palgrave MacMillan.

Kanbur, Ravi. 2001. Economic policy, distribution and poverty: The nature of the disagreements. *World Development* 29 (6): 1083–94.

Krueger, Ann. 1983. *Trade and employment in developing countries. Vol. 3, Synthesis and conclusions.* Chicago: University of Chicago Press.

Lee, Ha Yan, Luca Antonio Ricci, and Roberto Rigobon. 2004. Once again, is openness good for growth? NBER Working Paper no. 10749. Cambridge, MA: National Bureau of Economic Research, September.

Panagariya, A. 2002. Trade liberalization and food security: Conceptual links. In *Trade reforms and food security,* 25–42. Rome: Food and Agricultural Organization of the United Nations.

———. 2004. Opponent's comments on "Subsidies and trade barriers" by Kym Anderson. In *Global crises, global solutions,* ed. Bjørn Lomborg, 592–604. Cambridge: Cambridge University Press.

Ravallion, Martin. 2004a. Competing concepts of inequality in the globalization debate. In *Brookings trade forum 2004,* ed. Susan Collins and Carol Graham, 1–38. Washington, DC: Brookings Institution Press.

————. 2004b. Looking beyond averages in the trade and poverty debate. World Bank Policy Research Working Paper no. 3461. Washington, DC: World Bank, November.

Rodriguez, Francisco, and Dani Rodrik. 2000. Trade policy and economic growth: A skeptic's guide to the cross-national evidence. In *NBER macroeconomics annual 2000*, ed. Ben Bernanke and Kenneth Rogoff, 261–325. Cambridge: MIT Press.

Valdes, A., and A. F. McCalla. 1999. Issues, interests and options of developing countries. Paper presented at conference on Agriculture and the New Trade Agenda in the WTO Negotiations. 1–2 October, Geneva, Switzerland.

Winters, Alan L., Neil McCulloch, and Andrew McKay. 2004. Trade liberalization and poverty: The evidence so far. *Journal of Economic Literature* 42 (March): 72–115.

World Bank. Forthcoming. *The growth experience: Lessons from the 1990s.* Ed. Roberto Zagha. Washington, DC: World Bank.

I

Global (Cross-Country) Analyses

1

Why Are the Critics So Convinced That Globalization Is Bad for the Poor?

Emma Aisbett

1.1 Introduction

Economic globalization is a surprisingly controversial process. Surprising, that is, to the many economists and policymakers who believe it is the best means of bringing prosperity to the largest number of people all around the world. Proponents of economic globalization have had a tendency to conclude that dissent and criticism are the result of ignorance or vested interest (Bardhan 2003). They have argued that antisweatshop campaigners do not understand that conditions in the factories owned by multinationals tend to be better than those in comparable domestic firms; that environmentalists are denying the world's poor the right to develop freely; and that unionists in developed countries are protecting their interests at the expense of the workers in poorer parts of the world. Bhagwati (2000) provides a good example of the way that some proponents of globalization have reacted to critics:

> No one can escape the antiglobalists today. . . . This motley crew comes almost entirely from the rich countries and is overwhelmingly white, largely middle class, occasionally misinformed, often wittingly dishonest, and so diverse in its professed concerns that it makes the output from a monkey's romp on a keyboard look more coherent. (p. 134)

More recently, however, leading economists and policymakers, including Bhagwati (2004), have been advocating for "reasoned engagement" and "careful response" to some of the more mainstream critics of globalization (p. 4). There is a growing sense of the value of doing more than knock-

Emma Aisbett is a PhD candidate in the agricultural and resource economics department at the University of California, Berkeley.

ing down the straw men put forward by the extreme or the misinformed. As Stanley Fischer (2003) says:

The debate [over globalization] is untidy and ill-defined, and one could react by saying that it has no place in a professional setting like this one. But we cannot afford to ignore it, for the views and attitudes expressed in it will inevitably affect public policy—and the issues are critically important for the future economic growth and well-being of all the people of the globe. (p. 2)

The aim of this paper is to help explain both the "what" and the "why" of common criticisms of globalization's record on poverty and inequality. In particular, it addresses the question of why many people in rich countries believe that globalization has been bad for the poor in developing countries and has worsened inequality.[1]

The answer to this question consists essentially of two parts: first, that neither the theory nor the empirical evidence on globalization and poverty is unarguably positive; second, and more important, that people's interpretation of the available evidence is strongly influenced by their values and by their beliefs about the process of globalization.

Evidence for the first part of my argument is presented in sections 1.2 and 1.3. Section 1.2 discusses the large amount of empirical work that has tried to identify causal links between globalization and poverty and inequality. I argue here that the linkages between globalization policies and poverty outcomes remain theoretically unclear and difficult to test empirically, and that more nuanced empirical research is required to address the remaining concerns with regard to globalization. Section 1.3 discusses some key trends in poverty and inequality numbers over the current period of globalization. Here I argue that the wide range of poverty and inequality estimates, which arises from apparently minor methodological differences, leaves ample room for a difference in opinion about the achievements of the last twenty-five years.

Sections 1.4 and 1.5 comprise the second part of my answer. Section 1.4 shows that critics of globalization often have different conceptions of poverty and inequality than those preferred by economists. Section 1.5 argues that people are predisposed to thinking that globalization is bad for the poor because they view the power structures of globalization as being biased toward the already rich and powerful. Section 1.6 summarizes and concludes.

Before attempting to explain antiglobalization sentiment, it is worthwhile to clarify what is meant by "globalization" and "antiglobalization" in the context of this paper. That is the subject of the remainder of this section.

1. A recent survey conducted by the World Economic Forum (WEF; 2002) found that people in richer countries were more likely than people in poorer countries to believe that globalization benefited the poor less than the rich.

1.1.1 Globalization

Despite the fact that a definition of globalization has been attempted by hundreds of authors and distinguished speakers on the topic, the word continues to mean very different things to different people. In light of this, I do not attempt to provide any general definition of globalization; rather, I will merely explain what is meant by globalization in the context of this paper.

In this paper, *globalization* refers to global economic integration, or economic globalization. Economic globalization, including increases in trade, foreign investment, and migration, is widely agreed to be occurring through a combination of improvements in technology and decreased transportation costs, as well as deliberate policy choices on behalf of many national governments to liberalize their economies and participate in the development of global institutions. Thus, the policy aspect of economic globalization is a cumulative outcome that results from the choices of many individual countries to increase their integration with the global economy.[2]

Given that globalization may be viewed as the cumulative result of increased integration on behalf of many individual countries, we need to consider how individual countries become integrated into the global economy. There are two broad approaches to measuring the extent to which a country is integrated with the global economy. The first approach is to determine the level of restrictions placed on the movement of goods, services, and factors into and out of the country. Thus, liberalized capital markets, free movement of labor, and an absence of trade restrictions could all be considered indicators of an integrated economy. The second measure of a country's integration is the relative size of the flows of goods, services, factors, and profits into and out of the country. Although these two measures are often used interchangeably, they are not identical concepts and are not even highly correlated empirically (Harrison 1996). Consider export subsi-

---

2. This idea that globalization is the aggregate result of individual country liberalization is made by Prasad et al. (2003). Although it will not be a major issue in this paper, it is worth noting that the impact on a country of its own integration may be different from the impact of exogenous increases in globalization. Consider the case of Mexico. The impact of its own efforts at liberalization and integration may be to increase foreign trade and investment. At the same time, however, many other low- and middle-income countries have been integrating, which leads to more competition for foreign capital and export markets. Thus, exogenous increases in the level of global economic integration (i.e., economic globalization), and increases in Mexico's own level of integration, may have exactly opposite effects on the level of trade and investment in that country. Indeed, this example is not far from reality. One of the conclusions of the 2002 United Nations Conference on Trade and Development (UNCTAD) report (UNCTAD 2002, p. IX) is that middle-income countries such as those in Latin America and Southeast Asia will need to rapidly upgrade their skill-intensive manufactures if they are to stay ahead of competition from low-income countries that are becoming increasingly export oriented.

dies. Viewed from the first perspective, these programs are akin to tariffs and are decidedly contrary to the principle of economic globalization. Yet, viewed from the second perspective, these programs can be seen to greatly increase the level of integration achieved. Indeed, having read many arguments from both sides, it seems to me that this ambiguity is a major reason that some people claim that the East Asian tigers' success was based on pro-integration policies, while others claim the exact opposite.

The distinction between policies and outcomes is important to the globalization debate. Analysis of popular writings and opinion surveys suggests that most people are happy with increases in trade in principle, yet they view policies of unregulated free markets and minimal government involvement much less favorably.[3]

Another linguistic issue of relevance to understanding the globalization debate is that criticisms of globalization are often actually criticisms of a broader neoliberal policy agenda that globalization is believed to imply. Burtless (2004) makes this point when he describes the difference between what economists (typically proponents of globalization) and public health advocates (often critics) mean when they refer to globalization or liberalization:

> Whereas trade economists interpret liberalization to mean policies that eliminate trade and capital barriers at international borders, public health advocates consider the domestic policy changes that third world governments are obliged to accept in order to become full-fledged members of the IMF–World Bank–Davos club of nations. (p. 1)

1.1.2 Antiglobalization

Despite the popularity and convenience of the term, in the remainder of this paper I avoid referring to the "antiglobalization movement." There are two reasons for this. First, many of the concerns and positions that I discuss may be attributed to a far broader segment of the population than that which is actively involved in any movement. The use of such a label, and its application to street protesters, has a divisive effect between groups who in reality share many of the same concerns. In particular, it forces a wedge between academic economists and the concerned public.

Second, as has been noted by many leading authors, the so-called antiglobalization movement is not uniformly opposed to globalization as it is

3. For example, based on surveys of 18,797 people in nineteen countries, Globescan reports that majorities in all countries except the United States support opening up markets to poor countries. In the United States support for opening up to poor countries was premised on the supply of increased government support for those who lose their jobs as a result of increased imports. Similarly, in a report that brings together all the available evidence on public opinion in the United States, the Program on International Policy Attitudes (PIPA; 2002) finds that most Americans do agree with free trade in principle; however, their support is contingent on complementary policies to address social and environmental concerns as well as American job losses.

broadly defined.[4] It is a fact that the movement itself is global, and all the leading writers of the movement reject the antiglobalization label.[5] Naomi Klein, unofficial spokesperson of the movement, has this to say about the term: "The irony of the media-imposed label, 'anti-globalization,' is that we in this movement have been turning globalization into a lived reality, perhaps more so than even the most multinational of corporate executives" (quoted in Chihara 2002, p. 1).

But what about globalization as defined here? People may enjoy the World Wide Web and easy international travel, but what about the economic aspects of globalization? As will be argued in the following paragraphs, for the most part people are not opposed to the principle of global economic integration. They are, however, critical of the way in which it is currently progressing, and they do believe that the optimal level of integration will allow space for national sovereignty, democracy, and some government intervention to advance social and environmental agendas. We refer to these individuals as "critics of globalization" and reserve the label "antiglobalization" for people who would genuinely like to stop globalization dead in its tracks. Globalization's critics will be the focus of this paper.

1.2   Questionable Causation

As noted by Bardhan (2003), both sides of the globalization debate have had a tendency to claim an unreasonable degree of causation between liberalizing policies and observed trends in poverty and inequality. The claims of causation are so confounded that both sides claim the success of the Asian tigers as the result of their own policies, and the failure of many of the African states as the result of the opposite policies. Thus, globalization's proponents claim China's and Taiwan's growth in recent decades as the result of liberalization of their economies, while globalization's critics claim that these same countries have been able to capitalize on the opportunities afforded by globalization because of extensive government intervention both in the past and in the present.

Similarly, globalization's proponents claim that many of Africa's economic problems are due to lack of openness and excessive, inappropriate government intervention. Globalization's critics claim that Africa's woes come from other sources (including corrupt or incompetent governments), but the forced liberalization imposed by structural adjustment programs and other lending conditions has not delivered the promised growth. Instead globalization has only made living conditions worse for the poor as government services are cut back and instability is increased.

4. See, for example, Sen (2002), Kanbur (2001), Ravallion (2003), and Bhagwati (2004).
5. See, for example, Korten (2001).

An enormous research effort has been expended by economists in an attempt resolve these contradictory claims. This section will summarize the types of empirical research that have been conducted, and identify a set of stylized facts that have emerged from it. It then discusses why the empirical literature has not been as successful as many practitioners would hope in convincing skeptics of the benefits of globalization.

Before proceeding, it is important to make clear what the current section and the following section on measurement of poverty and inequality do and, more important, do not try to achieve. Neither section is in any way a comprehensive assessment of the literature that they are discussing. They do not aim to produce a statement of the type "overall, the empirical evidence supports the conclusion that globalization is good/bad for the poor."[6] Quite the contrary: their aim is to show how the empirical evidence to date leaves ample room for debate about the impact of globalization on the poor. Accordingly, the approach taken in the following sections is to highlight only a few key statistics and empirical methods, as well as their limitations and biases.

Reimer (2002) provides an excellent overview of the different empirical methods that have been employed in research on globalization and their findings. He categorizes the research methods under the following headings:

- *Cross-country regression analyses,* which test for correlations among trade, growth, income, poverty, and inequality measured at the national level
- *Partial equilibrium/cost-of-living analyses,* which are typically based on household expenditure data and emphasize commodity markets and their role in determining poverty impacts
- *General equilibrium studies,* which are generally based on disaggregated economy-wide social accounting matrices and account for commodity, terms-of-trade, and factor market effects
- The newest approach, *micro-macro syntheses,* which involve general equilibrium analysis coupled with some form of postsimulation analysis based on household survey data

One important method for analyzing the impacts of globalization is left off Reimer's list. I describe this category as microeconomic studies that test specific mechanisms (other than prices) through which globalization is be-

6. Readers who are interested in more comprehensive assessments of the empirical literature may consider one of the several high-quality survey papers, reports, and opinion pieces that have already been devoted to these questions. See, for example, International Monetary Fund (IMF; 1997, chap. 4); United Nations Development Programme (UNDP; 1999); McKay, Winters, and Kedir (2000); Reimer (2002); Bigman (2002); Berg and Krueger (2003); Bhagwati and Srinivasan (2002); Bourguignon et al. (2002); Prasad et al. (2003); Baldwin (2003); Goldberg and Pavcnik (2004); and Winters, McCulloch, and McKay (2004).

lieved to impact the poor. The findings of this literature have been summarized in a recent paper by two of the leading authors in this field, Goldberg and Pavcnik (2004).

While each empirical approach suffers from its own set of limitations, in combination, the above types of empirical research have been successful in providing several points on which a relatively broad consensus has been reached:[7]

1. Trade is correlated with, and often a source of, growth.

· 2. Growth is on average good for the poor.

3. U.S. and European Union (EU) agriculture and textile protectionism harms developing countries.

4. Foreign direct investment (FDI) is correlated with, and often a source of, growth.

5. Liberalization of markets for short-term capital can be detrimental and should be approached with caution.

6. Governments' safety nets can help to reduce negative impacts on the poor who lose as a result of liberalization and to increase acceptance of liberalization.

7. The Trade-Related Aspects of Intellectual Property Rights (TRIPs) agreement should be modified to limit negative impacts on provision of drugs to the poor.

8. Access to education, health, and credit are important factors in ensuring that the poor benefit from globalization. These factors also increase the growth potential from openness.

9. Poverty should be measured using education and health as well as income.

10. Excessive corporate power (market and political) is a concern.

11. Capture of market or political power by elites has negative implications for growth and welfare.

12. Political reform is needed in many developing countries.

It is particularly reassuring to observe that these points of consensus in the academic literature have supported the furtive emergence of a middle ground in the public debate over globalization. In reading publications from both sides, we observe an increasing number of participants who wish to move beyond competing and contradictory monologues and are willing to acknowledge some aspects of the argument presented by the other side. For example, Oxfam International is one of the leading nongovernmental organizations campaigning on free trade issues. Their briefing prepared for

7. See, for example, Harrison's introduction to this volume; IMF (1997, chap. 4); UNDP (1999); McKay, Winters, and Kedir (2000); Reimer (2002); Bigman (2002); Berg and Krueger (2003); Bhagwati and Srinivasan (2002); Bourguignon et al. (2002); Prasad et al. (chap. 11 in this volume); Baldwin (2003); Goldberg and Pavcnik (2004); Bolaky and Freund (2004); and Winters, McCulloch, and McKay (2004).

the Doha round of trade talks begins thus: "International trade can be a force for poverty reduction by reducing scarcity, and by creating livelihoods and employment opportunities, but this is not an automatic process. Liberalization is not a panacea for poverty any more than protectionism" (Oxfam 2001, p. 3).

From the other side, we have the *Economist* magazine, a publication established specifically to promote the free market. Their seventy-fifth birthday special issue on capitalism and democracy identified personal greed on behalf of company executives, a vacuum of ownership in publicly traded firms, and an unsavory degree of mutual vested interest between government and businesses as the major threats to capitalism and democracy (Emmott 2003).

Heartening as such progress is, there are a large number of unresolved issues that make it impossible to feel that the globalization debate is close to consensus. A summary of remaining disagreements over globalization, poverty, and inequality in developing countries is tabulated in the appendix. In the remainder of the current section, I consider some of the reasons why such disagreements persist despite the prodigious research effort that has been exerted by economists to resolve them. In essence I see three reasons for the limited success. First, these are very complex and difficult questions to answer. Second, the link between the empirical findings and the policy conclusions has until recently been given insufficient attention. And third, much of the empirical research has not understood the underlying concerns of the critics, and has therefore failed to address the more nuanced but no less pivotal parts of the debate, such as the issues presented in the appendix.

The literature on the impacts of globalization faces the same obstacles that the broader literature on growth faces. The trouble begins with the fact that there is no unambiguous theoretical outcome, and thus everything must be tested empirically (Winters 2000; Agénor 2002). The trouble continues because the observable outcomes—growth, inequality, and poverty—are functions of a very large number of both past and present variables, and they influence these other variables in return. In short, endogeneity plagues empirical research efforts on globalization.

The result is that it is very difficult to prove in the case of an individual country exactly which factor or combination of factors was responsible for its success or lack thereof. For this reason, it is important to consider the experience of a number of countries. In order to do that, comparable individual country case studies must be conducted, or some form of cross-country comparison made.[8] The latter method usually involves statistical analysis based on a cross-country regression model.

---

8. The former method was developed and applied very successfully in two projects, one by Little, Scitovsky, and Scott (1970) at the Organization for Economic Cooperation and Development (OECD) and one led by Bhagwati and Krueger for the National Bureau of Economic Research (NBER; Bhagwati and Srinivasan 2002).

Cross country regression studies have proved extremely useful for identifying correlations between relevant variables; however, they suffer some important methodological limitations when used for policy analysis (Deaton 1995; Ravallion 2003). Primary among these limitations are a lack of exogenous measures of openness, an inability to convincingly establish direction and strength of causality, and the economic simplifications required to use a linear regression framework. These limitations have led several leading economists to conclude that cross-country regressions should not be used as a basis for causal conclusions regarding the impacts of globalization (Bhagwati 2000; Bhagwati and Srinivasan 2002; Bardhan 2003; Ravallion 2003). These well-known limitations are also one of the reasons that critics of economic globalization remain unconvinced by the generally positive findings of such studies.

It is heartening to see that there is a growing acknowledgement of the limitations of a black-box approach to globalization and poverty, and increasing recognition among researchers of the importance of identifying the causal mechanisms through which globalization affects the poor. This approach is increasingly being represented by the contributions of this volume, as well as by Winters (2000, 2002; Winters, McCulloch, and McKay 2004) and the current United Nations University World Institute for Development Economics Research (UNU-WIDER) project on the Impact of Globalization on the World's Poor (UNU-WIDER 2004).

There is, however, a second reason that the empirical evidence to date has failed to convert critics of economic globalization into proponents. The reason is that the literature has not been well targeted toward addressing the remaining reservations that many people have about globalization. The mismatch between the questions currently being asked and the answers people want may be observed with reference to the list of outstanding disagreements in the appendix.

In my opinion, people do not need to be convinced that growth is generally good for the poor or that increased trade is generally good for growth. As will be shown in later sections of this paper, the evidence from reading criticisms of globalization is that people are more interested in the optimal policy mix to maximize the benefits to the poor while minimizing the negative impacts on any subgroup of the poor that is made worse off by such policies. They are also interested in ensuring that growth is economically, socially, and environmentally sustainable. Social sustainability, it is assumed, requires that inequality be kept under a certain limit.

Consider the case of the debate over free trade. Only a very small proportion of critics consider autarky to be an optimal trade policy. The vast majority agrees, like Oxfam, that trade can be beneficial. They disagree, however, with the conclusion that they perceive economists to have reached: that the optimal policy for a developing country is to unilaterally free trade without bargaining for any concessions from rich countries in

return. They are understandably skeptical that such a policy is preferable to the alternative position of a trade policy that includes some trade restrictions, some export support mechanisms, and some environmental, health, or labor regulations that may restrict trade.

Thus, the question in most critics' minds is not "to globalize or not to globalize?" but "what, and how much, to globalize?" This way of thinking may be viewed within the context of the broader debate over pro-poor growth. Both Kanbur (2001) and Ravallion (2003) mention this debate in their papers on globalization and poverty. As Ravallion (2003) says:

> According to some observers "such actions are not needed . . . Growth is sufficient. Period.". . . The basis of this claim is the evidence that poverty reduction has generally come with economic growth. But that misses the point. Those who are saying that growth is not enough are not typically saying that growth does not reduce absolute income poverty. . . . They are saying that combining growth-promoting economic reforms with the right [other] policies . . . will achieve more rapid poverty reduction than would be possible otherwise. (pp. 18–19)

1.3 Measurement of Poverty and Inequality

The purpose of this section, and section 1.4 after it, is to provide a taste of both the technical (this section) and philosophical (next section) issues in the measurement of poverty and inequality that are pertinent to the globalization debate. It is important to understand these issues for two reasons. First, trends in various measures of poverty and inequality are the bread and butter of participants on *both* sides of the globalization debate. Thus, if we wish to understand why the two sides disagree, it is important to understand these trends. That being said, the reader is reminded that, despite the claims of both sides, trends in either direction over the modern period of globalization (usually defined as the time since 1980) do not imply causation. This brings us to the second reason that it is important to understand the debate over poverty and inequality measurement. These measures are necessary inputs to any econometric study that does actually attempt to identify causal links between globalization and poverty or inequality. No matter how sophisticated the theoretical model or econometric method is, the fact remains: garbage in—garbage out.

The importance of improving measurement methodology beyond the current industry standard is argued by Deaton (2004), who says:

> There is no credibility to the claim that globalization has been good for the poor based on a calculation that applies badly measured distributional shares to (upwardly biased) measures of growth from the national accounts. The globalization debate is serious enough that we must genuinely measure the living standards of the poor, not simply assume them. We cannot prove that growth trickles down by assuming that growth

trickles down, nor argue that globalization has reduced poverty without measuring the living standards of the poor. (p. 40)

1.3.1   Poverty

Despite the existence of a multitude of different poverty measures, many of which may be technically superior, the discussion in this section is limited to the world poverty head count. This particular measure was chosen both because it is the simplest one and because it is arguably the most often quoted in the globalization debate. As will be obvious from the discussion that follows, the calculation of even this most simple of measures involves enough technical detail to confuse the inexpert and to promote a vigorous scholarly debate.

Table 1.1 provides a comparison of the most widely cited current estimates of the world poverty head count. It can be seen that even very rigorous authors have produced different estimates of the same statistic. The reasons for these very different results may be largely explained by a few key differences in method. We discuss these differences below. Also included in the discussion are the claims by some authors that all of the estimates in table 1.1 significantly underestimate the level of poverty.

Choosing a Poverty Line

The first step in generating a poverty head count is to choose a poverty line. Since 1991, the standard poverty line has been approximately US$1 per day, in purchasing power parity (PPP) terms. This line was originally chosen as being representative of the poverty lines in low-income countries (Chen and Ravallion 2000). It is also common to report poverty figures for a line set at twice this value, US$2 per day.

The World Bank's $1-per-day and $2-per-day poverty lines have been criticized for being arbitrary, and arbitrarily too low, which means that they underestimate the number of people living in poverty (Wade 2002; Reddy and Pogge 2003). The importance of the choice of poverty line to the estimated head count can be observed in table 1.1. It can be seen that the head count for the current $2-per-day line is more than twice that for the $1-per-day line. More important, the *upward* trend in the head count is more than ten times as high using the $2-per-day line. The significance of the choice of poverty line is also highlighted by the latest poverty estimates from the World Bank (Chen and Ravallion 2004). They find that the number of people living below $1.08 per day fell dramatically from 1981 to 2001, by just under 400 million (representing approximately a halving in the incidence of poverty as a fraction of world population). However, the number of people living between the $1.08 and $2.15 lines increased even more, by around 680 million. As a result, the estimated number living under the $2.15 poverty line actually increased by 285 million between 1981 and 2001.

Table 1.1   Comparison of recent world poverty estimates

1998 head count (billions)	1998 incidence (%)	Average change 1987–98 (millions per annum)	Total change 1987–98 (%)	Poverty line ($/day)	Source of mean	Currency conversion	Source
1.20	24.0	+1.4	-4.35	1.08	HHS	WBPPP93	Chen and Ravallion (2000), tables 2 and 3
2.80	56.0	+22.9	-5.02	2.15	HHS	WBPPP93	Chen and Ravallion (2000), tables 2 and 3
0.35	6.7	-3.3	-2.1	1.08	NAcc	WBPPP93	Sala-i-Martin (2002b), table 1
0.97	18.6	-20.0	-8.4	2.15	NAcc	WBPPP93	Sala-i-Martin (2002b), table 1
0.46	9.2	-30.8	-9.9	1.08	NAcc	WBPPP93	Bhalla (2003). table 1
0.37	7.4	-22.6	-7.4	1.15	NAcc	WBPPP96	Bhalla (2003). table 1

Notes: Average change = total change in the head count over the period 1987–98, divided by eleven years. HHS = household survey data. NAcc = national accounts data. WBPPP93 = World Bank purchasing power parity conversion using base year 1993; uses Elteto, Koves, and Szulc method. Chen and Ravallion (2000) are essentially responsible for generating the most recent World Bank figures. 1998 head count and Average change for Bhalla (2003) were calculated from his reported incidence figures, using the same population size as Chen and Ravallion (2000). Sala-i-Martin's incidence is based on the total world population rather than the population of developing countries, as used by the other authors.

While acknowledging that there was an element of arbitrariness to the original choice of $1 and $2 per day, Deaton (2001) argues that the data consistency losses from defining a new poverty line would outweigh any benefits obtained.

Estimating the Incomes of Different Groups within One Country

There are two main methods of estimating the economic well-being of the population of a country. The first is to use national accounts data to estimate the mean income, and household-level survey data to estimate the income distribution. The second is to use household survey data to directly calculate the incomes of each decile in the income distribution.

Deaton (2003) explains that the main difference between these two methods arises from the fact that the household surveys (HHSs) lead to a lower estimate of average income than the national accounts and that the difference between the two increases as incomes increase. This is true when comparing richer and poorer countries at the same time period, and when comparing the same countries over time. There are three main causes of this discrepancy. First, richer people tend to understate the income by more than poorer people. Second, richer people tend to respond less often to household income or expenditure surveys. Third, according to Deaton (2003), national accounts data tend to overestimate the growth rate of per capita income. On the other hand, Bhalla (2003) has argued vigorously that the national accounts estimates are far more accurate, and accuses the World Bank of biasing its estimates in order to obtain more funding.

The impact of the difference between these two methods is illustrated in table 1.1. It is clear that HHS-based estimates produce significantly more pessimistic estimates of both the total number of poor and the reductions in the number of poor.

Maintaining Consistency across Countries

The third contentious issue in the calculation of world poverty figures is the way in which incomes are compared across countries. The main criticism is that the consumption basket used to estimate PPPs does not reflect the consumption patterns of the poor (Wade 2002; Reddy and Pogge 2003; Deaton 2001). The baskets of goods and services used in all the World Bank's PPP calculations are based on a representative national consumption bundle, not the bundle of goods typically consumed by the poor. This means that because basic needs are relatively more expensive in poor countries the use of such broad-gauge PPP measures overestimates the purchasing power of the incomes of the poor in developing countries. Wade (2002) and Reddy and Pogge (2003) estimate this effect to be on the order of 30 to 40 percent.

A related issue in the comparison of incomes across countries is the way in which the prices are combined to produce PPP exchange rates. The

World Bank uses the Elteto, Koves, and Szulc (EKS) method, while the Penn World Tables are based on the Geary-Khamis (GK) method. According to Dowrick (2001) the GK method tends to overestimate the incomes of the poor, while the EKS method leads to a very slight underestimation. This issue is discussed further in the section on the calculation of inequality measures.

Maintaining Consistency across Time

The method used by the World Bank and the other authors in table 1.1 involves comparison between countries on PPP terms in some specified year, followed by country-by-country, year-to-year adjustments in real income based on national consumer price indexes (CPIs). The problem with this methodology, as noted by Deaton (2001), is that the use of a different base year causes changes in poverty estimates that overshadow the magnitude of any real trend. Among other things, this means that poverty head counts using different base years cannot be compared. As noted by Wade (2002), it was the comparison of head counts based on two different PPP base years that generated the much-cited claim by the World Bank that the poverty head count had decreased by 200 million over the period 1980–98.

In addition to the arbitrary changes in poverty head count that are brought on by updating the PPP base year, there may also be systematic biases. Reddy and Pogge (2003) argue that ongoing updating of the PPP base year will cause the overestimation of the incomes of the poor to get progressively worse as average incomes rise. This means that over time, as the base year is updated, the poverty head count will fall, irrespective of what is actually happening to the poor.

The preceding discussion has illustrated that the official World Bank poverty figures are simultaneously attacked from the left on the grounds that they outrageously underestimate the extent of poverty and overestimate the gains made in recent years, and attacked from the right on the grounds that they do exactly the opposite. Both the right and the left claim that the bank is manipulating its chosen methodology for political reasons. This is an unfortunate state of affairs, which makes it very difficult for disinterested participants in the globalization debate to form an objective opinion.

There are undoubtedly weaknesses in the current poverty accounting practices of the World Bank that leave it vulnerable to such criticisms. Some of these weaknesses are implicit in the attempt to summarize all the deprivation in the entire world into a single number, and will never be resolved. However, some of the weaknesses can be reduced as methodology continues to evolve and improve. A good first step would be to follow Deaton's (2001) recommendation that a locally validated set of PPP poverty lines be developed and then held fixed, thus eliminating the large variations brought on by changes in PPP base year.

1.3.2   Inequality

The numbers debate over global inequality has every bit of the complexity of that over poverty, plus one additional layer. That additional layer is the question of what sample best represents world inequality. Should we consider every citizen as a member of a single global income distribution? Or should we recognize the existence of national borders and talk about within-country and between-country components of inequality? The answer, of course, is that each measure has its different merits, and each will be preferable in different contexts.

This section will focus on world inequality calculated assuming that there are no borders, referred to from here on as "world inequality."[9] This measure has been chosen on the basis of two major merits. First, it is the concept most analogous to the world poverty head count, which was discussed under the previous heading. Second, it is the concept that most represents what globalization is all about. Indeed, one of the reasons that globalization has been associated with a rise in concern over global inequality could be that people are beginning to think more as global citizens. Consumers in rich countries see that the global economy connects them to the very poorest farmers in developing countries, and that makes them feel that they have the power, indeed the responsibility, to make the world a fairer place.

The one major disadvantage of the no-borders approach to calculating inequality is that it is possibly the least relevant to policy analysis. Thus, it is worth spending a paragraph to summarize a few broadly accepted facts about the other measures and their trends in recent decades.[10] To begin with, everyone agrees that the lion's share, of the order of two-thirds or more, of inequality in the world is due to between-country inequality, and that this share has changed little since 1980. Most experts would agree that since 1980 within-country inequality has increased in more countries than it has decreased. Most would also agree that between-country inequality has increased if all countries are given equal weight. On the other hand, many would also agree that between-country inequality has decreased if countries are weighted by population.[11] Finally, almost all would agree that

9. Recently two excellent papers (Sutcliffe 2004; Svedberg 2004) have been published that provide a more comprehensive picture of the debate over inequality in the age of globalization. These papers cover, among other points, the debate over population weighting in intercountry inequality estimates.

10. This paragraph is based on the reading of the following papers: Dowrick and Akmal (2005), Milanovic (2002), Sala-i-Martin (2002a, 2002b), Wade (2002), Ravallion (2003), Crook (2003), Galbraith (2003), Fischer (2003), and Loungani (2003).

11. This latter finding, however, is dependent on whether incomes are compared on exchange rate or PPP terms, with PPP the more widely accepted basis and the one that more often leads to the conclusion that inequality has fallen. Dowrick and Akmal (2005) argue that both exchange rate and PPP are biased and that, when the bias is removed from PPP, very little change is found in population-weighted between-country inequality over the period 1980–97.

the driving force underlying any inequality calculations over the period has been the fact that major economies, especially at the very poor end (China and India), but also at the very rich end (the United States and United Kingdom), experienced a combination of growth and increased within-country inequality.

World inequality, the measure that we are mostly concerned with in this chapter, is essentially the sum of between-country and within-country inequality. This means that the fact that India and China both grew and experienced increased internal inequality causes estimates of changes in world inequality to consistently lie between the estimates of changes in between-country inequality calculated using alternatively unit weights or population weights for each country.[12] It is, therefore, not surprising that some authors find that world inequality is increasing, while others find it is decreasing.

Although there are many variations in methodology for calculating world inequality, most of the variation in results arises from two sources, both of which were also important to the debate over poverty head count. The first is the use of national accounts data versus HHS data to calculate mean national income. The second is the use of the PPP versus exchange rate to convert between incomes in different countries.[13] The impact of these methodological differences on the results obtained can be seen in table 1.2, and in graphical form in figure 1.1. Note that although the results presented in table 1.2 and figure 1.1 are based only on the Gini coefficient, the qualitative conclusions of each of the methodologies are robust to the use of several common measures of inequality.

As was the case with the poverty estimates, the use of household survey data gives a significantly more pessimistic view of recent decades. Using HHS data only, Milanovic (2002, 2005) finds that world inequality *increased* at a rate of around 0.2 Gini points per year. Using national accounts data to find average incomes, Sala-i-Martin (2002a) finds that world inequality decreased at the rate of about 0.2 Gini points per year over the same period.[14] This is despite the fact that the two had very similar estimates for the initial inequality in 1988.

The work of Dowrick and Akmal (2005) and Dowrick (2001) illustrates

12. Estimates of a potential upward trend in world inequality are lower than those of between-country inequality because "world inequality" implicitly weights countries by population. On the other hand, because world inequality accounts for the rise in within-country inequality, the trend is generally higher than that suggested by population-weighted between-country inequality alone.

13. There are several methods for calculating PPP; however, most studies use the Penn World Tables PPP figures. These are based on the GK method. See Summers and Heston (1991) for details.

14. Note that the two authors also differ in the PPP conversion method. Sala-i-Martin uses the Penn World Tables data based on the GK method. Milanovic uses the EKS method. As is explained below, this difference also works to exaggerate the difference between the inequality trends identified by the two authors.

Table 1.2   Comparison of some recent world inequality estimates

Gini (start year)	Gini (end year)	Rate of change	No. of countries	Source of mean	Income conversion	Source
78.2 (1988)	80.5 (1993)	0.46	91	HHS	XR	Milanovic (2002), table 16
62.8 (1988)	66.0 (1993)	0.64	91	HHS	EKSPPP	Milanovic (2002), table 16
62.8 (1988)	64.5 (1998)	0.19	91	HHS	EKSPPP	Milanovic (2005)
62.7 (1988)	61.5 (1993)	−0.24	125	NAcc	GKPPP	Sala-i-Martin (2002a), table 1
62.7 (1988)	60.9 (1998)	−0.18	125	NAcc	GKPPP	Sala-i-Martin (2002a), table 1
64.2 (1978)	60.9 (1998)	−0.17	125	NAcc	GKPPP	Sala-i-Martin (2002a), table 1
63.8 (1980)	61.5 (1993)	−0.18	125	NAcc	GKPPP	Sala-i-Martin (2002a), table 1
65.9 (1980)	63.6 (1993)	−0.18	46	NAcc	GKPPP	Dowrick and Akmal (2005), table 5
77.9 (1980)	82.4 (1993)	0.37	46	NAcc	XR	Dowrick and Akmal (2005), table 5
69.8 (1980)	71.1 (1993)	0.15	46	NAcc	Afriat	Dowrick and Akmal (2005), table 5

Notes: Rate of change = total change in the Gini from start year to end year divided by number of years between. HHS = household survey data. NAcc = national accounts data. XR = exchange rate. EKSPPP = purchasing power parity calculated with the Elteto, Koves, and Szulc method. GKPPP = purchasing power parity using Penn World Tables data, based on the Geary-Khamis method. Afriat = an alternative PPP conversion designed to eliminate the biases typically present in GKPPP. See Dowrick and Akmal (2001) for details.

the sensitivity of inequality calculations to the choice of currency conversion when national accounts data are used to find average incomes. Dowrick and Akmal (2005) argue that both exchange rates and PPPs based on the GK method are biased means of conversion.[15] To correct for these biases, they recommend and apply a PPP measure based on an Afriat index which they argue is a true money-metric measure of relative utility. Not surprisingly, both the level and the trend in inequality based on Dowrick and Akmal's Afriat index lie between the corresponding values based on GK PPP and exchange rate. On balance, the Afriat index shows a very slight increase in inequality over the period 1980–93.

According to Sala-i-Martin (2002a), the major difference between his

15. Dowrick (2001) discusses the EKS method of calculating PPP in addition to the GK method. He finds that EKS measures of relative incomes are much closer to the "true" Afriat measures than GK measures. He also finds that whereas the GK measure leads to a downward bias in estimates of inequality between countries, the EKS measure leads to a slight upward bias.

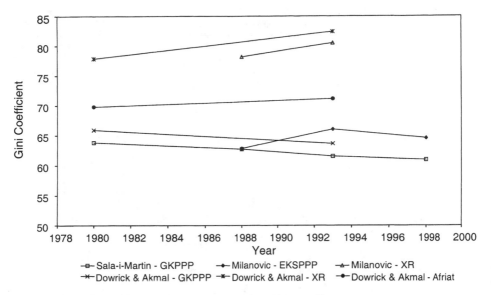

Fig. 1.1   Comparison of some estimates of world inequality
Note: See table 1.2 notes for explanation of abbreviations.

methodology and that of Dowrick and Akmal is that he includes a larger number of countries in his sample. Sala-i-Martin notes that the bias in the countries that are excluded from Dowrick and Akmal's sample leads to an *underestimate* of the increases in inequality over their chosen time period. This would suggest that if the larger sample of Sala-i-Martin were combined with the unbiased PPP conversion of Dowrick and Akmal, we would find that world inequality rose slightly over the period 1980–93.

1.4   Concepts of Poverty and Inequality

The central question in this paper is why some people believe that globalization is bad for the poor while others believe quite the opposite. The previous two sections have argued that part of the answer to this question is that the technical literature on globalization and poverty faces methodological issues, some of which simply may not be resolvable to the satisfaction of all sides. However, if technical issues were the only cause, then we would expect to see a world populated by people sitting on the globalization fence, who are awaiting further evidence before coming down on either. This is clearly not the world in which we live.

The following two sections propose two explanations for why the critics have been able to come to such strong conclusions based on the existing ev-

idence.[16] First, in the current section, I argue that there are subtle differences in values held by critics and proponents, which lead them to interpret the evidence differently. Specifically, these differences lead them to have different interpretations of value-laden phrases such as "worsening poverty" and "growing inequality." Then in section 1.5 I argue that critics and proponents interpret the technical evidence differently because they have different opinions on the "deep facts," that is, the fundamental processes underlying globalization.[17]

In arguing the importance of values as filters through which people process facts that are presented to them, I follow the tradition of economists and social thinkers such as Robbins (1932), Samuelson (1947), Graaff (1962), and Robinson (1964). More recently, Dasgupta (2005) says, "facts can be as subject to dispute as are values, in part because facts and values are often entangled" (p. 3).

The implication of people's inherently filtered interpretation of evidence is that, although economists should continue to make every effort to improve the quality of the facts on globalization and poverty, we should not expect that this strategy alone will ever end the debate. As Putnam (1993) writes, "It is all well and good to describe hypothetical cases in which two people 'agree on the facts and disagree about values,' but . . . when and where did a Nazi and an anti-Nazi, a communist and a social democrat, a fundamentalist and a liberal . . . agree on the facts?" (p. 146).

1.4.1   Poverty

This section seeks to identify and explain the concepts of poverty that are most often employed by critics of economic globalization. It will show that the concepts employed by critics tend to be ones that lead to a more pessimistic conclusion about the impact of globalization on poverty. This choice of concepts by critics could be viewed as simply a cynical means of supporting their prior position. However, this section will argue that their choice of definition of poverty is equally well explained by values and social preferences that many critics hold.

This section builds on the work of Ravi Kanbur (2001), who identified several dimensions along which conceptions of poverty tend to vary:

- Total number of poor versus poverty incidence
- Monetary versus multidimensional measures
- Level of aggregation
- Time horizon

16. Although the discussion in this paper focuses on why the critics have formed strong conclusions against globalization, the principles here could equally be used to explain to an audience of critics or skeptics why the proponents of globalization have been able to form such strong convictions on the topic.

17. Dasgupta (2005) describes "deep facts" as "the pathways that characterise social, political, and ecological systems" (p. 3).

Numbers versus Incidence

Both Ravallion (2003) and Kanbur (2001) observe that the relative importance of the *total number of poor* and the *incidence of poverty* is one of the major points of difference in the globalization debate. Academic economists and international development agencies such as the World Bank and UNDP rely almost entirely on incidence as the appropriate measure, while critics of economic globalization refer almost without exception to the total number of people living in poverty. The following "globalization facts and figures" reported by the International Forum on Globalization (IFG; 2001) illustrate this focus.

Excluding China, there are 100 million more poor people in developing countries than a decade ago.—The World Bank, Annual Review of Development Effectiveness, 1999

Since 1980, economic decline or stagnation has affected 100 countries, reducing the incomes of 1.6 billion people. For 70 of these countries, average incomes are less in the mid-1990s than in 1980, and in 43, less than in 1970.—United Nations Human Development Report, 1999

We can understand the different focus of the two groups very easily if we consider the advantages and disadvantages of the two concepts. If, for example, we want to make intercountry comparisons, then poverty incidence makes much more sense as a measure.[18] Poverty incidence also allows the poverty outcomes of a policy to be evaluated independent of the impact of population growth. These are all things that economists and development specialists wish to do. These poverty professionals also tend to believe that poverty incidence is a better indicator of the ease with which poverty could be eliminated in the next period.[19] Thus, a decrease in the poverty incidence is considered to be progress against poverty, even if the total number of poor has not changed or has risen slightly, because the country is now in a better position to fight poverty in the next period. It has also been argued by Sala-i-Martin (2002b) that a veil-of-ignorance argument suggests that poverty incidence is a more appropriate welfare measure than poverty head count. He asks where we would prefer our children to be born: "in a country of a million people with half a million poor (poverty rate of 50%) or in a country of two million people and 600,000 poor (a poverty rate of 33%)."

For people outside the economics profession, the utility of a poverty

18. It is possible, however, to conceive of alternative measures that could be used for intercountry comparisons. For example, one could compare "poverty reduction rates" in much the same way that GDP growth is used as the primary measure of overall economic performance.

19. Consider, for example, two countries that both have one million poor people. One country has only one thousand rich people, and the other has ten million rich people. It is obvious that the latter country is in a much better position financially to eradicate poverty.

measure as an analytical tool is less important. Their focus tends to be directly on the goal, and that goal is to minimize the number of people who are deprived of basic needs. Further, many would argue that there are ways in which the total number of people remaining poor is a better measure of how easy it will be to eradicate poverty in the future. This view is based on an environmental-limits or neo-Malthusian perspective.[20]

As it turns out, whether one uses total number of poor or poverty incidence does make a difference to the conclusions that one draws from an assessment of world poverty trends. Although there is significant variation in the estimates obtained using different methods or different time periods, all of the estimates show a decrease in the *incidence* of poverty since the 1980s.[21] The total *number* of extreme poor, however, has been variously found to increase (World Bank 2000–2001), stay the same (World Bank 2001), slightly decrease (Chen and Ravallion 2004), or significantly decrease (World Bank 2002).[22] Excluding China, or using a higher poverty line, produces evidence of a significant increase in the total number of poor (Chen and Ravallion 2004).[23]

Monetary versus Multidimensional Measures

Kanbur (2001) argues that critics of globalization tend to think of poverty as a multidimensional concept rather than something that can be fully captured by measures of average income or expenditure. In this regard, critics are now on the same side as the majority of development economists (Thorbecke 2003; Kanji and Barrientos 2002; Kanbur 2001). Kanbur (2001) notes that health and education outcomes are now agreed to be "on a par with income in assessing poverty and the consequences of economic policy" (p. 1085). Evidence of the importance now placed on health and education outcomes is provided by the UNDP's *Human Development Report 2003,* the World Bank's *World Development Report 2000,* and the World Bank and UNDP's joint efforts on the "Millennium Goals."

Though harder to quantify, *empowerment, participation,* and *vulnerability to shocks* are also gaining acceptance as important dimensions of poverty (Kanbur 2001; World Bank 2000–2001). The inclusion of these additional dimensions seems justified by the priorities of the poor themselves.

20. The argument is that if the creation of goods ultimately depends on environmental resources, and those resources are limited, then an increase in the number of poor people in the world is always a bad sign. Thus, this group tends to see poverty more as the result of lack of access to resources than as a lack of economic activity.
21. For discussions of the issues involved in calculating poverty estimates, and the different results obtained, see Wade (2002), Ravallion (2003), and Deaton (2001, 2002) as well as the original source articles cited.
22. Note that the World Bank (2002) estimate of a 200 million reduction in the number of poor is based on comparison of numbers generated by two incompatible methodologies (Wade 2002).
23. In this paragraph references to the number of extreme poor are based on a poverty line set at approximately $1 per day, while the higher poverty line referred to is $2.15 per day.

A major study, *Voices of the Poor: Can Anyone Hear Us?* was published by the World Bank in 2000 (Narayan et al. 2000). The authors found that poverty was indeed multidimensional and that illiteracy, illness, humiliation, absence of basic infrastructure, and lack of material well-being and physical assets (as opposed to income) formed the major issues.

The opinions of the poor also seem to suggest that the impact of globalization on their lives is less positive than measures of changes in their average income would suggest. Graham (2001) reports that the perceptions of the poor and middle-class of their welfare change from national integration and liberalization are systematically below what is suggested by their measured income change. Similarly, as Short and Wolfenson say in the foreword to *Voices of the Poor,* "What poor people share with us is sobering. The majority of them feel they are worse off and more insecure than in the past" (Narayan et al. 2000).

People's self-perceptions, of course, are always prone to subjectivity and bias. So what do external measures of poverty's other dimensions suggest about the impact of globalization? As proponents of globalization like to note, there have been significant improvements in literacy rates, life expectancy, and infant mortality over the last twenty-five years (e.g., Fischer 2003; Loungani 2003). As with the monetary measures, however, the use of numbers rather than incidence tells a somewhat less laudable story. For example, while the world rate of illiteracy fell by a third between 1980 and 2002, the total number of illiterate adults in the world decreased by a mere 1.4 percent over the same period.[24] Similar patterns hold for other measures, such as infant mortality and access to clean water and sanitation.

Moving beyond an analysis of trends, Wei and Wu (2002) find evidence from an econometric study using data from seventy-nine countries that a faster increase in trade openness is associated with a faster increase in life expectancy and a faster reduction in infant mortality. However, they find no corresponding evidence for financial integration. Also on the issue of health, Deaton (2004) argues that one's perception of the impact of globalization is also dependent on what one means by globalization. He suggests that the things economists tend to think of in regard to globalization, such as increased incomes and faster diffusion of health-related knowledge and technologies, are beneficial to the health of the poor. On the other hand, some of the institutional aspects of globalization, which are the focus of many critics' concerns, may not be so beneficial. In particular, he

24. These data are from the World Resources Institute's EarthTrends database. The world literacy rate rose from 69.3 percent in 1980 to 80.2 percent in 2002. The total number of illiterate in the world rose from 883 million in 1980 to a peak of 890 million in 1988 and has been falling steadily since then to around 871 million in 2002. This was helped in large part by China, in which the number of illiterate has been falling steadily from 222 million in 1980 to 145 million in 2002, and hampered by India, where the number has been rising steadily from 250 million in 1980 to 291 million in 2002.

suggests that the General Agreement on Trade in Services (GATS) may restrict the freedom of governments to shape their health delivery systems, and that the TRIPs agreement may make provision of drugs in poor countries, particularly for HIV and AIDS, more expensive than necessary.

With regard to voice and empowerment, proponents of globalization point out that the period of globalization has been accompanied by the spread of democracy (e.g., Fischer 2003; Micklethwait and Wooldridge 2000). In contrast, as will be explained in section 1.5, many critics believe that voice and empowerment are among the first casualties of globalization. They believe that globalization shifts decision making to higher and higher levels of government, well beyond the potential for meaningful democratic participation from the poor.[25] These two opinions are not, however, as incompatible as they at first appear. Proponents of globalization seem to be talking about whether the system in each country is fundamentally democratic, while critics of globalization are talking about the realities of voice and participation within those countries that are already ostensibly democratic.

Aside from the impact on democratic participation, there are two other major claims made against globalization on the basis of nonmonetary dimensions of poverty. The first is that it increases vulnerability to shocks, and the second is that reduced tariff revenues and neoliberal policies associated with globalization lead to cutbacks in government services important to the poor.

Kanbur (2001) provides a list of the type of services that people envisage as being harmed by globalization but that are not recorded in monetary measures of poverty:

> If the bus service that takes a woman from her village to her sister's village is canceled, it will not show up in these [monetary] measures. If the health post in the urban slum runs out of drugs, it will not show up. If the primary school text books disappear, or if the teacher does not show up to teach, it will not show up. (p. 1087)

Thankfully, there has been a large amount of research effort directed at evaluating the concerns over both vulnerability and government service provision. To attempt to summarize the conclusions of this research is to do a grave injustice to this extensive literature. However, for our purposes, with the help of Winters, McCulloch, and McKay (2004), we offer the following. First, there is agreement that capital account liberalization can lead to increased macroeconomic volatility in developing countries (Bhagwati 1998; Fischer 2003; Prasad et al. 2003). Similarly, there is evidence that the removal of government price support mechanisms can increase volatility of income for those dependent on the sale of agricultural commodities.

---

25. See IFG (2002). See also Bardhan and Mookherjee (2000), who claim that political centralization may exacerbate problems of capture in the presence of inequality.

However, the impact of other aspects of liberalization, such as trade liberalization, has been found to be sometimes stabilizing and sometimes destabilizing. Finally, there is little evidence to support the claim that trade liberalization and structural adjustment packages in developing countries lead to cutbacks in the provision of public goods for the poor (Winters, McCulloch, and McKay 2004).

Level of Aggregation and Time Horizon

It is often perplexing to economists to hear people refer to globalization 'worsening poverty' even in situations in which it is clear that the total number of people in poverty has fallen. Part of the explanation for this puzzling view is that many people consider the phrase "worsening poverty" to be apposite in any situation in which a significant number of already poor people are made poorer. Kanbur (2001) attributes the greater concern that critics of globalization have for those who lose from the process to a smaller geographical perspective, or lower level of aggregation, and different time horizon. He explains the smaller geographic perspective as follows: "For an NGO working with street children in Accra, or for a local official coping with increased poverty among indigenous peoples in Chiapas, it is cold comfort to be told, 'but national poverty has gone down'" (p. 1087).

With regard to time horizon, Kanbur suggests that critics of globalization have at once a shorter-term and a longer-term worldview than many of its proponents. The shorter-term view is the one that leads critics to feel particularly concerned about the loss of income by certain subgroups as a result of globalization-induced changes in the economy. This short-term view is contrasted with the medium-term perspective of economists. In the medium term it is argued that globalization will promote new industries, and better jobs will become available to replace those that had been lost.

According to critics of globalization, the pertinent question is whether the people who lost their livelihoods in the short term are likely to be the same ones who gain a new and better source of income in the medium term. In the case of middle-aged or older people, or where lack of education and poor geographical mobility limit access to new opportunities, it may be the case that the losers remain losers, for the rest of their lives.[26]

The problem with Kanbur's explanation based on geographical scope and time horizon is that it does not fully complete the picture. His examples of nongovernmental organization (NGO) workers and local officials working with the poor do not explain why large numbers of people who work in

26. Ravallion (2003) provides some empirical evidence in support of this concern. H claims that, when analyzing the poverty impact of economic integration, "it is quite commo to find considerable churning under the surface. Some people have escaped poverty while o ers have fallen into poverty, even though the overall poverty rate has moved rather li (p. 16).

office jobs in rich countries also appear to use the losses of certain sub-groups as their criterion for claiming that globalization has worsened poverty.

I propose a more basic explanation: that people simply do not like to see poor people being made worse off. This could be interpreted as an indication that critics of globalization support a Rawlsian notion of social welfare, as opposed to the utilitarian notion that is popular among economists. Another explanation is that although the rational side of most personalities will tend toward a utilitarian perspective, the social side of those same personalities will find personal tragedies such as the suicide of South Korean farmer Lee Kyung Hae at the World Trade Organization meeting in Cancun highly compelling. As behavioral economists are finding more and more, we are often not consistent in our framing of such complex values. More recent evidence from behavioral experiments suggests yet another potential explanation: the critics are simply displaying a very common human characteristic. After conducting experiments based on hypothetical allocation decisions (unrelated to globalization), Baron (1995) finds that

> People are reluctant to harm some people in order to help others, even when the harm is less than the forgone help (the harm resulting from not acting). The present studies use hypothetical scenarios to argue that these judgments go against what the subjects themselves would take to be the best overall outcome. (p. 1)

It seems fair to conclude, then, that the balance between greater good and personal losses is a dilemma to which there is no easy solution. Balancing stakeholder and national interests is the perennial challenge for policymakers. Part of the reason that globalization is so unpopular may be that, in order to get past the powerful stakeholders such as the owners of capital in protected industries, policymakers have had to shift the balance far toward being concerned with the greater national good. In such an environment, the voices of already marginalized groups such as peasants and indigenous peoples have almost no chance of being heard.

Seen in the worst light, those middle-class white kids protesting in the street in their wealthy countries are trying to stop something that has made many of the world's poor better off. Seen in the best light, they are trying to give a voice to those who otherwise have none, and pushing policymakers to think harder about how to soften those sharp edges of globalization.

1.4.2   Inequality

Critics of corporate globalization tend to consider the level of inequality to be an important component of social welfare, independent of its impact on poverty. If there is a trade-off between fairness and efficiency, they will lean toward fairness. Interestingly, the mounting evidence from be-

havioral economics research is that they are not alone. As Fehr and Schmidt (2000) find, "many people are strongly motivated by concerns for fairness and reciprocity" (p. 1). And as Rogoff (2004) says, "In the long run, global social welfare depends fundamentally on fairness and happiness" (p. 4).[27]

While the deep psychological reasons that people are concerned with fairness are still being unraveled, some argue that there is a practical basis for concern with inequality. Wade (2002) provides an example of the practical justification in his argument for why we should be concerned about exchange rate–based inequality between countries:

> It may, for example, predispose the elites to be more corrupt as they compare themselves to elites in remains why some people think that globalization leads to rich countries and squeeze their own populations in order to maintain a comparable standard of living. It may encourage the educated people of poor countries to migrate to rich countries, and encourage unskilled people to seek illegal entry.[28] It may generate conflict between states, and—because the market-exchange-rate income gap is so big—make it cheap for rich states to intervene to support one side or another in civil conflict. (p. 21)

In its *Global Trends 2015* report (IFG 2002, p. 30), the U.S. Central Intelligence Agency (CIA) also seemed to think inequality was worth worrying about. According to them, globalization would create

> an even wider gap between regional winners and losers than exists today. [Globalization's] evolution will be rocky, marked by chronic volatility and a widening economic divide . . . deepening economic stagnation, political instability and cultural alienation. [It] will foster political, ethnic, ideological and religious extremism, along with the violence that often accompanies it.

Given, then, that inequality is a common concern, the question still remains why some people think that globalization leads to more inequality and others think it leads to less. As with poverty, the explanation lies largely in differences in what people really mean by inequality and worsening inequality. Indeed, the debate over what type of inequality we should worry about is even more intense than that over poverty. The intensity of the debate seems to be fueled by the fact that inequality is a genuinely complex concept. Concepts of inequality vary significantly depending on the

---

27. In this instance Rogoff is referring to the "long run" as the time after which absolute poverty will have been eliminated. As he says in the same paper, "we can expect that as global income inexorably expands over the next century, issues of inequality, rather than subsistence, will increasingly take center stage in the poverty debate" (p. 1).

28. Straubhaar (quoted in IMF 1997, chap. 4) finds that net emigration from a poor country to a rich one tends to diminish when the wage differential between the two countries falls below 1:4.

person and on the framing of the issue presented to each person (Devooght 2003; Litchfield 1999).

In order to keep this paper a manageable length, I must once again apologize to an extensive literature (this time on the philosophical, axiomatic, and social bases for selecting inequality measures), and move on to the evidence that directly relates to globalization. In short, I will argue that critics of globalization tend to think in either absolute dollar terms or in terms of polarization between the top and bottom of the income distribution. They are also particularly concerned with the distribution of the gains from globalization. In contrast, proponents of globalization, and most academic economists, tend to use distributional measures of relative inequality, of which the Gini coefficient is the most popular.[29]

Inequality in the Absolute Gains from Globalization

According to both Kanbur (2002) and Ravallion (2003), emphasis on *absolute* as opposed to *relative* inequality is the source of much of the perception that globalization is increasing inequality.[30] In support of this, Ravallion quotes experimental evidence in which 40 percent of participants were found to think about inequality in absolute terms. To explain what he means by absolute inequality, he provides the following example. Consider an economy that has only two households, one with an income of $1,000 and the other with an income of $10,000. Distribution-neutral growth in the economy of 100 percent would double both incomes and leave the Gini coefficient unchanged. However, the poorer household now has $2,000 and the richer $20,000. This means that the richer household gained ten times as much as the poor household. Many people would not consider this a fair outcome and would probably describe it as an example of increased inequality, despite the fact that *relative* inequality is unchanged.

The example above is also relevant to the sweatshop debate. Consider the case of a multinational corporation that opens a factory in a developing country. The multinational provides better pay and conditions than similar local enterprises: say, a wage of $2.20 per day rather than $1.80 per day. For the poor and unskilled in the local community, taking a job in the new factory represents an improvement over their previous standard of living. Meanwhile, as a result of transferring to the new, cheaper location, the multinational makes cost savings of $18 per worker per day. Six dollars of this saving is spent on paying off the investment in the new factory, six dol-

29. Different statistics regarding the population over which inequality is being measured have also been used to advantage by both sides of the debate. This issue was discussed in subsection 3.2.
30. A pleasing development, perhaps in response to this observation, is that two recent surveys of the debate on inequality and globalization (Sutcliffe 2004; Svedberg 2004) include figures on and discussion of trends in absolute inequality.

lars is passed on to consumers, primarily in rich countries, and corporate executives collect six dollars as a bonus.

Despite the fact that the above situation clearly describes a Pareto improvement, many critics of globalization would consider it a bad outcome on the basis that it was unfair. They would rather see a greater share of the gains going to the poor workers. This issue is closely related to what Birdsall (2003) claims is the major reason for the popular perception that globalization is good for the rich and bad for the poor. According to her,

> We economists (and I put myself in that group) are missing the point. True, world poverty may be declining and global inequality no longer rising. But that does not mean that the global economy is fair or just. . . . Even relatively benign outcomes may belie fundamentally unequal opportunities in an unfair global game. (p. 3)

Combining the insights of Ravallion and Birdsall, we may conclude that many critics are concerned about inequality in absolute gains and in opportunities for gain from globalization.

Polarization and Top-Driven Inequality

Changes in inequality in absolute terms are no doubt important in the minds of many critics. However, a perusal of the internet suggests that there is a second concept of inequality that is also popular among critics of globalization. The statistics most often quoted in support of the negative impact of globalization on inequality are, in fact, measures of the *level* of *relative* inequality (compare *changes* in *absolute* inequality as discussed above). However, unlike economists' measures, which are based on the entire income distribution, the figures reported by critics of economic globalization usually refer simply to the polarization of the distribution.[31] That is, they focus only on the two ends of the distribution, which suggests a particular concern with top-driven inequality. Wade (2001) provides an excellent example of the figures quoted on polarization:

> Global inequality is worsening rapidly. . . . Technological change and financial liberalization result in a disproportionately fast increase in the number of households at the extreme rich end, without shrinking the distribution at the poor end. . . . From 1988 to 1993, the share of the world income going to the poorest 10 percent of the world's population fell by over a quarter, whereas the share of the richest 10 percent rose by 8 percent. (p. 72)

Statements such as this, which refer to changes in the relative incomes of the top and bottom deciles, are typical of the criticisms of economic glob-

---

31. The same two recent surveys of inequality and globalization (Sutcliffe 2004; Svedberg 2004) that gave attention to absolute inequality also include significant discussion of polarization measures. This shift toward more broadly appealing inequality concepts is to be applauded.

alization that originate in relatively rich countries. However, according to Graham (2001), top-driven inequality may also be important to the negative perceptions of globalization among the poor and middle class in poorer countries. Graham's argument is that by providing an ever-higher benchmark for comparison, top-driven inequality leads people to underestimate their own income gains.

Knowing that many people think of inequality in terms of absolute gains and polarization, rather than in terms of Gini coefficients, goes some way to explaining the confidence with which critics of economic globalization assert that it causes increased inequality. The empirical evidence does suggest that people do tend to gain from globalization in proportion to the amount of wealth they already had.[32] Moreover, as Sutcliffe (2004) points out, polarization measures have tended to increase in recent times even when the Gini coefficient is falling.[33]

1.5   Dissatisfaction with the Process of Globalization

> Capitalism is the astounding belief that the most wickedest of men will do the most wickedest of things for the greatest good of everyone.
> —John Maynard Keynes

> This powerful network, which may aptly, if loosely, be called the Wall Street–Treasury complex, is unable to look much beyond the interest of Wall Street, which it equates with the good of the world.
> —Jagdish Bhagwati (1998)

According to Bayesian learning theories, the conclusion that a person draws from a given set of information is highly dependent on the prior opinion of that person. Similarly, when faced with a number of conflicting information sources of unknown quality, a person will place the most weight on those sources that agree with their priors (Tenenbaum 2003). These theories provide a very substantial explanation for why, despite the vast research effort directed at proving whether globalization is good or bad for the poor, large differences in opinion remain. The purpose of this section is to explain why so many people form negative priors about the impact of globalization on the poor.

---

32. This, as Ravallion (2003) points out, is the correct way to interpret Dollar and Kraay (2001) and (2002).

33. This is particularly true for intercountry rather than true world inequality measures. This effect also increases as the polarization measure becomes more narrow, thereby reflecting a smaller proportion of the total income distribution. For example, according to Sutcliffe's (2004, p. 28) calculations, the ratio of the top to bottom 1 percent, 5 percent, and 10 percent of the world's population has at times risen even when the ratio of the top to bottom 20 percent was falling. This provides yet another opportunity for critics and proponents of globalization to disagree on trends.

The answer to our question begins with the observation that many critics view globalization as a process through which power is distilled upward and away from the poor, toward a global elite. As Kevin Danaher, author and public education director of the large nonprofit organization Global Exchange, writes:

> Within the global movement for changing how capital gets invested, there are two key questions being raised. First, who is sitting at the table when the investment decisions get made? Second, what are the values guiding the process?
>
> If the people sitting at the table are a mono-crop (wealthy, white males), then the policies coming from that decision-making process cannot reflect the needs and desires of the rest of us. . . . A mono-crop of pro-corporate voices at the decision-making table will shut out other sectors of society, such as workers, environmentalists, churches, community groups, and others. Thus "democracy" becomes an empty phrase because the diversity of voices that is essential for real democracy is blocked by those with power not wanting to share it. (Danaher 2001)

Although corporate executives are the most often envisaged members of the global elite, critics also see it as including technocrats, bureaucrats, and politicians.[34] McMurtry (2002) provides a lucid and impassioned example of concern over the concentration of power associated with globalization in his article "Why the Protesters Are Against Corporate Globalization":

> The ultimate subject and sovereign ruler of the world is the transnational corporation, operating by collective prescription and enforcement through the World Trade Organization in concert with its prototype the NAFTA [North American Free Trade Agreement], its European collaborator, the EU, and such derivative regional instruments as the APEC [Asia-Pacific Economic Cooperation], the MAI [Multilateral Agreement on Investment], the FTAA [Free Trade Area of the Americas], and so on.
>
> Together these constitute the hierarchical formation of the planet's new rule by extra-parliamentary and transnational fiat. (p. 202)

The second half of the answer to our question "Why do people form negative priors about the impact of globalization on the poor?" is that few noneconomists believe that this powerful, self-interested global elite will make decisions that maximize long-run benefits to the poor. Indeed, the assumption is more commonly that the elite will make decisions that are good for the elite, and that what is good for the elite is almost invariably bad for the poor.[35] Consider the following quotation from the World

34. For example, this is an ongoing theme in Korten's (2001) hugely successful book *When Corporations Rule the World,* an entire chapter of which is titled "Building Elite Consensus."
35. It is worth noting here that this is an area of important difference between critics of the current form of globalization and those who may be truly described as opposed to globalization. The first group includes organizations such as Oxfam International and Greenpeace. These groups are global themselves, and thus their position is that global governance can

Trade Organization (WTO) overview on the web site of Global Trade Watch.[36]

> The WTO and GATT Uruguay Round Agreements have functioned principally to pry open markets *for the benefit of* transnational corporations *at the expense of* national and local economies; workers, farmers, indigenous peoples, women and other social groups; health and safety; the environment; and animal welfare. In addition, the WTO system's rules and procedures are *undemocratic, un-transparent and nonaccountable and have operated to marginalize the majority of the world's people.* (emphasis added)

While these statements are somewhat lacking in balance, they do hint at a number of important policy questions that have attracted some academic interest but are deserving of much more. Of all these questions, the one on which the gap between public concern and academic interest has been the greatest is the role of big business. A reading of the many web sites set up to criticize globalization reveals that this issue is the most widely held concern of the general public with regard to globalization. However, if you don't have time to surf the Web, evidence of this may easily be found in the titles of the two best-selling antiglobalization books: David Korten's *When Corporations Rule the World* and Naomi Klein's *No Logo.* However, the role of imperfect competition in the context of international trade and theories of multinational firms is emphasized less today than it was twenty years ago. Although the importance of departures from perfect competition was emphasized in models of strategic trade and infant industries in the 1980s, in the 1990s economists generally emphasized the importance of global competition in removing instead of enhancing market power.

As the two book titles above suggest, people are concerned about both the political and the market power of transnational corporations. Concern about the political power of big business exists independently of concern over globalization.[37] However, critics believe globalization exacerbates the problem of corporate power in three ways. First, it facilitates the expansion of the richest and most powerful corporations into countries whose governments are more susceptible to capture and whose populations are far

---

work but that the influential global elite needs to be expanded to include civil society in a role as strong as that of big business. In contrast, the latter group, which includes most notably the IFG, tends to believe that democracy will deliver better policies than a combination of technocracy and lobby groups, even if the lobby groups are broadly balanced. They argue further that democracy cannot function when the representative group exceeds a certain maximum size, which is far smaller than the world population. Thus, they argue that global governance is inherently flawed and local, democratic self-determination is to be preferred.

36. http://www.citizen.org/trade/wto/index.cfm

37. A *Business Week*/Harris Poll published in the September 2000 edition of *Business Week* showed that 72–82 percent of respondents agree that business has gained too much power over too many aspects of American life, while 74–82 percent agreed that big companies have too much influence over government policy, politicians, and policymakers in Washington.

less empowered than those in their home countries. The most commonly cited examples of the problem are the labor conditions of footwear and clothing manufacturers, and damage to health and livelihoods of local populations in the vicinity of oil and mining operations. It is further claimed that protest and unrest by indigenous or labor groups is violently repressed by the national government directly or paramilitaries, and that the foreign corporation either actively supports the repression or complicity ignores it. Some of the most commonly cited cases involve Nike and the Gap in Indonesia, Coca-Cola in Colombia, Rio Tinto and Freeport Mc-Moran's joint venture in Irian Jaya (a reluctant part of Indonesia), and Shell in the Niger Delta.[38]

The second way in which globalization is believed to exacerbate problems of corporate power is that it involves the strengthening of supranational institutions, to which critics believe large corporations have disproportionate access. The WTO is the most often criticized international institution in this regard, and the TRIPs agreement is the most often criticized outcome of this perceived influence.[39] Third, globalization is believed to exacerbate the problem of excessive corporate political power because it is believed to make big business even bigger, and power is believed to be proportional to size.[40]

Proponents of globalization often hold a much more optimistic view of the impact of globalization on corporate political power. They argue that corporate input to policymaking can be constructive and that globalization actually decreases the likelihood of policy capture by industry. The latter point is supported by the observation that globalization is often associated with increased accountability and openness of national governments, and increased competition for national monopolies. In addition, it is argued that the costs of corruption and excessive regulation are higher in an open economy, leading to increased pressure for institutional reform (Bolaky and Freund 2004). There is also empirical evidence to support these proposed linkages (Ades and Di Tella 1999; Berg and Krueger 2003). Bardhan (2003, 2004) suggests that the forces identified by both sides of the debate are likely to be at work.[41] Consequently, he says, the effect of globalization on the political equilibrium will vary on a country-by-country basis, and he calls for more systematic empirical studies on the topic.

We turn now to the second major source of concern with corporate globalization, that is, increased market concentration. This issue, according to Kanbur (2001) is "undoubtedly the most potent difference in framework

---

38. To learn more about these claims, simply enter the company name and location in your favorite search engine. Alternatively, visit the high-quality site of the Global Policy Forum, http://www.globalpolicy.org/, where you can enter the key words in their Google-driven search facility or browse by category. The web site contains thousands of news articles as well as reports by both NGOs and UN committees.
39. See, for example, Bardhan (2003) and Deardorff (2003).
40. See, for example, Renner (2000).
41. See also Bardhan and Mookherjee (2000).

and perspective" in the globalization debate (p. 1089). Bardhan (2003) and Bhagwati (2002) also note that one of the fundamental differences between globalization's proponents and critics is that the former consider the impacts of market liberalization within a framework of perfect competition, while the latter consider it in the context of highly imperfect competition. Thus, while much economic research has considered the ability of globalization to reduce the market power held by previously monopolistic *domestic* firms, many critics see globalization as a mechanism by which the oligopolistic reach of the transnational corporations spreads to the farthest corners of the globe.

The important implication of the assumption of a world of imperfect competition is that it makes distortions in both factor and goods markets feasible.[42] Hence it is possible to believe that the poor are being exploited both in their role as suppliers of inputs, particularly labor, and in their role as consumers of finished products. A classic example of this belief was the debate in India in the mid-1990s. Many small farmers were suffering at the same time that many poor consumers were facing rapidly increasing food prices. The culprits, some claimed, were the rapidly expanding foreign agribusinesses that were acting as middle men in the food supply chain.[43]

Although it is unlikely that foreign agribusinesses were the primary cause of the consumer price hikes in the Indian example, there is some evidence that some large transnational corporations do have market power. Some major world markets are highly concentrated, and business executives continue to strive for greater market share under the belief that this is necessary in a globalized economy (Ghemawat and Ghadar 2000).[44] Ac-

---

42. For example, Sethi (2003) claims that "most modern economies operate under conditions of imperfect competition where corporations gain above-normal profits, i.e., market rent, from market imperfections. Therefore, corporations should be held accountable for a more equitable distribution of these above-normal profits with other groups, e.g., customers, employees, etc., who were deprived of their market-based gains because of market imperfections and corporate power" (p. 1). Deardorff (2003) attempts to provide an economic model describing the exploitative power that corporations are accused of exercising over labor.

43. For example, in a speech in late 1998, then Prime Minister Shri Atal Bihari Vajpayee said that

A major area of concern for all of us in the supply and distribution of essential commodities is the exploitative role of middlemen. This was evident even in the recent spurt in prices—the difference between wholesale and retail prices of onion, potatoes, pulses and edible oils was sometimes in the 200 per cent to 300 per cent band.

The worst irony is that increased purchase price for the consumer does not mean better sale price for the farmer. Prices of agriculture produce often fluctuate so wildly from year to year due to market manipulations by middlemen, that sustainable crop planning becomes a near impossibility. (quoted in *India News Online* 1998)

See also Shiva (2002) and Aragrande and Argenti (2001).

44. An example of such concentration can be seen in autos, where the top five firms account for almost 60 percent of global sales. In electronics, the top five firms have over half of global sales. And the top five firms have over 30 percent of global sales in airlines, aerospace, steel, oil, personal computers, chemicals, and the media. These figures are from Morgan Stanley Capital International and the International Data Corporation, quoted in the *Economist* ("A Game of Global Monopoly," March 27, 1993, Survey 17).

cording to a recent report from the FAO Committee on Commodity Problems (FAO 2003) market concentration and vertical integration are "growing realities" in grain and cereal markets, which can be traced in part to trade liberalization, aggressive export promotion policies, and privatization of government trading entities. Ghemawat and Ghadar (2000), however, argue that hard empirical evidence that globalization of an industry drives increased concentration of that industry is lacking. Bardhan (2003) suggests that the impact of globalization on market concentration is in need of more empirical investigation. However, he adds that even if the issue is validated empirically, protesters should be lobbying for better antitrust laws, not more trade restrictions.

1.6   Conclusion

This paper has attempted to explain why criticisms of globalization's impact on the poor continue to abound despite the general consensus that liberalization promotes growth and growth is good for the poor. The explanation consisted of four parts. First, many people view the empirical evidence in favor of globalization skeptically because they see globalization as a process through which power is concentrated upward and away from the poor. In particular, they see transnational corporations as gaining a disproportionate amount of both political and market power. Critics of globalization are also firmly of the opinion that corporations will use their increased power in ways that benefit themselves and harm the poor.

Although these concerns are not without basis, there are mediating factors that make it difficult to conclude that globalization is increasing corporate power or that increased corporate power is necessarily bad for the poor. On the first point it is important to remember that globalization exposes many previously powerful national corporations to outside competition, and requires greater transparency in government policymaking. On the second point, it may be that the efficiency benefits of large corporations outweigh any losses from increased market power. Thus, it would seem that there is room for more empirical research to determine whether the corporate globalization does indeed give the poor cause for concern.

The next part of the explanation focused on the multiplicity of meanings of the phrases "worsening poverty" and "increasing inequality." The discussion in regard to poverty followed on from Kanbur's (2001) work, which identified four major differences between the concepts of poverty employed by globalization's critics and proponents. These four dimensions are the total number of poor versus poverty incidence, monetary versus multidimensional measures, level of aggregation, and time horizon. I argued that although level of aggregation and time horizon do appear to be important distinctions, they are both emblematic of a more general con-

cern that the poor should not be the ones to bear the adjustment costs of globalization.

I then examined the implications of each of these different concepts for the assessment of the progress of the last twenty years. It was argued that invariably some groups of poor are adversely affected by globalization, even when a much larger number of poor are made better off. Thus, concern for negatively affected subgroups will always lead to a less favorable assessment of the impact of globalization. In the presence of strong population growth, looking at total number of poor rather than poverty incidence also leads to a predictably more pessimistic assessment. However, the implications of including nonmonetary dimensions of poverty are less clear. Many people clearly believe that liberalization will lead to negative impacts on nonmonetary dimensions of poverty, but the empirical evidence on this is mixed.

In regard to inequality I argued that economic research generally applies measures of the shape of the income distribution, while many of the criticisms of globalization are based on polarization and on changes in absolute inequality. The latter concept is related to the observation that the poor often do not have equal access to the opportunities presented by globalization (Birdsall 2003; Winters, McCulloch, and McKay 2004). Both polarization and absolute changes in inequality tend to indicate rising inequality more often than the measures of inequality preferred by economists.

The next section showed that there remain important unresolved methodological issues in the calculation of even the most fundamental poverty and inequality measures. Foremost among these issues are the use of household survey data versus national accounts data to estimate average national incomes, and the method of comparing incomes across countries and over time. Both of these issues have major implications for our assessment of the last twenty years. Until we reach a consensus on them, there will be empirical support for both optimistic and pessimistic views of the period of globalization.

Global trends over the last twenty years, however, are not the best facts on which to base claims about the benefits or otherwise of globalization. Thorough empirical work, which links specific policy measures to poverty outcomes, provides a far better basis. The empirical work to date has contributed to a broad acceptance that trade and FDI are growth promoting. Yet much work remains to show which policies can reduce the adjustment costs borne by the poor and maximize the share of the benefits they obtain from globalization.

Overall it seems that the difference of opinion between globalization's supporters and critics can be largely explained by differences in prior views and priorities, as well as current ambiguities in the empirical evidence. Rather than viewing criticism as a burden to be thrown off as quickly as

possible, policymakers and researchers alike could do well to heed its message: "good" isn't good enough. We owe it to the world's poor to do better.

Appendix

Summary of Remaining Disagreements

Strong Globalizers	*Cautious Globalizers*
Globalization is good for the poor.	Globalization is bad for the poor.
Inequality should not be a concern as long as poverty is decreasing. Relative inequality is the appropriate measure of inequality.	Absolute inequality should be a concern in its own right, regardless of poverty outcomes.
The proportion of the population living in poverty is the appropriate measure of poverty outcomes.	The absolute number of people living in poverty matters more than the proportion.
Current income-based measures are sufficient for answering most questions regarding the benefits of globalization.	Poverty measures should include empowerment and vulnerability.
More liberal trade is always better.	Total trade liberalization may not be the best means of promoting trade in the longer term, and even if it is, it may come at too great a cost in terms of social and environmental policies. Totally free trade is unlikely to be the optimal policy, and the optimal policy mix will be case specific.
It is optimal for developing countries to unilaterally liberalize their economies.	Developing countries should refuse to further liberalize their economies until the major economic powers genuinely improve access for developing-country exports.
The way in which growth is achieved makes little difference to distributional outcomes; therefore governments should employ policies that focus on maximizing growth.	Maximizing short-term growth is not necessarily the way to produce sustainable reductions in poverty.

Governments should place minimal controls on FDI in order to attract as much as possible.

Governments should place controls on FDI in order to maximize the welfare gain to the host country.

Policies that improve the profitability of large foreign corporations should be undertaken, because these corporations provide jobs for unskilled workers and bring in new technology.

Policies that improve the profitability of large foreign corporations should not be undertaken, because the poor and the environment inevitably pay for the extra profits gained.

Although the provision of safety nets is important, lack of safety nets should not be used as a reason for delaying liberalization.

Liberalization should not proceed until adequate safety nets are in place.

Government provision of essential services such as health, education, water, and power is inefficient and/or corrupt; therefore these activities should be privatized. This can be done without negative effects on the poor by provision of subsidies or vouchers.

Government provision of essential services is the only means of ensuring that all the poor have access to them at a reasonable standard. Privatization will have severe negative consequences for the poor.

Opening economies to foreign trade and investment improves competitiveness and eliminates inefficiencies caused by national monopoly power.

Opening economies to foreign trade and investment eliminates smaller local firms and further extends the oligopolistic power of the transnational corporations.

Large reductions in wages in previously protected sectors are merely evidence that these sectors were earning monopoly rents that they were sharing with their workers.

Large reductions in wages in previously protected sectors send many previously middle-class people toward poverty. It is evidence of the shift toward corporations in relative bargaining power that accompanies opening.

Opening reduces the potential for capture of economic and political power by local elites.

The evidence is that integration with world markets is associated with relative increases in the incomes of the very rich. This makes it difficult to believe that their economic and political power has shifted toward the lower income brackets. If anything, local elites must now share their power with international elites.

Political reform is necessary in many developing countries; liberalization will provide a catalyst for reform.

It is appropriate to have enforceable supernational trade and investment agreements. They will ultimately lead to an optimal outcome.

The effect on the political equilibrium will be case specific, and it is highly possible that liberalization will have detrimental effects.

Nation states should not relinquish power to international bodies, since democracy does not function at such a high level. *Or* Economically oriented international bodies such as the WTO need to be balanced by equally powerful international organizations whose primary concerns are social and environmental.

References

Ades, A., and R. Di Tella. 1999. Rents, competition, and corruption. *American Economic Review* 89 (4): 982–93.

Agénor, P.-R. 2002. Does globalization hurt the poor? World Bank Development Research Group Working Paper no. 2922. Washington, DC: World Bank.

Aragrande, M., and O. Argenti. 2001. *Studying food supply and distribution systems to cities in developing countries and countries in transition: Methodological and operational guide.* Rev. ed. Rome: Food and Agriculture Organization of the United Nations.

Baldwin, R. 2003. Openness and growth: What's the empirical relationship? NBER Working Paper no. W9578. Cambridge, MA: National Bureau of Economic Research.

Bardhan, P. 2003. Globalization and the limits to poverty alleviation. University of California, Berkeley, Department of Economics. Mimeograph. Available at http://globetrotter.berkeley.edu/macarthur/inequality/papers/BardhanGlobLimit.pdf.

———. 2004. The impact of globalization on the poor. In *Brookings trade forum 2004,* ed. S. Collins and C. Graham, 271–96. Washington, DC: Brookings Institution Press.

Bardhan, P., and D. Mookherjee. 2000. Capture and governance at local and national levels. *American Economic Review* 90 (2): 135–39.

Baron, J. 1995. Blind justice: Fairness to groups and the do-no-harm principle. *Journal of Behavioral Decision Making* 8:71–83.

Berg, A., and A. Krueger. 2003. Trade, growth and poverty: A selective survey. IMF Working Paper no. WP/03/30. Washington, DC: International Monetary Fund.

Bhagwati, J. 1998. The capital myth: The difference between trade in widgets and dollars. *Foreign Affairs* 77 (3): 7–13.

———. 2000. Globalization in your face: A new book humanizes global capitalism. *Foreign Affairs* 79 (4): 134–39.

———. 2002. Coping with antiglobalization: A trilogy of discontents. *Foreign Affairs* 81 (1): 2–5.

————. 2004. *In defense of globalization.* New York: Oxford University Press.
Bhagwati, J., and T. N. Srinivasan. 2002. Trade and poverty in the poor countries. *American Economic Review* 92 (2): 180–83.
Bhalla, S. 2003. Crying wolf on poverty: Or how the millennium development goal has already been reached. IIE Working Paper no. 0403. Washington, DC: Institute for International Economics.
Bigman, D. 2002. *Globalization and the developing countries: Emerging strategies for rural development and poverty alleviation.* The Hague: CAB Publishing.
Birdsall, N. 2003. Asymmetric globalization: Global markets require good global politics. *Brookings Review* 21 (2): 22–28.
Bolaky, B., and C. Freund. 2004. Trade, regulations, and growth. World Bank Development Research Group Working Paper no. W2409. Washington, DC: World Bank.
Bourguignon, F., D. Marin, A. J. Venables, L. A. Winters, F. Giavazzi, D. Coyle, P. Seabright, et al. 2002. Making sense of globalization: A guide to the economic issues. CEPR Policy Paper no. 8. London: Centre for Economic Policy and Research.
Burtless, G. 2004. Health in an age of globalization: A comment on Deaton. In *Brookings trade forum 2004,* ed. S. Collins and S. Graham, 111–23. Washington, DC: Brookings Institution Press.
Centre for Economic Policy and Research (CEPR). 2002. *Trade liberalization and poverty: A handbook.* London: CEPR and Department for International Development.
Chen, S., and M. Ravallion. 2000. How did the world's poorest fare in the 1990s? World Bank Development Research Group Working Paper no. W2409. Washington, DC: World Bank.
————. 2004. How have the world's poorest fared since the early 1980s? World Bank Policy Research Working Paper no. 3341. Washington, DC: World Bank, June.
Chihara, M. 2002. Naomi Klein gets global. *AlterNet,* September 25, http://www.alternet.org/story.html?StoryID=14175.
Crook, C. 2003. Global inequality and *The Economist:* A reply to James Galbraith. *openDemocracy,* September 15, http://www.opendemocracy.net/articles/ViewPop UpArticle.jsp?id=9&articleId=1485
Danaher, K. 2001. People's globalization vs. elite globalization. *International Socialist Review,* no. 19 (July-August), http://www.isreview.org/issues/19/Kevin Danaher.shtml.
Dasgupta, P. 2005. What do economists analyze and why: Values or facts. *Economics and Philosophy* 21:221–78.
Deardorff, A. 2003. What might globalization's critics believe? RSIE Discussion Paper no. 492. Ann Arbor: University of Michigan, Research Seminar in International Economics.
Deaton, A. 1995. Data and econometric tools for development analysis. In *Handbook of development economics,* ed. J. Behrman and T. N. Srinivasan, 1785–1882. Amsterdam: North-Holland.
————. 2001. Counting the world's poor: Problems and possible solutions. *World Bank Research Observer* 16 (2): 125–47.
————. 2003. Measuring poverty in a growing world (or measuring growth in a poor world). NBER Working Paper no. 9822. Cambridge, MA: National Bureau of Economic Research.
————. 2004. Health in an age of globalization. In *Brookings trade forum 2004,* ed. S. Collins and C. Graham, 83–130. Washington, DC: Brookings Institution Press.

Devooght, K. 2003. Measuring inequality by counting "complaints": Theory and empirics. *Economics and Philosophy* 19:241–63.

Dollar, D., and A. Kraay. 2001. Trade, growth and poverty. World Bank Development Research Group Working Paper no. 2615. Washington, DC: World Bank.

————. 2002. Growth is good for the poor. *Journal of Economic Growth* 7 (3): 195–225.

Dowrick, S. 2001. True international income comparisons: Correcting for bias in fixed price measures and exchange rate measures. Paper presented at the Economic Measurement Group Workshop, University of New South Wales. 30 March, Sydney, Australia.

Dowrick, S., and M. Akmal. 2005. Contradictory trends in global income inequality: A tale of two biases. *Review of Income and Wealth* 51 (2): 201–29.

Emmott, B. 2003. Radical birthday thoughts: A survey of capitalism and democracy. *Economist.* June 28.

Fehr, E., and K. Schmidt. 2000. Theories of fairness and reciprocity: Evidence and economic applications. IERE Working Paper no. 75. University of Zurich, Institute for Empirical Research in Economics.

Fischer, S. 2003. Globalization and its challenges. *American Economic Review* 93 (2): 1–30.

Food and Agriculture Organization (FAO). 2003. Major developments and issues in agricultural commodity markets. Report of the 64th Session of the Food and Agriculture Organization's Committee on Commodity Problems. 18–21 March, Rome, Italy. Available at http://www.fao.org/DOCREP/MEETING/005/Y8289e .HTM#P50_18344.

Galbraith, J. 2003. Globalization and inequality: *The Economist* gets it wrong. *open-Democracy,* September 11, http://www.opendemocracy.net/debates/article-7-30-1483 .jsp.

Ghemawat, P., and F. Ghadar. 2000. The dubious logic of megamergers. *Harvard Business Review* 78 (4): 65–74.

Goldberg, P., and N. Pavcnik. 2004. Trade, inequality, and poverty: What do we know? Evidence from recent trade liberalization episodes in developing countries. In *Brookings trade forum 2004,* ed. S. Collins and C. Graham, 223–69. Washington, DC: Brookings Institution Press.

Graaff, J. de V. 1962. *Theoretical welfare economics.* Cambridge: Cambridge University Press.

Graham, C. 2001. Stemming the backlash against globalization. Brookings Policy Brief no. 78. Washington, DC: Brookings Institution.

Harrison, A. 1996. Openness and growth: A time series, cross-country analysis for developing countries. *Journal of Development Economics* 48:419–47.

India News Online. 1998. Prime minister inaugurates chief ministers' conference to review the price situation. December 1–15. http://www.indianembassy.org/inews/ December98/4.htm.

International Forum on Globalization (IFG). 2001. Globalization: The facts and figures of poverty and inequality. *IFG Bulletin* 1, no. 3, http://www.thirdworld traveler.com/Globalization/Globalization_FactsFigures.html.

————. 2002. Alternatives to economic globalization: A better world is possible. San Francisco: Berrett-Koehler.

International Monetary Fund (IMF). 1997. *World economic outlook.* Washington, DC: International Monetary Fund.

Kanbur, R. 2001. Economic policy, distribution and poverty: The nature of the disagreements. *World Development* 29 (6): 1083–94.

————. 2002. Economics, social science and development. *World Development* 30 (3): 477–86.

Kanji, N., and S. Barrientos. 2002. Trade liberalization, poverty and livelihoods: Understanding the linkages. IDS Working Paper no. 159. Brighton, UK: Institute of Development Studies.

Korten, D. 2001. *When corporations rule the world.* San Francisco: Berrett-Khoeler.

Litchfield, J. A. 1999. Inequality: Methods and tools. PovertyNet. http://www.worldbank.org/poverty/inequal/index.html.

Little, I. M. D., T. Scitovsky, and M. Scott. 1970. *Industry and trade in some developing countries.* Oxford, UK: Oxford University Press.

Loungani, P. 2003. Inequality: Now you see it, now you don't. *Finance & Development* 40 (3): 22–23.

McKay, A., L. A. Winters, and A. M. Kedir. 2000. A review of empirical evidence on trade, trade policy and poverty. Background document for second Development White Paper. London: Department for International Development.

McMurtry, J. 2002. Why the protestors are against corporate globalization. *Journal of Business Ethics* 40:201–5.

Micklethwait, J., and A. Wooldridge. 2000. *A future perfect: The challenge and hidden promise of globalization.* New York: Crown Business.

Milanovic, B. 2002. True world income distribution, 1988 and 1993: First calculation based on household surveys alone. *Economic Journal* 112 (January): 51–92.

———. 2005. *Worlds apart: Measuring global and international inequality.* Princeton, NJ: Princeton University Press.

Narayan, D., R. Patel, K. Schafft, A. Rademacher, and S. Koch-Schulte. 2000. *Voices of the poor: Can anyone hear us?* New York: Oxford University Press/ World Bank.

Oxfam. 2001. Is the WTO serious about reducing world poverty? The development agenda for Doha. Washington, DC: Oxfam. http://www.oxfam.org/eng/pdfs/ pp0110_WTO_reducing_world_poverty.pdf.

Prasad, E., K. Rogoff, S. J. Wei, and M. A. Kose. 2003. Effects of financial globalization on developing countries: Some empirical evidence. IMF Working Paper no. 031703. Washington, DC: International Monetary Fund.

Program on International Policy Attitudes (PIPA). 2002. International trade. *Americans and the world digest.* Washington, DC: Program on International Policy Attitudes. http://www.americans-world.org/digest/global_issues/intertrade/ summary.cfm.

Putnam, H. 1993. Objectivity and the science-ethics distinction. In *The quality of life,* ed. M. C. Nussbaum and A. Sen, 143–57. Oxford, UK: Clarendon Press.

Ravallion, M. 2003. The debate on globalization, poverty and inequality: Why measurement matters. World Bank Development Research Group Working Paper no. 3038. Washington, DC: World Bank.

Reddy, S. J., and T. W. Pogge. 2003. How *not* to count the poor. Columbia University, Institute of Social Analysis. http://www.columbia.edu/~sr793/count.pdf.

Reimer, J. J. 2002. Estimating the poverty impacts of trade liberalization. Global Trade Analysis Project Working Paper no. 20. Purdue University, Department of Agricultural Economics.

Renner, M. 2000. Corporate mergers skyrocket. In *Vital signs 2000: The environmental trends that are shaping our world,* by L. R. Brown, M. Renner, and B. Halwell, 142–45. Washington, DC: Worldwatch Institute.

Robbins, L. 1932. *An essay on the nature and significance of economic science.* London: MacMillan.

Robinson, J. 1964. *Economic philosophy.* Harmondsworth, UK: Penguin.

Rogoff, K. 2004. Some speculation on growth and poverty over the twenty-first century. In *Brookings trade forum 2004,* ed. S. Collins and C. Graham, 305–11. Washington, DC: Brookings Institution Press.

Sala-i-Martin, X. 2002a. The disturbing "rise" of global income inequality. NBER Working Paper no. W8904. Cambridge, MA: National Bureau of Economic Research.

————. 2002b. The world distribution of income (estimated from individual country distributions). NBER Working Paper no. 8933. Cambridge, MA: National Bureau of Economic Research.

Samuelson, P. A. 1947. *Foundations of economic analysis.* Cambridge, MA: Harvard University Press.

Sen, A. 2002. Globalization and poverty. Lecture presented at Santa Clara University, California. 29 October. Available at http://www.scu.edu/globalization/speakers/senlecture.cfm.

Sethi, S. P. 2003. Globalization and the good corporation: A need for proactive coexistence. *Journal of Business Ethics* 43 (1–2): 21–31.

Shiva, V. 2002. Profits over people: How the World Food Summit in Rome last fortnight buried food rights, and clearly laid the contours of the future the powerful of the world are designing. *Frontline* 19 (13), http://www.globenet3.org/Articles/Article_Vandana.shtml.

Summers, R., and A. Heston. 1991. The Penn World Table (mark 5): An expanded set of international comparisons, 1950–1988. *Quarterly Journal of Economics* 106 (2): 327–68.

Sutcliffe, B. 2004. World inequality and globalization. *Oxford Review of Economic Policy* 20 (1): 15–37.

Svedberg, P. 2004. World income distribution: Which way? *Journal of Development Studies* 40 (5): 1–32.

Tenenbaum, J. 2003. Bayesian models of human learning and reasoning. Lecture presented at Northwestern University, Evanston, IL. 19 May. Available at http://www.cogsci.northwestern.edu/Bayes/1.mht!1_files/frame.htm.

Thorbecke, E. 2003. Conceptual and measurement issues in poverty analysis. Paper presented at World Institute for Development Economics Research Conference on Inequality, Poverty, and Human Well-Being. 30–31 May, Helsinki, Finland.

United Nations Conference on Trade and Development (UNCTAD). 2002. *Trade and development report, 2002.* Geneva: UNCTAD.

United Nations Development Programme (UNDP). 1999. *Human development report 1999: Globalization with a human face.* New York: Oxford University Press.

United Nations University World Institute for Development Economics Research (UNU-WIDER). 2004. The impact of globalization on the world's poor. Call for papers for the First Project Meeting on Conceptual Issues, 29–30 October. http://www.wider.unu.edu/ (accessed April 10, 2004).

Wade, R. 2001. Winners and losers. *Economist.* April 28.

————. 2002. Globalization, poverty and income distribution: Does the liberal argument hold? LSE Development Studies Institute Working Paper no. 02-33. London: London School of Economics, July.

Wei, S.-J., and Y. Wu. 2002. The life-and-death implications of globalization. IMF Discussion Paper. Washington, DC: International Monetary Fund.

Winters, L. A. 2000. Trade, trade policy and poverty: What are the links? CEPR Research Paper no. 2382. London: Centre for Economic Policy and Research.

————. 2002. Trade liberalization and poverty: What are the links? *World Economics* 25 (9): 1339–67.

Winters, L. A., N. McCulloch, and A. McKay. 2004. Trade liberalization and poverty: The evidence so far. *Journal of Economic Literature* 42 (March): 72–115.

World Bank. 2000–2001. *World development report 2000/2001: Attacking poverty.* Washington, DC: World Bank.

————. 2001. *World development indicators 2001*. Washington, DC: World Bank.
————. 2002. *Globalization, growth and poverty: Building an inclusive world economy*. Washington, DC: World Bank.
World Economic Forum (WEF). 2002. People around the world increasingly favor globalization but worry about jobs, poverty and environment: World Economic Forum survey of 25,000 citizens across 25 countries. Press release. February 1.

Comment   Xavier Sala-i-Martin

Emma Aisbett has written an interesting paper about why mainstream economists and the so-called critics of globalization seem to disagree about the economic impact of globalization. The central point of the paper is that the critics have some negative priors about globalization and academic research does not provide clear evidence that they are wrong. By not providing unequivocal results about aspects such as the evolution of poverty or inequality in the purported era of globalization, the critics can always point to some piece of empirical evidence that supports their preconceptions. Economists' lack of clarity, the author argues, is evident, for example, in the way poverty or inequality is defined or in the lack of robustness of econometric studies.

The first question one should ask is whether academic economists should engage in these debates. When I first asked myself this question, the book *Conversations with Economists* (Klamer 1984) came to my mind. In that book Robert Solow was asked about what was then the new classical macroeconomics based on general equilibrium models and rational expectations. His answer was "Suppose someone sits down where you are sitting right now and announces to me that he is Napoleon Bonaparte. The last thing I want to do with him is to get involved in a technical discussion of cavalry tactics at the Battle of Austerlitz. If I do that, I'm getting tacitly drawn into the game that he is Napoleon Bonaparte."

Of course, the classical economists Solow was referring to back in 1984 were making very valid points. So valid that general equilibrium models became standard practice in macroeconomic research over the following two decades . . . and three of their intellectual leaders—Robert Lucas, Finn Kydland, and Edward Prescott—ended up winning the Nobel Prize. But the fact that classical economists had valid points does not mean that everyone who criticizes standard economics has valid points also. The thrust of Solow's argument is still valid: economists should not engage in serious debates with every critic, every social and political movement. In this particular case, it is not clear whether academic research should

Xavier Sala-i-Martin is a professor of economics at Columbia University and a research associate of the National Bureau of Economic Research.

change its normal course simply because a number of protesters fail to understand international trade or cross-country econometrics.

What seems clear, however, is that should academic economists choose to engage in such debates, they should not lower their standards. Just because the critics have strange priors, we should not accept claims based on substandard methodological practices. The debate with the critics must be based on sensible theories and on accepted econometric methods. The reason I mention this is that the methodology used by the critics (as it is described in the paper) seems to be the following:

1. Define the globalization period.
2. Check whether poverty and inequality have increased or decreased during this period.
3. Conclude that globalization is good or bad, depending on whether poverty and inequality have decreased or increased.

This methodology has a number of serious problems. First, globalization is not a well-defined phenomenon and, as a result, the globalization period cannot be properly defined. The critics seem to suggest that the globalization period is the decades that follow 1980, but it is not clear why. What exactly happened to any measure of openness that warrants taking 1980 as the first year of the globalization period? The lack of a clear and unambiguous definition leads us to the absurd situation (which is patent in table 1.2 of the paper) where it seems that if one can show that inequality has increased in *any five-year period* after 1980, then one has shown that globalization is bad.[1]

The second problem with this methodology is that it fails to prove that the supposed increases (or declines) in inequality are due to globalization as opposed to the thousands of other things that occurred during the same period. Imagine that a bunch of protesters decide to form a movement called "critics of MTV." The movement has credible priors that MTV is bad for the economy (because it takes young citizens' time away from study and productive work, which significantly affects human capital, and it changes their attitudes toward sacrifice, competition, and risk taking, which impacts their productivity and their incentives to invest and become entrepreneurs). To prove the validity of their conjectures, the group defines the "MTV period" as the post-1980 period (MTV was created in 1981). They then go to the economics literature and find out that some measures of poverty and inequality have exploded during this period, and they conclude that their priors were correct: MTV is bad for the economy!

Would anyone take the "critics of MTV" seriously if they simply show

1. Table 1.2 reports a very influential paper by Milanovic (2001), in which worldwide inequality is estimated for 1988 and 1993. The increase in the value of the Gini coefficient during this five-year period has been widely quoted by the critics as evidence that globalization has adverse effects on the evolution of world income inequality.

this kind of empirical evidence to support their priors? I would think the answer is no. And if it were to be taken seriously, the group would actually have to fight the critics of globalization because they would both have presented *exactly the same empirical evidence.* And I suppose they would have to fight with the "critics of the personal computer," the "anti-Walkman" crowd, and the "opponents of the disposable camera" (all of which products were introduced in the early 1980s). The fact that these things have happened after 1980 is no evidence that MTV, Walkmans, disposable cameras, or globalization is bad (or good). I would assume that, at the very least, these groups should show whether the citizens of the countries that have experienced increases in poverty rates have access to MTV, whether they use Walkmans or disposable cameras, or, yes, whether the countries in which they lived have indeed globalized. Notice that this is very hard to do without an empirically useful definition of globalization, and it certainly cannot be done by simply (loosely) defining a "globalization period" and observing what happened during it.

Having said that, I will abstract from this problem for the rest of the paper, and pretend that we can actually talk about and measure the "globalization period" and analyze the evidence on poverty and inequality over the last couple of decades.

Aisbett is correct in pointing out that the definition of poverty is not clear: it is a multidimensional concept that goes beyond income; there are debates on how to adjust for purchasing power parity (PPP); and it is not clear whether one should measure income poverty or consumption poverty. Moreover, even if all these issues were to be resolved (that is, even if we agreed that we can use a monetary measure and that this measure should be adjusted by a particular system of PPP prices), it is still unclear what is the line that defines poverty. The two most widely used lines are what the World Bank calls "extreme poverty line" (which corresponds to $1 a day) and the "poverty line" ($2 a day). Of course, these lines are arbitrary . . . but any other lines would be also.

The fact that all these methodological questions exist does not mean, however, that anything goes in the debate on poverty. Yes, poverty is a multidimensional concept, but in order to show that "real" poverty has increased while "monetary" poverty has declined, one has to show a deterioration of these additional measures. And most of them show an overall improvement over the last two decades: life expectancy is up, education has increased, literacy rates have improved, starvation has gone down, access to water and sanitation has increased, and so on.

In terms of monetary poverty, the claim made by Aisbett is that it is not clear whether poverty has increased or declined because poverty rates (or incidence) seem to have declined clearly whereas the total number of citizens living below the poverty line may have increased. The problem, according to her, is that since the critics can pick and choose their favorite

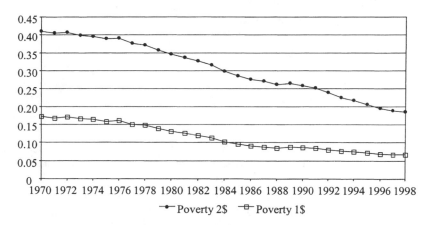

Fig. 1C.1   Poverty rates

measure, they can always argue that poverty has increased. There are two problems with this argument. First, people are not allowed to pick and choose a measure ex post, based on their prejudices. It might make little sense to use certain indexes to deal with particular questions. If, on the other hand, one asks whether we should be more concerned about poverty rates or head counts, a veil-of-ignorance argument used in Aisbett's paper suggests that rates are probably more important.

What is the evidence on the evolution of poverty rates? Let me show you the results that I got in some of my own research (I apologize for the self-cite). Figure 1C.1 shows the evolution of income poverty using $1-per-day and $2-per-day lines. The rates were cut by between one-half and two-thirds between 1970 and 1998: the $2-per-day declines from 0.4 to 0.18 and the $1-per-day falls from 0.17 to 0.06 over the same period. If we look at this more important measure of poverty, the world is certainly improving.

The problem, as suggested by Aisbett, is that in a world with rising population, poverty rates may fall at the same time that poverty numbers increase! And if one is allowed to pick and choose whether to look at rates or counts, one is essentially allowed to choose whether poverty increases or decreases. The problem with this line of reasoning is that poverty counts have also declined during the last two decades! Figure 1C.2 shows that the $1-per-day count fell from 600 million in 1976 to 350 million in 1998. The $2-per-day figures also show a reduction from 1.4 billion to about 1.0 billion during the same period.

Are these numbers crazy? Some people (from the World Bank) criticize them because I used income per capita from the national accounts to pin down the mean of the distribution as opposed to using the survey means (a method used by the World Bank). The reason is that the means of the surveys do not grow as fast as the income per capita as computed by the na-

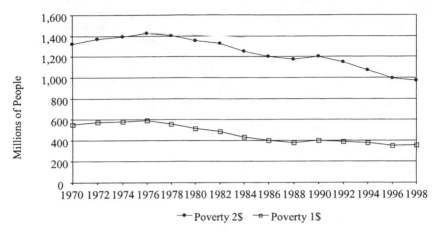

-●- Poverty 2$ -□- Poverty 1$

Fig. 1C.2   Poverty head counts

tional accounts. It is not entirely clear why these discrepancies exist. However, in a recent article published in the *Economist,* Martin Ravallion (research manager of the Development Research Group of the World Bank) argues that the World Bank $1-per-day numbers are comparable to my $2-per-day figures (Ravallion 2004). According to Ravallion, "The [World] Bank currently estimates that the world poverty rate fell from 33% in 1981 (about 1.5 billion people) to 18% in 2001 (1.1 billion), when judged by the frugal $1-a-day standard."[2] My conclusion is, therefore, that the most empirical evidence from academic researchers as well as the World Bank suggests that both poverty rates and counts have been declining dramatically over the last two decades, the two decades that the critics called the globalization period.

An interesting question is whether the poverty lines used make sense. The $1-a-day line is clearly arbitrary . . . but so would be any other line! The problem for the critics is that poverty rates fall for all conceivable poverty lines! To demonstrate this, figure 1C.3 shows cumulative distribution functions (CDFs) for 1970, 1980, 1990, and 1998. We see that the 1980 CDF curve stochastically dominates that of 1970, that the 1990 CDF curve stochastically dominates that of 1980, and that the 1998 CDF curve stochastically dominates that of 1990. In other words, poverty rates declined between 1970 and 1998 for every conceivable poverty line. Thus, engaging in debates about what exact poverty lines we should be considering when making statements about how poverty has evolved during the "globalization period" is not likely to change the conclusion that poverty rates have declined and that globalization is (I suppose) good for the poor.

2. Compare with my figures of 38 percent (1.4 billion) in 1981 and 18.5 percent (1.0 billion) in 1978 (Sala-i-Martin 2002).

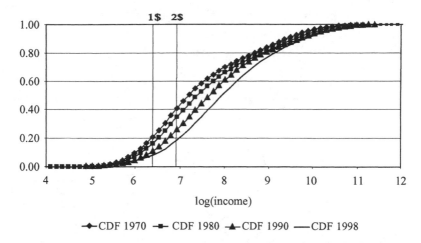

Fig. 1C.3   Evolution of the world distribution of income (cumulative distribution functions [CDFs])

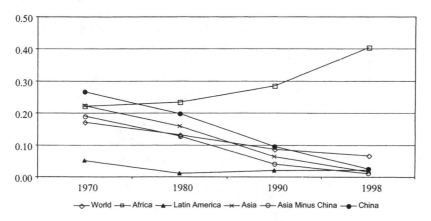

Fig. 1C.4   Poverty rates for world regions: $1 per day

A common practice among critics consists in suggesting that poverty actually increases if we exclude China (or China and India) from the analysis (Aisbett cites a report by the World Bank that does exactly that in section 1.4.1). This is true, but perhaps irrelevant: of course when we exclude those countries where poverty declines, poverty in the remaining countries increases. Which is not to say that we should ignore the regions of the world that witness deterioration of poverty rates and counts. The really important questions are (1) what regions of the world are witnessing a deterioration of poverty rates, (2) whether poverty is falling in China only, and (3) whether the cause of increasing poverty, wherever that happens, is globalization.

Figure 1C.4 displays poverty rates for Asia, China, Asia minus China,

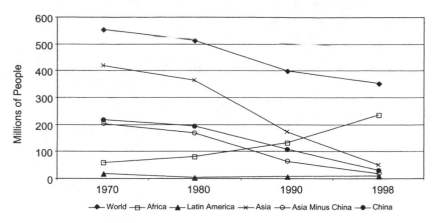

Fig. 1C.5   Poverty head counts for world regions: $1 per day

Latin America, and Africa. We see that poverty rates have declined substantially in China, but also in the rest of Asia (thus, it is not true that poverty declines only in China). We notice that, after falling during the 1970s, poverty rates stagnated in Latin America. The real problem occurs in Africa, where $1/day rates have almost doubled from a bit over 20 percent to just above 40 percent. Figure 1C.5 shows that poverty counts also declined in China, the rest of Asia, and Latin America, but have increased in Africa.

Of course, if one wants to use these data and argue that globalization causes poverty, one should show that East Asia, South Asia, and Latin America have experienced more globalization than Africa. One way to answer this question is to follow Dollar and Kraay (2000), who divide countries into those that globalized after 1980 and those that reduced their exposure to globalization and estimate the evolution of poverty in each of the two groups.[3] If we use a $1-per-day line, poverty counts fell by 309 million people within post-1980 globalizers and increased by 79 million in countries that failed to globalize (see table 1C.1). If we use the $2-per-day line, the numbers are –478 million and +80 million, respectively. Of course, which country should be assigned to which group remains a controversial issue, in part because we do not have an empirically useful definition of globalization, which is precisely why I mentioned earlier that this should be a priority of researchers of this field. If we had a good and empirically useful definition of globalization (and I have argued repeatedly that we do not) we could estimate a cross-country regression where the change of

---

3. See Dollar and Kraay (2000) for definitions. Of course, if we had a good and empirically useful definition of globalization (and I have argued repeatedly that we do not) we could estimate a cross-country regression where the change of poverty rates are the dependent variable and globalization is the explanatory variable.

Table 1C.1   Evolution of poverty rates and head counts

	Population	Poverty rates		Poverty head counts	
		$1/day	$2/day	$1/day	$2/day
A. Globalizers					
1970	1,615,775	0.251	0.608	405,323	981,661
1980	1,986,033	0.193	0.506	382,841	1,005,457
1990	2,373,008	0.094	0.334	223,615	792,142
1999	2,655,988	0.036	0.190	95,660	503,506
Change since 1970		−0.215	−0.418	−309,663	−478,155
Change during 1970s		−0.058	−0.101	−22,482	23,796
Change during 1980s		−0.099	−0.172	−159,226	−213,315
Change during 1990s		−0.058	−0.144	−127,955	−288,635
Change during 1980s + 1990s		−0.157	−0.317	−287,181	−501,950
B. Nonglobalizers					
1970	454,464	0.180	0.420	81,888	190,870
1980	589,005	0.106	0.324	62,395	191,053
1990	758,979	0.122	0.296	92,872	224,941
1999	906,102	0.178	0.299	161,087	271,272
Change since 1970		−0.002	−0.121	79,199	80,402
Change during 1970s		−0.074	−0.096	−19,493	183
Change during 1980s		0.016	−0.028	30,477	33,888
Change during 1990s		0.055	0.003	68,215	46,332
Change during 1980s + 1990s		0.072	−0.025	98,692	80,220

poverty rates is the dependent variable and globalization is the explanatory variable.

My next few points relate to the debate on the evolution of world income inequality. This debate resembles that of poverty: there is controversy on whether one should use national accounts data or survey data to pin down the means of the distributions; there are arguments on what index of inequality one should use; and there are debates on how or whether to adjust for PPP. This last debate is a bit bogus: the Robert Wade quotation in section 1.4.2 of the paper ("exchange rate inequality may predispose the elites to be more corrupt, as they compare themselves to the elites in rich countries") is an interesting example of creative ex post rationalization that seeks to justify one measure of inequality that increases (and therefore justifies one's prejudices). It should be clear that, in order for us to be able to measure inequality across objects, objects must be comparable. And, since PPP-unadjusted income data across countries are not comparable, inequality measures that use these data should not be considered.[4]

4. Besides, Wade's ingenious justification leaves unclear why the elites want to compare the amount of dollars they have rather than the size of their villas, the eccentricity of their parties, or the length of their boats. If the critics have to rely on this kind of creative and noncredible theorizing to argue that the world is deteriorating, they are in deep intellectual trouble.

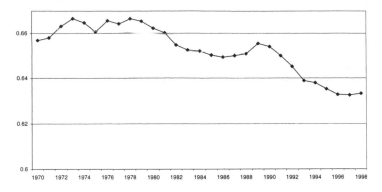

Fig. 1C.6   Global income inequality: Gini coefficient

If one uses PPP-adjusted income and anchors the mean of the distribution to GDP per capita, measured global inequality among individual incomes is clearly not "exploding." Figure 1C.6 displays the Gini coefficient I reported (Sala-i-Martin 2002). Worldwide inequality increases during the 1970s and declines over the following two decades. Having said this, I find it interesting to note that the Gini coefficient does not fall monotonically. Just as recessions occur in the middle of otherwise growth process, inequalities may suffer small short-term reversals. This should be a warning against extrapolating analysis of inequality over very short periods of time.[5]

The critics of globalization may suggest that this conclusion depends on the use of the Gini coefficient and that things might look different with other indexes. I show (Sala-i-Martin 2002) that this is not likely to be the case. I show that the mean logarithmic deviation, the Theil index, the Atkinson index with coefficient 0.5, the Atkinson index with coefficient 1, the variance of log income, the coefficient of variation, the ratio of the income of the top 20 percent to the bottom 20 percent of the population, and the ratio of the income of the top 10 percent to the bottom 10 percent of the population all evolve in a very similar fashion.

Aisbett suggests that the critics tend not to accept this evidence because their priors lead them to think of inequality in terms of polarization so an index like the ratio of top to bottom incomes is better than the Gini coefficient (most commonly used by academic economists) because the Gini puts too much weight on middle-of-the-distribution levels of income. To support this premise, she cites Wade again, who claims that the ratio of in-

---

5. This is of particular importance given the impact that Milanovic's (2001) evidence on growing income inequality "during the globalization period" had on public opinion: the study compared inequality in 1988 with that for 1993, a five-year period! (Why Milanovic 2002 reports a similar-sized decline in inequality over the following five-year period remains a mystery.)

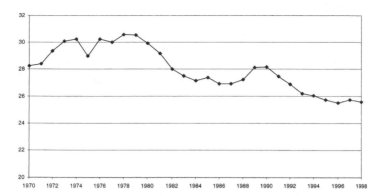

Fig. 1C.7   World income inequality: Ratio of top 10 percent to bottom 10 percent

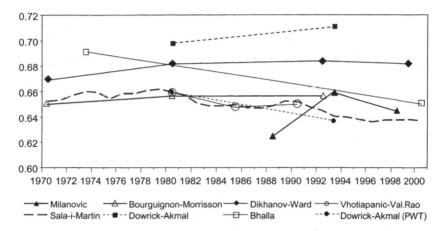

Fig. 1C.8   Gini estimates from other studies compared

come of the top 10 percent of the distribution to the bottom 10 percent increased dramatically between 1988 and 1993. Leaving aside the question of why this five-year period is of particular interest in terms of analyzing the economic impact of globalization, Wade exaggerates when he says that this actually increased. Figure 1C.7 shows that the behavior of the ratio of 10 percent top to bottom follows a trend very similar to other measures of inequality: it clearly did not "explode." It clearly did not even increase. It actually went from a value of more than 30 in 1978 to a bit over 25 in 1998!

The final question is whether these results are sensitive to different methodologies (such as the use of national accounts data rather than survey means to anchor the mean of the distribution). Figure 1C.8 shows the behavior of the Gini coefficient according to different studies. A quick look at the figure suggests that there is little or no evidence that global income inequality has exploded during the globalization period. Most measures

show either a small decline, a small increase, or no trend. Notice that the only large change in inequality occurs in the study by Milanovic (2001), who, as mentioned above, compares 1988 with 1993. The size of the increase is only matched by the size of the decline over the following half decade (which is reported in Milanovic 2002).[6]

My final thought relates to the criticism made in the paper of cross-country econometrics. The problem seems to be that, because the empirical evidence presented by this econometrics literature is not robust and consistent, the door is open for the critics to justify their priors that openness is bad for the growth of a nation. My reading of the literature is that it is true that there are researchers who show that openness is strongly and positively correlated with growth. It is also true that other researchers question the channel through which openness comes about (they conjecture that it may work more through institutions than through the channels explained by conventional trade theories). It is even true that other researchers question the robustness of these results and show that the correlation may be statistically insignificant. The problem with the critics is that there is little or no empirical evidence in the literature—robust or otherwise—showing that openness (globalization?) is negatively correlated with growth! While the "critics," therefore, can be reasonably skeptical about the claim that openness is unambiguously good for growth, they should be even more skeptical toward the claim that it is bad!

In sum, Emma Aisbett has written an interesting paper that raises more questions than answers as to whether the debate in which the "critics" want to engage is useful or is a complete waste of time.

References

Dollar, David, and Aart Kraay. 2000. Growth is good for the poor. Washington, DC: World Bank. Working Paper.
Klamer, Arjo. 1984. *Conversations with economists*. Totowa, NJ: Rowman and Allenheld.
Milanovic, Branko. 2001. True world income distribution, 1988 and 1993: First calculation based on household surveys alone. *Economic Journal* 112 (January): 51–92.
———. 2002. Worlds apart: The twentieth century's promise that failed. Washington, DC: World Bank. Unpublished Manuscript.
Ravallion, Martin. 2004. Pessimistic on poverty? *Economist.* April 10.
Sala-i-Martin, Xavier. 2002. The world distribution of income: Estimated from individual country distributions. NBER Working Paper no. 8993. Cambridge, MA: National Bureau of Economic Research, May.

6. Given that the two studies by Milanovic anchor the income distributions to the survey means rather than national accounts, and given that these large swings in the Gini coefficient seem implausible, these results should cast some doubt on the World Bank's methodology. Despite its implausibility, it is interesting to see that the huge increase in inequality between 1988 and 1993 reported by Milanovic has been widely cited by the critics as central evidence that globalization has caused a disturbing rise in global income inequality.

Stolper-Samuelson Is Dead
And Other Crimes of Both
Theory and Data

Donald R. Davis and Prachi Mishra

This conference volume asks what impact globalization has on poverty. What role are theorists to play in these discussions? A temptation is simply to write yet another model using newer and cooler techniques drawn from other fields, but we are skeptical about whether this is what the world really needs (at least at the moment). In this, we are on the side of Descartes, who in his *Discourse on Method* enjoins the researcher to proceed from the simple to the complex. We think that we need to start with the absolutely simplest models that we can and add complexity only as persistent empirical evidence forces us to do so. At least as a starting point, the null hypothesis should not be too complex.

Having argued that we should start with very simple models and add complexity only as necessary, let us head in the other direction and critique our fixation on the predictions of the simplest models. Models exist to make a point. Just as a toy hammer prepares a child to use a real hammer, our toy models provide us with insights that will be immensely useful when we turn to more complex problems. But when we need to pound in a nail, we don't want to use a toy hammer. And we should be equally cautious about spending all of our time testing toy theories or interpreting the data in terms of these theories. We shouldn't ignore them, discard them, or least of all mutilate them. But we do need to ask what the deep lesson is to be learned from the simple models and how one should go about using this insight in a more complex setting.

Donald R. Davis is the chairman of the department and professor of economics at Columbia University and a research associate of the National Bureau of Economic Research. Prachi Mishra is an economist in the research department at the International Monetary Fund.

The views expressed in this paper are those of the authors and should not be attributed to the International Monetary Fund, its executive board, or its management.

For theorists, this poses a clear problem. As we will see below, the data keep pushing us toward a world much less tidy than the elegant one where we spend most of our time theorizing. Why can't we live in a world more amenable to crisp models? For the data analyst, it likewise poses a problem. How do we make use of the real insights of the simple models in a world more complex by far?

One of the difficulties in reading empirical analyses for someone of theoretical proclivities is that the models under study are frequently alluded to only vaguely. What are the competing models of the world? What would lead us to believe one rather than another? When the prediction of one model is hard to find in the data, what are we to believe about the world? Too often one can't find a clear discussion.

Even if we trim down considerably the question of globalization and poverty to examine the relation between openness and wages, this is still a vast field with many different questions and difficult problems. What is the impact of liberalization by one country on wages of various groups in that country? What is the impact of liberalization by a large number of countries? What is the impact of different types of liberalization on wages? The approach that you would want will depend importantly on which question you want to answer.

Let's think for a while about the trading system as a whole. What model do you want to have in mind of the determinants of world trading patterns when we do this? Because we are now talking about world general equilibrium, we should realize that there are as many different potential models as there are models of any element of the economy. Trade economists spend most of their time working with just a small set of these when considering questions of trade patterns—Ricardo, Heckscher-Ohlin (-Vanek), specific factors, monopolistic competition, economic geography, dynamic models of accumulation, growth, and trade, and models of trade and technical change. If we ask which of these are relevant to the world we live in, surely the answer is—all of them! The question should rather be to establish in which contexts each is helpful and to establish magnitudes.

There are theory crimes and there are data crimes. Sometimes we manage both at the same time. We commit theory crimes constantly—toy models are entirely in the realm of theory crimes. But they are misdemeanors in the service of higher ideals, namely, developing our intuition about the workings of the models. Theory felonies occur when we are so entranced by the elegance of our toy models that we lose sight of the question we are trying to answer, indeed come to believe that we have provided an answer even when clearly central aspects of the problem are addressed inappropriately.

A prime example is the Stolper-Samuelson theorem. The year 1991 marked the fiftieth anniversary of the publication of the article by Wolfgang Stolper and Paul Samuelson that provided the first statement and proof of the Stolper-Samuelson theorem. To observe this golden jubilee,

international trade economists at the University of Michigan organized a conference in honor of this celebrated theorem. One of the highlights of the resulting volume (Deardorff and Stern 1994) was the original letter from the editor of the *American Economic Review*, which praised the paper for its "brilliant theoretical performance" but nonetheless rejected it for publication on the basis that it does not "have anything to say about any of the real situations with which the theory of international trade has to concern itself" (P. T. Homan, quoted in Deardorff and Stern 1994, xi). The conventional view of this referee report is that it is a howler, a monumental gaffe, a high-water mark on the seas of academic idiocy. Yet the present paper will argue that, in one of the theorem's central applications, the referee report got it about right.

It is time to declare Stolper-Samuelson dead. A theorem, of course, is immortal. It is a logical relation that existed before there were humans and will survive them, just as surely as the theorem of Pythagoras. And the Stolper-Samuelson theorem has the hallmarks of great economic theory: an issue of great substantive importance, elegant analytics, and surprising results. Yet an enormous problem arises when we try to apply the Stolper-Samuelson theorem, unthinkingly, specifically to the question of the consequences of trade liberalization for the poorest or least skilled in poor countries. In this context, Stolper-Samuelson has become a central reference point, indeed a mantra, a totem: "Stolper-Samuelson says that trade liberalization will raise the real income of the abundant (unskilled) labor in poor countries." Stolper-Samuelson, qua theorem, is not wrong, of course. But if we use it, as we so often have, as if it provides a reliable answer to this question of real human significance, then it is worse than wrong—it is dangerous.

Of course, the fact that the Stolper-Samuelson theorem fails to be robust to theoretical departures from its core assumptions is not news. Hence, we will spare the reader a catalog of alternative theoretical assumptions that vitiate Stolper-Samuelson. Rather, we hope to appeal to a selection of recent empirical work on the part of trade economists that suggests that the conventional way of thinking about applying Stolper-Samuelson is hopeless.

2.1   A Primer on Issues with Stolper-Samuelson

The aim of this section is to give trade and nontrade economists a simple common language both to understand the insights of Stolper-Samuelson and also to understand its shortcomings as a tool for examining the problems of trade liberalization in developing countries. To do so, we will aim to develop a transparent exposition of the Stolper-Samuelson theorem and add some amendments that build our intuition about dimensions of robustness of the theorem, but also steer the conversation toward the dimensions in which the *practical or real-world* use of the theorem breaks down.

Consider the case of a country that is small in the world market for two

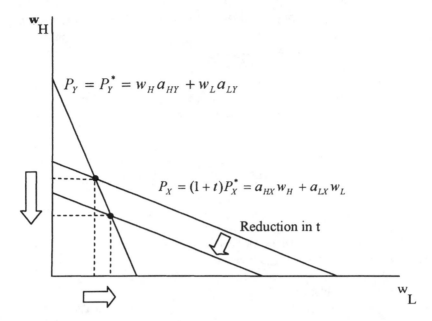

Fig. 2.1   Trade liberalization and factor prices: Stolper-Samuelson theorem

goods, X and Y. For simplicity, assume that X and Y are produced with fixed-coefficient technologies in the two inputs, say, skilled and unskilled labor (H and L). Perfect competition is assumed to reign in all goods and factor markets, and there are no geographical or sectoral barriers to mobility within a country. Let X be the skill-intensive good. Assume that *both goods are produced in this country in equilibrium* (fig. 2.1).

Under these conditions, price must equal unit cost. For the Y sector, this is easily written as

$$P_Y = w_H a_{HY} + w_L a_{LY}.$$

If we want to graph this in factor price space, we simply get

$$w_H = \frac{P_Y}{a_{HY}} - \frac{a_{LY}}{a_{HY}} w_L.$$

This is a simple linear equation with slope equal to minus the inverse of the skill intensity. Equivalently, the skill intensity is given as the slope of the normal to the unit cost curve (so the "flat" line is that of the skill-intensive X sector).

Even before we establish equilibrium factor prices, there are lessons to be learned here that are more general than the framework we are using. The first is that we need to pay attention to which goods price we are looking at—namely, the domestic price. Second is that here this price gives us the

revenue available to pay domestic factors of production. If the domestic price falls, *and the good continues to be produced under the same technology*, then some factor of production must receive less in compensation. If we think we see a good produced before and after a drastic trade liberalization, but we can't seem to find any factor that has had more than a trivial change in its factor return, then we had better look again. One possibility is that the goods on which we liberalized trade are not really the same as the goods we are producing, and so they had a zero or negligible effect on domestic prices of the goods we do produce. A second possibility would be some kind of "induced technical change" in which the unit input coefficients fall with liberalization so that wages can be maintained. If this change in the apparent unit input coefficients represented increased effort, then one should be cautious to note the losses in real income implied by the disutility of the added effort.

With the relative goods price and technology given exogenously, the single competitive cost condition above is insufficient to determine two factor prices. However, these can be determined given the corresponding unit cost condition for X:

$$w_H = \frac{P_X}{a_{HX}} - \frac{a_{LX}}{a_{HX}} w_L$$

Positive production of both goods requires that the associated zero-profit conditions intersect in the nonnegative orthant of factor price space and that the country's endowments lie in the range spanned by the two goods' factor intensities. For now we assume this to be true. Then the factor prices are determined by the intersection of the two zero-profit lines—that is, consistent with price equal to unit cost in both sectors.

The conventional argument that the unskilled in poor countries will benefit from trade liberalization requires just a few more steps. Assume that the poor country is an exporter of the unskilled-intensive good and importer of the skill-intensive good. Then $P_Y = P_Y^*$ and $P_X = (1 + t) P_X^*$, where P_X and P_X^* denote the domestic and foreign prices respectively of the skill-intensive good; P_Y and P_Y^* denote the same for the unskilled-intensive good. Removal of the tariff lowers the *domestic* price of the skill-intensive importable X without affecting that of the exportable Y. The reader can easily convince herself, based on this diagram or simple algebra, that the skilled wage falls in terms of both goods and the unskilled wage rises in terms of both goods (fig. 2.1).[1] This is the source of the conventional

---

1. The simplest way to see this graphically is to note how far the skilled wage would have fallen if the proportional decline in the price of X had fallen proportionally on both factors. Since equilibrium skilled wage with active production of both goods falls farther yet, clearly the real wage has fallen in terms of both goods. Correspondingly, the new equilibrium features a higher nominal unskilled wage here, hence also real wage, since the price of Y is unchanged and that of X fell.

statement that "trade theory" suggests that liberalization will raise the wages of the unskilled in unskilled abundant countries.

Before moving on to critiques of this conventional wisdom, we touch on a couple of additional topics. One is the role of nontraded goods. In this conventional setting, the prices of traded goods have already established the two factor prices (assuming both traded goods are always produced) as a function of the two domestic traded goods prices. Given these factor prices, cost minimization determines the price of nontraded goods, hence the demand in the nontraded sector, and local supply meets exactly that demand. Local demand shocks for nontraded have no effect on the equilibrium price of nontraded goods (i.e., they are met with a pure supply adjustment) so long as both traded goods continue to be produced. Hence a long tradition by trade economists of ignoring nontraded sectors—which are typically the majority of output!—in discussions of trade and factor prices.

We now introduce the concept of a noncompeting good. Up to now we have assumed that there is local production of all goods that are internationally traded. What happens if there is some good Z that is produced elsewhere (continue assuming we are small in world markets) but consumed here? We can call Z a noncompeting good because there is no local production and (by assumption) changes in tariffs on Z do not affect domestic prices of goods we do produce. In this case, the removal of a tariff on Z is a pure source of consumption gain for our consumers without affecting the product wages of skilled and unskilled in terms of X and Y. Both factors have higher real wages.

It is easiest to introduce the idea of intermediates here in a model in which the intermediate is a noncompeting good that also enters with a fixed coefficient (say one unit of intermediate per unit of output, say in the X sector). As before, let $P_X = (1 + t)P_X^*$ be the domestic price of the importable good. But now allow for an imported intermediate with price P_Z^* subject to a tariff t_Z. Then the domestic price must cover both payments to factors and the cost of intermediates; hence, we must amend the zero-profit condition of X to read

$$(1 + t)P_X^* = w_H a_{HX} + w_L a_{LX} + (1 + t_Z)P_Z^*.$$

That is, the domestic price now must suffice to pay both domestic factors plus the tariff-inclusive price of intermediates. Rearranging, this also yields

$$(1 + t)P_X^* - (1 + t_Z)P_Z^* = w_H a_{HX} + w_L a_{LX}.$$

The left-hand side is now the per-unit revenue associated with producing X, net of payments for intermediates, that can be used to compensate domestic factors. The important point to note is that t, the tariff on the domestically produced final product, and t_Z, the tariff on the imported intermediate, enter with opposite signs. A tariff on imports of the final good is

protective (yields more revenue to compensate domestic factors per unit output); a tariff on imports of the intermediate import is antiprotective (yields less revenue to compensate domestic factors per unit output). Or most simply of all, for an import competing producer, a tariff on final output is good news, while a tariff on intermediates is bad news. (Of course, if Z is steel and X is autos and both are domestically produced, then a tariff on Z is protective for steel but antiprotective for autos in the sense outlined here.) Figure 2.2 shows that the reduction in tariff on the intermediate good Z shifts the unit cost curve outward (since, given the price of X, for each value of w_L, w_H will have to rise), unlike the reduction in tariff on final good X. This would lead to an increase in the returns to high-skill labor and a decrease in the returns to low-skilled labor and hence an increase in wage inequality. Thus, it is possible that trade liberalization benefits the skilled labor in poor countries if liberalization takes place in the intermediates. The effect is exactly opposite to that shown in figure 2.1.

Nearly all of the theoretical elements of the Stolper-Samuelson framework are reasonable objects of scrutiny. We will emphasize some more than others, not because they are the only important ones but because, based on existing models and data work in international trade, these seem to be the most troublesome elements. No doubt other elements will need to be added later. We will especially emphasize those relevant for people who would like to do empirical work on trade liberalization in poor countries. We'll postpone until later speaking about imperfections in goods and factor

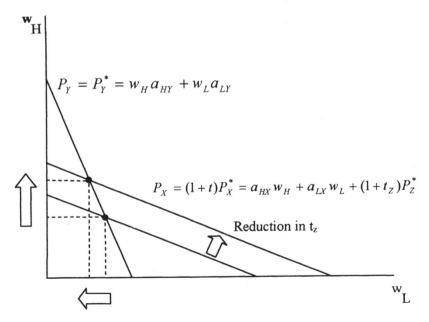

Fig. 2.2   Trade liberalization in intermediates and factor prices

markets, although these are also surely present in developing countries, because many very significant problems emerge for Stolper-Samuelson without worrying about these.

In thinking about problems of international trade, and specifically in thinking about Stolper-Samuelson, there is above all one whirlpool to which the siren song calls most strongly both to theorists and empiricists. This is the question of aggregation—most importantly here, the aggregation of goods. When we say that Stolper-Samuelson suggests that the unskilled in poor countries will benefit, the underlying model we have in mind is that we have two sectors, a skill- (or capital-) intensive importables sector and an unskilled-intensive exportables sector. In this world, indeed, the only potentially relevant tariff will be on the skill-intensive importable which is also produced locally, hence lower its domestic price, and yield precisely the effect conventionally described.

We have already alluded to many of the problems that may arise, both in theory and in data analysis, from thinking about our problem in these highly aggregated terms. There may be final goods that are noncompeting and hence enter our consumer price index but don't affect our product wages. If there are many such goods, it may be that some of these are more skill intensive than the goods we produce and some may be yet more unskilled intensive than the products we produce. In data analysis, changes in tariffs on truly noncompeting goods should be ignored in terms of effects on product wages. Unfortunately, the industry and tariff data that we have access to doesn't provide any way to distinguish between goods that compete with local production from goods that don't. We will see below that this is a potentially important problem for data analysis.

When we add to the case of more than two goods also the possibility that there are more than two countries, we encounter another type of problem. Even if we can continue to speak of our country as "unskilled abundant" in global terms, and if we can continue to speak of it producing two goods, it no longer follows which good will be the exportable one. As we will develop in more detail below, the pattern of trade will depend on a country's "local" rather than global factor abundance. That is, we need to be able to compare the country's factor abundance to that of others that produce the same sets of goods. Importantly, in our context, it is possible that it is tariffs on the unskilled-intensive good that are binding, and it is thus possible that trade liberalization lowers the price of the unskilled-intensive good produced locally, hurting those at the bottom of the ladder. In this type of world, trade is almost certain to hurt those at the very bottom of the ladder in some countries (unless the reduction in the consumer price index [CPI] from drops in tariffs on noncompeting goods sufficiently compensates for the fall in the real product wage).

The problem of aggregation of goods strikes again when we consider traded intermediates. We know that a large share of trade is in intermedi-

ates rather than final goods. As sketched theoretically above, tariffs on intermediate products used in an industry must be treated differently from tariffs on final outputs produced locally—indeed, they enter with the opposite sign in the using industry. It is at least disconcerting, then, that much of the literature on trade liberalization and wages in developing countries either ignores the question of imported intermediates or provides poor documentation of how it has been addressed. We are at least left worried about how to interpret results.

2.2   Do Rich and Poor Countries Produce the Same Goods?

By now there is overwhelming evidence that, whether at the level of industries used in a great deal of empirical work, or even at very fine levels of disaggregation at which tariffs are applied, the goods in the import basket are often quite different from the domestically produced goods. They differ *systematically* in the factor input composition, and they differ *systematically* in quality. Contrary to the way that we tend to treat them in both theoretical and data analyses, they are not perfect substitutes for the domestically produced goods. Often it may be more appropriate to think of them as noncompeting goods.

Let us spend a little time elaborating on this problem of aggregation. One area in which the problem of international aggregation of goods arose is in discussions of factor price equalization and measuring the factor content of international trade. In a pioneering study, Bowen, Leamer, and Sveikauskas (1987; hereafter BLS) assembled data on twelve productive factors for twenty-seven countries, calculated factor contents of trade, and compared these to predictions based on endowment differences. In calculating these factor contents for the central part of their paper, BLS committed the data crime of assuming that all countries use the U.S. technology matrix (although they also explored some deviations from this). Almost contemporaneously, Dollar, Wolff, and Baumol (1988; hereafter DWB) were examining correlations between industry factor input ratios and country factor input availability. Assuming that all countries produce the same goods and that there are no problems of aggregation, Rybczynski (or its multigood multifactor equivalent) predicts that the correlation should be zero. The actual correlation is much closer to unity.

Davis and Weinstein (2001) revisited the question of DWB.[2] Their initial intent was to make adjustments for cross-country productivity differences ignored by DWB and to demonstrate that, once this was done, we could have factor price equalization (FPE) adjusted for factor quality. The key idea was that FPE could be consistent with measured factor differences within an industry if that industry contained many goods and if capital-

2. See also Davis and Weinstein (2002).

abundant countries had their within-industry production on average skewed toward the more skill-intensive varieties. The key piece of evidence they hoped to provide was to show that the correlation between capital abundance and capital intensity within an industry arose only in traded goods, where the aggregation issue was more likely, but not in nontraded sectors, in which countries' consumption bundles would need to be much more similar. To their initial chagrin, Davis and Weinstein found that the correlation was essentially as strong in nontraded as traded sectors. This led them (and hopefully others!) to give up on trying to find a way to preserve any variant of "integrated equilibrium" as a useful way of thinking even about the subset of rich countries in the Organization for Economic Cooperation and Development (OECD). Moreover, it led them to think about a world with a high degree of specialization within the OECD, and a fortiori across a broader set of countries.

A very similar message emerges from the important work of Schott (2004). His work looks at price data at the most detailed available tariff categories for imports to the United States (in later years at the ten-digit harmonized system). What he finds is that, even at this extremely disaggregated level, there are enormous differences in import prices (across manufacturing industries by a mean factor of 24) and that the differences are systematically related to levels of development. It may be a matter of semantics whether we want to think of these as differences in quality or simply different goods—or probably more usefully as both. In combination with the earlier work, it strongly warns against thinking about imports as if all goods within a particular category compete closely with domestically produced varieties.

As we launch further into a discussion of the impact of trade on wages in the South, we have the benefit of a very extended discussion of related issues vis-à-vis the United States (and to a lesser extent Europe). This discussion helped us to learn (or rediscover) quite a bit about the workings of our toy models. However—with a few notable exceptions—we are much less convinced that the discussion told us a great deal about the impact of international trade on U.S. wages. Indeed, much of the writing had what, after the fact, can only seem to be a great air of unreality attached to it. An example and an important strand of the literature constituted the so-called factor content studies. These started out as empirical exercises that treated the implicit net factor content (often, though not always, using U.S. coefficients) as a net addition or subtraction from the local labor supplies. The empirical studies in turn inspired theoretical work, usually in a two-good context, about the conditions under which such factor content calculations are justified. It was often hard to know whether the greater unreality lay in the fiction that all imports were the same as their domestic counterparts (the assumption in virtually all of the analytic work) or the methods used

to calculate factor contents in the rare case that it was noted that imports and domestic goods are often not the same.

While it is easy to lash out at the studies that march forward as if it is fine to pretend that all countries produce the same goods, it is much harder to advise theorists or data analysts quite what they are to do with such an untidy world. Perhaps, though, a first step is to become more aware of the challenges that we face.

2.3   The Consequences of Moving to a More Complex World

Having set out our view that one of the great crimes in both theoretical and data work is the assumption that all countries produce the same goods, let us now spend a little time talking about how this might affect the way that we think about problems of trade liberalization and wages. A more formal discussion of this is in Davis (1996). However, we think that a verbal discussion of the results should suffice to make the major points. Following the injunction of Descartes, we will try to talk about this in the simplest possible framework. Consider a world with a large number of countries, no one of which is large enough to influence world prices. Assume that we are in a conventional Heckscher-Ohlin world in which the two factors are skilled and unskilled labor. Assume that there are many goods and that endowment differences are too large to support FPE. To start, assume all goods are final consumption goods (i.e., ignore intermediates). Again, for simplicity, assume that each of the resulting "cones" is formed by just two goods and that they are produced with fixed input ratios. How will this affect the standard theoretical results from the two-good FPE model, and how should it affect the way that we look at data exercises?

The first thing to note is that there are some appealing features of such a model. It matches well with the Davis-Weinstein results on breaks in (adjusted) FPE and is consistent with the Schott results when one notes that our statistical categories have grouped goods of different factor intensities (and possibly also different qualities) within the same industry. Moreover, it helps to make sense of one of the robust features of the data work— namely, that even countries that we think of as (unskilled) labor abundant may protect their most labor-intensive activities. In a standard Heckscher-Ohlin world, this would make no sense because this good would be an export, not an import! Here it makes perfect sense if we are looking at countries that are intermediate in labor abundance, since they may be importing goods from countries of both greater and less capital (skill) intensity. Protection of a labor-intensive sector by a country that is in global terms itself labor abundant is not an anomaly. One might then need a political economy account of why protection is higher in these sectors, but that is fine.

While there are some appealing features of this model, this does not at

all mean that it makes life simple for the researcher. Let's see why. An important fact about such a world is that, as in the standard Heckscher-Ohlin model, factor prices are determined by technology and domestic goods prices, but it is crucial to emphasize here that the relevant goods prices are those *produced* domestically because the factor prices emerge out of the binding zero-profit conditions of producers (and only those goods actually produced locally are relevant). Prices of imports not produced locally can figure importantly in the CPI, hence real wages, but they figure not at all in the product wages paid by producers. Hence, when we think about trade liberalization in this context, it is crucial to distinguish between competing goods (those produced locally) and noncompeting goods (those imported but not locally produced). Trade liberalization with respect to competing goods produces quasi-Stolper-Samuelson effects, while such liberalization with respect to noncompeting goods provides a pure consumption gain and no Stolper-Samuelson effects.

As noted, this is a huge headache for the empirical researcher. Assuming again that within an industry the statistical agencies have grouped together some goods that are competing and others that are noncompeting, then only some of these tariff changes should induce Stolper-Samuelson effects. But the empirical researcher is faced with the problem of deciding which goods are which—not an easy task! In this simple framework, though, theory does allow us to conjecture that the noncompeting goods are likely to come from countries very different (in endowments, but probably also in technology) from the country under study.

If we loosen the grip of our analysis just a little here, so countries are not purely small and tariffs on imports not produced locally do substitute (if poorly) for locally produced varieties, then this might help us to understand another seeming feature of the data exercises—that industry wage premia respond weakly to tariff changes (see the Blom et al. 2004 study of Brazil and the Feliciano 2001 study of Mexico). While this is not the perfect setting to discuss this, the basic point is pretty clear: if local political economy dictates the need to raise target factor prices, hence the relevant domestic goods price, and the only available target is a good that substitutes poorly for the local variety, then it will take a very large tariff to raise the price of the local good even a small amount. Taken in reverse, trade liberalization against a good that is a poor substitute for a local variety will affect local factor prices only weakly (because they affect the goods prices only weakly).

While we have been pointing to the evils of ignoring aggregation, thus far we have been focusing on the aggregation of different goods produced by different countries into a common industry category. We have not spoken as much about how the world changes when we allow for a world with large numbers—say, a continuum—of goods produced even within a country. Yet it is precisely in such models that a great deal of the most in-

teresting work has been done. This work finds its foundation in the papers of Dornbusch, Fischer, and Samuelson (1977, 1980; hereafter DFS). The most important contributions have come from Feenstra and Hanson (1996), Xu (2003), and Melitz (2003).

Feenstra and Hanson's work (1996) is often discussed as if it is primarily a paper about intermediate trade. As a substantive matter, that is how they developed it because they thought this was important to the case they focused on—namely, outsourcing from the United States to Mexico. For the analytics, though, the novel insight was not the consideration of intermediates but rather the use of a model with a continuum of goods to think about impacts on factor prices. The basic insight is pretty simple. In a two-good DFS (1980) world without trade costs, goods at the boundary of those produced in the United States and Mexico will be the most skill-intensive goods in Mexico and simultaneously the least skill-intensive goods in the United States. If accumulation in Mexico (due to capital inflows, domestic capital accumulation, population expansion, etc.) shifts the boundary to expand the range of goods produced in Mexico, the goods added on will shift relative labor demand in favor of skilled workers in Mexico and similarly in the United States. What is crucial to the example is not that these are intermediates (although that was very apt in this case) but rather that boundary goods are the most skill-intensive in one and the least skill-intensive in the other. Impacts of neutral accumulation on factor prices are likely to move the same direction in both countries.

While Feenstra and Hanson focus on the consequences of accumulation shifting the boundary good, Xu (2003) considers the case of trade liberalization. Trade liberalization now has several effects to consider (for convenience, ponder a case of symmetric liberalization). Liberalization reduces the interval of nontraded goods at the margin of comparative advantage. To continue the example, Mexico entirely stops producing some of its most skill-intensive nontraded goods (the most skill-intensive of all goods produced there) but expands production of some goods that previously were nontraded but are now the most skill-intensive products exported. At the same time, relative domestic prices of imports fall in each country, shifting relative demand in each country toward importables. Xu's focus is to establish the possibility for a unilateral liberalization that the expansion of the range of exportables previously not traded can dominate, shifting relative factor demand and factor prices in a way that enhances inequality.

It is worth pausing for a moment to ponder what it might look like if we were to merge the DFS (1980) model with the Davis (1996) or Davis and Weinstein (2001) approaches to trade relations—that is, to have a model that allows for a continuum of goods, breaks in FPE, and many countries. We don't know whether anyone has sought analytic results in a general equilibrium version of such a model. (The complexity even in the Xu set-

ting certainly suggests that such results will not come easily.) It is worth pondering nonetheless because this is a case where twoness is almost certainly the exception instead of the rule. The more general and surely more common case is that in which countries have two margins, one of greater and one of lesser (skill-capital-technological) intensity corresponding to countries above and below the country of interest. Whether both margins are crucial in a particular case may depend on the nature of the policy shock. A unilateral reform may more significantly involve both margins, whereas a bilateral free trade area (FTA) may have most of the adjustment on one margin (although in general equilibrium, the other may be affected as well). This might help to understand the contrast in experience between Mexico's early unilateral liberalization and the later opening to the North American Free Trade Agreement (NAFTA; see Robertson 2004).

Both Davis (1996) and Feenstra and Hanson (1996) offer explanations of how trade or investment can worsen the situation of those least well off in a poor country. Davis (1996) focuses on the mechanism whereby even a country that is labor abundant when compared to the world as a whole is an importer of the labor-intensive good it actually produces, leading liberalization to lower the domestic price of that good and thus wages for the poorer groups in that society. In Feenstra and Hanson, the mechanism is that expansion of total output in the poorer country leads it to add new goods at the margin to its production mix. In the case considered, the marginal goods shifted are at the expense of the Northern country. These become the most skill- or capital-intensive of the goods produced in the poorer country, which in turn shifts relative factor demand against unskilled labor there.

Topalova (chap. 7 in this volume) has suggested that liberalization in India may have worsened the situation of those least well off and emphasizes that a lack of geographical and sectoral mobility may have contributed to this. It is worth considering at least a very simple framework, consistent with a multicone world, that makes the point. Suppose the world consists of three countries, A (which we can consider the North or the rest of the world [ROW]), B, and C (where the latter are two groups within India). For simplicity, let this be an endowment economy where A has sugar, B (a relatively skilled group) has tea, and C (the unskilled) has jaggery.[3] When India's trade barriers are high, members of group B can trade with C or not trade at all. Tea with jaggery is not very attractive for a relatively well-off group, but it is better than only tea. When the trade barriers come down, all goods become in principle tradable. But members of group A only like sugar and tea, not jaggery. Members of group B like sugar and tea, but they will eat jaggery only when sugar is not available. Members of group C eat jaggery because it is cheap and would love to eat sugar except that even af-

---

3. Jaggery is a coarse unrefined sugar made from sugar cane juice.

ter liberalization it is too expensive. Moreover, with group B now having access to sugar, they want to sell less of their tea for jaggery, causing the relative price of jaggery to collapse. In effect, the initial trade barriers gave the poor a kind of monopoly power over B that disappears when B can trade with the rest of the world—leaving C worse off.

Having thought about this model with a continuum of goods but no apparent industries, it is worth thinking about what we should observe if each industry is itself composed of a continuum of goods of varying factor (technological) intensity. This forces us to think about the difference again between averages and margins. A statement that a particular industry, for example, is skill intensive is a statement about an average over an integral across all varieties in that industry using production weights. Yet adjustment is at the margins. An industry that is relatively unskilled intensive on average may yet be expected to have production over a range of skill intensities.

Melitz (2003) develops a model with heterogeneous firms defined by varying productivities. He shows how exposure to trade induces only the more productive firms to enter the export market and simultaneously forces the least productive firms to exit, leading to a rise in aggregate industry productivity. This model could be used to explain the findings in Goh and Javorcik (chap. 8 in this volume) for Poland and Mishra and Kumar (2005) for India. These papers find that reduction in tariffs is associated with an increase in wages within the industry. Trade liberalization could lead to an interfirm reallocation toward more productive firms and a rise in aggregate industry productivity, which gets passed on to industry wages.

Verhoogen (2004) reexamines the case of Mexico to question the existing interpretations of rising wage inequality there till the mid-1990s. His first observation is that the rise in the relative skilled wage *did not* come about due to a shift in relative demand across industries in favor of those using skilled workers more intensively. He shows that the shift in relative outputs in Mexico in the relevant period actually were in favor of unskilled and low-capital-intensity sectors. Instead he focuses on within-industry shifts. His hypothesis is that within industries, firms differ in productivity, with the more productive firms exporting (as in Melitz 2003), and that there is differentiation in product quality (Anderson, de Palma, and Thisse 1992). When new opportunities for trade arise—due in the case he examines to the sharp devaluation of the peso—these new opportunities are seized by these most productive firms. These firms produce a better-quality good for export than for the domestic market in order to appeal to richer developed-country consumers. Producing high-quality goods requires paying higher wages to all workers but especially to skilled workers, raising returns to all factors in those firms, but particularly to the most skilled. Here, the counterpart to the "technical change" argument that has been

used in the North is a "product shift" argument within industries that accounts for the within-industry shift in relative factor demand even as the across-industry shift would seem to point the other way.

It may seem odd that in a paper notionally devoted to theory one of the requests we have for empirical researchers is to spend more time describing the data and how they are handled. An example is the treatment of tariffs on intermediates. An elementary point is that a tariff on goods competing with a local producer's outputs provides protection, but a tariff on its inputs is antiprotective. But in many of the papers we look in vain for the words *intermediate* or *input-output* in a description of the impact of tariffs. We simply don't know how the issue of tariffs on intermediates has been addressed. But clearly the fact that it reverses the sign of the anticipated effect of a tariff should suffice to draw some discussion. We all know that the researcher did not get to design the data collection and that it may be less than ideal for the task at hand. Confess your data crimes and much will be forgiven. And much more will be learned.

2.4   Economics and Geography

One of the most important analytic developments in the study of trade of the 1990s is that of economic geography.[4] The analytic underpinnings are very simple: Dixit-Stiglitz production and costs of trade. While the models come in many variants, a large number of them yield provocative predictions about the nature of economic development and the difficulties faced by countries and international institutions in moving poor countries out of poverty. Trade liberalization need not help! Indeed, trade liberalization in these contexts has two faces. One is the improved access that you have to sell your products abroad. However, the other, particularly for a small country, is the possibility that the market becomes a site of consumption but not of production, at least of the crucial increasing-returns activities that yield high real wages. This certainly should not be interpreted as a blanket rationale for import substitution activities. But it does provide additional paths of serious inquiry into the costs and benefits of protection.

One of the more interesting analyses relevant to our problem is contained in Puga and Venables (1996). They consider a problem in which a country of the North, say Japan, has rising world demand for its products. Those products incorporate both high- and low-order activities. With the rising demand, wages rise in Japan, making it attractive to outsource some of the low-order activities to other locations. The question is to which

---

4. For monographs on the theory, see Fujita, Krugman, and Venables (1999) and Baldwin et al. (2003). Early work on the empirics includes Davis and Weinstein (1996, 1999). More recent empirical work includes Redding and Venables (2004), Hanson and Xiang (2004), and Davis and Weinstein (2004).

country the outsourcing will be done. If we are in a neoclassical world, then if there are many similarly situated countries—in terms of geography, policy, labor skill, and so on—each such similar country will get a similar share of the outsourcing. However, if we are instead in an "economic geography" world in which *local* sourcing of intermediate activities is crucial to the productivity in this outsourcing, then there will have to be both winners and losers. Some country or countries will receive this outsourcing and others will not. Those that do receive it will see demand for their labor rise and real wages rise, possibly very significantly; but this will not be so in the other countries.

These kinds of models present very significant problems in cross-country analyses. The cross-country analyses assume that outcomes are smooth in the policy variables. In the economic geography world, outcomes are lumpy.

In addition to the problems that these kinds of models present to the statistician, they present a yet greater problem to the policymaker. If the interaction of technology and geography dictates that Japan is going to outsource to just one country, then a dozen could pursue "good policies" yet only one emerge victorious.

2.5   Trade and Growth

The discussion to this point has treated theoretical considerations from the perspective of comparative statics. This is a very useful perspective, particularly for the purpose of understanding short- to medium-horizon impacts. However, it is ultimately limited, and perhaps decisively flawed, for three reasons. The first is simply that over any reasonable horizon, the magnitudes of growth impacts swamp magnitudes of comparative static impacts. The second, which is crucial here, is that the answers we receive as to the comparative static versus dynamic effects of liberalization need not be the same. Finally, when dynamic considerations exist—that is, in the world we actually inhabit(!)—one cannot really make sense even of comparative statics unless one has an eye on the dynamics that govern the movements of resources. All of these elements point to the need to explicitly consider links between trade liberalization and growth.

It is useful to start with a perfect competitive market view of trade and growth. Stiglitz (1970) considered such a world with a dynamic Heckscher-Ohlin model. In this model, autarkic differences in capital-labor ratios arose endogenously from deeper parameters reflecting rates of time discount. The patient country would accumulate a great deal of capital per worker in the autarkic steady state relative to the impatient country. Several key conclusions emerge from Stiglitz's work. The first is that trade leads to greater divergence in accumulation and specialization in production. The logic is quite simple. Assuming the initial differences in endow-

ments are not too large, FPE insures that factor returns must be equalized across the trading partners. Incipiently this raises the return to capital in the country already abundant in it and reduces it in the other country. Accumulation resumes in the capital-abundant country and decumulation sets in in the other country. Per capita incomes diverge. Since the rates of return must equal parametrically distinct national discount rates to be in a steady state, this can only arise if endowment differences become sufficiently great to break FPE (and under the assumption of barriers to capital flows that would be sufficient to arbitrage differences in factor returns). As noted, in the long run, the initial differences in per capita income would increase. Nonetheless, in this perfect-markets equilibrium, there are dynamic gains even for the country that in the long run will have a lower per capita income as a result of trade. The reason, of course, is that along the path to the new steady state it is possible to enjoy a higher level of consumption that more than compensates for the lower steady-state level of consumption.

A first path into dynamic questions of trade liberalization in imperfect markets may come from a consideration of models of learning by doing such as those of Robert Lucas (1988) and Alwyn Young (1991). The imperfection in question is that learning here enters as an external effect proportional to production. Lucas considers this in a two-country, two-good framework, where the goods are distinguished according to fundamental rates of learning opportunity. The first insight from the Lucas framework is that if learning is external, even transitory differences in comparative advantage can determine long-term growth opportunities. A country whose learning opportunities are diminished as a result of assignment by comparative advantage to slow-learning sectors may yet experience not only static but dynamic gains from trade as learning in the other country is passed on through lower prices. The central insight of Young is to place this squarely in a North-South context. He introduces the idea that learning is bounded and sequential. The North is further along in its learning path. The consequence is that it introduces a presumption that trade liberalization releases labor from sectors where learning is exhausted to be deployed in sectors where learning opportunities still exist, and vice versa for countries of the South. Because of the possibility of real income gains from the consumption side, this does not quite establish dynamic losses from trade, but it is certainly suggestive of this possibility, as comparative advantage dictates that production in the South be shifted toward sectors where learning is exhausted. Davis (1992) has argued that the restriction of this discussion to small dimensions in countries, goods, or both tends to understate the opportunities particularly for small countries to enjoy dynamic gains by specializing their learning in a small number of sectors. It is much easier to converge to the world productivity frontier in one or a few sectors than many.

The work of Grossman and Helpman (1991), building on work by Romer (1986) and Aghion and Howitt (1992), advanced greatly the discussion of the dynamics of trade and income. This is a rich body of work and can only be touched on here. The central issues of interest are that they consider the engine of growth to be innovation and imitation, which in turn are purposeful activities driven by the incentives that markets provide to firms. The traditional incentives to augment capital as in Stiglitz (1970) are here augmented by incentives to invest in knowledge. A fundamental element is that knowledge is nonrival (although it may be excludable). There are gains to the world (and potentially to all countries) from having to discover things only once. There are likewise gains to the world from having innovation take place where it is least costly. Of course, many of the prior concerns about the distribution of these gains across countries emerge yet again here. Moreover, with markets imperfect, both the level and the location of innovation can be nonoptimal (and possibly the level even too great!).

2.6 Conclusions

This volume is dedicated to understanding the impact of globalization on poverty in poor countries. This paper has tried to discuss the theory that is most relevant for such a discussion in the context of trade liberalization. Since the question of the impact of trade liberalization on the poor in poor countries is such an obviously important question, it is a major embarrassment to the profession that we understand it so poorly. This volume takes many important steps forward, but the need for further inquiry is manifest.

Certainly a starting point is to cast off the shibboleths of Stolper-Samuelson in its global form as a useful way to think about the world that we actually live in. Insights from growth theory and from the theory of economic geography, as well as more traditional theories, will be important in moving us forward.

The empirical work contained in this volume, in combination with other work outside, has been extraordinarily useful. Its use will be all the greater if we spend less time coming up with immediately tidy explanations and spend more time identifying the puzzling aspects of the problem. They should not be in short supply. For the studies of trade liberalization, the most pressing line for further inquiry should be understanding the extent and process of reallocation. This will need to be studied with detailed reference to institutions and local characteristics. Labor market rigidities may explain why declining industries find it hard to fire workers. But it is hard to understand why expanding industries are not drawing in many of these same workers. It is not clear yet that there is a fully consistent story.

There is an old joke about a drunkard who explains that although he lost

his keys in the park down the street he is looking for them here under the lamppost because the light is so much better. A lot of our theoretical and empirical work has a taste of this logic. And it is not entirely crazy, because our toy models do give us useful insights and the empirical work gives us some views of the data that might surprise and so inspire us. We hope, though, that we have made the case that in this untidy world of ours it might make sense to spend some time in the dark, on our knees, groping for the keys.

References

Aghion, Philippe, and Peter Howitt. 1992. A model of growth through creative destruction. *Econometrica* 60 (2): 323–51.
Anderson, Simon P., Andre de Palma, and Jacques-François Thisse. 1992. *Discrete choice theory of product differentiation.* Cambridge, MA: MIT Press.
Baldwin, Richard, Rikard Forslid, Philippe Martin, Gianmarco Ottaviano, and Frederic Robert-Nicoud. 2003. *Economic geography and public policy.* Princeton, NJ: Princeton University Press.
Blom, Andreas, Pinelopi Goldberg, Nina Pavcnik, and Norbert Schady. 2004. Trade policy and industry wage structure: Evidence from Brazil. *World Bank Economic Review* 18 (3): 319–44.
Bowen, Harry P., Edward E. Leamer, and Leo Sveikauskas. 1987. Multicountry, multifactor tests of the factor abundance theory. *American Economic Review* 77 (5): 791–809.
Davis, Donald R. 1992. Mutual dynamic gains from trade due to specialization in learning by doing. In Essays in the theory of international trade and economic growth. PhD diss., Columbia University.
———. 1996. Trade liberalization and income distribution. NBER Working Paper no. 5693. Cambridge, MA: National Bureau of Economic Research.
Davis, Donald R., and David E. Weinstein. 1996. Does economic geography matter for international specialization? NBER Working Paper no. 5706. Cambridge, MA: National Bureau of Economic Research.
———. 1999. Economic geography and regional production structure: An empirical investigation. *European Economic Review* 43 (February): 379–407.
———. 2001. An account of global factor trade. *American Economic Review* 91 (5): 1423–53.
———. 2002. What role for empirics in international trade? In *Bertil Ohlin: A centennial celebration (1899–1999),* ed. Ronald Findlay, Lars Jonung, and Mats Lundahl, 363–87. Cambridge, MA: MIT Press.
———. 2004. A search for multiple equilibria in urban industrial structure. NBER Working Paper no. 10252. Cambridge, MA: National Bureau of Economic Research.
Deardorff, Alan V., and Robert M. Stern, eds. 1994. *The Stolper-Samuelson theorem: A golden jubilee.* Ann Arbor: University of Michigan Press.
Dollar, David, Edward M. Wolff, and William J. Baumol. 1988. The factor-price equalization model and industry labor productivity: An empirical test across countries. In *Empirical methods for international trade,* ed. Robert C. Feenstra, 23–48. Cambridge, MA: MIT Press.

Dornbusch, Rudiger, Stanley Fischer, and Paul A. Samuelson. 1977. Comparative advantage, trade, and payments in a Ricardian model with a continuum of goods. *American Economic Review* 67 (5): 823–39.

———. 1980. Heckscher-Ohlin trade theory with a continuum of goods. *Quarterly Journal of Economics* 95 (2): 203–24.

Feenstra, Robert C., and Gordon H. Hanson. 1996. Foreign investment, outsourcing, and relative wages. In *The political economy of trade policy: Papers in honor of Jagdish Bhagwati*, ed. Robert C. Feenstra, Gene M. Grossman, and Douglas A. Irwin, 89–127. Cambridge, MA: MIT Press.

Feliciano, Zadia. 2001. Workers and trade liberalization: The impact of trade reforms in Mexico on wages and employment. *Industrial and Labor Relations Review* 55 (1): 95–115.

Fujita, Masahisa, Paul Krugman, and Anthony Venables. 1999. *The spatial economy: Cities, regions and international trade.* Cambridge, MA: MIT Press.

Grossman, Gene M., and Elhanan Helpman. 1991. *Innovation and growth in the global economy.* Cambridge, MA: MIT Press.

Hanson, Gordon H., and Chong Xiang. 2004. The home-market effect and bilateral trade patterns. *American Economic Review* 94 (4): 1108–29.

Lucas, Robert E., Jr. 1988. On the mechanics of economic development. *Journal of Monetary Economics* 22 (1): 3–42.

Melitz, Marc J. 2003. The impact of trade on intra-industry reallocations and aggregate industry productivity. *Econometrica* 71 (6): 1695–1725.

Mishra, Prachi, and Utsav Kumar. 2005. Trade liberalization and wage inequality: Evidence from India. IMF Working Paper no. WP 05/20. Washington, DC: International Monetary Fund.

Puga, Diego, and Anthony J. Venables. 1996. The spread of industry: Spatial agglomeration in economic development. *Journal of the Japanese and International Economies* 10 (4): 440–64.

Redding, Stephen, and Anthony J. Venables. 2004. Economic geography and international inequality. *Journal of International Economics* 62 (1): 53–82.

Robertson, Raymond. 2004. Relative prices and wage inequality: Evidence from Mexico. *Journal of International Economics* 64 (2): 387–409.

Romer, Paul M. 1986. Increasing returns and long-run growth. *Journal of Political Economy* 94 (5): 1002–37.

Schott, Peter K. 2004. Across-product versus within-product specialization in international trade. *Quarterly Journal of Economics* 119 (2): 647–78.

Stiglitz, Joseph E. 1970. Factor price equalization in a dynamic economy. *Journal of Political Economy* 78 (3): 456–88.

Verhoogen, Eric. 2004. Trade, quality upgrading and wage inequality in the Mexican manufacturing sector: Theory and evidence from an exchange-rate shock. Columbia University, Department of Economics. Mimeograph.

Xu, Bin. 2003. Trade liberalization, wage inequality, and endogenously determined nontraded goods. *Journal of International Economics* 60 (2): 417–31.

Young, Alwyn. 1991. Learning by doing and the dynamic effects of international trade. *Quarterly Journal of Economics* 106 (2): 369–405.

3

Globalization, Poverty, and All That
Factor Endowment versus Productivity Views

William Easterly

That globalization causes poverty is a staple of antiglobalization rhetoric. The Nobel Prize winner Dario Fo compared the impoverishment of globalization to the events of September 11, 2001: "The great speculators wallow in an economy that every year kills tens of millions of people with poverty—so what is 20,000 dead in New York?" (quoted in Levy and Peart 2001). The protesters usually believe globalization is a disaster for the workers, throwing them into "downward wage spirals in both the North and the South" (Cavanagh and Mander 2002). Oxfam (2004a) identifies such innocuous products as Olympic sportswear as forcing laborers into "working ever-faster for ever-longer periods of time under arduous conditions for poverty-level wages, to produce more goods and more profit." According to a best-selling book by William Greider (1997),

> in the primitive legal climate of poorer nations, industry has found it can revive the worst forms of nineteenth century exploitation, abuses outlawed long ago in the advanced economies, including extreme physical dangers to workers and the use of children as expendable cheap labor. (p. 34)

Oxfam complains that corporate greed is "exploiting the circumstances of vulnerable people," which it identifies mainly as young women, to set up profitable "global supply chains" for huge retailers like Wal-Mart. In China's fast-growing Guangdong Province, "young women face 150 hours

William Easterly is a professor of economics at New York University and codirector of the university's Development Research Institute.

I am grateful for comments from Ann Harrison, Aart Kraay, Don Davis, and participants in the National Bureau of Economic Research globalization workshop. Comments on related work at the Brookings Trade Forum were also helpful.

of overtime each month in the garment factories—but 60 per cent have no written contract and 90 per cent have no access to social insurance." Women at the bottom of these global supply chains must work "at high speed for low wages in unhealthy conditions" (Oxfam 2004b).

Even Western diplomats are scared by the effects of globalization on poor people: Jean-Paul Fitoussi, advisor to French prime minister Lionel Jospin, referred to "deregulated global markets" as "Frankenstein," who somehow must be brought "under control." Anthony Giddens, director of the London School of Economics and advisor to Tony Blair, said there was a "general realization" that "you cannot leave people unprotected before the global market" (quoted in Micklethwait and Wooldridge 2000). (But can you leave them unprotected before Group of Seven bureaucrats?)

Economists find such rhetoric hard to take, since the neoclassical model of growth identifies at least three ways in which globalization makes the poor of the world better off. Let us define globalization as the movement across international borders of goods and factors of production. Let us adopt the standard assumption of the neoclassical model that poor countries are poor because of lower capital per worker. Let us identify the world's poor as largely belonging to the group of unskilled workers in poor countries. Then globalization has three beneficial channels for poor workers: (a) it gives them access to inflows of capital, which will raise the marginal product of labor and thus wages (part of which can be taken in the form of increased health and safety benefits and shorter hours); (b) it gives them the opportunity to migrate to rich countries, where their wages will be higher; and (c) it gives them market access for their goods, raising the wages of unskilled workers in labor-abundant countries according to textbook trade theory.

Do the poor indeed benefit from globalization through these three channels? I review how these predictions arise from the neoclassical model's predictions when income differences between rich and poor countries are explained by factor endowments. If income differences are instead explained by productivity differences, then these simple predictions do not hold. Hence, it is important to decide to what extent factor endowment models explain the stylized facts as opposed to productivity models. I examine the actual behavior of poverty, inequality, and trade, trends in trade and factor flows, and factor returns to assess whether the factor endowment predictions come true.

I conclude that the clear theoretical channels between globalization and poverty featured by factor endowment models are not very helpful in understanding globalization outcomes. Unfortunately, many episodes seem to require productivity channels to accommodate the facts. Even more unfortunately, we know much less about how productivity channels work than we know about factor endowments.

3.1   The Channels by Which Globalization Affects Poverty in Standard Models

I define globalization as the free movement of capital, labor, and goods across national borders. When I discuss effects of globalization, I have in mind unhindered flows as compared to a situation with restricted flows or, in the extreme case, no flows at all. I look at these flows from the standpoint of the neoclassical growth model. Factor endowment models feature equal productivity levels across nations, while the productivity model is defined as differing productivity levels. These are polar cases, of course, as there are intermediate cases of differences in both factor endowments and productivity. I use the polar cases for pedagogical clarity.

3.1.1   Factor Movements

In the factor endowment model of neoclassical growth, free movement of factors tends to reduce poverty gaps between nations. In Factor World, income differences between countries are due to different capital-labor ratios. Rich nations have more capital per worker than poor nations. Rates of return to capital will be higher in poor nations than in rich nations, while wages will be higher in rich nations than poor nations.

The equations are as follows. Let Y_i, A_i, K_i, and L_i stand for output, labor-augmenting productivity, capital, and labor in country i (where i can either be rich, R, or poor, P).

$$Y_i = K_i^{\alpha}(A_i L_i)^{1-\alpha}$$

Let $k_i = K_i/L_i$ and $y = Y_i/L_i$. The rate of return to capital r and wage w in country i is

$$r_i = \frac{\partial Y_i}{\partial K_i} = \alpha k_i^{\alpha-1} A_i^{1-\alpha},$$

$$w_i = \frac{\partial Y_i}{\partial L_i} = (1-\alpha)k_i^{\alpha} A_i^{1-\alpha}.$$

I am going to use the wage of unskilled workers in poor countries as the indicator of poverty to be affected by globalization. I prefer this to the usual poverty head count numbers, as the latter indicator has a number of undesirable properties: (a) it is very sensitive to the poverty line chosen, and there is no clear guidance how to choose a poverty line; (b) it has an illogical discontinuity at the poverty line, implying a large leap in welfare with an ε movement across the poverty line, but little effect from even a substantial movement as long as one stays either below or above the poverty line.

The per capita income measure is potentially subject to the critique that increases in Gini coefficients could mean that income gains all accrue to the rich. Changes in Gini coefficients influence poverty outcomes just as

average income growth does (see the recent survey by Besley and Burgess 2003), so I will pay a lot of attention to Ginis. I will show in a moment that factor endowment models generally predict that globalization will lower inequality in poor countries, not increase it.

If $A_R = A_P = A$, then the per capita income ratio between the two countries when A is the same is

$$\frac{y_R}{y_P} = \left(\frac{k_R}{k_P}\right)^\alpha.$$

If there is free mobility of factors, then capital will want to migrate from rich to poor nations, while workers will want to migrate from poor to rich nations. This will decrease the capital-labor ratio in rich countries while increasing it in poor countries. These flows will continue until capital-labor ratios are equal across nations and factor prices are equal, which will steadily decrease income gaps between nations (reducing poverty in poor countries). Compared to the no-factor-mobility state, returns to capital will rise in rich countries and fall in poor countries. With factor mobility, wages will fall in rich countries and rise in poor countries. Poverty in the South falls for two reasons: (a) the migration of capital to poor countries raises wages in poor countries, and (b) the migration of unskilled labor from poor to rich nations raises the income both of the migrants (who will gain access to higher capital per worker in the North) and of those workers who remain behind (because capital per worker in the South increases with the departure of some Southern workers).

If everyone has raw labor but less than 100 percent of the population owns capital, then the capital rental–wage ratio is positively related to inequality. Hence, factor flows (globalization) will reduce inequality in poor countries and increase it in rich countries.

The predicted capital flows are very large. Denoting k_i^* as the capital-labor ratio in country i ($i = P$ or R) in the final equilibrium, and the unstarred values of k_i and y_i as the initial values, we have the following:

$$\frac{k_P^* - k_P}{k_R^*} = 1 - \left(\frac{y_P}{y_R}\right)^{1/\alpha}$$

$$k_P^* = k_R^*$$

$$\frac{k_P^* - k_P}{y_P^*}\frac{y_P^*}{k_P^*} = 1 - \left(\frac{y_P}{y_R}\right)^{1/\alpha}$$

$$\frac{y_P^*}{k_P^*} = \frac{r^*}{\alpha}$$

$$\frac{k_P^* - k_P}{y_P^*} = \frac{\alpha}{r^*}\left[1 - \left(\frac{y_P}{y_R}\right)^{1/\alpha}\right]$$

In the factor endowment model, even small differences in initial income trigger massive factor flows. If we assume a capital share of 1/3, a ratio of poor- to rich-country income of 0.8, and a marginal product of capital (r^*) of .15, then the cumulative capital inflows into the poor country will be 108 percent of the terminal equilibrium GDP in the poor country!

Suppose instead that income differences between nations are due to productivity differences rather than differences in capital per worker. Now both capital and labor will want to move to the rich country, unlike the opposite flows predicted in the factor endowment model. Unlike the latter case, the final outcome in a frictionless world would be a corner solution in which all capital and labor move to the rich country to take advantage of the superior productivity. Obviously there have to be some frictions such as incomplete capital markets, preference for one's homeland, rich country immigration barriers, costs of relocating to a new culture, and so on to avoid this extreme prediction. Pritchett (2004) argues that there may in fact be countries that could become "ghost countries" if factor mobility was unimpeded, just like the rural counties currently emptying out on the Great Plains in the United States.

In the productivity differences model, equating rates of return to capital across countries implies that the ratio of k_R to k_P is the same as the ratio of A_R to A_P. This will also be the ratio of relative per capita incomes *and* the ratio of relative wages under free capital mobility:

$$\frac{\partial Y_R}{\partial K_R} = \alpha k_R^{\alpha-1} A_R^{1-\alpha} = \frac{\partial Y_P}{\partial K_P} = \alpha k_P^{\alpha-1} A_P^{1-\alpha}$$

$$\frac{k_R}{k_P} = \frac{A_R}{A_P}$$

$$\frac{w_R}{w_P} = \left(\frac{k_R}{k_P}\right)^{\alpha}\left(\frac{A_R}{A_P}\right)^{1-\alpha} = \frac{A_R}{A_P} = \frac{y_R}{y_P}$$

If income differences are due to productivity differences, then opening up to capital inflows will have no effect on unskilled wages in the poor country. The relative income of the world's poor will remain unchanged with this form of globalization (free capital mobility).

Of course, this is a polar case. In the real world, the poor country could have lower wages and per capita incomes because of *both* lower productivity and lower capital-labor ratios. Assessing the degree to which productivity and factor endowments contribute to poverty is the key to assessing the predicted impact of capital mobility.

3.1.2   Trade Flows and Inequality

To discuss trade, we need to shift from the one-sector neoclassical growth model to the standard two-sector trade model in which sectors

differ in their capital intensity. In a two-sector model with a neoclassical production function, goods mobility will have the same effect as factor mobility even if factors cannot move. The capital-abundant rich nation will export capital-intensive goods, while the labor-abundant poor nation will export labor-intensive goods. The expansion of demand for labor and fall in demand for capital in the poor country (compared to autarky) will raise wages of unskilled labor and lower capital rentals. The reverse will happen in the rich country. If the equilibrium is for less than complete specialization, factor prices will move toward equality in the two countries just as in the factor mobility case. Increased trade will reduce poverty in the South because of the expansion in demand for labor that comes with the expansion of labor-intensive exports. Again, if the capital rental–wage ratio is positively related to inequality within the nation, trade will increase inequality in the rich country and decrease it in the poor country.

What if the absolute level of labor-augmenting productivity is different between the two countries? With productivity differences, the factor price equalization theorem still applies, but it now applies to effective labor $A_i L_i$. The wage per unit of effective labor will be equalized between the two countries under free trade, as will the rate of return to capital in the two countries. This means that the wage per unit of physical labor in the two countries will be different. The ratio of the wage per unit of physical labor in the higher-productivity (rich) country to the lower-productivity (poor) country will be A_R/A_P. This will also be the ratio of per capita incomes in the two countries.

The analysis of which country is more labor abundant will also differ from the equal-productivity case. If the relative scarcity of labor in the rich country is sufficiently offset by higher relative productivity, then the rich country will be "labor abundant" and will export "labor-intensive" goods. Compared to autarky, wages will increase in the rich country and decrease in the poor country. Trade increases poverty in this paradoxical example. In this case, trade will reduce inequality in the rich country and increase it in the poor country. Compared to autarky, trade causes divergence of per capita incomes in this unusual case.

If productivity differences are not so stark as to offset relative factor scarcity, the rich country will be capital abundant, and we will go back to the usual prediction that trade reduces poverty in the South. Trade will still increase inequality in the rich country and lower it in the poor country.

As noted by many previous authors, interesting interactions between trade and factor flows arise from the unconventional productivity view of comparative advantage. Whereas in the factor endowments model, trade and factor flows do the same things to factor prices and are effectively substitutes, trade and factor flows can be complements in the productivity model. For example, if the rich country is perversely labor abundant because of productivity advantages in the labor-intensive sector, then trade

will raise the wage in the rich country (relative to the poor country) and lead to more labor migration from poor to rich countries. This makes the rich country even more labor abundant, strengthening its comparative advantage in labor-intensive products.

Analogously, trade could lead to capital inflows into the capital-abundant poor country, if productivity differences lie in that direction. This is the opposite of what happens in the factor endowments model, in which exports from the poor country of labor-intensive goods lower the rate of return to capital, eliminating the capital inflows that would have otherwise responded to the high returns to scarce capital.

The bottom line is that the effect of trade on Southern poverty depends on relative productivity levels as well as factor endowments. Which way the effect goes is an empirical matter.

3.1.3   Introducing Land as a Third Factor

Of course, there is one factor that does not move—land and natural resources. Even if productivity is higher elsewhere, land prices could adjust to retain some capital and labor in the home country. This was an important factor in the nineteenth century. It seems less so now in today's urbanized world. If land and capital are perfect substitutes, then an economy could substitute away from land and not drive up the return to the other factors to make them want to stay. However, there are many countries where agriculture is important enough that land and natural resource availability is a potentially relevant sticky factor that prevents flight of all factors to high-productivity places.

Land acts much like productivity in its effect on the marginal products of capital and labor. Hence a land-rich place could attract both capital and labor, just as a high-productivity place does. This was a very important factor in the nineteenth-century wave of globalization. It still seems relevant today in that natural resources may attract capital and labor into areas that otherwise have low productivity.

The relevant equations including land (T) are the following. Let the production function including land be

$$Y_i = T_i^\alpha K_i^\beta (A_i L_i)^{1-\alpha-\beta}$$

Now let capital and labor freely move to equate rates of return to capital and wages. Let $t_i = T_i/L_i$ and $k_i = K_i/L_i$. The rate of return to capital and wage will be

$$\frac{\partial Y_i}{\partial K_i} = \beta t_i^\alpha k_i^{\beta-1} A_i^{1-\alpha-\beta},$$

$$\frac{\partial Y_i}{\partial L_i} = (1 - \alpha - \beta) t_i^\alpha k_i^\beta A_i^{1-\alpha-\beta}.$$

Obviously, both capital and labor will be attracted to the land-abundant places as well as the places with higher productivity. Since both capital and labor can move, you can show that capital-labor ratios in the two places will be equated. Labor will move to equate wages, which reflect both land abundance and productivity. If there were no productivity differences between places, land-labor ratios would also be equated.

The effect of globalization on poverty with different land endowments now depends on whether the poor nation is land poor or land rich. If the poor nation is land rich, then the only reason it could be poor under the factor endowments model is that it lacks capital. Thus, the poor country attracts capital inflows under globalization both because capital is scarce in the poor country and because land wealth implies a higher marginal product of capital. This will increase wages and reduce poverty in the South. This is the relevant case for poor countries with rich commodity endowments.

If the poor nation is land poor, then we would expect it to lose population under globalization until land-labor ratios are equated. There is still a catching-up effect of Southern to Northern wages. In general, free factor mobility suggests a catching up of poor to rich nations in either case.

With differences in productivity, population density will be higher in the higher-productivity places:

$$\frac{\frac{L_R}{T_R}}{\frac{L_P}{T_P}} = \left(\frac{A_R}{A_P}\right)^{(1-\alpha-\beta)/\alpha}$$

Per capita incomes will move toward equality as well, since labor moves in response to both relative land abundance and productivity. Hence, there will be convergence of per capita incomes if both labor and capital can move freely, in either the factor endowments or productivity models. The only remaining sign of higher productivity in the rich countries in equilibrium is that they will have attracted capital and labor away from the lower-productivity poor countries. Similarly, the only effect remaining in equilibrium of higher land abundance will be that land-abundant countries will wind up with more labor and capital.

Obviously these are extreme predictions that only apply under complete factor mobility. We will examine whether these predictions hold with one natural experiment of full globalization: free factor mobility within the United States.

3.1.4 Mobile Physical Capital and Immobile Human Capital

So far I have not considered human capital. An interesting case with human capital is the open economy version of the factor accumulation model by Barro, Mankiw, and Sala-i-Martin (1995; hereafter BMS). BMS allows

capital flows to equalize the rate of return to physical capital across countries, while human capital is immobile. Immobile human capital explains the difference in per-worker income across nations in BMS.

The poor countries' marginal product of capital is low because of scarce human capital, which offsets its normal elevation by abundant labor. Whether scarce human capital outweighs abundant labor is ambiguous for poor countries. Hence, globalization does not necessarily lead to physical capital inflows for the South, and thus does not necessarily raise wages of unskilled workers. This could be another reason why globalization does not always lead to capital flows from rich to poor nations, and thus capital mobility does not necessarily lower poverty. Here we have the unwelcome appearance of ambiguity even in the factor endowments model.

However, there are problems with the BMS model in that it explains income differences solely by human capital, problems so severe as to make it not really a viable factor endowments model. As pointed out by Romer (1995), the BMS model implies that both the skilled wage and the skill premium should be much higher in poor countries than in rich countries. To illustrate this, we specify a standard production function for country i as

$$Y_i = AK_i^\alpha L_i^\beta H_i^{1-\alpha-\beta}.$$

Assuming technology (A) is the same across countries and that rates of return to physical capital are equated across countries, we can solve for the ratio of the skilled wage in country i to that in country j, as a function of their per capita incomes, as follows:

$$\frac{\dfrac{\partial Y_i}{\partial H_i}}{\dfrac{\partial Y_j}{\partial H_j}} = \left[\frac{\dfrac{Y_i}{L_i}}{\dfrac{Y_j}{L_j}}\right]^{-\beta/(1-\alpha-\beta)}$$

Using the physical and human capital shares (.3 and .5 respectively) suggested by Mankiw (1995), the model implies that skilled wages should be five times greater in India than the United States (to correspond to a fourteenfold difference in per capita income). In general, the equation above shows that skilled wage differences across countries should be inversely related to per capita income if human capital abundance explains income differences across countries, à la BMS.

The skill premium should be seventy times higher in India than the United States. If the ratio of skilled to unskilled wage is about 2 in the United States, then the skilled-unskilled wage ratio in India should be 140. This would imply a fantastic rate of return to education in India, seventy times larger than the return to education in the United States.

If we relaxed the restriction of immobility of human capital in this case, we would get a reverse brain drain from rich to poor countries. If we

broaden globalization to include mobility of human capital, this would be yet another reason why poor countries should catch up to rich ones in the factor endowments model—because they attract both physical and human capital. This is obviously counterfactual, as human capital tends to flow to rich countries.

With productivity differences, we do not have these extreme predictions. If the income difference between the South and the North is explained largely by productivity, then lower productivity has an offsetting effect to the scarcity of skills in the South in their effects on the return to skill in the South. This would cancel the counterfactual prediction of reverse brain drain. The predicted effect on physical capital inflows to the South is ambiguous as it was before, and hence the effect on Southern poverty. If we allow human capital to move with lower productivity in poor countries, there could be a tendency for both physical and human capital to flee from poor countries, depressing wages and worsening poverty. If we allow all three factors—physical and human capital and unskilled labor—to move, we return to the extreme prediction of poor countries emptying out.

The central message of this section has been that globalization reduces world poverty if income differences are due to differences in factor endowments, while the effects of globalization are null or ambiguous if income differences are due to productivity differences. I summarize the different predictions in table 3.1. Different globalization episodes or different groups of countries could fall into either case, or somewhere in between. Hence, I now turn to the examination of stylized facts on globalization and poverty.

3.2   Empirical Evidence on Globalization and Poverty

In this section, I review the evidence on globalization and poverty. My method is to look for stylized facts that provide direct or indirect evidence for whether factor endowment differences or productivity differences explain globalization and poverty outcomes. I look first at the overall patterns of trade and factor flows, then at the behavior of relative international incomes and factor prices, and finally at the effect of globalization on domestic inequality. I then adduce evidence from factor movements within countries. The overall pattern tends to support the productivity differences view instead of the factor endowments view, with occasional exceptions. Hence, although there are some globalization episodes that have reduced poverty, the overall effect of globalization on poverty looks like it falls short of the expectations of the standard textbook models.

3.2.1   Empirical Evidence on Trade and Factor Flows across Countries

The migration of labor is overwhelmingly directed toward the richest countries. The three richest countries alone (the United States, Canada,

Table 3.1   **Predictions of theoretical models of globalization**

Model	Income differences due to factor endowments	Income differences due to productivity differences
Neoclassical model with free mobility of capital and labor	Capital moves from rich to poor nations; labor moves from poor to rich nations; equal capital-labor ratios between rich and poor; factor price equalization; higher unskilled wages and reduced poverty in the South; increased inequality in rich countries, reduced inequality in poor countries.	Both capital and labor move from poor to rich countries. Capital-labor ratio in rich to poor countries is the same as ratio of relative productivity. In frictionless world, corner solution of rich country with all capital and labor, poor country emptying out ("ghost countries")
Neoclassical model with free trade in goods	Rich nations export capital-intensive goods, poor nations will export labor-intensive goods; factor price equalization; higher unskilled wages and reduced poverty in the South; trade increases inequality in rich nation and reduces it in poor nation.	Ratio of wages in rich to poor countries will be given by the productivity ratio. Two cases: (1) Rich nation could export labor-intensive goods if productivity advantage offsets labor scarcity; then trade would reduce inequality in rich country and decrease wages in poor country, and trade would increase Southern poverty. (2) If productivity advantage not so extreme, then trade increases inequality in rich country, increases it in poor country, reduces poverty in South.
Neoclassical model including land with free mobility of factors	Land-rich place attracts both capital and labor; in the limit, land-labor ratios are equated across countries; convergence of per capita incomes.	Population density higher in high-productivity places; still have convergence of per capita incomes.
Neoclassical model with mobile physical capital and immobile human capital (Barro, Mankiw, Sala-i-Martin)	Physical capital may not flow to poor countries if human capital scarcity more than offsets unskilled labor abundance; however, model implies counterfactually high returns to skills in human capital–scarce poor countries than in human capital–abundant rich countries.	Returns to skills determined by relative productivity levels. High-productivity rich countries will have higher returns to skills than low-productivity poor countries.

and Switzerland) receive half of the net immigration of all countries reporting net immigration. Countries in the richest quintile are all net recipients of migrants. Only eight of the ninety countries in the bottom four-fifths of the sample are net recipients of migrants (Easterly and Levine 2001).

Embodied in this flow of labor are flows of human capital towards the rich countries, the famous brain drain. In terms of the simple models above, human capital movements are governed by the same predictions as physical capital movements.

I used Grubel and Scott's (1977) data to calculate that in the poorest fifth of nations, the probability that an educated person will immigrate to the United States is 3.4 times higher than that for an uneducated person. Since we know that education and income are strongly and positively correlated, human capital is flowing to where it is already abundant—the rich countries.

A more recent study by Carrington and Detragiache (1998) found that those with tertiary education were more likely to migrate to the United States than those with a secondary education in fifty-one out of the sixty-one developing countries in their sample. Migration rates for primary or less educated to the United States were less than migration rates for either secondary or tertiary in all sixty-one countries. Lower-bound estimates for the highest rates of migration by those with tertiary education from their data range as high as 77 percent (Guyana). Other exceptionally high rates of migration among the tertiary educated are Gambia (59 percent), Jamaica (67 percent), and Trinidad and Tobago (57 percent).[1] None of the migration rates for the primary or less educated exceed 2 percent. The disproportionate weight of the skilled population in U.S. immigration may reflect U.S. policy. However, Borjas (1999) notes that U.S. immigration policy has tended to favor unskilled labor with family connections in the United States rather than skilled labor. In the richest fifth of nations, moreover, the probability is roughly the same that educated and uneducated will emigrate to the United States. Borjas, Bronars, and Trejo (1992) also find that the more highly educated are more likely to migrate within the United States than the less educated.[2]

Capital also flows mainly to areas that are already rich, as famously pointed out by Lucas (1990). In 1990, the richest 20 percent of world population received 92 percent of portfolio capital gross inflows; the poorest 20 percent received 0.1 percent of portfolio capital inflows. The richest 20 percent of the world population received 79 percent of foreign direct investment; the poorest 20 percent received 0.7 percent of foreign direct investment. Altogether, the richest 20 percent of the world population received 88 percent of private capital gross inflows; the poorest 20 percent received 1 percent of private capital gross inflows.

The developing countries do receive net inflows of private capital, as shown in figure 3.1. However, the importance of capital inflows rises with the per capita income of the developing country, counter to the prediction of factor endowment models.

1. Note that these are all small countries. Carrington and Detragiache (1998) point out that U.S. immigration quotas are less binding for small countries, because, with some exceptions, the legal immigration quota is 20,000 per country regardless of a country's population size.
2. Casual observation suggests brain drain within countries. The best lawyers and doctors congregate within a few metropolitan areas like New York, where skilled doctors and lawyers are abundant, while poorer areas where skilled doctors and lawyers are scarce have difficulty attracting the top-drawer professionals.

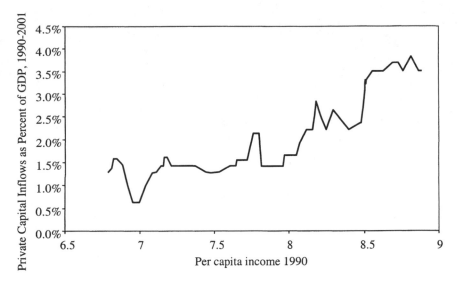

Fig. 3.1   Private capital flows to developing countries and per capita income, 1990–2001 (moving median of twenty observations)

Capital inflows to the poorest countries are primarily made up of foreign direct investment, as shown in figure 3.1. Even so, private foreign direct investment into the poorest region, Africa, is low and is mostly directed to natural resource exploitation (such as oil, gold, diamonds, copper, cobalt, manganese, bauxite, chromium, platinum). The correlation coefficient between foreign direct investment and natural resource endowment across African countries is .94 (Morriset). This tends to confirm the prediction for capital flows of the model including land and natural resources.

Moreover, these numbers do not reflect the movements of private capital out of developing countries outside of official channels—that is, capital flight. Fragmentary evidence suggests that capital flight is very important for poor regions. Collier, Hoeffler, and Patillo (2001) estimate that capital flight accounts for 39 percent of private wealth in both sub-Saharan Africa and the Middle East (see table 3.2). It is also important in Latin America (10 percent of wealth), but less so in South Asia and East Asia.

One measure often used to estimate capital flight is to cumulate the net errors and omissions data in the balance of payments accounts. There one finds evidence of large-scale outmigration of capital in absolute terms in East Asia, Russia, and Latin America (see table 3.3). As percent of GDP, the outflow of capital is very significant in the African countries. This tends to confirm the findings of Collier, Hoeffler, and Patillo (2001) for Latin America and Africa. The availability of more recent data since the East Asian crisis in my findings suggests that recent capital outflows out of East Asia are more dramatic than what those authors found earlier.

Table 3.2   Wealth and capital flight by region

Region	Public capital per worker	Private wealth per worker	Private capital per worker	Capital flight per worker	Capital flight ratio
Sub-Saharan Africa	1,271	1,752	1,069	683	0.39
Latin America	6,653	19,361	17,424	1,936	0.10
South Asia	2,135	2,500	2,425	75	0.03
East Asia	3,878	10,331	9,711	620	0.06
Middle East	8,693	6,030	3,678	2,352	0.39

Source: Collier, Hoeffler, and Patillo (2001).

Table 3.3   Top ten in cumulative negative errors and omissions

Absolute amounts (US$ billions)	Sum 1970–2002	% of GDP	Sum 1970–2002/ GDP 2002 (%)
China	−142	Liberia	−129
Russian Federation	−68	Mozambique	−82
Mexico	−27	Guinea-Bissau	−66
Venezuela	−17	Eritrea	−63
South Korea	−16	The Gambia	−45
The Philippines	−16	Ethiopia	−41
Argentina	−14	Zambia	−41
Brazil	−11	Bolivia	−35
Indonesia	−8	Burundi	−31
Malaysia	−8	Angola	−29

Source: World Development Indicators.

What does this picture of factor flows between rich and poor countries tell us? Although there are some poor country exceptions that attract capital inflows, in most poor countries *all* factors of production tend to move toward the rich countries. This supports the productivity differences view of globalization instead of the factor endowments view. The attractive force of higher productivity in the rich countries overturns the factor endowments predictions of convergence through capital flows and trade. Hence, we should not look for great things from globalization for reducing world poverty.

However, the flows of migrants are still relatively small out of the entire poor country population (3 million out of 5 billion), so we should not jump to the conclusion that the poor countries are just emptying out or that there is free labor mobility. The flows involved are actually too small to make much difference to either rich country or poor country incomes, hence the fact we will examine next: the relative stability of the relative income ratio of poor country to rich country in the era of globalization.

3.2.2   Evidence on Factor Returns within Countries

We have some evidence on the behavior of returns to skill and returns to physical capital within countries. Ross Levine and I (Easterly and Levine 2001) noted that skilled workers earn less, rather than more, in poor countries. We saw above that the BMS model of income differences due to human capital differences predicts that returns to skill would be much higher in poor countries. The facts do not support these predictions: skilled workers earn more in rich countries. Fragmentary data from wage surveys say that engineers earn an average of $55,000 in New York compared to $2,300 in Bombay (Union Bank of Switzerland 1994). Instead of skilled wages being five times higher in India than in the United States, skilled wages are 24 times higher in the United States than in India. The presence of higher wages across all occupational groups is consistent with a higher A in the United States than in India. The skilled wage (proxied by salaries of engineers, adjusted for purchasing power) is positively associated with per capita income across countries, as a productivity explanation of income differences would imply, and not negatively correlated, as a BMS human capital explanation of income differences would imply. The correlation between skilled wages and per capita income across forty-four countries is .81.

Within India, the wage of engineers is only about three times the wage of building laborers. Rates of return to education are also only about twice as high in poor countries—about 11 percent versus 6 percent from low income to high income (Psacharopolous 1994, p. 1332)—not forty-two times higher. Consistent with this evidence, we have also seen that the incipient flow of human capital, despite barriers to immigration, is toward the rich countries.

Returns to physical capital are much more difficult to observe across countries. Devarajan, Easterly, and Pack (2003) show some indirect evidence that private investment does not have high returns in Africa. They find that there is no robust correlation within Africa between private investment rates and per capita GDP growth. There is no correlation between growth of output per worker and growth of capital per worker. They also find with microevidence for Tanzanian industry that private capital accumulation did not lead to the predicted growth response (as shown by strongly negative total factor productivity residuals).

3.2.3   Empirical Evidence on Trade and Domestic Inequality

Does globalization increase inequality within poor countries, offsetting any positive income effect for the poor (or worsening a zero or negative income effect)? To test the effects of trade on inequality, I perform some stylized regressions. I do not attempt a full cross-country explanation of variations in domestic inequality; I also refrain from trying to establish

Table 3.4   Regression of log Gini coefficient on trade/GDP shares and interaction
terms and time trend (not shown), decade averages, 1960s–1990s

	Regression 1		Regression 2	
Fixed effects (within) regression	Coefficient	t-statistic	Coefficient	t-statistic
Constant	4.103	31.85	4.069	31.42
Log of trade share	−0.407	−4.90	−0.407	−4.93
Log of trade share interacted with developing-country dummy	0.400	4.47	0.364	3.99
Log of trade share interacted with commodity-exporting dummy			0.137	1.82
No. of observations	312		312	
No. of groups	112		112	
R^2	0.2142		0.2509	

causality, which is a massive task in itself. I stick to the more modest goal of assessing whether the bivariate associations go in the direction predicted by factor endowments or productivity differences. These results should be seen as additional stylized facts, not definitive findings of causal effects robust to third factors.

In table 3.4 I do fixed effects regressions of Gini coefficients on trade shares in GDP for a pooled cross-country, cross-time sample of decade averages for the 1960s, '70s, '80s, and '90s, for all countries (developed and developing) with available data. The source of my data for inequality is the Deininger and Squire inequality database, updated with World Development Indicator data from the World Bank. The source of the data on trade shares is the World Development Indicators. Since the theory predicts different signs on the inequality and trade relationship in rich and poor countries, I put in an interaction term that allows the slope to differ for developing countries.

The results suggest that trade reduces inequality in rich countries. The slope dummy on trade for developing countries is highly significant and of the predicted opposite sign. However, the net effect of trade in poor countries (the sum of the two coefficients) is to leave inequality unchanged. I checked whether the developing-country effect reflected commodity exporting, which is often associated with higher inequality, and also reflects the role of "land" in the factor endowments models. However, the developing-country slope dummy is robust to this control, so the contradiction to the predictions of factor price equalization holds. I also check robustness to a time trend for the Gini coefficient; although it is significant and negative, it doesn't change the results.

The pattern of results for rich countries suggests that some of the productivity-driven models of trade may be relevant. If we interpret the falling inequality as a fall in the capital rental–wage ratio (or as a fall in the skilled-

unskilled wage ratio for human capital), then more trade is actually good for the workers in rich countries. We could have the paradox that labor-augmenting productivity is so much higher in rich countries than in poor countries that rich countries are actually (effectively) labor abundant. Trade then decreases the capital rental–wage ratio. If this is true, then we might expect trade to increase inequality in the poor countries. Although there is a significant positive shift in the effect of trade on inequality in poor countries, the net effect turns out to be close to zero. There is a marginally significant slope dummy for commodity-exporting poor countries, in which more trade does increase inequality. These countries may reflect the effect of earnings from natural resources (what I called land in the models above), in which a land-abundant country has an increase in the land rental–wage ratio from opening up to trade. Thus, we could understand the increase in inequality with trade in commodity exporters, if inequality is driven by the land rental–wage ratio.

I next do cross-section regressions for the same relationship (see table 3.5). I regress two measures of inequality (the share of the top quintile and the Gini coefficient, both averaged over 1960–99) on the share of trade in GDP (tradeGDP, averaged over the same period), and the trade share interacted with the log of per capita income (lgdppc, averaged over the same period).[3] Interacting trade with income allows me to test whether the inequality-trade relationship changes between rich and poor countries, as predicted by the theory. I test robustness to including income and income squared to make sure that the trade-inequality relationship is not just proxying for the well-known cross-section Kuznets curve.

The results in the cross section are even stronger than in the fixed effects regression. Increased trade is now associated with higher inequality for poor countries (rather than zero effect as in the fixed effects regressions); the relationship reverses sign in the middle income range, and there is a negative relationship between trade and inequality among the rich countries (the same as in the fixed effects regressions).[4] Again, the empirical

3. The cross-country inequality data have been criticized by Atkinson and Brandolini (2001) as being inconsistent across countries in methodology and sample universe. The data set records whether the income distribution statistics refer to earnings, income, or expenditure. For income, they record whether it is gross income or net income. I use these classifications to adjust measures of inequality with estimated dummy variables for each category of survey methodology. I then subtract the coefficients on the dummies from the Gini coefficient or the top quintile share to adjust all statistics to their gross income equivalent. This procedure is far from perfect, as Atkinson and Brandolini (2001) point out, but it makes the best of a bad data situation. I then average whatever Gini coefficients (or top quintile shares) are available from 1960 to 2000 (most of them in the last two decades) to get one cross-section observation per country. The data on per capita income come from Summers and Heston as updated through 2000 by the Global Development Network Growth Database.

4. Entering dummies for primary exporting countries did not find any clear results—the primary export dummy was not significant, while the inverted U curve in trade share remained significant.

Table 3.5   Regressions with robust standard errors for inequality and trade

	Regression 1		Regression 2		Regression 3	
	Coefficient	*t*-statistic	Coefficient	*t*-statistic	Coefficient	*t*-statistic
A. Dependent variable: Share of top quintile in income averaged over 1960–99						
Constant	46.753	30.21	–10.702	–0.24	–1.350	–0.03
tradegdp	0.471	5.72			0.515	2.85
trade*lgdppc	–0.057	–6.26			–0.063	–3.01
lgdppc			18.211	1.62	11.689	1.06
lgdppc^2			–1.354	–1.94	–0.697	–0.99
No. of observations	106		106		106	
Prob > F	0.000		0.000		0.000	
R^2	0.235		0.164		0.244	
Income level at which derivative of inequality with regard to trade becomes negative		3,665				3,603
B. Dependent variable: Gini coefficient averaged over 1960–99						
Constant	39.844	27.8	–7.995	–0.17	6.172	0.14
tradegdp	0.517	5.19			0.400	2.14
trade*lgdppc	–0.059	–5.51			–0.045	–2.19
lgdppc			16.519	1.38	9.745	0.84
lgdppc^2			–1.256	–1.70	–0.675	–0.92
No. of observations	107		107		107	
Prob > F	0.000		0.000		0.000	
R^2	0.179		0.153		0.1854	
Income level at which derivative of inequality with regard to trade becomes negative		6,805				7,286

Note: Prob > F is the *p*-value of *F*-statistics.

evidence is just the opposite of what the factor price equalization story predicts—greater openness increases inequality in poor countries and decreases it in rich countries.

The results are robust to including income and income squared, which are not separately significant. Rather than proxying for the Kuznets curve, the trade-inequality relationship offers a possible substitute explanation for the cross-section Kuznets curve (since trade is correlated with income). Overall, the results indicate that understanding the trade and inequality relationship requires understanding the productivity differences associated with trade.

3.2.4   Trade and Growth

What if trade has an effect on productivity growth? The theory here is not very clear, but some argue that trade carries with it access to technol-

ogy. In this case, we would expect the poor countries to gain access to the superior technologies in the rich countries by trading with them, and hence trade could be a vehicle that reduces international inequality through convergence in productivity levels.

There is a huge empirical literature on trade and growth investigating this possibility, which has failed to establish a consensus for growth effects of trade. An old literature covered the correlation between export growth and GDP growth (Feder 1983; Ram 1985). That literature eventually failed to make the case for growth effects of trade because of the difficulty of establishing causality from export growth to GDP—after all, both will grow at the equilibrium productivity growth rate plus population growth in steady state. If productivity growth differs across countries, for whatever reason, there will be a spurious cross-section correlation.

The cross-country literature has revived the trade-growth debate with regressions of per capita growth on trade shares (usually insignificant) or some broad measure of trade policy (highly significant in Sachs and Warner 1995). However, the latter has been criticized as a trade argument for really being a general measure of bad policies and institutions (Rodriguez and Rodrik 2001).

Recently Dollar and Kraay (2004) have proposed the testing of a relationship between per capita growth and the *change* in the trade share. This takes us back almost to where we started—they regress GDP growth implicitly on trade growth (the latter interacted with trade share). They take some steps forward by including fixed effects, but again identification is unconvincing.

Stronger evidence for beneficial effects of trade comes from Frankel and Romer (1999), who did a regression of *levels* of per capita income on trade shares, using geographically determined "natural openness" as an instrument. The level effect could be consistent with a factor endowments view in which labor-intensive poor countries (who dominate the sample) benefit from higher trade through increased unskilled wages (which are proportional to per capita income, remember). It could also reflect a productivity effect, which would be common to both rich and poor countries.

As with all income-level regressions, the solution to the identification problem is not very convincing. One has to believe that the instrument does not affect income directly (doesn't everything affect income?). Also, the bivariate regression with income and trade does not consider competing determinants of income, such as institutions or education, which would then set up an even more complicated identification problem. Frankel and Romer's result is another useful stylized fact, in the same spirit as the stylized fact regressions presented here. It affects our priors about the beneficial effects of trade on long-run development, but it is not as convincing as establishing a causal relationship.

3.2.5   Migration, Income, and Population Density within Countries

The internal markets of countries are examples of "globalized" areas where there is free mobility of goods, capital, and labor. They are another interesting example of what we can expect from complete globalization.

Ross Levine and I (Easterly and Levine 2001) used the database of 3,141 counties in the United States to examine income concentration, population density, and migration within the United States. Migration goes from sparsely populated areas to densely populated areas. We find with county data for the United States that there is a statistically significant correlation of .20 between the in-migration rate of counties from 1980 to 1990 and the population density in 1980. Hence, labor is flowing to land areas where it is already abundant. In the model above, this is consistent with the high-density places being the high-productivity places. It is inconsistent with the simple factor endowment view in which labor would flow to where the labor-land ratio is low.

There is a strong correlation between per capita income of U.S. counties and their population density (correlation coefficient of .48 for the log of both concepts, with a t-statistic of 30 on the bivariate association).[5] This again is consistent with productivity differences between areas and inconsistent with income differences across regions being mainly determined by factor endowments. High-productivity places (which are the same as the high-income places) attract more labor relative to land. Of course, this income dispersion reflects either other factors or the incomplete transition of the migration process, since the equilibrium with free factor mobility is for equal regional incomes.

Sorting counties by GDP per square mile, we found a 50-and-2 rule: 50 percent of GDP is produced in counties that account for only 2 percent of the land, while the least dense counties that account for 50 percent of the land produce only 2 percent of GDP. Nor is this result just a consequence of the large unsettled areas of the West and Alaska. If we do the same calculation for land east of the Mississippi, we still have extreme concentration: 50 percent of GDP is produced on 4 percent of the land. The densest county is New York, New York, which has a GDP per square mile of $1.5 billion. This is about 55,000 times more than the least dense county east of the Mississippi ($27 thousand per square mile in Keweenaw, Michigan).

Obviously, another name for these concentrations is "cities." But even if we restrict the sample to metropolitan counties we see concentration: 50 percent of metropolitan GDP is produced in counties that account for only 6 percent of metropolitan land area.[6] There are also regional income differ-

5. Ciccone and Hall (1996) have a related finding for U.S. states.
6. Metropolitan counties are those that belong to a primary metropolitan statistical area (PMSA) or metropolitan statistical area (MSA) in the census classification of counties.

ences between metropolitan areas. Metropolitan areas in the densely populated Boston-to-Washington corridor have a per capita income that is $5,874 higher on average than other metropolitan areas. This is a huge difference: it is equal to 2.4 standard deviations in the metropolitan area sample. Although there may be differences in the cost of living, they are unlikely to be so large as to explain this difference. (The rent component of the cost of living may reflect either the productivity or the amenity advantages of the area—it seems unlikely that amenities are different enough among areas to explain these differences.)

This concentration is explained by the fact that most economic activity takes place in densely populated metropolitan areas. Urban economics is all about the productivity advantages of cities, which can reap the gains of economies of scale and externalities between people and businesses.

We also confirm the Barro and Sala-i-Martin (2003) finding for U.S. states: income per capita and in-migration are correlated. We do so with data on U.S. counties. Migration goes from poor counties to rich counties, with a statistically significant correlation of .21 between initial income and the in-migration rate. This makes sense if income differences reflect productivity differences, but not if they reflect different factor endowments. A regression of the in-migration rate for 1980–90 by county on population density in 1980 and income per capita in 1980 finds both to be highly significant.[7]

The transitional behavior of migration flows suggests a view that productivity differences between U.S. regions are important. However, they fail to illuminate why regional differences in income are still large after a long period of a "globalized" internal economy in the United States. We need different models, such as sorting of individuals and ethnic groups across regions, externalities within ethnic groups, and other types of poverty trap models I will not attempt to cover here.

3.2.6 Poor Areas

Not only riches are concentrated; so is poverty. Poverty is regionally concentrated in the United States, and these concentrations have an ethnic dimension as well. As figure 3.2 shows, there are four ethnic-geographic clusters of counties with poverty rates above 35 percent:

1. Counties in the West that have large proportions (>35 percent) of Native Americans
2. Counties along the Mexican border that have large proportions (>35 percent) of Hispanics
3. Counties adjacent to the lower Mississippi River in Arkansas, Missis-

---

7. The *t*-statistics are 8.2 for the log of population density in 1980 and 8.9 for the log of per capita income in 1979. The equation has an *R*-squared of .065 and 3,133 observations. The county data are from Alesina, Baqir, and Easterly (1999).

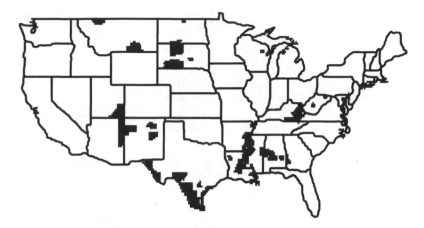

Fig. 3.2   Poverty in the "globalized" internal economy: Counties with a more than 35 percent poverty rate

sippi, and Louisiana and in the "black belt" of Alabama, all of which have large proportions of African Americans (>35 percent)
    4. Virtually all-white counties in the mountains of eastern Kentucky

The county data did not pick up the well-known inner-city form of poverty, mainly among blacks, because counties that include inner cities also include rich suburbs. (An isolated example of an all-black city is East St. Louis, Illinois, which is 98 percent black and has a poverty rate of 44 percent). Of course, poverty is concentrated in the inner city as well. An inner-city zip code in Washington, D.C., College Heights in Anacostia, has only one-fifth of the income of a rich zip code (20816) in Bethesda, Maryland. This has an ethnic dimension again, since College Heights is 96 percent black and the rich zip code in Bethesda is 96 percent white. In the Washington metropolitan area as a whole, there is a striking East-West divide between poor and rich zip codes (which again roughly corresponds to the black-white ethnic divide).[8] Borjas (1995, 1999) suggests there are strong neighborhood and ethnic externalities that may help explain poverty and ethnic clusters within cities. When 1990 census tracts are sorted by percent of black residents, the census tracts with the highest shares of blacks account for 50 percent of the black population but contain only 1 percent of the white population.[9] While this segregation by race and class could simply reflect the preferences of rich white people to live next to

---

8. Brookings Institution (1999) notes that this East-West geographic divide of the Washington, DC, area shows up in many socioeconomic variables like poverty rates, free and reduced-price school lunches, road spending, and so on.
    9. From the Urban Institute's Underclass Database, which contains data on white, black, and "other" population numbers for 43,052 census tracts in the United States.

each other, economists usually prefer to offer economic motivations rather than exogenous preferences as explanations of economic phenomena. Benabou (1993, 1996) stresses the endogenous sorting between rich and poor for the rich to take advantage of externalities like locally funded schools.

Poverty areas exist in many countries: northeast Brazil, southern Italy, Chiapas in Mexico, Balochistan in Pakistan, and the Atlantic provinces in Canada. Researchers have found externalities to be part of the explanation of these poverty clusters. Bouillon, Legovini, and Lustig (1999) find that there is a negative Chiapas effect in Mexican household income data, and that this effect has gotten worse over time. Households in the poor region of Tangail/Jamalpur in Bangladesh earned less than identical households in the better-off region of Dhaka (Ravallion and Wodon 1999). Jalan and Ravallion (2002) likewise found that households in poor counties in southwest China earned less than households with identical human capital and other characteristics in the rich Guangdong Province. Rauch (1993) likewise found with U.S. data that individuals with identical characteristics earn less in cities with low human capital than in cities with high human capital. All these examples represent the failure of almost complete globalization within countries to eliminate poverty.

3.3 Conclusions

Factor endowments and productivity differences are not mutually exclusive, because different situations will involve varying mixtures of factor endowment differences and productivity differences. However, productivity differences appear to be an important facet of many globalization and poverty episodes. Productivity differences are important to capture the flow of all factors of production toward the rich countries, the low returns to physical and human capital in many poor countries, and the perverse behavior of within-country inequality in reaction to trade flows. Even within the globalized economy of the United States, productivity differences seem necessary to comprehend the pattern of labor migration and persistent pockets of poverty.

Productivity differences to explain patterns of globalization and poverty are a nuisance! The neoclassical model based on factor endowments specifies very clear channels by which globalization would affect poverty (generally to reduce it). We have no such off-the-shelf models of productivity differences that would allow us to identify the channels by which globalization affects poverty. We need new models to understand the productivity channels that seem to be so important for so many globalization and poverty outcomes (often disappointing outcomes).

What are the lessons of this paper for whether globalization is something to be desired or feared? Should trade and financial reform promote glob-

alization? Ironically, both the critics and the promoters of globalization seem to share the same model—the factor endowments model. The critics fear that globalization will drive down wages and increase inequality in rich countries, while globalization's promoters promise that it will raise wages and decrease poverty and inequality in poor countries. Neither of these predictions comes true; the outcomes seem to favor instead the productivity-differentials model of income differences between countries. In the productivity view of the world, neither the worst fears of globalization detractors nor the glowing promises of globalization's advocates seem justified. Globalization is less important for the well-being of the poor than the (unfortunately more mysterious) process of productivity growth.

References

Alesina, Alberto, Reza Baqir, and William Easterly. 1999. Public goods and ethnic divisions. *Quarterly Journal of Economics* 114 (4): 1243–84.

Atkinson, Anthony B., and Andrea Brandolini. 2001. Promise and pitfalls in the use of "secondary" data-sets: Income inequality in OECD countries as a case study. *Journal of Economic Literature* 39 (3): 771–99.

Barro, Robert J., N. Gregory Mankiw, and Xavier Sala-i-Martin. 1995. Capital mobility in neoclassical models of economic growth. *American Economic Review* 85 (1): 103–15.

Barro, Robert J., and Xavier Sala-i-Martin. 2003. *Economic growth.* 2nd ed. Cambridge, MA: MIT Press.

Benabou, Roland. 1993. Workings of a city: Location, education, and production. *Quarterly Journal of Economics* 108:619–52.

———. 1996. Heterogeneity, stratification, and growth: Macroeconomic implications of community structure and school finance. *American Economic Review* 86 (3): 584–609.

Besley, Timothy, and Robin Burgess. 2003. Halving global poverty. *Journal of Economic Perspectives* 17:3–22.

Borjas, George J. 1995. Ethnicity, neighborhoods, and human capital externalities. *American Economic Review* 85 (3): 365–90.

———. 1999. *Heaven's door: Immigration policy and the American economy.* Princeton, NJ: Princeton University Press.

Borjas, George J., Stephen G. Bronars, and Stephen J. Trejo. 1992. Self selection and internal migration in the United States. *Journal of Urban Economics* no. 32:159–85.

Bouillon, César, Arianna Legovini, and Nora Lustig. 1999. Rising inequality in Mexico: Returns to household characteristics and the "Chiapas effect." Washington, DC: Inter-American Development Bank. Mimeograph.

Brookings Institution. 1999. *A region divided: The state of growth in greater Washington.* Washington, DC: Brookings Institution, Center on Urban and Metropolitan Policy.

Carrington, William J., and Enrica Detragiache. 1998. How big is the brain drain? International Monetary Fund Working Paper no. 98/102. Washington, DC: International Monetary Fund. July.

Cavanagh, John, and Jerry Mander, eds. 2002. *Alternatives to economic globalization: A better world is possible.* 2nd ed. San Francisco, CA: Berrett-Koehler.

Ciccone, Antonio, and Robert E. Hall. 1996. Productivity and the density of economic activity. *American Economic Review* 86 (1): 54–70.

Collier, Paul, Anke Hoeffler, and Catherine Patillo. 2001. Flight capital as a portfolio choice. *World Bank Economic Review* 15:55–80.

Devarajan, Shanta, William Easterly, and Howard Pack. 2003. Low investment is not the constraint on African development. *Economic Development and Cultural Change* 51 (3): 547–72.

Dollar, David, and Aart Kraay. 2004. Trade, growth, and poverty. *Economic Journal* 114 (493): F22–F49.

Easterly, William, and Ross Levine. 2001. It's not factor accumulation: Stylized facts and growth models. *World Bank Economic Review* 15 (2): 177–219.

Feder, Gershon. 1983. On exports and economic growth. *Journal of Development Economics* 12 (1–2): 59–73.

Frankel, Jeffrey, and David Romer. 1999. Does trade cause growth? *American Economic Review* 89:379–99.

Greider, William. 1997. *One world, ready or not: The manic logic of global capitalism.* New York: Touchstone.

Grubel, Herbert G., and Anthony Scott. 1977. *The brain drain: Determinants, measurement and welfare effects.* Ontario, Canada: Wilfrid Laurier University Press.

Jalan, Jyotsna, and Martin Ravallion. 2002. Geographic poverty traps? A micro model of consumption growth in rural China. *Journal of Applied Econometrics* 17 (4): 329–46.

Levy, David, and Sandra Peart. 2001. The secret history of the dismal science: Parasite economics and market exchange. Library of Economics and Liberty. http://www.econlib.org/library/Columns/LevyPeartdismal5.html.

Lucas, Robert E., Jr. 1990. Why doesn't capital flow from rich to poor countries? *American Economic Review Papers and Proceedings* 80:92–96.

Mankiw, N. Gregory. 1995. The growth of nations. *Brookings Papers on Economic Activity,* Issue no. 1:275–326.

Micklethwait, John, and Adrian Wooldridge. 2000. *A future perfect: The challenge and promise of globalization.* New York: Random House.

Morriset, J. 2000. Foreign direct investment in Africa: Policies also matter. World Bank Policy Research Working Paper no. 2481. Washington, DC: World Bank.

Oxfam. 2004a. Play fair at the Olympics: Respect workers' rights in the sportswear industry. Report in collaboration with the Clean Clothes Campaign and Global Unions. http://www.oxfam.org.uk/what_we_do/issues/trade/playfair_olympics _eng.htm.

———. 2004b. Trading away our rights: Women working in global supply chains. http://www.oxfam.org.uk/what_we_do/issues/trade/trading_rights.htm.

Pritchett, Lant. 2003. Boomtowns and ghost countries: Geography, agglomeration and population mobility. CGD Working Paper no. 36. Washington, DC: Center for Global Development, February.

Psacharopoulos, George. 1994. Returns to investment in education: A global update. *World Development* 22:1325–43.

Ram, Rati. 1985. Exports and economic growth: Some additional evidence. *Economic Development and Cultural Change* 33 (2): 415–25.

Rauch, James E. 1993. Productivity gains from geographic concentration of human capital: Evidence from the cities. *Journal of Urban Economics* 34:380–400.

Ravallion, Martin, and Quentin Wodon. 1999. Poor areas or only poor people? *Journal of Regional Science* 39 (4): 689–711.

Rodriguez, Francisco, and Dani Rodrik. 2001. Trade policy and economic growth: A skeptic's guide to the cross-national evidence. In *NBER macroeconomics annual 2000*, ed. Ben Bernanke and Kenneth S. Rogoff, 261–325. Cambridge, MA: MIT Press.

Romer, Paul. 1995. Comment on N. Gregory Mankiw, "The growth of nations." *Brookings Papers on Economic Activity,* Issue no. 1:313–20.

Sachs, Jeffrey, and Andrew Warner. 1995. Economic reform and the process of global integration. *Brookings Papers on Economic Activity,* Issue no. 1:1–95.

Summers, Robert, and Alan Heston. 1991. The Penn World Table (mark 5): An expanded set of international comparisons, 1950–1988. *Quarterly Journal of Economics* 106 (2): 327–68.

Union Bank of Switzerland. 1994. Prices and earnings around the globe. Zurich: Union Bank of Switzerland.

Comment   Aart Kraay

As usual, Easterly has written a paper full of interesting facts that challenge us to think differently, in this case about the links between globalization and poverty. Suppose we think of the world's poor as primarily being unskilled workers in poor countries. One can then think of three channels through which globalization, defined as the free movement of goods and factors across borders, can raise the incomes of the poor: (a) capital flows from rich to poor countries will raise the marginal product of unskilled workers in poor countries, (b) out-migration of unskilled workers from poor to rich countries will have similar effects, and (c) goods trade can act as a substitute for factor trade and again raise the return to relatively abundant unskilled labor in poor countries.

As always in economics, it is straightforward to write down models in which these three forces operate, and it is also easy to write down more complicated models in which the theoretical predictions are less clear-cut. Easterly nicely cuts through some of these conceptual ambiguities by observing that cross-country differences in factor endowments are a key feature of models in which the links from globalization to poverty reduction described above are likely to operate. The key empirical question therefore becomes how important cross-country differences in factor endowments are relative to cross-country differences in technology. Easterly marshalls an array of interesting stylized facts that, for the most part, points to technology differences rather than factor endowment differences as the main source of cross-country income differences. This in turn casts doubt on the tidy links between globalization and poverty reduction that one would ex-

Aart Kraay is a lead economist in the Development Research Group at the World Bank.

The views expressed here are the author's and do not necessarily reflect those of the World Bank, its executive directors, or the countries they represent.

pect if cross-country differences in factor endowments were important. In fact, under the strictest productivity view of income differences, globalization will reduce poverty only if it has direct effects on productivity. And on this count, Easterly concludes that both theory and empirical evidence give us little guidance.

In my discussion of this paper I would like to do three things. First, I would qualify somewhat Easterly's claim that the pattern of international capital flows is consistent with the existence of large productivity differences between rich and poor countries. Second, I would like to introduce an additional stylized fact that I think reinforces Easterly's case that the productivity view is empirically relevant. Third, I would like to suggest that the empirical evidence on the growth effects of one dimension of globalization, trade, is not as weak as Easterly suggests, and this provides a more hopeful conclusion about the links between globalization and poverty reduction than the one Easterly presents.

Sovereign Risk and North-South Capital Flows

One of Easterly's strongest indictments of the factor endowment view is his empirical observation that we do not see large flows of skilled labor and capital from rich countries (where they are relatively abundant) to poor countries (where they are relatively scarce). In the case of migration, the evidence suggests if anything that skilled workers migrate from poor to rich countries.[1] In the case of capital, the argument follows the classic "Lucas puzzle." Lucas (1990) observed that the return differences predicted by the neoclassical production function with equal technologies across countries and observed capital-labor ratios in rich and poor countries are implausibly large. It is tempting to conclude from these large return differences that North-South capital flows should be large and that the failure to observe such large flows is a failure of the theory. It is also tempting to conclude that the right "fix" for the theory is to assume that rich countries have higher productivity and that this explains the absence of large North-South capital flows. This is roughly the argument that Easterly uses to build his case for the productivity view.

But assuming productivity differences is not the only way to fix the problem. In a recent paper (Kraay et al. 2004) my coauthors and I quantify the importance of sovereign risk for international capital flows. One of the main results of that paper is the finding that just a little bit of sovereign risk can go a long way to bringing the theory closer to the data. In the absence of sovereign risk, both diminishing returns and production risk create in-

---

1. Easterly also argues that capital flows from poor to rich countries, based on the observation that rich countries account for the lion's share of capital inflows. For this issue it seems more appropriate to look at net than gross capital flows. Here I think the evidence would support the claim that North-South capital flows are at most small, and this is enough to make Easterly's point.

centives for capital to be spread across countries. In the absence of a countervailing force, capital-labor ratios would eventually be equalized across countries, implying very large international capital movements that we do not see in the data. We show that with no differences in technology and no sovereign risk poor countries should in the aggregate have net foreign asset positions equal to –300 percent of their wealth, while in reality the measured net foreign assets of poor countries are in the vicinity of –10 percent of their wealth. We next show that reasonable assumptions on the size of technology differences between rich and poor countries can narrow the gap between the theory and the data, but only up to a point. In particular we find that the theory still predicts that the South should have net foreign assets equal to –150 percent of wealth, or an order of magnitude more than we see in the data. However, if we also add a modest dose of sovereign risk—enough to generate the historical pattern of a major debt crisis roughly every thirty years—we find that the foreign assets of the South drop to only –20 percent of wealth, and this is much closer to what we see in the data.

In short, my point here is that it is possible to generate quite small North-South capital flows in simple world equilibrium models in which cross-country differences in capital-labor ratios combined with diminishing returns generate substantial return differences. I do not want to argue based on this that all is well with the factor endowment view, though. I only want to point out that simple back-of-the-envelope calculations of expected return differences across countries can give an incomplete picture of the incentives for international capital flows.

Growth and Poverty Reduction

I next want to introduce a further stylized fact that I think helps to bolster Easterly's case for the productivity view as opposed to the factor endowment view of the world. An important feature of the factor endowment view is that it predicts that globalization can have large effects on relative incomes within poor countries. The classic case is the textbook Stolper-Samuelson effect: increased trade will raise the relative price of the relatively abundant factor. If the poor are abundant unskilled workers in poor countries, increased trade will raise their wages and lower the return to the relatively scarce factors in poor countries. This is not to say that the factor endowment view implies that only relative incomes will change. For example, one can also think of models based on factor endowment differences where capital flows will also affect income levels. However, I do want to make the observation that changes in relative incomes are an important feature of the factor endowment view.

I now want to contrast this observation with the empirical fact that changes in relative incomes within countries account for only a tiny fraction of the cross-country variation in changes in poverty. This can be seen

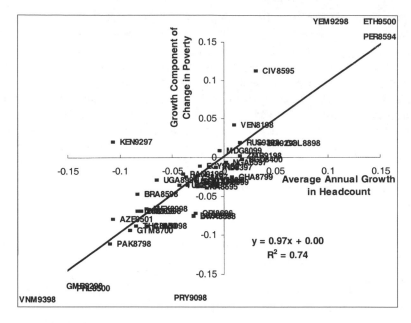

Fig. 3C.1   Growth and poverty reduction
Source: Kraay (2006).

most vividly in figure 3C.1, taken from Kraay (2006). On the horizontal
axis I have graphed the average annual percentage change in the head
count measure of poverty for a sample of developing countries. The head
counts are based on a $1-a-day poverty line, the changes are calculated
over the longest possible single period for each country, and the length of
the period varies with data availability for each country but averages about
ten years. On the vertical axis I plot the average annual percent change in
poverty that would hypothetically have occurred had relative incomes
within the country remained unchanged over the period. The striking feature of this picture is that this hypothetical change in poverty corresponds
very closely to the actual change in poverty. In particular the slope of the
regression line has a variance decomposition interpretation. The slope of
0.97 tells us that 97 percent of the variation of changes in the head count is
attributable to changes in average incomes, and only 3 percent is attributable to changes in relative incomes.

I think that this observation is relevant for the broader discussion of the
links between globalization and poverty in this book, for two reasons.
First, many of the theoretical linkages between trade and poverty emphasize the contribution of relative income changes to changes in poverty. But
in the data these relative income changes are actually quite small, and on
average they account for very little of the variation in changes in poverty.

This should warn us against placing too much emphasis on theoretical links between globalization and poverty that emphasize such relative income changes within countries. Second, I think that the observation that most poverty reduction comes through growth should focus our attention on the channels through which globalization may affect country growth rates directly. Here I agree with Easterly that we have relatively less guidance from theory. However, I think that the empirical evidence on the growth effects of one particular dimension of globalization—greater international trade—is stronger than Easterly suggests. I turn to this final point next.

Recent Empirical Evidence on the Growth Effects of Trade

Following the very influential Rodriguez and Rodrik (2000) critique of the cross-country empirical evidence on trade and growth, it has become commonplace to hear any observed correlation between trade and growth dismissed as either (a) a spurious artifact of omitted variable bias or simultaneity bias, or (b) irrelevant for policy. I think that such a dismissive view does not accurately capture the state of the empirical literature on trade and growth. I cannot attempt a comprehensive review of the evidence in this discussion. Rather, I would like to focus very selectively on a few recent papers that I think have made progress in addressing the limitations of the earlier literature and consistently turn up positive links between trade and growth that are harder to dismiss.

Much of the empirical literature on trade and growth has focused on partial cross-country correlations between trade and growth. As with all such cross-country regressions, it is difficult to adequately address concerns with omitted variables and reverse causation that potentially taint such partial correlations. A natural alternative is to rely on the within-country variation in trade and growth rates. Four recent papers—Dollar and Kraay (2002, 2004); Lee, Ricci, and Rigobon (2004); and Wacziarg and Welch (2003)—all adopt this approach.

The first three papers use regression analysis to look at the links between trade and the within-country variation in decadal or quinquennial growth rates, but they use very different identification strategies. The Dollar and Kraay papers use instrumental variables techniques, relying on standard internal instruments from the dynamic panel literature. In these two papers the identifying assumption is that shocks to growth in future decades are uncorrelated with the trade-GDP ratio in the current decade. Note that this identifying assumption allows for contemporaneous reverse causation—within a decade, higher growth might lead to higher trade for a variety of reasons. It also allows for contemporaneous omitted variables that matter for growth and are correlated with trade. Nevertheless, one can think of examples that undermine even this relatively stringent identifying assumption (as is so often the case in all empirical work!). An alternative is

provided by the Lee, Ricci, and Rigobon paper, which also allows for this contemporaneous reverse causation but achieves identification through heteroskedasticity. In particular, their approach relies on being able to find different splits of the data where the variance of shocks to growth is different, but one can safely assume that the slope coefficients in the regression are the same across these splits. Despite their use of very different identification strategies, is it striking that the three papers find growth effects of trade that are significant and quite similar in magnitude: a 10 percentage point increase in the trade-GDP ratio raises growth by somewhere between 0.25 and 0.45 percentage points.

Of course, one can always object that this finding is irrelevant for policy, because it links trade volumes and not trade policy to growth outcomes. The Lee, Ricci, and Rigobon paper also finds some evidence that a tariff index and a measure of import duties also raise growth, although the effects are less strongly significant. They also find quite strong evidence that the black market premium is strongly linked to growth, although they are careful not to oversell this result because reductions in the black market premium reflect more than just trade reforms.

More compelling evidence on the growth effects of trade policy reforms comes from Wacziarg and Welch (2003). These authors build on the earlier work of Sachs and Warner (1995) to develop a set of dates of trade liberalization. With these dates in hand, they compare average growth before and after trade liberalization, and they find that growth on average increases by between 0.5 and 1.5 percentage points per year. These are quite large growth effects, and Wacziarg and Welch are appropriately cautious not to attribute the entire increase in growth to trade reforms alone. As they clearly acknowledge, trade reforms are frequently accompanied by other, nontrade reforms, and isolating the partial effects of both trade and nontrade reforms is therefore difficult. One way they address this problem is to look at a smaller set of countries where they can identify a major class of domestic structural reforms, privatizations. Controlling for these concurrent reforms, they continue to find that growth increases substantially following liberalization dates.

A different strand of the trade and growth literature exploits the cross-country variation in trade and income levels, interpreting the results as evidence of very long-run effects. Frankel and Romer (1999) is the best-known of these papers, and it uncovered a causal long-run effect of trade on income using geographic remoteness as an instrument for trade. A drawback of such highly parsimonious regressions of per capita income on trade is that they ask a lot of the instrument: it has to be uncorrelated with many other possible determinants of income that are omitted from the regression. Controlling for other factors can therefore make the results more convincing, and this is exactly what Alcala and Ciccone (2004) do. They adopt the same levels specification as the Frankel and Romer paper, but

importantly they also introduce institutional quality into the regression, and instrument for it with a variety of variables capturing countries' colonial past.[2] In this augmented specification they continue to find strong long-run growth effects of trade.

Another recent paper, Rigobon and Rodrik (2004), seeks more ambitiously to isolate the long-run partial effects of rule of law, democracy, geography, and openness on per capita income, again exploiting cross-country variation in levels of these variables. They use the identification-through-heteroskedasticity approach, and they find an interesting mix of results. In their main specification they allow income to be a function of democratic institutions, rule of law, trade, and several exogenous geographic variables. In this core specification trade has a hard-to-explain *negative* and significant estimated causal impact on per capita income. However, in their first robustness check, they drop democracy from the regression and estimate a specification that is closer to that of Alcala and Ciccone (2004). When they do so, they now find a large *positive* and significant effect of trade on per capita incomes, consistent with the other paper's findings.

What do we learn from this? I have tried to argue here that in order to understand the first-order effects of globalization on poverty we need to focus on the growth effects of globalization. I have also argued that we have at least some empirical evidence to support the case that one particular dimension of globalization, increased international trade, does in fact have measurable growth benefits. I do not want to argue that the literature has succeeded in identifying the precise growth effects of narrowly defined trade policy reforms. The uncomfortable fact is that trade reforms are often accompanied by other reforms, and so we are unlikely to ever be able to precisely isolate their partial effects on growth. But the empirical evidence does suggest that countries that have chosen to participate in the process of globalization through trade reforms—often accompanied by other domestic reforms—have grown faster.

From the standpoint of poverty reduction, this additional growth is very welcome. In figure 3C.2 I want to emphasize that even the fairly modest estimated growth effects of trade discussed above are nontrivial relative to the growth rates required to achieve the Millennium Development Goal of halving poverty between 1990 and 2015. The vertical bars for each country represent an estimate of the average annual growth rate required to halve poverty over a twenty-five-year period, assuming no changes in relative incomes. Most of these required growth rates are clustered between 1 and 3 percent per year, and vary with the initial location and shape of the distri-

2. The paper contains two other important methodological innovations. The authors recalculate the original Frankel-Romer instrument based on more, and more recent, data, and they also measure trade as a fraction of purchasing power parity–adjusted GDP in order to have a cleaner measure of cross-country differences in real trade volumes relative to production.

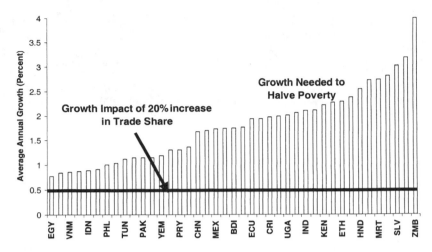

Fig. 3C.2   Growth required to halve poverty over twenty-five years

bution of income in the country. The horizontal line at 0.5 percent shows the estimated growth effect of trade (with all the caveats noted above) of a 20 percentage point increase in the trade-GDP ratio. Of course, one cannot conclude from this graph that narrow trade reforms in isolation will reduce poverty at the rate envisioned in the Millennium Development Goals. But we can say that the growth benefits of globalization have a nontrivial role in economic development and poverty reduction.

References

Alcala, Francisco, and Antonio Ciccone. 2004. Trade and productivity. *Quarterly Journal of Economics* 119 (2): 613–46.

Dollar, David, and Aart Kraay. 2002. Institutions, trade, and growth. *Journal of Monetary Economics* 50:133–62.

———. 2004. Trade, growth, and poverty. *Economic Journal* 114 (493): 22–49.

Frankel, Jeffrey A., and David Romer. 1999. Does trade cause growth? *American Economic Review* 89 (June): 379–99.

Kraay, Aart. 2006. When is growth pro-poor? Cross-country evidence. *Journal of Development Economics,* forthcoming.

Kraay, Aart, Norman Loayza, Luis Serven, and Jaume Ventura. 2004. Country portfolios. World Bank Policy Research Department Working Paper no. 3320.

Lee, Ha Yan, Luca Ricci, and Roberto Rigobon. 2004. Once again, is openness good for growth? *Journal of Development Economics* 75 (2): 451–72.

Lucas, Robert. 1990. Why doesn't capital flow from rich to poor countries? *American Economic Review* 80 (2): 92–96.

Rigobon, Roberto, and Dani Rodrik. 2004. Rule of law, democracy, openness, and income: Estimating the interrelationships. Manuscript, Sloan School of Management, MIT.

Rodriguez, Francisco, and Dani Rodrik. 2000. Trade policy and economic growth:

A skeptic's guide to the cross-national evidence. In *NBER macroeconomics annual 2000,* ed. Ben Bernanke and Kenneth Rogoff, 261–325. Cambridge, MA: MIT Press.

Sachs, Jeffrey D., and Andrew Warner. 1995. Economic reform and the process of global integration. *Brookings Papers on Economic Activity,* Issue no. 1:1–118.

Wacziarg, Romain, and Karen Horn Welch. 2003. Trade liberalization and growth: New evidence. Stanford University, Graduate School of Business. Working Paper.

Does Tariff Liberalization Increase Wage Inequality?
Some Empirical Evidence

Branko Milanovic and Lyn Squire

4.1 Introduction

The evidence reported and reviewed elsewhere in this volume suggests that increasing openness to trade is associated with higher growth and that growth can in turn explain much of the observed reduction in poverty (see in particular Harrison's introduction to this volume). A secondary question is whether the poor benefit as much as, more than, or less than other members of society as a result of trade liberalization. The relationship between trade liberalization and the distribution of income remains a hotly debated issue even though standard theory in the shape of the two-factor, two-country Heckscher-Ohlin model provides an unambiguous prediction: trade liberalization will increase the relative price of the abundant factor, which in the case of developing countries is usually taken to be unskilled labor. This in turn should reduce inequality.

As argued elsewhere in this volume, however, the Heckscher-Ohlin specification is a drastic simplification of a complex phenomenon, and relatively minor steps toward greater realism or a shift in focus toward different aspects of trade liberalization complicate matters (Davis and Mishra, chap. 2 in this volume). To take just one example, Feenstra and Hanson (1997) focus on a different form of "trade": the transfer of production from

Branko Milanovic is a senior associate in the Global Policy Program at the Carnegie Endowment for International Peace and an economist in the research department of the World Bank. Lyn Squire is president of Global Development Network.

This work was in part financed out of World Bank Research Grant PO85725 (project on Globalization and Middle Classes). Milanovic would also like to acknowledge the support of the McArthur Foundation. The authors are grateful to Gouthami Padam for assistance with data collection and to Ann Harrison, Doug Irwin, and participants of two National Bureau of Economic Research conferences for their comments and suggestions.

developed to developing countries. In their model, the wage gap between skilled and unskilled workers in developing countries increases, pointing toward increased inequality. Thus, plausible models can lead to quite different predictions.

Whenever theory leads to different predictions, empirical evidence is required to help us choose among alternatives. The available empirical literature, however, does not lead easily to robust conclusions. The combination of a complex phenomenon and data inadequacies renders empirical work both hazardous and partial. Different authors focus on different aspects of the phenomenon ranging from wage inequality to income inequality; they employ different specifications, sometimes relating levels of openness to levels of inequality and sometimes relating changes in openness to changes in inequality; and they use various alternative definitions of key variables, including the measure of openness, with some authors using quantities (trade volumes) and others using policies (tariff levels). The end result is that a careful interpretation of the existing literature requires attention to all these possible points of difference in the various studies.

The purpose of this paper is to present the results of a new empirical investigation of the relationship between trade liberalization and inequality, one that we hope addresses some of the concerns raised above. To this end, the paper draws on a review of the existing empirical literature to identify preferred ways of specifying the empirical model. One outcome of our review is that it leads to the use of two large databases on the distribution of wage income in various forms, sources that have not previously been tapped for this purpose.

The paper begins in section 4.2 with a review of existing empirical work in two critical dimensions: domain and specification. *Domain* refers to the measures of trade liberalization (volumes or policies) and of inequality (incomes or wages) under examination. It also refers to the focus of the study: whether it is a single-country or a multicountry study. *Specification* deals with the issue of whether variables should be measured in levels or in first differences. It also encompasses the important issue of interaction between variables. In section 4.3 we discuss the variables that we use in the empirical analysis. The estimation is presented in section 4.4 for interoccupational wage inequality and in section 4.5 for interindustrial wage inequality.

4.2   Review of the Empirical Literature

As noted in the introduction, the literature contains a diverse collection of empirical efforts to identify the relationship between trade liberalization and inequality. This diversity plagues the interpretation of results and comparisons across studies, but at the same time it provides a valuable source of material to guide the empirical specification estimated in this paper.

Our review covers fifteen papers completed within the last ten years. Of these, six point to a positive relationship between the chosen measure of openness and the chosen measure of inequality. Three indicate that openness increases inequality in low-income countries. Five studies find no impact on inequality. Only one paper points to declining inequality among the "globalizing countries" including the Organization for Economic Cooperation and Development (OECD). In addition, two other papers (Freeman 1995 and Richardson 1995) provide reviews of the then existing empirical literature and conclude that trade liberalization has a positive (increasing) albeit modest impact on inequality. What is surprising about this quick summary is that none of the studies indicate declining inequality in low-income countries, the one region where standard theory predicts such an outcome. The choice, then, seems to be between no impact and increased inequality.

Two qualifications are in order, however. First, the results are often quite fragile: small changes in specification or definition of variables can undermine statistical significance. And second, each of the fifteen studies focuses by necessity on only one aspect of the relationship between trade liberalization and equity. In principle, then, these apparently contradictory results could in fact be perfectly consistent. To explore this further, we examine the studies in each of two dimensions: domain, or the focus of the investigation, and specification, especially whether estimates are levels on levels, or changes on changes. At the end of our discussion of each dimension, we select our preferred option(s) for our subsequent empirical analysis.

4.2.1   Domain

Openness in the majority of papers is defined in terms of trade volumes. Only three papers use some indicator of policy to measure openness. And with respect to inequality, more papers analyze income inequality than wage inequality, with the latter typically being explored in the context of single-country studies exclusively in Latin America.

Income inequality in a cross-country sample is the subject of several papers. An early example is that by Edwards (1997). He regresses the change in the Gini index between the 1970s and the 1980s on a dummy indicating whether a country had engaged in trade liberalization as measured by the average black market premium or the average collected tariff ratio. He finds that trade reform did not significantly affect inequality. Other authors arriving at similar results—albeit using different specifications, time periods, and data—include Londono (2002) and Dollar and Kraay (2001). Barro (2000), however, finds that openness, as measured by trade volumes, is associated with higher levels of inequality in a panel of countries. He concludes: "Basically, the data reveal a long-term positive association between the levels of openness and inequality" (p. 5). Other authors, again

using different methods and variable definitions, concur. Spilimbergo, Londono, and Szekely (1999) and Lundberg and Squire (2003) also detect a link between openness and increased inequality.

Reconciling these results is difficult because they cover different countries and time periods (and could therefore be reflecting different relationships) and because they use different specifications and variable definitions. One possibility that emerges from other work is that country categorization may be important. Several authors (Ravallion 2002; Milanovic 2005; Savvides 1998) find that their preferred measure of openness increases inequality in low-income countries. Barro (2000) also finds the relationship more pronounced in poorer countries. In Spilimbergo, Londono, and Szekely (1999, p. 88) openness affects countries differently depending on their endowments: in capital-rich countries, openness reduces inequality, while in countries with abundant skilled labor, openness increases inequality. The authors argue that the former effect is driven by reduction of capital rents; the latter effect, however, is consistent with Heckscher-Ohlin.

The mix of countries in aggregate studies may therefore be the crucial factor leading to different results. Either way, this is a significant result, for two reasons. First, it runs counter to the prediction of conventional trade theory and raises obvious policy concerns. And second, it suggests that empirical work would benefit from some attempt to interact policy changes and initial conditions to capture the possibility of different effects at different levels of development, a point to which we return below.

Wage inequality is addressed by several authors in the context of specific Latin American countries. For example, Harrison and Hanson (1999) examine the extent to which the increase in wage inequality in Mexico was associated with the 1985 trade reform. They find that the reform did play a part but that other factors, including foreign direct investment, export orientation, and technological change, were also important. Regarding Mexico, Robertson (2000) argues that trade liberalization and "labor flexibilization" led to an erosion of rents in protected industries (which in the case of Mexico were less skilled) while foreign investments increased demand for highly skilled labor. The two effects resulted in widening wage distribution.

Beyer, Rojas, and Vergara (1999) find a similar effect of trade reform on wage inequality in Chile because skill-intensive, resource-based industries expanded following liberalization. Arbache, Dickerson, and Green (2003) find that following the extensive trade liberalization in Brazil in the 1990s, average wage in the traded sector fell compared to the nontraded sector (even after adjusting for education, experience, etc.) and that the only category that was spared a decline was the highly educated, because the returns to education went up. They argue that these results are consistent with the erosion of rents in the traded sector in the wake of liberalization,

and complementarity between skilled labor and new technology brought in by openness.

Behrman, Birdsall, and Szekely (2003) look at the impact of various policies (trade, financial liberalization, privatization, and tax reform) jointly or independently on wage differentials in Latin America during the last twenty years. This study's use of policy indicators (developed by the Inter-American Development Bank) rather than outcomes is very similar to the approach we shall adopt here. Behrman and coauthors conclude that more liberal trade regimes did not have an impact on wage differentials between different education categories. Financial liberalization and high-technology imports in the context of a liberal trade regime, however, contributed to the rising inequality. They conclude, "it is not increases in trade but changes in technology that are associated with growing wage gaps" (p. 30).

These studies suggest two overall conclusions for future empirical work. First, it is important to allow for each country's initial conditions, especially with respect to level of income and the prereform structure of protection, and the reduction in protection by sector in order to understand the impact of trade reform. And second, since trade reforms are seldom undertaken in isolation, allowance has to be made for other reforms. Most often, trade reforms come together, in a package with labor reforms. Disentangling the two effects—in addition to accounting for the effects of technological progress that may be nonneutral—is difficult.

Turning to the choice of variables, we select wage inequality rather than income inequality for both theoretical and empirical reasons. The link between policy reforms and wage inequality is likely to be much stronger than the link between policy reforms and inequality in total income. What happens to total income and its inequality is mediated by a number of other factors, including the role of social transfers (pension spending or family benefits), demographics of the population, family formation and mating, labor force participation, and so on. Since wage inequality is relatively immune to such factors, the link between policy and the distribution of wages should be much stronger than that between policy and the distribution of total income, and it should therefore be easier to detect empirically.

Moreover, labor is the main asset owned by the poor whether they are engaged as unskilled labor or informal workers in the urban areas or as landless laborers or small farmers in rural areas. The return to labor at low skill levels is therefore a critical determinant of poverty. Provided that there is some degree of informal-formal and urban-rural labor mobility, average wages in occupations or industries employing mainly low-skill or unskilled labor will reveal what is happening to the returns to the labor of the poor in general. Any worsening in the distribution of wages is therefore a strong indicator that the poor, both those in wage employment and those in various forms of self-employment, are not benefiting from trade liberalization

to the same extent as everyone else as far as the returns to labor are concerned. In effect, a worsening in the distribution of wages will be magnified when it is translated into the distribution of labor returns because of the large number of low-skill and unskilled workers not receiving a wage for their labor.

There is also an empirical reason for our choice. Inequality measures of total income are not available annually; we have inequality statistics for most countries only for a few years in a decade. The Deininger-Squire database, for example, gives on average an inequality statistic for one out of every five possible country/year combinations. In contrast, the two databases on wages that we use—Freeman and Oostendorp (2000) and the University of Texas Inequality Project database—have annual data for a large number of countries and years. This should increase the power of our empirical estimation and tests.

Trade liberalization can also be measured in many different ways. The primary choice is between policies (tariff reductions, elimination of nontariff barriers, etc.) and outcomes such as trade volumes that are a consequence of trade policies. Both approaches have been used in the literature. Most of the studies reviewed here used trade shares as their measure of globalization. Lundberg and Squire (2003) use the Sachs-Warner index, which, although linked to policies, has been criticized on the grounds that it captures more than trade policy. Edwards (1997) uses a variety of policy measures: average tariff, average quantitative restrictions (QR) coverage, and average black market premium. Savvides (1998) uses a specially created measure of protection covering both tariff and nontariff barriers compiled from United Nations Conference on Trade and Development (UNCTAD) data at the four-digit level of the Customs Cooperation Council Nomenclature. The measure is only available, however, for 1988. Finally, those studying wage inequality within a country are often able to make use of industry-specific tariff rates and quotas.

All of the various ways of specifying variables representing trade liberalization are useful and answer interesting questions. If trade volumes are chosen, then the study says something about the impact of trade volumes on inequality. And for some purposes that may be an interesting question. But, in our view, it does not say much about the impact of policy on inequality, primarily because trade volumes are not determined exclusively by policy. A wide range of factors will influence a country's trade volume: the country's geography, technology, demand conditions in importing countries, competitors' supply conditions, weather, and so on. Even attempts to control for these other factors will inevitably leave a residual that captures more than trade policies. We suspect that the widespread reliance on trade volumes in the empirical literature reflects the relative ease of obtaining data compared with the difficulty of achieving the same for trade policies. Since we are interested primarily in how pro-openness reforms

affect inequality, we prefer to focus on policies and thus place ourselves squarely in the policymakers' corner. We attempt to answer the question that many policymakers naturally formulate when they envisage trade reforms: "What will be the effect of liberalization reforms such as tariff reduction on wage differences between various occupations and industries?"

4.2.2   Specification

Turning to the econometric specification of the relationship to be estimated, we take two points from our review: first, although most researchers have regressed levels on levels, we believe that the work undertaken to date points to the importance of focusing on changes in both the dependent and the explanatory variables; and second, several studies suggest that the impact of policy change depends on the level of development and that therefore interactive relationships need to be incorporated.

The specification in most studies is a relationship between levels of inequality and levels of globalization. These studies generally have more success in finding statistically significant results. Thus, the studies that find a negative impact of globalization on inequality rely on regressions run in levels. For example, Barro (2000) regresses the Gini index on the share of trade in gross domestic product (GDP). Lundberg and Squire (2003) regress the Gini index on the Sachs-Warner measure of openness. On the other hand, the studies that regress changes in inequality on changes in globalization have a much more difficult time finding significant results. For example, Edwards (1997) uses the change in inequality between the 1970s and the 1980s as his dependent variable and a dummy indicating whether a country undertook trade reform as his explanatory variable. Dollar and Kraay (2001) use the growth in the income of the bottom 20 percent and changes in trade volume. Both sets of authors conclude that trade reform and/or changes in openness have no impact on inequality.

Interestingly, two papers undertake both levels-on-levels and changes-on-changes analyses. Milanovic (2005) finds that openness hurts poorer deciles in low-income countries when the analysis relates levels to levels, but he finds no measurable effect when he switches to changes on changes. Similarly, Harrison and Hanson (1999) find that high industry tariffs are associated with greater wage inequality when they conduct the analysis in levels but not in changes. This suggests that either there is no relationship between changes in openness and changes in inequality, or the data are not sufficiently fine to capture such a relationship.

This is an important observation because in our view changes-on-changes regression is the preferred specification. Trade liberalization is presumably a dynamic concept and a continuing one. Regressions of levels on levels, however, typically attempt to compare stable points of equilibrium. Consider this argument. Define liberalization for present purposes as trade openness measured by trade policies. Now imagine two countries,

one of which liberalized trade policy ten years ago and the other of which has literally just implemented its trade liberalization. One would imagine that resource reallocation, changes in factor prices, and other adjustments would have played out in the ten years following the reform in the first country, and the distribution of income would have arrived at a new stationary state. The relationship between policy and inequality could therefore be interpreted as an equilibrium. In the other country, however, trade policy will have changed but the economy, including inequality, will not have had a chance to adjust. If these two countries appear as two observations in a cross-country regression of levels on levels, it is very difficult to interpret the meaning of any results whether statistically significant or not. On the other hand, if the change in policy is related to the change in inequality after some common period of time in both countries, then the results, whatever they may be, are more easily interpreted. With this argument in mind, we focus our empirical work on variables measured in first differences. That is, we focus on *changes* in countries' policy stances and *changes* in inequality outcomes.

A second point that emerges clearly from the review as noted above is that the impact of liberalization may differ depending on the initial conditions of the liberalizing country. However, in the empirical work this approach is not always implemented. The implicit assumption is often that the effects of reforms are the same regardless of the initial level of policy openness or income. In other words, opening up an entirely closed economy by one reform point yields the same results as further opening an already open economy. We shall try to avoid this type of simplification by controlling for the initial level of openness and income and, of course, for other initial differences between economies. Similarly, reforms that are each represented by one policy variable are seen, for econometric convenience, to affect outcomes additively. This is a strong simplification: reforms might often act multiplicatively in that the absence of one type of reform negates the effects of another. We shall try to allow for this by including interaction terms.

4.3   Data Description

4.3.1   Inequality Measures

The first of the two large databases we use to derive inequality measures is that of Occupational Wages around the World (OWW).[1] The data cover the period from 1983 to 1999 and more than 150 countries. The coverage in all its dimensions, however, is problematic and fragmentary. Although

---

1. The OWW database is available at http://www.nber.org/oww/.

there are 156 countries in total, each country does not provide data (occupational wages) for every year. The yearly country coverage varies between 48 and 76. Occupations included also vary from country to country. Moreover, for a given country, even when the occupational coverage does provide the annual data, it is not necessarily uniform for each year.[2]

Furthermore, it should be noticed that each observation is an observation on "habitual" countrywide wages for a given occupation. Thus, some averaging is already built into the data. That, however, need not be a problem since, for example, the differences in earnings by skill levels are also based on averaging. There is, however, a difference in that the latter are obtained through a statistical analysis that covers a well-defined spectrum of wage earners (labor force survey) and controls for other relevant factors (gender, experience), while the International Labour Organization (ILO) data represent a mish-mash of average "habitual" wages for different underlying populations: some countries—for some years—report monthly wage rates, others report collectively bargained wages, yet others report hourly wages. At times men and women are combined, and at times only wages for men are reported. Freeman and Oostendorp (2000) overcome the problems of data comparability by "calibration," which is essentially a process of finding the adjustment coefficients (based on a regression analysis) for the data given in a "nonstandard" form, where the standard form is defined as the most common form being used in the data set—that is, monthly wages for male workers.[3]

The great advantage of the database (which incidentally also makes the calibration possible) is its size: in the Freedman-Oostendorp "summary" (compendium) of the ILO sources, there are more than 72,000 observations of average occupational wages.[4] For each of the three indexes of interoccupational wage inequality that we calculate (Gini coefficient, standard deviation, and absolute mean deviation from the median), inequality indexes are calculated only for the country/years that contain more than fifteen occupational wages (of the "calibrated" type). After this "filter" and a few others (dropping data for a number of small island economies and dependencies), we are left with 680 observations (country/years) covering the 1983–99 period and 118 countries. The average Gini is about 23.8, the median 21.7, with the standard deviation of about 10. A summary of the data is given in appendix table 4A.1. These inequality statistics can be regarded,

2. For example, the United States gives the data on 11 occupations in 1983 and 150 occupations in 1999.
3. They do several such calibrations and show (in an appendix) that the results (inequality statistics) do not depend on a particular calibration. For our calculations, we have used their suggested base-wage calibration, denoted xlwu in the OWW database.
4. The Freeman-Oostendorp database is indeed a "summary" of ILO data since the data on occupational wages have been collected by the ILO since 1924, while the Freeman-Oostendorp data begin with 1983.

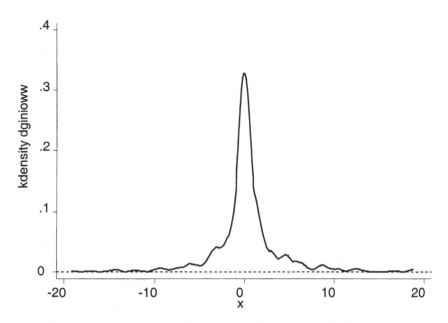

Fig. 4.1   Distribution of changes in occupational wage inequality (Dginioww; in percentage points, 1983–99)
Notes: There are 532 Dginioww observations. Changes are expressed in Gini points.

according to Freeman and Oostendorp, as indicators of both occupational wage inequality and skill premium.[5]

Figure 4.1 shows the distribution of annual changes in the calculated Gini coefficients (Dginioww) over the 1984–99 period. As we observe, the distribution is close to being symmetrical and normal, with the mean being slightly positive (0.17 Gini point) and a zero median.

The second large database of interindustrial wage differences was created by James Galbraith and associates and is known as the University of Texas Inequality Project (UTIP) database (see Galbraith and Kum 2003).[6] The original data come from United Nations Industrial Development Organization (UNIDO) statistics. The UNIDO statistics provide average manufacturing pay by industry. The number of industries (which provide their mean wages) varies between countries and years. On average, there are twenty-four industries per country/year (with the standard deviation of about seven). From these average industrial wages for a given country/year, Galbraith and his associates calculate the Theil index of inequality (variable Theil). The UTIP database covers on average about 90 countries an-

5. Implicitly, the greater the dispersion of interoccupational wages, the greater the return to skills.
6. The data are available at http://utip.gov.utexas.edu/.

Table 4.1   **Simple correlations between various inequality measures and inequality concepts**

	OWW average wage by occupation		
	Gini coefficient	Standard deviation	Absolute mean deviation from median
UTIP (average wage by industry) Theil	0.45*** (513)	0.48*** (513)	0.41*** (518)
OWW			
Gini coefficient		**0.96*** (723)**	**0.81*** (723)**
Standard deviation			**0.85*** (723)**

Notes: Number of observations given in parentheses. Each country/year represents one data point; that is, for each country/year, there is one inequality statistic. Null hypothesis: correlation = 0. Boldface indicates correlation coefficients calculated between various inequality measures from the same database.
***Significant at the 1 percent level.

nually over the period 1975–99.[7] In total, we use 1,651 Theil indexes from 141 countries (see appendix table 4A.2 for details). The average Theil is 5.5, the median 3.8, and the standard deviation 6.4. In about 10 percent of observations intersectoral wage differences are minimal with Theils less than 1. Many of these cases include developed countries (Nordic countries, the Netherlands) but also Algeria, Cuba, Iran, and (until the mid-1980s) China.[8]

Table 4.1 shows simple correlations between different inequality measures from the two databases. We have three inequality statistics from the OWW database (Gini coefficient, standard deviation, and absolute mean deviation from the median) and only one from UTIP (Theil coefficient). Different inequality statistics from the OWW database are obviously strongly correlated (see the figures shown in boldface). The correlation between Theil index from UTIP and Gini from the interoccupation inequality is much less—around 0.4 (see also figure 4.2). Still, it shows that higher skill premium is associated with greater intersectoral inequality. The cor-

7. The data are available at http://utip.gov.utexas.edu/. More recently, the database has expanded to the years prior to 1975. As of January 2004, the UTIP database has almost 3,200 country/year Theils and covers more than 150 countries.
8. It will be noticed that we do not use Gini coefficient here (although we would have liked to do so for a more direct comparison with the OWW data set). The reason is that the UTIP database does not provide individual mean industrial wages, which would allow us to calculate different inequality measures. The authors provide only the "finished" statistic—that is, the Theil index—and not the underlying data. This is not the case with the OWW database, where individual occupational wages by country/year are available and one can thus calculate various inequality indexes.

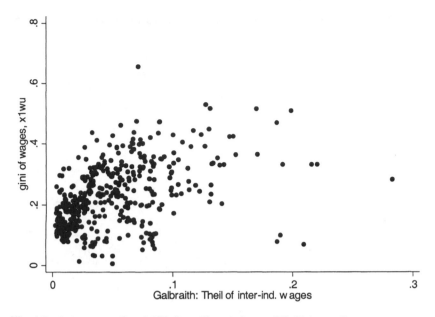

Fig. 4.2   Interoccupational (Gini) and interindustry (Theil) inequality

Notes: Calculated from 513 observations from 79 countries. Total number of observations is 723 (from 103 countries) for interoccupational inequality and 2,160 (from 141 countries) for interindustry inequality.

relation between the changes in the two measures (which we shall be using in our regressions) is virtually zero, however.

4.3.2   Import Liberalization Measures

For import liberalization, we use the World Bank measure of unweighted average tariff (variable Tarf) rate that covers the period from 1980 to 2000, includes 144 countries, and provides 1,255 observations (country/years) in total. The list of countries and number of country/years are shown in appendix table 4A.3. Over this period, the average tariff rate (calculated across the available countries) has been reduced from 28 percent to about 10 percent. Figure 4.3 shows how the distribution of average tariff rates by countries has shifted leftward, with the median, mean, and the standard deviation all significantly less today than in the early and mid-1980s.

The reduction has affected both rich and poor countries. The average tariff rate in poor countries (defined as those with GDP per capita less than $9,000 at international prices) was reduced from 33 percent to 13 percent; for the rich countries, the reduction was from 16 to 7 percent. The pattern of reduction for both poor and rich countries has been very similar to the one shown in figure 4.3: not only are average tariff rates less in 2000 than some twenty years ago, but the differences between the countries is much

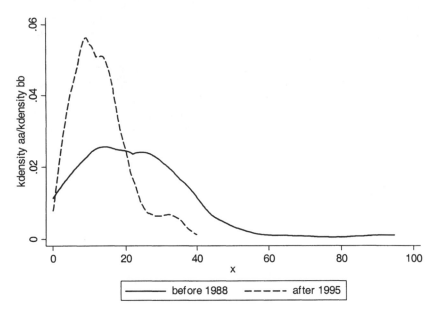

Fig. 4.3   Distribution of countries' average tariff rates in the periods 1980–88 and 1995–2000

Notes: Average tariff rate for a country over a period (1980–88 or 1995–2000) represents one observation. Number of countries is 106 for the first period and 132 for the second.

smaller too (in other words, the distribution of average tariff rates across countries is much more compressed now than in 1980).

One problem when trying to link tariff liberalization reforms to domestic outcomes such as wage distribution is that they are seldom undertaken in isolation. Most frequently, pro-openness trade reforms are accompanied by other "globalization" policies that may well affect labor market outcomes: for example, easier direct or portfolio investment by foreign residents or more liberal regulation of international labor flows. And just as frequently, trade reforms are accompanied by domestic reforms that impact directly on labor markets: "flexibilization" of the labor market, changes in the minimum wage legislation, more (or less) liberal severance pay, reform in the pension regimes, and so on. These accompanying domestic reforms often concern labor—whether they are "anti" or "pro" labor. Sometimes anti-labor legislation accompanies openness reforms because it is felt that liberalization in the foreign arena can be emptied of content (or cannot produce the desired results) if there is no improvement in the domestic legislation—that is, if the latter is deemed too restrictive. Mexico provides one such example (Robertson 2000; Hanson and Harrison 1999).

Alternatively, labor policies, at least for a segment of the labor force, can become more generous if that is the short-term cost the government needs

to pay in order to convince trade unions not to wreck the reforms. In that case, more generous severance pay, low-interest loans to start businesses, and early retirement schemes can all be used to reduce the resistance to reforms and to buy off potential losers. In addition to labor reforms, there may also be accompanying financial reforms: liberalization of interest rates, increased competition in the banking sector, and so on. All of this complicates any attempt to isolate the impact of trade reform on wage inequality. We shall therefore try to control for some of these other policies (labor markets, social transfers).

To measure labor market conditions, we use the Labor Market Data Base constructed by Martin Rama and Rachel Artecona (see Rama and Artecona 2002).[9] Their database has, at five-year intervals (year 1975, 1980, etc.), a number of labor-related measures such as social security contributions (in percentage of gross salary), unemployment rate, replacement rate in case of unemployment, and the like. For our purposes, we focus on two variables—share of labor force covered by collective agreements, and share of the unionized labor force—that allow us to capture the power of trade unions and organized labor.

4.4   Trade Liberalization and Occupational Wage Inequality

We look first at the level relationship between occupational wage inequality and mean tariff rate. Figure 4.4 shows that occupational wage inequality (or returns to education) tends to decrease with average income level of the country (panel A). This is of course what we expect since rich countries have a greater proportion of skilled labor. Likewise, the average tariff rate tends to be lower in richer countries (see panel B). Finally, returns to education increase in level of protection (panel C). This last point would seem to imply that protection is calibrated in such a way as to boost incomes of more skilled workers.[10] However, this relationship may be only apparent and due to the tendency of poorer countries to have, as we have just seen, higher average tariff rates. In fact, once we control for the difference in the returns to education that is due to income levels, the correlation between returns to education and protection vanishes (panel D). It is no longer statistically significant. We can conclude that in a cross-sectional setting, average level of protection and occupational wage inequality do not display any obvious relationship—once we adjust for the fact that poorer countries tend to have both higher returns to education and higher levels of protection.

But this does not necessarily imply that there is no relationship between the *changes* in mean tariff rate and *changes* in returns to education. The

9. The data have been kindly supplied by Martin Rama.
10. Which, by the way, would contradict the general finding of higher protection for less-skilled industries (see discussion above).

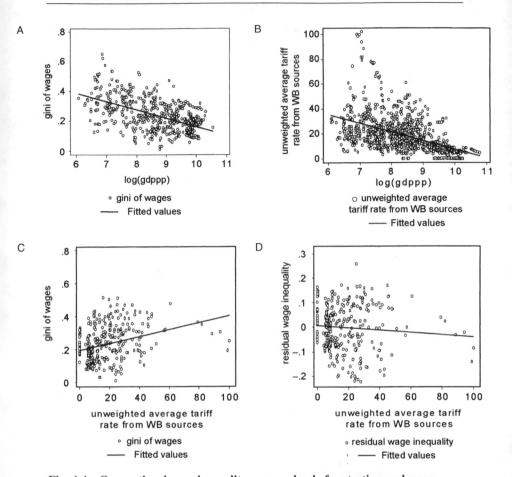

Fig. 4.4 Occupational wage inequality, average level of protection, and mean income: *A,* **occupational wage inequality and level of income;** *B,* **average tariff rate and level of income;** *C,* **occupational wage inequality and average tariff rate;** *D,* **occupational wage inequality (controlled for income) and average tariff rate**

correlation coefficient is –0.10 (see figure 4.5) and is significant at the 10 percent level. It suggests that there may be a weak negative (and uncontrolled for other variables) relationship such that a decrease in domestic protection (i.e., liberalization) is associated with an increase in returns to education.[11]

11. The two variables are run here and further below contemporaneously. However, since the data on mean tariff rates are often not available for all consecutive years, the Dtarf variable is defined in such a way as to include annual changes wherever available—that is, not only Tarf (t) – Tarf $(t – 1)$ but also Tarf(t) – Tarf$(t – 2)$ when Tarf$(t – 1)$ is not available. Thus, Dtarf is partly lagged (about 20 percent of observations refer to changes between years t and $t – 2$).

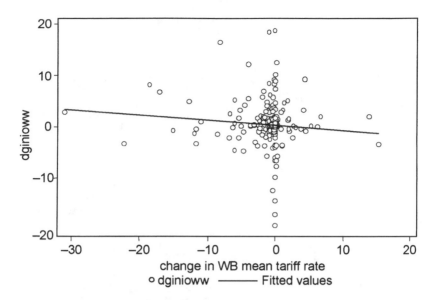

Fig. 4.5 **Relationship between change in mean tariff (Dtarf) and change in occupation wage inequality (Dginioww)**

Note: The regression coefficient remains negative and significant if outliers—that is, observations such that Dtarf ≤ –25—are eliminated.

Figure 4.6 shows the distribution of changes in occupational Ginis for country/years for which we have corresponding data on changes in protection (that is, figure 4.6 shows the distribution of Dginioww for our sample, not for all the observations of Dginioww that we have[12]). There is, on average, a tendency for occupational inequality to increase (the mean Gini change is +0.36, median +0.05), matching the tendency of tariff rates to go down over the last twenty years (in our sample, the average tariff change is –1.05 percentage points, the median –0.2). Thus, there is some prima facie evidence that decreases in protection and increases in occupational wage inequality may be related.

We look further at this relationship by breaking down changes in returns to education (Dginioww) across average protection changes (table 4.2). There is some evidence that deeper cuts in protection are associated with greater increases in occupational inequality. For example, when tariff protection goes down by more than 10 percentage points, occupational Gini increases on average by 1.45 points. When the reduction in protection is less (between 0 and 5 percentage points), the increase in wage inequality is

12. The shape of the two distributions, though, is almost exactly the same. The number of cases, however, is quite different. Our sample contains only 268 observations, while there is a total of 532 observations of changes in occupational inequality.

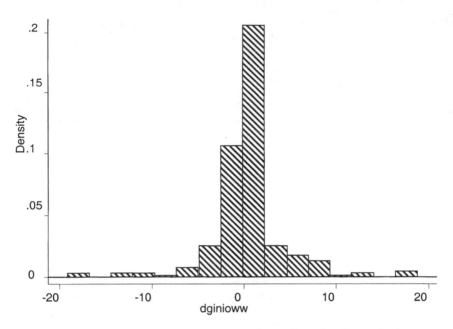

Fig. 4.6   **Distribution of changes in occupation inequality (when data on both occupational inequality and tariff changes are available)**

Table 4.2   Relationship between occupational wage inequality and protection
(average tariff rate)

Change in average tariff rate	Mean change in Dginioww (Gini points)	Standard deviation (Gini points)	No. of observations
Greater than –10 points (in absolute amounts)	+1.45	4.06	10
Between –5 and –10 points	+1.77	5.65	11
Between 0 and –5 points	+0.75	3.55	137
Zero	–0.79	4.50	70
Between 0 and +5 points	+0.43	3.91	34
Between +5 and +10 points	+0.68	1.15	3
Greater than +10 points	–0.73	3.78	2
Total	+0.36	4.00	268

also smaller (+0.75 Gini points). This relationship is not very strong and uniform, though. The change in Gini is, on average, positive even when average tariff rate goes up (by less than 10 percentage points). This in turn suggests that other factors must be at play too. Furthermore, in a number of cases where there was no change in mean tariff rate, average (and me-

Table 4.3   Relationship between interoccupational wage inequality and level of protection
(average tariff rate) in poor and rich countries

	Poor countries			Rich countries		
Change in average tariff rate	Mean change in Dginioww (Gini points)	Standard deviation (Gini points)	No. of observations	Mean change in Dginioww (Gini points)	Standard deviation (Gini points)	No. of observations
Decrease	+1.31	4.63	77	+0.44	2.56	82
No change	−2.71	6.64	18	−0.13	3.30	52
Increase	+0.29	4.21	30	+0.71	1.01	9
Total	+0.49	5.02	125	+0.25	2.80	143

Note: Poor countries are defined as those with GDP per capita less than $9,000 at international 1995 prices; rich countries are those above that threshold.

dian) wage inequality tended to go down. On balance, we conclude that, while there is some evidence that import liberalization is associated with increasing occupational wage inequality, this is unlikely to be the only factor that matters.

We next split the sample into rich and poor countries (table 4.3). We take $9,000 (in purchasing power parity, or PPP, at 1995 prices) as the cutoff point. This means that in 1980 about three-quarters of all countries in the world are regarded as poor (the proportion is about 70 percent in 2000). Since the data for the rich countries are, on average, more frequently available than for the poor, the cutoff point neatly splits our sample into about two halves.

The table illustrates that the same regularity applies to both poor and rich countries: decreases in protection are associated with higher wage inequality, but so are increases in protection (although the magnitudes are substantially lower). It is mostly when there is no change in mean tariff rate that we find shrinking occupational wage distribution. In effect, out of 122 cases when occupational inequality goes down, about one-third (39) involve situations with no change in mean tariff rate. Poor countries display in all cases (decrease, no change, or increase in protection) greater variability in outcomes. This is illustrated in figure 4.7, where we look at changes in occupational Gini when protection is reduced. The strongly spiked density function for the rich countries (dashed line) shows that reduced protection is accompanied by relatively small and very similar changes in rich countries' Ginis; in contrast, in poor countries, Gini changes (solid line) are much more spread out. The hypothesis of equality of the two distributions is soundly rejected (the Kolmogorov-Smirnov test is significant at less than 0.1 percent). This suggests that while average Dginioww for poor countries may, in response to liberalization, increase more than in rich countries (see table 4.3), the variability of outcomes will also be much greater and thus other variables (and possible measurement error) may play a more important part in explaining changes in wage inequality.

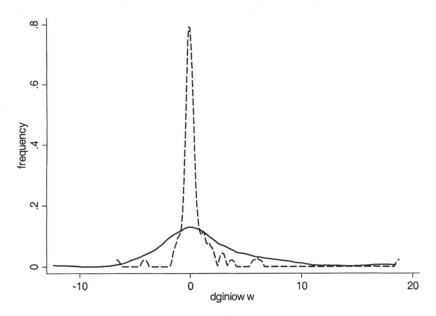

Fig. 4.7   Distribution of Dginioww in poor and rich countries when tariff protection goes down

Notes: Number of observations: 77 for poor countries, 82 for rich countries. Definition of poor and rich countries given in table 4.3 notes. Poor countries are shown by the solid line, rich countries by a dashed line.

In figure 4.8 we therefore focus on poor countries. We look at the change in their occupational wage Gini when tariff protection goes up or down. There are some notable differences: the "down" (solid) line both is thicker in the range Dginioww > 0 and has a much longer right-end tail. Thus, not only is the average Gini change greater when protection is lowered than when it is increased (as we know from table 4.3), but the distribution of Gini changes looks different.[13] There are many more instances of large increases in occupational wage inequality when protection is reduced than when protection is raised.

We now want to investigate how this simple relationship will hold when subjected to a more rigorous analysis. To do this, we estimate the following equation for the change in interoccupation (ΔIneq_O):

$$\Delta \text{Ineq}_O = \text{fct}(\Delta \text{average tariff, labor market conditions, income level})$$

or

$$\Delta \text{Ineq}_O = \text{fct}(\Delta t, s, y)$$

13. However, the Kolmogorov-Smirnov test cannot reject the hypothesis that the two distributions are the same (it is significant at *p* level is 0.22). The equality of means is rejected at the 10 percent level.

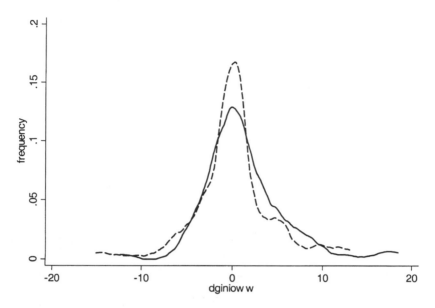

Fig. 4.8   Distribution of changes in interoccupational Gini in poor countries when protection goes up or down

Notes: "Down," denoted by the solid line, indicates the situation when mean tariff rate is reduced; "up," denoted by the dashed line, showed the situation when the mean tariff rate is increased.

A word about the estimation procedure. One might wish to allow changes in average protection level to affect inequality not only contemporaneously but through several time periods (introducing this as a lagged protection on the right-hand side). However, in that case our number of observations—whose low number is already an obstacle to better estimation—drops precipitously and the quality of results deteriorates. We thus assume that one or two years (to the extent that Dtarf also includes some two-year lagged observations) are a sufficient period of time for changes in protection to work their way through wage distribution. Endogeneity is unlikely in levels, and particularly so in a first-difference formulation as here, since change in interoccupational inequality is not likely to have much to do with change in protection. We therefore do not use instruments.[14] Furthermore, the use of first differences implies that idiosyncratic country effects are included.[15]

14. It is also difficult to find reasonable and workable instruments. We tried initial tariff level, on the assumption that reduction in tariffs bears some proportion to their initial levels, but the results were disappointing.

15. Behrman, Birdsall, and Szakely (2003) have the same formulation as here but present also the first-difference formulation of policy changes, or in other words the difference-of-differences formulation (with distributed lags over seven periods on the right-hand side). Their first-difference in levels formulation (table 2) is the same as ours.

Table 4.4   **Explaining interoccupational inequality, 1984–99 (%; dependent variable: annual change in Gini)**

	Regression 1	Regression 2	Regression 3
Δtariff	−0.118	−1.490	−5.707
	(0.097)	(0.033)**	(0.009)**
Ln (GDP per capita)	−0.060	0.448	0.456
	(0.816)	(0.236)	(0.320)
Δtariff · ln (GDP per capita)		0.168	0.688
		(0.057)	(0.008)**
Trade union members as % of labor force (TUMMBR)		0.002 (0.920)	
Percentage of workers covered by collective bargaining (TUCVGE)			−0.002 (0.855)
ΔTarf · TUMMBR		0.001	
		(0.915)	
ΔTarf · TUCVGE			−0.012
			(0.197)
Constant	0.651	−4.221	−4.132
	0.780	(0.205)	(0.331)
Adjusted R^2	0.005	0.02	0.06
F value (p)	1.6	1.7	2
	(0.19)	(0.15)	(0.1)
No. of observations	233	176	79

Note: Levels of significance, p values, given in parentheses.
**Significant at less than the 5 percent level.

Table 4.4 gives the results of the regressions for interoccupational wage inequality. We begin with a very parsimonious formulation where change in interoccupational inequality (Dginioww) is explained by change in average tariff rate (Dtarf) and income. None of the variables is found significant at the 5 percent level; however, Dtarf is negative and significant at the 10 percent level. The situation changes when we introduce the interaction term between the change in average tariff rate and level of income, and trade union membership or percentage of workers covered by collective bargaining agreements. Now, decrease in protection is strongly pro-inequality, with a 1 point decrease in average tariff rate associated with 5.7 percent annual increase in interoccupational inequality.

This pro-inequality effect, however, is reduced the richer the country (because of the positively signed interaction effect; see regression 3), and even for the very poor countries is less than it appears at first sight. Thus, in a very poor country with an income of PPP$1,000, a 1 point decrease in the average tariff rate will be associated with a Gini increase of only 1 percent. Around PPP$5,000 (using regression 3) the effect reverses and trade liberalization begins to be associated with a *decrease* in interoccupational inequality. For example, at the year 2000 mean value of lnGDP per capita

(8.4), the effect of the interaction term is stronger than the effect of change in tariff rate alone; in consequence, pro-openness reforms will be associated with a *decline* in measured interoccupational inequality in richer economies. Finally, note that the fact that labor market conditions are not statistically significant suggests that labor market conditions do not affect the change in the skill premium, while the fact that income is not significant in any formulation is consistent with industry-based (rather than skill-based) bargaining.

The results seem to provide some weak evidence that reduction in average tariff rate contributes to interoccupational wage inequality in poor countries, although the statistical properties of the regressions (most notably R^2) are not strong and the number of observations that we ultimately have to make the regressions is small (79 versus more than 500 observations on changes in interoccupational inequality and more than 1,000 observations on changes in average tariff rates). Therefore we have to take these results with a strong dose of caution.

4.5   Trade Liberalization and Interindustrial Wage Inequality

In figure 4.9 we inspect the relationship between interindustry wage inequality and several relevant variables (all in levels). Panel A shows that when a greater percentage of the labor force participates in collective bargaining, interindustrial wage differences are less. Panel B shows that interindustry wage differences increase as average tariff rate goes up. Now, low tariff rates are found—as we have seen before—more frequently in rich than in poor countries. So are high levels of unionization (collective bargaining). Thus, the two seem to be associated (panel C). This finding implies that some of the positive relationship between the average tariff rate and interindustry inequality from panel B may be due to the presence of high unionization. In other words, the upward slope detected in panel B may be due not to the existence of a real relationship between tariff rates and interindustry inequality but to the fact that countries with low tariffs also display high unionization—with the latter driving interindustry wage inequality down.

When we check for it, however, we find that this is not the case. As panel D shows, once we control for collective bargaining, the relationship between interindustry wage inequality and average level of tariff rates remains positive—in fact, it even becomes sharper. Protection thus indeed seems to drive interindustry wage differences up. We do a further check to make sure that the relationship is not due, in part, to a change in the sample.[16] This is

16. This happens because we have data on tariff rates and interindustry inequality for many more countries than is the case with collective bargaining. Thus, once we control for collective bargaining, the sample shrinks from 757 observations, as in panel B, to 286 observations in panel D.

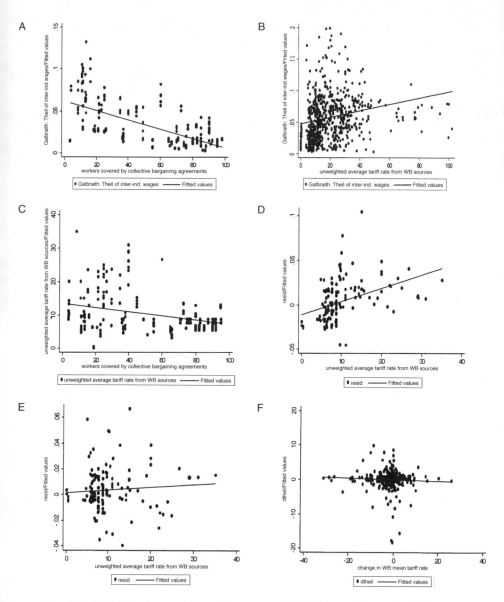

Fig. 4.9   Interindustry wage inequality, average level of protection, and unionism:
A, interindustry wage inequality and collective bargaining; *B*, average tariff rate and
interindustry wage inequality; *C*, collective bargaining and average tariff rate; *D*,
interindustry wage inequality (controlled for collective bargaining) and average tariff
rate; *E*, interindustry wage inequality (controlled for collective bargaining and level
of income) and average tariff rate; *F*, change in average tariff rate and change in
interindustry wage inequality

Table 4.5   Relationship between interindustry wage inequality and level of protection (average tariff rate) in poor and rich countries

	Poor countries			Rich countries		
Change in average tariff rate	Mean change in Theil (Theil points)	Standard deviation (Theil points)	No. of observations	Mean change in Theil (Theil points)	Standard deviation (Theil points)	No. of observations
Decrease	+0.02	2.56	219	+0.15	0.85	137
No change	+0.13	2.49	44	+0.05	0.60	72
Increase	−0.08	2.00	113	−0.32	3.41	23
Total	−0.01	2.39	376	+0.07	1.29	232

Note: Poor countries are defined as those with GDP per capita less than $9,000 at international 1995 prices; rich countries are those above that threshold.

not the case. When we run the relationship between the average tariff rate and interindustry wage differences (as in panel B) across the sample of country/years in panel D, the results do not change (graph not displayed here). Moreover, even after we control for *both* collective bargaining and income level,[17] the positive relationship between average tariff rates and interindustry wage differences remains (figure 4.9, panel E).

But the relationship between levels may not necessarily be indicative of the relationship between changes. And in effect, inspection of figure 4.9 (panel F) does show that there is a mild negative relationship between changes in average tariffs and changes in the Theil index of interindustry inequality. In table 4.5 we look at whether this relationship holds for poor and rich countries. We easily notice that for rich countries a decrease in protection is associated with an increase in interindustry wage inequality; and the reverse is true for the increase in protection. This in turn indicates that the protected sectors tended to be sectors with lower average wage (that is, less skilled). An increase in protection is associated with lower interindustry wage differences, implying again that higher tariffs will tend to protect sectors with lower average wage (presumably less skilled too). The same pattern, on average, holds for poor countries, although there the average changes are much less clear and the standard deviation much greater. Yet the fact that the same pattern is observable in poor countries as in rich countries (decreased protection associated with increased interindustry wage differences) would also tend to support the view that in poor countries too low-wage or lower-skill sectors tend to benefit from protection.

Figure 4.10 shows the change in interindustry Theil when protection is reduced. In rich countries, the effect does not vary much between the coun-

17. Since income level and interindustry inequality are negatively correlated.

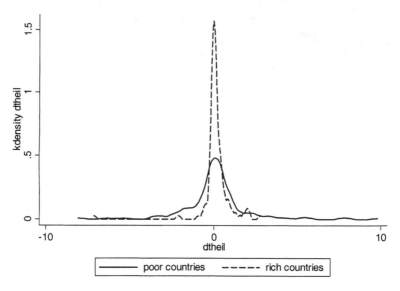

Fig. 4.10   Charge in interindustry Theil when average protection level goes down
Note: Definition of poor and rich countries given in table 4.3 notes.

tries and is bunched around zero with a longer right-end tail (which explains the positive sign of the average). For the poor countries, both right- and left-end tails are approximately equally long and the distribution is flatter.

The equation that we estimate for the change in interindustry inequality $(\Delta Ineq_I)$ can be written as

$$\Delta Ineq_I = \beta_0 + \beta_1 \text{ (change in average tariff)} + \beta_2 \text{ (labor market conditions)}$$
$$+ \beta_3 \text{ (change in labor market conditions)} + \beta_4 \text{ (income level)}.$$

Table 4.6 presents the results for interindustry wage inequality. The first, minimal, formulation shows that none of the variables is significant. In the second formulation, where we introduce the same two interaction terms as before (trade reform and income, and trade reform and union membership), the effect of change in protection on interindustry wage inequality becomes significant and negative. In other words, reduction in protection is associated with greater interindustry inequality: each percentage point of reduction in protection is associated with a 1.7 Theil point increase in interindustry inequality. This implies that as liberalization dissipates the rents from protection, the impact on the distribution of wages works, in relative terms, against those industries that engage more low-skill and unskilled workers. Since such workers will be drawn disproportionately from the ranks of the poor, the implication is that the poor who are engaged in

Table 4.6   Explaining interindustry inequality, 1976–99 (%; dependent variable: annual change in Theil)

	Regression 1	Regression 2	Regression 3
Δtariff	0.001	–1.731	–2.207
	(0.947)	(0)**	(0)**
Social expenditures as % of GDP	1.891	1.097	–2.487
	(0.08)	(0.558)	(0.21)
Ln (GDP per capita)		0.148	0.409
		(0.288)	(0.004)**
ΔTarf · ln (GDP per capita)		0.211	0.247
		(0)**	(0)**
Trade union members as % of labor force (TUMMBR)		–0.006	
		(0.268)	
Δtariff · TUMMBR		–0.005	
		(0.003)**	
Number of ILO conventions signed			0.007
			(0.006)**
Δtariff · number of ILO conventions signed			–0.002
			(0.044)**
Constant	–0.119	–1.224	–3.879
	(0.296)	(0.307)	(0.002)**
Adjusted R^2	0.0047	0.1232	0.127
F value (p)	1.56	4.98	5.91
	(0.2118)	(0.0001)**	(0)**
No. of observations	241	171	205

Note: Levels of significance, *p* values, given in parentheses.
**Significant at less than the 5 percent level.

wage employment benefit less from liberalization than their richer counterparts. Furthermore, provided there is at least some urban-rural and formal-informal labor mobility, the conclusion extends to the poor engaged in nonwage activities.

This effect, however, is less, or is overturned, at higher income levels (as the interaction term between income per capita and average tariff rate has a positive sign). At the median level of (ln) GDP per capita of the countries included in the sample (9.75), the interaction effect is greater than the direct effect of reform. We would thus expect to observe, at the median level of income and above, a decline in observed interindustry inequality even if proliberalization reforms alone tend to increase inequality between the industries. More exactly, the turning point would occur around the world median income, where (in the year 2000) we find countries such as Morocco, Ecuador, and Indonesia. For countries poorer than these we would observe trade reforms increasing interindustry inequality; for richer countries, we would observe a decrease in interindus-

try wage inequality. Similarly to what we found for interoccupational inequality, the effects are stronger and less ambiguous for poor than rich countries.

Reduction of the average tariff rate will tend to contribute to interindustry inequality more in countries with higher trade union density (see the interaction variable in regression 2). This suggests that union power is able to either limit tariff reduction for heavily unionized industries or introduce other, offsetting measures that protect their wages in some other way. It also suggests that union power tends to be concentrated in the higher-skill industries, thereby exacerbating the impact on wage inequality. The same result is observed in regression 3, where we replace trade union membership with the number of ILO conventions as the measure of union power.

4.6 Conclusions

The empirical results provide weak support for the hypothesis that a reduction of tariffs tends to be associated with an increase in interoccupational wage inequality (i.e., education premium) and somewhat stronger support that reduction in tariffs is associated with an increase in wage inequality between industries. The latter effect will be particularly strong in countries with a high density of trade unions. The implication is that the poor benefit less than the rich from liberalization but that their relative position could be improved by simultaneously taking measures to limit trade union power. Average country income plays an important role, though. Through its interaction with change in average tariffs, it offsets the effects of tariff reduction alone so that at income levels above the world median (that is, GDP per capita higher than PPP\$4,000 in 1995 international prices) the net effect reverses both for interoccupational and interindustry inequality.

Our results are obtained from the data covering approximately a twenty-year period from 1980 to 2000. The data come from three large and relatively recent databases of occupational inequality (OWW), interindustrial inequality (UTIP) and tariff rates (World Bank data). Although all three databases are rich in terms of the number of observations and do represent a major improvement in data availability, a user cannot escape the impression that there is still a nonnegligible noise in the data, perhaps not so much because the data supplied by different countries and in different periods are wrong but because the coverage of sectors and occupations and the definitions of wages are uneven and vary not only between countries but within countries as well. Thus, the data issues still represent an important obstacle to our ability to draw stronger conclusions regarding the effect of import liberalization on wage inequality in a cross-sectional setting.

Appendix

Table 4A.1   Summary of data from Occupational Wages around the World (OWW)

	Gini of interoccupational wages		
Country	Mean	Standard deviation	No. of observations
Algeria	0.1492	0.0305	8
Angola	0.3787	0.1196	3
Argentina	0.3545	0.1718	3
Australia	0.1543	0.0315	14
Austria	0.1852	0.0212	17
Azerbaijan	0.5310	0.0292	4
Bangladesh	0.2757	0.0537	9
Barbados	0.2283	0.0205	12
Belarus	0.1232	0.0058	5
Belgium	0.0900	0.0092	16
Belize	0.3173	0.0226	12
Benin	0.3863	0.0327	5
Bolivia	0.3843	0.0378	11
Botswana	0.2297	0.0032	2
Brazil	0.2348	0.0000	1
Bulgaria	0.1611	0.0000	1
Burkina Faso	0.3305	0.1400	8
Burundi	0.4175	0.0325	8
Cambodia	0.3751	0.1494	7
Cameroon	0.3866	0.0908	7
Canada	0.1341	0.0099	3
Cape Verde	0.2430	0.0001	2
Chad	0.5411	0.0548	4
Chile	0.3496	0.0053	3
China	0.1509	0.0371	10
Colombia	0.3649	0.0626	2
Zaire or Congo, Democratic Republic	0.4401	0.0000	1
Costa Rica	0.1315	0.0856	3
Côte d'Ivoire	0.3648	0.0854	4
Croatia	0.1930	0.0000	1
Cuba	0.1621	0.0121	6
Cyprus	0.2550	0.0143	16
Czech Republic	0.1339	0.0227	7
Denmark	0.1217	0.0199	10
Djibouti	0.3321	0.0000	1
Estonia	0.2191	0.0145	4
Ethiopia	0.3533	0.0000	1
Fiji	0.3099	0.0198	4
Finland	0.1343	0.0167	14
Gabon	0.3768	0.0562	5
Germany	0.2110	0.0101	17
Ghana	0.3607	0.0000	1
Honduras	0.3637	0.0316	9
Hong Kong	0.2078	0.0403	16
Hungary	0.2217	0.0378	6
Iceland	0.0972	0.0115	2
India	0.3247	0.1436	13
Iran, Islamic Republic of	0.1434	0.0000	1
Ireland	0.1913	0.0014	2
Italy	0.1498	0.0228	12
Japan	0.1995	0.0107	15

Table 4A.1 (continued)

Country	Gini of interoccupational wages		
	Mean	Standard deviation	No. of observations
Korea, Republic of	0.1979	0.0798	10
Kyrgyz Republic	0.3011	0.0153	4
Latvia	0.2558	0.0175	3
Lithuania	0.2328	0.0000	1
Luxembourg	0.1557	0.0000	1
Madagascar	0.1643	0.0536	2
Malawi	0.4522	0.0501	6
Mali	0.3167	0.0000	1
Mauritius	0.3060	0.0172	16
Mexico	0.0616	0.0602	8
Moldova	0.2055	0.0282	5
Mozambique	0.3055	0.0000	1
Netherlands, The	0.1164	0.0080	7
New Zealand	0.2060	0.0145	7
Nicaragua	0.3685	0.0263	6
Niger	0.3754	0.0000	1
Nigeria	0.3616	0.0570	6
Norway	0.1049	0.0242	16
Papua New Guinea	0.3164	0.0048	2
Peru	0.3525	0.0574	10
Philippines, The	0.0974	0.0357	9
Poland	0.1731	0.0446	2
Portugal	0.1398	0.0884	13
Puerto Rico	0.2071	0.0447	13
Romania	0.2139	0.0646	12
Russian Federation	0.2968	0.1173	8
Senegal	0.2644	0.0000	1
Seychelles	0.2593	0.0557	6
Sierra Leone	0.3099	0.0325	8
Singapore	0.3086	0.0199	15
Slovak Republic	0.1490	0.0149	5
Slovenia	0.2078	0.0160	4
South Africa	0.0982	0.0000	1
Sri Lanka	0.2299	0.0426	12
Sudan	0.2917	0.1540	6
Suriname	0.2336	0.0160	4
Swaziland	0.2911	0.0398	2
Sweden	0.1250	0.0349	9
Thailand	0.3057	0.0416	5
Togo	0.3372	0.0678	5
Trinidad	0.2502	0.0235	7
Tunisia	0.2143	0.1523	6
Turkey	0.1805	0.0489	4
Uganda	0.4810	0.0000	1
Ukraine	0.3049	0.0247	3
United Kingdom	0.1660	0.0170	14
United States	0.2097	0.0306	14
Uruguay	0.2578	0.0279	7
Venezuela	0.2622	0.0233	6
Yugoslavia	0.1760	0.0233	10
Zambia	0.3263	0.0569	7
Total	0.2370	0.1082	680

Note: Variable is xlwu from OWW.

Table 4A.2   Summary of data from University of Texas Inequality Project (UTIP)

Country	Theil index of interindustrial wage differences		
	Mean	Standard deviation	No. of observations
Albania	0.0736	0.1213	8
Algeria	0.0144	0.0156	15
Angola	0.3115	0.1041	2
Argentina	0.0512	0.0102	11
Armenia	0.2128	0.1351	5
Australia	0.0110	0.0036	23
Austria	0.0189	0.0065	25
Azerbaijan	0.0385	0.0238	5
Bahamas	0.0987	0.0191	3
Bahrain	0.4035	0.0000	1
Bangladesh	0.0349	0.0196	18
Barbados	0.0584	0.0172	23
Belgium	0.0167	0.0009	18
Belice	0.1059	0.0097	2
Benin	0.0744	0.0141	7
Bolivia	0.0711	0.0317	25
Bosnia and Herzegovina	0.0305	0.0124	2
Botswana	0.0585	0.0153	15
Brazil	0.0776	0.0097	5
Bulgaria	0.0250	0.0300	24
Burkina Faso	0.0328	0.0123	9
Burundi	0.0744	0.0297	13
Cameroon	0.1508	0.0907	20
Canada	0.0199	0.0039	25
Cape Verde	0.0052	0.0038	2
Central African Republic	0.0652	0.0279	17
Chile	0.0657	0.0193	25
China	0.0029	0.0010	7
Colombia	0.0393	0.0055	25
Congo, Republic	0.1144	0.0231	8
Costa Rica	0.0398	0.0188	15
Côte d'Ivoire	0.0737	0.0092	13
Croatia	0.0210	0.0103	11
Cuba	0.0046	0.0009	13
Cyprus	0.0363	0.0086	25
Czech Republic	0.0078	0.0049	9
Denmark	0.0066	0.0010	24
Dominican Republic	0.0792	0.0137	11
Ecuador	0.0495	0.0255	25
Egypt	0.0387	0.0228	25
El Salvador	0.0496	0.0349	17
Equatoria	0.0892	0.0178	2
Equatorial Guinea	0.0301	0.0084	9
Fiji	0.0512	0.0311	21
Finland	0.0107	0.0013	25
France	0.0160	0.0015	17
Gabon	0.1191	0.0410	7
Gambia, The	0.0374	0.0112	8
Germany	0.0108	0.0003	18

Table 4A.2 (continued)

Country	Theil index of interindustrial wage differences		
	Mean	Standard deviation	No. of observations
Ghana	0.1277	0.0363	16
Greece	0.0383	0.0125	25
Guatemala	0.1058	0.0826	21
Haiti	0.0458	0.0084	14
Honduras	0.0712	0.0321	16
Hong Kong	0.0112	0.0065	25
Hungary	0.0188	0.0186	25
Iceland	0.0435	0.0324	22
India	0.0838	0.0100	20
Indonesia	0.0751	0.0205	19
Iran, Islamic Republic of	0.0211	0.0205	18
Iraq	0.0244	0.0118	15
Ireland	0.0311	0.0185	24
Israel	0.0579	0.0144	22
Italy	0.0164	0.0049	24
Jamaica	0.1816	0.1185	15
Japan	0.0355	0.0172	25
Jordan	0.0779	0.0226	23
Kenya	0.0748	0.0143	24
Korea, Republic of	0.0151	0.0059	25
Kuwait	0.2466	0.1247	23
Kyrgyz Republic	0.0851	0.0236	6
Latvia	0.0087	0.0093	6
Lesotho	0.1055	0.0621	7
Libya	0.0324	0.0373	6
Lithuania	0.0713	0.0522	5
Luxembourg	0.0140	0.0034	20
Macedonia	0.0432	0.0225	10
Madagascar	0.0310	0.0182	14
Malawi	0.1128	0.0499	21
Malaysia	0.0313	0.0073	25
Malta	0.0110	0.0035	22
Mauritania	0.1845	0.0583	2
Mauritius	0.0750	0.0245	25
Mexico	0.0290	0.0099	25
Moldova	0.0318	0.0364	9
Mongolia	0.4423	0.4006	6
Morocco	0.0810	0.0145	24
Mozambique	0.1752	0.1233	7
Namibia	0.0314	0.0000	1
Nepal	0.0681	0.0284	9
Netherlands, The	0.0094	0.0025	25
New Zealand	0.0213	0.0150	22
Nicaragua	0.0205	0.0059	11
Nigeria	0.0390	0.0186	14
Norway	0.0095	0.0011	24
Oman	0.1121	0.0118	6
Pakistan	0.0544	0.0124	18

(continued)

Table 4A.2   (continued)

| Country | Theil index of interindustrial wage differences | | |
	Mean	Standard deviation	No. of observations
Panama	0.0669	0.0222	23
Papua New Guinea	0.0990	0.0309	15
Paraguay	0.0133	0.0000	1
Peru	0.0830	0.0351	12
Philippines, The	0.0655	0.0155	23
Poland	0.0158	0.0201	25
Portugal	0.0320	0.0064	15
Puerto Rico	0.0818	0.0398	15
Qatar	0.4041	0.0914	8
Romania	0.0103	0.0048	5
Russian Federation	0.0581	0.0090	6
Rwanda	0.0393	0.0092	6
Saudi Arabia	0.1847	0.0000	1
Senegal	0.0433	0.0299	23
Seychelles	0.0075	0.0036	11
Sierra Leone	0.1876	0.1344	2
Singapore	0.0434	0.0130	25
Slovak Republic	0.0163	0.0056	6
Slovenia	0.0165	0.0067	12
Somalia	0.0569	0.0258	6
South Africa	0.0616	0.0071	25
Spain	0.0287	0.0074	25
Sri Lanka	0.0526	0.0130	16
Suriname	0.0570	0.0221	19
Swaziland	0.0993	0.0456	20
Sweden	0.0077	0.0097	25
Syrian Arab Republic	0.0548	0.0566	24
Taiwan, China	0.0155	0.0031	23
Tanzania	0.0630	0.0263	13
Thailand	0.0945	0.0350	13
Togo	0.1050	0.0534	10
Trinidad	0.1579	0.0884	19
Tunisia	0.0896	0.0524	13
Turkey	0.0471	0.0189	24
Uganda	0.1739	0.1034	6
Ukraine	0.0347	0.0261	9
United Kingdom	0.0162	0.0022	25
United States	0.0312	0.0128	25
Uruguay	0.0481	0.0147	23
Venezuela	0.0484	0.0261	22
Yemen, Republic of	0.0670	0.0902	12
Yugoslavia	0.0847	0.0290	5
Zambia	0.0772	0.0147	6
Zimbabwe	0.0544	0.0298	24
Total	0.0548	0.0645	2,160

Table 4A.3   **Summary of unweighted average tariff rates from World Bank data**

Country	Average unweighted tariff rate		
	Mean	Standard deviation	No. of observations
Albania	17.00	0.00	1
Algeria	25.72	6.73	10
Argentina	18.33	8.05	16
Australia	8.17	3.37	11
Austria	7.05	1.34	11
Bahamas	31.37	1.37	3
Bahrain	5.20	2.63	6
Bangladesh	52.84	33.40	14
Barbados	16.02	4.11	6
Belarus	12.63	0.35	3
Belgium	7.05	1.34	11
Belize	14.66	4.86	5
Benin	33.75	14.30	11
Bolivia	12.58	4.20	16
Botswana	20.55	13.36	2
Brazil	31.89	16.33	20
Bulgaria	16.08	1.88	5
Burkina Faso	32.39	13.28	7
Burundi	29.80	14.94	4
Cambodia	35.00	0.00	1
Cameroon	21.77	5.83	7
Canada	6.74	2.08	9
Cape Verde	22.05	2.90	2
Central African Republic	21.80	6.81	4
Chad	15.75	0.07	2
Chile	14.75	6.57	16
China	33.48	11.59	12
Colombia	20.83	13.42	16
Zaire or Congo, Democratic Republic	23.66	4.76	8
Congo, Republic	19.72	7.44	5
Costa Rica	12.63	5.12	11
Côte d'Ivoire	24.85	3.54	18
Cuba	14.72	7.39	6
Cyprus	11.60	2.50	9
Czech Republic	6.14	1.03	11
Denmark	7.05	1.34	11
Dominican Republic	12.90	4.39	7
Ecuador	17.08	10.70	12
Egypt, Arab Republic of	34.79	8.81	10
El Salvador	11.86	5.83	11
Estonia	0.55	1.25	6
Ethiopia	30.30	1.62	5
Fiji	12.40	0.00	1
Finland	7.05	1.34	11
France	7.05	1.34	11
Gabon	20.16	0.77	5

(continued)

Table 4A.3   (continued)

| Country | Average unweighted tariff rate | | |
	Mean	Standard deviation	No. of observations
Gambia, The	13.55	0.07	2
Germany	7.05	1.34	11
Ghana	20.59	8.71	16
Greece	7.05	1.34	11
Guatemala	11.80	4.92	9
Guinea	21.14	24.54	7
Guyana	17.44	4.50	5
Haiti	16.43	9.79	3
Honduras	8.88	1.01	4
Hong Kong	0.00	0.00	21
Hungary	14.42	4.77	13
Iceland	5.97	2.83	10
India	56.49	25.21	14
Indonesia	20.73	9.12	13
Iran, Islamic Republic of	15.43	9.12	3
Ireland	7.05	1.34	11
Israel	7.78	0.74	9
Italy	7.05	1.34	11
Jamaica	16.10	4.47	13
Japan	6.08	0.62	12
Jordan	16.32	3.18	16
Kenya	32.25	10.18	15
Korea, Republic of	15.55	5.20	15
Kuwait	3.90	0.29	4
Latvia	5.23	0.67	4
Lebanon	13.13	5.89	4
Lesotho	17.40	0.00	1
Lithuania	4.14	0.38	5
Luxembourg	7.05	1.34	11
Madagascar	6.73	0.69	7
Malawi	19.71	4.69	16
Malaysia	12.59	2.94	13
Mali	15.66	2.50	5
Malta	7.54	0.96	5
Mauritania	22.42	6.38	10
Mauritius	31.02	6.88	13
Mexico	16.28	5.41	18
Mongolia	8.20	0.00	1
Morocco	28.15	8.34	17
Mozambique	15.74	1.25	5
Namibia	24.40	0.00	1
Nepal	17.73	4.27	9
Netherlands, The	7.05	1.34	11
New Zealand	6.99	3.67	8
Nicaragua	11.02	6.64	10
Niger	18.30	0.00	1
Nigeria	30.14	5.25	16
Norway	4.88	1.22	9

Country	Average unweighted tariff rate		
	Mean	Standard deviation	No. of observations
Oman	4.12	1.58	9
Pakistan	60.37	14.50	18
Panama	9.96	1.70	5
Papua New Guinea	17.06	5.43	5
Peru	26.48	13.34	19
Philippines, The	23.96	8.1	21
Poland	12.90	3.37	12
Portugal	7.05	1.34	11
Qatar	3.75	1.37	4
Romania	14.20	4.38	7
Russian Federation	11.24	2.48	5
Rwanda	34.53	5.69	4
Samoa	9.00	0.00	1
Saudi Arabia	9.58	4.36	12
Senegal	13.10	1.78	8
Sierra Leone	29.82	8.31	6
Singapore	0.30	0.16	15
Slovak Republic	7.10	0.91	5
Slovenia	11.00	0.69	3
Somalia	29.67	5.98	3
South Africa	11.86	6.43	13
Spain	7.05	1.34	11
Sri Lanka	24.52	8.09	13
Sudan	35.90	21.05	5
Suriname	24.82	10.15	5
Swaziland	15.10	0.00	1
Sweden	7.05	1.34	11
Switzerland	1.59	2.19	8
Syrian Arab Republic	20.57	13.34	6
Taiwan, China	17.94	9.31	13
Tanzania	25.58	5.03	14
Thailand	30.72	10.83	11
Togo	15.25	2.95	4
Trinidad	18.33	1.06	6
Tunisia	27.55	2.47	16
Turkey	21.26	9.32	12
Uganda	16.87	6.89	7
Ukraine	9.83	0.67	3
United Kingdom	7.05	1.34	11
United States	5.93	0.69	12
Uruguay	21.27	11.95	16
Venezuela	19.59	8.32	15
Vietnam	13.50	2.03	4
Yemen, Republic of	20.73	4.94	3
Yugoslavia	11.84	0.09	5
Zambia	20.17	7.85	9
Zimbabwe	16.39	6.23	11
Total	17.65	14.12	1,255

References

Arbache, Jorge Saba, Andy Dickerson, and Francis Green. 2003. Trade liberalization and wages in developing countries. University of Kent, Department of Economics. Working Paper. Available at www.ssrn.com.

Barro, Robert. 2000. Inequality and growth in a panel of countries. *Journal of Economic Growth* 5:5–32.

Behrman, Jere, Nancy Birdsall, and Miguel Szekely. 2003. Economic policy and wage differentials in Latin America. Center for Global Development Working Paper no. 29. Washington, DC: Center for Global Development, April. Available at http://www.cgdev.org/Publications/?PubID=29.

Beyer, Harald, Patricio Rojas, and Rodrigo Vergara. 1999. Trade liberalization and wage inequality. *Journal of Development Economics* 59:103–23.

Dollar, David, and Aart Kraay. 2001. Trade, growth, and poverty. Policy Research Working Paper no. 2615. Washington, DC: World Bank.

Edwards, Sebastian. 1997. Trade policy, growth and income distribution. *AEA Papers and Proceedings* 87 (2): 205–10.

Feenstra, Robert C., and Gordon A. Hanson. 1997. Foreign direct investment and relative wages: Evidence from Mexico's mequiladoras. *Journal of International Economics* 42:371–94.

Freeman, Richard B. 1995. Are your wages set in Beijing? *Journal of Economic Perspectives* 9 (3): 15–32.

Freeman, Richard B., and R. H. Oostendorp. 2000. Wages around the world: Pay across occupations and countries. NBER Working Paper no. 8058. Cambridge, MA: National Bureau of Economic Research.

Galbraith, James K., and Hyunsub Kum. 2003. Inequality and economic growth: A global view based on measures of pay. *CESinfo Economic Studies* 49 (4): 527–56.

Hanson, Gordon, and Ann Harrison. 1999. Trade and wage inequality in Mexico. *Industrial and Labor Relations Review* 52:271–88.

Harrison, Ann, and Gordon Hanson. 1999. Who gains from trade reform? Some remaining puzzles. *Journal of Development Economics* 59:125–54.

Londono, Juan Luis. 2002. Capital for equity in Latin America. Paper presented at Fourth annual World Bank Conference on Development Economics. June, Oslo, Norway.

Lundberg, Mattias, and Lyn Squire. 2003. The simultaneous evolution of growth and inequality. *Economic Journal* 113 (487): 326–44.

Milanovic, Branko. 2005. Can we discern the effect of globalization on income distribution? Evidence from household surveys. *World Bank Economic Review* 19 (1): 21–44.

Rama, Martin, and Raquel Artecona. 2002. A database of labor market indicators across countries. Washington, DC: World Bank. Unpublished manuscript.

Ravallion, Martin. 2002. Growth, inequality and poverty: Looking beyond averages. *World Development* 29 (11): 1803–15.

Richardson, David J. 1995. Income inequality and trade: How to think, what to conclude. *Journal of Economic Perspectives* 9 (3): 33–55.

Robertson, Raymond. 2000. Trade liberalization and wage inequality: Lessons from the Mexican experience. *World Economy* 23 (6): 827–49.

Savvides, Andreas. 1998. Trade policy and income inequality: New evidence. *Economics Letters* 61 (3): 365–72.

Spilimbergo, Antonio, Juan Luis Londono, and Miguel Szekely. 1999. Income distribution, factor endowment and trade openness. *Journal of Development Economics* 59:77–101.

Comment   Douglas A. Irwin

This chapter tackles a broad but topical subject—the cross-country empirical relationship between trade liberalization and within-country wage inequality, particularly in developing countries. This relationship, and hence the subject of this paper, is somewhat open ended because there is no strong theoretical result that influences our prior belief about what the relationship should be.

One could use the Stolper-Samuelson theorem to suggest that abundant factors of production should benefit from trade liberalization, but the mapping between this theorem and the messy complexity of developing countries is problematic, to say the least.

This chapter uses two measure of wage (not income) inequality, one relating to occupational wages and the other relating to industry wages. These inequality measures are related to a direct measure of a country's average tariff (not "openness" as measured by trade volumes and commonly employed in other studies).

The authors find weak evidence that a reduction in the average tariff rate is associated with higher interoccupational wage inequality in poor countries and somewhat strong evidence of an association with greater interindustry wage inequality. Although the authors are suitably cautious in interpreting their results, I would reinforce this caution. At one point, the authors write that a tariff reduction "contributes to" increased wage inequality. Since establishing a strong causal relationship between the two measures was not the primary object of the paper, I think "association" is a better characterization of the findings. Many factors drive wage inequality, and tariff policy is simply one (a measurable one) among many.

In addition, if there are difficulties in attributing changes in inequality within a country over a given time period to a particular policy measure, these difficulties are aggravated when considering the cross-country evidence. (The United States experienced growing wage inequality in the 1980s, and yet the average tariff did not change at all during the decade.)

At the same time, the results—their general tendency as well as their weakness—do not come as too much of a surprise. As Gordon Hanson's paper (chap. 10 in this volume) points out, six studies of six different countries all found the same general results—that greater openness leads to greater income/wage inequality. Thus, it appears that country studies have uncovered an empirical regularity.

This regularity, however, is itself a bit of a paradox. Given the Stolper-

Douglas A. Irwin is the Robert E. Maxwell '23 Professor of Arts and Sciences and a professor of economics at Dartmouth College, and a research associate of the National Bureau of Economic Research.

Samuelson theorem, which is drilled into the minds of every international economist, we would expect to see the skill premium fall for skilled workers in developing countries with trade liberalization. But perhaps someone should inform those workers that the skill premium increases with globalization. This is because Mayda and Rodrik (2005) examine surveys of pro- and antitrade views around the world and find that, in developing countries, higher levels of education are associated with antitrade views, consistent with Stolper-Samuelson. Yet, ironically, the evidence indicates that those with higher levels of education are precisely those benefitting from more trade.

Several broader points deserve mention as well.

- Sometimes I think we are missing the big picture. In low-income countries, about 60 percent of labor force is in agriculture; most of the rural poor are in agriculture. Yet our data sets usually cover just manufacturing or industry. I think if we are interested in inequality in developing countries, the urban-rural inequality or agriculture-nonagriculture wage gap is much more important than wage inequality within manufacturing (which could be a small part of the story). By focusing exclusively on manufacturing, we might be missing a big chunk of the economy and a big part of intranational wage inequality.

- A paper by Shang-Jin Wei and Yi Wu (2001) gets at this by measuring the urban-rural wage differential for 100 or so Chinese cities (urban areas and adjacent rural counties) over the period 1988–93. The central finding is that cities that experience a greater degree of openness in trade also tend to demonstrate a greater decline in urban-rural income inequality. Thus, globalization has helped to reduce, rather than increase, the urban-rural income inequality. What they suggest is that this pattern in the data suggests that inferences based solely on China's national aggregate figures (overall openness and overall inequality) can be misleading. What I would suggest is that raising rural, agricultural incomes is a key part of reducing inequality, and trade reforms (agricultural or land policy liberalization) may promote this process. Traditionally, trade policies have been strongly antiagrarian in developing countries.

To conclude, the literature on globalization and income inequality includes several country case studies. This paper attempts a cross-country examination of the relationship between tariff policy and inequality, and in some sense it confirms what we have learned from the country studies. Yet because these findings, for developing countries, conflict with the basic Stolper-Samuelson theorem prediction, there is a paradox waiting for more discussion and analysis in future work.

References

Mayda, Anna Maria, and Dani Rodrik. 2005. Why are some individuals (and countries) more protectionist than others? *European Economic Review* 49 (6): 1393–1430.
Wei, Shang-Jin, and Yi Wu. 2001. Globalization and inequality: Evidence from within China. NBER Working Paper no. 8611. Cambridge, MA: National Bureau of Economic Research, November.

My Policies or Yours
Does OECD Support for
Agriculture Increase Poverty
in Developing Countries?

Margaret McMillan, Alix Peterson Zwane,
and Nava Ashraf

The rural poor [in Mexico] growing maize for subsistence saw
their livelihoods destroyed by a flood of cheap U.S. imports.
—Oxfam briefing on agricultural subsidies, 2002

It must be acknowledged that unqualified assertions by many,
including the heads of some multilateral institutions, that subsidies and other interventions in agriculture in the OECD
countries are hurting the poor countries are not grounded in
facts. . . . The claim that the change will bring net gains to the
least developed countries as a whole is at best questionable
and at worst outright wrong.
—Economist Arvind Panagariya, 2002

5.1 Introduction

Rich countries are under increasing pressure from around the world to
end support to agriculture. Agricultural subsidies and price supports allow Organization for Economic Cooperation and Development (OECD)

Margaret McMillan is an associate professor of economics at Tufts University and a research associate of the National Bureau of Economic Research (NBER). Alix Peterson
Zwane is assistant cooperative extension specialist in the Department of Agricultural and Resource Economics at the University of California, Berkeley. Nava Ashraf is an assistant professor at Harvard Business School.

We thank Pongrat Aroonvatanaporn, Shilpa Phadke, Demian Sanchez, and Jesse Tack for
excellent research assistance and Mitali Das, Bill Easterly, Demian Sanchez, Matthias
Schuendeln, Tim Wise, participants in the NBER conferences, and especially Ann Harrison
and Will Masters for helpful comments and suggestions. All remaining errors are our own.

countries to sell their agricultural products on world markets at prices that are below the cost of production.[1] Critics claim that these policies inflict harm on poor countries by depressing world commodity prices.[2] They argue further that these policies are likely to hurt the poorest residents of the poor countries because poor people are often farmers. Thus, eliminating support for rich-country farmers will raise world prices and the incomes of the poor. Our goal in this paper is to evaluate these claims systematically by measuring the impact of OECD agricultural policies on poverty in developing countries.

Because of the diversity both within and among developing countries, the extent to which rich-country support policies translate into lower incomes in developing countries is an empirical question. Many least developed countries, especially in Africa, are net importers of food. As net food importers, they may be hurt by higher commodity prices (Panagariya 2002, 2004a; Valdes and McCalla 1999). Some countries may import cereals, such as maize and rice, but export other agricultural products, such as sugar or cotton. Higher prices for exports and imports will have net effects that are difficult to predict ex ante. Even within importing countries, the poorest members of society may be net sellers of food.

We begin our analysis with an investigation into the relationship between income per capita and the value of net cereal, food, and agricultural (food plus nonfood) exports for each of the three decades leading up to 2000. We find that—on average—the poorest countries have historically been net importers of cereals and food, the products most heavily supported by the OECD countries, just as they are today. That this pattern has not changed over the past thirty years casts some doubt on the notion that "dumping" turned exporters into importers. We also find that the poorest countries are—on average—net exporters of all agricultural products. However, with the important exception of cotton, the nonfood agricultural products are typically not the products supported by the OECD.[3]

What about the poor people in poor countries? To determine whether OECD policy hurts the poorest residents of the poor countries, we use a cross-country regression framework in which the head count poverty rate

---

1. Transfers to agricultural producers from consumers and taxpayers as a result of income and price support policies equaled $21,000 per farmer in the United States and $16,000 per farmer in the European Union (EU) in 1998–2000 (OECD 2001). This is almost 100 times greater than per capita incomes in the least developed countries.

2. James D. Wolfensohn, president of the World Bank, has stated that rich countries are "squandering" $1 billion a day on farm subsidies that hurt farmers in Latin America and Africa. Stanley Fischer, who was the deputy managing director of the International Monetary Fund (IMF) in the 1990s, has said the United States, Europe, and Japan pursue agricultural protection policies that are "scandalous" because of the harm they inflict on poor countries (Andrews 2002). Some also argue that these subsidies increase the volatility of commodity prices since support policies that are countercyclical with respect to domestic prices or shocks provide incentives for increased production when world prices are relatively low.

3. Panagariya (2004b) has recently made a similar point.

(or average income) is the dependent variable. Our innovation is to include as an explanatory variable a measure of rich-country support for the agricultural products produced in the developing country in question.[4] To our knowledge, this is the first use of this strategy to quantify the impacts of rich-country agricultural support policies on poor countries.[5] Also using this framework, we assess the relative importance of own-country characteristics and policies. We find no support in the cross-country analysis for the claim that—on average—OECD policies worsen poverty in developing countries.

To better understand the within-country distributional implications of rich-country agricultural subsidies, we complement our macro work with a case study of Mexican corn farmers using data at the farmer and household level. This case is instructive for several reasons. First, Mexico is often offered as a cautionary example of the impacts of agricultural trade liberalization on rural poverty. Second, the case of Mexico raises a number of issues, such as the importance of domestic policy, which can help to inform our cross-country analysis. Finally, we choose Mexico because rich nationally representative and previously unexploited data sets are available.[6]

Evidence from Mexico confirms the importance of domestic policies relative to international policies that affect commodity border prices, and highlights the importance of distributional issues masked by the cross-country analysis. In the mid-1990s the Mexican government initiated the liberalization of the corn sector in Mexico. As anticipated, this liberalization led to a sharp decrease in the producer price of corn and an increase in Mexican corn imports from the United States. Because this liberalization took place in the context of U.S. corn subsidies that lower border prices, the United States is sometimes held responsible for the price decline and increased poverty among Mexican corn farmers. Contrary to this

---

4. We introduce a new variable into a standard cross-country regression framework previously employed by others including Easterly and Levine (2003); Rodrik, Subramanian, and Trebbi (2002); Acemoglu, Johnson, and Robinson (2001); and Frankel and Romer (1999).

5. There is some evidence that terms of trade can affect incomes and poverty in developing countries. Sarel (1997) presents evidence that improvements in terms of trade are significantly negatively correlated with changes in income inequality in an ordinary least squares (OLS) regression. He argues that since "policies can rarely affect directly terms of trade dynamics," the implications of this finding are limited. However, policy changes in the OECD can directly affect the magnitude and nature of agricultural support, which in turn may affect commodity prices and developing countries' terms of trade. Acemoglu and Ventura (2002) present evidence that terms of trade may be quantitatively important for explaining cross-country income differences using an instrumental variables approach to account for the endogenous relationship between growth and changes in terms of trade.

6. Our data on Mexico come from INEGI (the Mexican Statistical Agency) and are drawn from two different surveys, the Encuesta Nacional de Empleo (ENE), an individual-level national employment survey, which includes a rich agricultural supplement, and the Encuesta Nacional de Ingresos y Gastos de los Hogares (ENIGH), a household-level income and expenditure survey. Both surveys were conducted both pre- and post-NAFTA, though not always for the same years.

popular view, our evidence suggests that U.S. corn subsidies have had a limited impact on the border price of corn. In addition, because the majority of the poorest corn farmers do not sell corn in the market, their incomes were not directly affected by the decline in the producer price of corn. By contrast, a majority of the medium-sized and large corn farmers do participate in the market. Medium-sized corn farmers experienced a sharp decline in real income, while the income of the largest corn farmers actually increased. Transfer payments to all corn farmers—also part of the corn market liberalization—increased but were structured so that benefits went disproportionately to the rich farmers.

Our results stand in stark contrast to the large body of literature that has been devoted to examining the *potential* impact of agricultural trade liberalization on developing countries using computable general equilibrium (CGE) models.[7] While the magnitudes of CGE estimates vary, agricultural trade liberalization is typically predicted to increase world commodity prices to the *overall* benefit of developing countries. For example, Beghin, Roland-Holst, and van der Mensbrugghe (2002) estimate that the removal of all agricultural subsidies and trade barriers could increase rural value added in low- and middle-income countries by $60 billion per year, which, as they note, exceeds most targets for development assistance by some 20 percent. Probably the most important reason for the differences in results is that other studies have not focused explicitly on poverty but rather on developing countries as a whole. Additionally, as pointed out by Panagariya (2004b), many studies combine liberalization by developing countries with liberalization by developed countries when estimating welfare impacts. We focus solely on the impacts of rich-country policies on poor countries and the poor residents of these countries.

In interpreting our results, a few caveats are in order. First, our measure of OECD policy is effectively the production-weighted average implicit export subsidy faced by each country in our sample. A variety of other OECD actions such as support for minor crops, import tariffs on products not produced domestically (e.g., coffee), phytosanitary regulations, and discretionary protection applied when imports rise may also be important for developing countries but are beyond the scope of this paper. Second, our measure of OECD policy does not include cotton, a key nonfood product that is heavily subsidized by the United States in a way that harms some very poor countries. Cotton is not included because the OECD calculates support only for the major commodities that make up the first 70 percent of the total value of agricultural production. However, in our view, the inclusion of

7. See, for example, OECD (2002); Economic Research Service/U.S. Department of Agriculture (ERS/USDA; 2002); Trueblood and Shapouri (1999); Hoekman, Ng, and Olarreaga (2002); and Beghin, Roland-Holst, and van der Mensbrugghe (2002). Note that some CGE-based studies of the Uruguay Round agreement found results consistent with the focus of this paper, such as Hertel, Masters, and Elbehri (1998).

cotton is unlikely to change our overall findings because it is only exported by a handful of the poorest countries and makes up a relatively small share of these countries' total agricultural production. Third, while we find that *on average* OECD support does not increase poverty and that *the majority* of poor Mexican corn farmers do not participate in the market, it may still be the case that many poor people are made poorer by these policies. Roughly 60 percent of the poorest Mexican corn farmers do not participate in the market. This means that 40 percent of the poorest corn farmers do participate in the market. For these people, the conclusions about the impacts of depressed corn prices are different. Such nuances help us to understand why different groups may have very different perspectives on these issues.

The remainder of this paper is organized as follows. Section 5.2 establishes the relationships between net exporter status and income for developing countries over time and in the cross section. Section 5.3 describes the data and estimation strategy used in the cross-country analysis and presents these results. Section 5.4 presents an analysis of the impact of a reduction in the price of corn on Mexico's corn farmers. Section 5.5 concludes.

5.2   Are the Poorest Countries Hurt by OECD Support for Agriculture?

We begin with an investigation into the relationship between income per capita (measured in constant 1985 dollars at purchasing power parity [PPP] exchange rates and collected from the Penn World Tables version 6.1) and the value of net cereal, net food, and net agricultural exports including nonfood products as a share of GDP (measured at current prices). This can be thought of as the fraction of current income earned from the sale of these products or spent to purchase these products. Because there are time series data on agricultural imports and exports, as well as income, it is possible to track the behavior of the cohort of developing countries over time.[8]

We identify the countries that may have been most affected historically by OECD agricultural policy as those that have spent (earned) the greatest fraction of income on imports (exports) of supported products. We are particularly interested in comparing how cereal importers differ from food or nonfood agricultural exporters because cereal prices are depressed by OECD agricultural support policies, while the prices of most other food products (with the important exceptions of dairy and sugar) and nonfood products (with the important exception of cotton) are largely unaffected by OECD support.

Figures 5.1, 5.2, and 5.3 present data on income earned from agricultural exports in three different ways. First, we use data from the Food and

---

8. Other authors have also presented data to highlight the diverse agricultural trade profile of developing countries (Valdes and McCalla 1999; Panagariya 2002, 2004a) but have emphasized cross-sectional patterns only. This snapshot of countries' trade positions may obscure long-run patterns in the data.

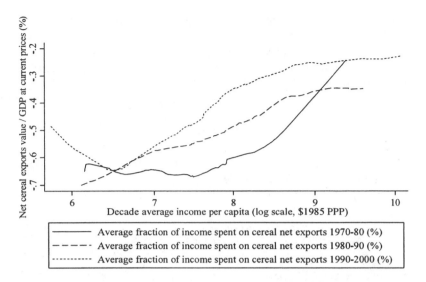

Fig. 5.1   Average income and net cereal exports by decade in a repeated cross section of developing countries

Agriculture Organization (FAO) to calculate the value of annual net cereal exports as a percentage of GDP for a sample of ninety-nine developing countries and take the average value of this number for the periods 1970–79, 1980–89, and 1990–2000.[9] We show the cross-sectional income profile for these three time periods in figure 5.1 by using a locally weighted regression of decadal average cereal export share on the decadal average of the log of income per capita (bandwidth = 0.8). We run the same regressions for food export share and present those results in figure 5.2. Figure 5.3 shows the regressions for agricultural export shares (including nonfood products such as green coffee and fibers).

Figure 5.1 shows that, in each decade, the poorest countries spend the largest percentage of their incomes on cereal imports, suggesting that they may experience net benefits as a result of depressed cereal prices. In fact, so few developing countries are net cereal exporters in any decade that the predicted net cereal export share is negative even at the highest income levels observed in the data.[10]

9. The sample includes three transition economies: Poland, Romania, and Hungary. The FAO definition of cereals includes wheat, paddy rice, barley, maize, popcorn, rye, oats, millet, sorghum, buckwheat, quinoa, fonio, triticale, canary seed, and mixed grains.

10. Among countries for which data are available, Thailand, Argentina, Nepal, Zimbabwe, South Africa, Uruguay, Pakistan, Kenya, and Guyana had positive average net export earnings from cereals in the 1970s. This list expanded to include Vietnam in the 1980s but lost Nepal and Kenya. In the 1990s, Guyana, Argentina, Thailand, Vietnam, Hungary, Paraguay, India, and Pakistan had positive net export earnings from cereals.

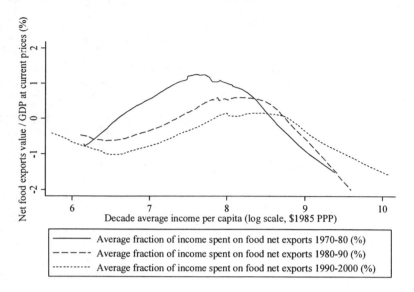

Fig. 5.2   Average income and net food exports by decade in a repeated cross section of developing countries

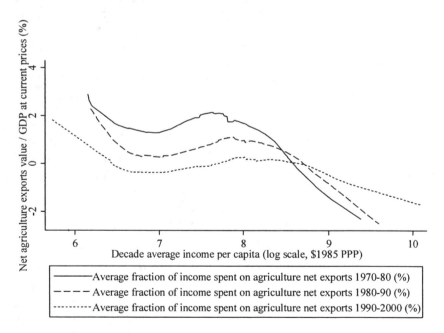

Fig. 5.3   Average income and net agriculture exports by decade in a repeated cross section of developing countries

Since 1970 the poorest countries have also experienced the smallest reduction in net expenditures on cereal exports as a share of GDP. To trace the average cereal export share of a given country experiencing economic growth, points should be connected not within years but across the regression lines, linking up the experience and behavior of a like country in the following decade. Thus, the fact that the regression lines are very close to each other at the lowest levels of income suggests that net export increases experienced at higher income levels largely bypassed the poorest countries in the postcolonial era.

These data suggest that depressed prices for food products may hurt middle-income countries but help the poorest and richest developing countries. As shown in figure 5.2, and unlike in the case of cereals alone, among non-OECD countries only middle-income countries earn income from food exports. The cross-sectional relationship between net earnings from all food exports as a share of GDP is nonmonotonic. This production category includes noncereal products that receive high levels of support in the OECD, including sugar, beef, and dairy products, as well as unsubsidized products such as cocoa and most fruits and vegetables.

The cross-sectional relationship between food export earnings share and income appears to be flattening over time. In the 1970s, a country with an income of $1,100 is predicted to have positive net food exports. A country with this level of income in the 1980s or 1990s is predicted to be a net food importer. The trend in these data appears to be toward zero net earnings from food exports. Although it is not shown here, this impression is even stronger when the sample size is enlarged to include twenty-one high-income OECD member countries.

Poor countries are most likely to be net exporters of agricultural products in total, as shown in figure 5.3.[11] We run the same regressions to create this figure, but we consider all agricultural products, including fibers, industrial seeds, green coffee, and tobacco. In this case we find a downward-sloping relationship between net export earnings and income. Relatively well-off developing countries import agricultural products as a whole. This suggests that depressed prices for nonfood agricultural products like cotton are particularly damaging to the poorest countries.

Figures 5.1, 5.2, and 5.3 together provide evidence that many poor countries import cereals but export agricultural products as a whole, and have been in this position throughout the postcolonial era. As we show in table 5.1,

11. In particular, this category of products includes cotton, an important export crop for several West African countries as well as Brazil, China, and India. Cotton is excluded from our regression analysis because, although production data are available from the FAO, support levels are not calculated for this crop. This support is certainly not trivial; about $2.3 million was provided as assistance to U.S. cotton growers in 2001–2 (International Cotton Advisory Committee 2002). The OECD calculates support only for the major commodities that make up the first 70 percent of the total value of agricultural production.

Table 5.1	Agricultural trade positions by country (sorted by income)				
			1990–2000 average percentage of income earned on net exports of:		
	Income per capita 2000, PPP$(1996)	Fraction of population below $1/day (most recent year)	Cereals	All food	All agriculture (food + nonfood)
Congo, Democratic Republic of the	322[a]		−0.54	−1.31	−0.88
Tanzania	482	0.49	−0.49	−0.50	1.50
Burundi[d]	523	0.55	−0.16	−0.61	0.98
Ethiopia[d]	635	0.23	−0.43	−0.52	
Guinea-Bissau	688		−2.23	−0.47	−0.88
Nigeria[d]	707	0.70	−0.32	−0.70	−0.68
Malawi[d]	784	0.42	−1.22	−1.11	4.70
Yemen, Republic of	817	0.10	−2.24	−5.29	−5.74
Madagascar[d]	836	0.49	−0.27	0.27	0.75
Togo[d]	870		−0.36	−0.72	1.08
Niger	875	0.61	−0.47	−0.48	−0.66
Sierra Leone	889[a]		−1.64	−2.63	−2.64
Zambia[d]	892	0.64	−0.59	−0.65	−0.51
Rwanda	895	0.36	−0.26	−1.03	−0.42
Chad	909		−0.21	0.28	1.67
Uganda[d]	941	0.85	−0.07	−0.34	1.36
Burkina Faso[d]	957	0.45	−0.66	−1.04	−0.71
Mali[d]	969	0.72	−0.25	0.10	1.95
Central African Republic[d]	992[b]	0.67	−0.24	−0.54	−0.24
Mozambique[d]	1,037	0.38	−0.75	−1.21	−1.47
Benin[d]	1,214		−1.21	−1.97	−0.29
Gambia, The[d]	1,217	0.26	−1.94	−4.38	−5.51
Kenya[d]	1,244	0.23	−0.31	−0.19	2.03
Angola	1,252[a]		−0.51	−2.22	−3.08
Cambodia	1,272[c]	0.34	−0.13	−0.57	−1.40
Sao Tome and Principe	1,314[a]			−1.27	−2.86
Mauritania	1,315[c]	0.26		−3.27	−4.06
Ghana[d]	1,351	0.45	−0.36	1.14	1.11
Nepal[d]	1,459	0.39	−0.02	−0.26	−0.49
Vietnam	1,522[a]	0.04	0.43	0.54	0.71
Comoros[d]	1,578		−1.17	−1.29	−1.51
Lesotho	1,592	0.36	−1.10	−5.07	−5.85
Senegal[d]	1,622	0.22	−1.30	−2.42	−2.43
Bangladesh[d]	1,684	0.36	−0.19	−0.48	−0.52
Nicaragua[d]	1,767	0.59	−0.59	−0.36	0.84
Congo, Republic[d]	1,808		−0.65	−2.22	−2.44
Côte d'Ivoire[d]	1,869	0.16	−0.61	4.07	5.93
Pakistan[d]	2,008	0.13	0.02	−0.29	−0.33
Cameroon[d]	2,042	0.32	−0.22	0.29	1.15
Honduras[d]	2,050	0.21	−0.42	1.06	2.85
Haiti[d]	2,349[b]		−1.30	−2.87	−2.91
India[d]	2,479	0.45	0.04	0.03	0.12
Zimbabwe[d]	2,486	0.56	−0.06	0.26	2.25

(*continued*)

Table 5.1 (continued)

	Income per capita 2000, PPP$(1996)	Fraction of population below $1/day (most recent year)	1990–2000 average percentage of income earned on net exports of:		
			Cereals	All food	All agriculture (food + nonfood)
Bolivia[d,e]	2,724	0.14	−0.33	0.14	0.58
Guinea[d]	2,831		−0.40	−0.74	−0.76
Papua New Guinea[d]	2,922[c]		−0.53	−0.11	0.80
Sri Lanka[d]	3,300	0.07	−0.35	−0.78	0.22
Philippines, The[d,e]	3,425	0.15	−0.25	−0.09	−0.21
Ecuador[d]	3,468	0.18	−0.18	1.98	2.41
Equatorial Guinea	3,604			−0.68	−1.58
Guyana	3,613[c]	0.03	1.97	6.36	6.18
Indonesia[d,e]	3,642	0.07	−0.16	−0.02	0.17
Jamaica[d]	3,693	0.00	−0.90	−0.91	−0.65
Morocco[d]	3,717	0.01	−0.44	−0.32	−0.63
China[d]	3,747	0.17	−0.06	0.04	0.01
Jordan[d]	3,895	0.00	−1.66	−3.52	−3.91
Guatemala[d,e]	3,914	0.16	−0.23	0.80	2.02
Cape Verde[d]	4,027		−1.34	−4.81	−5.73
Syria[d]	4,094		−0.28	−0.21	−0.09
Egypt[d]	4,184	0.03	−0.56	−1.09	−1.30
Romania[d]	4,285	0.02	−0.06	−0.28	−0.55
El Salvador[d]	4,435	0.31	−0.30	−0.71	0.29
Namibia	4,459[c]	0.35	−0.46	0.66	0.77
Peru[d]	4,589	0.18	−0.49	−0.74	−0.60
Paraguay[d,e]	4,684	0.15	0.05	1.29	1.39
Algeria[d]	4,896	0.01	−0.80	−1.85	−2.16
Cuba	5,087[a]		−0.52	1.75	1.68
Swaziland	5,227	0.08	−0.37	4.49	3.80
Dominican Republic[d]	5,270	0.00	−0.46	−0.18	0.03
Colombia[d,e]	5,383	0.08	−0.19	0.03	1.02
Fiji[d]	5,442[c]		−0.73	2.61	2.39
Lebanon	5,786		−0.72	−4.45	−6.11
Costa Rica[d,e]	5,870	0.02	−0.53	4.10	6.51
Iran	5,995	0.00	−0.39	−0.59	−0.70
Panama[d]	6,066	0.07	−0.29	0.48	0.35
Grenada[d]	6,178		−0.66	−3.72	−4.27
St. Lucia	6,330	0.25	−0.80	−0.15	−1.09
Venezuela[d]	6,420	0.14	−0.20	−0.54	−0.67
Belize	6,591		−0.35	5.16	4.37
Tunisia[d]	6,776	0.00	−0.45	−0.34	−0.65
Thailand[d,e]	6,857	0.02	0.46	1.07	1.41
St. Vincent[d]	7,148		0.40	2.70	2.09
Brazil[d,e]	7,190	0.08	−0.13	0.30	0.75
Dominica[d]	7,379		−0.65	2.80	0.25
South Africa[d,e]	7,541	0.11	−0.04	0.18	0.20
Botswana	7,550[c]	0.31	−0.58	−1.90	−2.67
Gabon[d]	8,402		−0.24	−1.27	−1.52
Mexico[d]	8,762	0.10	−0.17	−0.28	−0.28

Table 5.1   (continued)

| | Income per capita 2000, PPP$(1996) | Fraction of population below $1/day (most recent year) | 1990–2000 average percentage of income earned on net exports of: | | |
			Cereals	All food	All agriculture (food + nonfood)
Poland[d]	9,217	0.01	−0.08	0.14	−0.15
Uruguay[d,e]	9,622	0.00	0.63	2.27	2.31
Malaysia[d,e]	9,919	0.00	−0.40	1.36	1.89
Chile[d,e]	9,926	0.01	−0.13	0.84	1.00
Seychelles[d]	10,241		−0.90	−5.14	−6.16
Hungary[d]	10,439	0.00	0.29	1.89	1.83
Argentina[d,e]	11,006	0.08	0.56	1.82	2.42
Trinidad and Tobago[d]	11,175	0.04	−0.41	−1.09	−0.87
St. Kitts and Nevis	13,666			−1.06	−1.95
Mauritius[d]	13,932		−0.41	1.43	1.08
Cyprus[d]	16,063[b]	0.00	−0.72	−0.58	−0.32
Barbados[d]	16,415	0.00	−0.36	−1.30	−1.61
Singapore[d]	22,642[b]	0.00	−0.22	−1.75	−1.39
Hong Kong, China[d]	26,699	0.00	−0.15	−2.23	−2.87

Source: FAOSTAT, Penn World Tables, World Bank PovertyNet.
[a]Year of observation 1995.
[b]Year of observation 1998.
[c]Year of observation 1999.
[d]Indicates country included in regression analysis.
[e]Indicates Cairns Group member.

which ranks countries by current income per capita and summarizes the data from the latest decade that are presented graphically in figures 5.1 through 5.3, many poor countries, and even many middle-income countries, that export food products import cereals, particularly in the 1990s. Depressed commodity prices as a result of domestic support for agriculture in the OECD could lower the value of both imported products and exported products for these countries. While it is true that a majority of poor countries are net exporters of agricultural products today (see table 5.1), among the nonfood products cotton stands out as the only nonfood commodity whose price is likely to be significantly depressed by OECD agricultural support.

Of course, the experience of developing countries is diverse, and, because they are regressions, figures 5.1 through 5.3 obscure differences in countries' experiences at any income level. However, these results suggest that it is unlikely that broad agricultural liberalization, which is likely to result in higher world prices for cereals as well as dairy products, sugar, and cotton, will benefit the majority of the poorest countries.

Country-level average values of net cereal or food exports tell us little about what happens to the poor within a country. Even in countries that are net importers of food, the poor may be net exporters of food. Thus, a

poor country might be hurt by higher food prices while the poor within that country benefit from higher food prices. The remainder of the paper is devoted to this issue.

5.3 Does OECD Support Hurt the Poorest People in Poor Countries?

Even if the poorest countries are net importers of products protected and subsidized by OECD governments, it is possible that the poorest people within these countries are net sellers of these cheap imports. If this were the case, then OECD support that benefits the country as a whole could increase poverty in that same country. In fact, this is a common assumption based on the observation that poverty tends to be concentrated in rural areas. We begin this section by describing our approach to testing this hypothesis in a cross-country regression framework. This is followed by a description of our methodology for obtaining country-specific measures of OECD support and a description of our data. We conclude with a presentation of results.

5.3.1 Empirical Strategy

To test the claim that OECD support for agriculture hurts the poor, we begin by estimating the following equation:

(1) $$\log \mathrm{HP}_{it} = \alpha_i + \gamma \log \mathrm{OECDPOLICY}_{it} + \varepsilon_{it},$$

where HP is the head count poverty rate for country i at time t based on the \$1-a-day poverty line, α_i is a country fixed effect, ε is the disturbance term, and OECDPOLICY is a country-specific measure of OECD support that varies over time and whose construction we discuss in the next subsection. This simple specification allows us to preserve the largest number of observations for which data on poverty and OECD support are available. In this specification, γ represents the elasticity of poverty with respect to OECD support. Critics of OECD agricultural policy would expect γ to be positive and significant. To this basic equation we add additional controls for comparability with previous work and to test the notion that own-country policies are more important than OECD support as determinants of poverty.

One potential problem with this specification has to do with the endogeneity between OECD support and world commodity prices. OECD support is a function of commodity price fluctuations and domestic political considerations. Commodity price fluctuations can in turn be affected by OECD policy. Thus, in principle, we need to take care in the interpretation of γ. In other words, we could mistakenly attribute to OECD policy changes in poverty that are being driven purely by changes in commodity prices. Practically, this is a moot issue, since we find no significant relationship between OECD policy and poverty.

A second problem with this approach is the limited availability of the in-

tersection of poverty data and data on OECD support to agriculture. Because these data are sparse and since there is a strong association between average income and poverty reduction, we also consider the impact of OECD support on average income in developing countries by estimating the following equation:

$$(2) \qquad \log y_{it} = \delta_i + \beta \log \text{OECDPOLICY}_{it} + \sigma_{it},$$

where δ is a country fixed effect, σ is the disturbance term, and β represents the elasticity of poverty with respect to OECD policy. The only difference between equation (2) and equation (1) is that in equation (2) we now insert the log of average income per capita as the dependent variable.

One advantage to estimating equations (1) and (2) is that the time-invariant factors that affect poverty and income, such as institutions, geography, and structural measures of integration, are subsumed in the country fixed effects. We also control for time-variant global trends that may affect incomes, such as global weather shocks and energy prices using time fixed effects.

5.3.2   Data

Our main innovation is in constructing OECDPOLICY, a country- and year-specific measure of OECD support to agriculture. Therefore, we devote the majority of this section to describing both how the OECD computes commodity- and year-specific measures of distortionary support and how we aggregate these data into variables that can be included in the regression analysis. We then briefly describe the other variables used in our analysis.

Since 1987 the OECD has tracked support, by commodity, for agriculture in member countries. The U.S. Department of Agriculture (USDA) has calculated support by commodity and country for the period 1982–90. In order to use these data to develop the variable OECDPOLICY, we need to select a measure of domestic support and identify a means of aggregating support measures across commodities to develop a country-specific measure of other countries' agricultural policies.

The producer support estimate (PSE) is the most commonly used measure of domestic support for agriculture. The PSE measures the annual monetary value, at the farm gate, of gross transfers from consumers and taxpayers to agricultural producers arising from policy measures to support agriculture.[12] The PSE for a commodity is usually presented as a fraction of the value of total gross farm receipts for the commodity. This is re-

---

12. The PSE includes domestic subsidies to agriculture, barriers to market access, and export subsidies. It does not include food aid (OECD 2001). The PSE includes implicit payments, such as those that arise from commodity-specific price gaps created by trade barriers, but excludes gaps between domestic and border prices that may arise because of transportation costs, quality differences, or marketing margins.

ferred to as the "percent PSE" and measures the portion of farmer receipts attributable to policy.[13]

An alternative definition of trade-distorting support is the producer nominal protection coefficient (NPC), which is defined as the ratio between the average price received by producers (at farm gate) and the border price (net of transportation costs and marketing margins). This is conceptually equivalent to the implicit export subsidy necessary to export the observed quantity produced. An NPC equal to one implies that producers receive border prices for their output after adjusting for transportation costs and thus do not receive production-distorting signals from agricultural support policies. The NPC is calculated on a commodity-by-commodity basis for the OECD as a whole by taking a production-weighted average of producer prices and a common border price.

A third measure of support calculated by the OECD is the producer nominal assistance coefficient (NAC), which is defined as the ratio of the value of total gross farm receipts, including support, and production valued at world market prices, without support. The NAC is related to the PSE, but it calculates support independent of exchange rate effects. When the NAC is equal to one, receipts are entirely derived from the market.

All three measures of support for agriculture are highly correlated within countries and correlated across countries, both in aggregate and by commodity. In the main regression specifications discussed in this paper, we measure support for agriculture in the OECD by commodity using the NPC. However, our results are robust to alternative measures of support. Figure 5.4 reports the NPC by commodity for the OECD for the periods 1986–88 and 2000–2. Milk, sugar, and rice receive the highest levels of production-distorting support.

In order to estimate equations (1) and (2), we must identify which OECD support policies are relevant to country i in period t by matching support policies to countries in a way that reflects the relative importance of support by commodity for each country. That is, for a non-OECD country i, we must identify a set of weights to use to combine measures of the NPC for the following products: wheat, maize, rice, other grains, oilseeds, sugar, milk, beef, sheep meat, wool, pig meat, poultry, and eggs. These are the products for which the NPC is calculated by the OECD and USDA. We must also appropriately account for the fact that countries produce other agricultural products for which the NPC is equal to one.

---

13. The percent PSE has several potential shortcomings when considering how it might be used in econometric analysis (Masters 1993; Wise 2004). It is possible that total support for agricultural producers as measured by the PSE could be increased by policy changes, while the distortionary effects of support are reduced by changes in the policy mix used to support agriculture (e.g., if export subsidies were replaced with decoupled income or production support). This is because the PSE is made up of several categories of transfers that have differing impacts on production, consumption, and trade. Thus, the most common measure of support may not be the most appropriate for our analysis; we do not expect policies that do not affect trade to impact developing countries.

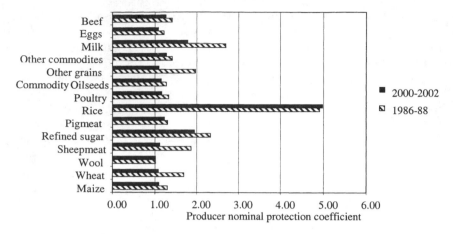

Fig. 5.4   **Producer nominal protection coefficients by commodity**

We create the variable OECDPOLICY as a weighted average of support provided by rich-country governments to growers of these products (or similar commodities that are likely substitutes for it) in each year for the period 1982–2000, where weights are defined by the share of each product in the developing country's agricultural output in 1970.[14] This approach should avoid the problem that current production choices are partly determined by current subsidy levels. In addition, some African countries have severely discriminated against agriculture in the past; we want to consider their potential exports (as measured by their sectoral structure in 1970) rather than their actual exports or production. For commodities that have a calculated NPC we use FAO data on 1970 total production of the following products: wheat, maize, rice, other grains (calculated as total cereals less wheat, maize, and rice), oilseeds (including cake and meal), sugar (refined, cane, and beet), milk (condensed, dry, and fresh), beef and veal, sheep meat (fresh), wool (greasy), pig meat, poultry meat, and eggs. For vegetables and melons, all roots and tubers, all fibers, coffee, cocoa, and all fruits, we set the NPC equal to one.[15]

14. Ideally, this approach would use developing-country agricultural sectoral composition in 1930—before the architecture of modern OECD farm policy was put in place. Data from this period may be of poor quality, however, to the extent that they exist.

15. By assuming an NPC of one for fibers we underestimate the value of OECDPOLICY for cotton producers. Even excluding cotton, bound tariffs for these products are not uniformly equal to zero in developed countries. Thus, our approach underestimates OECD-POLICY. However, tariffs for these products are much lower than bound tariffs for so-called program crops and those commodities for which the OECD calculates an NPC. There are also relatively few megatariffs for these products. For example, the World Trade Organization (WTO) bound tariffs reported by the United States include nineteen tariffs of 100 percent or higher. Only six of these are for products for which we assume an NPC of one, and these are minor products in the nuts and tobacco commodity group.

African countries, which have a relatively large fraction of historical agricultural production in roots and tubers and in coffee and cocoa, tend to have low levels of OECDPOLICY. Small countries that import essentially all their food needs also have low values of OECDPOLICY. Conversely, rice producers have high values of OECDPOLICY. Grain and oilseed exporters, such as Brazil, tend to have values of OECDPOLICY that fall in the middle of the distribution.

We note in table 5.1 the countries included in our regression analysis—a subset of the countries included in figures 5.1 through 5.3. Our largest sample includes seventy-five developing countries for the period 1982–2001. We also identify the countries that are members of the Cairns Group, currently considered to be among the most competitive agricultural exporters. Far more countries in our sample are net food and cereal importers than exporters, which is consistent with our discussion in section 5.2 of the experience of a larger sample of developing countries. Notably, however, the Cairns Group countries are not all historical exporters; Bolivia, Chile, and Indonesia were net importers of food and cereals in the 1970s, for example.

Our data on income per capita, measured in 1996 PPP dollars, come from the Penn World Tables, version 6.1. To control for global weather shocks that impact commodity prices we use a common measure of the El Niño–Southern Oscillation (ENSO) severity called the Southern Oscillation Index (SOI) anomaly.[16] Recent research has shown that ENSO severity can explain as much as 20 percent of annual commodity price variation (Brunner 2002). There is also a positive correlation between ENSO, as measured by the SOI anomaly, and GDP growth. Thus, we expect the coefficient on this variable to be positive.

Table 5.2 reports summary statistics for all of the variables used to estimate equations (1) and (2). We report these statistics for the entire sample and then separately for the Cairns Group and for historical food importers.[17] We define countries that were food and cereal exporters or importers based on data for the 1970s, the decade prior to our analysis. Food-importing countries have higher average incomes than the Cairns Group food exporters because several well-off island countries (e.g., Hong Kong and Singapore) are food importers. However, the variance of incomes in the Cairns Group is significantly lower among food importers. None of the poorest countries in the sample are in this group. These patterns are stable across the two decades that we consider.

16. The SOI anomaly measures deviations between air pressure differentials in the South Pacific and historical averages. For each year, we take the average of the SOI anomaly as measured in January and June. These data are available from the National Oceanic and Atmospheric Administration (NOAA).

17. In table 5.2 and in the regression analysis, Bolivia, Chile, and Indonesia are included only in the Cairns Group sample. They are not included in the historical food-importers sample.

Table 5.2   **Summary statistics for cross-country regressions**

	No. of observations	Mean	Standard deviation	Minimum	Maximum
A. All developing countries in pooled cross section 1982–2001					
Head count poverty rate ($1/day, PPP $1985)	225	20.23	20.61	0.00	87.67
Income per capita (PPP $1985)	1,485	3,357	3,098	341	20,591
OECDNPC	1,503	1.57	0.48	0.99	3.64
Log consumer price index	1,377	0.19	0.43	–0.12	4.77
Exports + imports/GDP	1,461	0.68	0.39	0.06	2.95
B. Cairns Group in pooled cross section 1982–2001					
Head count poverty rate ($1/day, PPP $1985)	72	9.85	8.87	0.00	47.04
Income per capita (PPP $1985)	281	4,105	1,702	1,580	8,724
OECDNPC	281	1.80	0.45	1.17	3.20
Log consumer price index	281	0.31	0.63	–0.01	4.77
Exports + imports/GDP	281	0.56	0.35	0.12	2.29
C. Cereal and food importers in pooled cross section 1982–2001					
Head count poverty rate ($1/day, PPP $1985)	74	24.20	26.11	0.00	87.67
Income per capita (PPP $1985)	613	3,834	4,065	437	20,591
OECDNPC	621	1.52	0.52	0.99	3.64
Log consumer price index	554	0.14	0.30	–0.12	4.33
Exports + imports/GDP	591	0.71	0.44	0.16	2.95
D. Other developing countries in pooled cross section 1982–2001					
Head count poverty rate ($1/day, PPP $1985)	85	25.41	18.58	0.00	72.29
Income per capita (PPP $1985)	611	2,500	2,064	341	11,783
OECDNPC	621	1.55	0.45	1.01	3.30
Log consumer price index	562	0.17	0.39	–0.10	4.64
Exports + imports/GDP	609	0.71	0.32	0.06	1.59

Source: World Development Indicators (trade share and CPI), Penn World Tables (income), and World Bank PovertyNet (head count), FAOSTAT, and SourceOECD (OECDNPC).

Notes: Cereal and food importers defined as countries that had negative values of net exports of cereals and food on average in 1970s. The average Southern Oscillation Index anomaly has an average value of –0.58 (standard deviation 1.18).

Because our specification includes country dummies, our measures of a country's own policies were chosen to reflect trade and macro policies that vary significantly over time within countries. Therefore, the variables we use to control for own-country policies are trade share (exports plus imports divided by GDP) and inflation. Table 5.2 shows that the Cairns Group countries are richer than the rest of the countries in the sample. They also have a significantly smaller share of the population below the poverty line. The trade share of GDP is actually lower for the Cairns Group, which is likely to be explained by the differences in GDP. OECD-POLICY is slightly higher for the Cairns Group, implying that these countries are slightly more vulnerable to OECD subsidies. The rate of inflation in the Cairns Group is nearly double that in the rest of the sample. This is

because nine of the fourteen Cairns Group countries are in Latin America, where inflation has been notoriously problematic.

5.3.3   Results

Tables 5.3 and 5.4 present the results of estimating equations (1) and (2), respectively. In both tables, the estimates are separated into three panels. Panel A presents results for the entire sample. There is good reason to believe that the coefficient on OECDPOLICY will vary across countries. Specifically, the effect of changes in commodity prices on poverty (income) is likely to depend on whether a country is a net importer or net exporter of the product in question. Therefore, in panels B and C we relax the assumption of a constant elasticity of poverty (income) with respect to OECD policy. In panel B we estimate equations (1) and (2) for members of the Cairns Group, and in panel C we estimate these equations for countries that are historical net food importers.

We begin by looking at the results of the estimation of equation (1) for the entire sample. The regressions in columns (1) and (2) report the simple correlation between OECDPOLICY and poverty. In column (1) we control only for country fixed effects; in column (2) we add time fixed effects. In columns (3) through (6) we add a measure of average income and a measure of weather fluctuations, and in columns (5) and (6) we add two measures of domestic policy: trade as a share of GDP and the log of inflation. The only robust result across specifications is the relationship between average income and poverty documented by Besley and Burgess (2003).

Imposing the assumption of a constant elasticity across countries is one reason that we might not find any relationship between OECD policy and poverty. We check this by estimating equation (1) separately in panel B for the Cairns Group, the group of countries pushing for agricultural liberalization and most expected to benefit from agricultural liberalization. The results in panel B are not much different from those in panel A. We turn next to the group of countries expected to lose as a result of higher food prices, historical food importers. Once again, the coefficient on OECD policy is insignificantly different from zero. For this subsample of countries, reducing inflation is associated with poverty reduction.

Why do we find no relationship between OECD policy and poverty? The most obvious explanation is the lack of data. Our entire sample consists of a little over 200 observations for most countries because the poverty data are only available for two or three years. We can partially address this issue by redefining our dependent variable to be average income per capita. To obtain the link between OECD policy and poverty, we can then rely on the link between average income and poverty documented by Besley and Burgess (2003) and evident in our table 5.3.

Table 5.4 reports the results of estimating equation (2). In panel A we report estimates for the whole sample. As in table 5.3, there is no evidence of

Table 5.3 **Poverty and OECD agricultural support: Cross-country evidence**

	(1)	(2)	(3)	(4)	(5)	(6)
	A. All developing countries					
Ln OECDPOLICY	0.140	2.439	3.036	3.036	2.203	2.120
	(0.885)	(1.684)	(1.446)**	(1.746)	(1.544)	(1.691)
Ln GDP per capita			−4.300	−4.300	−5.093	−5.135
			(2.104)**	(2.104)**	(2.426)**	(2.487)**
SOI anomaly				−0.326	−0.291	−0.291
				(0.155)**	(0.169)	(0.168)
Ln inflation					−0.382	−0.395
					(0.286)	(0.296)
Trade share						0.375
						(1.244)
No. of observations	223	223	217	217	211	211
R^2	0.67	0.69	0.72	0.72	0.73	0.73
	B. Cairns Group only					
Ln OECDPOLICY	1.307	1.427	1.346	1.346	0.931	0.464
	(1.781)	(1.693)	(0.976)	(0.976)	(1.081)	(1.361)
Ln GDP per capita			−3.570	−3.570	−3.590	−3.766
			(3.148)	(3.148)	(3.189)	(3.142)
SOI anomaly				−0.142	−0.135	−0.112
				(0.186)	(0.189)	(0.190)
Ln					−0.330	−0.347
					(0.411)	(0.426)
Trade share						0.574
						(0.981)
No. of observations	70	70	69	69	69	69
R^2	0.55	0.67	0.69	0.69	0.69	0.70
	C. Historical food-importers only					
Ln OECDPOLICY	−1.372	1.448	1.130	1.130	0.471	0.512
	(1.254)	(2.163)	(2.776)	(2.776)	(2.678)	(2.586)
Ln GDP per capita			−4.154	−4.154	−4.816	−4.842
			(2.088)**	(2.088)**	(2.031)***	(2.069)***
SOI anomaly				0.715	0.739	0.686
				(0.643)	(0.619)	(0.563)
Ln inflation					−0.622	−0.647
					(0.229)**	(0.228)**
Trade share						1.042
						(1.340)
No. of observations	74	74	74	74	72	72
R^2	0.83	0.88	0.91	0.91	0.92	0.92

Notes: Robust standard errors in parentheses. All estimates include country fixed effects. Estimates in columns (2)–(6) also include year dummies.

***Significant at the 1 percent level.

**Significant at the 5 percent level.

Table 5.4   Income and OECD agricultural support: Cross-country evidence

	(1)	(2)	(3)	(4)	(5)
		A. All developing countries			
Ln OECDPOLICY	0.102	0.136	0.136	0.131	0.128
	(0.043)**	(0.082)	(0.082)	(0.085)	(0.082)
SOI anomaly			0.033	0.033	0.030
			(0.012)***	(0.012)***	(0.013)**
Ln inflation				−0.006	−0.007
				(0.022)	(0.023)
Trade share					0.032
					(0.118)
No. of observations	1,410	1,410	1,410	1,299	1,282
R^2	0.97	0.98	0.98	0.98	0.98
		B. Cairns Group only			
Ln OECDPOLICY	0.176	0.469	0.469	0.462	0.323
	(0.117)	(0.256)	(0.256)	(0.255)	(0.243)
SOI anomaly			0.015	0.016	0.018
			(0.041)	(0.042)	(0.042)
Ln inflation				0.010	0.000
				(0.027)	(0.027)
Trade share					0.263
					(0.116)***
No. of observations	267	267	267	267	267
R^2	0.87	0.94	0.94	0.94	0.94
		C. Historical food importers			
Ln OECDPOLICY	0.123	0.168	0.168	0.204	0.213
	(0.060)**	(0.090)	(0.090)	(0.101)	(0.113)
SOI anomaly			0.036	0.023	0.018
			(0.016)**	(0.011)***	(0.013)
Ln inflation				−0.048	−0.045
				(0.021)***	(0.022)***
Trade share					−0.062
					(0.135)
No. of observations	582	582	582	524	507
R^2	0.98	0.98	0.98	0.98	0.98

Notes: Robust standard errors in parentheses. All estimates include country fixed effects. Estimates in columns (2)–(5) also include year dummies.
***Significant at the 1 percent level.
**Significant at the 5 percent level.

any robust relationship between OECD policy and average income per capita in developing countries. We do find that good weather has a small effect on average income (as previously documented by Brunner 2002). In panel B of table 5.4 we present the same sequence of regression results for the smaller sample of Cairns Group countries. Recall that some of these countries were actually food importers in the 1970s. These are the countries for

which we predict a negative correlation between OECDPOLICY and income per capita. Again, the sign on OECDPOLICY is opposite to what we'd predict, but the coefficient is so imprecisely measured that we cannot distinguish it from zero. We examine the impact of OECDPOLICY on historical food importers in panel C. This is the group for which we predicted a positive relationship between OECDPOLICY and income per capita. The sign on OECDPOLICY is as predicted, but again the result is insignificantly distinguishable from zero in all but one instance. There is a dichotomy between the Cairns Group sample and the historical food importers in that trade share is positively correlated with income for the Cairns Group but has no relationship to income for the historical food importers. By contrast, inflation is negatively correlated with income for historical food importers and does not appear to matter for the Cairns Group countries.

5.3.4   Discussion

In summary, we find no evidence in our regression analysis that—*on average*—OECD policies help or hurt the poor. Several caveats are in order. First, for each country, we are looking at a package of policies that includes all of the products produced by the developing country. It is possible for a country to be a net exporter of one commodity and a net importer of a second commodity, both of which are subsidized by the OECD countries. The effects of a price decline would have different effects in the different sectors, and we are unable to capture this in our current framework, which focuses on aggregate effects. Second, looking at average income might be misleading if—as many of the advocates for the poor suggest—the poor are the net sellers of these products and the relatively well-off are the net consumers of these same products. In this case, OECD policy, by depressing commodity prices, could make the poor worse off and the rich better off, leaving average income unchanged. We would capture this in our poverty regressions, but, as we mentioned, these data are sparse. Finally, the poverty data are likely to include government transfers in some cases and not in others. This is problematic because it makes it difficult to isolate the impact of OECD policy on poverty.

5.4   Do U.S. Corn Subsidies Hurt Poor Mexican Corn Farmers?

In this section of the paper, we evaluate the claim that U.S. support to corn farmers—by depressing Mexican producer prices—has been largely responsible for the increase in rural poverty in Mexico.[18] We begin by doc-

---

18. For example, in a recent policy brief Oxfam (2003) argues that NAFTA has been responsible for a surge in U.S. corn exports to Mexico and the associated decline in the real producer price of corn. Moreover, the brief argues that Mexican corn farmers are at a distinct disadvantage vis-à-vis U.S. corn farmers because of the huge subsidies paid out by the U.S. government. The result of this flood of cheap U.S. imports has been an increase in poverty of the 15 million Mexicans who depend on corn as a source of income.

umenting the decline in the Mexican producer price of corn. Next we consider the reasons for this decline: was it primarily Mexican policy or U.S. policy? We also consider the possibility that the majority of corn farmers living far from the border in states like Chiapas are sheltered from changes in the world price of corn. Finally, we analyze the impact of the decline in producer prices on Mexican corn farmers and their families.

Mexican corn is an ideal case study for our purposes for a number of reasons. Mexico is an importer of corn and has been for several decades. Corn is also a product heavily subsidized by the OECD countries and in particular the United States, a major trading partner of Mexico. We have national employment surveys and household data that include detailed information on corn expenditures and sources of income, including income received in the form of government transfers. These data are available for the period 1990–2000—the period over which the real Mexican producer price of corn declined by more than 50 percent. Thus, we can learn a great deal about the impact of depressed commodity prices on the poor by studying the case of Mexico. We also have time series data on regional producer prices and reference prices that allow us to explore the determinants of the decline in producer prices, including the extent to which producer prices move with world prices. We rely on existing work that examines the link between world corn prices and U.S. corn subsidies to estimate the relative importance of U.S. corn subsidies as a determinant of the Mexican producer price of corn.

As we discussed extensively in the first half of this paper, the impact of a price decline on poverty depends on whether the poor are net buyers or net sellers of the commodity in question. This is as true for households as it is for countries, but it has largely been ignored in discussions of the impact of corn trade liberalization on Mexico (see, for example, Nadal 2001 and World Bank 2004).[19]

Using nationally representative survey data for the years 1991 through 2000, we study the *actual* impact of a reduction in the price of corn on poverty among corn farmers in Mexico. Like de Janvry, Sadoulet, and Gordillo de Anda (1995), we are interested in identifying net sellers of corn. Because detailed data on income and expenditure are not recorded

19. Two papers written prior to the implementation of NAFTA do consider the possibility that poor Mexican corn farmers might actually be net consumers of corn. Using household survey data from 1990 for three states in Mexico, de Janvry, Sadoulet, and Gordillo de Anda (1995) find that the majority of small and medium-sized corn producers do not produce for the market. They predict therefore that most corn farmers' income will not be directly affected by the decline in the price of corn associated with NAFTA, while a significant share will benefit as consumers. Using a general equilibrium framework, Levy and van Wijnbergen (1995) quantify the impact on household welfare, the labor market, and the land market of liberalizing the Mexican corn sector. This paper makes the important point that even subsistence farmers who do not sell corn are likely to sell labor. Thus, to the extent that the drop in corn prices reduces rural wages, subsistence farmers are likely to be hurt by the liberalization of the corn sector.

in the same survey, making it difficult to identify households that are net sellers, we use information from the National Employment Survey to document over time by measures of living standard (size of land holdings) the share of corn farmers who report that they sell corn and the changes in these farmers' income. This exercise allows us to determine the share of the poorest corn farmers whose income has been directly affected by changes in the price of corn because they sell corn.

Of course, even if individual farmers' earnings from corn farming have fallen, it could be that total household expenditures on corn products have fallen by even more, in which case the household to which the corn farmer belongs would be a net beneficiary of the reduction in the price of corn. Since the National Employment Survey only tracks income from the respondents' primary job, we use household survey data to document, by measures of living standard, changes in income and expenditure on corn products of families with family members who report that their primary or secondary source of income is corn farming. While the household survey does not specifically ask for the amount of income derived from corn farming, it does ask whether the household members' primary source of income is corn farming. In addition, the survey asks each individual member of the household whether their income is derived from labor (work income), from business (profit income), from remittances both domestic and international (income from remittances), from government programs (income from transfers), or from other sources, such as rental income (other income). For those households that report that their primary source of income is corn farming, the work and profit share of income reported is derived primarily from corn farming. Thus, a comparison between changes in income and changes in expenditure on corn products allows us to determine whether households that rely on corn farming as a primary or secondary source of income (and in particular the poorest corn farmers) have on net benefited from a reduction in the price of corn.[20]

To determine the relative impact of domestic policy and international policy on the producer price of corn, we examine the extent to which U.S. subsidies have depressed Mexican producer prices, and we study the pattern of corn prices across time and across states. Our primary goal here is to determine the reason for the dramatic decline in the producer price of corn over the period 1986–2002. First, we consider the impact of domestic policy ("my policies") on the producer price by comparing Mexican producer prices to border prices pre- and post-1994, the year the North American Free Trade Agreement (NAFTA) between Canada, Mexico, and the United States was signed. We focus on NAFTA because it marks the be-

---

20. One complication that we do not address is the fact that corn is purchased in many different forms. Thus, it is harder to argue that the expenditure patterns are attributable solely or even primarily to NAFTA.

ginning of the liberalization of the corn market. Importantly, NAFTA encompasses both policies designed to align Mexican producer prices with world prices (such as tariff liberalization) and domestic policies designed to soften the negative consequences of this liberalization. We extend this analysis to a comparison of prices at the state level to determine whether—as some claim—states farthest from the border have been shielded from trade liberalization. To obtain an estimate of the impact of U.S. subsidies on border prices, or how much higher border price would be in the absence of U.S. subsidies ("your policies"), we rely on a recent survey of this issue by Wise (2004).

One important caveat is in order. Our data do not track the same households over time, and therefore we are unable to document what has happened to the income of farmers and households who relied heavily on corn farming prior to liberalization and who then switched out of corn farming into some other activity. To understand whether in fact our results suffer from a serious selection bias, we examine farmer (and corn-farming household) characteristics over time to determine whether these have changed substantially. In future work, we will use regression analysis and correct for selection bias.

The remainder of this case study is organized as follows. We first describe the policy environment in Mexico. Next we assess the relative importance of "my policies" (NAFTA) or "your policies" (U.S. corn subsidies) in determining the Mexican producer price of corn. We then consider the impact of these policies on poverty among Mexican corn farmers. We conclude with outstanding issues and directions for future research.

5.4.1   The Policy Environment in Mexico

This section of the paper is devoted to describing the package of policies known as NAFTA. The critics claim that NAFTA has exposed poor Mexican corn farmers to cheap U.S. imports. However, it is important to remember that NAFTA included several policy reforms beyond the removal of tariffs. It is also worth noting that NAFTA was freely agreed to by the Mexican government and thus should be counted among "my policies" in the parlance of this paper.

Since the implementation of NAFTA, tariffs on imported corn have been dramatically reduced. The Mexican over-quota bound tariff on corn has been reduced from 206.4 percent to 72.6 percent, and the tariff-rate quota (TRQ) has increased from 2.5 million metric tons to 3.36 million metric tons. At the same time, Mexico has converted its import licensing system to a transitional TRQ that will remain effective until 2008 with a 3 percent annual increase in quantity. Over the first six years of the agreement, an aggregate 24 percent of the tariff was eliminated. The remainder will be phased out by 2008.

NAFTA included several policy reforms beyond the removal of tariffs

that affected corn farmers. The reforms in the agricultural sector that most directly affected corn farmers are the removal of price supports and the implementation of direct income transfers. Other reforms that would have had an impact on corn farmers are an extension program aimed at raising productivity, changes in credit, and land reform. We discuss each of these below, drawing on a recent evaluation of the effect of NAFTA on Mexico's agricultural sector (Yunez-Naude and Barceinas Paredes 2002).

According to Yunez-Naude and Barceinas Paredes (2002), it is widely agreed that the most important domestic policy reform has been the elimination of price supports to producers of basic crops. The producer price of corn was supported through government procurement by CONASUPO (the National Basic Foods Company). The 1991 nominal rate of protection to corn was 77 percent, and the producer subsidy equivalent (PSE) amounted to $92 per tonne for white corn and $71 per tonne for yellow corn, compared to $28 in the United States and $21 in Canada. Consumer prices were also subsidized, but mainly for urban consumers through access to CONASUPO stores. In these government-run stores, consumers could purchase cheaper corn that the government had acquired from producers at inflated prices. However, few farmers live close enough to such stores to sell corn at the high support price and then buy their consumption needs at the low subsidized prices (de Janvry, Sadoulet, and Gordillo de Anda 1995).

CONASUPO's role in the corn market was substantially diminished in 1995 as a result of the Mexican peso crisis. The peso devaluation in 1995 allowed the Zedillo government to transform CONASUPO into a buyer of last resort and eliminate price supports to corn farmers. However, because of the drop in corn prices in 1996, the government of Mexico reinstated an intermediate scheme of price fixing whereby prices were fixed on a regional basis at a level between the guaranteed price and the international price. This scheme was abolished in 1999.[21]

Some Mexican corn producers currently receive a fixed subsidy per ton of marketable surplus under the Marketing Support Program. In order to participate in this program, producers must have a marketable surplus. Relatively few farmers (around 10 percent) fit this description (Zahniser and Coyle 2004). PROCAMPO was initiated in the winter of 1993–94, a few months before the beginning of NAFTA. The program was designed to supplement farmers' income and moved support in the direction of income transfers. Payments were based on area under cultivation. Its main purpose was to help farmers facing stiff competition from U.S. and Canadian farmers make a transition to more competitive crops. It is intended to

---

21. CONASUPO also subsidized tortilla processors and maize millers by selling to these processors the maize purchased from farmers at a price that would allow the processors a "reasonable" profit.

last until 2008, when full trade liberalization under NAFTA will be complete.

There are several other reforms that took place during the 1990s not specifically aimed at corn farmers but that would nevertheless impact them. The first is the Alliance for the Countryside (Alianza para el Campo). It includes PROCAMPO as well as other programs. One of the most important programs is PRODUCE, which is an extension program designed to increase productivity via improved technology. Liberalization of the agricultural sector also entailed the elimination of subsidized inputs such as seeds fertilizer and credit. Finally, the Salinas government amended the constitution in 1991 to liberalize property rights in the *ejidal* sector. Until this time, peasants who benefited from land redistribution, *ejidatarios,* were by law not allowed to associate, rent, or sell their land. The constitutional amendment abolished this provision and is expected to develop rural land markets by allowing farmers to participate in private credit markets and by promoting direct investment.

Based on the preceding discussion, it should now be clear that when we refer to NAFTA we are not simply referring to a removal of tariffs on imported corn. NAFTA was much broader than that. In what follows, we use NAFTA to represent domestic policy changes ("my policies") that impact the Mexican producer price of corn.

5.4.2   What Determines the Mexican Producer Price of Corn:
        My Policies or Yours?

There is no doubt that NAFTA is having an impact on United States–Mexico corn trade. Figure 5.5 confirms the findings of others that U.S. corn

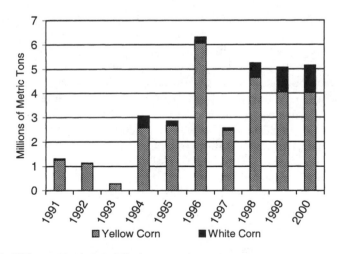

Fig. 5.5   U.S. corn exports to Mexico
Source: USDA (www.//www.ers.usda.gov/Briefing/Corn/trade.htm).

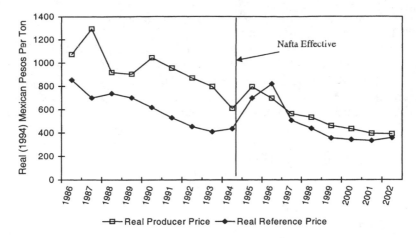

—▫— Real Producer Price   —◆— Real Reference Price

Fig. 5.6   Corn producer prices and world prices
Source: OECD Producer Support Estimate database.

exports to Mexico (the United States is the only country that exports significant amounts of corn to Mexico) have increased dramatically since the signing of NAFTA.[22] Moreover, prior to NAFTA, the United States exported virtually no white corn—the type of corn typically grown by Mexican corn farmers—to Mexico. However, as figure 5.5 shows, the amounts of both yellow and white corn exported from the United States to Mexico increased substantially after the signing of NAFTA.[23] As a share of Mexican corn production, U.S. imports increased from an average of 8.4 percent of total production in the eight years leading up to NAFTA to an average of 32.6 percent of total production in the eight years following NAFTA.

Figure 5.6 shows that the average real price paid to producers of corn in Mexico dropped significantly between 1986 and 2002. Part of the drop in Mexican producer prices has to do with the drop in the world price of corn; the Mexican producer price follows fairly closely the border price. In figure 5.6 we plot the annual average Mexican producer price in real 1994 pesos against the annual average border price, also reported in real 1994 pesos. The border price was obtained from the OECD's PSE database (http://www.oecd.org/dataoecd/33/54/32361406.xls) and reflects the cost of importing U.S. corn at the border, including freight charges to the border but not within Mexico. U.S. dollars are converted to pesos using an annual av-

22. See, for example, Zahniser and Coyle (2004).
23. The distinction between yellow corn and white corn is an important one. Mexican corn farmers primarily grow white corn, which is used to make food products. Yellow corn is typically used to feed animals. However, there is some substitutability between yellow and white corn. Food-grade yellow corn is used to make cornflakes, tortilla chips, beer, and other foods, and white corn can be used as animal feed (Zahniser and Coyle 2004).

erage of the official exchange rate. Both series are converted to 1994 pesos using the national consumer price index.

There are two important pieces of evidence to take away from figure 5.6. First, although the two price series moved closely together throughout the 1990s, 1996 was an exception. In 1996, the two series diverge as U.S. prices increase and Mexican prices drop. Indeed, in 1996 Mexican producers were actually taxed, and were receiving only 88 percent of the U.S. price for their product. Thereafter, the two series continue to move closely together. Second, prior to NAFTA, the gap between the Mexican price and the U.S. price is significantly greater than the gap post-NAFTA. Indeed, the average NPC (the ratio of the Mexican producer price to the border price) for the period 1986–95 is 1.61, while the average NPC for the period 1996–2002 is 1.17.[24]

We test the patterns suggested by figure 5.6 more formally in a regression framework and report these results in tables 5.5 and 5.6. For U.S. prices, we use the same price series shown in figure 5.6. For Mexican producer prices, we now use a separate price series for each of Mexico's thirty-two states. Our time series covers only 1991–2000 since these are the years for which we have price data at the state level. Also in tables 5.5 and 5.6, we explore the possibility that states further from the border, where the poorest corn farmers live, are less affected by changes in world prices and NAFTA. Following Nicita (2004), we assign states to four groups depending on their distance from the U.S. border.[25]

Table 5.5 presents the results of regressions of the real Mexican producer price for each state on real border prices. To eliminate the common time trend, we first difference both price series. In column (1) we report the results of the simple correlation between Mexican and U.S. prices. Not surprisingly, the correlation is positive. In column (2) we test whether this relationship has changed significantly as a result of NAFTA. The weak and negative sign on the interaction term is counterintuitive and suggests that the relationship between Mexican and U.S. prices weakened after NAFTA. However, in column (3), we introduce a control for the sudden shift in policy in 1996 and find that the coefficients on the NAFTA terms are now insignificantly different from zero. We interpret this as evidence that, except in 1996, Mexican and U.S. prices moved closely together both before and after NAFTA. In column (4), we restrict the sample by dropping 1996 and

24. The results are even more pronounced if we do not include 1995 in the pre-NAFTA average.
25. Border states are Baja California, Sonora, Chihuahua, Coahuila, Nuevo Leon, and Tamaulipas. Northern states are Sinaloa, Nayarit, Zacatecas, Aguascalientes, San Luis Potosi, and Durango. Central states are Jalisco, Colima, Michoacan, Guanajuato, Queretaro, Estado de Mexico, Hidalgo, Distrito Federal, Tlaxcala, Morelos, Puebla, and Veracruz. Southern states are Guerrero, Oaxaca, Chiapas, Tabasco, Campeche, Yucatan, and Quintana Roo.

Table 5.5 **Is globalization driving the trends in Mexican producer prices? (1991–2000; dependent variable: Mexican producer price in first differences)**

	(1)	(2)	(3)	(4)
Real U.S. price	0.204	0.322	0.322	0.313
	(4.00)***	(5.40)***	(5.37)***	(2.22)
USPrice · Nafta		−0.177	−0.045	
		(1.63)	(0.10)	
Nafta		37.142	64.000	
		(2.17)**	(2.71)***	
USPrice · Break			−0.706	
			(2.01)	
Breakdum			−10.272	
			(0.09)	
USPrice · North				0.068
				(0.38)
USPrice · Central				0.095
				(0.55)
USPrice · South				0.013
				(0.07)
North				23.243
				(0.85)
Central				30.863
				(1.15)
South				17.821
				(0.66)
Constant	−63.912	−95.931	−95.931	−76.424
	(7.38)***	(8.86)***	(8.82)***	(3.39)***
No. of observations	224	224	224	192
R^2	0.08	0.11	0.14	0.16

Notes: Robust *t*-statistics in parentheses. Mexican producer prices are annual by state and were obtained from SAGARPA. They were deflated to real 1994 prices using the national CPI. U.S. prices were obtained from the OECD Producer Support Estimate database and are the c.i.f. import price of corn not including transport or processing costs from the Mexican border to Mexican consumers. U.S. prices were converted to Mexican pesos using the annual average official exchange rate. Mexican and U.S. prices are in first differences to eliminate the common time trend. NAFTA is a dummy equal to 1 for the years 1996–2000. Results are robust to defining the NAFTA dummy equal to 1 also in 1995. The omitted category is border states. These are Baja California, Sonora, Chihuahua, Coahuila, Nuevo Leon, and Tamaulipas. Northern states are Sinaloa, Nayarit, Zacatecas, Aguascalientes, San Luis Potosi, and Durango. Central states are Jalisco, Colima, Michoacan, Guanajuato, Queretaro, Estado de Mexico, Hidalgo, Distrito Federal, Tlaxcala, Morelos, Puebla, and Veracruz. Southern states are Guerrero, Oaxaca, Chiapas, Tabasco, Campeche, Yucatan, and Quintana Roo.

***Significant at the 1 percent level.
**Significant at the 5 percent level.

Table 5.6   Is globalization driving the differential between Mexican and U.S. corn prices? (1991–2000; dependent variable: ratio of Mexican to U.S. corn price)

	(1)	(2)	(3)
Nafta	−0.440		−0.493
	(9.42)***		(6.37)***
North		−0.019	−0.078
		(0.35)	(0.79)
Central		0.033	−0.010
		(0.53)	(0.10)
South		0.020	0.001
		(0.22)	(0.09)
North · Nafta			0.093
			(0.87)
Central · Nafta			0.069
			(0.58)
South · Nafta			0.001
			(0.02)
Constant	⁻1.619	1.339	1.647
	(38.82)***	(32.49)***	(23.01)***
No. of observations	256	256	256
R^2	0.30	0.00	0.31

Notes: Robust t-statistics in parentheses, Mexican producer prices are annual by state and were obtained from SAGARA. U.S. prices were obtained from the OECD Producer Support Estimate database and are the c.i.f. import price of corn not including transport or processing costs from the Mexican border to Mexican consumers. U.S. prices were converted to Mexican pesos using the annual average official exchange rate. NAFTA is a dummy equal to 1 for the years 1996–2000. Results are robust to defining the NAFTA dummy equal to 1 also in 1995. The omitted category is border states. These are Baja California, Sonora, Chihuahua, Coahuila, Nuevo Leon, and Tamaulipas. Northern states are Sinaloa, Nayarit, Zacatecas, Aguascalientes, San Luis Potosi, and Durango. Central states are Jalisco, Colima, Michoacan, Guanajuato, Queretaro, Estado de Mexico, Hidalgo, Distrito Federal, Tlaxcala, Morelos, Puebla, and Veracruz. Southern states are Guerrero, Oaxaca, Chiapas, Tabasco, Campeche, Yucatan, and Quintana Roo.
***Significant at the 1 percent level.

test for the possibility that Mexican prices might follow more closely the world price in states closer to the border; we find no evidence of this.

In table 5.6, we test whether a relaxation of tariffs on imported corn reduced the wedge between the Mexican producer price of corn and the border price. In column (1), we do this by regressing the ratio of the Mexican price to the U.S. price on a NAFTA dummy. The results indicate that prior to NAFTA Mexican prices were 1.62 times the U.S. price and that post-NAFTA Mexican prices were only 1.18 times the U.S. price. These numbers are consistent with the simple calculations based on the annual data used to plot figure 5.6. In column (2) we test whether this differential is any smaller for states closer to the border and find no evidence of this. In col-

umn (3) we test whether the differential changed more (less) in states close to (far from) the border. Since the only term of any significance is the NAFTA dummy, we conclude that this is not the case.[26]

These results suggest that while the Mexican producer price has always moved in tandem with the world price, NAFTA squeezed the differential between Mexican producer prices and border prices. How much higher would the border price be if the United States were not subsidizing corn? Unfortunately, there is no consensus on this issue, as commodity prices are notoriously difficult to predict. However, though the estimates vary depending on the methodology, the bottom line seems to be that the magnitude of the price difference would actually be quite small. Wise (2004) summarizes these results and reports that the largest estimate of 2.9 percent comes from a study by the International Food Policy Research Institute (IFPRI). The smallest estimate (−3.0 percent) is from a study by the Agricultural Policy Analysis Center (APAC) and implies that removing U.S. subsidies would actually raise producer prices! In 2000, a 3 percent increase in the producer price of corn would increase the poorest farmers' monthly income by at most six pesos (Mex$6, or US$0.63).[27]

In summary, the sharp drop in Mexican producer prices over the period

26. Since these results are at odds with a recent publication by the World Bank (Fiess and Lederman 2004), we note a few differences between our study and the World Bank study. The World Bank study performs a cointegration analysis using monthly price data at the national level. They report that the results are unchanged if they use annual data. Like us, they find a high degree of comovement between U.S. prices and Mexican prices. However, unlike us, they report that the differential between Mexican and U.S. prices is the same pre- and post-NAFTA. They also plot their price series, but a comparison between our figure 5.6 and their figure 4 is difficult because they take logs of nominal prices whereas we plot levels of real prices. The most confusing thing about the World Bank study is the fact that they report that their results do not hold unless they include a dummy variable for the period 1995–97. They justify this on the grounds that this was a period of severe drought during which Mexico imported record amounts of U.S. corn. There are at least two problems with this. First, while it is true that Mexico imported record amounts of corn in 1996, this is not the case for 1995, nor is it the case for 1997 (see figure 5.1). Therefore, it is unclear why the dummy should take a value of one in 1995 and 1997. Second, the dummy variable captures half the post-NAFTA period, so to include it but not incorporate it in the constant term that the authors report to be the price differential seems misleading.

27. Finally, we consider the possibility that the steep decline in the real producer price might be partially due to the large devaluation of the Mexican peso in 1995. The direct effect of the devaluation would have been to offset the decline in tariffs on imported corn, thus protecting Mexican corn farmers. However, there are two indirect effects that must be considered. First is the inflation that was a by-product of the devaluation. Second is the strain on the government budget. We note that the average rate of inflation over the period 1986–94 was 43 percent, while the average rate of inflation from 1995 to 2000 was only 22 percent. Therefore, it is difficult to argue that the inflation was the root cause of farmers' problems. Additionally, the government has continued to support corn farmers, albeit not directly. These programs are expensive and have managed to keep farmers' real income (including transfers) from falling dramatically over the period 1990–2000. Based on this evidence, we conclude that the change in farmers' income from corn farming is directly tied to the changes in the price of corn at least partially brought on by NAFTA.

1990–2000 corresponds almost exactly to NAFTA's effective date. Although it is possible that Mexican producer prices would be higher if the United States did not subsidize corn, the magnitude of this effect seems small both in comparison to the effect of trade liberalization and in absolute terms. In addition, since there was no dramatic change in U.S. farm policy over this period, Mexican prices would have been higher throughout the entire period. Thus, it seems unlikely that U.S. corn subsidies are driving poverty in Mexico unless one takes the stand that U.S. corn farmers as an interest group were largely responsible for NAFTA.

5.4.3   How Did the Drop in Mexican Producer Prices Affect Poor Corn Farmers?

In this section we turn to analyzing the distributional consequences of the drop in producer prices that we documented in section 5.4.2. We can think of this analysis as answering two distinct questions. The first is the focus of this paper: who in poor countries bears the brunt of rich-country support to agriculture? The second is the focus of this volume: how does trade liberalization affect the poor?

Data

Our data on corn farmers come from the agricultural supplement of the Encuesta Nacional de Empleo (ENE) collected by the Instituto Nacional de Estadística, Geografía e Informática (INEGI) in Mexico. This survey covers 453,503 individuals in rural areas, is nationally representative, and was undertaken in 1991, 1993, 1995, 1996, 1997, 1998, 1999, and 2000. The agricultural supplement is rich in detail about crop production, land quality and size, wages, hired labor, dwelling characteristics, and total farm output—thus providing a detailed description of the production side of corn farming—as well as containing demographic, employment, and income information from the broader employment survey. This data set has rarely been exploited, and this study is the first, to our knowledge, to use the ENE agricultural component to analyze welfare effects on Mexico's rural sector. The data set is not a panel, as each subject is only interviewed once, but is a repeated cross section. INEGI did not, however, alter its sampling procedures over the years in question, so it is relatively safe to conclude that changes we see among sectors is due to compositional changes in the population, as opposed to compositional changes in the sample.

The ENE data, however, only include income from the respondents' primary occupation and do not include consumption data. To allow a broader analysis of welfare, we complement the ENE data with data from the Encuesta Nacional de Ingresos y Gastos de los Hogares (ENIGH). This survey covers 21,117 rural households and covers the years 1992, 1994, 1996, 1998 and 2000. These data are also nationally representative repeated cross

sections and do not follow the same households over time.[28] At the household level, the survey asks for a measure of total household income and income from transfers including remittances (domestic and international), and subsidies from PROCAMPO and other government programs. At the individual level, the survey asks each member of the household how much he or she earns and whether these earnings are derived from wages, the individual's own business enterprise, or other sources such as rental income. We aggregate individual incomes by household to come up with the following breakdown of the household's total income: profit income, work or labor income, income from remittances, income from transfers, and other. In addition, the survey asks whether a household's primary or secondary source of income is corn farming. The survey also has a detailed consumption module, which recounts household expenditure on food, including corn and corn products, education, health, housing, clothing, and so on.

Table 5.7 presents means of socioeconomic characteristics of the rural population from ENE for the entire sample period. All means were computed adjusting for population weights. For purposes of comparing corn farmers with the rest of the rural population, we have divided our summary statistics into four panels. Panel A reports statistics for all rural dwellers. Panel B reports statistics for all rural dwellers involved in agriculture, identified as those respondents who report that the industry of their primary occupation is agriculture. This category includes farm laborers as well as those who own or rent the land. Panel C reports statistics for farmers, where *farmer* is defined as someone who takes part in agricultural activities and owns, occupies, or rents land (as opposed to agricultural laborers). Finally, panel D reports statistics for a subset of the farmers in panel C who report that their primary occupation is the cultivation of corn and beans. In each panel, we report mean monthly income in real 1994 pesos. Income is defined as total household income, and the majority of respondents (97.5 percent) report that their income comes in the form of profits and family consumption. The measure of income in ENE does not include remittances or transfers. We also report mean age, years of schooling, hours worked, and total usable land occupied by the respondent. To determine the relative importance of corn farming, we report the percent of respondents in each year who claim that their primary occupation is corn

---

28. For the years 1992–2000, the conceptual framework of the survey is the same. Therefore, we are able to compare results across years. The survey is a stratified sample according to urban and rural location, and sampling is done to ensure that households are representative of geographic clusters, with the probability of being included proportional to cluster size. However, a comparison of national accounts data and the ENIGH survey data suggests that up to 60 percent of income goes unreported in the ENIGH survey. However, Damian (2001) and others report that this problem derives primarily from the difficulty of including the very wealthy Mexicans in the survey. Since our analysis focuses largely on the rural poor, we believe that our results are not significantly affected by this problem (Salas 2003).

Table 5.7 **Means of socioeconomic characteristics of rural dwellers across time**

	1991	1993	1995	1996	1997	1998	1999	2000
			A. All rural dwellers					
No. of observations	15,216	15,017	20,861	100,411	28,967	95,321	76,441	99,901
Real income (1994 pesos)	702.75	637.66	657.29	595.91	576.26	581.80	554.01	649.50
Age	33.18	33.77	33.82	33.60	34.34	34.31	34.72	34.60
Years of schooling	4.63	4.66	5.17	5.57	5.74	5.74	5.48	5.87
Hours worked	33.94	33.94	20.94	22.33	22.97	22.52	22.80	21.90
Total land (in hectares)	0.98	0.89	0.67	0.71	0.58	0.68	0.73	0.50
Involved in agriculture	0.32	0.32	0.28	0.26	0.28	0.27	0.28	0.24
Farmer	0.14	0.14	0.11	0.10	0.10	0.10	0.09	0.09
Corn occupation	0.20	0.15	0.15	0.13	0.14	0.13	0.14	0.10
Corn subsistence	0.11	0.12	0.09	0.08	0.07	0.08	0.08	0.07
Corn selling	0.02	0.02	0.02	0.02	0.02	0.02	0.02	0.01
			B. Rural dwellers involved in agriculture					
No. of observations	5,134	5,074	6,467	25,977	6,858	25,735	18,538	22,887
Real income (1994 pesos)	585.04	495.31	502.94	434.60	427.04	411.30	405.81	425.72
Age	35.25	35.74	35.73	35.58	36.32	36.04	36.40	36.67
Years of schooling	3.81	3.75	3.96	4.23	4.46	4.38	4.30	4.42
Hours worked	33.73	33.41	35.14	38.13	38.33	34.80	37.85	35.54
Total land (in hectares)	3.04	2.75	2.37	2.72	2.07	2.47	2.64	2.08
Corn occupation	0.63	0.46	0.54	0.50	0.49	0.48	0.50	0.40
Corn subsistence	0.35	0.36	0.32	0.30	0.26	0.29	0.29	0.27
Corn selling	0.05	0.05	0.06	0.08	0.08	0.07	0.07	0.06
			C. All farmers					
No. of observations	2,258	2,241	2,596	10,420	2,504	9,888	7,011	8,703
Real income (1994 pesos)	582.81	480.74	515.13	450.81	447.93	415.38	389.37	394.70
Age	46.56	47.67	46.79	47.11	48.82	48.20	47.98	48.50
Years of schooling	2.78	2.63	3.05	3.34	3.54	3.38	3.48	3.46
Hours worked	37.96	37.02	40.36	43.87	45.27	41.34	44.50	40.87
Total land (in hectares)	7.10	6.21	5.91	7.00	5.63	6.63	6.95	5.59
Corn occupation	0.62	0.46	0.64	0.59	0.60	0.60	0.61	0.54
Corn subsistence	0.81	0.82	0.80	0.76	0.72	0.78	0.75	0.73
Corn selling	0.12	0.12	0.14	0.20	0.22	0.19	0.18	0.16
			D. All corn farmers					
No. of observations	1,420	1,003	1,628	6,047	1,481	6,017	4,185	4,900
Real income (1994 pesos)	516.81	349.63	277.89	267.68	270.01	256.84	207.64	49.23
Age	47.85	48.73	47.35	47.58	50.11	48.97	48.50	49.23
Years of schooling	2.44	2.22	2.62	2.79	2.93	2.79	2.98	2.94
Hours worked	37.11	36.09	39.66	43.93	45.70	41.05	45.23	40.18
Total land (in hectares)	6.25	3.85	4.09	4.40	4.16	4.94	4.09	3.90
Corn occupation	1.00	1.00	1.00	1.00	1.00	1.00	1.00	1.00
Corn subsistence	0.86	0.90	0.91	0.85	0.84	0.90	0.87	0.88
Corn selling	0.15	0.16	0.16	0.25	0.27	0.23	0.24	0.22

Source: ENE 1991–2000.

Notes: "Farmer" is defined as someone who takes part in agricultural activities and owns, occupies, or rents land (as opposed to agricultural laborer). "Corn farmer" is defined as a farmer who identifies his primary occupation as the cultivation of maize and beans. "Corn subsistence" is the percentage of farmers who respond that their primary crop for subsistence is maize and beans. "Corn selling" is the percentage of farmers who respond that their main crop for selling is corn. Medians are not reported because they are virtually identical to means.

Table 5.8   Summary statistics for families with corn farmers

	1992	1994	1996	1998	2000
Real monthly corn consumption					
Value (1994 pesos)	77.50	62.87	73.44	61.05	55.20
As a share of food expenditures	0.20	0.16	0.19	0.19	0.17
As a share of total expenditures	0.10	0.07	0.11	0.10	0.09
Quantity (kilograms)	16.39	15.30	16.21	15.61	17.10
Real monthly income					
Income from work	221.57	228.14	209.99	172.43	179.98
Income from profits	479.06	420.24	327.12	339.03	355.92
Income other	21.93	6.62	10.90	10.32	13.11
Income from transfers (other)	102.19	143.43	175.70	145.97	206.64
Income from transfers (remittances)	83.14	98.99	109.97	88.13	100.69
No. of observations	1,141,718	1,249,234	1,368,191	1,204,051	990,784

Source: ENIGH 1992–2000.

Notes: Consumption figures include corn purchases, corn produced for household's consumption, and in-kind payments and gifts of corn. "Corn farmer" is defined as someone who reports that his or her primary occupation is the cultivation of corn and beans.

farming (Corn occupation), that their primary crop for subsistence is corn (Corn subsistence), and that their main crop for selling is corn (Corn selling).

These data highlight several important facts. The share of rural dwellers who consider themselves farmers has fallen from 14 percent of the rural population in 1991 to 9 percent of the rural population in 2000. Corn farmers make up 20 percent of the rural population in 1991 and only 10 percent of the rural population in 2000. Among farmers, a majority are corn farmers—although this dropped from 62 percent in 1991 to 54 percent in 2000. Three-quarters of all farmers say they grow corn as their primary crop for subsistence. However, very few farmers (between 12 percent and 22 percent) say that corn is their primary crop for selling.

Thus, most farmers are corn farmers, and this has not changed very much over the past ten years. This is important because it implies that there has not been a significant amount of diversification into other farming activities away from corn farming. Corn farmers have on average more land than the average rural dweller and are poorer than other farmers and than the rest of the population. The *average* real monthly income from corn farming in 2000 was only Mex$206 (US$21.79), or US$261.48 per year.[29] Finally, corn farmers also have less schooling and work longer hours than the rest of the rural population.

Table 5.8 presents means of real household variables for families in

29. The average annual exchange rates (Mexican pesos per dollar) beginning in 1990 are 2.84, 3.02, 3.1, 3.12, 3.39, 6.42, 7.6, 7.92, 9.15, 9.55, and 9.45.

which at least one individual identifies his or her primary occupation as the cultivation of corn and beans. In the top panel of table 5.9, we report real monthly household expenditure on corn, expenditure on corn as a share of total food expenditure, expenditure on corn as a share of total expenditure, and the quantity of corn purchased. Corn includes corn tortillas, grain, flour, *masa,* and starch; corn consumption includes corn purchases, corn produced for household consumption, and in-kind payments and gifts of corn. There are two important aspects of these data worth mentioning. First, we are not looking only at expenditure on corn grain but expenditure on corn grain and all derivative products, allowing us to capture the impact of imported grain on all of these products. In particular, our expenditure data include corn tortillas, whose price went up sharply during the 1990s for reasons unrelated to NAFTA. We include tortillas on the grounds that prices would have risen even more had the price of corn grain not fallen. Second, both our income and our expenditure data include the value of home consumption, in-kind payments, and gifts. Therefore, the change in consumption expenditure can be viewed as an upper bound on the increase in real income associated with the drop in the price of corn.

In the bottom panel of table 5.8, we report total real monthly household income as well as real monthly income derived from work (labor income), profits, government transfers, and remittances. Since the income reported in table 5.8 is household income and the income in table 5.7 is income derived from the respondents' primary occupation or individual income, the two numbers are not directly comparable. However, the income data from the national employment survey (ENE) derive primarily from profits and home consumption and would fall under "income from profits" at the household level. Therefore, by comparing the national employment survey income data with the ENIGH household survey income data we can get a sense for both how important profits from corn farming are and also how important supplementary sources of income are to corn-farming families. For example, in 1996 the profit share of income for corn-farming families was roughly Mex$327 per month. According to the national employment survey data, the average real income earned from corn farming by the corn farmer was roughly Mex$268 per month. This is equal to 82 percent of the profit share of income reported in the household data or 32 percent of the average corn-farming families' total real monthly income. Thus, profits from corn farming are on average the most important source of income for families of corn farmers, but work income and income from transfers are also important, at 23 percent and 19 percent of total income, respectively.

The means in table 5.8 reveal that—for the *average* corn-farming family—aggregate corn consumption and aggregate income have not changed remarkably between 1992 and 2000. Real monthly expenditure on corn fluctuates between Mex$77 and Mex$55 per month. The average family spends around 19 percent of its food budget on corn products and around

Table 5.9 **Means of corn farmer characteristics by standard of living across time**

	1991	1993	1995	1996	1997	1998	1999	2000
A. Small corn farmers (<5ha land)								
No. of observations	920	813	1,260	4,768	1,135	4,810	3,252	3,976
Real income (1994 pesos)	437.51	323.17	245.26	199.77	205.61	162.49	155.19	152.79
Age	46.64	48.98	46.51	46.90	49.77	48.56	48.05	48.52
Years of schooling	2.37	2.22	2.60	2.75	2.81	2.67	2.83	2.86
Hours worked	36.32	35.59	39.46	43.37	45.20	39.90	44.93	39.77
Total land (in hectares)	2.39	2.23	2.10	2.20	2.17	2.19	2.12	2.08
Corn subsistence	0.89	0.92	0.93	0.89	0.88	0.93	0.92	0.92
Corn main crop for selling	0.10	0.11	0.11	0.19	0.23	0.18	0.19	0.19
Do not produce to sell	0.67	0.77	0.73	0.65	0.68	0.68	0.63	0.63
Occasionally sell corn	0.16	0.13	0.12	0.13	0.13	0.12	0.10	0.10
Never sell corn	0.56	0.67	0.64	0.57	0.59	0.60	0.57	0.57
B. Medium corn farmers (5–15ha land)								
No. of observations	387	173	288	1,010	264	948	714	731
Real income (1994 pesos)	636.55	452.16	367.47	485.34	485.46	477.46	376.56	52.52
Age	51.55	47.56	52.71	50.44	50.91	51.19	50.50	52.52
Years of schooling	2.58	1.86	2.65	2.81	3.36	2.97	3.43	3.24
Hours worked	36.59	37.74	40.83	45.50	47.54	43.71	47.05	42.53
Total land (in hectares)	8.59	8.26	8.55	8.32	8.36	8.35	8.43	8.52
Corn subsistence	0.80	0.84	0.83	0.70	0.73	0.79	0.67	0.70
Corn main crop for selling	0.27	0.31	0.39	0.46	0.42	0.41	0.47	0.37
Do not produce to sell	0.33	0.47	0.35	0.23	0.35	0.29	0.24	0.33
C. Large corn farmers (>15ha land)								
No. of observations	96	17	59	240	63	259	219	193
Real income (1994 pesos)	845.46	529.43	649.68	753.77	743.45	1,031.82	725.53	949.71
Age	48.13	48.32	52.86	50.54	55.41	48.95	50.71	53.89
Years of schooling	2.50	4.76	4.00	3.66	3.83	4.08	4.53	3.66
Hours worked	45.75	41.78	42.19	51.20	52.74	50.94	44.92	41.39
Total land (in hectares)	34.15	28.40	44.71	38.88	33.97	37.46	32.22	32.31
Corn subsistence	0.78	0.49	0.75	0.49	0.36	0.62	0.51	0.58
Corn main crop for selling	0.16	0.69	0.47	0.58	0.62	0.61	0.54	0.37
Do not produce to sell	0.25	0.14	0.13	0.19	0.15	0.16	0.14	0.18

Source: ENE 1991–2000.

Notes: "Farmer" is defined as someone who takes part in agricultural activities and owns, occupies, or rents land (as opposed to agricultural laborer). "Corn farmer" is a farmer who identifies his primary occupation as the cultivation of corn and beans. "Corn subsistence" is the percentage of respondents who answer that their main crop for subsistence is corn. "Corn main crop for selling" is the percentage of respondents who answer the question "what is your main crop for selling?" as "corn." "Do not produce to sell" is the percentage of respondents who answer the question "what is your main crop for selling?" as "I don't produce to sell." "Occasionally sell corn" is the percentage of respondents who answer the question "how much of your subsistence crop do you sell?" with "corn." "Never sell corn" is the percentage of respondents who answer they do not produce to sell when asked "what is your main crop for selling?" but who answer "which of your subsistence crops do you sell?" with "corn." Medians are not reported because they are virtually identical to means.

10 percent of its total budget on corn products. The average family's real monthly income was Mex$907 (US$292) in 1992 and Mex$856 (US$90.58) in 2000. Note that, to the extent that these families purchase imported products, the peso values understate the drop in real income.

While expenditure on corn did not change significantly following NAFTA for the average corn-farming family, there has been a marked change in the composition of income. In 1992 the profit share of income was roughly 53 percent, and this fell to around 39 percent in 2000. The work share of income also fell from around 24 percent in 1992 to around 20 percent in 2000. The drop in these two sources of income was largely offset by an increase in income from transfers (11 percent in 1992 and 23 percent in 2000).

In the next two sections, we examine the data from the national employment surveys (ENE) and the household surveys (ENIGH) on corn farmers and families with corn farmers by standard of living, as measured by land holdings. Our primary goal is to determine how the drop in the price of corn has impacted the poorest corn farmers and the poorest corn-farming families in Mexico.

Results from the National Employment Surveys (ENE)

Here we analyze in more detail the subgroup of the rural population comprising those who identify themselves as corn farmers. Recall that these are individuals who own, occupy, or rent land (as opposed to agricultural laborers) and who claim that their primary occupation is the cultivation of maize and beans. We recognize that farm laborers are an important group of rural dwellers whose wages are likely to be affected by changes in the price of corn. We do not attempt to consider the welfare of these individuals here. Rather, our goal is to determine how the drop in the price of corn affected the poorest corn farmers in Mexico. To do this, we divide corn farmers into three groups—small, medium, and large—depending upon the size of each farmer's land. We then determine whether a majority of the poorest corn farmers, those with the smallest land holdings, are net buyers or net sellers of corn.

Table 5.9 reports corn farmer characteristics by total land holding across time.[30] The mean landholding of the smallest corn farmers (those with less than 5 ha [hectares] of land) is roughly 2 ha. This corresponds to the average land held by the poorest corn farmers identified by de Janvry, Sadoulet,

30. The advantages of splitting the sample based on landholding are that we do not have to worry about measurement issues associated with income and that we can directly compare our results to those of others who also classify corn farmers by landholding. In appendix table 5A.2, we report income-based, monthly per capita measures of poverty. By Mexican standards, only our average small corn farmer is classified as extremely poor. The medium corn farmers earn enough monthly income from corn farming to place them above both the extreme poverty line and the moderate or asset-based poverty line. However, in 2000, by international standards, the medium corn farmers would be considered moderately poor.

and Gordillo de Anda (1995) as "non-participants in the market" and by Levy and van Wijnbergen (1995) as "subsistence" farmers, who primarily farm rain-fed land. The mean landholding of the medium-sized corn farmers (those with between 5 and 15 ha of land) is roughly 8.5 hectares. The mean landholding of the largest corn farmers (those with more than 15 ha of land) is roughly 35 ha. For small, medium, and large corn farmers we report means of real income, age, years of schooling, hours worked, and landholding over time. In addition, we report the percent of the population who say that their main crop for subsistence is corn (Corn subsistence), the percent of the population who say that their main crop for selling is corn (Corn main crop for selling), and the percent of the population who say that they do not produce a crop to sell in the market (Do not produce to sell).[31]

For the poorest farmers (those with less than 5 ha of land), we report statistics for two additional variables. We do this because we are concerned that the poorest farmers (often called subsistence farmers) may occasionally sell corn but nevertheless report that they do not produce corn with the intent of selling. To determine the extent to which this takes place, we first report the percentage of poor farmers who answer the question "which of your subsistence crops do you sell?" with "corn." We label this "Occasionally sell corn." Next we determine the percentage of respondents who report that they never sell corn as the fraction of the poorest who report that they do not produce to sell but nevertheless answer that they sometimes sell the corn they grow for subsistence. We label this variable "Never sell corn." There is no need to do this for the medium and large corn farmers because we already know that a majority of these farmers do sell corn in the market.

A majority of the poor report that they do not produce to sell. In 1991, 67 percent of the small corn farmers reported that they did not produce to sell in the market. This figure peaks at 77 percent in 1993 and falls to 63 percent in 2000. An overwhelming majority of these same farmers, 89 percent in 1991 and 92 percent in 2000, do say that corn is their primary crop for subsistence. When we allow for the possibility that some of these farmers may sell corn on occasion, the percentages fall and we are left with a somewhat stronger conclusion. The majority of the poor report that they never sell corn in all of the eight years for which we have data. For example, in 1991, 56 percent of the poorest farmers report that they never produce to sell, and in 2000, 57 percent report that they never produce to sell.

By contrast, only around 33 percent of the medium-sized farmers and 16 percent of the large farmers say that they do not produce to sell. Therefore,

---

31. To keep the tables clear and manageable, we leave out the percentage of the population who report that they do not sell any of their subsistence crop. An analysis of this variable leads to the same conclusion that the majority of the poor report that they do not sell any of their subsistence crop.

the drop in the price of corn associated with NAFTA does not directly affect the income of the majority of the poorest corn farmers while it negatively impacts the income of a majority of the medium- and large-scale corn farmers. Although the employment survey does not ask about expenditure, those farmers who report that they do not sell are most certainly net buyers of corn. It is almost impossible to be completely self-sufficient because of the vagaries of the weather. Thus, among the poorest corn farmers, the majority are net buyers of corn and have thus *benefited* from any reduction in the price of corn associated with NAFTA. The opposite is true for the medium- and large-scale corn farmers.

Although it is not shown in the tables, we also analyzed the summary statistics by splitting the samples in panels A, B, and C into those who sell and those who do not sell. In all three cases, the corn farmers who report that they do not produce to sell are poorer, older, and less well educated, and have less land than the farmers who do produce to sell. Additionally, the corn farmers who report that they do not produce to sell also report that the majority of their income comes in the form of family consumption, while those who do produce to sell report that the majority of their income comes in the form of profits (table 5.10). With only one exception, all groups and subgroups of corn farmers saw their real income decline substantially between 1991 and 2000. Only large corn farmers experienced a substantial increase in their income between 1995 and 2000. If we split large farmers into those who produce to sell and those who do not produce to sell, we find that the larger corn farmers who do not produce to sell actually experienced a decline in their real income over the period 1991–2000. However, the increase in the incomes of those large farmers who do produce to sell is even more dramatic (from Mex$684 per month to Mex$1,162 per month) once we remove the large corn farmers who do not produce to sell.

In table 5.10, we check whether there has been a significant change in the characteristics and real income of corn farmers pre- and post-NAFTA. In terms of both magnitude and statistical significance, the most striking changes are the reduction in the real income of small farmers and the increase in the real income of large farmers. Between 1991 and 2000, small farmers' real monthly income dropped by roughly Mex$285, while large farmers' real income increased by around Mex$100. Between 1995 and 2000, small farmers' real income dropped by roughly Mex$93, while large farmers' real monthly income increased by around Mex$300.

The drop in the real income of the small farmers can be explained by the reduction in the price of corn. Although the majority of these farmers do not participate in the market, they do report that their most important source of income from their primary occupation is the value of home consumption. Thus, even for those farmers who do not participate in the market the imputed value of real income will have fallen.

Table 5.10   **Differences between corn farmers in 1991 and 2000**

Farmer characteristics and income (ENE)	Differences between 1991–92 and 2000			Differences between 1994–95 and 2000		
	Difference	*t*-statistic	*P*-value	Difference	*t*-statistic	*P*-value
A. All corn farmers						
Age	1.37	2.95	0.00	1.87	4.16	0.00
Years of schooling	0.50	6.20	0.00	0.31	4.08	0.00
Hours worked	3.07	5.41	0.00	0.52	1.05	0.30
Total land (in hectares)	−2.34	−7.07	0.00	−0.19	−0.65	0.52
Income (1994 pesos)	−310.46	−23.51	0.00	−71.54	−6.81	0.00

	Differences between 1991 and 2000			Differences between 1995 and 2000		
	Difference	*t*-statistic	*P*-value	Difference	*t*-statistic	*P*-value
B. Small corn farmers						
Real income (1994 pesos)	−284.72	−23.84	0.00	−92.47	−9.43	0.00
Age	1.88	3.31	0.00	2.01	3.94	0.00
Years of schooling	0.48	5.22	0.00	0.26	2.93	0.00
Hours worked	3.45	5.15	0.00	0.31	0.56	0.58
Total land (in hectares)	−0.31	−6.09	0.00	−0.03	−0.47	0.64
C. Medium corn farmers						
Real income (1994 pesos)	−271.79	−8.79	0.00	−2.71	−0.10	0.92
Age	0.97	1.03	0.31	−0.19	−0.19	0.85
Years of schooling	0.66	3.58	0.00	0.60	3.18	0.00
Hours worked	5.94	4.75	0.00	1.70	1.34	0.18
Total land (in hectares)	−0.07	−0.46	0.64	−0.03	−0.17	0.86
D. Large corn farmers						
Real income (1994 pesos)	104.25	1.03	0.30	300.03	2.09	0.04
Age	5.76	3.22	0.00	1.03	0.50	0.62
Years of schooling	1.16	3.27	0.00	−0.34	−0.77	0.44
Hours worked	−4.36	−1.86	0.06	−0.81	−0.33	0.74
Total land (in hectares)	−1.84	−0.49	0.62	−12.40	−1.70	0.09

Source: ENE 1991, 1995, 2000.
Notes: P-values indicate probability that difference is not equal to zero. "Corn farmer" is defined as a farmer who identifies his primary occupation in the cultivation of corn and beans.

The increase in the income of the large farmers is somewhat more puzzling. However, this could be explained by a number of factors. For example, it is consistent with Levy and van Wijnbergen's (1995) argument that irrigated farmers would experience an increase in net income because the gain they experience as a result of the drop in rural wages outweighs the loss they experience as a result of the reduction in the price of corn. We hope to explore in more detail the reasons for the gain in large farmers' real income in future work.

In summary, the majority of the poorest corn farmers did not sell corn

Table 5.11   **Income and consumption of families of corn farmers in 1992 and 2000 by standard of living**

	1992	1994	1996	1998	2000	Change 1992/2000	Change 1994/2000
A. Low-income corn-farming families							
Real monthly corn consumption (means)							
Value (1994 pesos)	77.15	71.63	79.97	62.73	53.70	−23.45***	−17.93***
As a share of food expenditures	0.28	0.24	0.28	0.26	0.22	−0.06	−0.01
As a share of total expenditures	0.15	0.12	0.17	0.14	0.13	−0.02	0.01
Quantity (kilograms)	17.31	18.86	18.74	17.73	19.68	2.37**	0.82
Real monthly income (means)							
Work income	78.97	99.34	114.35	86.93	89.24	10.27***	−10.10***
Profit income	240.94	242.68	191.42	151.28	114.30	−126.64***	−128.38***
Other income	2.15	1.28	1.25	1.92	1.68	−0.47	0.40
Income from transfers (other)	44.45	62.94	83.51	75.46	121.91	77.46***	58.98***
Income from transfers (remittances)	42.02	58.40	38.69	46.32	39.23	−2.79	−19.17***
No. of observations	438,613	365,409	445,568	470,569	352,983		
B. Middle-income corn-farming families							
Real monthly corn consumption (means)							
Value (1994 pesos)	75.93	63.49	80.64	67.49	62.58	−13.35***	−0.91
As a share of food expenditures	0.19	0.16	0.20	0.18	0.17	−0.03	0.00
As a share of total expenditures	0.10	0.07	0.10	0.09	0.08	−0.02	0.01
Quantity (kilograms)	15.71	15.59	17.85	16.57	18.60	2.90**	3.01**
Real monthly income (means)							
Work income	134.72	189.20	195.81	177.06	187.89	53.17***	−1.31
Profit income	468.93	370.02	255.29	291.64	192.61	−276.32***	−177.41***
Other income	4.30	9.42	13.85	10.52	13.20	8.90	3.78
Income from transfers (other)	111.56	87.33	145.60	110.04	215.28	103.72***	127.95***
Income from transfers (remittances)	97.17	78.50	101.16	60.93	111.61	14.44**	33.11***
No. of observations	324,016	407,348	469,429	353,566	329,765		
C. High-income corn-farming families							
Real monthly corn consumption (means)							
Value (1994 pesos)	79.31	55.63	59.47	52.82	48.83	−30.48***	−6.80**
As a share of food expenditures	0.12	0.09	0.11	0.11	0.10	−0.02	0.01
As a share of total expenditures	0.05	0.04	0.05	0.05	0.04	−0.01	0.00
Quantity (kilograms)	15.90	12.30	12.00	12.01	12.40	−3.49**	0.10**
Real monthly income (means)							
Work income	277.24	316.34	320.04	277.43	286.95	9.71**	−29.38**
Profit income	617.19	599.82	537.21	624.13	807.63	190.44***	207.81***
Other income	60.90	8.34	17.45	20.87	26.12	−34.78**	17.78**
Income from transfers (other)	163.15	253.37	296.93	270.22	294.48	131.33***	41.11***
Income from transfers (remittances)	20.19	147.74	190.17	167.40	159.44	39.25**	11.70***
No. of observations	372,611	475,855	450,238	373,118	298,706		

Source: ENIGH.

Notes: Consumption figures include corn purchases, corn produced for household's consumption, and in-kind payments and gifts of corn. "Corn farmer" is defined as someone who identifies his or her primary occupation as the cultivation of corn and beans. All means computed using population weights. The last two columns report the change in mean between 1992 and 2000 and then between 1994 and 2000.

***Significant at the 1 percent level.

**Significant at the 5 percent level.

in the market prior to NAFTA. Therefore, their income will not have been directly affected by the forces of globalization associated with NAFTA and the devaluation of the peso. By contrast, a majority of the medium and large corn farmers did sell corn in the market prior to NAFTA and continued to do so after the implementation of NAFTA. Thus, we conclude that the medium-sized corn farmers experienced a sharp decline in real income as a result of NAFTA. The income of the largest corn farmers has increased. Without additional information, it is not possible to attribute the increase in the incomes of the large corn farmers to globalization.

Results from the Household Surveys (ENIGH)

We turn now to the families of those individuals who identify their primary occupation as the cultivation of corn and beans. Specifically, we examine household expenditure on corn products and the sources of total household income. Ideally, we would like to have this information for the same individuals interviewed in the employment survey. This would allow us to understand whether the poorest families who say they do not sell any corn rely on other sources of income that might be indirectly affected by the price of corn, such as wage income derived from working on other people's corn farms. Unfortunately, the surveys were not conducted in this fashion. Therefore, we split our sample into three groups based on income from profits on the grounds that income from profits is very closely correlated with the size of the landholding. Thus, we take the families in the bottom tercile of the distribution of income from profits as the representative families of the corn farmers with less than 5 ha of land. Similarly, those in the middle of the distribution represent the families of the medium-sized corn farmers, and those in the top third of the distribution represent the families of the largest corn farmers (those with more than 15 ha of land).

Panel A of table 5.11 reveals that for the average low-income corn-farming family real monthly expenditure on corn decreased by around Mex$20 per month over the period 1994–2000. This amounts to around US$2 per month or US$24 per year for the poorest corn-farming families. We noted in the discussion of these data that this would be an upper bound on the benefits to the poorest corn-farming families as a result of the drop in the price of corn. This is because these families are so poor that they often cannot afford to buy corn and so will go without and because the consumption figures include the value of home consumption. For the poorest corn-farming families, the share of corn in food expenditure stayed roughly constant at around 25 percent, and the share of corn expenditure in total expenditure stayed roughly constant at around 15 percent.

On the income side, the big changes for the poorest families over the period are the drop in the profit share of income and the increase in transfers. Monthly income from profits was around Mex$130 higher in 1992 and 1994 than it was in 2000. On the other hand, transfer income increased

threefold over this same period. The share of income derived from corn farming drops only slightly. Since expenditure on corn changed only marginally and since work income was hardly affected, we conclude that the welfare of those families who do not sell corn in the market—the majority of the poorest corn farmers—has been largely unaffected by the drop in the price of corn. Moreover, these families have benefited from the income support programs associated with NAFTA.

Panel B of table 5.11 reveals a different story; the drop in the price of corn negatively impacted the majority of middle-income families. This is because the majority of these farmers do sell corn in the market. Total monthly expenditure on corn for these farmers has barely changed over time. As with the poorest corn farmers, work income has also not changed much over time. The profit share of income for the middle-income corn farmers fell by Mex$276 between 1992 and 2000 and by Mex$177 between 1994 and 2000. This represents a reduction in real income of almost 50 percent. This was almost entirely offset by the increase in government transfers (Mex$128) and the increase in remittances (Mex$33).

Panel C of table 5.11 demonstrates that both profit income and income from transfers increased substantially over this time period. Other sources of income were largely unaffected. Income from profits for the high-income corn farmers increased by Mex$190 between 1992 and 2000 and by Mex$208 between 1994 and 2000. This amounts to an increase in real income of roughly 33 percent. Thus, the majority of the high-income families benefited from changes in the Mexican corn market.

There are several other interesting trends that stand out in table 5.12. First, households from all income groups witnessed an increase in income associated with government transfers from programs like PROGRESA and PROCAMPO. The largest percentage increase was given to the poorest corn-farming families, whose income from transfers increased by 200 percent, going from Mex$44 a month to Mex$122 a month between 1992 and 2000. Although transfers to the middle- and upper-income corn-farming families increased by less in percentage terms (100 percent), in absolute terms these families receive substantially more than the poorest corn-farming families in transfer payments from the government. For example, in 2000, the average middle-income family received a monthly payment of Mex$215, while the average upper-income family received a monthly payment of almost Mex$300—roughly three times what the poor household received.

Second, the increase in transfer payments may explain part of the mysterious increase in corn production even though the real price of corn has fallen dramatically. Levy and van Wijnbergen (1995) discuss this possibility in great detail. Liberalization of the corn sector under NAFTA creates an incentive problem. Because many corn farmers will be hurt, the government has an incentive to compensate these farmers for their losses. Levy and van Wijnbergen estimate that the efficiency gains associated with

NAFTA would be substantial and that this revenue could be used to compensate the losers. However, compensating farmers pro rata to their corn production will create an incentive to continue to grow corn even in the face of falling market prices.

5.4.4 Discussion

While thought provoking, our analysis suffers from two important shortcomings. First, we consider only the first-order effects of price changes on income and consumption expenditure while ignoring both the partial equilibrium effects of food price changes on quantities demanded and supplied and the general equilibrium effects of the price changes on employment patterns, wages, the price of other factors, and technological innovation. Thus, our analysis is best thought of as a good approximation to what happened in the short run (see, for example, Barrett and Dorosh 1996).

We focus here on short-run impacts of globalization for two related reasons. First, using short-run changes seems to be most appropriate for studying the impact of price changes on the poor, who, as Barrett and Dorosh (1996) say, are "likely to be teetering on the brink of survival" and less able to take advantage of supply-side effects of price changes. And second, our primary goal is to understand whether globalization has affected the poorest corn farmers. In future work, we will incorporate the general equilibrium effects of changes in the price of corn. In particular, an important group that we have not considered here is farm workers. Though not technically corn farmers, these people are likely to be among the poorest of the rural population and their livelihoods significantly impacted by changes in the price of corn.

We are also—in part—limited by our data. Since our data sets are not panels but are repeated cross sections, there is a concern that our results might suffer from selection bias. The composition of small, medium, and large corn farmers could be changing over time, as could the structure of the larger corn-farming sector. This means that we could be picking up a compositional effect rather than the effect of globalization. It is clear from table 5.7 that the absolute number of families in which at least one person reports that his primary occupation is corn farming has fallen over the past decade. Therefore, it is possible that some poor corn farmers left corn farming for other, better-paying jobs and that those particular corn farmers could have been the most able, educated ones. Thus, the negative impact on corn farmers that we observe in the cross-sectional data over time could be partially a result of the corn farmers with the best outside opportunities (something that likely correlates well with present income) leaving corn farming. Any complete statement about changes in the overall welfare of corn farmers would need to take selection into account and to correct for it when studying the impact of globalization on poor corn farmers. It is also independently interesting to study which corn farmers were able to adjust and leave corn farming when the price of corn decreased, and which were

not able to leave but adjusted in other ways, possibly by increasing their production of corn.

However, our conclusion that the majority of the poorest corn farmers and their families have not been hurt by globalization is likely to hold regardless of the shortcomings of our analysis. This is because these people were so poor to begin with that it is hard to imagine them being worse off as a result of globalization. They were not selling corn in the market, and they did not rely heavily on income from work. Hence, for these people there is really only upside potential.

5.5   Conclusion

This paper documents the historical impacts of OECD agricultural policies on developing countries. We first provide evidence that the majority of poor countries are net importers of both cereals and food but net exporters of agricultural products as a whole. This has been true throughout the postcolonial era. Even middle-income countries that export food products are net importers of cereals, particularly in the 1990s. Thus, to the extent that OECD support policies depress the price of cereals and food, these programs benefit consumers in poor countries. Of course, even if a country is a net importer, competition from subsidized imports will hurt the net sellers of these products within the importing countries. However, there is a growing body of evidence—consistent with our evidence from Mexico—indicating that the poorest individuals in the poorest countries are actually net buyers of cereals and food and therefore benefit from lower food prices.[32]

Our econometric results are consistent with this evidence and suggest that in many food-importing developing countries, OECD support policies are not correlated with the poverty rate or with income, even after controlling for domestic policies such as openness to trade. Consequently, the results suggest that OECD agricultural policies do not have a uniform impact on developing-country incomes; net food-importing countries are likely to gain, while food exporters are likely to be hurt.

In the high-profile case of Mexico, we find that NAFTA reduced the wedge between the real producer price and the border price, making corn production less profitable. We also find that the poorest corn farmers are net food buyers, since they have little land per person and so are forced to earn cash income in other ways in order to buy food. Therefore, the reduction in corn prices was unambiguously good for the majority of the poorest corn farmers. However, we also find that middle-income corn farmers have been hit hard, as their real income from corn farming fell by more than 50 percent while the average income of the largest corn farmers increased by almost 40 percent. Although the price of corn is no longer di-

32. See, for example, Levinsohn and McMillan's piece on Ethiopia (chap. 13 in this volume).

rectly supported by the Mexican government, transfer payments to corn farmers at all levels of income increased substantially between 1991 and 2000. Because these payments are often tied to amount of land cultivated with corn, their increase may explain the puzzle of increasing corn production in the face of falling corn prices.

Our findings may be taken as a note of caution in the context of arguments for wholesale multilateral agricultural trade liberalization in industrial countries as a means of alleviating poverty in developing countries. The aggregate efficiency gains associated with trade liberalization, a topic not addressed in this paper, may mask negative impacts for many developing countries, particularly the poorest. Trade negotiators may need to consider means of protecting these countries from the negative effects of higher commodity prices, at least in the short run, and developing countries may find it advantageous to advocate for more far-reaching liberalization in the cotton, dairy, and sugar markets rather than in the markets for bulk grain commodities that they import.

Appendix

Table 5A.1   **Description of variables and data sources**

Variable name	Source	Description
Head count poverty rate	World Bank PovertyNet	Constant US$(1985); fraction of population with income less than $1 per day
Log average income per capita	Penn World Tables 6.1	Constant US$(1985), real GDP per capita
SOI anomaly	National Oceanic and Atmospheric Administration data, available at ftp:// ftp.ncep.noaa.gov/pub/cpc/wd52dg/ data/indices/soi	Southern Oscillation Index anomaly
OECDPOLICY	SourceOECD agriculture support estimates, available at http://oecd publications.gfi-nb.com/cgi-bin/OECD BookShop.storefront/EN/product/ 512002093C3 USDA Economic Research Service Trade Issues data, available at http://usda.mannlib.cornell.edu/	OECD average nominal protection coefficient. Data included in regression as weighted average across commodities where weights are production shares for major commodity classes. These commodity classes are wheat, maize, rice, other grains, oilseeds, sugar, milk, beef, sheep meat, wool, pig meat, poultry, eggs, coffee, cocoa, roots and tubers, fruits, and vegetables (including melons). Data available from OECD for period 1987–2000 and ERS/USDA for period 1982–87.

(continued)

Table 5A.1	(continued)

	FAOSTAT data on agricultural production of primary crops, available at http://faostat.fao.org/faostat/collections ?subset=agriculture	Data included in regression as weighted average across commodities where weights are production shares for major commodity classes listed above in 1970. Production share data from FAO.
Exports + import/GDP	World Development Indicators	Exports and imports in constant US$(1985) at market exchange rate. GDP is in PPP$(1985)
Ln (1 + inflation rate)	World Development Indicators	Log of rate of inflation plus one

Table 5A.2   **Rural poverty lines for Mexico**

Monthly per capita poverty lines (1994 pesos)	1994	1996	1998	2000
Food poverty/extreme poverty	43.29	87.61	117.52	139.78
Asset poverty/moderate poverty	82.78	159.21	208.76	254.50
$1/day poverty line	68.51	124.29	173.8	219.24
$2/day poverty line	137.02	248.58	347.6	438.48

Sources: ENIGH, ENE, World Bank (2004).

Notes: Food poverty is defined as the income required to purchase a food basket to satisfy minimum nutritional requirements. Asset poverty uses Engel coefficients to estimate the non-food component of income. Since our income data are in real 1994 pesos and the poverty line estimates were originally in 2000 pesos, we used the general CPI to convert the poverty lines to real 1994 pesos. Income from corn farming is only reported in the last three years because the available data for the earlier years do not correspond to the years available household data.

References

Acemoglu, D., S. Johnson, and J. A. Robinson. 2001. The colonial origins of comparative development: An empirical investigation. *American Economic Review* 91 (5): 1369–1401.

Acemoglu, D., and J. Ventura. 2002. The world income distribution. *Quarterly Journal of Economics* 17 (2): 659–94.

Andrews, E. L. 2002. Rich nations are criticized for enforcing trade barriers. *New York Times.* September 30.

Barrett, C. B., and P. A. Dorosh. 1996. Nonparametric evidence from rice in Madagascar. *American Journal of Agricultural Economics* 78:656–69.

Beghin, J., D. Roland-Holst, and D. van der Mensbrugghe. 2002. Global agricultural trade and the Doha Round: What are the stakes for North and South? Paper presented at the OECD–World Bank Forum on Agricultural Trade Reform, Adjustment, and Poverty. 23–24 May, Paris.

Besley, T., and R. Burgess. 2003. Halving global poverty. *Journal of Economic Perspectives* 17 (3): 3–22.

Brunner, A. D. 2002. El Nino and world commodity prices: Warm water or hot air? *Review of Economics and Statistics* 84 (1): 176–83.

Damian, A. 2001. *Adjustment, poverty and employment in Mexico.* Hampshire, UK: Ashgate.

de Janvry, A., E. Sadoulet, and G. Gordillo de Anda. 1995. NAFTA and Mexico's maize producers. *World Development* 23 (8): 1349–62.

Easterly, W., and R. Levine. 2003. Tropics, germs, and crops: How endowments influence economic development. *Journal of Monetary Economics* 50:3–39.

Economic Research Service/U.S. Department of Agriculture. 2002. World agriculture supply and demand estimates. http://usda.mannlib.cornell.edu/reports/waobr/wasde-bb/.

Fiess, N., and D. Lederman. 2004. Mexican corn: The effects of NAFTA. Trade Note 18. Washington, DC: World Bank International Trade Department, September.

Frankel, J., and D. Romer. 1999. Does trade cause growth? *American Economic Review* 89 (3): 379–99.

Hertel, T. W., W. A. Masters, and A. Elbehri. 1998. The Uruguay Round and Africa: A global, general equilibrium analysis. *Journal of African Economies* 7 (2): 208–34.

Hoekman, B., F. Ng, and M. Olarreaga. 2002. Reducing agricultural tariffs versus domestic support: What's more important for developing countries? World Bank Policy Research Paper no. 2918. Washington, DC: World Bank.

International Cotton Advisory Committee (ICAC). 2002. Production and trade policies affecting the cotton industry. Washington, DC: ICAC.

Levy, S., and S. van Wijnbergen. 1995. Transition problems in economic reform: Agriculture in the North American Free Trade Agreement. *American Economic Review* 85 (4): 738–54.

Masters, W. A. 1993. Measuring protection in agriculture: The producer subsidy equivalent revisited. *Oxford Agrarian Studies* 21 (2): 133–42.

Nadal, A. 2001. The environmental and social impacts of economic liberalization on corn production in Mexico. Study commissioned by Oxfam GB and WWF International. London: Oxfam.

Nicita, A. 2004. Who benefited from trade liberalization in Mexico? Measuring the effects on household welfare. Policy Research Working Paper no. 3265. Washington, DC: World Bank.

Organization for Economic Cooperation and Development (OECD). 2001. Agricultural policies in OECD countries: Monitoring and evaluation. Paris: OECD.

———. 2002. The medium-term impacts of trade liberalisation in OECD countries on the food security of non-member countries. Paris: OECD.

Oxfam. 2003. Dumping without borders: How U.S. agricultural policies are destroying the livelihoods of Mexican corn farmers. Oxfam Briefing Paper no. 50. London: Oxfam.

Panagariya, A. 2002. Trade and food security: Conceptualizing the linkages. Paper presented at the Conference on Trade, Agricultural Development, and Food Security: The Impact of Recent Economic and Trade Policy Reform. 11–12 July, Rome, Italy.

———. 2004a. Opponent's comments on "Subsidies and trade barriers" by Kym Anderson. In *Global crises, global solutions,* ed. Bjørn Lomborg, 592–604. Cambridge: Cambridge University Press.

———. 2004b. The tide of free trade will not float all boats. *Financial Times.* August 2.

Rodrik, D., A. Subramanian, and F. Trebbi. 2002. Institutions rule: The primacy of institutions over geography and integration in economic development. CID

Working Paper no. 97. Cambridge, MA: Harvard University, Center for International Development.

Salas, J. M. 2003. Poverty in Mexico in the 1990s. Syracuse University, Maxwell School of Citizenship and Public Affairs. Working Paper no. 257.

Sarel, M. 1997. How macroeconomic factors affect income distribution: The cross-country evidence. IMF Working Paper no. WP/97/152. Washington, DC: International Monetary Fund.

Trueblood, M., and S. Shapouri. 1999. Trade liberalization and the sub-Saharan African countries. ERS/USDA Food Security Assessment document GFA-11. Washington, DC: Economic Research Service, U.S. Department of Agriculture.

Valdes, A., and A. F. McCalla. 1999. Issues, interests, and options of developing countries. Paper presented at the World Bank Conference on Agriculture and the New Trade Agenda in WTO 2000 Negotiations. 1–2 October, Geneva.

Wise, T. A. 2004. The paradox of agricultural subsidies: Measurement issues, agricultural dumping, and policy reform. GDEI Working Paper no. 04-02. Medford, MA: Tufts University, Global Development and Environment Institute.

World Bank. 2004. *World development indicators.* CD-ROM.

Yunez-Naude, A., and F. Barceinas Paredes. 2002. Lessons from NAFTA: The case of Mexico's agricultural sector. Final Report to the World Bank. Washington, DC: World Bank, December.

Zahniser, S., and W. Coyle. 2004. U.S.-Mexico corn trade during the NAFTA era: New twists to an old story. ERS/USDA Electronic Outlook Report no. FDS-04D-01. Washington, DC: Economic Research Service, U.S. Department of Agriculture, May.

Comment   Mitali Das

McMillan, Zwane, and Ashraf (hereafter MZA) have written an interesting paper, which asks whether large agricultural subsidies in rich countries affect rural incomes in poor ones. Many observers will agree that an answer to this question is imperative in resolving the debate over and designing the appropriate WTO policy on OECD agricultural subsidies. The simplest story for a link is as follows: subsidies allow rich farmers to sell on the world market at below-cost prices; these are transmitted to producer prices in poor nations; and these in turn affect the incomes of the agrarian population. Under this transmission from rich farmers' subsidies to poor farmers' incomes, net exporters among poor nations would realize lower agrarian incomes while net importers would benefit from higher ones. MZA test this hypothesis empirically.

There are three key results of MZA that I note. First, MZA find that agriculture subsidies in OECD nations do indeed affect rural incomes in poor nations. They affect them in a nonlinear manner, but not in the expected manner: rural incomes among net importers are found to be de-

Mitali Das is an associate professor of economics at Columbia University.

creasing as OECD support increases, while rural income for net exporters is falling as OECD support for the commodities they grow increases. A second result I discuss is ancillary to the paper (admittedly, it is also not discussed by the authors) but is implied by a robustness test that MZA carry out. It suggests that once OECD subsidies are accounted for, growth (to misquote Dollar and Kraay 2002) is no longer good for the poor. Finally, a third finding is that in post-NAFTA Mexico, corn farmers' incomes fell substantially following the flood of heavily subsidized corn imports from the United States.

The first result is the most tenuous. It is logically inconsistent with the theoretical predictions of any reasonable model. Apart from poor data quality, measurement error, and small sample size (which MZA point to), the methodological implementation raises issues that very plausibly lead to the unexpected results. These are elaborated upon below.

The second result is less tenuous but is nevertheless surprising. It is overlooked in the paper but merits discussion for this simple reason: the approximate unit elasticity of the lowest quintile's income to average income is an empirical regularity that apparently withstands controls for country fundamentals (GDP, exports/imports, inflation rates), social development (secondary school enrollment, rule-of-law indexes), and financial-sector development; see Dollar and Kraay (2002). Yet MZA's inclusion of controls for OECD support policy attenuates this elasticity until it is indistinguishable from zero. While this is possible in principle, the paper is void of any discussion on this by-product of the empirical results. Explanations for this finding will be suggested here.

I am in general agreement with the third result. There is broad consensus about agrarian incomes in post-NAFTA Mexico, in both popular and academic circles.[1] The raw data in MZA support this consensus. Causality is still difficult to establish, however. There are two suggestions I will make. One is to supplement their descriptive statistics with minimal regression analysis or statistical tests of equality. The second is to balance the discussion of income losses with the economic gains due to NAFTA (DeLong 2000) and discuss net welfare gains.

A more detailed discussion of the first two results follows. To this end, it is useful to specify the model MZA estimate, which can be succinctly summarized as

(1)   Income of lowest quintile$_{it}$ = OECDpolicies$_{it}\beta_1$ + OECDpolicies$_{it}^2\beta_2$

$$+ X'_{it}\gamma + \varepsilon_{it},$$

where OECDpolicies represents a measure of the OECD subsidy policies that are relevant for (poor) nation i at time t, and X denotes controls.

---

1. See, e.g., "Dumping without Borders" (Oxfam 2003).

Result 1: From Rich Farmers' Subsidies to Poor Farmers' Incomes

To approximate OECD subsidies on the commodities produced in poor ones (i.e., to measure "OECDpolicies"), MZA adopt a quite reasonable approach, using a weighted average of the net protection coefficient (NPC) for each commodity produced by the rich nations. Commodities not produced get a zero NPC, and weights are the share of the commodity in the poor nation's output. Using this measure, instrumental variables estimates are derived from the model in equation (1). Estimates of β_1 and β_2 are found to be negative and positive respectively, leading to the unexpected U-shaped response of income of the lowest quintile to OECDpolicies mentioned earlier. Below, I suggest what could lead to this result, and I also suggest methodological changes that could recover the expected result.

Point A: Net Importers and Net Exporters

How in fact might OECD subsidies be viewed from a poor nation's perspective? It depends. For a net exporter, agrarian incomes are decreasing in OECD subsidies ($\beta_1 < 0$, $\beta_2 \leq 0$), while for a net importer the opposite ought to be true ($\beta_1 > 0$, $\beta_2 \geq 0$). Without separating net exporters from importers, therefore, a null hypothesis on β_1 and β_2 in equation (1) cannot be formulated. This is a potentially leading cause of confounding the estimates obtained in equation (1).

To address this, two approaches come to mind. One is to weight the NPC nonmonotonically (from -1 to 0 for importers and 0 to 1 for net exporters). This would fit nicely here because the relevant partial effect is evaluated at a particular level of OECDpolicies, which is negative for net importers and positive for exporters. With this specification, one could expect that the sign of the effect on the lowest quintile's income in net importers would be, in general, inverted from that for net exporters.[2] A limitation of this approach is that it would a priori require that the absolute effect of OECD policies is identical for net importers and exporters. An alternative is inclusion of an interaction between the subsidy variable and an indicator for exporter/importer status:

$$(2)\ \text{Income of lowest quintile}_{it} = \text{OECDpolicies}_{it}\beta_1 + \text{OECDpolicies}_{it}^2\beta_2$$
$$+ \text{NetEx}_{it} \cdot \text{OECDpolicies}_{it}\beta_3 + \text{NetEx}_{it}$$
$$\cdot \text{OECDpolicies}_{it}^2\beta_4 + X'_{it}\gamma + \varepsilon_{it},$$

where NetEx is an indicator for net exporters.

Here, the null hypotheses are $\{\beta_1 > 0, \beta_2 \geq 0, \beta_2 + \beta_4 \leq 0, \beta_1 + \beta_3 < 0\}$. Additionally, an interesting testable hypothesis is for symmetry in responses—that is, whether the reduction in poverty for net importers from

---

2. It would depend on the magnitude of the coefficient for the linear part.

a unit increase in OECDpolicies is equivalent in absolute magnitude to the increase in poverty for net exporters. Because net exporters' incomes are directly linked with reductions in price, while net importers' income might be less so, an asymmetric response could be expected. More generally, some evidence indicates that income gains in poor nations accrue largely to the upper quintile (Das and Mohapatra 2003).

I would recommend that MZA reestimate the alternative model in equation (2) and test each of these hypotheses directly.

Point B: Weighting Choices

Weights used in the MZA approach are the shares, *in 1970,* of the OECD-subsidized commodity in the poor nation's output. A potential problem with this dating approach is of misstating the true effect of OECD subsidies, because nations very likely adjust their crop allocation to the most profitable combinations over time. For instance, net exporters might appropriately shift away from commodities that are persistently heavily subsidized in OECD nations, because they lead to lower world prices and lowered profits.[3] Then, even if point A was irrelevant, the estimates would be statistically biased and inconsistent. Because crop allocation and planning do not generally adjust instantaneously to foreign subsidy levels, one suspects that current allocations are less likely to be determined by current subsidy levels (MZA) and more likely to be affected by previous subsidy levels.

To this end, I would recommend that MZA compare the 1970 shares of the commodities in the poor nations' output with more contemporaneous ones, to determine whether it is appropriate to proceed with 1970 shares in construction of the key variable OECDpolicies.

Result 2: Growth Is No Longer Good for the Poor?

I refer here to results obtained in table 5.8 (last column, first row).

To preserve comparability with other research on poverty, MZA perform a series of robustness tests. In particular, MZA include the set of controls from Dollar and Kraay (2002) where income of the lowest quintile is a function of average income, country fundamentals, social indicators, financial sector variable and region effects. The elasticity of the poor's income to average income is found to be stable (approximately unity) and robust to a wide range of specifications; see Dollar and Kraay (2002). This implies that the lowest quintile's income rises approximately one-for-one with income, and lays the basis for the "Growth is good for the poor" assertion.

3. As a heuristic point, India's export share of tea has reduced from 40 percent to approximately 13 percent between 1960 and 1992 (Indian Child).

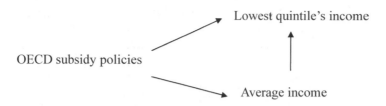

Fig. 5C.1   Possible attenuation of the regression coefficient of average income

Primarily because this finding is robust to many potential determinants of growth, it is surprising that the result attenuates (it is indistinguishable from zero) when MZA include the controls for OECDpolicies. The OECD policy variables themselves are by and large statistically significant, and they indicate that OECD support is more important than average income as a determinant of poverty. How shall we interpret this? Could OECD policies have sufficiently strong effects to wipe out the apparently robust relation between growth and poverty?

My intuition is pulled in two directions here.

On the one hand, in light of points A and B for result 1, instrumental variables estimates of table 5.8 could be biased, and the suggested pattern spurious. This is a plausible argument because the signs of the effects are contrary to what might be expected.[4]

On the other hand, even if the specific results of table 5.8 are inaccurate (because of, say, small samples), OECD policies could have strong enough effects to make growth irrelevant (or less important) for the lowest quintile's income. One reason is the sheer size of the rural population in less-developed nations, which the World Bank estimates to be 76 percent of the total population in poor nations (see MZA's table 5.1). Anecdotal evidence indicates that the rural population derives a large share of their income directly from crops; for example, in 2000 data, Mexican farmers indicated that 56 percent of their income was directly derived from corn and beans (MZA's table 5.11). In this way, a large fraction of income, for a large fraction of the population, depends directly on prices for the crops they grow. These prices affect not just the lowest quintile's income but average income as well (the share size of the rural population is well over 20 percent, as indicated above). A schematic for this scenario is shown in figure 5C.1.

What this schematic implies for regression analysis is that, where OECD policies and average income are both determinants of the lowest quintile's income and OECD subsidy policies are an important determinant of average income, the regression coefficient on the variable OECDpolicies could

---

4. The sums of the coefficients indicate that OECD policies lead to reductions in poverty or increases in lowest quintile's incomes, in all regions of the world except for Eastern and Central Europe.

simply denote the net effect (of the policies plus that of average income) on the lowest quintile's income. If OECD subsidy policies are negatively correlated with average income, as they should be for net exporters, the regression coefficient on average income will attenuate. This is one explanation for the finding in table 5.8.

However, MZA would also have to address net exporters and importers (result 1A) in order to precisely estimate whether OECD subsidy policies matter more than growth for poverty.

Conclusions

This paper is a good starting point in quantifying the impact of rich nations' food subsidies on poor nations' incomes. The importance of this topic is well understood in the policy literature, and MZA must be congratulated for analyzing a quite difficult and contentious policy issue. The empirical exercise raises challenges similar to those in other cross-country regression analyses, and it is further complicated by small samples. The usual interpretational issues arise, and causality is quite difficult to establish in the face of coincidental global and regional shocks.

Additional data could help resolve some of these problems. In particular, I would suggest the authors use larger samples to explore the premise that I outline in result 2: is a key determinant of the relation between lowest quintile's income and average income operating simply through policies such as the OECD subsidies?

The Mexico case study using microdata could potentially overcome many of these problems, so future work might focus on understanding the patterns of income growth and reduction using such micro-level data. This is an important area of research, so I look forward to reading more of the authors' research on the matter.

References

Das, M., and S. Mohapatra. 2003. Income inequality: The aftermath of stock market liberalization in emerging markets. *Journal of Empirical Finance* 10:217–48.

DeLong, J. B. 2000. NAFTA's (qualified) success. *Worldlink,* September/October. http://www.j-bradford-delong.net/Econ_Articles/Econ_Articles.html.

Dollar, D., and A. Kraay. 2002. Growth is good for the poor. *Journal of Economic Growth* 7 (3): 195–225.

Indian Child. India agricultural trade. http://www.indianchild.com/india_agricultural_trade.htm.

Oxfam. 2003. Dumping without borders: How U.S. agricultural policies are destroying the livelihoods of Mexican corn farmers. Oxfam Briefing Paper no. 50. London: Oxfam.

II

Country Case Studies of
Trade Reform and Poverty

6

The Effects of the Colombian Trade Liberalization on Urban Poverty

Pinelopi Koujianou Goldberg and Nina Pavcnik

6.1 Introduction

The recent wave of trade reforms in the developing world has been followed by an intense debate as to whether these reforms contributed to the increase in wage inequality observed in many developing countries during this period. While this debate has not delivered a unanimous answer, free trade advocates emphasize that even if trade liberalization increased inequality (thus worsening the *relative* position of some groups in the population), it may still have improved the *absolute* position of the entire population, thus reducing poverty. Proponents of this view accordingly advocate a shift of focus from relative to absolute measures of well-being.

Despite the importance of the above argument, there has been little work on the effects of trade policy on absolute measures of well-being, such as poverty. The scarcity of studies on this topic is primarily due to the difficulties associated with the measurement of poverty on one hand, and the identification of the trade policy effects on the other. The present paper takes a step toward filling this gap. While our analysis faces many of the challenges encountered in previous attempts to establish a link between trade liberalization and poverty reduction, we believe that the importance of the issue from a public policy point of view justifies the attempt to more closely study this link.

Our analysis focuses exclusively on the *urban* sector in Colombia, a

Pinelopi Koujianou Goldberg is a professor of economics at Yale University and a research associate of the National Bureau of Economic Research (NBER). Nina Pavcnik is an associate professor of economics at Dartmouth College and a research associate of the NBER.

We are grateful to Eric Edmonds, Ann Harrison, and Chang-Tai Hsieh for helpful comments. This research was supported in part by funding from the National Science Foundation Grant SES no. 0213459.

country that underwent major unilateral trade liberalization in the late 1980s and early 1990s following its 1981 accession to the General Agreement on Tariffs and Trade/World Trade Organization (GATT/WTO). The focus on the urban sector is dictated by the nature of the policy experiment we exploit to identify the relationship between openness and poverty reduction. The drastic tariff and nontariff barrier reductions between 1985 and 1992 were concentrated in the manufacturing sector, which is mainly located in urban areas. The average tariff in manufacturing dropped from 50 to 13 percent between 1984 and 1998; in contrast, the average tariffs in agriculture declined substantially less, from 26 to 12 percent. Given the relatively small magnitude of trade liberalization in rural areas, we do not expect the reforms to have had as significant an impact on rural poverty, at least not in the short or medium run. Furthermore, the wide use of domestic production and export-oriented agricultural policies by developed countries suggests that agricultural prices in the developing world would be potentially affected more by a multilateral liberalization of agricultural trade, such as the one currently debated in the Doha WTO negotiations, than a unilateral trade liberalization episode in a single country. Hence, although poverty is particularly problematic in rural areas, we confine our analysis to the urban sector. According to World Bank estimates, poverty rates in urban Colombia lie well above the poverty rates in developed countries, even though they are consistently lower than in rural areas.[1]

Methodologically, we rely on a partial equilibrium approach to identify the link between poverty and trade liberalization in the short or medium run. To be more specific, we focus on the effects of trade liberalization on urban poverty via the *labor income channel*. We examine whether the trade reforms led to changes in employment conditions and wages in the short to medium run, which may have affected poverty. The obvious shortcoming of this approach is that we are not able to deliver an overall assessment of the effect of trade liberalization on poverty. By focusing on the labor income channel, we abstract from the effects that trade policy may have had on poverty through the consumption or household production channels.[2] Given that trade policy affects goods prices and that both consumption and household production decisions are a function of these prices, these channels are potentially important. This is demonstrated, for example, in two recent studies that have adopted a general equilibrium approach to as-

1. In particular, the 2002 World Bank Poverty Assessment report for Colombia reports a poverty rate of 55 percent for the urban sector in 1999, while the poverty rate in the rural sector is 79 percent. The national poverty rate is reported at 64 percent. The corresponding numbers for the "extreme" poverty rate in 1999 are 14 percent, 37 percent, and 23 percent respectively. We discuss the precise definitions of these poverty rates and their measurement in section 6.4.1.
2. For a discussion of the channels through which trade liberalization affects poverty see Goldberg and Pavcnik (2004) and Winters, McCulloch, and McKay (2004).

sess the poverty effects of trade reforms (Porto 2006 and Chen and Raval-lion 2004b).

In addition, we potentially ignore one of the most important channels through which trade may affect poverty, namely growth. There is fairly robust evidence that growth reduces poverty (see Ravallion 2004, pp. 5–6 and figure 2) in the long run. However, the relationship between openness and growth has been more contentious. Given that establishing a clear link between free trade and growth has been empirically elusive (see Hallak and Levinsohn 2004 and Winters, McCulloch, and McKay 2004 for recent overviews), there is little hope that one could credibly demonstrate a relationship between free trade and poverty via the growth channel, especially since the growth effects of trade liberalization probably spread over several years.

On the positive side, the partial equilibrium approach does not require the strong assumptions inherent in the general equilibrium framework (see Goldberg and Pavcnik 2004 for a detailed discussion). Furthermore, the partial equilibrium approach allows us to link poverty (or at a minimum some of the variables that are highly correlated with it) to trade liberalization using plausibly exogenous variation in trade policy over time, so that identification of the pure trade policy effects is arguably more compelling. Finally, there is still little known about the short- and medium-run effects of trade reforms. Given that the adjustment costs associated with trade liberalization are potentially high, a study of the short- or medium-run effects is important from a policy point of view, especially since the negative stance toward free trade is often attributed to the negative effects that reforms are expected to have in the short run.

Our analysis proceeds as follows. We start by providing a brief overview of the policy experiment and the data we exploit in our empirical analysis. Next, we discuss how we measure poverty and compare our poverty measures to those used by the World Bank and Colombian policymakers. Based on these measures we then describe who is poor in urban Colombia. The purpose of this exercise is to establish whether poverty is correlated with particular conditions (e.g., unemployment, employment in sectors that experienced large tariff cuts, work in the informal sector, compliance with minimum wages) that are likely to be affected by trade liberalization. If it is, then the next step in the analysis is to examine whether the trade reforms did indeed have an impact on these conditions. The advantage of this step-by-step approach is that it allows us to infer not only whether trade liberalization had an impact on poverty, but also the specific channels through which this impact was realized. Finally, in the last step of the empirical analysis, we make an attempt to directly relate our poverty measures among the employed to trade liberalization, in order to assess the overall effect of the trade reforms on urban poverty via the labor income channel.

To preview our results, we find strong and robust evidence that urban poverty is highly correlated with certain conditions such as unemployment, employment in the informal sector, and wages below the minimum wage standard. However, we find little to no evidence that any of these conditions were affected by the recent trade liberalization in a significant manner. Perhaps not surprisingly, we then also fail to find any direct correlation between poverty and trade reforms in urban Colombia using a partial equilibrium approach. While it is premature to draw any general conclusions regarding the relationship between trade liberalization and poverty in developing countries based on a single-country study, our results seem to point to growth and general equilibrium effects as being potentially more important in reducing poverty.

6.2   The Policy Experiment: The Colombian Trade Liberalization

Starting in 1985 Colombia experienced gradual trade liberalization that culminated in 1990–91. As we have argued in our earlier work, several features of this trade liberalization episode make it attractive from an empirical point of view.[3]

First, because Colombia had not participated in the tariff-reducing negotiation rounds of the GATT/WTO, it used tariffs as one of the primary trade protection tools prior to the reforms.[4] A big part of the Colombian trade liberalization consisted of reducing tariffs to levels comparable to those observed in other WTO members. The main advantage of tariffs relative to nontariff barriers to trade (NTBs) as a measure of trade policy is that they are easy to measure and comparable across years.[5] NTBs were also reduced as part of the reforms. Unfortunately, industry-level information on NTBs is not consistently available on an annual basis. Fortunately, the existing data suggest that tariff levels (and their changes) are positively correlated with NTB levels (and their changes), so tariff changes are likely to provide fairly accurate measures of the overall trade policy changes (although the coefficients on tariffs in our regressions might overstate the pure tariff effect).

A second appealing feature of the Colombian trade reforms is that they affected not only the average level of protection but also its structure. Indicatively, although the correlation of industry tariffs between 1984 and 1986 was 0.94, the correlation between 1984 and 1992 (a year following the

---

3. See Attanasio, Goldberg, and Pavcnik (2004) and Goldberg and Pavcnik (2003, 2005) for a detailed description of the reforms and for tables and figures with descriptive statistics on the tariff and nontariff barrier reductions.
4. Colombia became a GATT member in 1981 but chose to make use of the developing-country exemption regarding tariff cuts (article XVII of GATT).
5. In particular, NTBs are measured by coverage ratios, which are notoriously problematic measures of the trade restrictiveness of NTBs.

peak of trade reform activity) was only 0.55. The changing structure arises from the fact that the reforms had a differential impact on each sector: sectors with initially high levels of protection (such as textiles and apparel) experienced the largest tariff cuts; in contrast, in sectors with lower pre-reform protection levels, the tariff cuts were more modest. It is this cross-sectional variation in tariff reductions that we exploit in order to identify the trade policy effects. In addition, this change in the trade protection structure was accomplished over the course of several years, which provides ample variation over time in the data for the purpose of identifying the trade policy effects.

Finally, because the main objective of the Colombian government was to bring industry tariffs to an almost uniform level in accordance with WTO guidelines, policymakers were less prone to succumb to industry pressure or lobbying. This implies that tariff changes can be plausibly considered exogenous.

These features of the Colombian trade reforms suggest that the cross-sectional variation in tariff changes provides an appealing policy experiment to study how trade policy changes have affected the Colombian economy. There are, however, two potential caveats associated with such an exercise. First, although tariff changes arguably provide accurate measures of the recent liberalization in Colombia, the "opening" of the Colombian economy might have also affected other trade-related variables that are not captured by tariffs. To address this concern we exploit changes in industry imports and/or exports over time as additional measures of exposure to trade. The use of quantity measures such as imports and exports is naturally controversial, as such variables are endogenous to trade policy changes.[6] The advantage of using them is that any changes in trade policy that we may have missed by exclusively focusing on tariffs will probably lead to changes in the import and export volumes so that these variables may more accurately represent the cumulative effect of trade policy changes. Along the same lines, we have considered including foreign direct investment (FDI) in the analysis, especially as there is strong evidence that FDI has had strong distributional effects in Mexico (see in particular Feenstra and Hanson 1996, 1997). Unfortunately, FDI data are not available for Colombia at the industry level. However, FDI inflows in Colombia have been small relative to Mexico, so it is unlikely that they have had any significant impact on the labor market.

The second caveat is that the cross-sectional variation of tariff changes is useful only to the extent that we study outcomes that are likely to differ by industry (e.g., industry employment, wages). This is precisely the reason that we focus on partial equilibrium effects of trade policy changes. We ab-

---

6. To alleviate these endogeneity concerns we employ lagged values of imports or exports rather than their current values.

stract from economy-wide implications of tariff policy changes, because, while there is no doubt that economy-wide effects are important in the general equilibrium, we do not have a way of separating these trade-induced effects from other economy-wide shocks without imposing strong identification assumptions.

6.3   The Household Survey Data

Our ultimate empirical goal is to link the trade policy changes described above to poverty measures or to economic variables that are highly correlated with poverty. To construct these variables we rely on the June waves of the Colombian National Households Survey (NHS), which are administered biannually by the Colombian National Statistical Agency (DANE). We focus on the June waves because these waves include a special module on the informal sector of the economy (defined as the sector that does not comply with labor market regulations). Given that the informal sector accounts for 50 to 60 percent of urban employment and given that informality is a priori likely correlated with poverty, including information on those employed in the informal sector in a study of urban poverty is particularly important. To construct poverty measures we rely on the income information provided in the NHS. While expenditure survey data may be preferable for measuring poverty, the household expenditure survey in Colombia is available for only one year, so it is not possible to analyze the *evolution* of poverty using the expenditure data.

Our data cover urban areas in the years 1986, 1988, 1990, 1992, 1994, 1996, and 1998. This fourteen-year period covers several trade liberalization episodes. We construct several variables that control for household and individual demographics such as age, gender, marital status, family size, whether a person is a household head, education, literacy, geographical location, whether a person was born in urban area, and how long the person has resided in current residence. Based on the information on highest completed grade, we classify individuals by education as those with no complete schooling, complete primary school, complete secondary school, and complete university degree.

In addition, the survey contains detailed information on employment characteristics and wages. Individuals who are older than eleven are classified into three categories: inactive, unemployed, and employed.[7] For all categories, the NHS reports income from sources other than earnings. For unemployed individuals, the survey reports the one-digit International Standard Industrial Classification (ISIC) code of the industry

---

7. DANE classifies individuals aged twelve and older as inactive if they are not employed and are not actively seeking work. The primary activity of inactive individuals is usually being a student, a homemaker, or a pensioner.

in which the individuals used to work and the industry in which they are looking for new work. There is a total of nine single-digit ISIC industries.

For those who are employed, the survey reports earnings, occupation, type of employer (i.e., private company, government, private household, self-employed, unpaid family worker), and the two-digit ISIC code of the industry in which the individuals are employed. There is a total of thirty-three two-digit ISIC industries per year.[8] Based on the information on the reported earnings and the number of hours worked normally in a week, we construct hourly and monthly wages. We also create controls for whether an individual works for a private company, government, or a private household, and whether he or she is an employer or self-employed. Furthermore, the survey reports whether the worker's employer contributes to the worker's social security fund. The employer's compliance with the social security legislation (and thus labor market regulation) provides an excellent indicator for whether a worker is employed in the formal sector. Finally, based on the information on monthly minimum wage standard, we generate an indicator for whether a worker's monthly earnings are below minimum wage standard.[9]

The main disadvantage of our data is that we do not have information on unionization. However, Edwards (2001) and anecdotal evidence suggest that unions do not have significant power in most Colombian industries (with the possible exception of the public sector and the petroleum industry).

6.4   Who Is Poor in Urban Colombia

6.4.1   Measurement of Poverty

Poverty Lines

An operational definition of poverty presents many conceptual and measurement problems (see Ravallion 2004 for a detailed discussion). One of the most important ones is the distinction between *absolute* and *relative* poverty. In the first case, the measurement of poverty relies on a poverty line that has a fixed real value—the $1-per-day poverty line at 1993 purchasing power parity (PPP), which is representative of poverty lines used in poorest countries, provides an example of such a fixed line. In contrast, the measurement of relative poverty relies on a line that increases with the mean income. The two measures have very different implications for the assessment of the impact of trade reforms on poverty. To see why, consider

---

8. We have tariff information for twenty-one of these industries (although tariffs are likely to be zero in the industry categories for which no tariffs are reported—i.e., services).
9. Information on monthly minimum wages is from Maloney and Nunez (2003).

the extreme case in which the (relative) poverty line moves proportionately with mean income. A trade policy that raises all incomes by the same proportion will in this case leave relative poverty unchanged. Still, the policy has raised—in absolute terms—the incomes at the bottom of the income distribution, reducing the (absolute) poverty of the lowest-income individuals.

We focus on absolute poverty for several reasons. First, the value judgment underlying the use of the relative poverty line is that well-being should be measured in relative terms only. This view seems extreme, especially when applied to low- or middle-income developing countries such as Colombia; while relative standing is certainly important for welfare, it is hard to argue that absolute standards of living are irrelevant in a country like Colombia. Second, when a relative measure of poverty is adopted, the question of how trade policy has affected poverty becomes equivalent to the question of how trade policy has affected inequality. The latter question has been researched extensively in the literature—see, for example, Attanasio, Goldberg, and Pavcnik (2004) for a detailed analysis of how the trade reforms have affected inequality in Colombia. However, the existing literature has mostly abstracted from the link between absolute poverty and trade policy.

Obviously, any measure of absolute poverty depends crucially on the setting of the fixed poverty line. DANE calculates its own poverty line based on some minimum calorie and nutrition requirements for an individual of average age. Urban poverty lines differ across cities. DANE further distinguishes between two poverty lines: the "extreme" poverty line and the regular poverty line, which according to the World Bank is 2 to 2.5 times higher than the extreme one (see World Bank 2002, p. 100, for a detailed description). Unfortunately, DANE does not make its poverty data publicly available, and the World Bank (2002) reports DANE poverty lines only for selected years. Moreover, it is not clear whether the consumption basket used in the DANE poverty calculations remains fixed over time; a changing consumption basket would complicate comparisons of poverty across years even further. For these reasons, we decided to adopt the "international" poverty lines that are based on multiples of the $1-per-day (in 1993 PPP terms) measure. Details on how this line was chosen are provided in Chen and Ravallion (2001, 2004a).[10] In the context of Colombia, this line will be expressed in 1995 Colombian pesos.

To make sure that our empirical results are not due to the particular choice of the poverty line, we consider several multiples of the $1-per-day

10. Following Chen and Ravallion, we actually use the $1.08-per-day (in 1993 PPP terms) line and its multiples, although this line is usually referred to as the "$1-per-day" poverty line.

measure ($2, $3, $4, $5, and $7) and conduct extensive sensitivity analysis. In addition, we compare individuals in the bottom 10 percent and 20 percent of the per capita income distribution in urban Colombia in 1986 to those who fare better. The income for the bottom 10 percent of the income distribution lies somewhere between the $2 and $3 poverty line; for the bottom 20 percent of the income distribution, the income is between $3 and $4 per day. Overall, we consider eight distinct measures of poverty (six measures based on multiples of the $1-per-day line, and two measures based on the income distribution). These measures should cover the entire spectrum of plausible poverty measures.

Household Income Per Person

Household income is measured in the NHS on a monthly basis as the sum of the incomes of all individuals in the household. Income of employed individuals consists of reported wages or earnings from self-employment. The earnings of individuals who work as unpaid family workers are set to zero. In addition, the survey asks all individuals older than eleven (irrespective of their employment status) whether they have received income from other sources (such as interest payments, dividends, rents, pensions, public assistance, etc.). All monetary values are expressed in 1995 pesos.

To obtain per capita household income we adjusted the household income by the number of household members. To this end, we experimented with two alternative adult-equivalency formulas:

1. The first formula follows Deaton and Paxson (1997), who compute adult equivalency as $(N_a + \alpha N_c)^\theta$, where N_a is number of adults in a household, N_c is number of children (defined as individuals aged fifteen or less), α is adult equivalency scale, and θ is an economies-of-scale parameter. The parameters α and θ can take on the values 1, .75, and .5. This yields nine measures of per capita household income. This is the formula most commonly used in developing countries, although there is no consensus on the particular values of the parameters α and θ.

2. The second formula is the Organization for Economic Cooperation and Development (OECD) formula for adult equivalence: $1 + .7(N_a - 1) + .5N_c$ (based on World Bank Poverty Manual, online document, page 21).

Because there is little agreement in the development literature as to which equivalency formula is more appropriate, we have computed per capita income based on alternative equivalency and scale parameters, and examined the correlations across these alternative definitions. The results are reported in appendix table 6A.1 and suggest that alternative measures of per capita income are highly correlated, with the correlations ranging from 0.92 to 1. In general, the income measures seem more sensitive to

changes in the scale parameter θ than changes in the adult equivalency parameter α. As a further robustness check we have also computed poverty head count ratios using the $1- and $2-per-day measures for alternative adult equivalency formulas. The results are presented in appendix table 6A.2. While the exact head count ratio varies with the values of α and θ (as with table 6A.1, the estimates are more sensitive to the economies-of-scale parameter than the adult equivalency parameter), the time trends regarding the evolution of the poverty head count ratios are similar across alternative per capita income definitions. Hence, it is unlikely that different income measures will yield different conclusions regarding the effects of trade policy on poverty.

Given the high correlation coefficients across income definitions in table 6A.1 and the similar time trends in the poverty head count ratios, we chose to focus on a per capita income measure based on α = 1 and θ = 1 (in other words, simple per capita household income without any adult equivalency adjustment) for the rest of the analysis. This is consistent with the approach taken in Chen and Ravallion (2001, 2004a) and the World Bank Poverty Report (World Bank 2002).

Poverty Head Count Ratios

Based on the per capita income measure discussed above, we computed various poverty head count ratios, each corresponding to a different poverty line. Our estimates are displayed in table 6.1.

To assess whether the numbers in table 6.1 appear reasonable, we compared the head count ratios we obtained based on the $2-per-day measure to those reported by the World Bank using the same measure (World Bank

Table 6.1   Poverty head count ratios

	1984	1986	1988	1990	1992	1994	1996	1998
$1	.025	.025	.018	.014	.018	.011	.022	.028
$2	.069	.067	.057	.051	.058	.037	.055	.073
$3	.158	.157	.139	.129	.130	.100	.127	.159
$4	.263	.259	.243	.241	.239	.182	.214	.248
$5	.366	.377	.336	.344	.341	.278	.311	.346
$7	.528	.541	.516	.513	.508	.431	.474	.489
DANE poverty			.55			0.48[a]		0.55[b]
DANE extreme poverty			.17			0.1[a]		0.14[b]

Notes: As in Chen and Ravallion (2001), $1-a-day line in 1993 PPP is $1.08-a-day line (same applies to its multiples). All estimates are computed using survey weights. The first column refers to the poverty line used in the computation of poverty rates in each row. The DANE poverty rate and extreme poverty rate are from World Bank (2002, table 2) based on DANE poverty lines. These rates are available only for selected years (1988, 1995, 1998).

[a]Number is for 1995.

[b]Number is for 1999.

2002, table 2, p. 12). Our estimates seem very close to those reported by the World Bank.[11]

Table 6.1 exhibits several interesting features. First, note that the poverty rates based on the $1-per-day measure are extremely small. This is not surprising given that Chen and Ravallion (2001) suggest that the $1 line is indicative of poverty lines used in poor countries, and not of middle-income countries such as Colombia. Second, while the $2-per-day line is presumably more appropriate for Colombia, note that the poverty rates computed based on this line are still well below the poverty rates reported by the World Bank based on DANE poverty lines. This suggests that the standard of living considered acceptable by Colombians is substantially higher than the one corresponding to the $2-per-day measure. The urban poverty rates computed by the World Bank based on DANE poverty lines (available for selected years only in the World Bank Poverty Report; World Bank 2002, table 2, p. 12) are displayed at the bottom of table 6.1. A comparison of these rates to the ones we have computed based on multiples of $1-per-day poverty lines suggests that the extreme poverty rate corresponds roughly to a definition of poverty that uses the $3-per-day measure as the poverty line; the regular poverty rate corresponds roughly to the definition that uses the $7-per-day measure. It is worth noting that these poverty lines, which are viewed as the appropriate benchmarks by Colombian policymakers, suggest that poverty is still substantial in urban areas.[12]

A final feature of table 6.1 worth noting is that even though the magnitudes of poverty rates differ depending on what poverty lines we use, they all exhibit similar time trends. In all cases, poverty steadily declines between 1984 and 1994 and rises thereafter. Hence, it seems safe to conclude that no matter what poverty definition we adopt, our empirical results concerning the effects of trade policy on poverty will not depend on the particular choice of the poverty line.

6.4.2   Descriptive Results: Who Is Poor

Before investigating the relationship between trade policy and poverty, we use the household survey data to describe which households are most

11. In particular, for 1988 we estimate the poverty rate based on the $2-per-day measure to be 5.7 percent, while the World Bank reports a figure of 5 percent for the same year. The World Bank estimate for 1995 is 3 percent. While we do not have data for that particular year, our estimates for 1994 (3.7 percent) and 1996 (5.5 percent) seem in line with their estimates. Similarly, we do not have data for 1999, but our poverty estimate for 1998 (7.3 percent) is roughly in line with the World Bank estimate of 5 percent for 1999. Overall, it seems that our estimates are slightly higher than those reported in the World Bank report, but given that the World Bank uses a different wave of surveys (September instead of June) and that the years they use in their calculations differ from those we have available in our survey waves, the numbers seem to match up quite well.

12. These estimates are also in line with Porto's (2006) poverty numbers for Argentina, which imply extensive urban poverty when the internal Argentinean poverty line is used, especially in the period covering the Argentinean financial crisis.

Table 6.2   **Poverty head count ratios by household head characteristics**

	$1	$2	$3	$4	$5	$7	Bottom 10%	Bottom 20%
Employment								
Inactive	.028	.078	.151	.246	.360	.516	.115	.196
Unemployed	.188	.310	.477	.594	.704	.814	.388	.527
Employed	.016	.052	.141	.245	.363	.531	.091	.184
Education								
No school	.042	.118	.261	.405	.553	.726	.185	.323
Elementary	.022	.061	.149	.263	.393	.577	.100	.197
Secondary	.011	.018	.053	.087	.150	.296	.030	.065
University	.006	.006	.008	.014	.037	.077	.007	.011
Age								
≤20	.043	.115	.154	.261	.339	.572	.145	.176
21–30	.026	.064	.145	.264	.400	.567	.098	.193
31–40	.030	.083	.190	.296	.421	.581	.131	.236
41–50	.023	.063	.159	.264	.373	.548	.104	.203
51–60	.020	.051	.130	.213	.328	.486	.083	.163
>60	.030	.084	.169	.232	.331	.481	.106	.179
Female	.030	.084	.169	.267	.379	.523	.125	.208
Male	.024	.063	.154	.258	.376	.545	.103	.198

Notes: Households are grouped by the characteristics of the head of the household. Column headings refer to the poverty line used in the calculations of the head count ratio in each column. Bottom 10% (20%) refers to the individuals living in the bottom 10% (20%) of the income distribution in 1986. All figures are based on 1986 data, the first year of data with all relevant variables. All estimates are computed using survey weights.

affected by poverty. Correlations between poverty and various demographic and employment-related characteristics can give us a preliminary idea as to how likely it is that trade policy has had an impact on Colombian urban poverty.

Table 6.2 presents the fraction of individuals classified as poor in 1986 by the following characteristics of household head: employment status, education, age, and gender. As with our earlier tables, the magnitudes of the poverty rates differ depending on the poverty line used in the calculations, but the comparisons across different household groups exhibit the same patterns. We therefore focus most of our discussion on the $3-per-day measure.

The most interesting pattern emerging from table 6.2 is that poverty is highly correlated with unemployment. For example, for the $3-per-day measure, our calculations suggest that 47.7 percent of individuals living in households with an unemployed household head are poor; for the $7-per-day line this proportion is as high as 81.4 percent. Clearly, one cannot contemplate a poverty reduction in urban Colombia without addressing the issue of unemployment.

Having said that, it is worth noting that even among the employed, the poverty rates are not negligible. The $3-per-day line implies that 14 percent

of individuals living in households with an employed household head live in poverty; if one uses the $7-per-day line as the benchmark, as Colombian policymakers do, then the poverty rate among the employed becomes 53 percent. These are sizable numbers!

The patterns revealed in table 6.2 are also evident in table 6.3, in which we examine the same correlations in a regression framework; this allows us to obtain correlations between poverty and employment-related variables *conditional* on demographics such as education, age, and so on. Consistent with the results based on the unconditional means in table 6.2, the estimates indicate that lack of education is associated with a higher probability of being poor. More important, we again find that, even conditional on education, poverty is highly correlated with unemployment (inactive is the base group). A comparison of the R-squares from regressions with and without employment indicators further suggests that employment status (i.e., employed, unemployed, inactive) has substantial explanatory power. For example, conditional on demographic and educational indicators, employment indicators account for 3.1 percent of the overall variance in poverty and 29 percent of the explained variance in poverty in the case of the $3-a-day poverty line.

As noted earlier, poverty rates among the employed are not negligible either. We therefore turn our attention next to poverty among individuals living in households with an employed head of household. Which demographics and employment characteristics of such households are correlated with poverty? This question is addressed in tables 6.4 and 6.5. As before, we present our results both as unconditional correlations (table 6.4) and in a regressions framework that conditions on various demographics (table 6.5).

First, the results in table 6.4 suggest that poverty rates vary by industry of employment: at the one-digit ISIC level, the sectors of construction and of wholesale and retail trade are associated with the highest poverty rates. Using the $3-per-day line, we find that 19 percent and 18.4 percent of individuals living in a household where the household head is employed in these two sectors respectively live in poverty; the financing, insurance, and business sector presents the lowest poverty rates (7 percent), while manufacturing is somewhere in the middle (11.5 percent). A further breakdown of employment by two-digit ISIC code shows that poverty rates also vary across two-digit ISIC codes. This variation is likely to be relevant for the assessment of the effects of trade policy on poverty; if tariff reductions are disproportionately concentrated on industries with higher poverty rates, leading to a decline in relative prices and potentially wages in these sectors, then trade liberalization may have adverse effects on poverty in the short run.

Second, no matter what poverty definition one adopts, poverty rates are substantially higher for individuals living in households where the

Table 6.3   Poverty and household head characteristics (regression results)

	$1	$2	$3	$4	$5	$7	Bottom 10%	Bottom 20%
Age	-0.0005	-0.0018**	-0.0032***	-0.0061***	-0.0101***	-0.0120***	-0.0028***	-0.0043***
	(0.367)	(0.030)	(0.004)	(0.000)	(0.000)	(0.000)	(0.005)	(0.001)
Age squared	0	0	0	0.0000**	0.0001***	0.0001***	0	0
	(0.423)	(0.228)	(0.231)	(0.037)	(0.000)	(0.000)	(0.114)	(0.161)
Male	0.0016	-0.0041	-0.0018	0.012	0.0268**	0.0331***	-0.0062	0.0123
	(0.679)	(0.499)	(0.833)	(0.216)	(0.011)	(0.002)	(0.396)	(0.176)
Married	-0.0092**	-0.0288***	-0.0443***	-0.0616***	-0.0654***	-0.0391***	-0.0367***	-0.0603***
	(0.004)	(0.000)	(0.000)	(0.000)	(0.000)	(0.000)	(0.000)	(0.000)
Elementary	-0.0237***	-0.0671***	-0.1152***	-0.1446***	-0.1704***	-0.1593***	-0.0946***	-0.1330***
	(0.000)	(0.000)	(0.000)	(0.000)	(0.000)	(0.000)	(0.000)	(0.000)
Secondary	-0.0333***	-0.1031***	-0.1988***	-0.2981***	-0.3959***	-0.4364***	-0.1538***	-0.2476***
	(0.000)	(0.000)	(0.000)	(0.000)	(0.000)	(0.000)	(0.000)	(0.000)
University	-0.0359***	-0.1054***	-0.2247***	-0.3445***	-0.4808***	-0.6219***	-0.1640***	-0.2815***
	(0.000)	(0.000)	(0.000)	(0.000)	(0.000)	(0.000)	(0.000)	(0.000)
Household size	-0.0004	0.0077***	0.0240***	0.0398***	0.0462***	0.0511***	0.0145***	0.0299***
	(0.495)	(0.000)	(0.000)	(0.000)	(0.000)	(0.000)	(0.000)	(0.000)
Unemployed	0.1559***	0.2441***	0.3026***	0.2990***	0.2861***	0.2121***	0.2778***	0.2960***
	(0.000)	(0.000)	(0.000)	(0.000)	(0.000)	(0.000)	(0.000)	(0.000)
Employed	-0.0124***	-0.0168***	-0.0147*	-0.0163	-0.0195*	-0.0307***	-0.0191**	-0.0242**
	(0.004)	(0.010)	(0.098)	(0.118)	(0.084)	(0.007)	(0.014)	(0.013)
R^2_1	.009	.035	.075	.122	.160	.199	.054	.095
R^2	.050	.076	.106	.144	.176	.209	.090	.121
No. of observations	16,933	16,933	16,933	16,933	16,933	16,933	16,933	16,933

Notes: p-values are reported in parentheses. Column headings indicate the poverty line used to create the poverty indicator in a given column. Bottom 10% (20%) refers to the individuals living in the bottom 10% (20%) of the income distribution in 1986. R^2_1 refers to R^2 from a regression that does not include employment and unemployment indicators. All figures are based on 1986 data, the first year of data with all relevant variables. Number of observations refers to number of households in 1986 data.

***Significant at the 1 percent level.

**Significant at the 5 percent level.

*Significant at the 10 percent level.

Table 6.4   **Head count ratios by household head characteristics for households with employed household head**

	$1	$2	$3	$4	$5	$7	Bottom 10%	Bottom 20%
Agriculture and hunting	.020	.046	.167	.292	.377	.509	.100	.215
Forestry and logging	.000	.000	.063	.337	.337	.337	.000	.337
Fishing	.000	.094	.172	.172	.172	.480	.094	.172
Coal mining	.000	.000	.071	.071	.233	.527	.071	.071
Petroleum and natural gas	.000	.000	.014	.034	.090	.205	.000	.034
Metal ore mining	.000	.000	.000	.000	.000	.229	.000	.000
Other mining	.119	.143	.306	.634	.778	.778	.195	.336
Food	.008	.038	.117	.237	.361	.538	.081	.168
Textile, apparel, leather	.011	.031	.120	.216	.344	.553	.063	.152
Wood	.006	.044	.129	.242	.460	.607	.086	.170
Paper	.015	.015	.048	.120	.215	.375	.023	.059
Chemical	.008	.026	.093	.167	.276	.440	.058	.127
Non-metallic mineral products	.022	.076	.162	.241	.458	.680	.099	.173
Basic metal industry	.000	.021	.146	.215	.419	.576	.021	.204
Machinery and equipment	.014	.030	.115	.235	.327	.533	.061	.165
Other manufacturing	.006	.033	.107	.154	.263	.426	.064	.107
Electricity, gas, steam	.000	.052	.123	.194	.303	.449	.059	.167
Water works and supply	.000	.063	.099	.219	.368	.600	.085	.146
Construction	.013	.058	.191	.326	.488	.675	.109	.246
Wholesale trade	.004	.004	.054	.118	.137	.324	.009	.063
Retail trade	.030	.099	.190	.299	.409	.560	.145	.244
Restaurants and hotels	.026	.063	.177	.291	.414	.612	.123	.227
Transport and storage	.015	.039	.122	.233	.351	.531	.082	.167
Communication	.000	.000	.053	.073	.163	.313	.000	.073
Financial institutions	.000	.000	.007	.016	.075	.214	.002	.009
Insurance	.000	.000	.000	.000	.091	.177	.000	.000
Real estate and business	.003	.011	.081	.192	.302	.441	.034	.105
Public administration	.000	.007	.044	.136	.232	.449	.015	.068
Sanity	.000	.000	.100	.300	.581	.759	.050	.235
Social and community services	.001	.008	.048	.105	.183	.285	.025	.068
Recreation and culture	.013	.053	.131	.209	.357	.490	.089	.187
Household and personal services	.029	.093	.243	.366	.492	.664	.158	.298
International bodies	.000	.000	.000	.000	.525	.525	.000	.000
Agriculture	.019	.046	.164	.291	.373	.505	.098	.217
Mining	.041	.049	.125	.247	.350	.465	.081	.144
Manufacturing	.011	.034	.115	.215	.347	.535	.067	.152
Utilities	.000	.056	.114	.202	.325	.500	.068	.160
Construction	.013	.058	.191	.326	.488	.675	.109	.246
Wholesale and retail trade	.029	.090	.184	.292	.401	.561	.138	.236
Transport	.014	.037	.118	.224	.340	.519	.077	.161
Financing, insurance, business	.002	.007	.053	.126	.219	.355	.022	.069

(*continued*)

Table 6.4   (continued)

	$1	$2	$3	$4	$5	$7	Bottom 10%	Bottom 20%
Community, social, personal services	.013	.046	.135	.230	.340	.497	.083	.174
Formal	.001	.013	.081	.127	.286	.456	.036	.111
Informal	.026	.080	.186	.298	.419	.586	.131	.237
Paid above minimum wage	.000	.008	.068	.154	.273	.450	.030	.097
Paid below minimum wage	.074	.215	.410	.577	.697	.832	.315	.502
Unpaid family worker	.187	.271	.385	.670	.707	.966	.385	.445
Private-sector employee	.005	.027	.125	.240	.374	.557	.064	.167
Government employee	.001	.006	.044	.120	.216	.389	.019	.073
Domestic employee	.022	.083	.310	.424	.528	.736	.168	.345
Self-employed	.041	.115	.224	.340	.453	.608	.174	.279

Note: See notes to table 6.2.

household head works in the informal (rather than the formal) sector. Third, a wage below the minimum wage standard is an excellent predictor of poverty: 41 percent of individuals living in a household where the household head is paid below the minimum wage live in poverty (according to the $3-per-day line).[13] While this is not surprising (obviously a poverty definition based on an income measure will be highly correlated with wage-related variables), it serves as a confirmation that individuals receiving minimum wages in their primary employment do not have other sources of income that would considerably improve their financial situation. Finally, poverty depends on the type of employer: unpaid family workers and members of their household are most likely to be poor, while government employees fare the best.

These empirical patterns are confirmed in the regression analysis conducted in table 6.5. The table reports results from regressions based on the $3-per-day and $4-per-day poverty lines respectively; additional results based on alternative poverty definitions can be found in appendix tables 6A.3, 6A.4, and 6A.5. Apart from confirming the robustness of the aforementioned correlations, the regression results allow us to assess the explanatory power of various characteristics of employed household heads in explaining poverty. First, the two-digit ISIC industry indicators (retail is the omitted one) are jointly significant. Comparisons of the R-squares across specifications that do and do not include industry indicators suggest that, conditional on demographic characteristics, industry indicators account

13. Minimum wages in Colombia are set at the national level. The monthly minimum wage over our sample period (expressed in 1995 pesos) lies well above the poverty lines used by DANE; in particular, it is about 4 times the extreme poverty line ($3 per day) and 1.7 times the regular poverty line ($7 per day).

Table 6.5   Poverty and household head characteristics for households with employed head ($3- and $4-per-day poverty line)

	$3-a-day poverty line					$4-a-day poverty line				
	(1)	(2)	(3)	(4)	(5)	(1)	(2)	(3)	(4)	(5)
Agriculture and hunting	0.0012	0.0023	0.0234	0.0390*	0.0344*	0.0007	-0.004	0.0209	0.0397	0.0301
	(0.952)	(0.908)	(0.215)	(0.054)	(0.091)	(0.978)	(0.870)	(0.354)	(0.101)	(0.218)
Forestry and logging	-0.0704	-0.0502	-0.0049	-0.0075	-0.0058	0.1372	0.1561	0.2099	0.2022	0.2032
	(0.600)	(0.707)	(0.968)	(0.955)	(0.965)	(0.391)	(0.329)	(0.156)	(0.204)	(0.202)
Fishing	0.1522	0.1392	0.1444	0.129	0.1248	0.0307	0.0181	0.024	0.0067	0.0029
	(0.300)	(0.342)	(0.287)	(0.376)	(0.391)	(0.861)	(0.917)	(0.882)	(0.969)	(0.987)
Coal mining	-0.1230*	-0.0938	-0.0584	-0.0702	-0.0623	-0.2227**	-0.1951**	-0.1532*	-0.1681*	-0.1617*
	(0.095)	(0.202)	(0.391)	(0.337)	(0.394)	(0.011)	(0.026)	(0.060)	(0.055)	(0.065)
Petroleum and natural gas	-0.1076*	-0.0921	-0.0352	-0.0561	-0.055	-0.1529**	-0.1385**	-0.0707	-0.0997	-0.0991
	(0.062)	(0.109)	(0.508)	(0.327)	(0.336)	(0.026)	(0.044)	(0.266)	(0.145)	(0.147)
Metal ore mining	-0.2165	-0.2283	-0.1114	-0.1449	-0.1604	-0.3501	-0.3618	-0.2219	-0.2761	-0.2898
	(0.351)	(0.324)	(0.603)	(0.529)	(0.486)	(0.207)	(0.191)	(0.387)	(0.316)	(0.293)
Other mining	0.1351*	0.1186	0.0764	0.1715**	0.1413*	0.3191***	0.3203***	0.2696***	0.3566***	0.3444***
	(0.074)	(0.125)	(0.286)	(0.022)	(0.066)	(0.000)	(0.001)	(0.002)	(0.000)	(0.000)
Food	-0.0802***	-0.0562***	-0.0258*	-0.0323**	-0.0263*	-0.0741***	-0.0526***	-0.0166	-0.0246	-0.0209
	(0.000)	(0.000)	(0.079)	(0.041)	(0.099)	(0.000)	(0.005)	(0.345)	(0.194)	(0.274)
Textile, apparel, leather	-0.0704***	-0.0577***	-0.0388***	-0.0367***	-0.0351***	-0.0813***	-0.0688***	-0.0465***	-0.0464***	-0.0448***
	(0.000)	(0.000)	(0.001)	(0.003)	(0.005)	(0.000)	(0.000)	(0.001)	(0.002)	(0.003)
Wood	-0.0629***	-0.0640***	-0.0410**	-0.0339*	-0.0390*	-0.0716***	-0.0711***	-0.0438*	-0.0416*	-0.0446*
	(0.002)	(0.002)	(0.030)	(0.094)	(0.055)	(0.003)	(0.003)	(0.052)	(0.085)	(0.067)
Paper	-0.0994***	-0.0738***	-0.0439*	-0.0548**	-0.0476*	-0.1159***	-0.0919***	-0.0565*	-0.0699**	-0.0641*
	(0.000)	(0.007)	(0.086)	(0.046)	(0.083)	(0.000)	(0.005)	(0.065)	(0.033)	(0.051)
Chemical	-0.0610***	-0.0227	0.0039	-0.0108	0.0029	-0.0589**	-0.0214	0.0064	-0.0072	0.0057
	(0.005)	(0.307)	(0.849)	(0.621)	(0.898)	(0.024)	(0.422)	(0.795)	(0.785)	(0.831)

(continued)

Table 6.5 (continued)

	$3-a-day poverty line					$4-a-day poverty line				
	(1)	(2)	(3)	(4)	(5)	(1)	(2)	(3)	(4)	(5)
Non-metallic mineral products	-0.0322	-0.0002	0.0085	0.0191	0.0294	-0.0456	-0.0142	-0.0042	0.0075	0.0172
	(0.226)	(0.995)	(0.733)	(0.473)	(0.271)	(0.152)	(0.658)	(0.888)	(0.814)	(0.590)
Basic metal industry	-0.0502	-0.0243	0.0066	-0.0044	0.0027	-0.0767	-0.0522	-0.0155	-0.0293	-0.0235
	(0.314)	(0.626)	(0.887)	(0.930)	(0.956)	(0.198)	(0.380)	(0.778)	(0.621)	(0.692)
Machinery and equipment	-0.0772***	-0.0541***	-0.0179	-0.0302*	-0.0255	-0.0688***	-0.0459**	-0.0029	-0.0202	-0.0155
	(0.000)	(0.002)	(0.268)	(0.082)	(0.146)	(0.001)	(0.028)	(0.879)	(0.330)	(0.459)
Other manufacturing	-0.0551	-0.0525	-0.0409	-0.0483	-0.0481	-0.1052**	-0.1028**	-0.0892**	-0.0982**	-0.0981**
	(0.160)	(0.179)	(0.258)	(0.214)	(0.216)	(0.025)	(0.028)	(0.039)	(0.035)	(0.035)
Electricity, gas, steam	-0.0684*	-0.0312	0.0008	-0.0148	-0.0028	-0.0996**	-0.0647	-0.0268	-0.0442	-0.0346
	(0.061)	(0.393)	(0.980)	(0.683)	(0.939)	(0.022)	(0.138)	(0.508)	(0.308)	(0.427)
Water works and supply	-0.0799	-0.0413	0.0072	-0.0214	-0.0095	-0.0818	-0.0454	0.0121	-0.0214	-0.0117
	(0.122)	(0.424)	(0.881)	(0.676)	(0.853)	(0.185)	(0.462)	(0.833)	(0.728)	(0.849)
Construction	-0.0395***	-0.0394***	-0.0176	-0.0178	-0.0213*	-0.0217	-0.0224	0.0042	0.0006	-0.0033
	(0.001)	(0.001)	(0.106)	(0.127)	(0.069)	(0.121)	(0.109)	(0.744)	(0.963)	(0.816)
Wholesale trade	-0.0819**	-0.0638*	-0.025	-0.0491	-0.0443	-0.0764*	-0.0595	-0.0135	-0.0426	-0.0389
	(0.029)	(0.089)	(0.472)	(0.188)	(0.235)	(0.088)	(0.183)	(0.745)	(0.340)	(0.384)
Restaurants and hotels	-0.0274*	-0.0244	-0.0082	0.0044	0.0015	-0.0375**	-0.0344*	-0.0162	-0.0046	-0.0069
	(0.081)	(0.120)	(0.575)	(0.778)	(0.922)	(0.046)	(0.067)	(0.353)	(0.807)	(0.715)
Transport and storage	-0.0643***	-0.0579***	-0.0225**	-0.0421***	-0.0417***	-0.0766***	-0.0714***	-0.0293**	-0.0536***	-0.0542***
	(0.000)	(0.000)	(0.034)	(0.000)	(0.000)	(0.000)	(0.000)	(0.021)	(0.000)	(0.000)
Communication	-0.0985**	-0.9696*	-0.0254	-0.0444	-0.0368	-0.1585***	-0.1314***	-0.0788*	-0.1027**	-0.0966*
	(0.019)	(0.096)	(0.513)	(0.286)	(0.377)	(0.002)	(0.009)	(0.089)	(0.039)	(0.053)
Financial institutions	-0.0999***	-0.0581**	-0.0307	-0.0489**	-0.0337	-0.1459***	-0.1058***	-0.0736***	-0.0932***	-0.0800***
	(0.000)	(0.011)	(0.146)	(0.029)	(0.139)	(0.000)	(0.000)	(0.004)	(0.001)	(0.003)
Insurance	-0.1031**	-0.0694	-0.0369	-0.0626	-0.0504	-0.1510**	-0.1180**	-0.0796	-0.1091*	-0.0979
	(0.046)	(0.185)	(0.447)	(0.223)	(0.334)	(0.015)	(0.059)	(0.170)	(0.076)	(0.116)

	(1)	(2)	(3)	(4)	(5)	(6)	(7)	(8)	(9)	(10)
Real estate and business	-0.0582***	-0.0402**	-0.0149	-0.0328*	-0.0266	-0.0430**	-0.0171	0.0028	-0.0167	-0.0126
	(0.001)	(0.019)	(0.346)	(0.052)	(0.119)	(0.034)	(0.184)	(0.884)	(0.409)	(0.535)
Public administration	-0.1071***	-0.0766***	-0.0227	-0.0529***	-0.0445***	-0.1159***	-0.0871***	-0.0231	-0.0598***	-0.0531***
	(0.000)	(0.000)	(0.107)	(0.000)	(0.004)	(0.000)	(0.000)	(0.169)	(0.001)	(0.004)
Sanity	-0.1179**	-0.0771	-0.0284	-0.0598	-0.0467	-0.0365	0.002	0.0599	0.0235	0.0342
	(0.022)	(0.135)	(0.553)	(0.244)	(0.363)	(0.554)	(0.974)	(0.295)	(0.701)	(0.578)
Social and community services	-0.0766***	-0.0454***	-0.0105	-0.0261*	-0.0168	-0.0836***	-0.0541***	-0.0128	-0.0314*	-0.0237
	(0.000)	(0.001)	(0.404)	(0.052)	(0.220)	(0.000)	(0.001)	(0.395)	(0.051)	(0.146)
Recreation and culture	-0.0644**	-0.0467*	-0.0283	-0.022	-0.0181	-0.0890***	-0.0713**	-0.0495*	-0.0452	-0.0409
	(0.015)	(0.080)	(0.251)	(0.405)	(0.497)	(0.005)	(0.025)	(0.094)	(0.153)	(0.200)
Household and personal services	0.0459***	0.0405***	0.0237**	0.0572***	0.0527***	0.0572***	0.0518***	0.0316***	0.0690***	0.0648***
	(0.000)	(0.000)	(0.020)	(0.000)	(0.000)	(0.000)	(0.000)	(0.009)	(0.000)	(0.000)
International bodies	-0.0775	-0.0277	0.0275	-0.0149	0.0022	-0.1026	-0.0561	0.0095	-0.038	-0.0243
	(0.683)	(0.883)	(0.875)	(0.937)	(0.991)	(0.650)	(0.804)	(0.866)	(0.866)	(0.914)
Family worker				0.2807***	0.2656***				0.3211***	0.3084***
				(0.004)	(0.007)				(0.006)	(0.009)
Self-employed				0.1052***	0.0915***				0.1087***	0.0971***
				(0.000)	(0.000)				(0.000)	(0.000)
Informal		0.0664***	0.0202***		0.0342***		0.0626***	0.0072		0.0284***
		(0.000)	(0.001)		(0.000)		(0.000)	(0.342)		(0.001)
Paid below minimum wage			0.3195***					0.3818***		
			(0.000)					(0.000)		
R^2	.106	.113	.238	.122	.124	.156	.160	.278	.167	.168
No. of observations	13,035	12,943	12,932	13,035	12,943	13,035	12,943	12,932	13,035	12,943

Note: p-values are reported in parentheses. Column headings indicate the poverty line used in the calculations of the head count ratio in each column. All regressions also include controls for age, age squared, gender, whether a person is married, education indicators, and household size. All figures are based on 1986 data, the first year of data with all relevant variables. Number of observations refers to number of households.

***Significant at the 1 percent level.

**Significant at the 5 percent level.

*Significant at the 10 percent level.

for 1.5 percent of the overall variance and 14 percent of the explained variance in poverty among households with employed heads. These regressions suggest that industry affiliation is correlated with poverty. Thus, if trade policy affects industry wages and trade policy changes differed across industries, the reforms may have in principle impacted the poverty rate. Second, the results in table 6.5 also point to an important role for informality and minimum wage in explaining poverty. Conditional on demographics and industry indicators, informality accounts for .7 percent of the overall variance and 6 percent of the explained variance in poverty. Conditional on demographics, industry indicators, and informality, the "below the minimum wage" indicator accounts for 12.5 percent of the overall variance and 53 percent of the explained variance in poverty (when the $3-per-day measure is used).

6.4.3 Summary

Our descriptive analysis yields several findings that motivate our further work. First, poverty in urban Colombia is highly correlated with unemployment. A natural question is therefore whether the trade liberalization has had a significant impact on unemployment. However, poverty rates among the individuals living in households with employed heads are also high, ranging from 14 percent to 53 percent depending on the poverty line used. Within this group, poverty is highly correlated with employment of the household head in the informal sector and a wage below the minimum wage standard. The industry of employment also seems to matter. Given these patterns, it is natural to ask how the trade reforms affected the probability of a worker working in the informal sector, and whether trade liberalization affected compliance with minimum wage legislation. Furthermore, trade policy could also have affected poverty through its effects on worker wages. We take up these questions in the next section.

6.5   Trade Policy and Poverty

6.5.1   The Evolution of the Aggregate Poverty Rate:
The Aggregate Trends

Before investigating the relationship between trade liberalization and poverty, it is useful to examine some aggregate trends in the evolution of poverty rates over our sample period. A clear pattern emerging from table 6.1 is that no matter what poverty definition one adopts, poverty rates seem to steadily decline between 1984 and 1994–95 and increase thereafter. By 1998 the poverty rates are close to the rates observed in 1984. The usual explanation offered in the literature for the 1996–98 increase in urban poverty is the recession (see World Bank 2002). The reasons for the steady decline of urban poverty between 1984 and 1995, however, are less clear.

Given that 1985–94 was the period of trade reforms, it is tempting to attribute the decrease of urban poverty to the changes initiated by the reforms. To obtain a preliminary idea of what factors lowered the poverty rate between 1984 and 1994 we start our analysis by asking whether the decline in the poverty rate was primarily driven by a decline in unemployment or a decline in the poverty rate within the set of unemployed individuals. In particular, we decompose the decline in the poverty rate between 1986 and 1994, ΔP_t, into two components, the reduction in unemployment (the *between* component) and the reduction of poverty within the unemployed (the *within* component):[14]

$$\Delta P_t = P_t - P_\tau = \sum_j \Delta U_{jt} p_{j\cdot} + \sum_j \Delta p_{jt} U_{j\cdot},$$

where j indicates the employment status of the household head (inactive, employed, or unemployed), U_{jt} indicates the share of individuals living in households with status j in year t, p_{jt} is the poverty rate within status j at time t, $U_{j\cdot} = .5(U_{jt} + U_{j\tau})$, and $p_{j\cdot} = .5(p_{jt} + p_{j\tau})$.[15]

The results are displayed in table 6.6. The top of the table includes all individuals, while the middle part of the t `le focuses only on those living in households whose household head is in the labor force (thus excluding the inactive category). What is striking about the decomposition in table 6.6 is that the within component accounts for over 90 percent of the decline in the poverty rate between 1994 and 1986. Hence, the decline in the poverty rate between 1986 and 1994 is explained mostly by an improvement in the position of household heads within each of our employment categories, rather than by movements out of unemployment. This is a rather surprising result, as we would have expected the decline in poverty to be associated with a decline in unemployment. The contribution of the within component is also significant for explaining the increase in the poverty rate between 1994 and 1998, although its magnitude is smaller than the one for the 1986–94 period. Thus, the results for the second subperiod of our sample (1994–98) are more consistent with the anecdotal claim that the increase in poverty during the late 1990s is due to the recession, as they suggest a larger role of the between component (movement into unemployment).

We next focus on poverty changes among the individuals living in households with employed household heads. In particular, we have further decomposed the decline in the poverty rate among the individuals living in households with an employed household head into within and between

14. In this decomposition, we focus on 1986 rather than 1984 because 1986 is the first year in our data with all available variables.

15. This decomposition is similar to the one often used in the literature on skill upgrading in order to decompose the increase in the share of skilled workers into a within-industry and between-industries component.

Table 6.6   Decomposition of changes in head count ratios

	Head count ratio			Change 1994–1986					Change 1998–1994				
	1986	1994	1998	Total	Within	Within (share)	Between	Between (share)	Total	Within	Within (share)	Between	Between (share)
All individuals	.157	.100	.159	−.057					.059				
Decomposition by inactive, employed, unemployed					−.053	.944	−.003	.056		.049	.832	.010	.168
Individuals in households with household head in labor force	.158	.103	.161	−.055					.058				
Decomposition by employed, unemployed					−.051	.929	−.004	.071		.046	.795	.012	.205
Individuals in households with employed household head	.141	.093	.137	−.048					.044				
Decomposition by													
Two-digit ISIC industry					−.049	1.028	.001	−.028		.044	.993	.000	.007
Informal sector					−.045	.940	−.003	.060		.038	.867	.006	.133
Paid below minimum wage					−.029	.601	−.019	.399		.021	.474	.023	.526

Note: Head count ratios are based on $3-a-day poverty line.

components for each of the variables highly correlated with poverty: industry affiliation, employment in the informal sector, and a wage below the minimum wage. The results from these decompositions are displayed at the bottom of table 6.6, and they exhibit the same pattern as the ones regarding unemployment: the within component dominates the between component in every case. With respect to industry affiliation and informality in particular, the share of the within component exceeds 90 percent, while for the minimum wage it is smaller but still significant (60 percent). Hence, the decline in poverty occurred predominately through improvements in the position of individuals at their current jobs, rather than changes in their employment.[16]

What does the above analysis imply about the role of trade policy in reducing poverty? Given that the trade policy changes were concentrated in the early period, when the between movements are small, it seems unlikely that any effect that trade liberalization may have had on poverty was driven *primarily* by movements of people out of categories associated with high poverty (e.g., unemployment, informality) and into categories with lower poverty (employment, formal-sector employment, minimum wage). It is possible, however, that trade policy affected poverty by impacting the wages of employees within the above-defined categories. In addition, trade liberalization could be relevant for explaining the between component of poverty changes, small as this may be. We therefore turn now to a more systematic investigation of the relationship between trade liberalization and poverty.

6.5.2   Trade Policy and Unemployment

The high incidence of poverty among the unemployed leads to the question of how trade liberalization has affected unemployment. Unfortunately, this is not a question that can be answered convincingly with the available data. Ideally, one would like to identify the relationship between trade policy and unemployment by relating detailed industry tariff changes to changes in industry unemployment. However, the lack of detailed data on industry affiliation of the unemployed in the NHS precludes such an analysis. The unemployed workers who were previously employed report the last industry of employment at the one-digit ISIC level. Similarly, the unemployed individuals who were not previously employed report the industry in which they are seeking employment at the one-digit ISIC level. This leads to nine industry observations per year, and only six of these nine

16. We have also replicated the analysis in table 6.6 focusing only on individuals that are in the labor force and using their own employment characteristics for decomposition (rather than the characteristics of the household head). This addresses the concern that numbers in table 6.6 might understate the between movements, if secondary breadwinners are more likely to lose jobs during a recession. Although (as expected) the between component increases somewhat, the within component continues to play the dominant role.

industries have available tariffs. Most important, most of the time-variation in tariffs occurred within the manufacturing industries, which are now treated as a single sector.

Nevertheless, given the importance of unemployment in explaining poverty in urban Colombia, we conduct two exercises to obtain a *rough* idea about the role of trade policy in affecting unemployment.

The first exercise is to examine whether the change in the probability of being unemployed over the time of trade reform was greater for workers employed in traded-good sectors (such as manufacturing) than for workers with the same observable characteristics in nontraded-good sectors (such as wholesale and retail trade, restaurants, hotels, construction, etc.). This exercise was conducted in one of our previous papers (Attanasio, Goldberg, and Pavcnik 2004, section 8). In particular, we regressed an indicator for whether an individual was unemployed, on one-digit ISIC industry indicators (the omitted category was wholesale trade, retail trade, and restaurants and hotels [ISIC 6]), an indicator for a year following the trade reform, the interaction of industry indicators with the year indicator, and a set of worker characteristics (age, age squared, male, married, head of the household, education indicators, literate, lives in Bogota, born in urban area, time in residence, urban birth interacted with time in residence). If the probability of being unemployed increased (decreased) relatively more over time in manufacturing relative to a sector such as wholesale and retail trade and restaurants and hotels (i.e., the coefficient on the interaction of the manufacturing indicator with year indicator were positive [negative] and significant), this could provide some indirect (and suggestive) evidence that trade reforms were associated with increases (decreases) in the probability of unemployment.

To summarize the results from that exercise, we found no evidence that the probability of unemployment changed significantly in the manufacturing sector relative to most nontraded-good sectors between 1984 and 1998, even though the manufacturing sector experienced drastic tariff declines. Given that the comparison of years 1984 and 1998 could have potentially missed short-term adjustments to trade reform, we also considered the unemployment adjustment in periods right before and after the major tariff declines by focusing on changes in unemployment between 1988 and 1992. The coefficient on the interaction of the manufacturing indicator with the post-trade-reform year indicator indicated in this case a decrease in the probability of becoming unemployed in the manufacturing sector relative to the wholesale and retail trade sector. It is not clear, however, whether this decline was due to the trade reforms per se or to the exchange rate depreciation in 1990–91 that lowered the demand for nontraded goods relative to traded goods. This decrease, however, seems short-lived. In the long run (i.e., 1984–98), we do not find any evidence that the probability of unemployment changed in traded sectors relative to nontraded sectors.

Table 6.7   **Unemployment and trade exposure**

	(1)	(2)
Tariff	.006	.042
	(0.596)	(0.454)
Lagged imports		0.00003**
		(0.003)
Lagged exports		–0.00002
		(0.773)
Industry indicators	Yes	Yes
Year indicators	Yes	Yes
R^2	0.073	0.073
No. of observations	304,393	304,393

Notes: p-values based on standard errors that are clustered on industry are reported in parentheses. All regressions also include controls for age, age squared, gender, whether a person is married, head of the household, education indicators, household size, literacy indicator, whether a person lives in Bogota, whether a person was born in urban area, time in current residency, and the interaction of urban birth with time in currency residency. Tariff, lagged imports, and lagged exports are for one-digit ISIC industry of previous employment (or industry in which a person is looking for work for the first-time job seekers). Industry indicators are on one-digit ISIC level. Observations refers to number of employed or unemployed individuals, which includes those in industries that did not report tariffs but where tariffs were likely (and were thus assumed) to be zero.
**Significant at the 5 percent level.

The second exercise is to directly relate the probability of becoming unemployed to trade-related variables, such as tariffs, lagged imports, and lagged exports. These variables refer to the (one-digit SIC) industry in which the currently unemployed person used to work (or, for the first-time job seekers, the industry in which a person is looking for work). In particular, we regress an indicator of whether an individual is unemployed on his or her demographic characteristics (listed in the note to the table), one-digit industry dummies, year dummies, one-digit SIC tariff rates, lagged imports and lagged exports. For industries for which National Planning Department (DNP) does not report tariffs we set the tariff rate equal to zero.[17] When interpreting the results of this regression it is important to keep in mind that we only have variation in tariff rates in nine one-digit ISIC industries, some of which never actually experienced tariff changes. Hence, due to the high level of aggregation, we may not have sufficient variation in the data to identify the link between trade-related variables and unemployment, even though such a link might be evident at a finer level of aggregation.

The results are presented in table 6.7 and show no association between tariff and unemployment. Furthermore, there is no evidence that there is a

17. This is probably not a bad assumption because all these industries are services.

relationship between exports and unemployment. We do find, however, that as (lagged) imports increase, the probability of becoming unemployed increases. Overall, the evidence seems mixed and inconclusive. Although, as emphasized above, the results are only suggestive given the high level of aggregation and the potential endogeneity of some of the variables we employ on the right-hand side (such as imports or exports), it seems fair to say that whatever effects the trade reforms may have had on unemployment, they were not substantial enough to be evident in the raw data, at least not at the one-digit SIC level of aggregation. Even at a more disaggregate level, the stability of industry employment shares we observe over this period does not seem to support the idea that trade liberalization had a significant impact on unemployment. Specifically, in Attanasio, Goldberg, and Pavcnik (2004) we computed the employment shares by two-digit SIC industry for periods before and periods after the trade reforms. The changes were found to be surprisingly small, suggesting that despite the magnitude of tariff cuts and the extent of the overall reform, there was neither increased nor decreased unemployment at the industry level.

In sum, the above two exercises do not provide strong evidence that trade policy affected the probability of becoming unemployed in either direction.

So far, our analysis has concentrated on the question of whether unemployed individuals are unemployed because of trade-related reasons. A somewhat different question, yet one that is relevant for the poverty discussion, is whether, within the set of unemployed individuals, those who became unemployed because of trade-related reasons fare worse, in the sense of being poorer than the rest. This could be the case, for example, if individuals who were laid off from industries facing intense import competition have a harder time finding a new job, so that they remain unemployed for a longer period of time, or if increased import competition had affected their earnings in the past, when they were employed, leading to lower interest income when they became unemployed. Unfortunately, it is not possible to answer these questions definitively without panel data that would allow us to track individuals over time, trace their earnings, and compute unemployment hazard rates. But as before, we can obtain a rough idea about the empirical relevance of the above considerations by trying to link poverty within the unemployed directly to trade-related variables. In unreported regressions, we have regressed the likelihood of being poor among the unemployed on tariffs, lagged imports, lagged exports, industry indicators, and the aforementioned individual demographic characteristics. The results were again mixed and not robust across different definitions of poverty.

Overall, although poverty in urban Colombia is clearly highly correlated with unemployment, we do not find any strong and conclusive evidence that the trade reform activity affected unemployment in either direction.

6.5.3   Trade Policy and Informality

Having found no evidence of a link between trade liberalization and changes in unemployment at the industry level, we next turn to the question of whether the trade reforms affected poverty within the set of employed individuals. Given that within the set of employed individuals poverty rates were particularly high for those working in the informal sector, we start by examining whether trade liberalization led to worker reallocation across the formal and informal sectors.

In a previous paper (Goldberg and Pavcnik 2003) we presented evidence that the tariff declines in Colombia were associated with an increase in the probability of being employed in the informal sector, although the effects were small and applied only to the period preceding the labor market reform (but not thereafter).[18] Moreover, we have found that informal work is associated with lower benefits and worse working conditions, and that informal workers face lower wages than workers with the same *observable* characteristics in the formal sector. Of course, these correlations do not necessarily imply that informal workers are worse off than formal workers, given that there may be sorting into the informal sector based on unobservable characteristics—for example, workers may self-select into the informal sector because they value the flexible hours that informal employment offers. Nonetheless, given that our descriptive results in section 6.4.2 suggest that a nonnegligible share of informal workers are not just worse off than formal workers in terms of monetary compensation but actually poor (especially when one considers the higher poverty lines), the concern arises that trade policy may have contributed to poverty by leading to a reallocation of labor toward the informal sectors.[19]

To examine this possibility more thoroughly we repeat the analysis of our earlier paper (that focused on a pooled sample of employed individuals) both for the entire sample and for subgroups of employed who might a priori face a higher likelihood of being pushed into the informal sector when the economy opens up to import competition. In particular, in table 6.8 we regress an indicator of whether an employed individual works in the informal sector on demographic characteristics (listed in the note to the table), industry indicators, year dummies, tariffs, and the interaction of tariffs with an indicator for whether the time period was covered by labor market reform. This approach is similar to the two-stage approach we have employed in our earlier work, and the results are similar. Column (1) of the

18. In 1990, Colombia instituted a labor market reform that significantly reduced the cost of hiring and firing workers (Kugler 1999; Edwards 2001).
19. For a detailed analysis of the arguments why this may happen and a formal model linking trade liberalization with changes in informal employment, see Goldberg and Pavcnik (2003).

Table 6.8 **Informal employment and tariffs**

	Employees and self-employed							Employees						
	(1)	(2)	(3)	(4)	(5)	(6)	(7)	(8)	(9)	(10)	(11)	(12)	(13)	(14)
Tariff	−0.064*	−0.053*	−0.072*	−0.073*	−0.05	0.027	−0.088***	−0.069**	−0.043	−0.084*	−0.073	−0.061*	0.026	−0.111***
	(0.054)	(0.098)	(0.054)	(0.099)	(0.155)	(0.397)	(0.000)	(0.044)	(0.187)	(0.058)	(0.133)	(0.062)	(0.416)	(0.000)
Tariff · post-labor reform	0.351***	0.328***	0.407***	0.364	0.495**	0.396**	0.022	0.312**	0.260*	0.463**	0.373	0.383**	0.385**	−0.018
	(0.002)	(0.003)	(0.002)	(0.101)	(0.012)	(0.015)	(0.754)	(0.045)	(0.075)	(0.021)	(0.145)	(0.015)	(0.019)	(0.836)
Sample	All	Men	Women	Unskilled	Skilled	Large firm	Small firm	All	Men	Women	Unskilled	Skilled	Large firm	Small firm
Year indicators	Yes	Yes	Yes	Yes	Yes	Yes	Yes	Yes	Yes	Yes	Yes	Yes	Yes	Yes
Industry indicators	Yes	Yes	Yes	Yes	Yes	Yes	Yes	Yes	Yes	Yes	Yes	Yes	Yes	Yes
R^2	0.342	0.324	0.373	0.319	0.302	0.13	0.132	0.29	0.262	0.336	0.282	0.196	0.126	0.133
No. of observations	100,131	57,668	42,463	70,049	30,082	37,786	62,205	76,770	45,279	31,491	52,547	24,223	37,615	39,038

Notes: p-values, based on standard errors that are clustered on industry, are reported in parentheses. All regressions also include controls for age, age squared, gender, whether a person is married, head of the household, education indicators, household size, literacy indicator, whether a person lives in Bogota, occupation indicators, type of employer indicators, whether a person was born in urban area, time in current residence, and the interaction of urban birth with time in current residency. Number of observations refers to number of employed individuals.

***Significant at the 1 percent level.

**Significant at the 5 percent level.

*Significant at the 10 percent level.

table corresponds to the specification we have used in our earlier work, except for the fact that our sample now includes unpaid family workers. It confirms our previous findings and suggests that higher tariff reductions are associated with a higher probability of being employed in the informal sector, but only in the period prior to the labor reform. In columns (2) through (7) we repeat the estimation separately for each of the following subgroups: men, women, unskilled workers, skilled workers, workers employed in large firms (eleven or more people) and workers employed in small firms (less than eleven people).[20] It is often alleged that women and unskilled workers are the most likely to switch to informal employment during trade reforms. The results in table 6.8 seem to provide some support for this claim, as the increase in informality *prior* to the labor market reform is more likely to occur among women than men (compare columns [2] and [3]) and among unskilled than skilled workers (compare columns [4] and [5]), even though both of these estimates lie within each other's confidence intervals. Note also that the results in columns (6) and (7) indicate that the increases in informality associated with the tariff declines prior to the labor reform occur mostly in small establishments (employing less than eleven people). Columns (8) through (14) repeat the analysis that excludes the self-employed, and they yield similar findings.

Table 6.9 extends the analysis by including, in addition to tariffs, lagged imports and exports as measures of trade exposure. The results regarding the effects of the tariff declines remain robust (although we now find evidence of increases in informality associated with the tariff declines in both large and small firms prior to the labor reform). What is interesting is that the results for exports suggest that higher exports are associated with lower probability of working in the informal sector. This result is mainly driven by large firms. The negative association between exports and informal employment is consistent with anecdotal evidence suggesting that large export firms are more likely to offer more permanent jobs, higher benefits, and better working conditions, possibly out of concern for public scrutiny.

Overall the results are in line with the evidence presented in our earlier work, suggesting that the Colombian tariff reductions were associated with a slight increase in informal employment, but only in the period preceding the labor market reform. Given that the poverty rate is higher in the informal sector, one would then have expected an increase in the aggregate poverty rate.[21] This is clearly not the case; the aggregate poverty rate decreases during the 1986–95 period. Moreover, the decomposition in table 6.6 suggests not only that the role of between movements was limited, but also that to the extent that worker reallocation across the formal and in-

20. Our definition of large firms is driven by the survey question (which does not distinguish among the size of establishments that employ more than eleven people).
21. Of course, this is only true to the extent that the wages paid to informal workers did not simultaneously increase.

Table 6.9   Informal employment and trade exposure

	Employees and self-employed							Employees						
	(1)	(2)	(3)	(4)	(5)	(6)	(7)	(8)	(9)	(10)	(11)	(12)	(13)	(14)
Tariff	-0.12260**	-0.08814	-0.16836***	-0.12162*	-0.09094	-0.10357**	-0.09546***	-0.14604**	-0.08469	-0.24276***	-0.14308*	-0.10869*	-0.10414**	-0.12807**
	(0.014)	(0.125)	(0.001)	(0.067)	(0.108)	(0.028)	(0.001)	(0.017)	(0.182)	(0.000)	(0.081)	(0.088)	(0.024)	(0.010)
Tariff · post–labor reform	0.37414***	0.37878***	0.38164***	0.38038**	0.51134**	0.53342***	0.03056	0.38202***	0.35282**	0.49539***	0.45294**	0.43403**	0.52382***	0.02524
	(0.000)	(0.000)	(0.000)	(0.029)	(0.014)	(0.001)	(0.671)	(0.001)	(0.011)	(0.000)	(0.021)	(0.018)	(0.001)	(0.748)
Lagged imports (I)	0.00011	0.00008	0.00011	0.00001	0.00022	0.00011	-0.00006	0.00005	0.00005	0.00001	-0.00009	0.00017	0.00011	-0.00018
	(0.115)	(0.544)	(0.569)	(0.940)	(0.212)	(0.116)	(0.476)	(0.382)	(0.717)	(0.973)	(0.391)	(0.272)	(0.108)	(0.126)
I · post–labor reform	0.00010***	0.00013*	0.0001	0.00020**	0.00002	0.00004	0.00008	0.00013***	0.00014*	0.00015	0.00025**	0.00004	0.00004	0.00018**
	(0.001)	(0.051)	(0.644)	(0.044)	(0.832)	(0.482)	(0.137)	(0.000)	(0.057)	(0.546)	(0.019)	(0.596)	(0.492)	(0.025)
Lagged exports (E)	-0.00029***	-0.00032***	-0.00024*	-0.00034***	-0.00025***	-0.00049***	-0.00004	-0.00034***	-0.00034***	-0.00036**	-0.00040***	-0.00025**	-0.00048***	-0.00007
	(0.002)	(0.001)	(0.055)	(0.016)	(0.001)	(0.000)	(0.464)	(0.001)	(0.006)	(0.031)	(0.008)	(0.000)	(0.000)	(0.407)
E · post–labor reform	-0.00019**	-0.00017*	-0.00024**	-0.00014	-0.00016	-0.00036***	-0.00004	-0.00025**	-0.00019**	-0.00041***	-0.00022	-0.00019	-0.00036***	-0.0001
	(0.018)	(0.056)	(0.012)	(0.221)	(0.193)	(0.000)	(0.264)	(.011)	(0.049)	(0.003)	(0.106)	(0.159)	(0.000)	(0.190)
Sample	All	Men	Women	Unskilled	Skilled	Large firm	Small firm	All	Men	Women	Unskilled	Skilled	Large firm	Small firm
Year indicators	Yes	Yes	Yes	Yes	Yes	Yes	Yes	Yes	Yes	Yes	Yes	Yes	Yes	Yes
Industry indicators	Yes	Yes	Yes	Yes	Yes	Yes	Yes	Yes	Yes	Yes	Yes	Yes	Yes	Yes
R^2	0.343	0.325	0.373	0.32	0.303	0.132	0.132	0.29	0.263	0.337	0.283	0.196	0.127	0.133
No. of observations	100,131	57,668	42,463	70,049	30,082	37,786	62,205	76,770	45,279	31,491	52,547	24,223	37,615	39,038

Note: See notes to table 6.8.
***Significant at the 1 percent level.
**Significant at the 5 percent level.
*Significant at the 10 percent level.

formal sectors contributed to the poverty reduction, this happened by workers moving out of the informal and into the formal sector. This is precisely the opposite of the effect attributed to tariff reductions. Hence, it appears that the tariff-induced changes in informal employment not only did not contribute to the poverty reduction witnessed during this period but, if anything, went in the opposite direction. It is important to keep in mind, however, that the estimated effects are small and disappear once the labor market reform becomes effective.[22]

6.5.4 Trade Policy and Compliance with Minimum Wage Legislation

A different channel through which trade liberalization could have affected poverty is by increasing the noncompliance of firms with minimum wage legislation.[23] Noncompliance is definitely an issue in Colombia; according to our calculations, the percentage of earners receiving wages below the minimum wage standard ranges from 17 percent to 30 percent in individual years, with no clear time trend evident in the data. It is interesting to note, however, that noncompliance peaks in 1992, a year following the most drastic tariff reductions.

To examine whether noncompliance was affected by the trade reforms we employ the same approach as before and regress an indicator for whether an employed individual receives a wage above the minimum wage on demographic characteristics (see notes to table 6.10 for details), industry indicators, year dummies, and various measures of trade exposure. Although our preferred trade exposure measure is tariffs, we also consider lagged imports and exports. We estimate this relationship on a sample of employees (excluding self-employed and unpaid family workers) and experiment with different subsamples of these workers. To summarize the results, shown in table 6.10, there is no evidence that tariff declines are associated with changes in the compliance with minimum wage standard in the sample as a whole (columns [1] and [10]) or in various subsamples of workers.[24] We also find no association between (lagged) exports and noncompliance in the sample as a whole (column [10]). However, higher (lagged) imports are associated with greater noncompliance with minimum wage laws in the overall sample (column [10]), and this relationship holds in most subsamples of the data. Reassuringly, this relationship holds among the

22. Although tariffs are our preferred measure of exposure to trade, the results for exports suggest that because Colombian exports increased between 1986 and 1994, higher exports could have in principle contributed to 1994–1986 poverty reductions through reallocations of workers from informal to formal sector. However, as emphasized before, the reallocation (i.e., between) component of poverty declines accounts for a very small part of poverty reduction between 1986 and 1994.

23. Maloney and Nunez (2003) provide details on minimum wage legislation in Colombia.

24. Negative association between tariffs and noncompliance among men and in small firms in columns (4) and (9), respectively, is not robust to inclusion of lagged imports and exports.

Table 6.10   Noncompliance with minimum wage laws and trade exposure

	(1)	(2)	(3)	(4)	(5)	(6)	(7)	(8)	(9)	(10)	(11)	(12)	(13)	(14)	(15)	(16)	(17)	(18)
Tariff	-0.014	-0.063	-0.017	-0.027*	-0.014	-0.017	-0.018	-0.006	-0.082*	-0.01114	-0.04061	-0.00069	-0.03012	0.02421	-0.02442	0.00419	-0.00055	-0.0518
	(0.266)	(0.170)	(0.299)	(0.054)	(0.674)	(0.298)	(0.435)	(0.821)	(0.052)	(0.511)	(0.500)	(0.966)	(0.120)	(0.664)	(0.246)	(0.846)	(0.985)	(0.289)
Lagged imports										0.00010***	0.00005	0.00005*	0.00008***	0.00022*	0.00014***	0	0.00003	0.00017***
										(0.007)	(0.461)	(0.061)	(0.000)	(0.065)	(0.001)	(0.829)	(0.114)	(0.003)
Lagged exports										-0.00003	0.00017	0.00011*	-0.00011	0.00022	-0.00015	0.00025**	0.00003	0.00014
										(0.736)	(0.159)	(0.057)	(0.284)	(0.408)	(0.268)	(0.001)	(0.713)	(0.372)
Sample	All	Informal	Formal	Men	Women	Unskilled	Skilled	Large firm	Small firm	All	Informal	Formal	Men	Women	Unskilled	Skilled	Large firm	Small firm
Year indicators	Yes	Yes	Yes	Yes	Yes	Yes	Yes	Yes	Yes	Yes	Yes	Yes	Yes	Yes	Yes	Yes	Yes	Yes
Industry indicators	Yes	Yes	Yes	Yes	Yes	Yes	Yes	Yes	Yes	Yes	Yes	Yes	Yes	Yes	Yes	Yes	Yes	Yes
R^2	0.208	0.197	0.075	0.165	0.207	0.182	0.094	0.099	0.189	0.208	0.197	0.075	0.166	0.207	0.183	0.094	0.099	0.189
No. of observations	82,183	35,930	32,006	48,914	33,269	58,114	24,069	34,679	33,690	82,183	35,930	32,006	48,914	33,269	58,114	24,069	34,679	33,690

Notes: p-values based on standard errors that are clustered on industry are reported in parentheses. All regressions also include controls for age, age squared, gender, whether a person is married, head of the household, education indicators, household size, literacy indicator, whether a person lives in Bogota, occupation indicators, type of employer indicators, whether a person was born in urban area, time in current residency, and the interaction of urban birth with time in current residency. Number of observations refers to number of employed individuals with all required data. The number of observations is lower in columns (2), (3), (9), and (10) because the information on informality is not available in 1984. These regressions exclude self-employed and unpaid family workers.

***Significant at the 1 percent level.

**Significant at the 5 percent level.

*Significant at the 10 percent level.

unskilled workers, but not among the skilled workers (for whom the minimum wage legislation is less likely to be binding).

What does this imply about the role of trade policy in reducing poverty? Given that the massive trade liberalization of the late 1980s and early 1990s led to an increase in imports, the results in table 6.10 seem to suggest that, if anything, trade liberalization should have led to lower compliance with minimum wages, and hence to an increase in poverty. Hence, our results regarding the effects of trade liberalization on poverty via the minimum wage channel are similar to the ones we obtained regarding the informality channel: in both cases we find some evidence that trade liberalization affected the relevant variables (compliance with minimum wage laws in the first case, employment in the informal sector in the second case), but in both cases the direction of the effect suggests that trade liberalization should have led to an increase in poverty. Thus, it seems safe to conclude that the poverty reduction we observe between 1986 and 1994 cannot be attributed to trade-policy-induced changes in informality or to minimum wage compliance.

6.5.5   Trade Policy and Poverty: A Direct Assessment

Our empirical analysis so far has failed to find any strong link between the Colombian trade liberalization and variables that could be related to the poverty reduction between 1986 and 1994. This is consistent with the results in table 6.6 that show that the poverty reduction occurred mostly through within-group changes in poverty rates rather than movement of people between groups, regardless of whether the groups are defined in terms of employment, informality, or compliance with minimum wage laws. What remains as a residual explanation is the possibility that trade liberalization affected poverty by directly affecting worker wages.

In earlier work (Goldberg and Pavcnik 2005; Attanasio, Goldberg, and Pavcnik 2004) we have examined the impact of the Colombian trade liberalization on *relative* wages and found that the trade reforms have contributed to an *increase* in relative wage dispersion. This evidence was based on analyzing the response of industry wage premia to the tariff declines; specifically, our work showed that industry wage premia declined more in sectors that experienced the largest tariff cuts. Given that these sectors were sectors that had lower wage premia prior to the trade reforms and employed a higher share of unskilled workers (in industries like textiles and apparel, footwear, wood and wood products), the decline in the wage premia further widened the gap between the rich and poor.[25] Furthermore, our work found some suggestive evidence that the well-documented increase in the economy-wide skill premium over that period could be partly due to

25. The terms *skilled* and *unskilled* were defined based on education. In particular, we define as "unskilled" workers who have at most primary education.

the trade reforms. In particular, we documented that the largest increases in the share of skilled workers in each sector occurred in the sectors that had the largest tariff cuts. Hence, there are indications that the skill-biased technological change may have been in part induced, or at a minimum reinforced, by the trade reforms.

Given these previous results on the effects of the trade reforms on relative wages, trade liberalization would have had to have a large positive effect on *absolute* wages in order to reduce poverty. As we pointed out in the introduction, this effect would have been most likely realized through growth. However, the effect of trade policy changes on aggregate growth cannot be identified, as they cannot be separated from other policy changes and events that may have concurrently affected growth.

We therefore resort to the same partial equilibrium identification strategy we used in the earlier exercises to examine whether the trade policy changes can be directly linked to changes in the poverty rates by sector of employment. This identification strategy relies on the fact that the tariff reductions in the Colombian trade reforms affected industries differentially. Given our earlier results, we would be surprised if we found any effects. Nevertheless, examining the link between trade liberalization and poverty reduction in a direct way serves as a check that we haven't missed any other important channels through which the trade reforms may have affected poverty at the industry level.

In table 6.11, we regress an indicator for whether an employed individual is poor on individual characteristics, two-digit ISIC industry dummies, year dummies, and trade exposure measures.[26] While we do not find any *robust* evidence regarding the effects of tariff declines on poverty, higher imports are associated with higher poverty rates at the sectoral level, while higher exports are associated with lower poverty rates (although the latter results depend in part on the poverty line we use). Furthermore, we find that, conditional on imports and exports, lower tariffs are associated with a higher probability of being poor when the lower poverty lines ($1, $2, and $3 per day) are used.

This evidence on the direct relationship between trade liberalization and poverty among the employed at the sectoral level is consistent with our earlier findings concerning the effects on informality and minimum wage compliance, and most likely partly driven by them. In all cases the empirical analysis suggests that either trade liberalization had no effects on poverty, or—to the extent that it had any—these effects went in the direction of increasing poverty.

---

26. For a discussion of the analysis of the same relationship for unemployed individuals, see end of section 6.5.2.

Table 6.11 Poverty and trade exposure among employed individuals

	$1	$2	$3	$4	$5	$7	$1	$2	$3	$4	$5	$7
Tariff	−0.007	−0.008	−0.011	−0.005	0.01	0.021*	−0.00822*	−0.01042*	−0.01900**	−.015	.002	.018
	(0.167)	(0.199)	(0.131)	(0.537)	(0.217)	(0.086)	(0.097)	(0.088)	(0.026)	(0.203)	(0.889)	(0.419)
Lagged imports							0.00001**	0.00002***	0.00002	0.00003***	0.00006**	0.00008**
							(0.018)	(0.001)	(0.158)	(0.002)	(0.012)	(0.032)
Lagged exports							−0.00002	−0.00004	−0.00009**	−0.00012*	−0.00012*	−0.00008
							(0.482)	(0.300)	(0.014)	(0.089)	(0.091)	(0.516)
Year indicators	Yes	Yes	Yes	Yes	Yes	Yes	Yes	Yes	Yes	Yes	Yes	Yes
Industry indicators	Yes	Yes	Yes	Yes	Yes	Yes	Yes	Yes	Yes	Yes	Yes	Yes
R^2	0.022	0.057	0.099	0.138	0.171	0.217	0.022	0.057	0.099	0.138	0.171	0.217
No. of observations	97,798	97,798	97,798	97,798	97,798	97,798	97,798	97,798	97,798	97,798	97,798	97,798

Notes: p-values based on standard errors that are clustered on industry are reported in parentheses. Column heads indicate the poverty line used to create the poverty indicator in a given column. All regressions also include controls for age, age squared, gender, whether a person is married, head of the household, education indicators, household size, literacy indicator, whether a person lives in Bogota, occupation indicators, type of employer indicators, whether a person was born in urban area, time in current residency, and the interaction of urban birth with time in current residency. Number of observations refers to number of employed individuals that had nonmissing household income (and thus nonmissing measure of poverty).

***Significant at the 1 percent level.

**Significant at the 5 percent level.

*Significant at the 10 percent level.

6.6   Conclusions

Between 1985 and 1995 Colombia experienced massive trade liberalization. At the same time urban poverty declined by approximately 10 percent. The chronological coincidence of trade liberalization and poverty reduction raises the question of whether the former has contributed to the latter. In this paper we have tried to establish a link between the trade reforms and the changes in urban poverty, approaching the task from many different angles.

To summarize our findings, we fail to find evidence of such a link. Our descriptive results establish that poverty in urban areas is highly correlated with unemployment, employment in the informal sector, and noncompliance with minimum wages. The poverty rates among the employed also differ by industry, suggesting a potential role of industry affiliation in explaining poverty. However, we find no evidence that the trade reforms impacted any of the above variables in a significant way. To the extent that we find any effects, the effects are small and go in the wrong direction, suggesting that the trade reforms may have contributed to an increase in urban poverty. Perhaps more surprisingly, we find that most of the reduction in urban poverty between 1986 and 1994 is accounted for by within-group changes in poverty rather than movements of people out of groups with high poverty rates, such as the unemployed, informal-sector workers, and below minimum wage earners. Given these patterns, it is not surprising that we also fail to find any evidence of a direct link between the trade reforms and the poverty reductions by sector.

These results contrast with the ones reported in chapter 7 in this volume by Petia Topalova, who examines the effects of the Indian trade liberalization on poverty and finds that trade liberalization led to an increase in poverty in those regions that were more affected by the trade reforms. What accounts for the difference between the two sets of results? Before we try to answer this question it is worth noting the many similarities between the two papers in terms of methodological approach. Both papers use microdata to investigate the impact of trade reforms; both papers exploit plausibly exogenous variation in trade policy, measured by sizable tariff reductions; and finally, both papers exploit the fact that the tariff reductions differed by sector. In the Topalova paper this differential tariff reduction by sector translates into regional variation in the degree of trade liberalization given that different sectors are concentrated in different regions of the country, and she exploits the latter to identify the effects of the trade policy reform. Note also that both studies focus on a trade policy experiment (tariff reductions) whose immediate effect is to intensify import competition rather than expanding exports. Given these similarities, it is not surprising that the two papers yield similar results regarding many issues, such

as the extent of labor mobility (which in both cases is documented to be low) and the decrease of relative wages in sectors or regions that were hit harder by the tariff declines. Yet the two studies differ in their findings regarding the effect of increased openness on poverty.

While the reasons for this difference cannot be pinned down with certainty without further investigation, the most plausible explanation hinges on the differential impact of the two liberalization episodes on agriculture. Agricultural trade liberalization in Colombia was limited; given that most of the poor are concentrated in the rural areas, it is not a surprise that their fates were not altered (at least not in the short run) by a trade liberalization wave that affected mostly the manufacturing sector in the urban areas. In contrast, the Indian trade liberalization included significant tariff reductions in the agricultural sector, which are explicitly accounted for in Topalova's comprehensive study. Interestingly, Topalova documents that the poverty increase was concentrated in rural areas and agricultural sectors. The results of the two papers taken together seem thus to suggest that liberalization of the *agricultural* sector may have a significant effect on poverty in the short and medium run. There will certainly be many opportunities to put this claim to the test in the near future as many developed countries consider reforming their domestic agricultural policies in ways that would certainly impact the developing world. Furthermore, Topalova's results indicate that the issue of labor mobility may be a first-order concern when it comes to assessing the effects of trade liberalization on poverty; one of the reasons that people in areas affected by tariff reductions become poorer is that they do not move to regions or sectors that are better off. Similarly, in the case of Colombia, the decline of relative wages of unskilled workers is partly explained by the fact that these workers do not move quickly enough to industries with higher wages. Taking measures to increase labor mobility could potentially ease adjustment to trade reforms and mitigate some of the potentially adverse effects of trade liberalization in the short and medium run.

We are still left with the question of how to explain the Colombian poverty decline between 1986 and 1994. The residual explanation left to us is that there was an economy-wide increase in absolute wages, pronounced enough to compensate for the worsening of the relative position of individuals at the left tail of the income distribution. Whether this increase was brought about through the trade reforms is a question we cannot answer, given that the trade policy changes coincide with other reforms (c.g., labor market reform) and other events that may have also affected wages. But it seems fair to conclude that to the extent trade liberalization had any role at all in the decline of poverty during that period, this was through the operation of general equilibrium effects, the potential effects of lower tariffs on the prices of consumer goods, and the potential impact of free trade on growth.

Appendix

Table 6A.1   **Correlation of per capita household income measures based on different adult equivalency scales**

	α = 1, θ = 1	α = 0.75, θ = 1	α = 0.5, θ = 1	α = 1, θ = .75	α = 0.75, θ = .75	α = 0.5, θ = .75	α = 1, θ = .5	α = 0.75, θ = .5	α = 0.5, θ = .5	OECD
α = 1, θ = 1	1.00									
α = 0.75, θ = 1	1.00	1.00								
α = 0.5, θ = 1	.99	1.00	1.00							
α = 1, θ = .75	.98	.99	.99	1.00						
α = 0.75, θ = .75	.98	.98	.99	1.00	1.00					
α = 0.5, θ = .75	.97	.98	.98	1.00	1.00	1.00				
α = 1, θ = .5	.93	.94	.94	.98	.99	.99	1.00			
α = 0.75, θ = .5	.93	.94	.94	.98	.98	.99	1.00	1.00		
α = 0.5, θ = .5	.92	.93	.94	.98	.98	.99	1.00	1.00	1.00	
OECD	.99	.99	.99	1.00	1.00	1.00	.97	.97	.97	1.00

Table 6A.2   **Sensitivity of head count ratios to adult-equivalency scales**

α	θ	1984	1986	1988	1990	1992	1994	1996	1998
		A. $1-per-day poverty line							
1	1	.025	.025	.018	.014	.018	.011	.022	.028
0.75	1	.021	.023	.016	.012	.015	.010	.020	.024
0.5	1	.019	.020	.013	.011	.013	.009	.018	.022
1	0.75	.016	.018	.011	.010	.012	.008	.017	.019
0.75	0.75	.015	.017	.011	.009	.011	.008	.015	.019
0.5	0.75	.014	.015	.010	.008	.010	.007	.014	.017
1	0.5	.012	.014	.009	.007	.009	.007	.014	.015
0.75	0.5	.012	.013	.009	.007	.009	.007	.013	.015
0.5	0.5	.012	.013	.009	.006	.008	.007	.013	.014
OECD		.017	.018	.011	.010	.011	.008	.017	.020
		B. $2-per-day poverty line							
1	1	.069	.067	.057	.051	.058	.037	.055	.073
0.75	1	.054	.055	.043	.038	.043	.028	.045	.058
0.5	1	.041	.042	.034	.026	.035	.020	.038	.048
1	0.75	.032	.035	.028	.020	.027	.016	.031	.036
0.75	0.75	.029	.031	.023	.017	.024	.014	.027	.033
0.5	0.75	.025	.027	.020	.015	.019	.013	.024	.030
1	0.5	.021	.023	.016	.013	.015	.011	.021	.025
0.75	0.5	.020	.022	.015	.013	.014	.011	.020	.024
0.5	0.5	.018	.020	.013	.012	.013	.010	.019	.023
OECD		.034	.035	.028	.020	.027	.016	.031	.038

Table 6A.3 Poverty and household head characteristics for households with employed head ($1- and $2-per-day poverty line)

	$1-a-day poverty line					$2-a-day poverty line				
	(1)	(2)	(3)	(4)	(5)	(1)	(2)	(3)	(4)	(5)
Agriculture and hunting	-0.0018 (0.824)	-0.0006 (0.942)	0.004 (0.624)	0.0122 (0.140)	0.0122 (0.143)	-0.0293** (0.035)	-0.0269* (0.054)	-0.0135 (0.301)	0.0008 (0.957)	-0.0007 (0.957)
Forestry and logging	-0.0368 (0.500)	-0.0304 (0.577)	-0.00205 (0.700)	-0.0135 (0.804)	-0.0127 (0.814)	-0.1208 (0.189)	-0.1055 (0.250)	-0.0767 (0.371)	-0.0708 (0.436)	-0.0693 (0.446)
Fishing	-0.0401 (0.503)	-0.0434 (0.467)	-0.0425 (0.465)	-0.0488 (0.411)	-0.0492 (0.407)	0.0689 (0.494)	0.0596 (0.553)	0.0629 (0.503)	0.0504 (0.613)	0.0479 (0.631)
Coal mining	-0.0269 (0.369)	-0.0179 (0.551)	-0.01 (0.734)	-0.0073 (0.807)	-0.0053 (0.859)	-0.0894* (0.077)	-0.0676 (0.180)	-0.0451 (0.339)	-0.0474 (0.343)	-0.0419 (0.403)
Petroleum and natural gas	-0.0209 (0.372)	-0.0162 (0.489)	-0.0034 (0.883)	-0.0018 (0.939)	-0.0014 (0.952)	-0.0710* (0.072)	-0.0596 (0.130)	-0.0235 (0.523)	-0.0301 (0.442)	-0.0294 (0.452)
Metal ore mining	-0.0251 (0.791)	-0.0283 (0.764)	-0.0017 (0.985)	0.0015 (0.988)	-0.0013 (0.989)	-0.0927 (0.561)	-0.1014 (0.523)	-0.0268 (0.857)	-0.0358 (0.820)	-0.0461 (0.770)
Other mining	0.0715** (0.020)	0.027 (0.392)	0.0173 (0.574)	0.0850*** (0.005)	0.036 (0.251)	0.0435 (0.401)	0.0096 (0.856)	-0.0172 (0.730)	0.0724 (0.158)	0.0281 (0.593)
Food	-0.0214*** (0.001)	-0.0140** (0.029)	-0.0073 (0.246)	-0.0036 (0.578)	-0.0021 (0.745)	-0.0562*** (0.000)	-0.0384*** (0.000)	-0.0192** (0.060)	-0.0181* (0.094)	-0.014 (0.198)
Textile, apparel, leather	-0.0209*** (0.000)	-0.0167*** (0.001)	-0.0125** (0.011)	-0.0084* (0.095)	-0.0077 (0.130)	-0.0623*** (0.000)	-0.0532*** (0.000)	-0.0414*** (0.000)	-0.0355*** (0.000)	-0.0348*** (0.000)
Wood	-0.0157* (0.057)	-0.0152* (0.067)	-0.0101 (0.213)	-0.005 (0.546)	-0.005 (0.527)	-0.0459*** (0.001)	-0.0448*** (0.001)	-0.0302** (0.021)	-0.0229* (0.098)	-0.0244* (0.079)
Paper	0.0013 (0.904)	0.0092 (0.413)	0.0158 (0.149)	0.0179 (0.110)	0.0196* (0.080)	-0.0522*** (0.006)	-0.0332* (0.079)	-0.0143 (0.419)	-0.0168 (0.371)	-0.0119 (0.526)
Chemical	-0.0128 (0.151)	-0.0014 (0.874)	0.0044 (0.617)	0.006 (0.506)	0.0089 (0.327)	-0.0545*** (0.000)	-0.0268* (0.079)	-0.0101 (0.479)	-0.0146 (0.330)	-0.0059 (0.698)

(continued)

Table 6A.3 (continued)

	$1-a-day poverty line					$2-a-day poverty line				
	(1)	(2)	(3)	(4)	(5)	(1)	(2)	(3)	(4)	(5)
Non-metallic mineral products	-0.0168	-0.0074	-0.0056	0.0022	0.0044	-0.0344*	-0.0112	-0.0057	0.0064	0.013
	(0.120)	(0.497)	(0.598)	(0.837)	(0.688)	(0.059)	(0.543)	(0.740)	(0.726)	(0.478)
Basic metal industry	-0.0278	-0.0197	-0.0129	-0.0107	-0.009	-0.0684**	-0.0489	-0.0293	-0.0319	-0.0269
	(0.172)	(0.331)	(0.516)	(0.596)	(0.658)	(0.046)	(0.152)	(0.359)	(0.346)	(0.428)
Machinery and equipment	-0.0187***	-0.011	-0.0029	-0.0012	0.0004	-0.0664***	-0.0479***	-0.0249**	-0.0290**	-0.0245**
	(0.008)	(0.122)	(0.673)	(0.865)	(0.954)	(0.000)	(0.000)	(0.026)	(0.015)	(0.041)
Other manufacturing	-0.0123	-0.0112	-0.0088	-0.0098	-0.0095	-0.0517*	-0.0497*	-0.0425*	-0.0464*	-0.0462*
	(0.441)	(0.480)	(0.573)	(0.536)	(0.547)	(0.054)	(0.063)	(0.090)	(0.081)	(0.082)
Electricity, gas, steam	-0.0225	-0.0113	-0.0042	-0.0026	0.0001	-0.0602**	-0.0327	-0.0124	-0.0176	-0.0096
	(0.130)	(0.449)	(0.774)	(0.863)	(0.996)	(0.016)	(0.191)	(0.596)	(0.479)	(0.701)
Water works and supply	-0.0286	-0.0169	-0.0062	-0.0068	-0.0042	-0.0415	-0.0129	0.0178	0.0049	0.013
	(0.174)	(0.423)	(0.763)	(0.744)	(0.841)	(0.241)	(0.717)	(0.592)	(0.889)	(0.711)
Construction	-0.0173***	-0.0166***	-0.0115**	-0.0092*	-0.0093*	-0.0446***	-0.0444***	-0.0304***	-0.0274***	-0.0296***
	(0.000)	(0.001)	(0.014)	(0.054)	(0.052)	(0.000)	(0.000)	(0.000)	(0.001)	(0.000)
Wholesale trade	-0.0104	-0.0049	0.0038	0.0018	0.0029	-0.0586**	-0.0453*	-0.0207	-0.0325	-0.0294
	(0.496)	(0.750)	(0.800)	(0.907)	(0.848)	(0.023)	(0.078)	(0.388)	(0.202)	(0.249)
Restaurants and hotels	-0.0118*	-0.0106*	-0.0086	0.0001	-0.0002	-0.0334***	-0.0311***	-0.0218**	-0.0081	-0.099
	(0.064)	(0.097)	(0.169)	(0.993)	(0.974)	(0.002)	(0.004)	(0.031)	(0.454)	(0.358)
Transport and storage	-0.0100**	-0.0079*	-0.0001	-0.0018	-0.0015	-0.0473***	-0.0427***	-0.0203***	-0.0297***	-0.0296***
	(0.031)	(0.089)	(0.983)	(0.702)	(0.747)	(0.000)	(0.000)	(0.006)	(0.000)	(0.000)
Communication	-0.0223	-0.0136	-0.0037	-0.0022	-0.0005	-0.0686**	-0.0473*	-0.0193	-0.0256	-0.0205
	(0.191)	(0.426)	(0.824)	(0.897)	(0.978)	(0.017)	(0.099)	(0.473)	(0.369)	(0.472)
Financial institutions	-0.0196**	-0.0073	-0.0012	-0.0006	0.0024	-0.0609***	-0.0305*	-0.0133	-0.0203	-0.0107
	(0.032)	(0.434)	(0.894)	(0.948)	(0.792)	(0.000)	(0.051)	(0.365)	(0.187)	(0.493)
Insurance	-0.022	-0.0122	-0.0051	-0.0069	-0.0046	-0.0614*	-0.0373	-0.0168	-0.0292	-0.0218
	(0.297)	(0.567)	(0.807)	(0.740)	(0.827)	(0.084)	(0.299)	(0.617)	(0.407)	(0.541)

	(1)	(2)	(3)	(4)	(5)	(6)	(7)	(8)	(9)	(10)
Real estate and business	−0.0211***	−0.0157**	−0.0101	−0.0116*	−0.0102	−0.0647***	−0.0519***	−0.0359***	−0.0444***	−0.0408***
	(0.002)	(0.024)	(0.138)	(0.092)	(0.140)	(0.000)	(0.000)	(0.001)	(0.000)	(0.000)
Public administration	−0.0237***	−0.0144**	−0.0023	−0.0035	−0.0016	−0.0706***	−0.0479***	−0.0138	−0.0275***	−0.0218**
	(0.000)	(0.020)	(0.699)	(0.566)	(0.797)	(0.000)	(0.000)	(0.156)	(0.008)	(0.037)
Sanity	−0.0299	−0.0174	−0.0066	−0.0083	−0.0053	−0.0955***	−0.0650*	−0.0342	−0.0493	−0.0403
	(0.155)	(0.407)	(0.747)	(0.693)	(0.800)	(0.007)	(0.066)	(0.302)	(0.160)	(0.252)
Social and community services	−0.0216***	−0.0123**	−0.0045	−0.0029	−0.0009	−0.0609***	−0.0380***	−0.0160*	−0.0208**	−0.0147
	(0.000)	(0.026)	(0.402)	(0.601)	(0.877)	(0.000)	(0.000)	(0.066)	(0.024)	(0.116)
Recreation and culture	−0.0099	−0.0046	−0.0006	0.0058	0.0068	−0.0475***	−0.0348*	−0.0232	−0.0138	−0.0115
	(0.358)	(0.674)	(0.958)	(0.591)	(0.528)	(0.009)	(0.057)	(0.175)	(0.445)	(0.528)
Household and personal services	0.0049	0.0037	−0.0002	0.0091**	0.0086*	0.004	0.0004	−0.0104	0.0138*	0.0103
	(0.269)	(0.400)	(0.965)	(0.040)	(0.054)	(0.593)	(0.956)	(0.140)	(0.080)	(0.167)
International bodies	−0.0243	−0.0095	0.0026	−0.0011	0.0025	−0.0585	−0.0219	0.0129	−0.0087	0.0026
	(0.752)	(0.902)	(0.972)	(0.989)	(0.974)	(0.653)	(0.866)	(0.915)	(0.946)	(0.984)
Family worker				0.0814**	0.0785**				0.2146***	0.2047***
				(0.042)	(0.050)				(0.001)	(0.002)
Self-employed				0.0392***	0.0365***				0.0837***	0.0746***
				(0.000)	(0.000)				(0.000)	(0.000)
Informal	0.0197***		0.0091***		0.0068**	0.0492***	0.0198***		0.0229***	
	(0.000)		(0.001)		(0.019)	(0.000)	(0.000)		(0.000)	
Paid below minimum wage			0.0723***				0.2030***			
			(0.000)				(0.000)			
R^2	.017	.020	.063	.031	.031	.058	.066	.179	.080	.082
No. of observations	13,035	12,943	12,932	13,035	12,943	13,035	12,943	12,932	13,035	12,943

Note: See notes to table 6.3.

***Significant at the 1 percent level.

**Significant at the 5 percent level.

*Significant at the 10 percent level.

Table 6A.4 Poverty and household head characteristics for households with employed heads ($5- and $7-per-day poverty line)

	$5-a-day poverty line					$7-a-day poverty line				
	(1)	(2)	(3)	(4)	(5)	(1)	(2)	(3)	(4)	(5)
Agriculture and hunting	-0.0066	-0.0098	0.0154	0.0299	0.0218	-0.0293	-0.0309	-0.009	-0.0001	-0.0072
	(0.805)	(0.714)	(0.540)	(0.262)	(0.417)	(0.279)	(0.256)	(0.730)	(0.998)	(0.792)
Forestry and logging	0.0221	0.04	0.0947	0.0828	0.0838	-0.1113	-0.0941	-0.0472	-0.0626	-0.0613
	(0.900)	(0.820)	(0.566)	(0.636)	(0.633)	(0.534)	(0.599)	(0.783)	(0.726)	(0.731)
Fishing	-0.0888	-0.1008	-0.0951	-0.1113	-0.1149	-0.016	-0.0273	-0.0219	-0.0339	-0.0378
	(0.645)	(0.601)	(0.599)	(0.562)	(0.549)	(0.935)	(0.889)	(0.907)	(0.862)	(0.847)
Coal mining	-0.1778*	-0.1518	-0.1092	-0.1268	-0.1207	-0.065	-0.0397	-0.0031	-0.0241	-0.0164
	(0.066)	(0.116)	(0.228)	(0.188)	(0.211)	(0.509)	(0.686)	(0.973)	(0.806)	(0.867)
Petroleum and natural gas	-0.1637**	-0.1499**	-0.081	-0.114	-0.1133	-0.1876**	-0.1742**	-0.1153	-0.1477*	-0.1468*
	(0.030)	(0.047)	(0.253)	(0.130)	(0.133)	(0.015)	(0.023)	(0.117)	(0.054)	(0.056)
Metal ore mining	-0.4671	-0.4772	-0.3349	-0.398	-0.4103	-0.1367	-0.1471	-0.0259	-0.0813	-0.097
	(0.125)	(0.117)	(0.241)	(0.190)	(0.176)	(0.659)	(0.635)	(0.931)	(0.793)	(0.754)
Other mining	0.3441***	0.3538***	0.3020***	0.3792***	0.3763***	0.1780*	0.1875*	0.1442	0.2062**	0.2043**
	(0.001)	(0.001)	(0.002)	(0.000)	(0.000)	(0.078)	(0.070)	(0.146)	(0.041)	(0.048)
Food	-0.0730***	-0.0519**	-0.0152	-0.0267	-0.0223	-0.0393*	-0.0213	0.0102	-0.0022	0.0008
	(0.000)	(0.013)	(0.435)	(0.200)	(0.287)	(0.059)	(0.315)	(0.614)	(0.916)	(0.969)
Textile, apparel, leather	-0.0496***	-0.0369**	-0.0143	-0.0171	-0.0146	0.0127	0.0257	0.0452***	0.0389**	0.0424**
	(0.002)	(0.023)	(0.347)	(0.296)	(0.373)	(0.438)	(0.120)	(0.004)	(0.020)	(0.011)
Wood	0.0137	0.0168	0.0445*	0.0417	0.0414	0.0124	0.0139	0.0379	0.0349	0.0324
	(0.607)	(0.530)	(0.076)	(0.117)	(0.122)	(0.647)	(0.608)	(0.146)	(0.199)	(0.235)
Paper	-0.1134***	-0.0905**	-0.0545	-0.0704*	-0.0647*	-0.1126***	-0.0903**	-0.0593**	-0.0781**	-0.0710*
	(0.002)	(0.013)	(0.109)	(0.052)	(0.074)	(0.002)	(0.014)	(0.093)	(0.034)	(0.055)
Chemical	-0.0580**	-0.0209	0.0078	-0.0095	0.0043	-0.0511*	-0.0133	0.0119	-0.0124	0.0054
	(0.043)	(0.474)	(0.775)	(0.743)	(0.882)	(0.080)	(0.655)	(0.677)	(0.674)	(0.856)
Non-metallic mineral products	0.0383	0.0698**	0.0799**	0.0879**	0.0990***	0.0896**	0.1156***	0.1246***	0.1293***	0.1374***
	(0.272)	(0.048)	(0.016)	(0.012)	(0.005)	(0.012)	(0.001)	(0.000)	(0.000)	(0.000)

Basic metal industry	0.0073	0.0306	0.0679	0.0516	0.0573	0.0034	0.026	0.058	0.0389	0.0459
	(0.912)	(0.640)	(0.269)	(0.430)	(0.381)	(0.959)	(0.696)	(0.363)	(0.558)	(0.490)
Machinery and equipment	-0.0612***	-0.0382*	0.0055	-0.0158	-0.01	-0.02	0.0019	0.0394*	0.0164	0.0231
	(0.007)	(0.096)	(0.800)	(0.490)	(0.666)	(0.386)	(0.934)	(0.079)	(0.482)	(0.327)
Other manufacturing	-0.0646	-0.0621	-0.0484	-0.0581	-0.0578	-0.0432	-0.0406	-0.0285	-0.0379	-0.0373
	(0.209)	(0.227)	(0.315)	(0.257)	(0.259)	(0.410)	(0.437)	(0.569)	(0.468)	(0.474)
Electricity, gas, steam	-0.0854*	-0.0523	-0.0138	-0.0337	-0.0243	-0.0351	-0.0031	0.0301	0.0064	0.0179
	(0.074)	(0.276)	(0.760)	(0.481)	(0.612)	(0.471)	(0.950)	(0.520)	(0.895)	(0.715)
Water works and supply	-0.0603	-0.0257	0.0328	-0.0038	0.0055	-0.0324	0.001	0.051	0.0128	0.0244
	(0.473)	(0.704)	(0.607)	(0.955)	(0.935)	(0.638)	(0.989)	(0.440)	(0.853)	(0.724)
Construction	0.0096	0.0084	0.0351**	0.0306**	0.0263*	0.0559***	0.0563***	0.0801***	0.0726***	0.0696***
	(0.530)	(0.585)	(0.015)	(0.047)	(0.089)	(0.000)	(0.000)	(0.000)	(0.000)	(0.000)
Wholesale trade	-0.1121**	-0.0960*	-0.0492	-0.0805	-0.0768	-0.0941*	-0.0784	-0.0382	-0.0688	-0.064
	(0.023)	(0.051)	(0.287)	(0.101)	(0.118)	(0.060)	(0.118)	(0.426)	(0.170)	(0.201)
Restaurants and hotels	-0.0196	-0.016	0.003	0.0112	0.0096	0.0059	0.009	0.026	0.0305	0.0281
	(0.343)	(0.439)	(0.879)	(0.589)	(0.644)	(0.778)	(0.668)	(0.197)	(0.149)	(0.186)
Transport and storage	-0.0652***	-0.0607***	-0.0179	-0.0437***	-0.0447***	-0.0398***	-0.0354**	0.0013	-0.0225	-0.0234
	(0.000)	(0.000)	(0.204)	(0.004)	(0.003)	(0.009)	(0.021)	(0.928)	(0.141)	(0.127)
Communication	-0.1759***	-0.1501***	-0.0966*	-0.1237**	-0.1178**	-0.1018*	-0.0768	-0.031	-0.06	-0.0526
	(0.001)	(0.006)	(0.061)	(0.024)	(0.032)	(0.069)	(0.170)	(0.563)	(0.284)	(0.348)
Financial institutions	-0.1451***	-0.1063***	-0.0735***	-0.0959***	-0.0823***	-0.1083***	-0.0686**	-0.0404	-0.0688**	-0.0506*
	(0.000)	(0.000)	(0.009)	(0.001)	(0.006)	(0.000)	(0.025)	(0.168)	(0.023)	(0.098)
Insurance	-0.1111	-0.0758	-0.0368	-0.0719	-0.0571	-0.1744**	-0.1370*	-0.1035	-0.1431**	-0.1230*
	(0.102)	(0.271)	(0.569)	(0.288)	(0.405)	(0.012)	(0.050)	(0.123)	(0.038)	(0.079)
Real estate and business	-0.0192	-0.0048	0.0255	0.0053	0.0086	0.0233	0.0351	0.0612***	0.0430**	0.0451**
	(0.387)	(0.831)	(0.226)	(0.810)	(0.701)	(0.304)	(0.125)	(0.005)	(0.058)	(0.048)
Public administration	-0.1120***	-0.0846***	-0.0195	-0.0596***	-0.0530***	-0.0241	0.0012	-0.0568***	0.0179	0.0249
	(0.000)	(0.000)	(0.299)	(0.003)	(0.009)	(0.224)	(0.953)	(0.004)	(0.380)	(0.226)
Sanity	0.0429	0.0795	0.1384**	0.099	0.1094	0.1289*	0.1644**	0.2147***	0.1739**	0.1868***
	(0.527)	(0.242)	(0.030)	(0.143)	(0.106)	(0.062)	(0.017)	(0.001)	(0.012)	(0.007)

(continued)

Table 6A.4   (continued)

	$5-a-day poverty line					$7-a-day poverty line				
	(1)	(2)	(3)	(4)	(5)	(1)	(2)	(3)	(4)	(5)
Social and community services	-0.0750***	-0.0479***	-0.0059	-0.0263	-0.0197	-0.0632***	-0.0373**	-0.0013	-0.0241	-0.0162
	(0.000)	(0.007)	(0.723)	(0.139)	(0.273)	(0.000)	(0.039)	(0.938)	(0.182)	(0.376)
Recreation and culture	-0.0596*	-0.0407	-0.0187	-0.0187	-0.0124	-0.0608*	-0.0403	-0.0212	-0.028	-0.0192
	(0.087)	(0.246)	(0.571)	(0.592)	(0.723)	(0.086)	(0.258)	(0.534)	(0.431)	(0.592)
Household and personal services	0.0681***	0.0638***	0.0429***	0.0790***	0.0757***	0.0814***	0.0777***	0.0605***	0.0902***	0.0868***
	(0.000)	(0.000)	(0.001)	(0.000)	(0.000)	(0.000)	(0.000)	(0.000)	(0.000)	(0.000)
International bodies	0.1997	0.2438	0.3106	0.2602	0.2734	0.1292	0.172	0.2289	0.1777	0.194
	(0.422)	(0.326)	(0.183)	(0.294)	(0.270)	(0.610)	(0.497)	(0.345)	(0.482)	(0.442)
Family worker				0.2643**	0.2521*				0.2537*	0.2388*
				(0.041)	(0.052)				(0.055)	(0.070)
Self-employed				0.1016***	0.0902***				0.0814***	0.0674***
				(0.000)	(0.000)				(0.000)	(0.000)
Informal		0.0590***	0.0026		0.0273***		0.0570***	0.0092		0.0332***
		(0.000)	(0.757)		(0.004)		(0.000)	(0.289)		(0.001)
Paid below minimum wage			0.3889***					0.3292***		
			(0.000)					(0.000)		
R^2	.192	.196	.292	.200	.201	.233	.236	.299	.238	.239
No. of observations	13,035	12,943	12,932	13,035	12,943	13,035	12,943	12,932	13,035	12,943

Note: See notes to table 6.3.

***Significant at the 1 percent level.

**Significant at the 5 percent level.

*Significant at the 10 percent level.

Table 6A.5   Poverty and household head characteristics for households with employed head (bottom 10 and 20 percent)

	Bottom 10%					Bottom 20%				
	(1)	(2)	(3)	(4)	(5)	(1)	(2)	(3)	(4)	(5)
Agriculture and hunting	−0.0335*	−0.0332*	−0.0148	0.0056	0.0005	−0.0137	−0.0187	0.0063	0.0278	0.0159
	(0.053)	(0.055)	(0.356)	(0.745)	(0.979)	(0.539)	(0.402)	(0.759)	(0.213)	(0.478)
Forestry and logging	−0.1807	−0.1604	−0.1209	−0.1157	−0.1138	0.1996	0.2223	0.2763**	0.2686*	0.2703*
	(0.114)	(0.159)	(0.250)	(0.306)	(0.313)	(0.177)	(0.131)	(0.040)	(0.067)	(0.065)
Fishing	0.009	−0.0034	0.0013	−0.0149	−0.0184	0.0904	0.0758	0.0818	0.0649	0.0603
	(0.943)	(0.978)	(0.991)	(0.904)	(0.882)	(0.576)	(0.638)	(0.578)	(0.686)	(0.707)
Coal mining	−0.0808	−0.0516	−0.0207	−0.0262	−0.0186	−0.1712**	−0.1384*	−0.0963	−0.1131	−0.1043
	(0.198)	(0.410)	(0.720)	(0.673)	(0.765)	(0.035)	(0.087)	(0.192)	(0.160)	(0.195)
Petroleum and natural gas	−0.1043**	−0.0888*	−0.0392	−0.051	−0.0499	−0.1138*	−0.0965	−0.0286	−0.0572	−0.0564
	(0.034)	(0.069)	(0.385)	(0.293)	(0.304)	(0.073)	(0.127)	(0.620)	(0.363)	(0.370)
Metal ore mining	−0.1607	−0.1719	−0.0701	−0.0867	−0.1008	−0.2751	−0.2884	−0.1488	−0.1965	−0.2151
	(0.417)	(0.383)	(0.700)	(0.658)	(0.606)	(0.282)	(0.258)	(0.523)	(0.438)	(0.396)
Other mining	0.0902	0.067	0.0304	0.1278**	0.0909	0.1778**	0.1694**	0.1188	0.2177***	0.1940**
	(0.162)	(0.309)	(0.617)	(0.045)	(0.164)	(0.033)	(0.047)	(0.127)	(0.008)	(0.022)
Food	−0.0638***	−0.0399***	−0.0133	−0.0143	−0.0085	−0.0758***	−0.0485***	−0.0123	−0.0231	−0.0161
	(0.000)	(0.003)	(0.283)	(0.288)	(0.529)	(0.000)	(0.005)	(0.440)	(0.184)	(0.358)
Textile, apparel, leather	−0.0731***	−0.0604***	−0.0439***	−0.0381***	−0.0367***	−0.0896***	−0.0750***	−0.0527***	−0.0526***	−0.0506***
	(0.000)	(0.000)	(0.000)	(0.000)	(0.001)	(0.000)	(0.000)	(0.000)	(0.000)	(0.000)
Wood	−0.0549***	−0.5030***	−0.0328**	−0.0249	−0.0268	−0.0725***	−0.0728***	−0.0454**	−0.0406*	−0.0458**
	(0.002)	(0.002)	(0.040)	(0.147)	(0.121)	(0.001)	(0.001)	(0.027)	(0.068)	(0.041)
Paper	−0.0821***	−0.0565**	−0.0304	−0.036	−0.0291	−0.1294***	−0.1007***	−0.0651**	−0.0804***	−0.0724**
	(0.000)	(0.016)	(0.161)	(0.123)	(0.213)	(0.000)	(0.001)	(0.019)	(0.008)	(0.017)
Chemical	−0.0574***	−0.0199	0.0032	−0.0058	0.0067	−0.0628***	−0.0194	0.0082	−0.0077	0.0082
	(0.002)	(0.293)	(0.853)	(0.755)	(0.724)	(0.009)	(0.427)	(0.714)	(0.749)	(0.738)

(continued)

Table 6A.5 (continued)

	Bottom 10%					Bottom 20%				
	(1)	(2)	(3)	(4)	(5)	(1)	(2)	(3)	(4)	(5)
Non-metallic mineral products	-0.0454** (0.046)	-0.014 (0.540)	-0.0064 (0.762)	0.0077 (0.733)	0.0171 (0.453)	-0.0615** (0.036)	-0.0254 (0.389)	-0.0153 (0.570)	-0.0051 (0.861)	0.0066 (0.823)
Basic metal industry	-0.1153*** (0.007)	-0.0894** (0.035)	-0.0624 (0.111)	-0.0679 (0.107)	-0.061 (0.147)	-0.038 (0.490)	-0.0088 (0.873)	0.028 (0.576)	0.0124 (0.820)	0.0204 (0.708)
Machinery and equipment	-0.0806*** (0.000)	-0.0580*** (0.000)	-0.0264* (0.054)	-0.0320** (0.030)	-0.0280* (0.060)	-0.0781*** (0.000)	-0.0514*** (0.007)	-0.0083 (0.635)	-0.0264 (0.167)	-0.0205 (0.288)
Other manufacturing	-0.0466 (0.164)	-0.0437 (0.189)	-0.0336 (0.274)	-0.0395 (0.231)	-0.039 (0.236)	-0.1001** (0.020)	-0.0970** (0.024)	-0.0833** (0.034)	-0.0926** (0.030)	-0.0923** (0.031)
Electricity, gas, steam	-0.0821*** (0.008)	-0.0451 (0.147)	-0.0172 (0.549)	-0.0267 (0.386)	-0.0154 (0.619)	-0.0716* (0.074)	-0.03 (0.455)	0.008 (0.826)	-0.0128 (0.749)	0.0007 (0.986)
Water works and supply	-0.0602 (0.172)	-0.0217 (0.622)	0.0205 (0.613)	0.0003 (0.995)	0.0116 (0.791)	-0.0805 (0.157)	-0.0371 (0.513)	0.0206 (0.691)	-0.0163 (0.773)	-0.0029 (0.960)
Construction	-0.0516*** (0.000)	-0.0516*** (0.000)	-0.0329*** (0.000)	-0.0293*** (0.003)	-0.0328*** (0.001)	-0.0329** (0.011)	-0.0322** (0.012)	-0.0057 (0.629)	-0.0091 (0.478)	-0.0126 (0.327)
Wholesale trade	-0.0767** (0.017)	-0.0586* (0.066)	-0.0247 (0.401)	-0.0428 (0.176)	-0.0381 (0.228)	-0.1043** (0.012)	-0.0840** (0.042)	-0.0378 (0.315)	-0.683* (0.096)	-0.063 (0.125)
Restaurants and hotels	-0.0256* (0.057)	-0.0223* (0.095)	-0.0084 (0.495)	0.0072 (0.590)	0.0047 (0.725)	-0.0357** (0.039)	-0.0321* (0.064)	-0.0125 (0.431)	-0.0007 (0.968)	-0.004 (0.816)
Transport and storage	-0.0535*** (0.000)	-0.0471*** (0.000)	-0.0161* (0.073)	-0.0305*** (0.002)	-0.0301*** (0.002)	-0.0739*** (0.000)	-0.0671*** (0.000)	-0.0249** (0.031)	-0.0494*** (0.000)	-0.0497*** (0.000)
Communication	-0.0986** (0.006)	-0.0699** (0.050)	-0.0313 (0.342)	-0.0427 (0.227)	-0.0355 (0.316)	-0.1203*** (0.009)	-0.0879* (0.056)	-0.0352 (0.403)	-0.0609 (0.184)	-0.0525 (0.253)
Financial institutions	-0.0801*** (0.000)	-0.0388** (0.046)	-0.0149 (0.405)	-0.0273 (0.152)	-0.0133 (0.493)	-0.1236*** (0.000)	-0.0766*** (0.002)	-0.0442* (0.054)	-0.0676*** (0.006)	-0.0503** (0.045)
Insurance	-0.0828* (0.061)	-0.0497 (0.265)	-0.0214 (0.603)	-0.0409 (0.348)	-0.0298 (0.500)	-0.1292** (0.023)	-0.091 (0.114)	-0.0524 (0.319)	-0.0847 (0.135)	-0.0705 (0.219)

	(1)	(2)	(3)	(4)	(5)	(6)	(7)	(8)	(9)	(10)
Real estate and business	-0.0754*** (0.000)	-0.0580*** (0.000)	-0.0359*** (0.008)	-0.0491*** (0.001)	-0.0437*** (0.003)	-0.0737*** (0.000)	-0.0533*** (0.005)	-0.0233 (0.176)	-0.0458** (0.014)	-0.0386** (0.040)
Public administration	-0.0999*** (0.000)	-0.0694*** (0.000)	-0.0225* (0.059)	-0.0439*** (0.001)	-0.0359*** (0.006)	-0.1242*** (0.000)	-0.0899*** (0.000)	-0.0258* (0.091)	-0.0647*** (0.000)	-0.0553*** (0.001)
Sanity	-0.1182*** (0.007)	-0.0775* (0.078)	-0.0351 (0.387)	-0.0581 (0.183)	-0.0457 (0.295)	-0.0509 (0.371)	-0.005 (0.930)	0.0531 (0.306)	0.13 (0.819)	0.0278 (0.623)
Social and community services	-0.0738*** (0.000)	-0.0428*** (0.000)	-0.0124 (0.245)	-0.0216* (0.059)	-0.0128 (0.269)	-0.0842*** (0.000)	-0.0491*** (0.001)	-0.0077 (0.573)	-0.0287* (0.053)	-0.0182 (0.227)
Recreation and culture	-0.0587*** (0.010)	-0.0414* (0.068)	-0.0253 (0.228)	-0.0149 (0.508)	-0.0113 (0.616)	-0.0690** (0.018)	-0.0486* (0.098)	-0.0268 (0.317)	-0.0225 (0.441)	-0.0177 (0.547)
Household and personal services	0.0154* (0.099)	0.0107 (0.249)	-0.0037 (0.665)	0.0272** (0.003)	0.0236** (0.011)	0.0527*** (0.000)	0.0469*** (0.000)	0.0267** (0.015)	0.0651*** (0.000)	0.0601*** (0.000)
International bodies	-0.0716 (0.658)	-0.0224 (0.890)	0.0257 (0.863)	-0.007 (0.965)	0.009 (0.955)	-0.0959 (0.646)	-0.0401 (0.847)	0.0258 (0.892)	-0.0271 (0.896)	-0.0077 (0.970)
Family worker				0.3476*** (0.000)	0.3338*** (0.000)				0.3113*** (0.004)	0.2933*** (0.007)
Self-employed				0.1086*** (0.000)	0.0958*** (0.000)				0.1156*** (0.000)	0.0989*** (0.000)
Informal	0.0656*** (0.000)		0.0253*** (0.000)		0.0318*** (0.000)		0.0744*** (0.000)	0.0189*** (0.006)		0.0396*** (0.000)
Paid below minimum wage			0.2779*** (0.000)					0.3822*** (0.000)		
R^2	.082	.092	.225	.106	.108	.129	.137	.279	.144	.146
No. of observations	13,035	12,943	12,932	13,035	12,943	13,035	12,943	12,932	13,035	12,943

Note: See notes to table 6.3.

***Significant at the 1 percent level.

**Significant at the 5 percent level.

*Significant at the 10 percent level.

References

Attanasio, O., P. Goldberg, and N. Pavcnik. 2004. Trade reforms and wage inequality in Colombia. *Journal of Development Economics* 74:331–66.

Chen, S., and M. Ravallion. 2001. How did the world's poorest fare in the 1990s? *Review of Income and Wealth* 47:283–300.

———. 2004a. How have the world's poorest fared since the early 1980s? World Bank Policy Research Working Paper no. 3341. Washington, DC: World Bank.

———. 2004b. Welfare impacts of China's accession to the World Trade Organization. *World Bank Economic Review* 18 (1): 29–57.

Deaton, A., and C. Paxson. 1997. Poverty among children and the elderly in developing countries. Princeton University, Research Program in Development Studies. Working Paper.

Edwards, S. 2001. The economics and politics of transition to an open market economy: Colombia. Paris: OECD.

Feenstra, R., and G. Hanson. 1996. Foreign investment, outsourcing and relative wages. In *Political economy of trade policy: Papers in honor of Jagdish Bhagwati,* ed. R. C. Feenstra, G. M. Grossman, and D. A. Irwin, 89–127. Cambridge, MA: MIT Press.

Feenstra, R., and G. Hanson. 1997. Foreign direct investment and relative wages: Evidence from Mexico's maquiladoras. *Journal of International Economics* 42: 371–93.

Goldberg, P., and N. Pavcnik. 2003. The response of the informal sector to trade liberalization. *Journal of Development Economics* 72:463–96.

———. 2004. Trade, inequality and poverty: What do we know? In *Brookings trade forum 2004,* ed. S. Collins and C. Graham, 223–69. Washington, DC: Brookings Institution Press.

———. 2005. Trade protection and wages: Evidence from the Colombian trade reforms. *Journal of International Economics* 66:75–105.

Hallak, J. C., and J. Levinsohn. 2004. Fooling ourselves: Evaluating the globalization and growth debate. NBER Working Paper no. 10244. Cambridge, MA: National Bureau of Economic Research.

Kugler, A. 1999. The impact of firing costs on turnover and unemployment: Evidence from the Colombian labour market reform. *International Tax and Public Finance Journal* 6 (3): 389–410.

Maloney, W., and J. Nunez. 2003. Measuring the impact of minimum wages: Evidence from Latin America. NBER Working Paper no. 9800. Cambridge, MA: National Bureau of Economic Research.

Ravallion, M. 2004. Competing concepts of inequality in the globalization debate. In *Brookings trade forum 2004,* ed. S. Collins and C. Graham, 1–38. Washington, DC: Brookings Institution Press.

Porto, G. 2006. Using survey data to assess the distributional effects of trade policy. *Journal of International Economics,* forthcoming.

Winters, A., N. McCulloch, and A. McKay. 2004. Trade liberalization and poverty: The evidence so far. *Journal of Economic Literature* 62:72–115.

World Bank. 2002. Colombia poverty report. Washington, DC: World Bank. Available at http://lnweb18.worldbank.org/external/lac/lac.nsf/Countries/Colombia/CC081B1813AF278985256BA300824DE6?OpenDocument.

Comment   Chang-Tai Hsieh

This paper by Goldberg and Pavcnik measures the effect of trade liberalization in Colombia on poverty reduction. There are two central facts that motivate this paper. First, Colombia undertook a substantial liberalization of its trade regime in the early 1990s: the average tariff rate in the manufacturing sector fell from 50 percent in 1984 to 13 percent in 1998. Second, there was an economic boom in Colombia over the same time period that had the effect of lowering poverty. For example, the head count ratio fell by 5 percentage points from 1984 to 1994.

The paper presents three pieces of evidence to measure the causal link between trade liberalization and poverty reduction. First, using successive cross-sectional data sets from Colombia's national household survey, the authors show that poverty is associated with unemployment, with informal employment (measured as somebody working in a firm that does not pay social security taxes), with pay lower than the minimum wage, and with work in low-wage industries (such as personal services). Second, the paper uses a between-within decomposition widely used in the skill-biased technical change literature to show that the decline in poverty is not due to changes in cross-sectional correlates of poverty. Specifically, the authors show that changes in the unemployment rate, in the share of workers in the informal sector, in the fraction of workers paid the minimum wage, or in the share of workers in low-wage industries are not responsible for the decline in poverty. Finally, the core of the paper exploits the differential impact of the tariff decline across industries to measure the effect of trade liberalization. Specifically, the authors show that the extent of tariff decline in an industry is not associated with unemployment, informality, industry, or fraction of workers paid less than the minimum wage. The paper thus concludes that there is little evidence that the poverty decline was due to trade liberalization.

There are two things I find puzzling about this paper. First, it's not clear to me why the paper focuses most of its attention on the correlates of poverty rather than on poverty itself: there is only one table in the paper that measures the link between poverty and trade liberalization. Before looking at the correlates of poverty, one should first determine whether the poverty decline was associated with the trade liberalization. In addition, the correlates of poverty that the paper focuses on seem to be weak correlates. The R-squares from the cross-sectional regression of poverty on the indicators of poverty (informality, unemployment, etc.) seem quite low. Thus, by focusing on variables that have limited power to explain poverty, the research design seems set up to find no effect of trade policy. The low

Chang-Tai Hsieh is an associate professor of economics at the University of California, Berkeley, and a faculty research fellow of the National Bureau of Economic Research.

explanatory power of the cross-sectional regression is particularly puzzling since the measure of poverty is basically based on income, the explanatory variables include all the variables typically included in a Mincerian wage regression, and we know that a standard Mincerian wage regression typically yields R-squares of 20 to 30 percent.

Second, using their simple accounting decomposition, the authors show that the decline in poverty cannot be attributed to changes in their correlates of poverty. Given this fact, however, the core of the paper—the correlation between the extent of trade liberalization and changes in the correlates of poverty—seems beside the point. Put differently, if we already know that changes in the correlates of poverty are not important in explaining the poverty decline, why are we bothering to measure the extent to which trade liberalization is associated with changes in the correlates of poverty?

Finally, more broadly, it seems difficult to make the case that one can use the differential impact of the trade reform across industries to measure its effect on poverty. There are (at least) two reasons for this. First, if the magnitude of job creation and destruction is at least as high in Colombia as it is in the United States, it seems difficult to pick up the effect of a sectoral shock by looking at workers in a given industry. For example, it could well be the case that trade liberalization was responsible for large losses for many people in protected sectors. However, if unemployment spells were short for most people, it would be difficult to pick up this effect from the cross-industry correlation of poverty and trade liberalization. One way to deal with this problem might be to use the differential regional impact of the trade reform, with the argument that interregional migration is lower than intersectoral movement.

Second, Colombia underwent many other policy reforms at exactly the same time. For example, it underwent a banking reform and labor market reform in 1990, liberalization of foreign direct investment and of the capital account in 1991, and a significant social security reform in 1993. It seems likely that many of these reforms would have a differential effect across industries. For example, social security reform presumably would have a different effect in industries that, prior to the reform, were paying social security taxes relative to firms that were not. The question, obviously, is the extent to which the differential effect of these other reforms is correlated with the differential impact of trade liberalization.

Trade Liberalization, Poverty, and Inequality
Evidence from Indian Districts

Petia Topalova

7.1 Introduction

After the Second World War, India, along with other developing countries, chose a strategy of import substitution as a means of industrializing. In the past two decades, however, many countries have begun to favor global economic integration, and in particular trade liberalization, as a development strategy. Although there is a general presumption that trade liberalization results in a higher gross domestic product (GDP), much less is known about its effects on income distribution. The distributional impacts of trade are particularly important in developing countries, where income inequality is typically pronounced and there are large vulnerable populations. If economic integration leads to further growth in income inequality and an increase in the number of poor in developing economies, the benefits of liberalization may be realized at a substantial social cost unless additional policies are devised to redistribute some of the gains from the winners to the losers.

Standard economic theory (Heckscher-Ohlin model) predicts that gains to trade should flow to abundant factors, which suggests that in developing countries unskilled labor would benefit most from globalization. The rising skill premium in the United States is often cited in support of standard trade theory. However, recently these sharp predictions have been

Petia Topalova is an economist at the International Monetary Fund.

I am indebted to Abhijit Banerjee, Esther Duflo, Sendhil Mullainathan, and Nina Pavcnik. This paper also benefited from discussions with Robin Burgess, Shawn Cole, Eric Edmonds, Ivan Fernandez-Val, Rema Hanna, Ann Harrison, Andrei Levchenko, and the participants in the development lunches at the Massachusetts Institute of Technology and the National Bureau of Economic Research Conference on Globalization and Poverty.

challenged.[1] According to the new theories, trade liberalization could reduce the wages of unskilled labor even in a labor-abundant country, thereby widening the gap between the rich and the poor. Moreover, even if global economic integration induces faster economic growth in the long run and substantial reductions in poverty, the adjustment might be costly, with the burden falling disproportionately on the poor (Banerjee and Newman 2004). Due to the ambiguity of the theory, the question of how trade liberalization affects poverty and inequality remains largely an empirical one.

Recent empirical work has attempted to address the question, focusing mostly on the effect of trade liberalization on within-country income inequality. Studies using cross-country variation typically find little relationship between trade liberalization and levels or rates of change of inequality.[2] However, these studies face significant problems: cross-country data may not be comparable, sample sizes are small, and changes in liberalization may be highly correlated with other variables important to income processes. A promising alternative is to use microevidence from household and industry surveys. Several studies examine the relationship between trade reforms and skill premia, returns to education, industry premia, and the size of informal labor markets. However, the findings of these studies are typically based on correlations and may not always be given a causal interpretation. And while there is some evidence on the effect of liberalization on industrial performance and wage inequality, the literature has so far ignored the next logical step: the impact of these performance changes on poverty.

This paper investigates the impact of trade reforms on poverty and inequality in Indian districts. Does trade liberalization affect everyone equally, or does it help those who are already relatively well off while leaving the poor behind? How does it affect income distributions within rural and urban areas? And is the effect of liberalization felt equally across regions in India?

India presents a particularly relevant setting in which to seek the answers to these questions. First, India is the home of one-third of the world's poor.[3] Second, the nature of India's trade liberalization—sudden, comprehensive, and largely externally imposed—facilitates a causal interpretation of the findings. India liberalized its international trade as part of a major set of reforms in response to a severe balance-of-payments crisis in 1991. Extremely restrictive policies were abandoned: the average duty rate declined

1. See Davis (1996), Feenstra and Hanson (1997), Stiglitz (1970), Cunat and Maffezzoli (2001), Banerjee and Newman (2004), and Kremer and Maskin (2003).
2. See Edwards (1998), Lundberg and Squire (2003), Rama (2003), Dollar and Kraay (2002), and Milanovic (2002).
3. Based on 2001 World Bank estimates. See http://www.worldbank.org/research/pov monitor/.

by more than half, and the percentage of goods importable without license or quantitative restriction rose sharply. The lower average tariffs, combined with changes in the tariff structure across industries, provide ample variation to identify the causal effects of trade policy on income processes.

Coincident with these tariff reductions were significant changes in the incidence of poverty and income inequality. To determine whether there is a causal link between liberalization and changes in poverty and inequality, this paper exploits the variation in the timing and degree of liberalization across industries, and the variation in the location of industries in districts throughout India. The interaction between the share of a district's population employed by various industries on the eve of the economic reforms and the reduction in trade barriers in these industries provides a measure of the district's exposure to foreign trade. In a regression framework, this paper establishes whether district poverty and inequality are related to the district-specific trade policy shocks. Because industrial composition is predetermined and trade liberalization was sudden and externally imposed, it is appropriate to causally interpret the correlation between the levels of poverty and inequality and trade exposure. Of course, if there were migration across districts in response to changes in factor prices, an analysis comparing districts over time may not give the full extent of the impact of globalization on inequality and poverty in India. However, the analysis still gives a well-defined answer to the question of whether inequality and poverty increased more (or less) in districts that were affected more by trade liberalization.

The study finds that trade liberalization led to an increase in poverty rate and poverty gap in the rural districts where industries more exposed to liberalization were concentrated. The effect is quite substantial. According to the most conservative estimates, compared to a rural district experiencing no change in tariffs, a district experiencing the mean level of tariff changes saw a 2 percent increase in poverty incidence and a 0.6 percent increase in poverty depth. This setback represents about 15 percent of India's progress in poverty reduction over the 1990s.

It is important to note that this exercise does not study the level effect of liberalization on poverty in India but rather the relative impact on areas more or less exposed to liberalization. Thus, while liberalization may have had an overall effect of increasing or lowering the poverty rate and poverty gap, this paper captures the fact that these effects were not equal throughout the country, and certain areas and certain segments of the society benefited less (or suffered more) from liberalization.

The finding of any effect of trade liberalization on regional outcomes is puzzling in the trade theorist's hypothetical world, where factors are mobile both across geographical regions within a country and across industries. Factor reallocation would equate incidence of poverty across regions. In a closely related study (Topalova 2004b), I present evidence that the

mobility of factors is extremely limited in India. The geographical inequalities are explained by the lack of relocation: migration is remarkably low, with no signs of an upward trend after the 1991 reforms. In the study I further examine the mechanisms through which trade liberalization affected poverty and inequality, establishing that the lack of geographical mobility is combined with a lack of intersectoral mobility. Changes in relative output prices led to changes in relative sector returns to sector-specific factors. As those employed in traded industries were not at the top of the income distribution on the eve of the trade reform, the reduction in income caused some to cross the poverty line or fall even deeper into poverty.

This study is related to several strands of literature. First, it fits into the recent large empirical literature on the effects of trade reforms on wage inequality. This literature has largely dealt with the experience of Latin American countries: Cragg and Epelbaum (1996), Revenga (1996), Hanson and Harrison (1999), Feliciano (2001), Goldberg and Pavcnik (2001), and Attanasio, Goldberg, and Pavcnik (2004). Currie and Harrison (1997) study the effect of trade liberalization in Morocco. These papers typically find small effects of trade on wage inequality of workers in the manufacturing sector. This paper extends this type of analysis by focusing not only on the effect of trade reforms on relative wages in manufacturing but on regional outcomes in general, thus capturing how trade effects seeped from the directly affected manufacturing and agricultural workers to their dependents, as well as people involved in nontraded-goods sectors.

This is also one of the first studies to examine the link between trade liberalization and poverty. So far Porto (2004) and Goldberg and Pavcnik (2004) have analyzed the relationship between trade and poverty in the case of Argentina and Colombia respectively. Porto's approach has the advantage of providing a general equilibrium analysis of the relationship between trade liberalization and poverty, by simultaneously considering the labor market and consumption effects of trade liberalization, but his results rely on simulations based on cross-sectional data. Goldberg and Pavcnik (2004), exploiting cross-sectional and time series variation at the industry level, find little evidence of a link between the Colombian trade reforms and poverty. Yet, as the study focuses on urban areas and people involved in manufacture, it may be missing the really poor. This paper relates plausibly exogenous changes in trade policy to poverty and inequality, studying both manufacturing and agricultural workers in both urban and rural areas. In addition, by defining the district as the unit of observation, it overcomes important selection and composition effects that studies at the industry level may face. Finally, the paper contributes to the literature on industry wage premia and their relation to trade protection.

The remainder of the paper is organized as follows. Section 7.2 describes the Indian reforms of 1991 focusing on trade liberalization, while section

7.3 presents the data used in the analysis. In section 7.4 the empirical strategy is explained, and the results follow in section 7.5. Section 7.6 concludes.

7.2   The Indian Trade Liberalization

India's postindependence development strategy was one of national self-sufficiency and stressed the importance of government regulation of the economy. Cerra and Saxena (2000) characterized it as both inward looking and highly interventionist, consisting of import protection, complex industrial licensing requirements, pervasive government intervention in financial intermediation, and substantial public ownership of heavy industry. In particular, India's trade regime was among the most restrictive in Asia, with high nominal tariffs and nontariff barriers, including a complex import licensing system, an actual user policy that restricted imports by intermediaries, restrictions of certain exports and imports to the public sector (canalization), phased manufacturing programs that mandated progressive import substitution, and government purchase preferences for domestic producers.

It was only during the second half of the 1980s, when the focus of India's development strategy gradually shifted toward export-led growth, that the process of liberalization began. Import and industrial licensing were eased, and tariffs replaced some quantitative restrictions, although even as late as 1989–90 a mere 12 percent of manufactured products could be imported under an open general license; the average tariff was still one of the highest, greater than 90 percent (Cerra and Saxena 2000).

However, the gradual liberalization of the late 1980s was accompanied by a rise in macroeconomic imbalances—namely, fiscal and balance-of-payments deficits—which increased India's vulnerability to shocks. The sudden increase in oil prices due to the Gulf War in 1990, the drop in remittances from Indian workers in the Middle East, and the slackened demand of important trading partners exacerbated the situation. Political uncertainty, which peaked in 1990 and 1991 after the poor performance and subsequent fall of a coalition government led by the second largest party (Janata Dal) and the assassination of Rajiv Gandhi, the chairman of the Congress Party, undermined investor confidence. With India's downgraded credit rating, commercial bank loans were hard to obtain, credit lines were not renewed, and capital outflows began to take place.

To deal with its external payments problems, the government of India requested a standby arrangement from the International Monetary Fund (IMF) in August 1991. The IMF support was conditional on an adjustment program featuring macroeconomic stabilization and structural reforms. The latter focused on the industrial and import licenses, the financial sector, the tax system, and trade policy. On trade policy, benchmarks

for the first review of the standby arrangement included a reduction in the level and dispersion of tariffs and a removal of a large number of quantitative restrictions (Chopra et al. 1995). Specific policy actions in a number of areas—notably industrial deregulation, trade policy and public enterprise reforms, and some aspects of financial-sector reform—also formed the basis for a World Bank Structural Adjustment Loan, as well as sector loans.

The government's export-import policy plan (1992–97) ushered in radical changes to the trade regime by sharply reducing the role of the import and export control system. The share of products subject to quantitative restrictions decreased from 87 percent in 1987–88 to 45 percent in 1994–95. The actual user condition on imports was discontinued. All twenty-six import licensing lists were eliminated, and a negative list was established (Hasan, Mitra, and Ramaswamy, 2003). Thus, apart from goods in the negative list, all goods could be freely imported (subject to import tariffs; Goldar 2002). In addition to the easing of import and export restrictions, there were drastic tariff reductions (figure 7.1, panels A and B). Average tariffs fell from more than 80 percent in 1990 to 37 percent in 1996, and the standard deviation of tariffs dropped by 50 percent during the same period. The structure of protection across industries changed (figure 7.1, panel G). Panel H of figure 7.1 shows the strikingly linear relationship between the prereform tariff levels and the decline in tariffs the industry experienced. This graph reflects the guidelines according to which tariff reform took place, namely reduction in the general level of tariffs, reduction

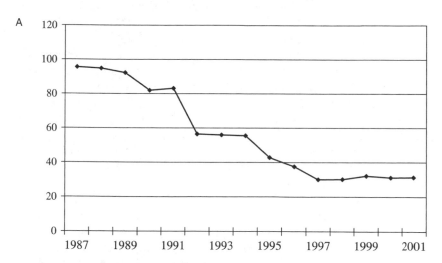

Fig. 7.1   Evolution of tariffs in India: *A,* average nominal tariffs; *B,* standard deviation of nominal tariffs; *C,* tariffs by broad industrial category; *D,* tariffs by industrial use–based category; *E,* share of free HS lines by broad industrial category; *F,* share of free HS lines by industrial use–based category; *G,* correlation of industry tariffs in 1997 and 1987; *H,* tariff decline and industry tariffs in 1987

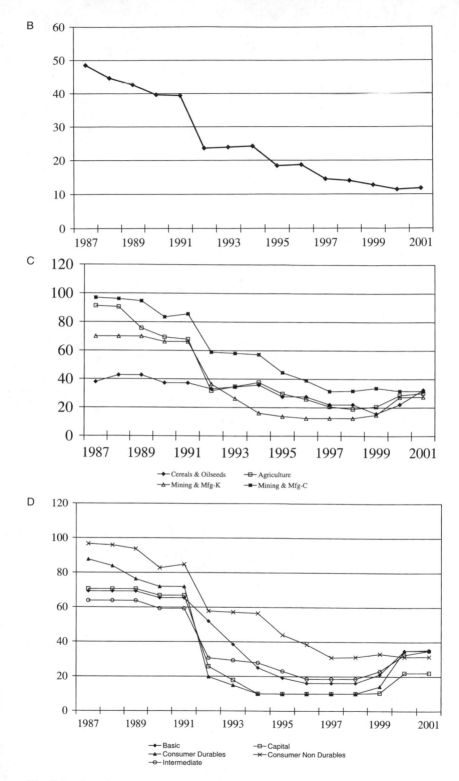

Fig. 7.1 (cont.)

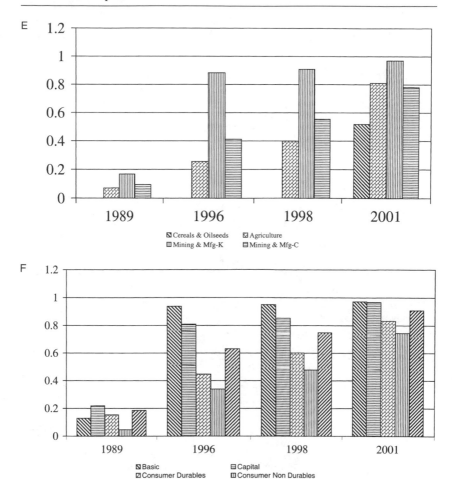

Fig. 7.1   (cont.) Evolution of tariffs in India: *A*, average nominal tariffs; *B*, standard deviation of nominal tariffs; *C*, tariffs by broad industrial category; *D*, tariffs by industrial use–based category; *E*, share of free HS lines by broad industrial category; *F*, share of free HS lines by industrial use–based category; *G*, correlation of industry tariffs in 1997 and 1987; *H*, tariff decline and industry tariffs in 1987

of the spread or dispersion of tariff rates, simplification of the tariff system, and rationalization of tariff rates, along with the abolition of numerous exemptions and concessions.[4] Agricultural products, with the exception of cereals and oilseeds, faced an equally sharp drop in tariffs, although the nontariff barriers (NTBs) of these products were lifted only in the late 1990s (figure 7.1, panels C–F). There were some differences in the magni-

4. The guidelines were outlined in the Chelliah report of the Tax Reform Commission constituted in 1991.

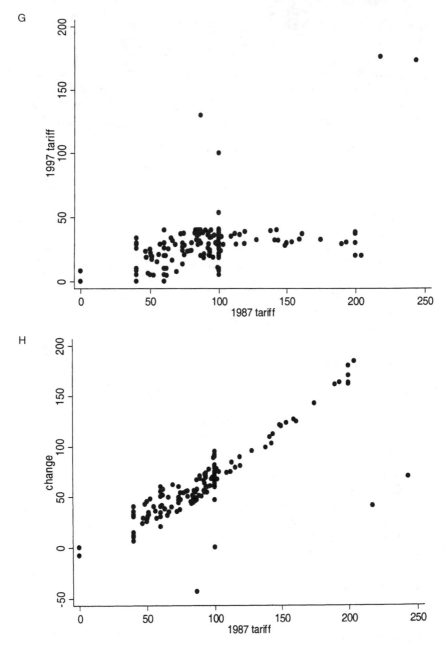

Fig. 7.1 (cont.)

tude of tariff changes (and especially NTBs) according to industry use type: consumer durables, consumer nondurables, capital goods, and intermediate and basic goods (figure 7.1, panels D and F). Indian authorities first liberalized capital goods, basic goods, and intermediates, while consumer nondurables and agricultural products were slowly moved from the negative list to the list of freely importable goods only in the second half of the 1990s. The Indian rupee was devalued 20 percent against the dollar in July 1991 and further devalued in February 1992. By 1993, India had adopted a flexible exchange rate regime (Ahluwalia 1999).

Following the reduction in trade distortions, the ratio of total trade in manufactures to GDP rose from an average of 13 percent in the 1980s to nearly 19 percent of GDP in 1999–2000 (fig. 7.2). Export and import volumes also increased sharply from the early 1990s, outpacing growth in real output (fig. 7.2). India's imports were significantly more skilled-labor intensive than India's exports and remained so throughout the 1990s, as shown in figure 7.3, which plots cumulative export and import shares by skill intensity in 1987, 1991, 1994, and 1997.

India remained committed to further trade liberalization, and since 1997 there have been further adjustments to import tariffs. However, at the time the government announced the export-import policy in the Ninth Plan (1997–2002), the sweeping reforms outlined in the previous plan had been undertaken and pressure for further reforms from external sources had abated.

7.3   Data

The data for this analysis were drawn from three main sources. Household survey data are available from the 1983–84, 1987–88, 1993–94, and 1999–2000 (thick) rounds of the Indian National Sample Survey (NSS). The NSS provides household-level information on expenditure patterns, occupation, industrial affiliation (at the three-digit National Industrial Classification [NIC] level), and various other household and individual characteristics. The surveys usually cover all states in India and collect information on about 75,000 rural and 45,000 urban households.[5] Using these data, I construct district-level measures of poverty (measured as head count ratio and poverty gap) and inequality (measured as the standard deviation of the log of per capita expenditure and the logarithmic deviation of per capita expenditure).[6] Following Deaton (2003a, 2003b), I adjust these estimates in two ways. First, I use the poverty lines proposed by Deaton as opposed to the ones used by the Indian Planning Commission,

---

5. The NSS follows the Indian census definition of urban and rural areas. To be classified as urban, an area needs to meet several criteria regarding size and density of the population, and the share of male working population engaged in nonagricultural pursuits.

6. The poverty measures are explained in detail in section 7.4.2. The head count ratio represents the proportion of the population below the poverty line, while the poverty gap index is the normalized aggregate shortfall of poor people's consumption from the poverty line.

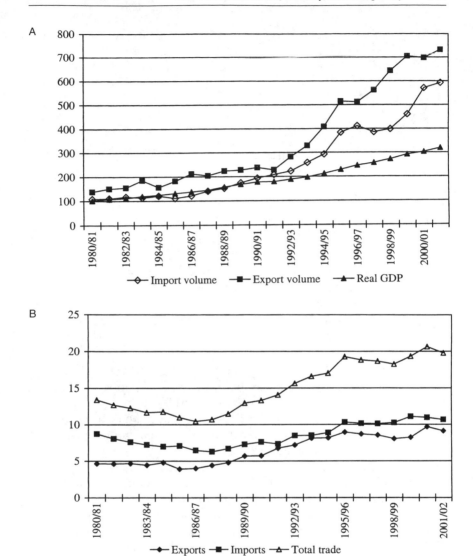

Fig. 7.2   **Evolution of India's trade: *A*, export, import, and output indexes (1978– 79 = 100); *B,* merchandise trade (in percent of GDP)**

which are based on defective price indexes over time, across states, and be- tween the urban and rural sectors. The poverty lines are available for the sixteen bigger states in India and Delhi to which I restrict the analysis.[7] In

7. Poverty lines were not available for some of the smaller states and union territories, namely Arunachal Pradesh, Goa, Daman and Diu, Jammu and Kashmir, Manipur, Meghalaya, Mizo- ram, Nagaland, Sikkim, Tripura, Andaman and Nicobar Islands, Chandigarh, Pondicherry, Lakshwadweep, Dadra Nagar, and Haveli. The results are not sensitive to the inclusion of these states, with poverty lines assumed to be the same as those of the neighboring states.

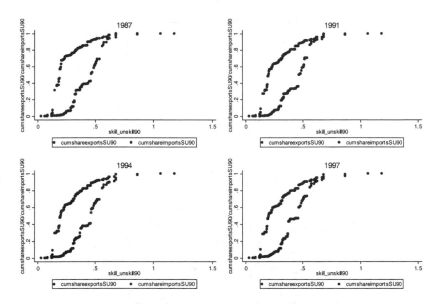

Fig. 7.3   Pattern of Indian trade, XM shares on skilled-unskilled ratio 90

addition, the 1999–2000 round is not directly comparable to the 1993–94 round. The 1999–2000 round introduced a new recall period (seven days) along with the usual thirty-day recall questions for the household expenditures on food, pan, and tobacco. Due to the way the questionnaire was administered, there are reasons to believe that this methodology leads to an overestimate of the expenditures based on the thirty-day recall period, which in turn affects the poverty and inequality estimates. To achieve comparability with earlier rounds, I follow Deaton and impute the correct distribution of total per capita expenditure for each district from the households' expenditures on a subset of goods for which the new recall period questions were not introduced. The poverty and inequality measures were derived from this corrected distribution. Throughout the 1990s there were substantial changes in the administrative division of India, with districts' boundaries changing as new districts were carved out of existing ones. As I compare districts over time, I construct consistent time series of district identifiers using census atlases and other maps of India. These were also used to match the NSS and census district definitions.

For industrial data, I use the Indian census of 1991, which reports the industry of employment at the three-digit NIC code for each district in India. Because the census does not distinguish among crops produced by agricultural workers, I use the forty-third round of the NSS to compute agricultural employment district weights. There are about 450 industry codes, of which about 190 are traded agricultural, mining, or manufacturing industries.

Finally, I use tariffs to measure changes in Indian trade policy. While NTBs have historically played a large role in Indian trade policy, data are not available at a disaggregated enough level to allow the construction of a time series of NTBs across sectors.[8] Instead, I construct a database of annual tariff data for 1987–2001 at the six-digit level of the Indian Trade Classification Harmonized System (HS) code based on data from various publications of the Ministry of Finance. I then match 5,000 product lines to the NIC codes, using the concordance of Debroy and Santhanam (1993), to calculate average industry-level tariffs. The few available data on NTBs come from various publications of the Directorate General of Foreign Trade as well as the 1992 study of the Indian trade regime by Aksoy (1992).

7.4 Empirical Strategy

The Indian liberalization was externally imposed and comprehensive, and the Indian government had to meet strict compliance deadlines. The period immediately before the reform and the five-year plan immediately following give rise to an excellent natural experiment. India's large size and diversity (India was divided into approximately 450 districts in twenty-seven states at the time of the 1991 census) allow for a cross-region research design. The identification strategy is straightforward: districts whose industries faced larger liberalization shocks are compared to those whose industries remained protected. Gordon Hanson employs a similar strategy in his study of the effect of globalization on labor income in Mexico in chapter 10 of this volume.

However, unlike Hanson's, the identification strategy of this paper exploits variation in the "initial" industrial composition across districts in India and the timing of liberalization across industries. I construct a measure of district trade exposure as the average of industry-level tariffs weighted by the workers employed in that industry in 1991 as a share of all registered workers. The variation in industrial composition will generate differential response of the district-level trade exposure to the exogenous changes in tariffs. In a regression framework, the baseline specification takes the following form:

$$(1) \qquad y_{d,t} = \alpha + \beta \cdot \text{Tariff}_{d,t} + \gamma_t + \delta_d + \varepsilon_{d,t},$$

where $y_{d,t}$ is district-level outcome such as measures of poverty and inequality, and $\text{Tariff}_{d,t}$ is the district exposure to international trade. The coefficient of interest, β, captures the average effect of trade protection on

---

8. In addition, the experience of other developing countries shows that NTB coverage ratios are usually highly correlated with tariffs; thus, estimates based on tariffs may capture the combined effect of trade policy changes (Goldberg and Pavcnik 2004). This relationship seems to hold in the case of India as well, based on the patchy data available.

regional outcomes. The inclusion of district fixed effects (δ_d) absorbs unobserved district-specific heterogeneity in the determinants of poverty and inequality, while the year dummies (γ_t) control for macroeconomic shocks that affect all of India equally.

The above methodology will capture the short- to medium-run effect of trade liberalization in a specific district. Note that in the presence of perfect factor mobility across regions, one would expect no effect of liberalization on regional outcomes. If workers can easily migrate in response to adverse price changes, the effect of liberalization captured in β would be zero. A further advantage of this identification strategy is that it will uncover the general equilibrium effect of trade liberalization within a geographical unit. Previous studies have focused on the effect of trade opening on manufacturing workers, who, in developing countries, typically represent a small fraction of the population, though often a large share of income. This strategy will capture the effect of trade liberalization not only on manufacturing and agricultural workers but also on their dependents and individuals in allied sectors.

It is important to emphasize that this empirical strategy cannot tell us anything about the first-order effect of trade on poverty. First, trade liberalization is likely to have effects common across India, through prices, availability of new goods, faster growth, and so on.[9] Second, it would be very difficult to draw a causal lesson using only time variation in trade liberalization and poverty levels, since the Indian economy was subject to numerous other influences over the period studied. This study, based on regional variation, does not reflect these effects and does not seek to answer questions about overall levels. Instead, it answers the question of whether all districts derived similar benefits (or suffered similar costs) from liberalization or whether some areas suffered disproportionately. This is an important question for policymakers, who might need to devise additional policies to redistribute some of the gains from the winners to those who do not win as much in order to minimize potential social cost of inequality.

The balance of this section addresses two potential complications. First, the process of trade liberalization is explored in detail, including the possibility that liberalization was correlated with other factors that affect regional poverty and inequality. Second, the measures used to quantify poverty and inequality are described, including careful attention to possible problems with the data, and their solution.

7.4.1   Endogeneity of Trade Policy

There are strong theoretical reasons (Grossman and Helpman 2002) to believe that in the absence of external pressure, trade policy is an endoge-

---

9. To a certain extent the effect of cheaper goods should be reflected in the deflators for the poverty lines.

nous outcome to political and economic processes. As the empirical strategy of this paper exploits the interaction of regional industrial composition and differential degree of liberalization across industries to identify the effect of trade liberalization on poverty and inequality, understanding the source of variation in the tariff levels is of utmost importance. In particular, there are two dimensions that suggest that endogeneity of trade policy may be a concern. First, the initial decrease in tariffs might have been just a continuation of a secular trend. The timing of trade reform might have reflected Indian authorities' perception of domestic industries as mature enough to face foreign competition, and labor and credit markets as flexible enough to ease the intersectoral reallocation that would ensue. Second, the cross-sectional variation in levels of protection might be related to economic and political factors. The relatively less efficient industries might have enjoyed a higher degree of protection; the political strength of labor as well as business is also often cited as a determinant of trade protection. If less productive industries or industries with higher lobbying ability are more concentrated in poorer areas, then one might see a positive correlation between district poverty rates and the district level tariffs. These two concerns are addressed in sequence below.

As already discussed in section 7.2, the external crisis of 1991 opened the way for market-oriented reforms in India, such as trade liberalization. The Indian government required IMF support to meet external payment obligations, and was thus compelled to accept the conditions that accompanied the support. Given several earlier attempts to avoid IMF loans and the associated conditionalities, the large number of members of the new cabinet who had been cabinet members in past governments with inward-looking trade policies and the heavy reliance on tariffs as a source of revenues, these reforms came as a surprise (Hasan, Mitra, and Ramaswamy 2003). According to a study on the political economy of economic policy in India, the new policy package was delivered swiftly in order to complete the process of changeover so as not to permit consolidation of any likely opposition to implementation of the new policies: "The strategy was to administer a 'shock therapy' to the economy. . . . There was no debate among officials or economists prior to the official adoption. . . . The new economic policy did not originate out of an analysis of the data and information or a well-thought-out development perspective" (Goyal 1996).[10]

Varshney (1999) describes the political environment in which the trade reforms were passed. Mass political attention at the time was focused on

10. This view is confirmed in a recent interview with Dr. Raja Chelliah, one of the masterminds of the reforms, who said, "We didn't have the time to sit down and think exactly what kind of a development model we needed. . . . There was no systematic attempt to see two things; one, how have the benefits of reforms distributed, and two, ultimately what kind of society we want to have, what model of development should we have?" (July 5, 2004, http://in .rediff.com/money/2004/jul/05inter.htm).

internal politics (ethnic conflict in particular), and trade reforms pushed through by a weak coalition government apparently escaped general attention, in contrast to the failed reform attempts of the much stronger Congress Party in 1985. As late as 1996, fewer than 20 percent of the electorate had any knowledge of the trade reform, while 80 percent had opinions on whether India should implement caste-based affirmative action. While some liberalization efforts (for example, privatization) were diluted or delayed due to popular opposition, trade liberalization was generally successful. As Bhagwati wrote, "Reform by storm has supplanted the reform by stealth of Mrs. Gandhi's time and the reform with reluctance under Rajiv Gandhi" (Bhagwati 1993).

There are several reasons why trade policy remained part of elite politics. Trade constitutes a relatively small part of GDP in India. Although tariffs were vastly reduced, consumer goods and agricultural products were initially not liberalized. And although there surely is an important link between mass welfare and trade policy, even when trade is a small share of the national product, these links are subtle and not yet established empirically.

Even if the timing of the sharp drop in average tariffs (fig. 7.1) appears exogenous, there is significant variation in the tariff changes across industries, which could confound inference. More precisely, it is important to understand whether the changes in tariffs reflected authorities' perceptions of industry's ability to compete internationally, or the lobbying power of the industry. Ideally, this concern could be alleviated by knowledge of the true intentions of Indian policymakers or, failing that, through a detailed study of the political economy behind tariff changes in India over the period. In the absence of objective and detailed analyses of such policy changes, the data may be examined for possible confounding relationships.

First, I examine to what extent tariffs moved together. An analysis of the tariff changes of the 5,000 items in the data set for 1992–96, the Eighth Plan, and for 1997–2001, the Ninth Plan, suggests that movements in tariffs were strikingly uniform until 1997 (fig. 7.4). During the first five-year plan that incorporated the economic reforms of 1991, India had to meet certain externally imposed benchmarks, and the majority of tariff changes across products exhibited similar behavior (either increased, decreased, or remained constant). After 1997, tariff movements were not as uniform. This suggests that policymakers were more selective in setting product tariffs during 1997–2001, and the problem of potential cross-sectional endogenous trade protection is more pronounced.

Second, there is no evidence that policymakers adjusted tariffs according to industry's perceived productivity during the Eighth Plan (i.e., until 1997). In a related study (Topalova 2004a), I tested whether current productivity levels predict future tariffs—a relationship one would expect if policymakers were indeed trying to protect less efficient industries. I found that the correlation between future tariffs and current productivity, and fu-

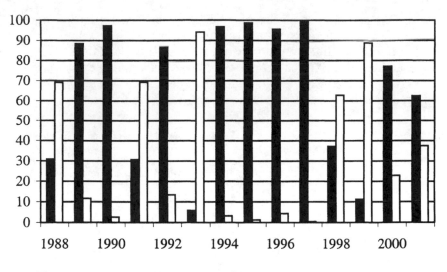

■ % Items with tariff reductions □ % Items with tariff increases

Fig. 7.4   Direction of tariff changes

ture tariffs and current productivity growth, is indistinguishable from zero for the 1989–96 period. For the period after 1997, however, future tariff levels seem to be negatively and statistically significantly correlated with current productivity. This evidence and the evidence on uniformity in tariff movements until 1997 suggest that it may not be appropriate to use trade policy variation after 1997. This study thus focuses on the 1987–97 period.

A third check uses data from the Annual Survey of Industries (ASI) to test for political protection. Even if the change in industry tariffs appears uncorrelated with the initial productivity of the industry, tariffs may be correlated with politically important characteristics of the firm. Using data from the ASI (which covers manufacturing and mining sectors), and following the literature on political protection, I regress the change in tariffs between 1987 and 1997 on various industrial characteristics in 1987.[11] These characteristics include employment size (a larger labor force may lead to more electoral power and more protection), output size, average wage (policymakers may protect industries where relatively low-skilled or vulnerable workers are employed), concentration (as measured by the average factory size, this captures the ability of producers to organize political pressure groups to lobby for more protection), and share of skilled

11. I use 1987 as the prereform year since the data on prereform poverty and inequality come from the forty-third round of the NSS, which was collected in 1987. The results are robust to using 1988 or 1990 as the prereform year.

workers. The results are presented in table 7.1, panel A. Tariff changes are not correlated with any of the industry characteristics.

Because agricultural workers are not included in the ASI data but comprise a large share of India's population, I conduct a similar exercise using data from the 1987 NSS. I estimate for all industries the average per capita expenditure, wage, poverty rate, and poverty depth at the industry level,

Table 7.1   Tariff declines and prereform industrial characteristics (dependent variable: Tariff1987 – Tariff1997)

	(1)	(2)	(3)	(4)	(5)	(6)	(7)	(8)
			A. Evidence from the ASI					
Log real wage	0.037							
	(0.062)							
Share of nonproduction workers		0.312						
		(0.399)						
Capital-labor ratio			0.013					
			(0.025)					
Log output				0.019				
				(0.020)				
Factory size					0.000			
					(0.000)			
Log employment						−0.002		
						(0.016)		
Growth log output 1982–87							−0.038	
							(0.061)	
Growth log employment 1982–87								0.024
								(0.083)
R^2	0.093	0.096	0.091	0.096	0.094	0.090	0.092	0.091
No. of observations	135	135	135	135	134	135	135	135
			B. Evidence from the NSS, rural and urban pooled					
Log per capita expenditure	−0.040							
	(0.051)							
Log wage		−0.002						
		(0.033)						
Poverty rate			0.019					
			(0.113)					
Poverty depth				−0.205				
				(0.339)				
R^2	0.06	0.07	0.06	0.06				
No. of observations	315	274	315	315				

Notes: Robust standard errors in parentheses. All regressions include indicators for industry use type: capital goods, consumer durables, consumer nondurables, and intermediate. In panel A, regressions are weighted by the square root of the number of factories. Data are from the 1987 ASI and cover mining and manufacturing industries. In panel B, regressions are weighted by the square root of the number of workers in each industry in the 1987 NSS. Urban and rural sample are pooled, and an indicator for urban is included. Separate regressions for the urban and rural sample exhibit similar patterns. Note that cereal and oilseed cultivation has been treated as a nontraded industry, because imports of these agricultural products were canalized (restricted only to state trading monopolies) until 2000.

and I check whether there is a correlation between these industry characteristics and tariff declines. The results, presented in table 7.1, panel B, show no significant relationship between tariff changes and these measures of workers' wellbeing, once controls for industry use type are included.

A possible explanation for these results can be found in Gang and Pandey (1996). They conducted a careful study of the determinants of protection across manufacturing sectors across three plans, 1979–80, 1984–85, and 1991–92, showing that none of the economic and political factors are important in explaining industry tariff levels in India.[12] They explain the phenomenon with the hysteresis of policy: trade policy was determined in the Second Five-Year Plan and never changed, even as the circumstances and natures of the industries evolved.

The evidence presented here suggests that the differential tariff changes across industries between 1991 and 1997 were as unrelated to the state of the industries as can be reasonably hoped for in a real-world setting.

One big exception to the otherwise haphazard pattern of tariff reductions comprises two major agricultural crops: cereals and oilseeds. Throughout the period of study, the imports of cereals and oilseeds remained canalized (only government agencies were allowed to import these items), and no change in their tariff rates was observed (the tariff rate for cereals was set at zero). Thus, they were de facto nontraded goods. The delay in the liberalization of these major agricultural crops was due to reasons of food security. However, the cultivators of these crops were also among the poorest in India. This brings some additional complications to the analysis, which are discussed at length in the following sections.

7.4.2   Measurement and Basic Patterns of Poverty and Inequality

Measuring poverty and inequality is not a trivial task. For poverty, I use both the head count ratio (HCR) and the poverty gap. The former, which I refer to as the poverty rate, represents the proportion of the population below the poverty line. While the HCR is widely used, it does not capture the extent to which different households fall short of the poverty line, and it is highly sensitive to the number of poor households near the poverty line. Thus, I also analyze the poverty gap index, defined as the normalized aggregate shortfall of poor people's consumption from the poverty line.[13]

---

12. In other developing countries, protection tends to be highest for unskilled, labor-intensive sectors. See Goldberg and Pavcnik (2001), Hanson and Harrison (1999), and Currie and Harrison (1997) for evidence from Colombia, Mexico, and Morocco, respectively.

13. Both the HCR and the poverty gap are members of the Foster-Greer-Thorbecke class of poverty measures, defined as $P_\alpha = \int_0^z [(z-y)/z]^\alpha f(y)dy$, where z is the poverty line and incomes are distributed according to the density function $f(y)$. The head count ratio is calculated by setting α to be 0, and the poverty gap by setting α to be 1. Since the survey design changed for the 1999–2000 round of the NSS, in order to obtain internally consistent measurements of poverty and inequality, the per capita expenditure data were adjusted at the district level, following Deaton (2003a, 2003b; Deaton and Tarozzi 2005).

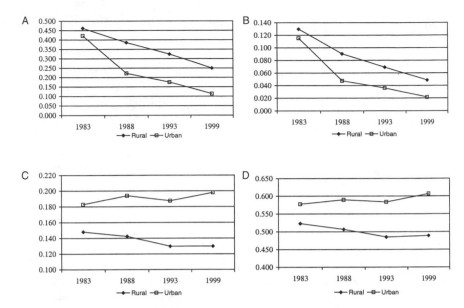

Fig. 7.5   Trends in urban and rural poverty and inequality: *A,* **evolution of the head count ratio;** *B,* **evolution of the poverty gap;** *C,* **evolution of the log deviation of consumption;** *D,* **evolution of the standard deviation of log consumption**

Notes: Deaton's adjusted poverty lines and price indexes were used (Deaton 2003a, 2003b; Deaton and Tarozzi 2005). The 55th-round data were adjusted for the change in questionnaire design.

Figure 7.5 plots the evolution of poverty in India, and indicates a substantial decline over the past two decades.

I chose two measures of inequality, the standard deviation of log consumption and the mean logarithmic deviation of consumption,[14] both because they are standard measures and because similar values are obtained when they are estimated from either the microdata or the estimated distributions. In contrast to poverty's steady decline, inequality follows a more complicated pattern. Although it registered a substantial decline between 1987 and 1993, both measures record a break in that trend and a slight increase in inequality after 1993 in rural India. In urban India, after a period of decline, inequality rose between 1993 and 1999.

As mentioned above, the measure of trade policy is the tariff that a district faces, calculated as the 1991 employment-weighted average nominal

---

14. The mean deviation of consumption is part of the family of generalized entropy coefficients. It is calculated according to the following formula:

$$I(0) = \int \frac{y}{\mu} \log\left(\frac{\mu}{y}\right) f(y)dy,$$

where μ is mean income.

ad valorem tariff at time t.[15] Appendix table 7A.1 provides summary statistics of the variables included in the analysis at the district level, including a breakdown of the workers across broad industrial categories. In the average rural district about 80 percent of main workers are involved in agriculture, of whom 87 percent are involved in cultivation of cereals and oilseeds.[16] Mining and manufacturing account for about 6 percent of the workers, and the remaining 12 percent are involved in services, trade, transportation, and construction. In urban India, agricultural workers represent only 19 percent, of which 73 percent are cultivators of cereals and oilseeds. Manufacturing and mining workers account for another fifth of the urban population, and the remaining three fifths comprise workers in services and the like.

The district level tariffs are computed as follows:

$$\text{Tariff}_{d,t} = \frac{\sum_i \text{Worker}_{d,i,1991} \cdot \text{Tariff}_{i,t}}{\text{Total Worker}_{d,1991}}$$

$\text{Tariff}_{d,t}$ is a scaled version of district tariffs. In this measure, workers in nontraded industries are assigned zero tariff for all years. These are workers in services, trade, transportation, and construction as well as all workers involved in the growing of cereals and oilseeds. The latter assumption is justified by the fact that all product lines of these two industries were canalized (imports were allowed only to the state trading monopoly) as late as 2000.[17] Furthermore, the tariffs of all product lines under the growing-of-cereals industry are zero throughout the entire period of interest.

One concern with the use of $\text{Tariff}_{d,t}$ is that it is very sensitive to the share of people involved in nontraded industries, the majority of whom are the cereal and oilseed growers. Since agricultural workers are usually at the bottom of the income distribution, $\text{Tariff}_{d,t}$ is correlated with initial poverty levels. The interpretation of results based on this measure may be unclear if there were (for other reasons) convergence across districts. In particular, poorer districts, which have a large fraction of agricultural workers, may experience faster reduction in poverty due to mean reversion or convergence. These districts may also record a lower drop in tariffs, since initially

15. As described in the data section (7.3), the 1991 population and housing census is used to compute employment by industry for each district. The employment data are available for the urban and rural sectors separately by industry at the three-digit NIC level for all workers except agricultural workers. To match agricultural workers to the tariff data, I compute district employment weights from the forty-third round of the NSS (July 1987–June 1988).

16. The 1991 Indian census divides workers into two categories: main and marginal workers. Main workers include people who worked for six months or more during the year, while marginal workers include those who worked for a shorter period. Unpaid farm and family enterprise workers are supposed to be included in either the main worker or marginal worker category, as appropriate.

17. These products also have minimum support prices fixed by the government of India.

the Tariff$_{d,t}$ measure is low. Thus, one might find a spurious negative relationship between tariffs and poverty and erroneously conclude that trade liberalization led to a relative increase in poverty at the district level. Alternatively, if workers in nontraded activities are on a different growth path than those in traded industries, Tariff$_{d,t}$ might capture this differential growth rather than the effect of trade policies. To overcome this shortcoming, I instrument Tariff$_{d,t}$ with TrTariff$_{d,t}$, defined as

$$\text{TrTariff}_{d,t} = \frac{\sum_i \text{Worker}_{d,i,1991} \cdot \text{Tariff}_{i,t}}{\sum_i \text{Worker}_{d,i,1991}}.$$

TrTariff$_{d,t}$, nonscaled tariffs, ignores the workers in nontraded industries. It weighs industry tariffs with employment weights that sum to one for the share of people in traded goods in each district. Thus, a district that has 1 percent workers in traded industries and another district where 100 percent of workers are in traded industries will have the same value of TrTariff$_{d,t}$ if, within the traded industries, the industrial composition is the same. Since the variation in TrTariff$_{d,t}$ does not reflect the size of the traded sector within a district, the non-scaled tariff would overstate the magnitude of any effect trade policy might have. Yet TrTariff$_{d,t}$ forms a good instrument, as it is strongly correlated with the scaled tariffs and overcomes the correlation with district initial poverty that is there by construction in Tariff$_{d,t}$. Table 7.2 presents the results from the first stage. Following equation (1), I estimate the following specification:

(2) $\text{Tariff}_{d,t} = \alpha + \beta \cdot \text{TrTariff}_{d,t} + \gamma_t + \delta_d + \varepsilon_{d,t},$

with γ_t and δ_d defined as above. Columns (1) and (3) present the correlation between the scaled and nonscaled tariffs. There is a very strong relation-

Table 7.2	First stage: Relationship between scaled and nonscaled tariffs (dependent variable: Tariff)			
	Rural		Urban	
	(1)	(2)	(3)	(4)
TrTariff	0.356***	0.633***	0.407***	0.687***
	(0.090)	(0.089)	(0.091)	(0.150)
TrTariff · Post		0.288***		0.214*
		(0.051)		(0.118)
R^2	0.84	0.86	0.91	0.91
No. of observations	728	728	724	724

Notes: All regressions include year and district dummies. Standard errors (in parentheses) are corrected for clustering at the state year level. Regressions are weighted by the square root of the number of people in a district.

***Significant at the 1 percent level.

*Significant at the 10 percent level.

ship between the nonscaled and scaled tariffs in both urban and rural India.

Another instrument is suggested by figure 7.1, panel G: tariff changes are linearly related to initial tariffs. One important principle in the tariff changes was to standardize the tariffs (reduce the standard deviation). A natural consequence of this is that the higher the tariff initially, the greater the reduction. Thus, I use preform unscaled tariffs times a post dummy, in addition to the unscaled tariffs, as instruments for tariff reduction, namely:

(3) $\text{Tariff}_{d,t} = \alpha + \beta \cdot \text{TrTariff}_{d,t} + \theta \cdot \text{Post}_t \cdot \text{TrTariff}_{d,1987} + \gamma_t + \delta_d + \varepsilon_{d,t}$

Columns (2) and (4) of table 7.2 include the interaction of the initial unscaled tariff and a postliberalization dummy. The interaction of the nonscaled tariffs times a post dummy is also strongly correlated with the scaled tariffs and adds explanatory power in all rural subsamples. In the urban sector, the relationship is not as strong.

Data on outcome variables are available for three years—1987, 1993, and 1999—while tariff data are available annually. It is not known how soon national policy changes affect regional outcomes, although there is probably some lag. If the 1993 outcomes were matched to the 1991 tariffs, 1993 would count as a pre year, while if they were matched to the 1992 tariffs, it would be a post year. To avoid this problem, 1993 is omitted from the analysis. I use the earliest available data, 1987, for the preform tariff measure, and the 1997 data as the post measure.

7.5 Results

I estimate four versions of equation (1): the ordinary least squares (OLS) relationship using $\text{Tariff}_{d,t}$; a reduced form using $\text{TrTariff}_{d,t}$; instrumenting for c using $\text{TrTariff}_{d,t}$; and finally instrumenting for $\text{Tariff}_{d,t}$ with both $\text{TrTariff}_{d,t}$ and with $\text{TrTariff}_{d,1987} \cdot \text{Post}_t$, where Post_t is a dummy equal to 1 in year 1999. Since the dependent variable is an estimate, I weight the observations by the square root of the average number of households in a district across rounds. Year dummies are included to account for macroeconomic shocks and time trends that affect outcomes equally across India, while district fixed effects absorb district-specific time-invariant heterogeneity. Outcomes of districts within a state might be correlated, since industrial composition may be correlated within a state; thus, I cluster the standard errors at the state year level. The results for the four outcomes of interest are presented in table 7.3: those for rural India in columns (1)–(4) and those for urban India in columns (5)–(8). Each panel gives the results for a different dependent variable. Columns (1) and (5) give the OLS relationship, columns (2) and (6) the reduced form, and columns (3), (4), (7), and (8), the instrumental variables (IV) results. In columns (4) and (8), I use both the unscaled tariffs and the preform unscaled tariffs times a postreform dummy as an instrument.

Table 7.3   Effect of trade liberalization on poverty and inequality in Indian districts

	Rural				Urban			
	Tariff (1)	TrTariff (2)	IV-TrTariff (3)	IV-TrTariff, Init TrTariff (4)	Tariff (5)	TrTariff (6)	IV-TrTariff (7)	IV-TrTariff, Init TrTariff (8)
	A. Dependent variable: Poverty rate							
Tariff measure	−0.287**	−0.297***	−0.834***	−0.687***	−0.215	−0.065	−0.156	−0.403
	(0.118)	(0.084)	(0.250)	(0.225)	(0.190)	(0.156)	(0.353)	(0.275)
No. of observations	725	725	725	725	703	703	703	703
	B. Dependent variable: Poverty gap							
Tariff measure	−0.129***	−0.114***	−0.319***	−0.206***	−0.084	−0.032	−0.076	−0.131
	(0.038)	(0.021)	(0.073)	(0.075)	(0.052)	(0.046)	(0.101)	(0.087)
No. of observations	725	725	725	725	703	703	703	703
	C. Dependent variable: StdLog consumption							
Tariff measure	−0.086	−0.094	−0.265	−0.161	0.092	0.108	0.257	0.213
	(0.154)	(0.082)	(0.228)	(0.183)	(0.094)	(0.115)	(0.295)	(0.250)
No. of observations	725	725	725	725	703	703	703	703
	D. Dependent variable: Log deviation of consumption							
Tariff measure	−0.016	−0.020	−0.057	−0.020	0.034	0.090	0.215	0.172
	(0.066)	(0.042)	(0.115)	(0.071)	(0.062)	(0.066)	(0.174)	(0.144)
No. of observations	725	725	725	725	703	703	703	703

Notes: All regressions include year and district dummies. Standard errors (in parentheses) are corrected for clustering at the state year level. Regressions are weighted by the square root of the number of people in a district.

***Significant at the 1 percent level.

**Significant at the 5 percent level.

In rural India, for both measures of poverty, there is a strong statistically significant negative relationship between district-level tariffs and poverty. The decline in tariffs as a result of the sharp trade liberalization appears to have led to a relative increase in the poverty rate and poverty gap in districts whose exposure to liberalization was more intense. The average district experienced a 5.5 percentage point reduction in the scaled district tariffs. The point estimates of the various specifications are similar and suggest that this 5.5 percentage point drop would lead to an increase in the poverty rate of 3.2 to 4.6 percentage points, and a 1.1 to 1.8 percentage point increase in the poverty gap. Given that poverty rate in the average district decreased by 12.7 percentage points and that poverty gap decreased by 4 percentage points during the entire decade, the effects of exposure to liberalization are rather large. Surprisingly, there is no statistically significant relationship between trade exposure and poverty in urban India. Although the point estimates are still negative, the magnitude of the coefficients is much smaller than in rural India. There is no statistically significant relationship between trade liberalization and either measure of inequality for the average district in either rural or urban India.

7.5.1   Why Rural?

The empirical literature on trade liberalization so far has focused predominantly on the manufacturing sector and urban areas because these were the areas most commonly affected by trade liberalization (Goldberg and Pavcnik 2004). Thus, it is rather surprising that the effect of trade liberalization on districts is more pronounced in rural India than in urban India.[18] A close look at the evolution of tariff barriers and NTBs in figure 7.1 suggests an explanation. Agriculture was not omitted from the 1991 reforms in India. Tariffs of agricultural products fell in line with tariffs of manufacturing and other goods. While quantity restrictions and licensing requirements on both the import and export of agricultural products (out of a concern for food security) were removed later than on other goods, the share of agricultural products that could be freely imported jumped from 7 percent in 1989 to 40 percent in 1998. Between 1998 and 2001 this number reached more than 80 percent.

In addition, the agricultural tariffs and NTBs are strongly correlated. The postliberalization data (the fifty-fifth round of the NSS) was collected from mid-1999 to mid-2000, right when the bulk of the removal of NTBs was taking place. Thus, the tariff measure may be capturing the effect of both tariff barriers and NTBs and reflect the short-term effect of the change in relative price of agricultural products on the extensive rural pop-

---

18. On the other hand, rural areas are where the poor people in India are concentrated. On the eve of the 1991 reforms, both poverty rates and poverty depth were almost double in rural areas (40 versus 22.8 percent poverty rate and 9 versus 4.7 percent poverty depth).

ulation. I construct separate measures of agricultural tariffs and mining and manufacturing tariffs that a district faces and regress district poverty and inequality on these measures of trade policy. Appendix table 7A.2 reveals that the results are driven by agricultural tariffs.[19] There is little relationship between mining and manufacturing tariffs and district outcomes, although, due to the large standard errors of the point estimates, I can not reject for any of the outcomes and for any of the subsamples that the effect of mining and manufacturing tariffs and of agricultural tariffs is the same. The finding is not that surprising; manufacturing and mining workers represent only 6 percent of workers in the typical rural district—thus, it is plausible that even if trade liberalization had a sizable effect on their well-being or relative earnings, it would not be reflected in district-level outcomes.

Furthermore, people involved in agriculture are the most vulnerable, often with little access to insurance devices. There is no shortage of press accounts of farmers committing suicide in the face of adverse shocks in India. Manufacturing workers, on the other hand, tend to be relatively richer than agricultural workers: significant decline in income may not be enough to push them below the poverty line.

7.5.2 Robustness

The effects of liberalization identified in this paper could be incorrect if measures of trade liberalization were correlated with omitted time-varying variables that affect poverty and inequality. In this section, I first examine whether districts with different initial industrial compositions were on different growth paths. I then determine whether preexisting conditions within districts are correlated with subsequent tariff changes. Finally, I measure whether initial (1987) conditions other than industrial composition in districts are correlated with subsequent changes in poverty and, if so, whether they are driving the results.

To address the concern that districts with different industrial composition may be experiencing different time trends in poverty and inequality that are (spuriously) correlated with tariff changes, I perform a falsification test. In particular, I test whether changes in poverty and inequality in the two periods prior to the reform (from 1983 to 1987) are correlated with measures of trade liberalization from 1987 to 1997.[20] I use the four specifications (OLS, reduced form, and both IV specifications), but now using 1983 and 1987 outcomes as pre and post, rather than the 1987 and 1999 outcomes. The results are presented in table 7.4. In both urban and rural

19. Note that the magnitudes of the coefficients in appendix table 7A.2 are not interpretable, as the measures of agricultural and mining and manufacturing tariffs are not scaled by the share of population employed in the particular sector.
20. Note that the analysis can be performed only at the region level, as district identifiers are not available in the thirty-eighth round of the NSS.

Table 7.4   Prereform test: Correlation between prereform trends in outcomes and tariff change

	Rural				Urban			
	OLS (1)	RF (2)	IV-TrTariff (3)	IV-TrTariff, Init TrTariff (4)	OLS (5)	RF (6)	IV-TrTariff (7)	IV-TrTariff, Init TrTariff (8)
A. Dependent variable: Poverty rate								
Tariff change	0.065 (0.571)		0.842 (0.851)	0.746 (0.762)	−0.092 (0.373)		0.274 (0.563)	0.375 (0.576)
TrTariff change		0.333 (0.326)				0.148 (0.289)		
R^2	0.001	0.033			0.002	0.004		
No. of observations	62	62	62	62	60	60	60	60
B. Dependent variable: Poverty gap								
Tariff change	0.007 (0.197)		0.114 (0.273)	0.091 (0.240)	−0.079 (0.117)		−0.194 (0.238)	−0.170 (0.211)
TrTariff change		0.045 (0.108)				−0.015 (0.128)		
R^2	0.000	0.003			0.013	0.016		
No. of observations	62	62	62	62	60	60	60	60
C. Dependent variable: StdLog consumption								
Tariff change	0.178 (0.131)		0.008 (0.287)	−0.119 (0.260)	−0.055 (0.170)		0.180 (0.320)	0.025 (0.260)
TrTariff change		0.003 (0.114)				0.097 (0.160)		
R^2	0.027	0.000			0.002	0.004		
No. of observations	62	62	62	62	60	60	60	60
D. Dependent variable: Log deviation of consumption								
Tariff change	0.074 (0.071)		−0.023 (0.141)	−0.094 (0.119)	−0.102 (0.107)		0.118 (0.213)	0.041 (0.169)
TrTariff change		−0.009 (0.055)				0.064 (0.108)		
R^2	0.011	0.000			0.013	0.004		
No. of observations	62	62	62	62	60	60	60	60

Notes: Standard errors (in parentheses) are corrected for clustering at the state level. Regressions are weighted by the square root of the number of people in the region. Dependent variables are Outcome1983 minus Outcome1987.

areas, there seems to be no correlation between tariff changes and the pre-reform trend in any of the outcomes.

In tables 7.5 and 7.6, I investigate the possibility that the results might be driven by convergence or omitted variables.[21] I control for time-varying effect of various prereform district characteristics as well as initial levels of outcomes, by including the interaction of these initial characteristics and a postliberalization dummy, estimating:

$$(4) \qquad y_{d,t} = \alpha + \beta \cdot \mathrm{Tariff}_{d,t} + \theta \cdot \mathrm{Post}_t \cdot X_{d,1987} + \gamma_t + \delta_d + \varepsilon_{d,t}$$

In all specifications I include in $X_{d,1987}$ initial industrial composition in the district (namely, percentage of workers in agriculture, manufacturing, mining, trade, transport, and services; workers in construction are the omitted category), percentage literate, and the share of scheduled caste and scheduled tribes population. I sequentially add as controls the initial level of the log of mean per capita expenditure in the district, the prereform trend in the outcome variable (the difference between its 1983 and 1987 value), and finally the initial value of the dependent variable itself instrumented by its value in 1983. I also allow for differential time trends in district outcomes across states with pro-employer, pro-worker, and neutral labor laws by including post times labor law fixed effects.[22] In columns (1)–(4), I use only $\mathrm{TrTariff}_{d,t}$ as an instrument for $\mathrm{Tariff}_{d,t}$, while in columns (5)–(8), I instrument the scaled tariff with both $\mathrm{TrTariff}_{d,t}$ and the initial level interacted with a postliberalization dummy. Columns (4) and (8) include the instrumented value of the lagged dependent variable, where the 1983 level is used as an instrument for the 1987 level.[23]

The inclusion of district initial characteristics does not substantially change the results at the district level. Controlling for initial per capita expenditure or prereform outcome reduces the size of the point estimates (from 0.8 to 0.44 for poverty rate and from 0.32 to 0.12 for poverty gap when the nonscaled tariff is the only instrument, and from 0.68 to 0.45 for poverty rate and from 0.21 to 0.12 for poverty gap when both the nonscaled tariff and its initial level are used as instruments). It may be that some of the variation in poverty depth and incidence that equation (1) attributed to trade liberalization was in fact due to convergence. According to these corrected estimates, the decline in tariffs increased relative poverty incidence by about 2 and poverty gap by 0.6 percentage points in the average district.

I also address the concern that some other reforms concurrent with trade

21. I present the analysis only for the rural sample from now on, as the effect of trade liberalization in the urban sector cannot be precisely estimated.
22. Indian states are classified as having pro-worker, neutral, or pro-employer labor laws by Besley and Burgess (2004).
23. Including the actual value would be equivalent to regressing changes on levels: if there is mean reversion and measurement error, the coefficient could be biased. In fact, the size of the coefficient on the initial level of the outcomes suggests implausibly strong convergence.

Table 7.5   Effect of trade liberalization on poverty and inequality in rural India controlling for initial characteristics and other reforms (district level)

	IV-TrTariff				IV-TrTariff, Init TrTariff			
	(1)	(2)	(3)	(4)	(5)	(6)	(7)	(8)
A. Dependent variable: Poverty rate								
Tariff Measure	−0.607***	−0.434**	−0.441	−0.444**	−0.418***	−0.426***	−0.522**	−0.456***
	(0.232)	(0.217)	(0.281)	(0.208)	(0.141)	(0.163)	(0.206)	(0.134)
Logmean		0.469***	0.340***			0.469***	0.338***	
		(0.035)	(0.044)			(0.034)	(0.041)	
Trend			−0.322***				−0.322***	
			(0.067)				(0.067)	
Lagged 43				−0.419***				−0.417***
				(0.123)				(0.120)
B. Dependent variable: Poverty gap								
Tariff Measure	−0.235***	−0.175***	−0.196**	−0.118*	−0.121**	−0.124**	−0.177**	−0.118***
	(0.075)	(0.066)	(0.090)	(0.069)	(0.062)	(0.063)	(0.080)	(0.041)
Logmean		0.161***	0.126***			0.162***	0.126***	
		(0.015)	(0.013)			(0.015)	(0.013)	
Trend			−0.319***				−0.318***	
			(0.064)				(0.064)	
Lagged 43				−0.576***				−0.576***
				(0.144)				(0.131)
C. Dependent variable: StdLog consumption								
Tariff Measure	−0.192	−0.244	−0.268	−0.057	−0.083	−0.078	−0.175	0.006
	(0.258)	(0.260)	(0.249)	(0.232)	(0.197)	(0.203)	(0.187)	(0.202)
Logmean		−0.140***	−0.047			−0.136***	−0.045	
		(0.035)	(0.040)			(0.035)	(0.041)	
Trend			−0.635***				−0.635***	
			(0.063)				(0.063)	
Lagged 43				−0.382				−0.410
				(0.278)				(0.261)
D. Dependent variable: Log deviation of consumption								
Tariff Measure	−0.009	−0.037	−0.095	0.044	−0.005	−0.004	−0.079	0.020
	(0.131)	(0.120)	(0.098)	(0.108)	(0.081)	(0.082)	(0.074)	(0.097)
Logmean		−0.078***	−0.031*			−0.077***	−0.030	
		(0.018)	(0.018)			(0.019)	(0.019)	
Trend			−0.584***				−0.584***	
			(0.100)				(0.100)	
Lagged 43				−0.570*				−0.547*
				(0.309)				(0.309)

Notes: No. of observations = 725. All regressions include year, district dummies, and state labor law year dummies, as well as preform literacy, share of SC/ST population, and industrial structure, which are interacted with a post dummy. Regressions are weighted by the square root of the number of people in a district or region. The data are from the 43rd and 55th rounds of the NSS. Standard errors (in parentheses) are corrected for clustering at the state year level. In columns (1)–(4), the district tariff is instrumented by the nonscaled tariff. In columns (5)–(8), the district tariff is instrumented by the nonscaled tariff and the interaction of prereform nonscaled tariff and a post dummy. In columns (4) and (8) the level of the lagged dependent variable is instrumented with the value of the dependent variables in 1983.

***Significant at the 1 percent level.
**Significant at the 5 percent level.
*Significant at the 10 percent level.

Table 7.6   Effect of trade liberalization on poverty and inequality in rural India controlling for initial characteristics and other reform (district level)

	IV-TrTariff				IV-TrTariff, Init TrTariff			
	(1)	(2)	(3)	(4)	(5)	(6)	(7)	(8)
A. Dependent variable: Poverty rate								
Tariff Measure	-0.573***	-0.446**	-0.428	-0.447**	-0.413***	-0.402***	-0.495**	-0.445***
	(0.222)	(0.201)	(0.274)	(0.202)	(0.149)	(0.152)	(0.203)	(0.129)
Logmean		0.485***	0.353***			0.486***	0.350***	
		(0.034)	(0.043)			(0.033)	(0.040)	
Trend			-0.310***				-0.310***	
			(0.068)				(0.068)	
Lagged 43				-0.441***				-0.441***
				(0.135)				(0.133)
FDI opened	-0.051	-0.215***	-0.134*	-0.152***	-0.055	-0.216***	-0.132*	-0.152***
	(0.059)	(0.057)	(0.073)	(0.055)	(0.059)	(0.054)	(0.069)	(0.052)
License industries	0.008	0.050	0.069	0.020	0.012	0.051	0.067	0.021
	(0.059)	(0.077)	(0.074)	(0.074)	(0.059)	(0.075)	(0.074)	(0.073)
Bank branches per capita	3,802***	1,013	1,285	1,293	3,787***	1,001	1,304	1,291
	(789)	(766)	(861)	(1,125)	(771)	(770)	(894)	(1,117)
B. Dependent variable: Poverty gap								
Tariff Measure	-0.224***	-0.181***	-0.190**	-0.118	-0.122*	-0.117*	-0.169**	-0.115***
	(0.073)	(0.069)	(0.093)	(0.073)	(0.066)	(0.063)	(0.082)	(0.042)
Logmean		0.166***	0.128***			0.168***	0.129***	
		(0.017)	(0.015)			(0.017)	(0.014)	
Trend			-0.313***				-0.312***	
			(0.063)				(0.063)	
Lagged 43				-0.604***				-0.607***
				(0.160)				(0.147)
FDI opened industries	-0.008	-0.064***	-0.028	-0.039**	-0.011	-0.066***	-0.028	-0.040***
	(0.018)	(0.020)	(0.024)	(0.016)	(0.019)	(0.021)	(0.024)	(0.015)
License industries	-0.002	0.012	0.021	0.005	0.000	0.014	0.022	0.005
	(0.017)	(0.021)	(0.021)	(0.019)	(0.017)	(0.021)	(0.022)	(0.019)
Bank branches per capita	1,213***	260	330	115	1,204***	242	324	110
	(232)	(224)	(267)	(366)	(224)	(219)	(268)	(342)
C. Dependent variable: Log deviation of consumption								
Tariff Measure	-0.175	-0.213	-0.244	-0.066	-0.061	-0.063	-0.162	0.004
	(0.255)	(0.260)	(0.251)	(0.228)	(0.201)	(0.208)	(0.193)	(0.204)
Logmean		-0.147***	-0.050			-0.142***	-0.048	
		(0.036)	(0.038)			(0.036)	(0.039)	
Trend			-0.622***				-0.622***	
			(0.069)				(0.068)	
Lagged 43				-0.316				-0.356
				(0.324)				(0.295)
FDI opened industries	-0.089*	-0.040	-0.054	-0.054	-0.092*	-0.045	-0.057	-0.051
	(0.049)	(0.049)	(0.052)	(0.053)	(0.049)	(0.050)	(0.051)	(0.052)
License industries	0.067	0.054	0.033	0.037	0.070	0.059	0.035	0.035
	(0.042)	(0.045)	(0.051)	(0.052)	(0.044)	(0.046)	(0.052)	(0.051)
Bank branches per capita	1,119	1,964*	1,249	1,090	1,109	1,922*	1,226	1,081
	(1,057)	(1,091)	(964)	(1,032)	(1,075)	(1,109)	(962)	(1,042)
D. Dependent variable: Log deviation of consumption								
Tariff Measure	-0.002	-0.022	-0.089	0.040	0.008	0.007	-0.070	0.021
	(0.119)	(0.116)	(0.097)	(0.104)	(0.081)	(0.083)	(0.076)	(0.095)
Logmean		-0.078***	-0.029*			-0.077***	-0.028*	
		(0.018)	(0.017)			(0.018)	(0.017)	

Table 7.6   (continued)

	IV-TrTariff				IV-TrTariff, Init Tr Tariff			
	(1)	(2)	(3)	(4)	(5)	(6)	(7)	(8)
Trend			−0.579***				−0.579***	
			(0.102)				(0.102)	
Lagged 43				−0.492				−0.463
				(0.404)				(0.388)
FDI opened industries	−0.055**	−0.029	−0.039	−0.023	−0.056**	−0.030	−0.039	−0.025
	(0.023)	(0.022)	(0.026)	(0.033)	(0.023)	(0.023)	(0.026)	(0.032)
License industries	0.044**	0.037**	0.024	0.013	0.044**	0.038**	0.025	0.015
	(0.017)	(0.018)	(0.023)	(0.027)	(0.018)	(0.019)	(0.024)	(0.026)
Bank branches per capita	258	704	423	251	257	696	418	253
	(510)	(518)	(436)	(458)	(509)	(519)	(436)	(455)

Note: See notes to table 7.5.
***Significant at the 1 percent level.
**Significant at the 5 percent level.
*Significant at the 10 percent level.

liberalization may be driving the results. In particular, in 1991 the government of India increased the number of de-licensed industries and specified a list of industries for automatic approval for foreign direct investment (FDI).[24] Substantial reforms were initiated in the financial and banking sector as well. Following the same methodology as in the construction of district tariffs, I construct district employment-weighted share of license-industries and district employment-weighted share of industries that are open to FDI.[25] The number of bank branches per capita in a district captures the potentially confounding effect of banking reforms.[26]

In table 7.6, I replicate the specifications presented in table 7.5 including these time-varying district-level measures of reforms. The effect of trade liberalization on poverty is completely insensitive to the additional controls. There is no correlation between poverty and the number of bank branches per capita or share of industries under a license. A larger share of industries open to FDI, however, is associated with faster reduction in poverty. As globalization is typically defined as not only trade liberalization but also opening to foreign investment, it is important to emphasize

24. Foreign investment was tightly regulated prior to 1991. Foreign companies needed to obtain specific prior approval from the Indian government, and foreign investment was limited to 40 percent. In 1991, the government created a list of high technology and high investment-priority industries with automatic permission for foreign equity share up to 51 percent. Over the 1990s this list was gradually expanded.

25. Data on policies regarding industrial delicensing and opening to FDI were compiled from various publications of the Reserve Bank of India *Handbook of Industrial Statistics.*

26. The Indian government heavily regulates private and public banks, as it considers the banking system an integral tool in its efforts to meet a number of social goals, such as poverty reduction. Indeed, Burgess and Pande (2005) have shown that rural bank branch expansion over the 1980s led to reduction in poverty.

this finding. It also reconciles Hanson's conclusion in chapter 10 of this volume, which employs similar methodology, that more globalized areas in Mexico experienced a larger increase in labor income with the finding that trade liberalization slowed poverty reduction in more exposed districts in India. Hanson's definition of exposure to globalization takes into account the share of maquiladora value added in state GDP, the share of FDI in state GDP, and the share of imports and exports in state GDP, while the main findings of this study concern the consequences of tariff liberalization.

In appendix table 7A.3 I investigate the role of imports versus exports, in addition to FDI, by including the district employment-weighted industry imports and exports. I use 1987 import/export data for the prereform period, and the 1993–97 annual average for the postreform period. Since imports and exports are the endogenous response to trade policy, exchange rate shocks, foreign demand, and so on, these regressions do not warrant a causal interpretation, yet they illustrate that imports are associated with higher, and exports with lower, incidence of poverty. These correlations are in line with the findings in Goldberg and Pavcnik's study in chapter 6 of this volume. Goldberg and Pavcnik investigate the effect of Colombia's trade liberalization on urban unemployment, informality, minimum wage compliance, and poverty, by exploiting variation in the timing and magnitude of tariff reductions across manufacturing sectors. While they find no robust relationship between tariff changes and various labor market outcomes, higher exposure to import competition is associated with greater likelihood of unemployment, informality, and poverty, while higher exports correlate with lower informality, lower poverty, and better minimum wage compliance.

7.6   Discussion and Conclusion

So far this paper has established that, whatever the India-wide effects of trade liberalization were, rural areas with a high concentration of industries that were disproportionately affected by tariff reductions experienced slower progress in poverty reduction. However, for these areas, there was no discernible effect on inequality.

The regionally disparate effects of liberalization are not consistent with standard trade theory. In the hypothetical world of a standard trade model, with perfect factor mobility across regions, labor would migrate in response to wage and price shocks, equalizing the incidence of poverty across regions. Estimating equation (1) would yield an estimate of β equal to zero, indicating that the local intensity of liberalization has no effect on local poverty.

The interpretation of estimates of equation (1) as effects of liberalization on regional outcomes is correct only if labor is immobile across geograph-

ical districts within India in the short to medium run—that is, if each district represents a separate labor market. While this represents an immediate departure from standard trade theory, the assumption is realistic for the case of India: the absence of mobility is striking. Moreover, the pattern of migration has remained remarkably constant through time, with no visible increase after the economic reforms of 1991.

Table 7.7 presents some estimates of migration for urban and rural India based on the three rounds of the NSS (1983, 1987, and 1999) that included questions on the migration particurlars of household members. Overall migration is not low; 20 to 23 percent of rural and 31 to 33 percent of urban residents have changed location of residence at least once in their lifetime. Most migrants are women relocating at marriage: around 40 percent of females in rural and urban India report a change in location, versus 7 percent of men in rural and 26 percent of men in urban locations. However, the migration most relevant for this study is short-run movement (within the past ten years) of people across district boundaries or within district across different sectors (i.e., from an urban area to a rural one, or vice versa). Only 3 to 4 percent of people living in rural areas reported changing either district or sector within the past ten years. Again, the percentage of women so doing is double the share of men. For people living in urban areas, the percentage of migrants is substantially higher. Yet less than 0.5 percent of the population in rural and 4 percent of the population in urban areas moved for economic considerations (or employment).

These low migration figures, combined with a second characteristic of India's economy—namely, the large and growing disparities in income across Indian states—challenge the standard theoretical framework. Ahluwalia (2002), Datt and Ravallion (2002), Sachs, Bajpai, and Ramiath (2002), Bandyopadhyay (2003), and others document significant differences in the level of state GDP per capita and growth rate of state output.

Even if there is little migration across districts, there could be high levels of reallocation within districts across industries. In a related study (Topalova 2004b) I examine whether, as standard trade theory predicts, there is intersectoral reallocation of labor and capital. There is no evidence of significant reallocation in the sample of all Indian states, although in the sample of Indian states with flexible labor laws, employment is positively correlated with industry tariffs.[27] This correlation is consistent with previous findings of faster growth of output and employment (Besley and Burgess 2004) and a higher elasticity of labor demand with respect to output price in states with flexible labor laws (Hasan, Mitra, and Ramaswamy

27. Besley and Burgess (2004) classify Indian states as pro-worker, pro-employer, or neutral, based on amendments of the Industrial Disputes Act. Hasan, Mitra, and Ramaswamy (2003) combine these categories with the ranking of the investment climate in Indian states from a survey of managers conducted by the World Bank, in order to classify states as having flexible or inflexible labor laws. Topalova (2004b) adopts the Hasan et al. classification.

Table 7.7   Migration patterns

	All			Male			Female		
	1983	1987	1999	1983	1987	1999	1983	1987	1999
A. Rural									
Place of birth different from place of residence	0.209	0.232	0.244	0.072	0.075	0.069	0.351	0.399	0.427
Moved within the past 10 years	0.094	0.102	0.097	0.047	0.048	0.040	0.144	0.160	0.156
Moved within the past 10 years, excluding migration within the same district and within the same sector (i.e., rural and urban to rural and urban)	0.029	0.032	0.036	0.020	0.021	0.021	0.039	0.044	0.051
Moved within the past 10 years from urban to rural	0.011	0.013	0.013	0.010	0.011	0.011	0.012	0.015	0.016
Moved within the past 10 years because of employment, excluding migration within the same district and within the same sector	0.005	0.005	0.004	0.008	0.009	0.007	0.002	0.002	0.001
B. Urban									
Place of birth different from place of residence	0.316	0.329	0.333	0.270	0.268	0.256	0.366	0.396	0.418
Moved within the past 10 years	0.182	0.185	0.174	0.168	0.164	0.151	0.198	0.209	0.199
Moved within the past 10 years, excluding migration within the same district and within the same sector (i.e., rural and urban to rural and urban)	0.131	0.132	0.131	0.125	0.121	0.118	0.138	0.144	0.146
Moved within the past 10 years from rural to urban	0.080	0.080	0.076	0.073	0.070	0.065	0.087	0.091	0.089
Moved within the past 10 years because of employment, excluding migration within the same district and within the same sector	0.044	0.042	0.033	0.074	0.071	0.058	0.010	0.011	0.006

2003). My study (Topalova 2004b) also examines whether these differences in the institutional environment and microeconomic flexibility affected the impact of liberalization: the most pronounced effects on poverty occurred in areas with inflexible labor laws (those that saw no change in industrial structure in response to trade liberalization) while inequality rose as a result of trade liberalization in areas with flexible labor laws.

My study (Topalova 2004b) further investigates whether the adjustment came through the price system, by looking at the effect of tariff changes on wages and wage premia, and finds substantial adjustment in wages and industry premia, including industry premia of agricultural workers. In chapter 8 in this volume Goh and Javorcik find that in Poland, workers in sectors with the largest tariff declines experienced the highest increase in wages; in India, these workers suffered the highest relative decrease in wage premia. Goh and Javorcik posit that in Poland's case, firms responded to higher import competition by increasing productivity and rewarded the increased labor productivity with higher wages. I find similar results in India (Topalova 2004a): microevidence suggests that firms in industries that were relatively more liberalized experienced higher productivity and productivity growth. However, in India, these trade-induced productivity increases were probably not shared with the workers or were insufficient to offset the relative downward pressure on factor returns.

The mechanisms discussed above are consistent with a specific factor model of trade in which labor is the specific factor in the short run. Rigid labor markets fostered by labor market regulations in parts of India prevented the reallocation of factors in the face of trade liberalization in those areas. Changes in relative output prices led to changes in relative sector returns to the specific factors. As those employed in traded industries were not at the top of the income distribution on the eve of the trade reform, the relative fall in wages contributed to the slower poverty reduction. This effect was aggravated by the slower overall growth in registered manufacturing employment in areas with inflexible labor laws, which retarded the pull out of poverty of the poorest subsistence farmers. In contrast, areas in which reallocation was easier and growth was faster (because of labor laws) were shielded from the effect of trade liberalization. In those areas, the changes in the income distribution seem to have taken place in the high end, as some workers tapped into the benefits of liberalization, thereby increasing the consumption inequality.

This is the first study (to my knowledge) to document such a relationship between trade liberalization and poverty within a developing or developed country. The findings are important from a policy perspective as an increasing number of developing countries pursue policies of trade liberalization, hoping to boost economic growth, raise living standards, and reduce poverty. This paper does not measure the overall effect of trade liberalization on income growth and poverty alleviation. There was a sub-

stantial reduction in poverty in India over the 1990s, which trade reforms may have boosted or slowed down. This paper establishes that different regions within India experienced differential effects of trade liberalization. Those areas that were more exposed to potential foreign competition did not reap as much of the benefit (or bore a disproportionate share of the burden) of liberalization in terms of poverty reduction.

A critical component to the findings of this study, as well as the study on Colombia in this volume, is the absence of labor mobility in the short to medium run. Workers do not relocate from sectors that should be contracting to those that should be expanding fast enough, thus impeding one of the main mechanisms that generate benefits from trade. Enhancing labor mobility will likely minimize the adjustment costs to trade opening. This study presents some evidence to this effect: the impact of trade on relative poverty in India was most pronounced in areas with inflexible labor laws, where labor mobility was hindered. If some of the immobility of labor is institutionally driven, then complementary measures to trade opening, such as labor market reform, can ease the shock of liberalization and minimize its unequalizing effects.

Appendix

Table 7A.1   **Summary statistics**

Variable	Rural			Urban		
	No. of observations	Mean	Standard deviation	No. of observations	Mean	Standard deviation
	A. 38th round 1983					
Poverty rate	368	0.429	0.173	372	0.439	0.147
Poverty gap	379	0.117	0.067	372	0.122	0.051
Standard deviation of log consumption	379	0.497	0.061	372	0.540	0.065
Logarithmic deviation	379	0.137	0.037	372	0.163	0.042
Tariff	n.a.	n.a.			n.a.	n.a.
TrTariff	n.a.	n.a.			n.a.	n.a.
Agricultural tariff	n.a.	n.a.			n.a.	n.a.
Mining and manufacturing tariff		n.a.	n.a.		n.a.	n.a.
	B. 43rd round 1987					
Poverty rate	379	0.368	0.196	366	0.248	0.168
Poverty gap	379	0.088	0.064	366	0.057	0.050
Standard deviation of log consumption	379	0.456	0.085	366	0.501	0.113
Logarithmic deviation	379	0.120	0.046	366	0.149	0.076
Poverty gap change in the 1980s	379	−0.029	0.062	364	−0.064	0.049

Table 7A.1   (continued)

	Rural			Urban		
Variable	No. of observations	Mean	Standard deviation	No. of observations	Mean	Standard deviation
Poverty rate change in the 1980s	379	−0.061	0.164	364	−0.191	0.145
Standard deviation change in the 1980s	379	−0.040	0.081	364	−0.038	0.115
Log deviation change in the 1980s	379	−0.017	0.048	364	−0.013	0.080
Tariff	364	0.081	0.080	362	0.172	0.085
TrTariff	364	0.883	0.096	362	0.891	0.083
Agricultural tariff	364	0.822	0.142	362	0.782	0.090
Mining and manufacturing tariff	364	0.914	0.043	362	0.923	0.576
Log mean per capita expenditure	379	5.065	0.252	366	5.389	0.274
Percent literate	364	0.368	0.137	362	0.591	0.094
Percent SC/ST	364	0.293	0.161	362	0.154	0.064
Percent farmers	364	0.816	0.103	362	0.194	0.101
Percent manufacturing	364	0.056	0.045	362	0.191	0.088
Percent mining	364	0.005	0.014	362	0.013	0.041
Percent service	364	0.065	0.037	362	0.264	0.073
Percent trade	364	0.032	0.020	362	0.217	0.045
Percent transport	364	0.013	0.011	362	0.073	0.025
		C. 50th round 1993				
Poverty rate	366	0.313	0.179	354	0.191	0.098
Poverty gap	366	0.067	0.052	354	0.039	0.027
Standard deviation of log consumption	366	0.428	0.088	368	0.539	0.056
Logarithmic deviation	366	0.105	0.048	368	0.166	0.038
Tariff	364	0.072	0.074	362	0.156	0.079
TrTariff	364	0.778	0.095	362	0.812	0.082
Agricultural tariff	364	0.632	0.130	362	0.635	0.089
Mining and manufacturing tariff	364	0.825	0.054	362	0.837	0.063
		D. 55th round 1999				
Poverty rate	364	0.241	0.138	360	0.145	0.108
Poverty gap	364	0.048	0.035	360	0.029	0.027
Standard deviation of log consumption	364	0.463	0.106	360	0.529	0.091
Logarithmic deviation	364	0.116	0.042	360	0.157	0.054
Tariff	364	0.026	0.022	362	0.060	0.030
TrTariff	364	0.306	0.060	362	0.317	0.044
Agricultural tariff	364	0.236	0.076	362	0.212	0.052
Mining and manufacturing tariff	364	0.341	0.022	362	0.336	0.030

Notes: SC = scheduled caste; ST = scheduled tribe; n.a. = not available.

Table 7A.2   Sectoral tariffs and poverty and inequality in rural and urban India

	Rural			Urban		
	(1)	(2)	(3)	(4)	(5)	(6)
A. Dependent variable: Poverty rate						
Agricultural tariff	−0.219***		−0.213***	−0.242**		−0.240**
	(0.071)		(0.070)	(0.097)		(0.102)
Mining and manufacturing tariff		0.277	0.221		−0.154	−0.148
		(0.318)	(0.297)		(0.163)	(0.154)
No. of observations	725	725	725	703	703	703
B. Dependent variable: Poverty gap						
Agricultural tariff	−0.081***		−0.080***	−0.066**		−0.065**
	(0.021)		(0.020)	(0.027)		(0.029)
Mining and manufacturing tariff		0.062	0.041		−0.072	−0.071
		(0.123)	(0.113)		(0.049)	(0.047)
No. of observations	725	725	725	703	703	703
C. Dependent variable: StdLog consumption						
Agricultural tariff	−0.110*		−0.110*	0.060		0.060
	(0.064)		(0.062)	(0.091)		(0.092)
Mining and manufacturing tariff		0.030	0.002		0.000	−0.001
		(0.220)	(0.208)		(0.131)	(0.129)
No. of observations	725	725	725	703	703	703
D. Dependent variable: Log deviation of consumption						
Agricultural tariff	−0.037		−0.035	0.053		0.053
	(0.025)		(0.025)	(0.066)		(0.066)
Mining and manufacturing tariff		0.073	0.064		0.024	0.022
		(0.109)	(0.111)		(0.076)	(0.074)
No. of observations	725	725	725	703	703	703

Notes: All regressions include year and district dummies. Standard errors (in parentheses) are corrected for clustering at the state year level. Regressions are weighted by the square root of the number of people in a district.

***Significant at the 1 percent level.

**Significant at the 5 percent level.

*Significant at the 10 percent level.

Table 7A.3 Imports, exports, and poverty in rural India (dependent variable: poverty rate)

	(1)	(2)	(3)	(4)	(5)	(6)	(7)	(8)
Imports of all traded industries	0.010							
	(0.006)							
Imports of agriculture		0.009		0.007		0.017*		0.016*
		(0.012)		(0.013)		(0.009)		(0.009)
Imports of mining/manufacture			0.008***	0.009***			0.006	0.006
			(0.003)	(0.003)			(0.004)	(0.004)
Exports of all traded industries	−0.002*				−0.002			
	(0.001)				(0.001)			
Exports of agriculture		−0.0003		−0.001		−0.001		−0.001
		(0.0018)		(0.002)		(0.001)		(0.001)
Exports of mining/manufacture			−0.002**	−0.002*			−0.002*	−0.001*
			(0.001)	(0.001)			(0.001)	(0.001)
FDI-opened industries	−0.215***	−0.230***	−0.247***	−0.251***	−0.164***	−0.169***	−0.187***	−0.188***
	(0.060)	(0.061)	(0.055)	(0.057)	(0.056)	(0.054)	(0.051)	(0.048)
License industries	0.048	0.064	0.056	0.055	0.020	0.034	0.031	0.029
	(0.070)	(0.076)	(0.072)	(0.072)	(0.065)	(0.071)	(0.070)	(0.069)
Bank branches per capita	782	863	963	957	861	1,059	941	981
	(685)	(727)	(710)	(697)	(1,013)	(1,099)	(1,115)	(1,101)
Logmean	0.504***	0.500***	0.503***	0.502***				
	(0.035)	(0.033)	(0.033)	(0.033)				
Lagged 43					−0.511***	−0.468***	−0.508***	−0.495***
					(0.128)	(0.142)	(0.137)	(0.142)

Notes: No. of observations = 725. All regressions include year, district dummies, and state labor law year dummies, as well as prereform literacy, share of SC/ST population, and industrial structure, which are interacted with a post dummy. Regressions are weighted by the square root of the number of people in a district or region. The data are from the 43rd and 55th rounds of the NSS. Standard errors (in parentheses) are corrected for clustering at the state year level. In columns (1)–(4), the district initial per capita expenditure interacted with a post dummy is included. In columns (5)–(8), the level of the lagged dependent variable, instrumented with the value of the dependent variables in 1983, and interacted with a post dummy, is included.

***Significant at the 1 percent level.

**Significant at the 5 percent level.

*Significant at the 10 percent level.

References

Ahluwalia, Montek. 1999. India's economic reforms: An appraisal. In *India in the era of economic reforms,* ed. J. Sachs, A. Varshney, and N. Bajpai, 26–80. New Delhi: Oxford University Press.

———. 2002. State-level performance under economic reforms in India? In *Economic policy reforms and the Indian economy,* ed. Anne O. Krueger, 91–122. Chicago: University of Chicago Press.

Aksoy, M. A. 1992. The Indian trade regime. World Bank Working Paper Series no. 989. Washington, DC: World Bank.

Attanasio, Orazio, Pinelopi Goldberg, and Nina Pavcnik. 2004. Trade reforms and wage inequality in Colombia. *Journal of Development Economics* 74 (2): 331–66.

Bandyopadhyay, Sanghamitra. 2003. Convergence club empirics: Some dynamics and explanations of unequal growth across Indian states. STICERD Discussion Paper no. DARP 69. London: Suntory and Toyota International Centres for Economics and Related Disciplines.

Banerjee, Abhijit, and Andrew Newman. 2004. Inequality, growth and trade policy. Massachusetts Institute of Technology, Department of Economics, and University College London, Department of Economics. Unpublished Manuscript.

Besley, Timothy, and Robin Burgess. 2004. Can labor regulation hinder economic performance? Evidence from India. *Quarterly Journal of Economics* 119 (1): 91–134.

Bhagwati, Jagdish. 1993. *India in transition: Freeing the economy.* New York: Oxford University Press.

Burgess, Robin, and Rohini Pande. 2005. Do rural banks matter? Evidence from the Indian social banking experiment. *American Economic Review* 95 (3): 780–95.

Cerra, Valerie, and Sweta Saxena. 2000. What caused the 1991 currency crisis in India? IMF Working Paper no. 00/157. Washington, DC: International Monetary Fund, October.

Chopra, Ajai, Charles Collyns, Richard Hemming, Karen Parker, Woosik Chu, and Oliver Fratzscher. 1995. India: Economic reform and growth. IMF Occasional Paper no. 134. Washington, DC: International Monetary Fund, December.

Cragg, Michael Ian, and Mario Epelbaum. 1996. Why has wage dispersion grown in Mexico? Is it the incidence of reforms or the growing demand for skills? *Journal of Development Economics* 51 (1): 99–116.

Cunat, Alejandro, and Marco Maffezzoli. 2001. Growth and interdependence under complete specialization. Bocconi University Working Paper no. 183. Bocconi University (Milan), Department of Economics.

Currie, Janet, and Ann Harrison. 1997. Sharing the costs: The impact of trade reform on capital and labor in Morocco. *Journal of Labor Economics* 15 (3, part 2): 44–71.

Datt, Gaurav, and Martin Ravallion. 2002. Is India's economic growth leaving the poor behind? *Journal of Economic Perspectives* 16 (3): 89–108.

Davis, Donald. 1996. Trade liberalization and income distribution. NBER Working Paper no. 5693. Cambridge, MA: National Bureau of Economic Research.

Deaton, Angus. 2003a. Adjusted Indian poverty estimates for 1999–2000. *Economic and Political Weekly.* January 25, 322–26.

———. 2003b. Prices and poverty in India, 1987–2000. *Economic and Political Weekly.* January 25, 362–68.

Deaton, Angus, and Alessandro Tarozzi. 2005. Prices and poverty in India. Chap.

17 in *The great Indian poverty debate,* ed. A. Deaton and V. Kozel. New Delhi: Macmillan.

Debroy, B., and A. T. Santhanam. 1993. Matching trade codes with industrial codes. *Foreign Trade Bulletin* 24 (1): 5–27.

Dollar, David, and Aart Kraay. 2002. Growth is good for the poor. *Journal of Economic Growth* 7 (3): 195–225.

Edwards, Sebastian. 1998. Openness, productivity and growth: What do we really know? *Economic Journal* 108 (447): 383–98.

Feenstra, Robert, and Gordon Hanson. 1997. Foreign direct investment and relative wages: Evidence from Mexico's maquiladoras. *Journal of International Economics* 42 (2): 371–93.

Feliciano, Zadia. 2001. Workers and trade liberalization: The impact of trade reforms in Mexico on wages and employment. *Industrial and Labor Relations Review* 55 (1): 95–115.

Gang, Ira, and Mihir Pandey. 1996. Trade protection in India: Economics vs. politics? Departmental Working Paper no. 199616. Rutgers University, Department of Economics.

Goldar, Bishwanath. 2002. Trade liberalization and manufacturing employment. ILO Employment Paper no. 2002/34. Geneva: International Labor Organization.

Goldberg, Pinelopi, and Nina Pavcnik. 2001. Trade protection and wages: Evidence from the Colombian trade reforms. NBER Working Paper no. 8575. Cambridge, MA: National Bureau of Economic Research, November.

———. 2004. Trade, inequality, and poverty: What do we know? Evidence from recent trade liberalization episodes in developing countries. NBER Working Paper no. 10593. Cambridge, MA: National Bureau of Economic Research, June.

Goyal, S. K. 1996. Political economy of India's economic reforms. New Delhi: Institute for Studies in Industrial Development. Working Paper, October.

Grossman, Gene, and Elhanan Helpman. 2002. *Interest groups and trade policy.* Princeton, NJ: Princeton University Press.

Hanson, Gordon, and Ann Harrison. 1999. Trade and wage inequality in Mexico. *Industrial and Labor Relations Review* 52 (2): 271–88.

Hasan, Rana, Devashish Mitra, and K. V. Ramaswamy. 2003. Trade reforms, labor regulations and labor demand elasticities: Evidence from India. NBER Working Paper no. 9879. Cambridge, MA: National Bureau of Economic Research, August.

Kremer, Michael, and Eric Maskin. 2003. Globalization and inequality. Harvard University, Department of Economics. Unpublished Manuscript.

Lundberg, Mattias, and Lyn Squire. 2003. The simultaneous evolution of growth and inequality. *Economic Journal* 113 (487): 326–44.

Milanovic, Branko. 2002. Can we discern the effect of globalization on income distribution? Evidence from household budget surveys. World Bank Research Paper no. 2876. Washington, DC: World Bank.

Porto, Guido. 2004. Trade reforms, market access and poverty in Argentina. World Bank Policy Research Working Paper no. 3135. Washington, DC: World Bank.

Rama, Martin. 2003. Globalization and the labor market. *World Bank Research Observer* 18 (2): 159–86.

Revenga, Ana. 1996. Employment and wage effects of trade liberalization: The case of Mexican manufacturing. *Journal of Labor Economics* 15 (3): 20–43.

Sachs, Jeffrey, Nirupam Bajpai, and Ananthi Ramiath. 2002. Understanding regional economic growth in India. CID Working Paper no. 88. Cambridge, MA: Center for International Development, March.

Stiglitz, Joseph. 1970. Factor price equalization in a dynamic economy. *Journal of Political Economy* 78 (3): 456–88.

Topalova, Petia. 2004a. The effect of trade liberalization on productivity: The case of India. IMF Working Paper no. 04/28. Washington, DC: International Monetary Fund. February.

———. 2004b. Factor immobility and regional effects of trade liberalization: Evidence from India. Massachusetts Institute of Technology, Department of Economics. Manuscript, October.

Varshney, Ashutosh. 1999. Mass politics or elite politics? India's economic reforms in comparative perspective. In *India in the era of economic reforms,* ed. J. Sachs, A. Varshney, and N. Bajpai, 222–60. New Delhi: Oxford University Press.

Comment   Robin Burgess

This is a pathbreaking paper. The literature on trade liberalization has tended to look at productivity and growth effects in the narrow domain of manufacturing. Where distributional impact has been considered, the focus again has been on inequality in the wages of manufacturing workers. The welfare effects of trade liberalization have received scant attention. Yet arguably this is what policymakers are interested in as they weigh their options.

The implications of having limited rigorous evaluation in this area of policy are serious. Too often the debates on liberalization and globalization degenerate into a battle between opposing ideologies based on flimsy evidence. Examples of positive or negative effects are marshaled alongside supportive theories to defend a given position. The poor evidence base also implies that debates occur at a general level. Instead of focusing on the advisability of pursuing particular elements within a liberalization reform package the debate tends to become polarized into camps for and against liberalization.

The reason that limited progress has been made in evaluating the welfare effects of trade liberalization has to do with data. Finding repeated observations on poverty and inequality and linking them to exposure to trade liberalization has proven problematic. This paper breaks this deadlock by exploiting the fact that India has repeated household surveys, which enables the author to construct district-level measures of rural and urban poverty and inequality. The household surveys span a period of rapid trade liberalization. Exposure of a district to trade liberalization is determined by prereform industrial structure. Having a higher share of employment in a sector that has experienced tariff reductions implies that it is more exposed to falls in trade protection. By regressing district trade exposure captured by employment-weighted tariff rates on district poverty and inequal-

Robin Burgess is associate professor of economics and director of the Economic Organization and Public Policy Program at the London School of Economics, and a faculty research fellow of the National Bureau of Economic Research.

ity, the author is able to get a sense of whether districts with industrial structures, which made them more exposed to tariff reductions, experienced more or less poverty or inequality reduction than districts that were less exposed.

What Topalova finds is fascinating. Districts that were more exposed to tariff reductions experienced lower falls in rural poverty. Urban poverty was unaffected by tariff reductions. Rural and urban inequality were also unaffected. The paper convincingly demonstrates that these results are robust independent of the specification used. The author is careful to point out that these are relative, within-India results—she cannot say anything about the overall effects of trade liberalization on poverty and inequality. The paper also devotes considerable attention to establishing the exogeneity of tariffs and to ensuring that poverty and inequality are correctly measured at the district level.

Where the paper is weaker is in establishing the mechanisms through which trade liberalization affects rural (and not urban) poverty. When the author breaks out tariff rates she finds that it is agricultural tariffs (and not manufacturing and mining tariffs) that are driving the results. This is an interesting finding, in particular as India was different from other liberalizing countries as it reduced tariffs in agriculture as well as in other sectors. And this finding is of central importance, given that agricultural tariff reductions will be a core issue in upcoming trade rounds.

However, it was not at all clear to me how tariff reductions impacted rural poverty. Are these effects coming through cheaper agricultural imports driving down prices and wages? And, if so, do we see different effects depending on the mix of rural households in a district that are net consumers or net producers of food and agricultural labor? The author finds some evidence of a positive correlation between agricultural imports and rural poverty, which takes us some way in this direction. I nonetheless would have liked to have seen more work linking tariff reductions and imports to specific characteristics of districts that would mediate their impact on rural poverty. This type of analysis would greatly strengthen the paper and help us begin to understand why the effects are rural specific. I also felt that a little more attention could have been given to reconciling the fact that we see no effect on rural inequality, even though rural poverty is affected.

The question of why urban poverty was unaffected is also not clear, given that other work by the author has shown positive effects on manufacturing productivity of tariff reductions. We would also expect wage and price effects linked to trade liberalization to affect urban residents. Pointing to the overall small size of the manufacturing sector affected by tariff reductions is important, but clearly the paper is only scratching the surface here. Given that tariff reductions in other countries have tended to focus on nonagricultural sectors, this is clearly an area where the analysis could be deepened.

The author uses tariff data for 1987–97 and, in effect, is using household survey rounds before and after the major trade liberalization in 1991 to look at effects on poverty and inequality. She interprets the coefficient on her district trade exposure coefficient as the short- or medium-run effects of trade liberalization. This then raises the question of what will happen in the longer term, as terms-of-trade shocks die down. As more recent data come in it would be interesting to see whether the negative impacts of district trade exposure on rural poverty weakens over time.

We know that rural and urban district poverty rates have been falling over the period of the analysis. The final question left open by the paper concerns understanding what is leading poverty to fall more in some districts than in others. The author's preliminary analysis of the correlation between poverty and openness to foreign direct investment goes in this direction. Looking at what has been driving the growth in services that may be less affected by trade liberalization but are likely to be an important part of the poverty reduction story is another way that this work could be extended to give us a more complete picture of the links between liberalization and poverty in Indian districts.

Related work by the author finds that the most pronounced effects on poverty occurred in areas with inflexible labor laws (Topalova 2004). This suggests that rigid labor markets fostered by state-specific labor regulations prevented the reallocation of labor in the face of trade liberalization, thus retarding the pull out of poverty of the poorest subsistence farmers. In contrast, in flexible labor areas, where reallocation was easier and growth was faster, the impact of trade liberalization on poverty was negligible. This highlights how the impact of trade liberalization may be heterogeneous depending on the functioning of labor institutions in different parts of India. Domestic policies pursued by state governments clearly have a bearing on the impact of trade liberalization on the welfare of citizens under their jurisdiction. In particular, labor mobility is emerging as a key theme in understanding why the impact of a common trade liberalization reform varies across different regions of a country like India.

As with all pathbreaking work, this paper raises more questions than it answers. I can see a host of researchers pursuing the questions posed by this important paper in coming years. The paper is an important example of a rising body of work that attempts to use microeconomic variation within countries to evaluate the impact of macroeconomic policies. A huge amount of work has gone into building the household, industrial structure, and trade data sets that underpin this paper. And the author has analyzed these data in a careful and meticulous manner. The policy payoff from using careful microeconomic data analysis of this type to examine the welfare effects of trade liberalization is enormous. The paper has begun to illuminate the mechanisms through which reductions in trade protection affect the welfare of rural and urban residents in India, and the author is able to

look at liberalization in a disaggregated manner. For example, she finds that tariff reductions and openness to foreign direct investment have opposing effects on rural poverty rates. She is also able to control for other factors, like financial liberalization, in her regressions, thus adding to the robustness of her results. This type of analysis, where different elements of a liberalization package are examined, is a major advance on cruder approaches that identify liberalization only via year dummies.

Trade liberalization is an important area of policy on which we had very little concrete evidence on welfare effects before the arrival of this paper. In my view the type of analysis of which this paper is a sterling example will transform the way we do international economics and bring a large chunk of the field into applied microeconomics. As this paper clearly demonstrates, this will be a welcome development both in terms of improving our ability to understand the impact of trade liberalization and in terms of being able to design it to enhance citizen welfare.

References

Topalova, Petia. 2004. Factor immobility and regional effects of trade liberalization: Evidence from India. Massachusetts Institute of Technology, Department of Economics. Unpublished Manuscript.

Trade Protection and Industry Wage Structure in Poland

Chor-ching Goh and Beata S. Javorcik

8.1 Introduction

Rapid trade liberalizations undertaken by many developing and transition countries during the past decade have inspired heated public discussions. Proponents of trade liberalization posit that for developing countries, many of which are small economies with abundant labor, opening would lead to rising wages. They point to the substantial increases in average real wages that have been taking place in open economies in the developing world over the last several decades as evidence that trade does indeed increase demand for the abundant factor—in this case, labor—much like trade theory would predict. In contrast, opponents of trade liberalization speak about the uneven distribution of gains from openness to trade and resulting increases in wage inequality. They also claim that liberalization will lead to a "race to the bottom" in wages and, as a consequence, to impoverishment of workers.

There exists little conclusive evidence about the effects of trade liberalization on wages. Two shortcomings of the early literature have been the use of average industry wage data, which are assumed to be independent of characteristics of workers in the industry, and the focus on outcomes (e.g., exports, imports, prices) instead of policy measures (e.g., tariffs). Only re-

Chor-ching Goh is a senior economist in the East Asia's Poverty Reduction and Economic Management Department at The World Bank. Beata S. Javorcik is a senior economist in the Trade Team of the Development Economics Research Group at The World Bank.

We wish to thank Irene Brambilla, Penny Goldberg, Ann Harrison, Nina Pavcnik, Guido Porto, and Ana Revenga for helpful suggestions and Pierella Paci, Jerzy Rozanski, and Jan Sasin for making the data available to us. We would also like to thank Federica Saliola for preparing the information for appendix B. The views expressed in the paper are those of the authors and should not be attributed to The World Bank.

cently have researchers begun to utilize policy variables, such as tariffs, to examine the impact of liberalization on industry wage premiums, which measure the portion of wages that cannot be explained by a worker's or a firm's characteristics but can be explained by a worker's industry affiliation. However, the conclusions of such studies have been mixed. On the one hand, Revenga (1997) and Goldberg and Pavcnik (2005) provide evidence suggesting that trade liberalization erodes the wages of workers in previously protected sectors. On the other hand, Pavcnik et al. (2004) find no significant relationship between liberalization and industry wage premiums, and Gaston and Trefler (1994) show that liberalization is associated with a higher industry wage premium.

In this paper, we investigate the relationship between trade liberalization and wages to understand the channel through which trade liberalization affects the wage structure and, indirectly, the linkage between trade and poverty. Unlike the existing studies, which are based on U.S. or Latin American data, this paper focuses on Poland, a central European country undergoing the transition from planned to market economy. Factor endowments in Poland differ from those in the countries previously examined. The share of the population aged fifteen to seventy-five with a college education, 10.7 percent in 1999, is lower than that in the United States, yet unlike many Latin American countries Poland attained universal literacy among the population due to its socialist legacy. Poland's proximity to the European Union market combined with its high level of human development may make it better positioned relative to Latin American countries to absorb new technologies and reap productivity gains from trade liberalization. Thus, it may not be surprising that the relationship between trade liberalization and wages in Poland differs from that found in studies focusing on Latin America.

We are interested in the impact of trade liberalization on wages because it has important implications for income inequality and poverty. Industries differ in the composition of workforce, with some having a higher proportion of skilled labor than others. If trade liberalization erodes wages, and if tariff reduction is greater in sectors with a disproportionate percentage of unskilled labor, as was the case in Poland, then the unskilled could experience a greater decline in earnings. As in other countries, educational attainment is a powerful predictor of poverty status in Poland. For instance, while fewer than 0.6 percent of households headed by a person with a college education were subject to hard poverty in 2001, the same was true of 12 percent of households headed by an individual with a secondary vocational degree and 18 percent of households whose head had only primary education. As is evident from table 8.1, the figures for medium poverty were equally striking. Moreover, this pattern persisted throughout the whole period of our study, 1994–2001 (Topinska and Kuhl 2003).

The effect of trade liberalization on income distribution and poverty is

Table 8.1   **Hard and medium poverty in Poland in 2001**

	Poverty head count (%)	
Education of household head	Hard poverty	Medium poverty
Tertiary	0.57	1.29
Secondary general	3.75	6.96
Secondary vocational	12.16	19.01
Primary	17.72	26.76
Total	9.60	15.17

Source: Topinska and Kuhl (2003).

likely to be larger in Poland than in other countries due to the rigidity of the Polish labor market and the slow change in the regional distribution of economic activities (see appendix table 8A.1). Thus, even a moderate change in wages across industries is likely to exacerbate the existing regional disparities in incomes and poverty incidence illustrated in figure 8.1.

The rigidity of Poland's labor regulations is an advantage in our analysis: with the limited labor mobility across sectors in the short and medium term, a worker's industry affiliation is the immediate channel through which the effects of trade liberalization will be felt. As illustrated in figure 8.2, employers in Poland are more restricted in their hiring and firing decisions relative to their counterparts in the United Kingdom, Turkey, Russia, Brazil, Colombia, or Mexico, to name just a few. Figure 8.2 presents the index of hiring and firing flexibility compiled by the Global Competitiveness Report (GCR), published jointly by the Geneva-based World Economic Forum and the Center for International Development at Harvard University in 1996. It is a country-specific measure that quantifies the average response to the survey question "Is hiring and firing of workers flexible enough?" It takes on the value of 6 for a very flexible labor market and 1 in the case of the most rigid ones. Since it is based on the views of "business practitioners" in each country, it captures not only laws on the books but also their enforcement. According to this index, Singapore and Hong Kong had the most flexible labor markets, while Poland ranked twenty-fifth out of forty-nine countries. While for Singapore and Hong Kong the index value was above 5, the United Kingdom, Brazil, the Czech Republic, and Russia (among other countries) had an index above 4; the index for Poland was equal to 3.6. A similar picture emerges from figure 8.3, which presents the index on the flexibility of individual dismissal compiled by Djankov et al. (2001).[1] Unlike the GCR index in the previous figure, this index is based on the existing regulations rather than their enforcement. In addition to being limited by rigid labor markets, which hinder worker real-

1. We are grateful to Simeon Djankov for providing us with the index.

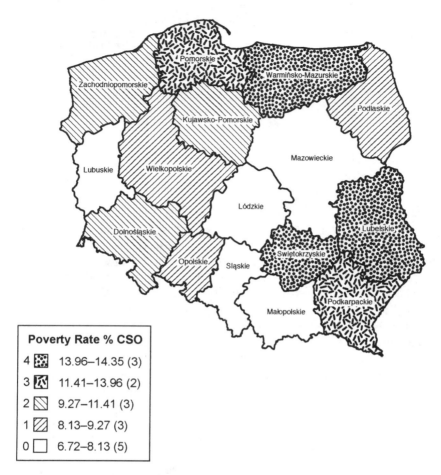

Poverty Rate % CSO

4	▨	13.96–14.35 (3)
3	▨	11.41–13.96 (2)
2	▨	9.27–11.41 (3)
1	▨	8.13–9.27 (3)
0	☐	6.72–8.13 (5)

Fig. 8.1   Regional incidence of poverty in Poland in 2001
Source: Topinska and Kuhl (2003).

location across sectors, labor mobility across regions is limited in Poland due to a housing shortage and prohibitive rent costs (for evidence see Deichmann and Henderson 2004; Przybyla and Rutkowski 2004). The absence of labor mobility, especially in the short and medium term, is also found in other studies in this volume, namely in Topalova's work on India (chap. 7) and Goldberg and Pavcnik's paper on Colombia (chap. 6).

The second advantage of choosing Poland as the subject of our analysis is the fact that the changes in its tariffs can be treated as exogenous, as they were stipulated by the Association Agreement between the European Community and Poland signed in 1991. This agreement predetermined the schedule of tariff reductions that took place during the period of interest, 1994–2001. Moreover, since the goals of the agreement were free movement

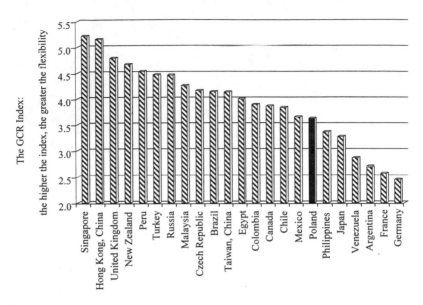

Fig. 8.2   Rigidity of Poland's labor market in international comparison: Index I
Source: World Economic Forum (1996).

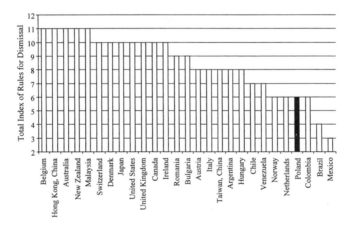

Fig. 8.3   Rigidity of Poland's labor market in international comparison: Index II
Source: Djankov et al. (2001).

of goods between the two entities and Poland's accession to the European Union, all tariffs on manufactured products (with the exception of processed food) were brought down to zero by 2001. Poland's trade liberalization was rapid and encompassed a drastic reduction in tariffs, which went from over 20 percent in leather manufacturing and over 15 percent in wood, nonmetallic, rubber, and plastic products in 1991 to zero within a decade.

We investigate the relationship between trade liberalization and wages in an expanded Mincerian wage equation. We pool together information from Labor Force Surveys conducted during the 1994–2001 period into one regression. Controlling for worker-, firm-, sector-, and location-specific characteristics as well as year and industry fixed effects, we expand the wage equation to include tariff variables. The analysis covers fourteen manufacturing sectors, including electricity production. Given the nature of the specification used, our attention is restricted to employed individuals, and thus we do not consider the implications of trade liberalization for unemployment.

We find that workers in industries with lower tariffs tend to have higher wages. This result is robust to including year and industry fixed effects, industry exports, imports, concentration, and capital accumulation, in addition to controlling for detailed worker characteristics. The result is consistent with a reduction in tariffs leading to increased competitive pressures in the liberalizing industry that forces companies to restructure and improve their productivity, which in turn results in the gains being shared with employees. This interpretation is in line with the findings of many studies that established a positive association between trade liberalization and productivity.[2] To further support this interpretation we employ firm-level data for the period 1996–2000 to demonstrate that trade liberalization indeed resulted in the increased productivity in liberalizing sectors. The robust and significant relationship between a reduction in tariffs and an increase in wages is also consistent with the stylized fact that there is much inefficiency in a planned economy; a sector that is exposed to greater foreign competition during the transition becomes more efficient and productive. Another possible explanation for the finding is that trade liberalization makes imported inputs cheaper, which enhances the profitability of the firms relying on such inputs. The findings of Amiti and Konings (2005) appear to support this hypothesis, but because of the aggregated nature of our industry classification, we are not able to investigate this hypothesis in depth.

Further, our findings do not suggest any erosion of wages of the unskilled (i.e., race to the bottom in wages) from trade liberalization, as they hold when we exclude skilled workers from the sample. Moreover, our data indicate that industries with a greater reduction in tariffs are also those with higher proportions of the unskilled.

This study is organized as follows. The next section presents some facts on Poland's trade liberalization. It is followed by a description of the empirical strategy and the data employed in the analysis. Then we present the estimation results. The last section concludes.

---

2. See Harrison (1994) for Côte d'Ivoire, Krishna and Mitra (1998) for India, Kim (2000) for Korea, Pavcnik (2002) for Chile, and Fernandes (2003) for Colombia.

8.2   Trade Liberalization in Poland

In September 1989 Poland's first non-Communist government since the end of World War II assumed power, taking over the economy with a large budget deficit and triple-digit inflation. On January 1, 1990, the government implemented a bold reform program (the "Balcerowicz plan") aimed at stabilizing the economy and beginning the process of economic liberalization and privatization. During the initial period of transition (1990–91) Poland experienced a deep recession, followed by a strong recovery, with the average annual growth rate of gross domestic product (GDP) equal to almost 5 percent during the 1992–2000 period.

Transition to a market economy completely revolutionized Poland's international trade. The country moved from a centrally planned system of exports and imports conducted by state trading agencies under the arrangements of the Council for Mutual Economic Assistance to a free market where local producers suddenly become subject to the forces of competition. In 1991, trading under the Council for Mutual Economic Assistance collapsed, and in December of the same year Poland signed an Association Agreement with the European Community, which was a prelude to its future membership in the European Union (EU). In July of 1995 Poland joined the World Trade Organization (WTO). Severe recessions in Poland's traditional export markets coupled with lowering of tariffs in Western European countries resulted in massive reorientation of Polish international trade from East to West.

The Association Agreement signed by Poland (and other central and eastern European countries) stipulated asymmetric phase-out of import tariffs with the goal of free trade in industrial goods by 2001. As a result, in 1999 the average Polish tariff on imports from the EU, the European Free Trade Association (EFTA), and Central European Free Trade Agreement (CEFTA) countries was brought down to 6.5 percent, as compared to the most-favored-nation (MFN) rate of 15.6 percent and the 34.6 percent rate applied to non-WTO members. The rapid liberalization of trade in manufacturing products was not, however, accompanied by similar changes in agricultural goods. While in 1999 the simple average applied MFN rate on manufacturing products was equal to 11.1 percent, the corresponding figure for agriculture was 34.2 percent. The difference largely reflects the tariffication of variable levies agreed upon by Poland during the Uruguay Round. As Poland was a nonmarket economy for the base years of 1986–88, selected in the Uruguay Round for estimating tariff equivalents of nontariff barriers prohibited on agricultural products, Poland applied the generally much higher EU tariff rates as the basis for tariffication, and thus considerably increased its protection of the agricultural sector (WTO 2000).

Panels A and B of figure 8.4 show the reduction in sectoral tariffs applied

A

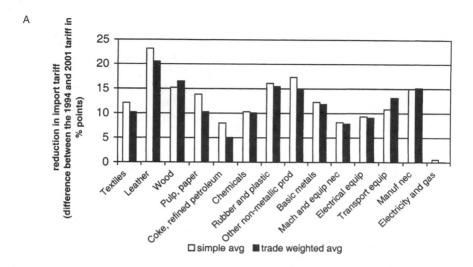

B

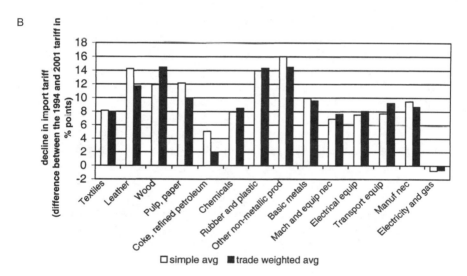

Fig. 8.4   Reduction in Poland's import tariffs between 2001 and 1994: *A,* **trade liberalization vis-à-vis the EU;** *B,* **trade liberalization vis-à-vis the world**
Source: World Bank's WITS database (http://192.91.247.38/tab/WITS.asp).

to imports from the EU and from the world, respectively, between 1994 and 2001. The largest reduction, of 23 percentage points, was observed in leather and leather products, followed by a 15 percentage point or higher reduction in other nonmetallic products, rubber and plastic products, wood and wood products, and other manufacturing. The smallest change was registered in tariffs on electricity and natural gas, which were low to

begin with. By 1999 all industrial products from the EU were entering Poland duty free, with the exception of food, beverages, and tobacco products; motor vehicles; and petroleum and petroleum products. However, imports from the world were still subject to tariffs. As of 1999, about three-quarters of Poland's exports and imports were conducted under preferential trading arrangements and thus subject to preferential tariffs.

As detailed in appendix B, the Association Agreement predetermined the speed and extent of trade liberalization, which allows us to treat tariff changes as exogenous. Since many agricultural products and processed foods, beverages, and tobacco were excluded from the liberalization specified in the agreement and/or remained subject to quantitative restrictions, we will not include them in the analysis.

8.3   Related Literature

The theoretical context for our analysis is provided by the specific-factors model. The model focuses on the short run and assumes that factors of production are immobile across sectors. Given the rigidities present in Poland's labor market, this model constitutes a suitable basis for thinking about the relationship between trade and wages in the Polish context. The model predicts a positive association between protection and industry wages. Protection reduces imports, and reduced imports increase labor demand, which in turn increases wages. This mechanism raises wages in the protected industry relative to the economy-wide average wage.

The second channel through which trade and protection affect wages is imperfectly competitive factor markets. For example, unions may extract part of the rents from protection in the form of more jobs rather than higher wages. Unionization is not a material issue in our analysis because the power of trade unions has been substantially weakened during the transition process. Trade union density in Poland has dropped from 80 percent of the workforce in 1989 to 14 percent in 2002. The highest trade union density was observed in mining (43.8 percent) and nontradable sectors such as transport (27.3 percent) and education (27.5 percent; Boeri and Garibaldi 2003).

The third channel through which trade and protection affect wages is imperfectly competitive product markets. Trade and protection affect the strategic interaction between firms, which in turn affects firm performance and wages. For example, if trade protection promotes entry into an industry by enhancing the profitability of existing firms, and if new entrants face setup costs, then protection promotes inefficient entry and raises average production costs (Horstmann and Markusen 1986).

Another strand of literature particularly relevant to a transition economy, like Poland, which until 1990 was heavily protected and not subject to market forces and competition, is the literature on trade liberalization and

productivity. Inefficiencies and lower productivity associated with an increase in trade protection have been illustrated in the literature using the computable general equilibrium models (for example, Cox and Harris 1985; Brown, Deardorff, and Stern 1992). There is also strong evidence from the findings of firm-level studies that reduction in trade protection results in productivity improvement. The competition effect from imports has been documented by many empirical studies (Roberts and Tybout 1997). For instance, Pavcnik (2002) finds that the productivity of plants in the import-competing sectors grew 3 to 10 percent faster than the productivity in the nontraded goods sector during trade liberalization in Chile, suggesting that exposure to international competition forces previously shielded plants to improve their performance. Fernandes (2003) demonstrates that trade liberalization in Colombia has increased plant-level productivity, primarily through gains in within-plant productivity. Other studies reaching similar conclusions include Harrison (1994) for Côte d'Ivoire, Krishna and Mitra (1998) for India, Kim (2000) for Korea, and Hay (2001) and Muendler (2005) for Brazil.

8.4   Data and Methodology

8.4.1   Labor Force Survey

The analysis is based on the data collected through the Polish Labor Force Survey (LFS). The survey has been conducted four times each year since the fall of 1992, and we have access to selected quarters of the surveys during the period 1992–2001. Unfortunately, it is not possible to employ all eleven years in the analysis, because the 1992 and 1993 surveys were based on a different industry classification. Thus, our analysis covers the period 1994–2001. We use the second quarter of years 1993 through 2001, except in years 1999 and 2001, for which only information for the first quarter was available to us.

The survey sample is representative of the country's population. Sampling for the LFS follows the two-stage household sampling. First, the stratification is based on voivodships (administrative districts), and primary sampling units are sampled from each stratum with diversified sampling probability, proportional to the number of households in a primary sampling unit. Second, a determined number of households are selected randomly from each primary sampling unit, depending on the size of primary sampling units. For example, eight households are sampled from primary sampling units from rural municipalities, and five households are sampled from primary sampling units from large cities.

Between 1993 and 1998, the sample was interviewed only in the middle month of the quarter, whereas after 1999 a uniform number of randomly selected households was interviewed in every week of the thirteen weeks

throughout the quarter. In each quarter about 24,000 households were interviewed, amounting to about 40,000 individuals sampled. Members of households aged above fifteen were asked questions on their employment status, type of employer, sector of employment, monthly earnings, weekly hours worked, and personal characteristics. Unfortunately, wage information on the self-employed is not available, because the self-employed were not asked questions about earnings. Employees make up about 70 percent of the sample in the survey, the self-employed represent another 25 percent, and the remaining 5 percent are unpaid family workers. Employment sectors are classified according to a variant of the European NACE classification system, which includes thirty-four sectors, fourteen of which pertain to manufacturing activities.

8.4.2   Empirical Framework

We investigate the relationship between trade liberalization and wages by estimating a reduced-form model with the logarithm of real hourly wages being the dependent variable. The real hourly wage is calculated by deflating the reported monthly wage to 1992 zlotys using the Consumer Price Index from the IMF's *International Financial Statistics* and dividing it by the number of hours worked in the reporting week multiplied by the number of weeks (4.2). Our sample is restricted to individuals of ages 15–75 inclusive, employed in the manufacturing and electricity sectors. We estimate the following wage equation (1) by pooling all workers from the 1994–2001 Labor Force Surveys:

$$(1) \qquad \ln w_{it} = \alpha + \mathbf{X}_{it}\beta + \delta \text{Tariff}_{jt} + \lambda_j + \delta_t + \varepsilon_{it},$$

where $\ln w_{it}$ is the log of real wages of worker i employed in industry j and observed in the LFS in year t. Note that the data set is not a true panel but consists of repeated cross sections. $\mathbf{X}_{it}$ is the vector of worker characteristics, which include age, age squared, marital status, gender, a dummy for the educational attainment category, a dummy for the occupation category, a dummy for employment in the private sector, a dummy for the geographic region (voivoidship), and a dummy for the size of the city where the worker lives. Tariff_{jt} represents the average tariff applied to imports of industry j's products in year t. The fixed effect for the worker's industry affiliation is denoted by λ_j, and δ_t is the year fixed effect. Year fixed effects are included to absorb economy-wide shocks that may affect wages, while industry dummies control for sector-specific effects, such as prevalence of labor unions. The standard errors are clustered on industry-year combinations.

Tariff_{jt} is defined as the simple average of tariffs on products of industry j imported at time t. We use tariffs vis-à-vis the EU as well as tariffs pertaining to imports from the world. We experiment with trade-weighted average tariffs, and the results are similar to those for the simple averages;

therefore we report only the latter. The tariff data come from the World Bank's World Integrated Trade Solution (WITS) database.

We estimate the effects of tariff changes on workers' wages while controlling for the individual worker's characteristics as well as for other potential influences (e.g., geographic and sectoral variables). Later, we also allow returns to schooling to vary by years. To eliminate a potential omitted-variable bias, we also include such controls as the Herfindahl index, measuring concentration in the industry, capital accumulation in the industry, stock of foreign direct investment (FDI) in the sector, and sectoral imports and exports. We use lagged values to avoid potential simultaneity bias. The Herfindahl index pertains to the four largest firms in the sector and is calculated based on firm-level data from the Amadeus database covering the period 1994–2001. The information on capital accumulation comes from various issues of the *Polish Statistical Yearbook*. The FDI figures are from the Foreign Trade Research Institute (various issues). Trade data come from the United Nations COMTRADE database.

8.5   Descriptive Statistics

Before proceeding to the empirical results, we briefly discuss the summary statistics. As presented in table 8.2, the average age of workers in our sample was thirty-eight in 1994 and increased to about thirty-nine in 2001. Average hours of work remained quite steady at about forty-one hours throughout the period, with the exception of 2001, when a decline to thirty-nine was registered. About three-quarters of workers in our sample were married, and females constituted less than half of the sample (45 to 47 percent) throughout the period. In 1994, only 24 percent of workers were employed in the private sector, but by 2001 this figure increased to 48 percent. The real average hourly wage increased by about 50 percent between 1994 and 2001.

The educational attainments increased during the period considered. The proportion of workers with primary school education or less fell from 13.57 percent to 10.24 percent. The shares of workers with general secondary education or vocational education have remained constant at 7 percent and 35 percent, respectively. The percentage of workers with tertiary education rose—the share of those with university degrees increased from 12.68 to 15.47 percent.

Table 8.3 presents the distribution of labor across industries in each year during the 1994–2001 period. The figures reflect structural changes taking place in the economy during this period, namely a fall in agricultural and mining employment and a rise of service sectors, which until 1990 had been underdeveloped. As for the latter, a particularly strong expansion was observed in wholesale and retail trade (43 percent growth), hotel services (71 percent growth), and financial, banking, and real estate services (43 per-

Table 8.2   **Summary statistics**

	1994	1995	1996	1997	1998	1999	2000	2001
Real hourly wage (in PLN)	1.05	1.07	1.15	1.24	1.31	1.33	1.44	1.51
	(.57)	(.58)	(.64)	(.74)	(.70)	(.78)	(1.0)	(1.2)
Age	38.0	38.3	38.5	38.3	38.2	38.6	38.6	39.3
	(9.7)	(9.8)	(9.8)	(10.0)	(10.1)	(10.2)	(10.1)	(10.6)
Weekly hours worked	41.6	41.9	41.9	41.9	41.6	41.1	40.5	39.3
	(7.9)	(7.7)	(7.5)	(7.4)	(7.3)	(6.9)	(8.2)	(9.4)
Married (%)	78	77	76	75	75	75	75	74
Female (%)	45	46	47	46	46	47	47	47
Working in private sector (%)	24	26	30	34	38	40	41	48
Highest education level								
attained (% by categories)								
Primary or less	13.57	13.5	12.7	11.79	10.85	10.73	10.03	10.24
Basic vocational	34.83	34.78	35.24	35.95	35.78	35.12	35.09	34.23
General secondary	7.65	7.39	6.86	6.64	6.63	6.67	6.68	7.27
Two-year college or								
secondary vocational	31.26	31.57	31.71	32.29	32.96	33.34	32.78	32.79
University	12.68	12.76	13.5	13.32	13.77	14.14	15.43	15.47
Size of city (% by categories)								
100,000 or more people	33.9	32.6	32.0	30.4	29.3	29.1	27.8	29.4
Less than 100,000 people	35.8	37.3	38.5	38.7	37.5	38.1	39.4	38.6
Village	30.3	30.1	29.5	30.9	33.2	32.8	32.8	32.0
No. of observations	14,733	15,059	14,528	14,391	14,437	12,917	9,724	10,099

Notes: Standard deviations in parentheses. The sample is restricted to those between fifteen and seventy-five years old, employees only. PLN denotes Polish zloty. Real hourly wages are expressed in logarithmic form.

cent). Employment in manufacturing industries remained relatively stable with the exception of plastic and rubber products, which registered an 89 percent growth, whereas machinery contracted, halving its share.

The changes in the economic structure have also affected the role of unions in the Polish economy. Mining and machinery sectors used to be industries with strong union presence, but the large fall in employment in these industries contributed to erosion of unions in Poland, as was the case in many other European countries where sectors with the highest numbers of union members had contracted (Boeri and Garibaldi 2003). Unionization has also become weaker because of privatization and the increase in the number of smaller enterprises. Historically, 100 percent of large state-owned enterprises (250+ employees) and 75 percent of medium-sized state-owned enterprises (50–250 employees) had two or more unions. After being privatized, however, only 5 percent of large private companies had unions. Moreover, unions are totally absent in newly created small private companies (Gardawski et al. 1998). Thus, unionization was not a significant force in Poland during the period of our analysis.

Within each industry, we observe changes in the composition of the la-

Table 8.3   Distribution of employment by industries, 1994–2001

	1994	1995	1996	1997	1998	1999	2000	2001
Agriculture, fishery	0.044	0.037	0.033	0.032	0.033	0.032	0.029	0.024
Mining	0.047	0.044	0.039	0.036	0.036	0.032	0.025	0.021
Manufacturing								
Food, beverages, tobacco	0.053	0.054	0.055	0.053	0.052	0.054	0.051	0.052
Textiles	0.041	0.046	0.042	0.042	0.042	0.040	0.039	0.037
Leather	0.008	0.008	0.007	0.008	0.008	0.006	0.006	0.006
Wood	0.019	0.017	0.017	0.020	0.018	0.018	0.018	0.025
Paper products	0.009	0.010	0.010	0.010	0.011	0.010	0.010	0.012
Petroleum	0.004	0.004	0.003	0.003	0.003	0.004	0.002	0.003
Chemical	0.014	0.013	0.017	0.014	0.012	0.013	0.014	0.012
Rubber/plastic	0.007	0.007	0.008	0.009	0.010	0.011	0.011	0.014
Nonmetallic	0.016	0.017	0.018	0.018	0.014	0.013	0.016	0.015
Metal	0.038	0.040	0.039	0.035	0.035	0.036	0.034	0.034
Machinery	0.027	0.028	0.024	0.025	0.022	0.023	0.023	0.017
Electrical appliances	0.014	0.012	0.014	0.014	0.013	0.013	0.014	0.017
Transport equipment	0.019	0.018	0.019	0.021	0.020	0.018	0.016	0.016
Other	0.018	0.015	0.017	0.017	0.017	0.015	0.014	0.020
Services								
Utilities	0.025	0.028	0.029	0.027	0.025	0.023	0.027	0.026
Construction	0.077	0.072	0.068	0.074	0.077	0.076	0.079	0.072
Wholesale and retail trade	0.094	0.101	0.101	0.100	0.108	0.109	0.108	0.134
Hotels and restaurants	0.012	0.013	0.013	0.013	0.012	0.012	0.012	0.020
Transport and communication	0.073	0.078	0.074	0.080	0.080	0.074	0.076	0.072
Financial, real estate, and business activities	0.045	0.051	0.057	0.052	0.055	0.062	0.058	0.064
Public administration	0.066	0.066	0.072	0.073	0.072	0.068	0.074	0.070
Education, health, and social work	0.188	0.183	0.194	0.194	0.192	0.207	0.209	0.185
Other community, social, and personal service activities	0.044	0.038	0.030	0.032	0.032	0.033	0.033	0.032
All sectors	1.000	1.000	1.000	1.000	1.000	1.000	1.000	1.000

bor force. As illustrated in table 8.4, which presents the share of unskilled workers in each industry, with the exception of the paper and pulp manufacturing and social and communal services sectors, where there have been increases in the shares of unskilled workers, the other industries registered declines of different magnitudes. Sectors such as construction, agriculture, wood product manufacturing, and textile manufacturing experienced a limited fall (3 to 5 percent) in the shares of unskilled workers, whereas industries such as banking and financial services and rubber and plastic product manufacturing observed larger declines (44 percent and 57 percent, respectively) over time.

Table 8.4   **Share of unskilled labor (workers with primary or less schooling), by industries, 1994–2001**

	1994	1995	1996	1997	1998	1999	2000	2001
Agriculture, fishery	0.335	0.357	0.346	0.309	0.336	0.323	0.313	0.283
Mining	0.140	0.141	0.121	0.105	0.114	0.094	0.113	0.104
Manufacturing								
Food, beverages, tobacco	0.191	0.182	0.194	0.169	0.159	0.154	0.130	0.158
Textiles	0.166	0.138	0.147	0.143	0.129	0.129	0.161	0.108
Leather	0.217	0.200	0.190	0.179	0.129	0.135	0.180	0.167
Wood	0.218	0.204	0.223	0.174	0.156	0.230	0.211	0.199
Paper products	0.156	0.154	0.142	0.149	0.116	0.096	0.228	0.191
Petroleum	0.183	0.197	0.137	0.128	0.146	0.125	—	0.091
Chemical	0.120	0.162	0.191	0.159	0.124	0.120	0.113	0.100
Rubber/plastic	0.169	0.168	0.258	0.234	0.134	0.183	0.073	0.118
Nonmetallic	0.265	0.237	0.199	0.230	0.209	0.199	0.185	0.172
Metal	0.162	0.152	0.150	0.132	0.120	0.132	0.096	0.101
Machinery	0.101	0.107	0.076	0.059	0.060	0.086	0.074	0.052
Electrical appliances	0.135	0.127	0.108	0.081	0.090	0.125	0.114	0.103
Transport equipment	0.133	0.122	0.102	0.098	0.105	0.092	0.083	0.094
Other	0.168	0.148	0.174	0.156	0.133	0.104	0.109	0.140
Services								
Utilities	0.113	0.143	0.125	0.109	0.097	0.086	0.096	0.102
Construction	0.163	0.171	0.153	0.167	0.151	0.153	0.153	0.149
Wholesale and retail trade	0.088	0.090	0.092	0.075	0.083	0.078	0.068	0.080
Hotels and restaurants	0.147	0.212	0.158	0.119	0.066	0.097	0.125	0.109
Transport and communication	0.140	0.147	0.135	0.123	0.117	0.122	0.102	0.105
Financial, real estate, and business activities	0.086	0.064	0.079	0.075	0.067	0.070	0.048	0.067
Public administration	0.069	0.054	0.041	0.045	0.042	0.032	0.036	0.036
Education, health, and social work	0.106	0.108	0.105	0.100	0.091	0.091	0.079	0.075
Other community, social, and personal service activities	0.123	0.139	0.134	0.118	0.116	0.132	0.165	0.173

As is evident from figure 8.5, sectors with a higher proportion of unskilled workers experienced a larger reduction in import tariffs between 1994 and 2001. The correlation between the unskilled labor share and the change in tariff is –0.644. The sector with the largest decrease (23 percentage points) in the average tariff vis-à-vis the EU is leather manufacturing, in which the shares of unskilled labor were 22 percent and 17 percent in 1994 and 2001, respectively. In contrast, the machinery and equipment industry had the smallest decrease (8 percent) in tariff, and the shares of unskilled labor were 11 percent and 5 percent in 1994 and 2001, respectively.

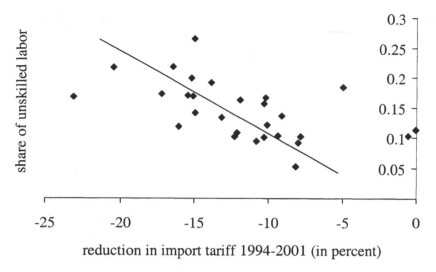

Fig. 8.5   Share of unskilled labor and tariff reduction (1994–2001)

8.6   Empirical Results

Table 8.5 presents the full set of explanatory variables in our basic wage model, which includes year and industry dummies. Our sample encompasses manufacturing (except for the food, beverage, and tobacco sector, excluded because of the concerns regarding nontariff barriers and tariffs not being predetermined), and the electricity sector. The coefficients on the worker characteristics are generally significant, with the exception of a dummy for employment in the private sector. The coefficients also have their expected signs. Older workers tend to earn more. Female workers with similar characteristics earn on average less than their male counterparts; married workers tend to earn more, possibly due to marriage signaling stability; the returns to schooling also have their expected signs, with significantly higher returns for a tertiary education. There are also wage premiums enjoyed by workers living in larger cities.

Moving on to the variables of interest, the results suggest that industry tariffs are negatively correlated with workers' hourly wages, controlling for an individual worker's characteristics, geographic variables, and employment in the private sector. Both the coefficient on tariffs vis-à-vis the European Union as well as the coefficient on tariffs vis-à-vis the world are negative and statistically significant at the 5 and the 1 percent level, respectively. This finding indicates that workers in more liberalized sectors earn more, controlling for all observable characteristics of the worker, the job, and the industry. This finding is robust to including year and industry fixed effects. In this basic specification, a 10 percentage point decline in the industry tariff vis-à-vis the EU is associated with a 2.5 percent increase in

Table 8.5 Effects of trade protection on wages: A basic model, 1994–2001 (dependent variable: log hourly real wage)

	(1)	(2)
Simple average tariff vis-à-vis European Union	−0.254**	
Simple average tariff vis-à-vis the world		−0.336***
Age	0.015***	0.015***
Age squared	−0.0001***	−0.0001***
Married dummy	0.070***	0.070***
Female dummy	−0.143***	−0.143***
Dummy: employed in private sector	0.009	0.009
Occupation		
Professionals	−0.216***	−0.216***
Technicians	−0.249***	−0.249***
Clerks	−0.354***	−0.354***
Service workers	−0.407***	−0.407***
Skilled agricultural workers	−0.455***	−0.455***
Craft workers	−0.362***	−0.362***
Plant and machine operators	−0.328***	−0.328***
Elementary occupations	−0.463***	−0.463***
City size		
50K–1 million population	−0.048***	−0.048***
20–50K population	−0.052***	−0.052***
10–20K population	−0.102***	−0.102***
5–10K population	−0.070***	−0.070***
2–5K population	−0.099***	−0.099***
<2K population	−0.164***	−0.165***
Village dummy	−0.091***	−0.091***
Education dummy		
Two-year college	−0.166***	−0.166***
Secondary technical	−0.253***	−0.252***
Secondary general education	−0.259***	−0.259***
Vocational education	−0.307***	−0.306***
Primary educated	−0.366***	−0.366***
Less than primary	−0.448***	−0.448***
Voivoidship dummies	Yes	Yes
Year dummies	Yes	Yes
Industry dummies	Yes	Yes
No. of observations	28,732	28,732
R-squared	.410	.410

Notes: The sample is restricted to those between fifteen and seventy-five years old, employees only, in the manufacturing and electricity sectors. Omitted categories of dummies: city (population above 100 thousand), education (four- or five-year college degree), occupation (managers).

***Significant at the 1 percent level.
**Significant at the 5 percent level.

wages of workers employed in the industry. For tariffs on imports from the world the corresponding increase in wages is 3.4 percent.

Next, we add to the basic model controls for industry concentration, sectoral imports, and exports to demonstrate that our results are robust to the inclusion of additional controls. In the top half of table 8.6, we present the results for the simple average of import tariffs in a given industry vis-à-vis the EU. In the bottom half, we present results employing tariffs vis-à-vis the world. Because the coefficients on worker characteristics remain very similar to those in the basic specification, this and the following tables will present only the effects of our variables of interest—tariffs and sector-specific characteristics. The specification in column (1) includes the lagged value of Herfindahl index, which captures industry concentration, in addition to all variables present in the basic specification. Controlling for the industry concentration does not change our earlier conclusion that lower trade protection is associated with higher wages. In column (2), we include lagged Herfindahl index and lagged imports (expressed in logarithmic form). In the top portion, with tariffs on imports from the EU, we employ figures pertaining to trade with the EU. Similarly, when tariffs vis-à-vis the world are used, trade figures pertain to trade with the world. As before, tariffs are negatively correlated with wages. In column (3), we include lagged exports (expressed in logarithmic form) in addition to the variables listed in the previous column. As before, lower tariffs are associated with higher wages, and the effect is significant at the 1 or the 5 percent level. As for other industry-specific variables, only lagged exports appear to be statistically significant. The positive coefficient on exports suggests that export-oriented industries offer a wage premium to workers employed there.

To ensure that our tariff variables do not simply proxy for the increased ability of sectors to export, we conduct two checks. First, we calculate the correlation between the annual changes in industry tariffs vis-à-vis the EU (or the world) and the annual changes in exports to the EU (or the world). The correlations are quite low –.02 (.12). For imports, the corresponding figures are –.04 (.06). Second, we estimate two additional specifications: one with contemporaneous imports and exports but without tariffs, and another one with contemporaneous imports, exports, and tariffs. If tariffs simply proxy for the sector's ability to export, the tariff variable should lose its significance. This is not the case, though. While contemporaneous exports are positively correlated with industry wages, the coefficient on tariffs remains negative, similar in magnitude to the earlier regressions and statistically significant at the 1 percent level. As before, industry imports do not appear to have a statistically significant effect on wages.

To address the concern that there may be other sector-specific time-varying factors affecting wages, we experiment with additional controls, such as capital accumulation, stock of FDI, and the share of unskilled labor. The first two variables are expressed in logarithms. The last variable

Table 8.6   **Effects of trade protection on wages with additional trade-related measures (dependent variable: log hourly real wage)**

	The basic model (specified in table 8.5) plus additional control variables				
	(1)	(2)	(3)	(4)	(5)
Simple average tariff vis-à-vis	−0.306***	−0.259**	−0.257**		−0.327***
European Union	(.110)	(0.110)	(0.104)		(0.094)
Lagged Herfindahl index (i.e., concentra-	−0.065	−0.097	−0.085	−0.076	−0.111
tion within an industry)	(0.062)	(0.083)	(0.062)	(0.053)	(0.047)
Lagged imports		0.016	−0.003		
		(0.017)	(0.015)		
Lagged exports			0.057***		
			(0.014)		
Contemporaneous imports				−0.003	−0.002
				(0.011)	(0.010)
Contemporaneous exports				0.063***	0.065***
				(0.014)	(0.014)
Year dummies	Yes	Yes	Yes	Yes	Yes
Industry dummies	Yes	Yes	Yes	Yes	Yes
No. of observations	25,798	25,413	25,413	25,798	25,798
R-squared	.410	.412	.413	.410	.411
Simple average tariff vis-à-vis	−0.357***	−0.290***	−0.249**		−0.317***
the world	(0.081)	(0.105)	(0.099)		(0.091)
Lagged Herfindahl index (i.e., concentra-	−0.064	−0.088	−0.077	−0.039	−0.089
tion within an industry)	(0.057)	(0.092)	(0.063)	(0.054)	(0.055)
Lagged imports		0.018	0.008		
		(0.018)	(0.015)		
Lagged exports			0.050***		
			(0.016)		
Contemporaneous imports				0.016	−0.009
				(0.024)	(0.025)
Contemporaneous exports				0.069***	0.065***
				(0.017)	(0.017)
Year dummies	Yes	Yes	Yes	Yes	Yes
Industry dummies	Yes	Yes	Yes	Yes	Yes
No. of observations	25,798	25,413	25,413	25,798	25,798
R-squared	.410	.413	.413	.410	.411

Notes: The table only presents selected variables of interest. All columns include the entire set of variables in the basic model specified in table 8.5 with additional control variables specified in respective columns. The sample is restricted to those between fifteen and seventy-five years old, employees only, in the manufacturing and electricity sectors. Robust standard errors in parentheses.

***Significant at the 1 percent level.

**Significant at the 5 percent level.

has been calculated based on the Labor Force Survey. All three controls enter as first lags. Additionally, in all specifications we include the lagged value of industry concentration. Results using tariffs vis-à-vis the EU are presented in the upper portion of table 8.7, and those using tariffs vis-à-vis the world are in the lower portion. In column (1), controlling for capital accumulation and the industry concentration, we still find that lower tariffs are associated with higher wages. Also, there is a mildly positive correlation between capital accumulation and wages. In column (2), we control for the

Table 8.7   **Effects of trade protection on wages with additional sector-specific variables (labor shares, capital accumulation, and foreign direct investment) (dependent variable: log hourly real wage)**

	The basic model (specified in table 8.5) plus additional control variables		
	(1)	(2)	(3)
Simple average tariff vis-à-vis	−0.212*	−0.577***	−0.624***
European Union	(0.122)	(0.153)	(0.114)
Lagged Herfindahl index (i.e., concentration	−0.046	−0.007	−0.362
within an industry)	(0.050)	(0.106)	(0.204)
Lagged capital accumulation	0.032**		−0.012
	(0.014)		(0.019)
Lagged foreign direct investment		0.008	−0.003
		(0.007)	(0.009)
Lagged unskilled labor shares			0.673***
			(0.214)
Year dummies	Yes	Yes	Yes
Industry dummies	Yes	Yes	Yes
No. of observations	25,798	13,307	11,181
R-squared	.410	.421	.415
Simple average tariff vis-à-vis the world	−0.279***	−0.510***	−0.513***
	(0.099)	(0.120)	(0.096)
Lagged Herfindahl index (i.e., concentration	−0.049	0.013	−0.302
within an industry)	(0.047)	(0.099)	(0.208)
Lagged capital accumulation	0.028*		−0.017
	(0.014)		(0.021)
Lagged foreign direct investment		0.001	−0.002
		(0.008)	(0.009)
Lagged unskilled labor shares			0.637***
			(0.217)
Year dummies	Yes	Yes	Yes
Industry dummies	Yes	Yes	Yes
No. of observations	25,798	13,307	11,181
R-squared	.410	.421	.415

Note: See notes to table 8.6
***Significant at the 1 percent level.
**Significant at the 5 percent level.
*Significant at the 10 percent level.

industry's concentration and FDI stock in the sector, and similarly we find a negative and significant relationship between tariffs and wages. However, FDI stock does not appear to have any significant effect on wages. In column (3), we control for capital accumulation, FDI, industry concentration, and the share of unskilled labor. The effect of tariff on wages is still significantly negative, suggesting that workers in sectors with a greater extent of liberalization benefit from higher wages, even after controlling for observable individual, sectoral, and geographical characteristics.

As a robustness check, we repeat the above analyses by allowing returns to schooling to change over time. To do so, we combine our seven education categories into three groups—tertiary, secondary, and primary or less—and interact each education group with year dummies. The results are very similar. Table 8.8 presents the basic specification with additional controls such as capital accumulation, stock of FDI, and the share of unskilled labor. Ceteris paribus, workers in more liberalized sectors receive higher wages.

As another robustness check, not reported here, we reestimate all the specifications, correcting standard errors for clustering on industries rather than industry-year combinations. Doing so does not change the conclusions of the paper.

Finally, we exclude skilled workers (i.e., those with university education) from our sample and present the estimation results of the subsample of unskilled workers in table 8.9 and table 8.10. The findings are very similar to those for the full sample in terms of the magnitudes of the impact from tariff reduction and the significance levels. The findings indicate that a reduction in the tariff is associated with wage increases for unskilled workers, after controlling for sector- and worker-specific characteristics. Thus, reductions in trade barriers appear to have benefited the unskilled in terms of an increase in wages.

In summary, our results suggest that lower trade protection in Poland has been associated with higher wages for the employed. These findings are consistent with those of Gaston and Trefler (1994) based on cross-sectional data for the United States. Below we discuss four potential explanations for our results. The first potential explanation is that output mix has shifted toward the production of labor-intensive goods, raising the return to labor relative to other factors of production. Since trade protection was greatest prior to trade reform in labor-intensive sectors, this could explain why workers in the sectors that had a reduction in protection appear to experience higher wages. If this was the story, we would expect to see a shift in the pattern of production or employment toward labor-intensive industries. The data presented in tables 8.3 and 8A.1 demonstrate, however, that this was not the case.

The second potential explanation is that a reduction in tariffs has been associated with an increase in firms' ability to export. However, as demon-

Table 8.8   Effects of trade protection on wages allowing for time-varying returns to schooling (dependent variable: log hourly real wage)

	The basic model (specified in table 8.5) plus additional control variables		
	(1)	(2)	(3)
Simple average tariff vis-à-vis	−0.226*	−0.594***	−0.640***
European Union	(0.120)	(0.149)	(0.110)
Lagged Herfindahl index (i.e., concentration	0.045	0.005	−0.356*
within an industry)	(0.049)	(0.105)	(0.201)
Lagged capital accumulation	0.032**		−0.013
	(0.014)		(0.018)
Lagged foreign direct investment		0.008	0.003
		(0.007)	(0.009)
Lagged unskilled labor shares			0.629***
			(0.213)
Year dummies	Yes	Yes	Yes
Industry dummies	Yes	Yes	Yes
No. of observations	25,798	13,307	11,181
R-squared	.407	.418	.411
Simple average tariff vis-à-vis the world	−0.282***	−0.524***	−0.528***
	(0.098)	(0.116)	(0.104)
Lagged Herfindahl index (i.e., concentration	−0.048	0.026	−0.294
within an industry)	(0.046)	(0.099)	(0.206)
Lagged capital accumulation	0.028**		−0.018
	(0.014)		(0.020)
Lagged foreign direct investment		0.001	−0.002
		(0.008)	(0.009)
Lagged unskilled labor shares			0.592***
			(0.216)
Year dummies	Yes	Yes	Yes
Industry dummies	Yes	Yes	Yes
No. of observations	25,798	13,307	11,181
R-squared	.407	.418	.411

Notes: The table only presents selected variables of interest. All columns include the entire set of variables in the basic model specified in table 8.5 except that returns to schooling are now time-varying. The sample is restricted to those between fifteen and seventy-five years old, employees only, in the manufacturing and electricity sectors. Robust standard errors in parentheses.
***Significant at the 1 percent level.
**Significant at the 5 percent level.
*Significant at the 10 percent level.

strated earlier, there is hardly any correlation between annual changes in industry tariffs and industry exports. Moreover, as illustrated in table 8.6, controlling for contemporaneous exports does not lead to a decline in the significance level or the magnitude of the estimated effect of tariffs.

The third possibility is that trade liberalization increases firm produc-

Table 8.9   **Subsample of unskilled workers: Effects of trade protection and various trade measures on wages (dependent variable: log hourly real wage)**

	The basic model (specified in table 8.5) plus additional control variables				
	(1)	(2)	(3)	(4)	(5)
Simple average tariff vis-à-vis European Union	−0.271*** (0.103)	−0.216** (0.106)	−0.215** (0.097)		−0.290*** (0.089)
Lagged Herfindahl index (i.e., concentration within an industry)	−0.045 (0.064)	−0.082 (0.084)	−0.07 (0.062)	−0.048 (0.054)	−0.080 (0.049)
Lagged imports		0.019 (0.016)	−0.0004 (0.014)		
Lagged exports			0.055*** (0.015)		
Contemporaneous imports				0.004 (0.01)	0.004 (0.010)
Contemporaneous exports				0.058*** (0.014)	0.060*** (0.014)
Year dummies	Yes	Yes	Yes	Yes	Yes
Industry dummies	Yes	Yes	Yes	Yes	Yes
No. of observations	24,370	24,012	24,012	24,370	24,370
R-squared	0.349	0.351	0.352	0.350	0.350
Simple average tariff vis-à-vis the world	−0.313*** (0.078)	−0.232** (0.099)	−0.193** (0.095)		−0.257*** (0.088)
Lagged Herfindahl index (i.e., concentration within an industry)	−0.045 (0.060)	−0.069 (0.094)	−0.058 (0.064)	−0.0077 (0.051)	−0.047 (0.053)
Lagged imports		0.023 (0.017)	0.013 (0.014)		
Lagged exports			0.048*** (0.016)		
Contemporaneous imports				0.030 (0.023)	0.009 (0.024)
Contemporaneous exports				0.055*** (0.016)	0.052*** (0.017)
Year dummies	Yes	Yes	Yes	Yes	Yes
Industry dummies	Yes	Yes	Yes	Yes	Yes
No. of observations	24,370	24,012	24,012	24,370	24,370
R-squared	0.350	0.352	0.352	0.350	0.350

Note: See notes to table 8.6.

***Significant at the 1 percent level.

**Significant at the 5 percent level.

tivity and profitability through access to cheaper or better intermediate inputs. While the high level of aggregation in our industry classification prevents us from testing this hypothesis explicitly, empirical support for this hypothesis has been presented by Amiti and Konings (2005). Using plant-level data from Indonesia, Amiti and Konings find that benefits arising from lower tariffs on intermediate inputs are higher than those arising from

Table 8.10   Subsample of unskilled workers: Effects of trade protection and sector-specific characteristics on wages (dependent variable: log hourly real wage)

	The basic model (specified in table 8.5) plus additional control variables		
	(1)	(2)	(3)
Simple average tariff vis-à-vis	−0.171	−0.494***	−0.541***
European Union	(0.110)	(0.138)	(0.104)
Lagged Herfindahl index (i.e., concentration	−0.025	0.025	−0.234
within an industry)	(0.049)	(0.099)	(0.200)
Lagged capital accumulation	0.034**		−0.015
	(0.014)		(0.018)
Lagged foreign direct investment		0.006	0.002
		(0.007)	(0.009)
Lagged unskilled labor shares			0.537**
			(0.249)
Year dummies	Yes	Yes	Yes
Industry dummies	Yes	Yes	Yes
No. of observations	24,370	12,646	10,621
R-squared	0.350	0.366	0.358
Simple average tariff vis-à-vis the world	−0.223**	−0.438***	−0.448***
	(0.090)	(0.109)	(0.089)
Lagged Herfindahl index (i.e., concentration	−0.028	0.043	−0.180
within an industry)	(0.047)	(0.094)	(0.203)
Lagged capital accumulation	0.030**		−0.020
	(0.014)		(0.020)
Lagged foreign direct investment		−0.00003	−0.002
		(0.007)	(0.009)
Lagged unskilled labor shares			0.505*
			(0.251)
Year dummies	Yes	Yes	Yes
Industry dummies	Yes	Yes	Yes
No. of observations	24,370	12,646	10,621
R-squared	0.350	0.366	0.358

Note: See notes to table 8.6.
***Significant at the 1 percent level.
**Significant at the 5 percent level.
*Significant at the 10 percent level.

a reduction in output tariffs. Their analysis suggests that a 10 percentage point fall in tariffs increases plant productivity by 1 percent due to lower output tariffs; however, importing firms enjoy an 11 percent gain as a result of lower input tariffs.

The final possibility is that trade liberalization has led to increased competitive pressures in industries, thus forcing firms to restructure and improve their productivity. This argument is in line with results of many firm-

level studies (e.g., Pavcnik 2002; Fernandes 2003; and Muendler 2005) that find that trade liberalization leads to higher productivity. This channel is even more plausible in the context of a transition economy, like Poland, where local firms were sheltered from any kind of competition until 1990. To provide further evidence on the plausibility of this channel, we use firm-level data for the same period to demonstrate that trade liberalization led to a higher total factor productivity in Polish firms. To make this exercise as comparable as possible to the industry premium results, we use the same aggregation of industries and a comparable time period (1996–2000). Full details are provided in appendix C.

Strictly speaking, our results cannot be interpreted as evidence of trade liberalization leading to poverty reduction, because, unlike Topalova (chap. 7) and Goldberg and Pavcnik (chap. 6) in their work in this volume, we do not directly examine the effects of trade liberalization on poverty. Although we do find that employed individuals enjoyed favorable outcomes as a result of trade liberalization, we have not looked into those who were not in wage employment.

8.7 Conclusions

In this study, we examine the relationship between changes in tariffs and wages during Poland's trade liberalization in 1994–2001. Our results indicate that a worker's wages are higher in industries with a larger reduction in trade protection, after controlling for the individual worker's characteristics, such as age, education, gender, marital status, geographic variables, and employment in the private sector. Our findings are robust to controlling for industry-level exports and imports, degree of concentration, capital accumulation, FDI stock, and the share of unskilled workers employed. Moreover, they are not affected by controlling for unobserved but time-invariant industry characteristics.

This result is consistent with the argument that reduction in trade protection brings about higher competition from imports, which can enhance worker productivity and industry performance. The robust and significant relationship between a reduction in tariffs and an increase in wages is also consistent with the stylized fact that there is much inefficiency in a planned economy; a sector that is exposed to greater foreign competition during the transition becomes more efficient and productive. Another possible explanation is that trade liberalization improves access to cheaper or better intermediate inputs, which could enhance profitability.

In addition, we find that industries with a larger reduction in tariffs are also those with higher shares of unskilled labor. When we exclude skilled labor from our sample, the results still hold. Thus, there is no evidence of trade liberalization leading to an erosion of wages of the unskilled or the so-called race to the bottom.

Appendix A

Table 8A.1   Distribution of male employment by industries and by broad regions, 1994–2001

	Poland	Districts along the western border	Interior/center districts	Capital city (Warsaw)	Districts along the eastern border	Northern coastal districts
			A. 1994			
Agriculture, mining, fishery	31.39	28.87	33.05	4.6	44.15	20.49
Services sector	45.86	45.63	42.44	77.89	38.12	57.94
Manufacturing	22.75	25.5	24.51	17.51	17.73	21.57
Food, beverages, tobacco	17	10	20	13	23	18
Textiles	7	5	11	1	3	4
Leather	2	2	2	1	3	2
Wood	11	10	10	6	12	12
Paper products	3	2	4	11	2	4
Petroleum	2	3	1	0	1	1
Chemical	5	7	4	8	4	3
Rubber/plastic	3	2	3	2	4	1
Nonmetallic	6	6	6	6	9	3
Metal	16	21	15	9	10	8
Machinery	11	14	9	9	9	11
Electrical appliances	5	5	5	12	3	4
Transport equipment	8	5	4	10	12	19
Other	7	7	6	11	6	7

B. 2001

Agriculture, mining, fishery	24.92	20.61	27.28	4.02	37.52	13.31
Services sector	51.98	54.52	48.12	76.84	44.39	60.92
Manufacturing	23.10	24.87	24.60	19.14	18.09	25.77
Food, beverages, tobacco	19	13	22	13	27	20
Textiles	5	4	9	4	3	1
Leather	2	1	2	0	2	1
Wood	10	11	8	5	11	12
Paper products	4	3	5	9	3	6
Petroleum	1	2	1	1	1	1
Chemical	5	6	4	6	3	5
Rubber/plastic	4	4	5	6	6	3
Nonmetallic	6	6	6	2	6	2
Metal	16	23	14	15	11	12
Machinery	9	12	8	12	9	7
Electrical appliances	5	5	4	12	3	4
Transport equipment	7	6	4	9	9	19
Other	7	4	10	7	6	7

Source: Labor Force Surveys.

Note: All figures are given in percents.

Appendix B

Association Agreement between the European Communities and the Republic of Poland

Article 10 of the Europe Agreement signed in 1991 between Poland and the European Community stipulated the schedule of liberalization with respect to manufacturing products (Harmonized System chapters 25–97). This schedule did not cover Harmonized System chapters 1–24, which encompass agricultural products, processed foods, beverages, and tobacco products. The provisions of Article 10 were as follows:

1. Customs duties on imports applicable in Poland to products originating in the Community listed in Annex IVa shall be abolished on the date of entry into force of this Agreement.

Annex IVa covered selected nonagricultural products from the following headings of the Harmonized System (HS): 25, 26, 27, 28, 29, 30, 38, 40, 44, 45, 47, 48, 49, 50, 51, 52, 53, 68, 71, 72, 74, 75, 78, 79, 80, 81, 84, 85, 86, 87, 88, 90, 97.

2. Customs duties on imports applicable in Poland to products originating in the Community which are listed in Annex IVb shall be progressively reduced as specified in that Annex.

Annex IVb covered selected tariff lines pertaining to motor vehicles (HS 8703, 8704, 8706, and 8707). It specified that customs duties on imports applicable in Poland to these products originating in the Community shall be eliminated according to the following schedule:

- On 1 January 1994 they will be reduced to six-sevenths of the basic duty.
- On 1 January 1996 they will be reduced to five-sevenths.
- On 1 January 1998 they will be reduced to four-sevenths.
- On 1 January 1999 they will be reduced to three-sevenths.
- On 1 January 2000 they will be reduced to two-sevenths.
- On 1 January 2001 they will be reduced to one-seventh.
- On 1 January 2002 they will be reduced to zero.

It also specified a suspension of customs duties within the limit of an annual preferential tariff quota for a certain number of cars starting from January 1, 1993.

3. Customs duties on imports applicable in Poland to products originating in the Community other than those listed in Annexes IVa and IVb shall be progressively reduced, and abolished by the end of the seventh year at the latest from the entry into force of this Agreement according to the following timetable:

- Three years after the date of entry into force of this Agreement each duty shall be reduced to 80 percent of the basic duty.
- Four years after the date of entry into force of this Agreement each duty shall be reduced to 60 percent of the basic duty.
- Five years after the date of entry into force of this Agreement each duty shall be reduced to 40 percent of the basic duty.
- Six years after the date of entry into force of this Agreement each duty shall be reduced to 20 percent of the basic duty.
- Seven years after the date of entry into force of this Agreement the remaining duties shall be eliminated.

Provisions of the Europe Agreement with respect to agricultural products (HS chapters 1–24) were covered in chapter II, which specified that

- Customs duties on imports applicable in Poland to products originating in the Community listed in Annex XI shall be reduced on the date of entry into force of the Agreement by 10 percentage points.

Annex XI pertained to selected products from the following HS chapters: 01, Live Animals; 04, Dairy Produce, Birds' Eggs, Natural Honey, Edible Products of Animal Origin, not Elsewhere Specified or Included; 06, Live Trees and Other Plants, Bulbs, Roots and the Like, Cut Flowers and Ornamental Foliage; 07, Edible Vegetables and Certain Roots and Tubers; 08, Edible Fruit and Nuts, Peel of Citrus Fruits or Melons; 10, Cereals; 12, Oil Seeds and Oleaginous Fruits, Miscellaneous Grains, Seeds, and Fruit, Industrial or Medicinal Plants, Straw and Fodder; 15, Animal or Vegetable Fats and Oils and Their Cleavage Products, Prepared Edible Fats, Animal or Vegetable Waxes; 18, Cocoa and Cocoa Preparations; 19, Preparations of Cereals, Flour, Starch or Milk, Pastrycooks' Products; 20, Preparations of Vegetables, Fruit, Nuts or Other Parts of Plants; 22, Beverages, Spirits, and Vinegar; 23, Residues and Waste From the Food Industries, Prepared Animal Fodder.

- The Community and Poland shall grant each other the concessions referred to in Annexes Xa (imports of bovine animal), Xb (some products of chapters 01, 02—Meat and Edible Meat Offal, 04), Xc (some products of chapters 07, 08, 20) and XI on a harmonious and reciprocal basis, in accordance with the conditions laid down therein.

Annex Xa specified that "In case the number of animals fixed in the framework of the balance sheet arrangements foreseen in Regulation (EEC) No. 805/68 are lower than a reference quantity, a global tariff quota equal to the difference between that reference quantity and the number of animals fixed under the balance sheet arrangements will be opened to imports from Hungary, Poland, and Czechoslovakia." Trade in agricultural goods was to remain subject to quantitative restrictions, which according to Article 20 were to be gradually abolished.

- Poland shall abolish at the latest by the end of the fifth year from the entry into force of the Agreement the quantitative restrictions on imports originating in the Community listed in Annex IX in accordance with the conditions established in that Annex.

Annex IX covered Beverages, Spirits, and Vinegar (HS chapter 22).

Appendix C

Evidence of Trade Liberalization and Changes in Firm Productivity

In order to shed some light on the channel through which trade liberalization may influence industry premiums, we examine the impact of tariff reductions on the productivity of Polish firms. This exercise is based on an unbalanced panel data set of 5,090 firms operating in Poland during the period 1996–2000. The information comes from Amadeus, a commercial database compiled by Bureau van Dijk, which contains comprehensive information on companies operating in thirty-five European countries, including Poland.[3]

The analysis proceeds in two stages. First, we estimate a production function separately for each sector to get measures of the total factor productivity (TFP):[4]

$$\ln Y_{it} = \alpha + \beta_1 \ln L_{it} + \beta_2 \ln K_{it} + \beta_2 \ln M_{it} + \mu_t + \varepsilon_{it},$$

where Y_{it} represents sales of firm i in year t, deflated by the sectoral deflator taken from the Poland's *Statistical Yearbooks*, L_{it} is the number of employees, K_{it} is the value of fixed assets, and M_{it} is the value of materials used. K_{it} and M_{it} are deflated by the GDP deflator. The equation also contains year dummies.

Then we relate the annual changes in TFP to the changes in industry import tariffs:

$$\Delta \ln \text{TFP}_{ijt} = \phi \Delta \text{tariff}_{jt} + \mu_j + u_{it},$$

3. Unfortunately, the version of Amadeus to which we have access does not include the 2001 figures and is missing employment data from before 1996, which restricts our analysis to the 1996–2001 period.

4. Due to a small number of observations we combine textiles and leather products into one sector when estimating the production function. We also combine coke and petroleum manufacturing with chemicals.

Table 8C.1   **Total factor productivity and trade liberalization: Estimation on first differences (dependent variable: total factor productivity)**

	All sectors		Manufacturing only	
	(1)	(2)	(3)	(4)
Simple average tariff vis-à-vis	−2.073**	−1.7611*	−2.0733*	−2.0987*
European Union	(0.989)	(1.0075)	(1.0026)	(0.9898)
Lagged Herfindahl index (i.e., concentration		−1.1178		0.0908
within an industry)		(0.7906)		(1.2733)
Industry dummies	Yes	Yes	Yes	Yes
Simple average tariff vis-à-vis the world	−1.9361**	−1.7026*	−1.8098**	−1.7552**
	(0.8329)	(0.8448)	(0.8307)	(0.8065)
Lagged Herfindahl index (i.e., concentration		−1.24		−0.2852
within an industry)		(0.7724)		(1.1204)
Industry dummies	Yes	Yes	Yes	Yes

Notes: The number of observations is equal to 6,039 in columns (1) and (2) and 2,420 in columns (3) and (4). The observations pertain to the period 1996–2000. Standard errors (in parentheses) clustered by industry.
**Significant at the 5 percent level.
*Significant at the 10 percent level.

where TFP_{ijt} is the total factor productivity estimated in the first stage for firm i operating in sector j in year t and tariff$_{jt}$ is the tariff on imports of industry j's products in year t. In addition to the fourteen manufacturing sectors considered in the paper, we also experiment with including all sectors and setting tariffs on services sectors to zero. Estimating the equation in first differences allows us to eliminate unobserved time-invariant characteristics of industry j. Since some industries may be experiencing faster TFP growth due to, for instance, faster technological progress we also include industry fixed effects in the estimation. We report robust standard errors corrected for clustering by industry. To make the analysis as comparable as possible to the industry premium exercise, we employ exactly the same industry classification and use the same tariff figures (with the exception of the sample also encompassing services industries).

The estimation results, presented in table 8C.1, give support to our hypothesis that trade liberalization is associated with higher productivity at the firm level. We find a negative and statistically significant coefficient on the tariff variable both in the sample encompassing all sectors and in the manufacturing subsample. The results hold for both trade liberalization vis-à-vis the EU and tariffs vis-à-vis the world. The results are also robust to including in the regression a lagged measure of industry concentration (Herfindahl index).

References

Amiti, Mary, and Jozef Konings. 2005. Trade liberalization, intermediate inputs and productivity. Evidence from Indonesia. CEPR Discussion Paper no. 5104. London: Centre for Economic Policy Research.

Boeri, Tito, and Pietro Garibaldi. 2003. How far is Warsaw from Lisbon? Bocconi University, Department of Economics. Unpublished manuscript.

Brown, Drussila K., Alan Deardorff, and Robert Stern. 1992. A NAFTA: Analytical issues and a computational assessment. *World Economy* 15 (1): 11–30.

Cox, David, and Richard Harris. 1985. A quantitative assessment of the economic impact on Canada of sectoral free trade with the United States. *Canadian Journal of Economics* 19 (3): 377–94.

Deichmann, Uwe, and Vernon Henderson. 2004. Urban and regional dynamics in Poland. Washington, DC: World Bank. Unpublished manuscript.

Djankov, Simeon, Rafael La Porta, Florencio Lopez-de-Silanez, Andrei Shleifer, and Juan Carlos Botero. 2001. The Regulation of Labor. Mimeo, Washington, DC: World Bank.

Fernandes, Ana. 2003. Trade policy, trade volumes, and plant-level productivity in Colombian manufacturing industries. World Bank Policy Research Working Paper no. 3064. Washington, DC: World Bank.

Foreign Trade Research Institute. Various issues. *Foreign investments in Poland.* Warsaw: FTRI.

Gardawski, J., B. Gaciarz, W. Panków, and A. Mokrzyszewski. 1998. Rozpad bastionu? Zwiazki zawodowe w gospodarce prywatyzowanej [Fall of a bastion? Labor unions in privatized economy]. Monograph. Warsaw: Instytut Spraw Publicznych and Ebert Foundation.

Gaston, Noel, and Daniel Trefler. 1994. Protection, trade, and wages: Evidence from U.S. manufacturing. *Industrial and Labor Relations Review* 47:575–93.

Goldberg, Pinelopi, and Nina Pavcnik. 2005. Trade, wages and the political economy of trade protection: Evidence from the Colombian trade reforms. *Journal of International Economics* 66 (1): 75–105.

Harrison, A. 1994. Productivity, imperfect competition, and trade reform: Theory and evidence. *Journal of International Economics* 36 (1–2): 53–73.

Hay, Donald A. 2001. The post-1990 Brazilian trade liberalization and the performance of large manufacturing firms: Productivity, market share and profits. *Economic Journal* 111:620–41.

Horstmann, Ignatius, and James Markusen. 1986. Up the average cost curve: Inefficient entry and the new protectionism. *Journal of International Economics* 20 (3–4): 225–47.

Kim, Euysung. 2000. Trade liberalization and productivity growth in Korean manufacturing industries: Price protection, market power and scale efficiency. *Journal of Development Economics* 62 (1): 55–83.

Krishna, Pravin, and Devashish Mitra. 1998. Trade liberalization, market discipline and productivity growth: New evidence from India. *Journal of Development Economics* 56 (2): 447–62.

Muendler, Marc-Andreas. 2005. Trade, technology and productivity: A study of Brazilian manufacturers, 1986–1998. University of California, San Diego. Unpublished manuscript.

Pavcnik, Nina. 2002. Trade liberalization, exit, and productivity improvements: Evidence from Chilean plants. *Review of Economic Studies* 69:245–76.

Pavcnik, Nina, Andreas Blom, Pinelopi Goldberg, and Norbert Schady. 2004.

Trade liberalization and industry wage structure: Evidence from Brazil. *World Bank Economic Review* 18 (3): 319–44.

Przybyla, Marcin, and Jan Rutkowski. 2004. Poland: Regional dimensions of unemployment. Washington, DC: World Bank. Unpublished manuscript.

Revenga, Ana. 1997. Employment and wage effects of trade liberalization: The case of Mexican manufacturing. *Journal of Labor Economics* 15 (3): 20–43.

Roberts, Mark, and James Tybout, eds. 1997. *Industrial evolution in developing countries: Micro patterns of turnover, productivity and market structure.* New York: Oxford University Press.

Topinska, Irena, and Karol Kuhl. 2003. Poverty in Poland: Profile, 2001, and changes, 1994–2001. Warsaw University. Unpublished manuscript.

World Economic Forum. 1996. *Global competitiveness report.* Geneva: World Economic Forum.

World Trade Organization. (WTO). 2000. Trade policy review: Poland 2000. Geneva: World Trade Organization.

Comment   Irene Brambilla

Most exercises that deal with quantifying the effects of a trade liberalization episode on wages (or other economic variables) face the common challenge of how to isolate the effect of changes in trade policy from other simultaneous changes in the economy. This issue is particularly relevant in the case of developing countries, as trade liberalization is usually part of a more complex reform program that may include the privatization of public enterprises, deregulation of the economy, restructuring of the tax and pension systems, and a decrease in the bargaining power of unions. In addition, oftentimes these reforms have occurred in the context of a currency crisis or an external debt renegotiation and have involved a reduction in inflation, stabilization of the exchange rate, and balancing of the budget. In the case of Poland, the reforms have been motivated by the transition from a planned to a market economy, also a clear case in which trade liberalization has been part of a broader program of structural reforms.

Several studies—including this one—take advantage of the across-industry variation in the change in tariffs in the attempt to identify the impact of trade liberalization on wages separately from other economic forces. Gaston and Trefler (1994) focus on the United States, Feliciano (2001) on Mexico, Goldberg and Pavcnik (2005) on Colombia, and Pavcnik et al. (2004) on Brazil. It can be the case, however, that changes in trade policy are correlated with other structural changes across industries, or even macroeconomic factors, that are omitted in the empirical specification.

Irene Brambilla is an assistant professor of economics at Yale University and a faculty research fellow of the National Bureau of Economic Research.

Unions that were relatively more influential than others, for example, could have negotiated higher benefits in terms of both higher wages and higher protection for their industry. Changes in exchange rates are likely to affect industries asymmetrically according to their openness. Additionally, there is a possibility of reverse causality if, for example, tariffs are set to protect industries where wages are lower. Goh and Javorcik make use of Poland's accession to the European Union to claim that the *after-reform* tariff levels are exogenously set by the accession to the common market (free trade between members and a common *given* tariff for nonmembers).

In the case of Poland, there is a *timing* dimension that supports the separate identification of the trade liberalization effects more strongly. The process of macro stabilization and liberalization of the economy began at the beginning of 1990 (including the elimination of a centrally planned system of imports and exports), whereas the tariff phase-out period to join the European Union did not begin until 1994. This timing difference provides two potential advantages that may be worth exploring in the paper. First, presumably by 1994 the initial macro shocks were under control and a large part of the transition to a market economy had taken place already. The authors consider the period 1994–2001 in their analysis. The changes in wages during their time frame are not subjected to the initial wave of reforms that occurred during 1990–1993, which might have affected industries in a nonsymmetric (and potentially correlated with tariffs) way. Second, the phase-out was nonsimultaneous across industries, with some industries liberalizing at different points in time, providing time variation in addition to industry variation in the changes in trade policy.

The authors use a series of cross sections from 1994 and 2001 from a Labor Force Survey that provide information on wages and workers' characteristics to run a wage regression. Individual wages are explained by the usual observed worker characteristics (age, marital status, education, gender, occupation category, private-sector dummy) plus the tariff in the industry to which that worker is affiliated. Time, industry, and region dummies, and several controls at the industry level—such as concentration, foreign direct investment, stock of capital, and imports and exports—are also included in the regression. Throughout different specifications, they find that industries with greater tariff reductions are associated with larger wages. The coefficient on the tariff level ranges from −0.24 to −0.68 (tables 8.5 through 8.8) and is always statistically significant, which implies an increase in wages of 2.4 to 6.8 percent for a 10 percent decrease in the tariff level of that industry. These results are robust to a change in the specification of the model, not presented in the current version of the paper, where industry premiums were computed as a first step and later regressed on industry tariff levels.

It would be informative to analyze the magnitudes implied by the actual reductions in tariffs in more depth. In the main specification of table 8.5,

when using the tariffs vis-à-vis the European Union, wages increase by 2.6 percent when tariffs decline by 10 percent. From figure 8.4, the decrease in tariffs range from 1 percent to 23 percent when all sectors are included, and from reductions of 8 to 23 percent when the electricity and gas sector is excluded. This implies increases in wages from 0.26 percent (electricity and gas) or 2.08 percent (machinery—the smallest decrease in tariffs when electricity and gas is excluded) to 6 percent (leather). When considering the changes in the external tariff (vis-à-vis the rest of the world), the changes in wages range from a decrease of 0.34 percent (electricity and gas) or an increase of 1.7 percent (machinery—when electricity and gas is excluded) to an increase of 5.4 percent (nonmetallic products other than rubber and plastic).

Most strikingly, the findings reveal a negative relation between wages and tariffs, even after controlling for industry effects, a result that is at odds with the specific-factors model and with some previous findings of studies of liberalization episodes and wages.[1] More specifically, Goldberg and Pavcnik (2005) find a positive association between tariff and wages in the case of Colombia. They show that the association becomes negative when industry effects are not included. Gaston and Trefler (1994) find a negative association between tariff and wages in a cross section of U.S. manufacturing industries, but the cross-sectional nature of their data does not allow for industry effects.

The authors attribute this somewhat surprising result to increases in productivity in those sectors that liberalized more, which in turn led to an increase in profits that was partly shared with workers through higher wages. They mention two sources of increases in productivity—a gain in efficiency due to the increased competition from imports, and easier and cheaper access to imported intermediate inputs—and briefly explore this hypothesis empirically by showing that their own estimates of total factor productivity at the industry level depend positively on the magnitude of the reduction in tariffs.

An additional contributing factor that might be worth exploring is the fact that as a sector expands it may need to hire workers whose characteristics are less specific to what is required in that industry. If workers are not homogeneous in dimensions that are not captured by the variables included in the wage regression—for example, the degree in which they are suitable for a particular industry—they are likely to receive different wages, and their movement across sectors will affect average wages. As a sector expands, the firms in that sector need to hire workers who are less likely to be trained or specialized to work there. These workers receive a lower wage than incumbent workers, which drives average wages in the ex-

---

1. The wage regression implies some degree of immobility across industries. The specific-factors model is the natural theoretical construction to associate to the empirical exercise.

panding sector down. The opposite happens in the contracting sector, where firms lay off the less suitable workers and average wages increase.

References

Feliciano, Z. 2001. Workers and trade liberalization: The impact of trade reforms in Mexico on wages and employment. *Industrial and Labor Relations Review* 55 (1): 95–115.

Gaston, N., and D. Trefler. 1994. Protection, trade and wages: Evidence from U.S. manufacturing. *Industrial and Labor Relations Review* 47 (4): 575–93.

Goldberg, P., and N. Pavcnik. 2005. Trade, wages, and the political economy of trade protection: Evidence from the Colombian trade reforms. *Journal of International Economics* 66 (1): 75–105.

Pavcnik, N., A. Blom, P. Goldberg, and N. Schady. 2004. Trade policy and industry wage structure: Evidence from Brazil. *World Bank Economic Review* 18 (3): 319–44.

Globalization and Complementary Policies
Poverty Impacts in Rural Zambia

Jorge F. Balat and Guido G. Porto

9.1 Introduction

During the last decade, Zambia adopted several economic reforms, including macroeconomic stabilization measures, trade liberalization, export promotion, and the elimination of marketing boards in maize and cotton. These reforms were expected to be beneficial in terms of national welfare, diversity in consumption, and productivity growth. The effects on the distribution of income and poverty were more uncertain, and positive impacts at the household level were harder to secure. In fact, poverty in Zambia increased during the 1990s. In this paper, we have two main objectives: to investigate the links between trade, complementary policies, and poverty observed in Zambia during the last decade, and to explore how new trade alternatives may bring about poverty alleviation in the future.

International trade introduces new opportunities and new hazards. Households are affected both as consumers and as producers or income earners. As consumers, households are affected when there are changes in the prices of goods consumed by the family. As income earners, households are affected when there are responses in wages and in agricultural income. In this paper, we examine the two sides of the globalization-poverty link.

Jorge F. Balat is a consultant to the trade unit of the Development Research Group of the World Bank. Guido G. Porto is an economist at the trade unit of the Development Research Group of the World Bank.

We are indebted to A. Harrison for her support. The discussion among participants at the National Bureau of Economic Research conference on Globalization and Poverty was very useful. We wish to specially thank our discussant, M. Slaughter, for his very useful comments and suggestions. Conversation with W. Easterly helped us clarify our understanding of some important issues; we thank him for his insights. Support from F. Yagci at the World Bank and the Zambia DTIS is greatly appreciated. All errors are our responsibility. The views expressed here are our own and do not necessarily correspond to those of the World Bank or its clients.

Since rural poverty is widespread in Zambia, we focus our analysis on rural households.

We carry out a series of separate poverty exercises related to the consumption and income impacts. On the income side, we are interested in exploring some of the dynamic effects of international trade on rural areas and agricultural activities. By facilitating access to larger international markets and by boosting nontraditional export sectors, trade provides incentives for rural households to move from subsistence to market-oriented agriculture. To capture these effects, we identify relevant agricultural activities, by providing a detailed description of household productive activities, and we estimate the income differential generated by market agriculture over subsistence agriculture using matching methods. These estimates provide a quantification of the income gains that may arise due to access to international markets and to the expansion of nontraditional exports. In addition, these income differentials across traded and nontraded agricultural activities may indicate the existence of distortions and/or supply constraints that prevent farmers from taking full advantage of profitable trading opportunities. Exploring these distortions and constraints is important to fully understand the links between globalization and poverty.

On the consumption side, we look at the effects of the removal of maize subsidies. There are two critical observations that support our somewhat narrow focus. On the one hand, Zambian households devote a very large fraction of total expenditure to food and, within food items, to maize; on the other, one of the major agricultural reforms comprised the elimination of the maize marketing board. In addition, we can use this experiment to look at the role of complementary policies. Concretely, the increase in the price of maize was expected to cause large welfare effects. But it triggered substitution effects toward cheaper varieties of maize that were only possible when the government facilitated entry into the small-scale mill industry. This is an instance in which complementary policies allowed households to smooth some of the welfare impacts of the increase in maize prices. However, the government restricted maize imports by small mills, or gave preference over publicly imported maize to industrial mills, and this hurt consumers in times of production shortages.

The paper is organized as follows. In section 9.2, we describe the trends in poverty observed in Zambia during the 1990s, we review the major reforms adopted during this period, and we characterize trends in traditional (mining) and nontraditional (agriculture) exports. In section 9.3, we look at sources of income, and we estimate income differential gains in market agriculture. In section 9.4, we study the expenditure patterns of Zambian households, and we explore the welfare costs of the elimination of consumption subsidies on maize. Section 9.5 concludes.

9.2   Trade and Poverty in Zambia

Zambia is a landlocked country located in southern central Africa. Clockwise, its neighbors are the Congo, Tanzania, Malawi, Mozambique, Zimbabwe, Botswana, Namibia, and Angola. In 2000, the total population was 10.7 million inhabitants. With a per capita gross domestic product (GDP) of only $302 in U.S. dollars, Zambia is one of the poorest countries in the world and is considered a least developed country. The goal of this section is to provide a brief characterization of trade and poverty in Zambia.

9.2.1   Poverty

Zambia faces two poverty ordeals: it is one of the poorest countries in the world, and it suffered from increasing poverty rates during the 1990s. The analysis of the trends in poverty rates can be done using several household surveys. There are four of them in Zambia: two Priority Surveys, collected in 1991 and 1993, and two Living Conditions Monitoring Surveys, in 1996 and 1998. All the surveys were conducted by the Central Statistical Office (CSO) using the sampling frame from the 1990 Census of Population and Housing.

The Priority Survey of 1991 is a Social Dimension of Adjustment (SDA) survey. It was conducted between October and November. The survey is representative at the national level and covers all provinces and rural and urban areas. A total of 9,886 households was interviewed. Questions on household income, agricultural production, nonfarm activities, economic activities, and expenditures were asked. Own-consumption values were imputed after the raw data were collected. Other questions referred to household assets, household characteristics (demographics), health, education, economic activities, housing amenities, access to facilities (schools, hospitals, markets), migration, remittances, and anthropometry.[1]

The 1996 and 1998 Living Conditions Monitoring Surveys expanded the sample to around 11,750 and 16,800 households, respectively. The surveys included all the questions covered in the Priority Survey of 1991 and expanded the questionnaires to issues of home consumption and coping strategies; they also gathered more comprehensive data on consumption and income sources.

Table 9.1 provides some information on poverty dynamics. In this paper, we use the head count as our measure of poverty. The head count is the proportion of the population with an income below the poverty line, which is defined as the monetary value of a basket of goods that would allow a person to achieve a minimum caloric requirement (the food poverty line) and

1. The 1993 Priority Survey was conducted during a different agricultural season and is therefore not comparable.

Table 9.1   Poverty in Zambia (head count)

	1991	1996	1998
National	69.6	80.0	71.5
Rural	88.3	90.5	82.1
Urban	47.2	62.1	53.4

Source: Own calculations based on the 1991 Priority Survey and the 1996 and 1998 Living Conditions Monitoring surveys.
Note: The head count is the percentage of the population below the poverty line.

a minimum nonfood expenditure (like housing or clothing).[2] In 1991, the poverty rate at the national level was 69.6 percent. Poverty increased in 1996, when the head count reached 80 percent, and then declined toward 1998, with a head count of 71.5 percent. In rural areas, poverty is widespread; in these areas the head count was 88.3 percent in 1991, 90.5 percent in 1996, and 82.1 percent in 1998. Urban areas fared better, with a poverty rate of 47.2 percent in 1991, 62.1 percent in 1996, and 53.4 percent in 1998 (fig. 9.1).

In table 9.2, a more comprehensive description of the poverty profile, by provinces, is provided for 1998. Zambia is a geographically large country, and provinces differ in the quality of land, weather, access to water, and access to infrastructure. The capital (Lusaka) and the Copperbelt area absorbed most of the economic activity, particularly when mining and copper powered the growth of the economy. The Central and Eastern provinces are cotton production areas. The Southern Province houses the Victoria Falls and benefits from tourism. The remaining provinces are less developed.

There were significant differences in the poverty rates across regions. All provinces showed aggregate poverty counts higher than 60 percent, except for Lusaka, the capital (48.4 percent). Poverty in Copperbelt was 63.2 percent, and in the Southern Province, 68.2 percent. The highest head count was observed in the Western Province, where 88.1 percent of the total population lived in poverty. The other provinces showed head counts in the range of 70 to 80 percent. Poverty was much higher in rural areas than in urban areas. Even in Lusaka, a mostly urban location, rural poverty reached over 75 percent. In the Western Province, 90.3 percent of the rural population lived in poverty in 1998. Urban poverty was lower, never exceeding 70 percent of the population (including the Western Province).

2. The food poverty line is computed with data on the caloric requirement of the diet of different individuals (males, females, adults, and children), on the caloric content of different food items (maize, milk, cassava), and on the prices of these goods. An allowance for other expenses like housing, education, clothing, and so on is added to this amount to estimate the poverty line. This is usually done by looking at the expenditure patterns of households in the neighborhood of the food poverty line.

Fig. 9.1   Typical dwelling in rural Zambia

Table 9.2   Poverty profile in 1998 (head count)

	Total	Rural	Urban
National	71.5	82.1	53.4
Central	74.9	82.3	60.5
Copperbelt	63.2	82.1	57.5
Eastern	79.1	80.6	64.4
Luapula	80.1	84.6	52.4
Lusaka	48.4	75.7	42.4
Northern	80.6	83.3	66.4
North-Western	74.3	77.4	54.1
Southern	68.2	73.0	51.8
Western	88.1	90.3	69.5

Source: Own calculations based on the 1998 Living Conditions Monitoring Survey.
Note: The head count is the percentage of the population below the poverty line.

9.2.2   Major Reforms

The Republic of Zambia achieved independence in 1964. A key characteristic of the country is its abundance of natural resources, particularly mineral deposits (like copper) and land. Due to high copper prices, the new republic did quite well in the initial stages of development. Poverty and inequality, however, were widespread, and this raised concerns among the

people and the policymakers. Soon the government began to adopt interventionist policies, with a much larger participation of the state in national development. Interventions included import substitution, price controls of all major agricultural products (like maize), and nationalization of manufacturing, agricultural marketing, and mining.

In the 1970s and 1980s, the decline in copper prices and the negative external conditions led to stagnation and high levels of external debt. A crisis emerged, and a structural adjustment program was implemented between 1983 and 1985. Riots in 1986 forced the government to abandon the reforms in 1987. A second International Monetary Fund (IMF) program failed in 1989, when the removal of controls in maize led to significant price increases.

In 1991, a new government was elected. Faced with a sustained, severe recession and with a meager future, the new government began economy-wide reforms including macroeconomic stabilization, exchange rate liberalization, fiscal restructuring, removal of maize subsidies, decontrol of agricultural prices, privatization of agricultural marketing, and trade and industrial policy. Table 9.3, reproduced from McCulloch, Baulch, and Cherel-Robson (2001), describes the major reforms adopted during the 1990s.

A major component of the reforms of the 1990s was the elimination of the marketing boards in maize and cotton. Before 1994, intervention in cotton markets was widespread. It involved setting prices for sales of certified cotton seeds, pesticides, and sprayers; providing subsidized inputs to producers; facilitating access to credit; and so on.[3] From 1977 to 1994, the Lint Company of Zambia (Lintco) acted as a nexus between local Zambian producers and international markets. Lintco had a monopsony in seed cotton markets and a monopoly in inputs sales and credit loans to farmers.

These interventions were eliminated in 1994, when markets were liberalized. Soon after liberalization, Lintco was sold to Lonrho Cotton, and a domestic monopsony was formed. Subsequent entry led to geographical monopsonies rather than national oligopsonies since firms segmented the market geographically. By 1997, the expansion of the cotton production base attracted new entrants. Competition ensued, supplanting the localized monopsonies.

At present, most cotton production in Zambia is carried out under outgrower schemes. There are two systems utilized by different firms: the farmer group system and the farmer distributor system. In the latter, firms designate one individual or farmer as the distributor and provide inputs. The distributor prepares individual contracts with the farmers. He is also in charge of assessing reasons for loan defaults, being able, in principle, to

---

3. For more details on cotton reforms in Zambia, see Food Security Research Project (2000) and Cotton Development Trust (2002).

Table 9.3   Major economic reforms in Zambia, 1989–98

Year	Stabilization policy and key events	Agricultural price and marketing	Trade reforms	Parastatal reform and privatization
1989	Decontrol of all consumer prices (except maize).	Abolition of national maize marketing board.		
1990	Policy Framework Paper agreed with IMF.	Demonopolization of agricultural marketing; maize meal subsidy withdrawn.		
1991	IMF suspends disbursements in June. Inflation soars. Election of MMD in October.		Removal of most export controls; removal of ban on maize exports.	
1992	Introduction of treasury bill financing; decontrol of borrowing and lending rates; introduction of "bureau de change" for exchange rate determination.	Severe drought; removal of mealie meal subsidy; removal of fertilizer subsidy.	Simplification and compression of tariff rates; increase in the tariff preference for goods from COMESA.	
1993	Introduction of cash budgeting.	Failed attempt to reform agricultural marketing.		Privatization act passed; Zambia Privatization Agency formed.
1994	Capital account liberalization.	Launch of the Agricultural Credit Management Programme.		
1995		Privatization of the milling industry; launch of WB agricultural-sector investment program.	Removal of 20 percent uplift factor applied to import values.	Dissolution of the Zambia Industrial and Mining Corporation (ZIMCO).
1996	MMD win elections, but UNIP boycott elections.			Acceleration of privatization program.
1997	Donors withdraw balance of payment support.			
1998	Copper prices adversely affected by East Asian crisis.			Negotiations on Zambia Consolidated Copper Mines (ZCCM) sale fall through.

Source: McCullogh, Baulch, and Cherel-Robson (2001) and Litchfield and McCullogh (2003).
Notes: MMD = Movement for Multiparity Democracy; UNIP = United National Independence Party; COMESA = Common Market for Eastern and Southern Africa.

condone default in special cases. He is in charge of renegotiating contracts in incoming seasons. In the farmer group system, small-scale producers deal with the ginneries directly, purchasing inputs on loan and repaying at the time of harvest. Both systems seem to work well.

Fueled by high copper prices and exports, during the 1970s and 1980s Zambia maintained large systems of maize production and consumption subsidies. They were administered by marketing boards. External shocks (the collapse of copper prices) and inappropriate domestic policies made marketing boards unsustainable and led to their elimination in the reforms of the 1990s. The removal of the distortions was supposed to bring about aggregate welfare gains. In practice, the effects on household welfare critically depended on complementary policies like the provision of infrastructure and the introduction of competition policies.[4]

In 1993, the government began reforming the maize pricing and marketing system, eliminating subsidies, and removing international trade restrictions. The most important reforms consisted of the removal of all price controls (including panterritorial and panseasonal pricing) and the decentralization of maize marketing and processing. At present, the marketing board has been fully eliminated. However, as of 2001, the government implemented a floor price for production of maize.

9.2.3   Trade Trends

Zambia's major trading partners are the Common Market for Eastern and Southern Africa (COMESA), particularly Zimbabwe, Malawi and the Congo, South Africa, the European Union (EU) and Japan. The main imports comprise petroleum, which accounted for 13.2 percent of total imports in 1999; metals (iron, steel), for 16.9 percent; and fertilizers, for 13 percent. Other important import lines include chemicals, machinery, and manufactures.

Zambian exports have been dominated by copper. In fact, since independence and up to 1990, exports consisted almost entirely of copper, which accounted for more than 90 percent of total export earnings. Only recently has diversification into nontraditional exports become important. The details are in table 9.4, which reports the evolution and composition of exports from 1990 to 1999. In 1990, metal exports accounted for 93 percent of total commodity exports. Nontraditional exports, such as primary products, agroprocessing, and textiles, accounted for the remaining 7 percent. From 1990 to 1999, the decline in metal exports and the increase in nontraditional exports are evident. In 1999, for example, 61 percent of total exports comprised metal products, while 39 percent were nontraditional exports. Within nontraditional exports, the main components are

4. For a description of the early reforms in maize marketing and pricing, see World Bank (1994).

Table 9.4   Exports, 1990–99 (millions of U.S. dollars)

	1990	1995	1996	1997	1998	1999	Annual growth rate (%) Actual 1990–99	Annual growth rate (%) Projected 1999–2010
Metal exports	1,168	1,039	754	809	630	468		
Nontraditional exports	89	178	226	315	308	298		
Primary agriculture	15	24	38	91	62	73	22	13
Floricultural products	1	14	18	21	33	43	52	13
Textiles	9	39	40	51	42	37	17	13
Processed and refined foods	6	25	34	31	49	33	24	17
Horticultural products	5	4	9	16	21	24	19	13
Engineering products	20	39	37	42	32	23	2	8
Semiprecious stones	8	8	11	15	12	14	21	13
Building materials	4	5	8	12	9	10	11	8
Other manufactures	0	1	1	3	3	7		11
Petroleum oils	11	11	6	2	7	6	–7	7
Chemical products	3	2	3	8	7	6	8	–4
Animal products	2	1	2	3	4	4	8	16
Wood products	1	1	2	3	3	3	13	8
Leather products	1	2	2	2	3	2	8	16
Nonmetallic minerals	2	1	1	1	1	1		13
Garments	3	0	0	0	0	0	–20	23
Handicrafts	0	0	0	0	0	0	29	11
Reexports	0		4	4	4	3		
Scrap metal	0		11	6	4	6		0
Mining	0			4	12	3		
Total commodity exports	1,257	1,217	981	1,123	937	766	–5	11
Metal share of total (%)	93	85	77	72	67	61		

Source: Bank of Zambia and IMF.

primary products, floricultural products, textiles, processed foods, horticulture, textiles, and animal products.

The last column of table 9.4 reports some informal export growth projections for some of the nontraditional categories. Notice that agriculture is expected to grow at a high rate over the decade, contributing to nearly 20 percent of total exports, up from less than 2 percent in 1990. For COMESA and the Southern Africa Development Community (SADC), cotton, tobacco, meat, poultry, dairy products, soybeans, sunflower, sorghum, groundnuts, paprika, maize, and cassava are promising markets. For markets in developed countries (the EU, the United States), coffee, paprika, sugar, cotton, tobacco, floriculture, horticulture, vegetables, groundnuts, and honey comprise the best prospects for export growth.

Exports are largely liberalized. There are no official export taxes, charges, or levies. Further, export controls and regulations are minimal.

Maize exports, however, are sometimes subject to bans for national food security reasons. In 2002, for instance, the export ban on maize was in place. There are some export incentives, from tax exemptions to concessions to duty drawback. For example, an income tax of 15 percent (instead of the standard 35 percent rate) is granted to exporters of nontraditional goods who hold an investment license. Also, investments in tourism are sometimes exempted from duties.

9.3   Income

We are most interested in exploring the effects of trade on the income of Zambian households. By affecting wages and cash agricultural income, trade opportunities are likely to have large impacts on household resources and on poverty. As argued by Deaton (1997) and others, the short-run effects of price changes can be assessed by looking at income shares. In table 9.5, we report the average income shares for different sources of income. At the national level, the main sources of income are income from home consumption (28.3 percent), income from nonfarm businesses (22.3 percent), and wages (20.8 percent). Regarding agricultural income, the sale of food crops accounts for 6.3 percent of total income, while the sale of cash crops accounts for only 2.5 percent. Livestock and poultry and remittances account for 5.5 and 4.9 percent of household income, respectively.

There are important differences in income sources between poor and nonpoor households. While the share of own-production is 33.3 percent in the average poor household, it is 19.1 percent in nonpoor families. In con-

Table 9.5	Sources of income (%)								
	National			Rural			Urban		
	Total	Poor	Nonpoor	Total	Poor	Nonpoor	Total	Poor	Nonpoor
Own production	28.3	33.3	19.1	42.5	42.9	42.0	3.3	4.4	2.4
Sales of food crops	6.3	7.6	3.8	9.1	9.5	7.6	1.4	1.7	1.1
Sales of nonfood crops	2.5	3.0	1.3	3.8	4.0	2.9	0.1	0.1	0.1
Livestock and poultry	5.5	6.8	2.9	8.1	8.7	5.9	0.8	1.0	0.7
Wages	20.8	14.4	32.9	6.9	5.9	10.3	45.3	40.3	49.4
Income, nonfarm	22.3	20.9	24.9	16.8	16.3	18.3	32.0	34.7	29.7
Remittances	4.9	5.0	4.8	5.3	5.0	6.1	4.3	4.9	3.9
Other sources	9.5	9.0	10.3	7.5	7.7	6.9	12.8	13.0	12.7
Total	100.0	100.0	100.0	100.0	100.0	100.0	100.0	100.0	100.0

Source: Own calculations based on the 1998 Living Conditions Monitoring Survey.
Note: The table reports income shares.

trast, while wages account for 32.9 percent of the total income of the non-poor, they account for only 14.1 percent of the income of the poor. The shares of the income generated in nonfarm businesses are 20.8 and 25 percent in poor and nonpoor households, respectively. The poor earn a larger share of income from the sales of both food and cash crops, and lower shares from livestock and poultry.

It is interesting to compare the different sources of income across rural and urban areas. In rural areas, for instance, 42.5 percent of total income is accounted for by own production; the share in urban areas is only 3.3 percent. The share of nonfarm income in rural areas is 16.7 percent, which should be compared with a 32.1 percent in urban areas. In rural areas, the shares from food crops, livestock, wages, and cash crops are 9.1, 8.1, 6.9, and 3.8, respectively. In urban areas, in contrast, wages account for 45.3 percent of household income, and the contribution of agricultural activities is much smaller.

The description of income shares is also useful because it highlights the main channels through which trade opportunities can have an impact on household income. We can conclude that, in rural areas, households derive most of their income from subsistence agricultural and nontradable services (nonfarm income). Cash crop activities and agricultural wages comprise a smaller fraction of total household income. In our analysis of the differential impacts of trade on household income, we focus on these last farm activities, for they are more likely to be directly affected by international markets.[5]

We explore the poverty alleviation effects of growth in nontraditional exports. If trade leads to higher prices for agricultural goods or higher wages, then there is a first-order impact on income given by the income shares described in table 9.5. But changes in the extensive margin should be expected, too. In rural areas, this involves farmers switching from subsistence to market-oriented agriculture. For instance, small-scale producers of own food are expected to benefit from access to markets by producing higher-return cash crops, such as cotton, tobacco, groundnuts, or nontraditional exports such as vegetables.

It is this attempt to identify and estimate second-round effects of increased market opportunities in rural areas that distinguishes this paper from most of the current literature. Starting with the pioneering work of Deaton (1989, 1997), estimation of first-order effects in consumption and income has become widespread. Techniques to estimate substitution in consumption are also available (Deaton 1990). But estimation of supply responses has proved much more difficult. The survey in Winters, McCul-

---

5. Notice that there may be spillover effects if trade causes growth in income and this leads to higher expenditures on nontradable good and services. We are unable to capture these effects in the data.

loch, and McKay (2004) highlights these issues and reports some of the available methods and results. In this paper, we capture supply responses using matching methods: by matching households in subsistence agriculture with households in market agriculture, we are able to estimate the average income differential generated by market-oriented activities. We do this for different crops as follows.

In rural areas, there are two main channels through which new trade opportunities can affect household income.[6] On the one hand, households produce agricultural goods that are sold to agroprocessing firms. This involves what we call cash crop activities. On the other hand, household members may earn a wage in a large-scale agricultural farm. This means that workers, instead of working in home plots for home production or cash crops, earn a wage in rural (local) labor markets. In this paper, we focus on these two types of activities.

We begin by identifying meaningful agricultural activities for the poverty analysis. Due to regional variation in soil, climate, and infrastructure, the relevant sources of income may be different for households residing in different provinces. To see this, we report in table 9.6 the main sources of household income in the rural areas of the nine Zambian provinces. For each agricultural product, the table shows the average share of total income accounted for by a given activity, the mean household income conditional on having positive income in a given activity, and the sample size, the number of households that are active in that particular agricultural activity.

Looking at income shares first, we observe that in the Central, Eastern, and Southern provinces, the most relevant cash crop is cotton. Poultry and livestock are also important sources of income, particularly in the Southern Province. Tobacco is a promising crop in the Eastern Province, and hybrid maize in the Central Province. In the Copperbelt Province, the most relevant products are vegetables and hybrid maize; in Luapula, they are groundnuts and cassava; in the Northern Province, cassava and beans; and in the North-Western Province, cassava. In all the provinces, livestock and poultry are two good sources of agricultural income.

A key aspect of international trade is that it opens up markets for new products. This implies that some relatively minor sources of income may become quantitatively more important as nontraditional exports grow. Notice, however, that in order to extract meaningful information from the Living Conditions Monitoring Survey, we face the practical constraint of sample sizes in our analysis. The data on the number of households reporting positive income and the average value of income for different agri-

---

6. See Porto (2005) for a descriptive household production model with these features. This model builds on previous work by Singh, Squire, and Strauss (1986), Barnum and Squire (1979), and Benjamin (1992).

Table 9.6   Income shares, average income, and sample sizes, by province

	Central	Copperbelt	Eastern	Luapala	Lusaka	Northern	North-Western	Southern	Western	Total
Cotton										
Share of income	8.4	0	9.5	0	0.8	0	0.1	2.8	0.2	3.1
Mean of income	50,688	12,808	24,791		58,447	167	10,134	37,016	12,827	32,254
Sample size	177	1	370	0	24	1	9	91	11	684
Vegetables										
Share of income	1.1	2.8	0.3	0.2	1.2	0.7	0.5	1.7	0.3	0.8
Mean of income	18,774	7,560	3,291	3,951	42,630	3,811	2,071	4,468	10,872	7,108
Sample size	68	87	46	27	53	100	92	151	18	642
Tobacco										
Share of income	0.2	0.1	2.3	0	0	0	0.1	0.2	0.1	0.5
Mean of income	41,472	2,434	58,529	715	833	1,001	2,348	103,252	38,609	40,590
Sample size	10	11	67	8	1	8	21	8	5	139
Groundnuts										
Share of income	0.9	0.7	2.4	2	0.2	1.4	1.1	0.4	0.2	1.2
Mean of income	6,101	8,605	4,024	8,510	16,268	3,941	7,343	5,746	2,733	5,316
Sample size	107	53	290	184	22	259	97	92	31	1,135
Paprika										
Share of income	0	0	0.1	0	0	0	0	0	0	0
Mean of income	30,579	1,609	14,116			250				13,767
Sample size	4	2	4	0	0	1	0	0	0	11
Industrial maize										
Share of income	6.1	2	0.7	0.3	1.7	0.6	0.3	1.4	0.5	1.3
Mean of income	60,377	24,162	21,075	20,160	37,910	9,617	14,924	36,458	8,929	33,897
Sample size	152	68	56	18	73	53	33	114	34	601

(*continued*)

Table 9.6 (continued)

	Central	Copperbelt	Eastern	Luapala	Lusaka	Northern	North-Western	Southern	Western	Total
Cassava										
Share of income	0.3	0.2	0.1	4.1	0	2.4	2.2	0.1	1.3	1.2
Mean of income	4,148	1,970	30,753	7,532	7,910	4,084	5,162	12,060	3,760	5,438
Sample size	43	18	9	242	3	331	214	13	71	944
Maize										
Share of income	4.4	3.1	3.2	0.5	1.1	0.9	3.8	0.9	2.6	2.2
Mean of income	13,603	14,25	10,069	4,575	14,210	5,758	7,179	9,463	7,013	9,209
Sample size	122	114	186	56	49	108	332	103	142	1,212
Rice										
Share of income	0	0	0.3	0.1	0	0.1	0	0	1.2	0.2
Mean of income	0	1,250	4,614	6,664		3,884	1,502		8,040	5,762
Sample size	0	1	39	9	0	31	3	0	48	131
Millet										
Share of income	0.9	0.1	0.2	0.3	0	1.3	0	0	0.2	0.4
Mean of income	4,821	1,402	4,253	2,338		2,727	1,574	2,250	3,161	2,965
Sample size	26	12	29	48	0	222	7	1	33	378
Sorghum										
Share of income	0.1	0.2	0	0	0.1	0.2	0.5	0	0.2	0.1
Mean of income	3,409	5,220	838	1,209	35,209	1,938	4,473		3,002	3,166
Sample size	17	17	4	12	5	45	60	1	16	177
Beans										
Share of income	0.2	0.1	0	0.5	0	2	0.8	0	0	0.5
Mean of income	6,486	1,922	6,388	9,668	8,631	11,007	3,679	2,679	2,412	8,598
Sample size	18	17	12	49	2	219	95	8	3	423

Soybeans										
Share of income	0.4	0	0.4	0.1	0	0	0	0	0	0.1
Mean of income	26,102	3,611	6,277	6,250	5,427	3,958	868	652	0	10,989
Sample size	19	3	30	1	2	6	2	2	0	65
Sweet potatoes										
Share of income	0.9	2.8	0.1	1	0	0.3	1.6	0.1	0.5	0.7
Mean of income	5,837	5,547	2,800	1,820	1,746	2,082	3,841	2,546	5,292	3,658
Sample size	57	154	26	110	9	124	159	29	29	697
Irish potatoes										
Share of income	0	0.1	0	0.1	0	0	0.3	0.1	0	0.1
Mean of income	9,987	8,935	2,494	5,810	333,333	2,443	4,321	25,420	0	8,135
Sample size	5	6	7	6	1	6	31	13	0	75
Sunflowers										
Share of income	0.1	0	0.5	0	0	0.1	0.1	0.2	0	0.1
Mean of income	12,656	4,167	4,834	750	7,738	3,424	1,100	5,770	0	5,472
Sample size	17	1	38	1	4	13	5	45	0	124
Livestock										
Share of income	2.9	1.3	4.3	0.6	3.8	2	2.3	8	6.9	3.8
Mean of income	16,126	11,606	11,910	11,808	14,285	8,701	12,955	44,612	14,936	19,442
Sample size	165	63	342	51	149	215	133	409	177	1,704
Poultry										
Share of income	6.4	2.2	4.5	2.7	5.9	3.4	2.8	4.6	6.7	4.3
Mean of income	3,329	6,530	2,550	2,061	5,967	1,940	2,220	3,762	1,501	2,778
Sample size	476	228	766	476	291	731	510	637	365	4,480

Source: Own calculations based on the 1998 Living Conditions Monitoring Survey.

Note: Income shares are in percentages, and mean of income are in monthly kwachas.

cultural products reported in table 9.6 give a sense of the potential relevance of those products. Based on this information, we identify the following meaningful agricultural products: cotton, vegetables (including beans), tobacco (in the Eastern Province only), groundnuts, hybrid maize, cassava, sunflowers, livestock, and poultry.

We turn now to a description of the methods that we use. Our aim is to estimate the differential income generated by market agricultural activities vis-à-vis subsistence agriculture, and to explore the poverty alleviation effects of allowing for an expansion of cash market activities among Zambian farmers. We use matching methods based on the propensity score. There is a large literature on matching methods. Original pieces include Rubin (1977) and Rosenbaum and Rubin (1983). More recently, Heckman, Ichimura, and Todd (1997, 1998) and Heckman et al. (1996) extended and assessed these methods. Dehejia and Wahba (2002) provided a practical examination of propensity score-matching methods using the data in Lalonde (1986).

We perform separate matching exercises, one for each of the cash agricultural products previously identified in table 9.6 (i.e., cotton, tobacco, hybrid maize, groundnuts, vegetables, cassava, sunflowers, and rural labor markets).[7] We estimate a probit model of participation into market agricultural, which defines the propensity score $p(\mathbf{X})$, for a given vector of observables $\mathbf{X}$. Subsistence farmers are matched with market farmers based on this propensity score, and the income differential is estimated using kernel methods. Details follow.

Let y_h^m be the income per hectare in market agriculture (e.g., cotton) of household h. Let y_h^s be the home-produced own consumption per hectare. Define an indicator variable M, where $M = 1$ if the household derives most of its income from cash agriculture. In practice, most Zambian households in rural areas produce something for own consumption. As a consequence, we assign $M = 1$ to households that derive more than 50 percent of their income from a given cash agricultural activity. Households that derive most of their income from home production are assigned $M = 0$. The propensity score $p(\mathbf{X})$ is defined as the conditional probability of participating in market agriculture

$$p(\mathrm{X}) = P(M = 1 \,|\, \mathrm{X}).$$

We are interested in estimating the average income differential of those involved in cash market agriculture. This can be defined as

$$\tau = E[y_h^m - y_h^s \,|\, M = 1].$$

---

7. We do not consider the case of livestock and poultry because, first, it seems reasonable to assume that this activity requires larger initial investments and, second, because Zambia has not dealt with the problem of animal disease yet.

The main assumption of matching methods is that the participation into market agriculture can be based on observables. This is the ignorability of treatment assignment. More formally, we require that y_h^m, $y_h^s \perp M \mid \mathbf{X}$. When the propensity score is balanced, we know that $M \perp \mathbf{X} \mid p(\mathbf{X})$. This means that, conditional on $p(\mathbf{X})$, the participation in market agriculture M and the observables $\mathbf{X}$ are independent. In other words, observations with a given propensity score have the same distribution of observables $\mathbf{X}$ for households involved in market agriculture as in subsistence. The importance of the balancing property, which can be tested, is that it implies that

$$y_h^m, y_h^s \perp M \mid p(\mathbf{X}).$$

This means that, conditionally on $p(\mathbf{X})$, the returns in market agriculture and in subsistence are independent of market participation, which implies that households in subsistence and in cash agriculture are comparable.

In general, the assumption that participation depends on observables can be quite strong. In Zambia, the decision to be involved in market agriculture seems to depend on three main variables: access to markets, food security, and tradition in subsistence agriculture. Farmers need market access to sell their agricultural products. In Zambia, many farmers reveal strong preferences to secure food needs before engaging in market agriculture. This behavior is probably affected by issues of risk aversion and lack of insurance. Tradition in agriculture may be the consequence of risk aversion, but it may be related to know-how and social capital in food agriculture. We capture these effects by including in the propensity function several key control variables like regional (district) dummies, the size of the household, the demographic structure of the family, the age and the education of the household head, and the availability of agricultural tools. We believe these variables $\mathbf{X}$ comprise a comprehensive set of observables to explain the selection mechanism.

It is possible to argue that there are still important unobservables that can generate biases in the results. An example would be, for instance, rainfall or temperature, which we could capture with the district dummies. Soil quality differences are important. We control for this by doing separate matching exercises in different agroclimatic regions. This means, for instance, that cotton farmers will be compared only with farmers producing food crops in cotton-growing areas. We do the same for tobacco and other products. But there will be other unobservables that we are unable to control for (like, for instance, unobserved farming activities). This is true, of course, for all matching exercises. Nevertheless, we believe that we have a reasonable model of the selection process, one that will allow us to extract useful estimates of the income gains in cash market agriculture. Table 9.7 reports the results of the estimation of the probit model for the most important cash agriculture crops.

Table 9.7 **Probit estimates: Selection into market agriculture**

	Cotton	Tobacco	Groundnuts	Vegetables	Maize	Wages
Constant	−1.338	−4.233	−2.210	−0.331	−0.777	2.264
	(0.796)	(1.821)	(0.709)	(0.734)	(0.988)	(0.919)
Married	−0.135	0.892	0.289	−0.466	−0.250	0.470
	(0.254)	(0.614)	(0.187)	(0.200)	(0.177)	(0.154)
Male	0.357	0.506	−0.364	0.365	0.275	−1.241
	(0.242)	(0.485)	(0.188)	(0.223)	(0.193)	(0.152)
Age	0.009	0.094	−0.016	−0.031	0.005	−0.100
	(0.027)	(0.070)	(0.019)	(0.024)	(0.021)	(0.049)
Age squared	0.000	−0.001	0.000	0.000	0.000	0.001
	(0.000)	(0.001)	(0.000)	(0.000)	(0.000)	(0.001)
Primary	0.448	−0.012	0.055	0.158	0.164	0.054
	(0.154)	(0.306)	(0.122)	(0.150)	(0.114)	(0.160)
High school (jr.)	0.390	0.134	0.295	0.427	0.277	0.375
	(0.203)	(0.676)	(0.149)	(0.168)	(0.133)	(0.170)
High school (sr.)	0.255	−0.591	−0.418	0.523	0.405	0.964
	(0.361)	(0.877)	(0.387)	(0.279)	(0.226)	(0.254)
Higher education	0.774	0.000	−0.318	1.006	1.450	1.127
	(0.889)	(0.000)	(0.687)	(0.431)	(0.449)	(0.407)
HH males	−0.183	0.884	0.309	−0.005	−0.058	0.966
	(0.342)	(0.769)	(0.246)	(0.293)	(0.237)	(0.323)
HH age 8–12	−0.151	−0.495	0.469	−0.462	0.692	0.626
	(0.529)	(1.248)	(0.419)	(0.515)	(0.401)	(0.498)
HH age 13–18	−0.121	0.070	0.082	−0.047	0.156	0.668
	(0.461)	(0.960)	(0.347)	(0.399)	(0.347)	(0.446)
HH age 19–45	0.092	−1.594	0.351	−0.550	0.399	1.259
	(0.399)	(1.011)	(0.322)	(0.398)	(0.304)	(0.368)
HH age 46+	−0.025	−0.425	0.532	−0.449	−0.044	2.610
	(0.466)	(1.025)	(0.336)	(0.434)	(0.362)	(0.544)
HH ill	−0.814	0.271	−0.526	−0.075	0.060	−0.402
	(0.340)	(0.552)	(0.236)	(0.293)	(0.238)	(0.302)
Distance food market	0.007	0.013	−0.003	−0.003	0.004	−0.014
	(0.004)	(0.007)	(0.002)	(0.003)	(0.002)	(0.004)
Distance mill	0.012		0.000	−0.007	0.000	−0.038
	(0.006)		(0.003)	(0.005)	(0.003)	(0.015)
Distance inputs	−0.003	0.005	−0.001	0.000	−0.005	0.000
	(0.003)	(0.007)	(0.002)	(0.002)	(0.002)	(0.002)
Distance water		0.096	−0.104	−0.168	−0.149	
		(0.261)	(0.088)	(0.113)	(0.082)	
Tools	0.603	−0.618	−0.069	0.375	0.411	
	(0.147)	(0.441)	(0.177)	(0.169)	(0.124)	
Owner	−0.121	−1.142	0.056	−0.104	−0.418	−1.555
	(0.400)	(0.586)	(0.292)	(0.273)	(0.226)	(0.177)
Land	0.030	0.362	0.077	0.014	0.142	0.058
	(0.024)	(0.094)	(0.024)	(0.026)	(0.016)	(0.018)
No. of observations	914	294	2,138	1,746	2,053	2,280
Treated	141	37	159	118	265	139
Nontreated	773	257	1,979	1,628	1,788	2,141
Pseudo R^2	0.21	0.31	0.17	0.26	0.34	0.50

Notes: Table shows probit estimates of the probability of producing cash crops. Regressions also include district dummies not shown in the table. Standard errors in parentheses. Married, male, age, age squared, and education dummies (primary, high school junior, high school senior, and higher education) refer to household head. HH males is the share of males in the household. HH age 8–12, HH age 13–18, HH age 19–45, and HH age 46+ are the shares of household members between ages 8 and 12, 13 and 18, 19 and 45, and over 46, respectively. HH ill is the share of ill members in the households. Distance food market, Distance mill, Distance inputs, and Distance water are distances (in kilometers) to the nearest food market, mill, crop inputs market, and water, respectively. Owner is a dummy that equals 1 if the household owns its farm.

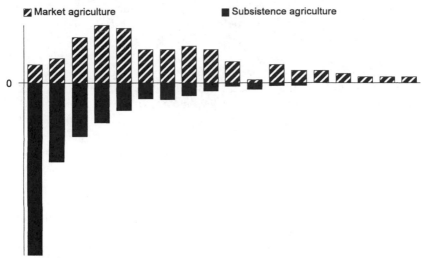

Fig. 9.2   Propensity score in cotton

Note: The graph shows the proportion of market agriculture households and subsistence agriculture households for different values of the propensity score.

In all our exercises, the balancing condition is tested following the procedure suggested by Dehejia and Wahba (2002). In all the cases, except for paprika and sunflowers, the balancing property is satisfied. This is a minor requirement that we impose in our procedure (we cannot test the ignorability requirement). In addition, as suggested by Dehejia and Wahba (2002) and Heckman, Ichimura, and Todd (1997, 1998), we graph histograms of the propensity score for those in market and those in subsistence. For the case of cotton, for example, such a plot is reported in figure 9.2. These graphs are important because they reveal the usefulness of the estimated propensity score as a predictor of the selection process. Since we are matching farmers on the basis of these propensity scores, we would like to find that the predicted probability for those farmers in subsistence is similar to the predicted probabilities for those farmers actually doing cash agriculture. In other words, this graph shows the number of subsistence farmers that can be meaningfully matched with cotton farmers. In figure 9.2, for instance, we find sufficient overlaps in the propensity scores.[8] This means that, at least in the region of common support of the propensity score, there are enough comparison units to match each cotton producer.[9]

8. Similar results are found in most of the other agricultural activities considered in this paper.

9. It is recommended that farmers in the region of noncommon support be excluded from the sample. We followed this suggestion in the estimation of the average effects.

There are two models that we want to explore, the constrained household model and the unconstrained household model. In the latter, households are assumed not to face significant constraints in terms of land, family labor supply, or inputs. This means that it would be possible for the household to plant an additional hectare of, say, cotton or cassava. In this case, the relevant quantity to estimate is the income that could be earned in cash activities. No income would be forgone by expanding cash crop activities. In contrast, in the constrained household model, land or labor imposes a limitation to farming activities. If a family were to plant an additional acre of cotton, then an acre of land devoted to own consumption (and other relevant resources) should be released.

It is unclear which model better explains the situation in Zambia. In some regions, land availability seems not to be a real constraint and farmers could in principle use additional hectares at no cost. In some places, labor supply and labor discipline seem to be a more important limitation. Access to seeds and inputs is relatively widespread in the case of cotton due to the outgrower scheme (see section 9.2). Other crops, such as hybrid maize, may require purchases of seeds in advance, something that may be difficult for many farmers. Fertilizers may also be expensive, but governmental subsidy programs in place may help ease the constraints. In any case, it is our belief that important lessons can be learned from the comparison of the results in the two models. The constrained model would give a sense of the short-run benefits of moving away from subsistence to market agriculture. The unconstrained model would reveal the additional benefits to Zambian farmers of helping release major agricultural constraints.

Results are reported in table 9.8. The first two columns correspond to the gains per hectare in the constrained model. In the next two columns, the constrained household is assumed to expand cash agricultural activities by the average size of the plots devoted to each of these activities. The following two columns report the gains per hectare in the unconstrained model; this model is directly comparable to that in the first two columns. The last two columns report the gains in the unconstrained model in the hypothetical situation in which the farmer moves from subsistence to market but devotes the average area to the market crop.

We begin by describing the case of cotton, the major market crop in some provinces (fig. 9.3). In the constrained model, farmers growing cotton are expected to gain 18,232 kwachas (Kw), on average, more than similar farmers engaged in subsistence agriculture. The gain is equivalent to 19.9 percent of the average expenditure of a representative poor farmer. To get a better sense of what these numbers mean, notice that the food poverty line in 1998 was estimated at Kw32,233 per month and the poverty line at Kw46,287 per month (per adult equivalent). Further, since the exchange rate in December 1998 was around Kw2,200, the gains are equivalent to just over US$8 (at 1998 prices).

Table 9.8   Income gains in market agriculture

	Constrained model (per hectare)		Constrained model		Unconstrained model (per hectare)		Unconstrained model	
	Total (in kwachas)	% of expenditure	Total (in kwachas)	% of expenditure	Total (in kwachas)	% of expenditure	Total (in kwachas)	% of expenditure
Cotton	18,232 (7,456)	19.9	21,878 (8,947)	23.9	51,569 (6,731)	56.4	61,883 (8,077)	67.7
Tobacco	80,661 (26,336)	88.2	64,529 (21,069)	70.6	119,124 (28,402)	130.3	95,299 (22,722)	104.2
Groundnuts	−11,717 (9,120)	−12.8	−4,452 (3,466)	−0.05	49,165 (5,606)	53.8	18,683 (2,130)	20.4
Vegetables	40,852 (25,381)	44.7	15,524 (9,645)	17.0	89,451 (25,257)	97.8	33,991 (9,597)	37.2
Maize	50,933 (11,341)	55.7	50,933 (11,341)	55.7	100,800 (9,989)	110.2	100,800 (9,989)	110.2
Cassava	a	a	a	a				
Sunflower	a	a	a	a				
Wages	95,307 (10,525)		95,307 (10,525)	104.2	117,305 (10,089)		117,305 (10,089)	128.3

Notes: Table shows results from propensity score matching of market agriculture farmers and subsistence farmers using kernel methods. Standard errors (in parentheses) are estimated with bootstrap methods. The constrained model (per hectare) assumes that the household has to give up one hectare of land to produce an additional hectare of a given cash crop (such as cotton). The constrained model assumes that the farmer moves from subsistence to market agriculture and allocates the average plot size of each cash crop (e.g., 1.2 hectares in the case of cotton). The unconstrained models assume that the farmer can allocate additional land to the cash crops without giving up subsistence production.

aNot calculated (see text).

Fig. 9.3   Cotton farm in eastern Zambia

So far, we have assumed that farmers give up one hectare of own consumption to produce an additional hectare of cotton. But the actual gains will depend on the area of cotton planted. One alternative exercise is to allow farmers to plant the average size of a typical cotton plot, which is estimated at 1.2 hectares. In this case, the constrained model generates a gain of Kw21,878. This is equivalent to 23.9 percent of the income of the poor. This model is perhaps more meaningful than the one-hectare exercise. It is important to notice that the average size of the land plots allocated to home production ranges from 1.5 to 5 hectares, with an unconditional average of around 2 hectares. This means that, on average, households would be able to substitute away from own-consumption activities and toward cotton-growing activities.

Our findings highlight important gains from switching to cotton. However, the magnitudes do not look too high, particularly given the relevance of cotton as an export commodity. One explanation for this result is that we have been working with the constrained model, according to which a farmer must forgo income to earn cotton income. If some of these constraints were eliminated, so that households could earn extra income from cotton without giving up subsistence income, gains would be much higher. We estimate these gains with the mean cotton income, conditional on pos-

itive income and on being matched with a subsistence farmer.[10] The expected gain from planting an additional hectare of cotton would be Kw51,516 (or approximately Kw10,273 per equivalent adult). These are larger gains, equivalent to around 56.4 percent of the average expenditure of poor households in rural areas. If the farmer were to grow the average size of cotton crops in Zambia (i.e., 1.2 hectares), then the gains in the unconstrained model would be Kw61,883, which is roughly equal to 67.7 percent of the average expenditure of the poor.

Another commercial crop with great potential in international markets is tobacco. In the constrained model, the gain per hectare of switching from subsistence agriculture to tobacco would be Kw80,661 monthly, or roughly 88.2 percent of average total household expenditure. Since, on average, 0.8 hectares are allocated to tobacco, the household would gain Kw64,529 if this plot size were planted. In the unconstrained model, the gain would be Kw119,124, around 130 percent of the total expenditure of an average poor household. If the average of 0.8 hectares were planted (without any constraints), the income gains would reach Kw95,299, approximately doubling expenditure. Growing tobacco seems to be an important vehicle for poverty alleviation.

Results for vegetables and groundnuts, two crops often mentioned as good prospects for nontraditional exports, reveal that no statistically significant gains can be expected in the constrained model. In the data, there is evidence of higher earnings in planting vegetables and lower earnings in planting groundnuts, but neither is statistically significant. Instead, gains can be realized if the constraints are released. For vegetables, the gain per hectare would be Kw89,451, or Kw33,991 if the average plot size devoted to this crop is planted. This is 37.2 percent of total average household expenditure. In the case of groundnuts, these gains would be equivalent to only 20 percent of the expenditure of households in poverty.

One key crop in Zambia is maize, which is grown by the vast majority of households. Farmers grow local varieties and hybrid maize. The former is mainly devoted to own consumption and is not considered suitable for world markets. Hybrid maize is, instead, potentially exportable. In table 9.8, we find that a farmer who switches from purely subsistence activities to produce (and sell) hybrid maize would make an additional Kw50,933. This gain, which is statistically significant, is equivalent to 55.7 percent of the expenditure of the poor. This is the expected gain, on average, since the average plot allocated to hybrid maize is estimated at precisely one hectare. If we assume that an additional hectare of maize is planted in a model with-

10. This matching implies two things. First, it means that the balancing property between cotton growers and subsistence farmers is satisfied. Second, it means that if a cotton farmer is too different from subsistence farmers, so that a match does not exist, then the income of this farmer is not used in the estimation of the average gain.

out household constraints, the income differential would be Kw100,800, or around the average expenditure of poor households.

These are important results. To begin with, we find support for the argument that claims that income gains can be achieved through the production and sale of hybrid maize. In addition, since most Zambian farmers across the whole country grow (or grew) maize, there is a presumption that they are able to produce it efficiently and that some of the constraints faced in other crops—such as know-how, fertilizer use, and seed usage—may not be present. In those regions in which cotton and tobacco, major exportable crops, are not suitable agricultural products (due to weather or soil conditions), the production of hybrid maize appears as a valid alternative.

Other crops identified as potentially exportable are cassava and sunflowers. These turn out to be irrelevant cases. The data were not good enough to allow for a meaningful evaluation of the benefits from exports. Either sample sizes were too small or the balancing conditions required to apply matching methods were not satisfied. This does not mean that there will be no gains from developing these markets but rather that the data are not suitable for our analysis. Finally, we have decided not to pursue the investigation of the cases of livestock and poultry, mainly because they involve significant initial investments. In addition, disease control is critical in these activities, and it is unclear whether Zambia will manage to achieve the standards needed to compete in international markets.

There is an additional exercise that we perform. If larger market access is achieved, rural labor markets may expand and workers may become employed and earn a wage. We can learn about the magnitudes of the income gains of moving from home plot agriculture to rural wage employment in agriculture by comparing the average income obtained in these activities. Concretely, we compare the average monthly wages of those workers employed in rural labor markets with the own consumption per working household member in subsistence agriculture.[11] In table 9.8, we estimate a gain of Kw95,307 per month in the constrained model (so that individuals would have to leave farming activities at home to work at a local large farm). In the unconstrained model (i.e., a model in which the worker becomes employed but keeps working in subsistence during the weekends), the gains would be Kw117,305. These gains range from 104.2 percent to 128.3 percent of the total expenditure of the average poor household in rural areas.

As in the cases of cotton, tobacco, and maize, the magnitudes of these gains suggest that rural employment in commercial farms could be a good instrument for poverty alleviation. There is evidence that, by fostering the development of larger-scale agricultural activities, international trade op-

---

11. This is computed as the ratio of reported own consumption and the total number of household members who work in subsistence agriculture.

portunities can help rural farmers to move out of poverty through rural labor markets, employment, and wage income.

It is important to show some evidence that the kind of switching that we are describing can actually take place. A careful answer to this question requires a panel data set that would allow us to track farmers who switched from subsistence to market agriculture, and compare their welfare before and after the switch. Unfortunately, this type of data is not available in Zambia. However, an overview of farm dynamics can be provided by comparing the evolution of the shares of income derived from cash agriculture at different time periods. Concretely, we estimate the average share of income generated by market agriculture in 1996 and 1998 at different points of the income distribution. We use nonparametric regressions (Fan 1992; Pagan and Ullah 1999). Figure 9.4 displays the results: the solid line represents the average shares in 1998, while the broken line corresponds to the averages in 1996. The graph reveals a clear switch toward market agriculture during the 1996–98 period. Among the poorest farmers, for instance, the share of income derived from cash agriculture increased from around 2 to 8 percent to over 20 percent. From the middle to the top of the income distribution, the increase in shares is of roughly 10 percentage points.

This analysis clearly indicates that the increase in market agriculture is correlated with the observed increase in exports of nontraditional agricultural products. This implies that the expansion of these activities is not due

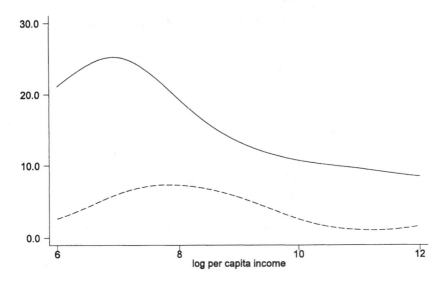

Fig. 9.4   Income shares derived from cash agriculture 1991–98

Notes: The graph shows the average shares of income derived from cash market agriculture. The solid and dotted lines represent the shares estimated with 1998 and 1996 data, respectively. The averages are estimated with nonparametric locally weighted regressions (Fan 1992).

simply to a contraction of other traditional sectors such as copper. Also, copper production is mainly an urban phenomenon affecting more urban employment than rural activities.[12]

Our interpretation of the results so far is as follows. We provided evidence of an increase in nontraditional exports that is concurrent with an increase in income shares coming from nontraditional agricultural goods. This implies that, faced with new trade opportunities, some Zambian farmers have switched from subsistence farming to cash market agriculture. This switch is only partial, since many farmers continue to produce some food for own consumption, but figure 9.4 reveals that switching is indeed a possibility. In addition, we showed that there are still income gains that could potentially be realized from further switching to market agriculture. The combination of these farm dynamics with the evidence of income gains estimated in table 9.8 suggests a natural role of trade and markets as vehicles for poverty alleviation.

The fact that there are income gains to be realized in market agriculture means that there are severe distortions and constraints in rural Zambia. We think of export opportunities as a way of releasing some of these constraints by providing markets for Zambian products. Access to international markets seems to be a basic prerequisite for successful poverty alleviation. But this is not enough. The realization of the gains associated with export opportunities will become feasible with complementary domestic policies. These may include extension services to farmers (transmission of information and know-how about producing a crop, crop diversification, and fertilizer and pesticide use), the provision of infrastructure and irrigation, the development of stronger financial and credit markets, and the provision of education (both formal education and labor discipline) and better health services.

It is easy to see why complementary policies matter. More educated households will be more prepared to face international markets and to adopt new crops and production techniques. If credit is made accessible to rural farmers, a larger fraction of them will be able to cover any necessary initial investment (in seeds, fertilizer, tools) needed to substitute subsistence production for cotton production (for instance). If better infrastructure is provided, transaction and production costs will be lower, facilitating trade of cash crops. And if better marketing opportunities arise, farmers will be "closer" to the market.

It is very hard, due to data limitation, to empirically investigate the role of these complementary policies.[13] In rural areas in Africa, though, many of the relevant issues can be illustrated by extension services in agriculture.

---

12. Notice, however, that there might be spillover effects through migration or remittances.
13. The analysis that follows was motivated by a suggestion from M. Slaughter to include a more detailed study of one policy.

These are services provided by the government (and by some agricultural intermediaries) that give farmers information and support on a variety of topics. These include information about markets, prices, buyers, and sellers; education on technology adoption, crop diversification, and crop husbandry; information on fertilizer use, seeds, and machinery; and many other aspects of everyday topics that may take place in the process of agricultural production. In consequence, we believe that a lot can be learned about the role of complementary policies by looking at the impacts of extension services on farm productivity. This is only an example of the role of those policies, but one that, we believe, makes a clear point about what can be done to help farmers take full advantage of new market opportunities.

To look at extension services and farm productivity, we use data from the Zambian Post-Harvest Survey. These data are collected annually by the CSO in Zambia. The survey is a farm survey: farmers are asked about production, yields, input use, basic household characteristics and demographics, and the like. One important question for our purposes is whether the household received extension services. Using this information, we estimate a simple model of cotton productivity. The dependent variable is yield of cotton per hectare of cultivated land. We control for some important determinants of agricultural production, such as input use, the size of the farm, the age of the household head, year dummies, and district dummies. More important, we include a dummy variable for whether the household received extension services.

Results are reported in table 9.9. As expected, we find that cotton yields respond positively to the use of pesticides. The age and sex of the household head are not significant determinants of agricultural productivity. Instead, there is some evidence that smaller farmers are more productive. The last row of table 9.8 reports the main result that we want to highlight: we

Table 9.9   **Extension services and market agricultural productivity**

Yield per hectare	Coefficient	Standard error
Constant	5.761	0.238
Head male	0.077	0.052
Head age	−2.67E–04	0.008
Head age (squared)	−3.33E–06	8.05E–05
Small	0.159	0.046
Pesticide	2.250	0.725
Pesticide (squared)	−3.160	1.810
Extension services	0.084	0.040
No. of observations	2,187	
R^2	0.17	

Source: Own calculations based on Post-Harvest Surveys.
Note: The regression includes year and district dummies.

find that households that have received extension services are on average more productive in market agriculture than households that have not received extension services. In fact, receiving agricultural extension services increases production per hectare by 8.4 percent! This corroborates the idea that education, information, and marketing services are key factors driving the best practice supply responses that are needed to secure gains from international trade.[14]

9.4   Expenditures

In this section, we investigate some of the consumption effects of price reforms in Zambia. We begin by describing the structure of expenditure. Table 9.10 reports the average budget shares spent by Zambian households in different goods in 1998. As expected, most of the budget was spent on food, with a national average share of 67.5 percent. The average was higher in rural areas (reaching 73.6 percent) and lower in urban areas (56.6 percent). Further, the poor spent a larger share of total expenditure on food than the nonpoor. At the national level, for instance, 71.7 percent of the total expenditure of an average poor family was devoted to food, while for nonpoor households the average was 59.2 percent.

Other goods accounting for a significant share of total expenditure were personal items, housing, transportation, alcohol and tobacco, and education. However, these average shares were always below 10 percent. The usual differences between urban and rural households, and between the poor and the nonpoor, were observed. For instance, nonpoor households tended to spend a larger fraction of expenditure on clothing, personal items, housing, and transportation. Budget shares on education and health were not different across poor and nonpoor households. Comparing rural and urban households, we find that rural households consumed more food, and urban households more personal items, housing, transportation, and education. Shares spent on clothing, health, and alcohol and tobacco were not very different.

There is one fundamental lesson that can be learned from table 9.10. In Zambia, as in many low-income developing countries, the largest fraction of household expenditure is spent on food. In consequence, the largest impacts of trade policies and economic reforms on the consumption side will be caused by changes in the prices of food items. Expenditures on nonfood items are relatively less important in terms of total expenditure, the welfare impacts being lower as a result.

Maize is the main food item consumed in Zambia. There are four main types of maize for consumption: home-produced maize, mugaiwa, roller

---

14. For a more detailed analysis of cotton reforms and farm productivity, see Brambilla and Porto (2005).

Table 9.10   **Average budget shares (%)**

	National			Rural			Urban		
	Total	Poor	Nonpoor	Total	Poor	Nonpoor	Total	Poor	Nonpoor
Food	67.5	71.8	59.3	73.6	74.6	70.3	56.6	63.1	51.2
Clothing	5.6	4.8	7.1	5.6	5.2	7.0	5.5	3.6	7.1
Alcohol and tobacco	3.6	2.9	4.9	3.7	3.0	6.0	3.3	2.3	4.1
Personal goods	7.1	6.8	7.6	5.7	6.1	4.5	9.5	9.1	9.9
Housing	4.5	4.2	5.0	2.9	3.0	2.4	7.3	7.7	6.9
Education	2.5	2.6	2.3	1.9	2.1	1.0	3.6	3.9	3.3
Health	1.4	1.3	1.6	1.3	1.3	1.5	1.7	1.5	1.7
Transport	4.2	3.2	5.9	3.4	3.1	4.3	5.5	3.6	7.1
Remittances	1.3	0.7	2.4	1.0	0.7	1.9	1.9	0.8	2.8
Other	2.4	1.7	3.9	0.9	0.8	1.2	5.1	4.2	5.9
Total	100.0	100.0	100.0	100.0	100.0	100.0	100.0	100.0	100.0

Source: Own calculations based on the 1998 Living Conditions Monitoring Survey.

maize, and breakfast meal. Roller meal and breakfast meal comprise industrial maize produced by large-scale mills (fig. 9.5). Both are finely ground maize, but roller meal is a lower-quality staple. Mugaiwa is the meal composed of maize grain that is ground by small-scale hammermills. Sometimes farmers (especially women) take the peel off the grain before taking it to the hammermill, leading to a tastier maize meal (fig. 9.6).

Table 9.11 shows that maize consumption indeed accounts for a large share of expenditure. In 1998, 18.5 percent of the average budget went to maize outlays at the national level; the corresponding figures in rural and urban areas were 21 percent and 14.2 percent. The total expenditure on maize was relatively balanced between home production, industrial maize, and mugaiwa. However, it is clear that households in rural areas spent a larger share on home-produced maize and on mugaiwa than households in urban areas, which spent more on industrial maize. There were important provincial differences in maize shares. In Lusaka, which includes the capital city, the average household devoted a moderate share to maize, mostly to industrial varieties. In Luapula and in the Northern Province, the shares spent on maize were much lower. This is because these regions specialize in growing cassava rather than maize (and, in Luapula, fishing is a key economic activity). In the remaining provinces, maize was the main staple.

Zambia adopted large reforms in the maize sector during the 1990s. Before 1993, maize marketing was controlled by a maize marketing board, which set prices for maize grain and maize meal. In particular, breakfast and roller meals were heavily subsidized. In 1993, the government eliminated all price controls. Given the importance of maize as a food expenditure in Zambia, in what follows we investigate the consumption effects of the elimination of these large consumption subsidies.

Fig. 9.5 Roller and breakfast meal maize

Fig. 9.6   Preparing mugaiwa maize

Fig. 9.6   (cont.)

Fig. 9.6   (cont.)

Table 9.11   Maize consumption, by province (%)

	Central	Copperbelt	Eastern	Luapala	Lusaka	Northern	North-Western	Southern	Western	Total
Total maize	22.5	17.6	29.3	3.7	14	5.6	14.9	25.2	32.9	18.5
Rural	26.3	22.9	30.5	2.9	25.1	4.7	14.6	28.6	33.4	21
Urban	16.1	15.7	17.7	9.7	11.9	10.8	17.2	12.9	27.7	14.2
Home production	7.6	1.6	14.7	1.1	0.9	2	6.8	5.2	12	5.4
Rural	11.6	4.8	16	1.2	5.2	2.1	7.5	6.5	13	8.2
Urban	0.9	0.4	2.5	0.6	0.1	0.9	2.2	0.5	2	0.5
Industrial	5.2	12.9	3.4	1	10.7	1.2	2.7	6.7	7.4	6.5
Rural	2.4	9.3	3.2	0.4	7.7	0.7	2.2	6.4	6.9	3.8
Urban	10	14.1	4.8	5.1	11.3	4.4	6.5	8	12.6	11.1
Mugaiwa	9.6	3.1	11.2	1.6	2.4	2.4	5.3	13.3	13.6	6.6
Rural	12.3	8.7	11.2	1.3	12.1	1.9	4.9	15.8	13.6	9
Urban	5.1	1.1	10.5	3.9	0.5	5.5	8.5	4.4	13.2	2.5

Source: Own calculations based on the 1998 Living Conditions Monitoring Survey.

Note: The table reports budget shares (over total expenditure).

The government subsidized maize to consumers by regulating maize milling and sales. Large-scale mills located in urban centers distributed industrial maize (breakfast and roller meal) throughout the country and controlled most of the market for maize meal. Small-scale mills (hammermills) were not allowed to participate in maize marketing. Their function was to mill own-produced grain for home consumption. Because of the subsidies to production and industrial maize, it was often cheaper for rural consumers to sell their harvested maize and buy cheap milled maize.

When the marketing board was eliminated, consumer prices for breakfast and roller maize increased significantly. However, the government liberalized the small-scale hammermill sector, allowing mills to enter the market. This facilitated the growth of consumption of mugaiwa, a cheaper form of maize meal, where households would bring grain to the small hammermills for grinding services. The introduction of competition in the milling industry allowed for the availability of cheaper varieties of meal maize, and consumers were able to ameliorate the negative impacts of the elimination of the subsidies.

There is a caveat, though. In times of production shortages, Zambia resorts to imported maize to satisfy food needs. Traditionally, industrial large-scale mills, as opposed to hammermills, have been able to import maize or have been granted preferential access to publicly imported grain (Mwiinga et al. 2002). These constraints on small-scale mills can force households to consume larger shares of industrial maize and lower shares of mugaiwa meal, with consequent welfare costs in terms of food security.

We turn next to the investigation of the consumption effects of the reforms.[15] When the marketing board was eliminated, industrial maize became too expensive for many households.[16] Not only did the removal of the subsidy cause higher costs, but the privatized mill industry could have acted as a monopoly, leading to prices well above marginal costs. With large average budget shares spent on industrial maize (table 9.10), such price increases would have significant welfare costs for Zambian consumers. For instance, a 100 percent increase in prices with a budget share of 15 percent among poor households in urban areas would lead to a welfare loss of 15 percent of initial total household expenditure.

To assess the impacts of these reforms on consumers, we would like to estimate a system of demand for different varieties of maize and use the structural parameters of demand to carry out an evaluation of the policy

---

15. Due to lack of data on input use and transport costs at the household level, we do not investigate the welfare losses caused by the elimination of support prices to producers, which is therefore left as a topic for future research.

16. Anecdotal evidence indicates that, in 1991, when the Zambian government first attempted to get rid of the marketing board as recommended by the IMF, prices of industrial maize in urban areas rose by as much as 100 percent. This led to riots and demonstrations that forced the government to reverse the initial reform.

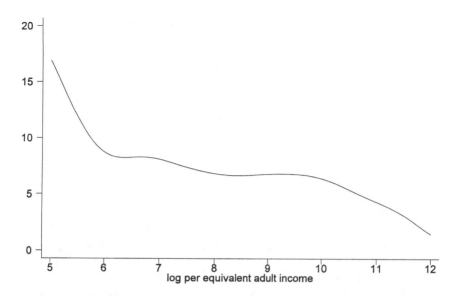

Fig. 9.7   Share of maize meals in rural Zambia before reforms (1991)

Notes: The graph shows the average budget share spent on industrial maize in rural areas. The averages are estimated with nonparametric locally weighted regressions (Fan 1992).

changes. In the case of Zambia, data constraints make it impossible to carry out a comprehensive examination of the dynamics of maize demand. It is possible, however, to provide a simpler analysis of the costs of the removal of the subsidies by looking at budget shares. As shown by Deaton (1989), the effect of a price change can be approximated by budget shares.

For our purposes, there are three relevant budget shares: on maize own consumption, on breakfast and roller maize (industrial maize), and on mugaiwa maize. We are interested in capturing the extent of substitution responses in the consumption of different types of maize. We can do this by estimating the average budget share, conditional on the level of household expenditure. To estimate these averages nonparametrically, we use Fan's (1992) locally weighted regressions. We estimate a regression function for 1991 (before the maize reforms) and another for 1998 (after the reform).

Figure 9.7 plots the nonparametric averages by level of per-adult-equivalent expenditure for rural Zambia in 1991. In the Priority Survey, we only have information on the share spent on industrial maize. Expenditure on mugaiwa was negligible, since the milling industry was not liberalized, and the expenditure on own consumption was not disaggregated into individual components. In any case, it is possible to observe that the share of industrial maize expenditure declines with income (as predicted by Engel's law). For the poorest households, the shares reach 14 percent of the bud-

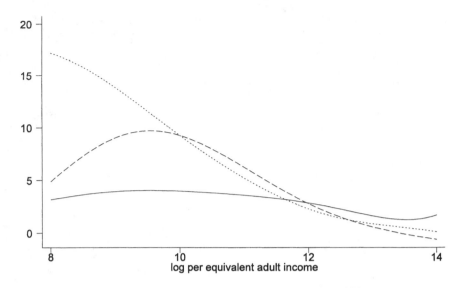

Fig. 9.8   Share of maize meals in rural Zambia after reforms (1998)

Notes: The graph shows the average budget shares spent on maize. The solid line represents the share of industrial maize; the broken line, the share of own consumption; and the dotted line, the share spent on mugaiwa. The averages are estimated with nonparametric locally weighted regressions (Fan 1992).

get. These large fractions are explained in part by the prevalence of the consumer subsidies.

Figure 9.8 estimates the Fan (1992) regressions after the reforms. The Living Conditions Monitoring Survey for 1998 includes data on many types of maize consumption. Thus, we can describe the whole pattern of household expenditures. The solid line represents the average budget share spent on industrial maize (breakfast and roller); the broken line, the share spent on own consumption; and the dotted line, the share spent on mugaiwa. We observe that the most important source of maize meal in 1998 is mugaiwa, particularly for poorer households (which show shares of over 15 percent of total expenditure). The share of own consumption increases with income at the bottom of the distribution, and then declines with it as income grows. In contrast, the share of industrial maize is relatively constant at all income levels.

This analysis clearly shows how rural households have substituted away from industrial maize and toward mugaiwa maize. Estimates by Mwiinga et al. (2002) indicate that the price of mugaiwa maize (which includes grain expenses plus milling services) is only about 60 to 80 percent of the price of industrial maize. The pattern of substitution reported by Zambian households thus reveals the benefits brought about by the possibility of having

access to this cheaper source of maize meal. For this to be possible, liberalization of the market was critical. Moreover, it is even possible for consumers to benefit from the overall reforms (elimination of marketing board and concurrent liberalization of mills) if, due to the deregulation, mugaiwa prices declined (much) below the price of industrial maize before the reform.[17]

As already mentioned, there are some restrictions on small mills imposed by the government. Since Zambia substantially relies on maize for food security, the country must resort to imports in times of production shortages. Typically, the government would grant special privileges to large-scale mills to import maize. They were allowed to import maize, or they were given preferential access to government-imported maize. This implies that local maize shortages, like those observed in 2001–2, would be accompanied by a shortage of mugaiwa. As a result, consumers would be forced to purchase more expensive industrial maize. The estimated averages give us a sense of the important welfare effects that this type of regulation can impose on poor rural households.

9.5   Conclusions

In this paper, we have investigated some of the impacts of international trade and economic reforms on rural households in Zambia. This is a low-income country, with widespread and prevalent poverty at the national and regional levels. In rural areas, poverty is still higher. In this context, efforts devoted to finding ways to alleviate poverty should be welcome. In Zambia, the government and international institutions have long been actively searching for programs and policies to improve the living standards of the population. Concretely, a set of reforms was implemented during the 1990s, including liberalization, privatization, and deregulation of marketing boards in agriculture. Further, farmers and firms were encouraged to look more closely at international markets.

After episodes of economic reform, households are affected both as consumers and as income earners. Consequently, we have looked at these two aspects of the globalization-poverty link. On the income side, we have estimated income gains from market agriculture vis-à-vis subsistence agriculture. On the consumption side, we have investigated the effects of the elimination of the consumer subsidies on maize that were caused by the elimination of the maize marketing board.

International trade and export growth would bring about an increase in the demand for traded goods produced by Zambian farmers. These include cotton, tobacco, hybrid maize, vegetables, and groundnuts. Further, rais-

17. Unfortunately, there are no data on mugaiwa prices before the reform with which to better assess this outcome.

ing the demand for rural labor would increase rural wages as well. Our results indicate that rural Zambians would gain substantially from expanding world markets, particularly in terms of cotton, tobacco, and maize income as well as wage income.

For this to be feasible, Zambia needs to have access to international markets. On the one hand, this requires the liberalization of world agricultural markets. But complementary policies would also be essential. On the production side, these include extension services (information), infrastructure (transport), irrigation, access to credit and finance, education, and health services.

The elimination of consumer subsidies on the main staple, maize, caused large welfare losses in rural households. Here, complementary policies were shown to have important effects as well. On the one hand, the liberalization of the milling industry allowed for the surge and development of the consumption of mugaiwa maize, a cheaper source of maize meal. This allowed for a strong substitution pattern in consumption whereby households would consume less of the expensive industrial maize varieties and more of the cheaper mugaiwa. On the other hand, the restrictions on imports of maize by small mills limited the extent of substitution that was feasible in times of maize production shortages.

We end with our main conclusion. Globalization and domestic reforms complement each other: the benefits from globalization can be fully exploited only if complementary measures are simultaneously taken, and the benefits from domestic reforms may not happen without global markets.

References

Barnum, H., and L. Squire. 1979. A model of an agricultural household: Theory and evidence. World Bank Occasional Paper no. 27. Washington, DC: World Bank.

Benjamin, D. 1992. Household composition, labor markets, and labor demand: Testing for separation in agricultural household models. *Econometrica* 60:287–322.

Brambilla, I., and G. Porto. 2005. Farm productivity and market structure: Evidence from cotton reforms in Zambia. Growth Center Discussion Paper no. 919. New Haven, CT: Yale University.

Cotton Development Trust. 2002. *Cotton news.* Lusaka, Zambia: Cotton Development Trust.

Deaton, A. 1989. Rice prices and income distribution in Thailand: A nonparametric analysis. *Economic Journal* 99:1–37.

———. 1990. Price elasticities from survey data. *Journal of Econometrics* 44:281–309.

———. 1997. *The analysis of household surveys: A microeconometric approach to development policy.* Baltimore, MD: Johns Hopkins University Press.

Dehejia, R., and S. Wahba. 2002. Propensity score matching methods for non-experimental causal studies. *Review of Economic Studies* 84 (1): 151–61.

Fan, J. 1992. Design-adaptive nonparametric regression. *Journal of the American Statistical Association* 87 (420): 998–1004.

Food Security Research Project. 2000. Improving smallholder and agribusiness opportunities in Zambia's cotton sector: Key challenges and options. Working Paper no. 1. Lusaka, Zambia: Food Security Research Project.

Heckman, J., H. Ichimura, J. Smith, and P. Todd. 1996. Sources of selection bias in evaluating social programs: An interpretation of conventional measures and evidence on the effectiveness of matching as a program evaluation method. *Proceedings of the National Academy of Sciences* 93 (23): 13416–20.

Heckman, J., H. Ichimura, and P. Todd. 1997. Matching as an econometric evaluation estimator: Evidence from evaluating a job training programme. *Review of Economic Studies* 64 (4): 605–54.

———. 1998. Matching as an econometric evaluation estimator. *Review of Economic Studies* 65 (2): 261–94.

Lalonde, R. 1986. Evaluating the econometric evaluations of training programs. *American Economic Review* 76 (4): 604–20.

Litchfield, J., and N. McCulloch. 2003. Poverty in Zambia: Assessing the impacts of trade liberalization in the 1990s. Sussex University, Poverty Research Unit. Mimeograph.

McCulloch, N., B. Baulch, and M. Cherel-Robson. 2001. Poverty, inequality and growth in Zambia during the 1990s. Paper presented at World Institute for Development Economics Research Development Conference. 25–26 May, Helsinki, Finland.

Mwiinga, W., J. Nijhoff, T. Jayne, G. Tembo, and J. Shaffer. 2002. The role of Mugaiwa in promoting household food security. Policy Synthesis no. 5. Lusaka, Zambia: Food Security Research Project.

Pagan, A., and A. Ullah. 1999. *Nonparametric econometrics.* New York: Cambridge University Press.

Porto, G. 2005. Informal export barriers and poverty. *Journal of International Economics* 66:447–70.

Rosenbaum, P., and D. Rubin. 1983. The central role of the propensity score in observational studies of causal effects. *Biometrika* 70 (1): 41–55.

Rubin, D. 1977. Assignment to a treatment group on the basis of a covariate. *Journal of Educational Statistics* 2 (1): 1–26.

Singh, I., L. Squire, and J. Strauss, eds. 1986. *Agricultural household models: Extensions, applications and policy.* Baltimore, MD: Johns Hopkins University Press.

Winters, A., N. McCulloch, and A. McKay. 2004. Trade liberalization and poverty: The evidence so far. *Journal of Economic Literature* 42:72–115.

World Bank. 1994. *Zambia poverty assessment.* Washington, DC: World Bank.

Comment   Matthew J. Slaughter

The conference for the proceedings of this book was held in Massachusetts. I drove to this conference with my wife and our two boys, and en route we

Matthew J. Slaughter is an associate professor of business administration at the Tuck School of Business, Dartmouth College, and a research associate of the National Bureau of Economic Research.

stopped at Plymouth Plantation, along the Massachusetts coast. We did this because our older boy Nicholas (and by osmosis his little brother Jacob) has been studying the Pilgrims in school. The Plantation is a living-history museum, whose main attraction is a thriving replica of the community of Jamestown established by the Mayflower settlers in the 1620s.

The museum curators assume the roles of real settlers, with astonishing accuracy in terms of dress, accent, and knowledge of actual events. You can talk with these settlers as you wander around their dwellings and infrastructure. During our visit I learned that the settlers' economic livelihood consisted of two main activities. One was agriculture, largely for self-sufficiency. The other was hunting small game, in particular beaver, whose pelts were exported back to Europe as a key intermediate input needed to make what at that time were some of the finest fur hats in the world. In exchange, settlers imported almost all their nonagricultural consumption goods such as furniture, farm implements, and armaments for self-defense.

I am reporting this not to bore you with my knowledge of first-grade civics (although I can report that Nicholas's classmates were keen to see our souvenirs, especially the small amount of plantation dirt and rocks we were permitted to take). No, this segue is instructive because the economic ties forged by the Plymouth settlers nearly 400 years ago are precisely the sort of economic ties that Zambians have been seeking to forge, as analyzed by this very interesting paper of Balat and Porto. Indeed, for any of you familiar with Plymouth Plantation, see if you are struck as I was by the similarity of the plantation grounds to the photographs of rural Zambia that Balat and Porto included with their paper.

The Jamestown Pilgrims survived those harsh early years largely because of their global engagement. Their consumption basket was sufficiently wide and deep thanks to their ability to become part of a global production network, mediated by multinational firms. These are classic gains from trade that we all teach and extol: greater production specialization on the production side according to comparative advantage, combined with greater consumption possibilities thanks to removing the constraint of consuming one's own production. At issue in this paper is whether citizens of Zambia have been able to reap such gains in recent years.

The authors' focus on Zambia is well matched to the twin themes of this conference volume of globalization and poverty. On the latter subject, Zambia in recent decades has sadly been one of the poorest countries on the planet. The 2000 per capita GDP of Zambia was US$302. This astonishingly low average was spread across most of the population of 10.7 million: as table 9.1 reports, the national poverty rate was 69.6 percent in 1991, 80 percent in 1996, and 71.5 percent in 1998. Today in 2005 there are deep discussions to reinvigorate efforts to reduce world poverty, and high on many lists is the policy prescription for "greater global engagement." This policy plank is widely acknowledged to be necessary but not sufficient,

with ongoing puzzlement about exactly what mix of opening borders and other changes works best.

Zambia is thus Exhibit A for the challenges facing the development community, and the work in this paper is an important contribution to existing knowledge. The authors bring careful data analysis to bear on two issues arising from Zambia's substantial policy liberalizations over the 1990s. One issue is whether individual producers gained from the new production opportunities that liberalization introduced to sell output on markets—including international markets—rather than producing just for own consumption. The other issue is how consumers were affected by the removal of price controls on maize, the largest single item in the typical household consumption basket. As a trade economist, I especially like the juxtaposition of these issues as they constitute the numerator and denominator of the real-income impacts that freer trade can generate in the benchmark Heckscher-Ohlin trade models through the celebrated Stolper-Samuelson mechanism.

For each of the two issues, there is a main finding. First, by comparing the income earned by own-production farmers with their observationally equivalent (as best the data allow such matches to be made) farmers selling output into markets (and/or working for wage on larger-scale farms), the authors argue that substantial income gains *could have been* earned by Zambian producers who pursued the new market opportunities after liberalization. Second, by examining relative prices across the four different qualities of maize available in Zambia, the authors find that substitution toward relatively cheap varieties *could have been* an important mechanism for cushioning the welfare impact of liberalization-induced price increases in higher-quality varieties. For both these results, the authors stress that "complementary policies," above and beyond trade liberalization, *could have been* an important factor in facilitating such switches. On the production side, such complementary policies probably included capital market access and extension services on crop quality and husbandry. On the consumption side, they probably included allowing market entry of new maize producers to meet shifting demand.

I have two general comments on the authors' careful work, both of which suggest future research directions. Both comments build on the italicized verb clauses of the previous paragraph, which are flagged on purpose.

The first general comment is that we need to know not just whether producers and consumers *could have* responded to liberalization policies in the ways just summarized. We also need to know *whether in fact* such shifts have happened in experiences like that of Zambia.

In general equilibrium models of trade, the focus tends not to be on how exactly national productive resources get reallocated from the autarky production point to its free-trade counterpart. That is okay for some ques-

tions. But in the real world the "how exactly" part is very important. Do existing firms continue and just change their product mix? Alternatively, do existing firms shut down and new firms start up in new industries? Are there important geographic shifts that accompany the industry shifts? On the consumption side, do families need to travel great distances to find new options? Unfortunately, the data of Balat and Porto are inherently unsuited to answer these sorts of "how exactly" questions, in large part because they have repeated cross sections rather than a true panel that tracks over time the same people and/or firms. Those interested in this essential line of research need more evidence on how production and consumption shifts actually do (and do not) happen.

My second general comment is that we need to know more about the role of what the authors call "complementary policies." Yes, there is a wide range of such policies that *could* help trigger the gains from trade liberalization; but which ones *actually* work?

Again, this is clearly a tall order that data limitations prevent the authors from addressing. They try with their analysis of farming extension services, where table 9.9 shows that receiving extension services is correlated with higher-productivity farms. This is suggestive, at best. Without any information on how selection into receiving extension services actually occurs, the identifying assumption that it is exogenous to farm performance cannot really be favored over the completely opposite story that governments choose to allocate scarce extension-services resources to what appear to be (arguably unobservably to the econometrician) high-performing producers.

There is much international research lately, contentious and otherwise, concluding that freer trade is probably a necessary reform but is unlikely a sufficient reform to trigger economic growth. But this deepens our need for institutional details like that raised in this study. We need case studies of what was tried where, and to what degree of success. The analogy of the practice of medicine comes to mind. Most clinical treatments that we take as conventional wisdom today gained this status only thanks to long histories of inductive trial and error. For the most vulnerable citizens of the world, like those of Zambia, more careful research like that in this paper is needed to make policy less a matter of trial and error.

Globalization, Labor Income, and Poverty in Mexico

Gordon H. Hanson

10.1 Introduction

There is now an immense body of literature on how globalization affects labor markets. Early research centered on the United States (Freeman 1995; Richardson 1995), motivated in part by an interest in understanding what caused marked changes in the U.S. wage structure during the 1980s and 1990s (Katz and Autor 1999). A common theme in this work is that globalization—especially in the form of global outsourcing—has modestly but significantly contributed to increases in wage differentials between more- and less-skilled workers (Feenstra and Hanson 1999, 2003). A small effect for international trade is perhaps unsurprising, given the large size of the U.S. economy and the still limited role that trade plays in U.S. production and consumption (Feenstra 1998; Freeman 2003). Later research shifted attention to other countries and to the developing world in particular, which in the 1980s began to lower barriers to trade and capital flows aggressively. The tendency for rising wage inequality to follow globalization is not limited to the United States or other rich countries. Expanding trade and capital flows have been associated with increases in the relative demand for skilled labor in many economies, including Chile (Pavcnik 2003), Colombia (Attanasio, Goldberg, and Pavcnik 2004), Hong Kong (Hsieh and Woo 2005), Mexico (Feenstra and Hanson 1997),

Gordon H. Hanson is a professor of economics in the Graduate School of International Relations and Pacific Studies and in the Department of Economics at the University of California, San Diego, and a research associate of the National Bureau of Economic Research (NBER).

I thank Julie Cullen, Esther Duflo, Ann Harrison, Jim Levinsohn, and participants in the NBER Conference on Globalization and Poverty for helpful comments. Jeffrey Lin provided excellent research assistance.

and Morocco (Currie and Harrison 1997), to list just a few recent examples.[1]

In most research to date, the focus has been on the relationship between globalization and earnings inequality. Fewer studies have examined how globalization affects income levels. This comes as something of a surprise, given the long-standing interest of developing-country research in how changes in policy affect the well-being of the poor. The relative lack of attention on the impact of globalization on poverty is perhaps partly attributable to methodology. The most established empirical techniques for identifying the effects of economic shocks, such as globalization or technological change, on earnings relate to estimating changes in the relative demand for labor of different skill types (Katz and Autor 1999). The lack of attention may also reflect a U.S. bias in the type of questions being asked. The strong emphasis in U.S. literature on why earnings inequality has increased may have spilled over into research on other countries, partially crowding out other issues.

In this paper, I examine how the distribution of income changed in Mexico during the country's decade of globalization in the 1990s. Taking the income distribution as the unit of analysis makes it possible to examine changes both in the nature of inequality—reflected in the shape of the distribution—and in the level of income—reflected in the position of the distribution. Mexico is worthy of study because over the last two decades the country has aggressively opened its economy to the rest of the world. This process began with a unilateral liberalization of trade in 1985, continued with the elimination of many restrictions on foreign capital in 1989, and culminated with the North American Free Trade Agreement (NAFTA) in 1994 (Hanson 2004).[2]

There is relatively little work on the impact of trade liberalization on poverty in Mexico. One notable exception is Nicita (2004), who applies data from the Mexico's National Survey of Household Income and Expenditure to techniques developed by Deaton and Muellbauer (1980) and Porto (2003) to construct an estimate of how tariff reductions have affected household welfare. This exercise involves estimating the impact of tariff changes on domestic goods' prices, the impact of changes in goods' prices on the wages of different skill groups, and income and price elasticities of demand for different goods, and then combining these estimates to form an estimate of the change in real income due to tariffs. During the 1990s, tariff

---

1. See Winters, McCulloch, and McKay (2004) and Goldberg and Pavcnik (2004) for surveys of the literature on globalization and income in developing countries.

2. See Chiquiar (2003) for a discussion of recent policy changes in Mexico. For other work on the labor market implications of globalization in Mexico, see Ariola and Juhn (2003), Cragg and Epelbaum (1996), Fairris (2003), Feliciano (2001), Revenga (1997), Hanson and Harrison (1999), and Robertson (2004). See Hanson (2004) for a review of this literature. For work on trade reform and wage inequality in Latin America, see Behrman, Birdsall, and Szekely (2003).

changes appeared to raise disposable income for all households, with richer households enjoying a 6 percent increase and poorer households enjoying a 2 percent increase. These income gains imply a 3 percent reduction in the number of households in poverty. Income gains are larger in regions that are close to the United States, where tariff-induced price changes are larger.

The approach in Nicita (2004) exploits cross-time variation in tariff levels to estimate how tariff changes are passed along into prices. The advantage of this approach is that it produces estimates of how changes in trade policy affect the *level* of real household income. One disadvantage is that it ignores other contemporaneous shocks that are also related to globalization, such as greater foreign investment and expanding global production networks in Mexico. The existence of other shocks reflects a common problem in evaluating the impact of trade liberalization. Trade reform is not a random event, but instead typically results as part of a government reaction to economic pressures that force it to abandon a preexisting set of policies. In Mexico, as in many other countries, when the government lowered import tariffs it also eliminated nontariff barriers, eased restrictions on foreign investment, deregulated industries, and privatized state-owned enterprises and agricultural cooperatives. Problematically, industries subject to larger reductions in tariffs may also have been subject to larger changes in other policies. Unless one carefully controls for these other policy changes—which is difficult to do given that many of the policy instruments being changed are either unobserved (e.g., the bureaucratic process for approving foreign direct investment) or hard to measure (e.g., nontariff barriers)—then one may misattribute income changes to import tariffs that are in fact associated with other policy shocks.

In this paper, I compare changes in the distribution of labor income in the 1990s between Mexican regions that were more or less exposed to globalization. As section 10.2 discusses, geographic variations in proximity to the United States and in natural resource supplies have helped make some Mexican regions much more exposed to foreign trade and investment than others. I take states with high exposure to globalization to be the treatment group and states with low exposure to globalization to be the control group (leaving states with intermediate exposure out of the analysis). I then apply a difference-in-difference strategy by comparing the change in the income distribution for high-exposure states to the change in income distribution for low-exposure states.[3] By comparing changes in the lower tail of the distributions across regions, I am able to measure the differential change in poverty across regions during Mexico's globalization decade

---

3. Implicit in the analysis is the assumption is that labor is sufficiently immobile across regions of Mexico for region-specific labor-demand shocks to affect regional differentials in labor income.

(subject to a common national shock in both regions). To provide a bench-mark for comparing poverty levels, I define the poverty threshold as the labor income needed to sustain a family of four at minimum consumption levels.[4]

The advantage of my approach relative to Nicita (2004), Porto (2003), and other work in the tradition of Deaton and Muellbauer (1980) is that I am able to consider a broader set of shocks related to globalization. The disadvantage of my approach is that I can only make statements about the *relative* regional change in poverty associated with globalization. Given the severe estimation problems in identifying the impact of trade reform on household income, no single approach is likely to be entirely satisfactory. My approach and that of Nicita (2004) should thus be seen as complementary.

The analysis is complicated by several issues, three of which stand out. One is that income distributions change both because the characteristics of the underlying population of individuals change and because the returns to these characteristics change. To identify the effects of globalization, I would like to examine changes in returns to characteristics (in my case, interregional differences in these changes) while holding the distribution of characteristics constant. To perform this exercise, I apply nonparametric techniques from DiNardo, Fortin, and Lemieux (1996) and Leibbrandt, Levinsohn, and McCrary (2005), which I describe in section 10.3. I also compare results from this approach to results from a more standard parametric approach, both of which are presented in section 10.4. A second issue is that other shocks in the 1990s may also have had differential effects on regions with high versus low exposure to globalization. The potential for these shocks to contaminate the analysis is an important concern, which I address by way of discussing qualifications to my results in section 10.5.

A third issue has to do with measurement. There are many components to income, including labor earnings, capital returns, rental income, government transfers, gifts, and remittances from family members abroad. Surveys that measure each of these components carefully, such as Mexico's National Survey of Household Income and Expenditure, are not representative across the regions of the country (Cortés et al. 2003), which makes it impossible to apply my estimation strategy to these data. Surveys that are representative across Mexico's regions, such as the Census of Population and Housing, measure labor income with relatively high precision, but lack complete data on other income categories. To ensure that my data are regionally representative, I use the Mexican census, and to minimize the impact of measurement error, I focus the analysis on labor income. Excluding other sources of income has the obvious drawback of

4. Since I estimate the shape of the entire distribution, other thresholds are straightforward to consider.

limiting the analysis to labor earnings rather than to the full distribution of income.[5]

To preview the results, states with high exposure to globalization began the 1990s with higher incomes than low-exposure states, even after controlling for regional differences in the observable characteristics of individuals. During the 1990s, low-exposure states had slower growth in labor income than high-exposure states. This took the form of a leftward shift in the income distribution of low-exposure states relative to high-exposure states. The results of this income shift were (1) a decrease in average labor earnings of 10 percent for individuals from states with low exposure to globalization relative to individuals from states with high exposure to globalization, and (2) an increase in the incidence of wage poverty (the fraction of wage earners whose labor income would not sustain a family of four at above-poverty consumption levels) in low-exposure states of 7 percent relative to that in high-exposure states.

10.2   Regional Exposure to Globalization

10.2.1   Data Sources

Data for the analysis come from two sources. In 1990, I use the 1 percent microsample of the XII Censo General de Poblacion y Vivienda, 1990, and in 2000 I use a 10 percent random sample of the 10 percent microsample of the XIII Censo General de Poblacion y Vivienda, 2000. The sample is working-age men with positive labor earnings. I focus on men, since labor force participation rates for women are low and vary considerably over time, ranging from 21 percent in 1990 to 32 percent in 2000. This creates issues of sample selection associated with who supplies labor outside the home. Compounding the problem, many women who report zero labor earnings may work in the family business or on the family farm. For men, problems of sample selection and measurement error also exist, but they appear to be less severe. Their labor force participation rates vary less over time, rising modestly from 73 percent in 1990 to 74 percent in 2000. Still, differences in labor force participation over time and across regions could affect the results reported in section 10.4. In section 10.3, I discuss strategies to correct for self-selection into the labor force.

10.2.2   The Opening of Mexico's Economy

In Mexico, the last two decades have not been a quiet period. Since 1980, the country has had three currency crises, bouts of high inflation, and sev-

---

5. One interesting extension to the analysis in this paper would be to use Mexico's National Survey of Household Income and Expenditure to estimate the empirical relationship between labor income and poverty. One could then use this mapping to evaluate how the changes in labor income that I estimate (using data from the Census of Population and Housing) may have affected poverty.

Table 10.1   Percent of Mexico's population with per capita income below threshold
             needed to achieve minimum caloric intake

Area	1992	1994	1996	1998	2000
Urban households	10.2	7.2	20.1	16.4	9.8
Rural households	29.5	30	43.3	43.8	34.1

Source: Cortés et al. (2003).

eral severe macroeconomic contractions, the most recent of which occurred in 1995 following a large devaluation of the peso that precipitated
the country's conversion from a fixed to a floating exchange rate. The liberalization of the country's trade and investment policies has been, in part,
a response to this turmoil. Mexico's currency crises and ensuing contractions have had very negative consequences on the country's poor. Table
10.1 shows that poverty rates rose sharply after the 1995 peso crisis.

Mexico's economic opening began in 1982, when the government responded to a severe balance-of-payments crisis by easing restrictions on
export assembly plants known as *maquiladoras*. In 1985, Mexico joined the
General Agreement on Tariffs and Trade (GATT), which entailed cutting
tariffs and eliminating many nontariff barriers. In 1989, Mexico eased restrictions on the rights of foreigners to own assets in the country. In 1994,
NAFTA consolidated and extended these reforms. Partly as a result of
these policy changes, the share of international trade in Mexico's gross domestic product (GDP) has nearly tripled, rising from 11 percent in 1980 to
32 percent in 2002. Mexico is now as closely tied to the U.S. economy as it
has been at any point in its history. In 2002, the country sent 89 percent of
its exports to and bought 73 percent of its imports from the United States.[6]

Mexico's maquiladoras, shown in figure 10.1, have been instrumental in
the country's export conversion. Between 1983 and 2002, real value added
in maquiladoras grew at an average annual rate of 11 percent, making it the
most dynamic sector in the country. In 2002, these export assembly plants
accounted for 45 percent of Mexico's manufacturing exports and 28 percent of the country's manufacturing employment (up from 4 percent in
1980). Their concentration in northern Mexico accounts in part for the differential regional impact of globalization in the country. A brief history of
Mexico's trade policy reveals the origins of northern Mexico's advantage
in export production.

In the 1940s, Mexico adopted a strategy of import substitution industrialization. To import most manufacturing products, firms had to obtain a
license from the government and pay moderate to high tariffs. In 1965,

6. Concomitant with its economic opening, Mexico privatized state-owned enterprises,
deregulated entry restrictions in many industries, and used wage and price restraints to com-
bat inflation.

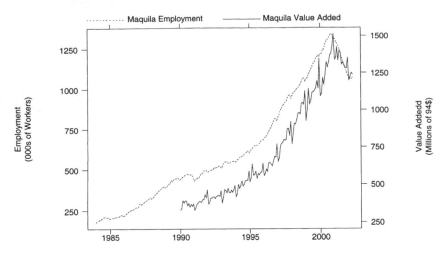

Fig. 10.1   Employment and value added in Mexico's maquiladoras

Mexico softened its import substitution strategy by allowing the creation of maquiladoras (Hansen 1981).[7] Firms could import free of duty the inputs, machinery, and parts needed for export assembly operations, as long as they exported all output. To ensure that firms abided by this rule, they were required to buy a bond equal to the value of their imports that would be returned to them once they had exported all their imported inputs in the form of final goods (hence the term *in-bond assembly plants*). In contrast to other firms in the country, maquiladoras could be 100 percent foreign owned. Bureaucratic restrictions on maquiladoras kept the sector small until 1982, when the government streamlined regulation of the plants.

Initially, maquiladoras were required to locate within twenty miles of an international border or coastline. In 1972, the government relaxed these rules and allowed maquiladoras to locate throughout the country. However, the plants continued to concentrate near the United States. As seen in figure 10.2, 83 percent of maquiladora employment is still located in states on the U.S. border. Proximity to the U.S. market is motivated in part by a desire to be near U.S. consumers, to whom maquiladoras export most of their production, and in part by a desire to be near U.S. firms, who often manage Mexican maquiladoras out of offices based in U.S. border cities.

U.S. trade policies initially gave maquiladoras an advantage over other Mexican producers in exporting to the U.S. market. Prior to NAFTA, a

7. The original motivation for this program was to create employment opportunities for Mexican workers returning to the country after working in the United States as temporary farm laborers under the Bracero Program. The U.S. government ended the Bracero Program in 1964, and the Mexican government was concerned that the returning workers would raise unemployment in border states.

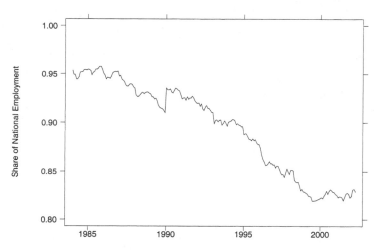

Fig. 10.2   Share of maquiladora employment in border states

U.S. firm that made components, shipped them to a plant in Mexico for assembly, and then reimported the finished good only paid U.S. import duties on the value of Mexican labor and raw materials used in assembly. NAFTA ended this special status for maquiladoras by giving all Mexican firms duty-free access to the U.S. market.[8] Yet, as seen in figure 10.1, NAFTA did little to stunt the growth of maquiladoras. In a purely legalistic sense, NAFTA did mean the end of the maquiladora regime; it eliminated the in-bond arrangement under which maquiladoras operated. However, Mexico's low wages continue to give the country a comparative advantage in the assembly of manufactured goods for the U.S. economy.

10.2.3   Regional Exposure to Globalization

Mexico's trade and investment reforms have dramatically increased the openness of its economy. These policies appear to have affected some parts of the country much more than others. Figure 10.3 plots the share of state GDP accounted for by value added in maquiladoras during the 1990s against distance to the United States. For three of the six states that border the United States (Baja California, Chihuahua, Tamaulipas), the maquiladora share of GDP is over 18 percent. For two of the three others (Coahuila, Sonora) it is over 8 percent. In the rest of the country, the maquiladora share of GDP is below 5 percent.

While maquiladoras are a large part of Mexico's exports, they are by no

8. With NAFTA, all firms in Mexico obtained duty-free access to the U.S. market as long as they comply with NAFTA rules of origin. NAFTA also exposes maquiladoras to rules of origin (from which they had been exempt previously), but now it also allows the plants to sell goods on the Mexican market.

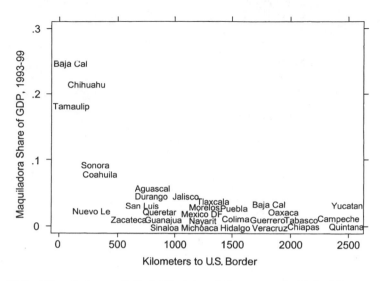

Fig. 10.3   Maquiladora activity in Mexico and distance to the United States

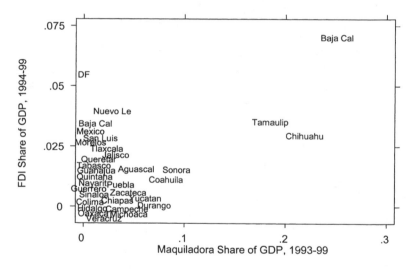

Fig. 10.4   Maquiladora activity and FDI in Mexico

means the whole story. Export production also occurs in states with relatively large supplies of skilled labor, which have attracted multinational
auto companies (as in Aguascalientes) and electronics producers (as in
Jalisco). Figure 10.4 plots the share of foreign direct investment (FDI) in
state GDP against the share of maquiladora value added in state GDP,
both averaged over the 1990s. While border states show up as high in both
categories, other states have attracted FDI in forms besides maquiladoras.

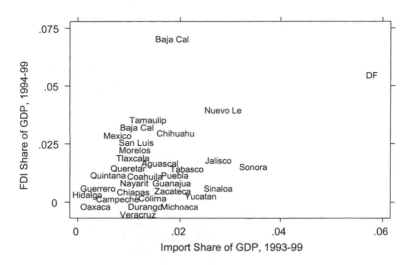

Fig. 10.5   FDI and imports in Mexico

These include states in which Mexico's most important industrial cities are located (Mexico City, Federal District; Monterrey, Nuevo Leon; Guadalajara, Jalisco).

Beyond FDI and maquiladoras, some states are exposed to globalization by virtue of having ports and being large importers. This is seen in figure 10.5, which plots FDI as a share of state GDP against imports as a share of state GDP.[9] A few states, such as Yucatan and Sinaloa, have high imports while attracting little in the way of FDI.

To categorize states as having high or low exposure to globalization, I use the three measures described in figures 10.3–10.5: the share of maquiladora value added in state GDP, the share of FDI in state GDP, and the share of imports in state GDP (each averaged over the period 1993–99). Using all three measures is important, since with the exception of FDI and imports they are relatively weakly correlated across states, as reported in table 10.2. Table 10.3 reports the globalization measures for Mexico's thirty-two states, where states are sorted according to their average rank across the three measures. I select as states with high exposure to globalization those whose average rank across the three measures is in the top third (and that have at least one individual rank in the top third), and I select as states with low exposure to globalization those whose average rank is in the bottom third (and that have no single rank in the top third).

Of the seven states with high exposure to globalization, five share a border with the United States; of the ten states with low exposure to global-

9. In Mexico, there are no data on exports at the state level (other than data on maquiladora exports).

Table 10.2   Correlation matrix for measures of exposure to globalization across Mexican states in the 1990s

	Maquiladora value added/ state GDP	Foreign direct investment/ state GDP	Imports/ state GDP	Share of state population migrating to U.S., 1995–2000
Maquiladora value added/state GDP				
Foreign direct investment/state GDP	0.381			
Imports/state GDP	–0.008	0.582		
Share of state population migrating to U.S., 1995–2000	–0.129	–0.371	–0.257	

Notes: Shares of state GDP (maquiladora value added, foreign direct investment, imports) are averages over the period 1993–99. Correlations are weighted by state share of the national population (averaged over 1990 to 2000).

ization, five are in southern Mexico. Historically, Mexico's north—with its more abundant mineral deposits, lower population densities, and closer proximity to the United States—has been relatively rich, while Mexico's south—with its higher population densities and larger indigenous community—has been relatively poor. It is well known that since Mexico's economic opening the border region has enjoyed relatively high wage growth, widening regional wage differentials in the country (Hanson 2004). However, the recent success of the border region follows a period in which Mexico's poorer regions had been catching up. Chiquiar (2005) finds that from 1970 to 1985, the fifteen years preceding Mexico's entry into the GATT, there was convergence in per capita GDP levels across Mexican states, and that after 1985 this process broke down. For the period 1985–2001, there is strong divergence in state per capita GDP levels. Chiquiar's results are reproduced in figure 10.6. Mexico's globalization decade thus follows a period during which income differences between high-exposure states and low-exposure states had been closing.

Finally, it is important to note that exposure to globalization is not simply a proxy for the opportunity to migrate to the United States. Contrary to popular belief, migration to the United States is not especially common among residents of Mexican states on the U.S. border. Mexico's high migration states are in agricultural regions in central and western Mexico, which have dominated migration to the United States for most of the last century (Durand, Massey, and Zenteno 2001). Most of these states have low exposure to FDI or to trade, as seen in figures 10.7 and 10.8, which plot the fraction of the state population migrating to the United States over the period 1995–2000 against the share of FDI in state GDP or the share of imports in state GDP. This suggests that high exposure to globalization does not indicate high exposure to emigration.

Proximity to the United States explains part of regional differences in

Table 10.3   Categorizing Mexican states by exposure to globalization in the 1990s

State	Average rank	Share of state GDP		
		FDI	Imports	Maquiladoras
High exposure to globalization				
Baja California	30	0.070	0.018	0.246
Chihuahua	28	0.030	0.018	0.214
Nuevo Leon	28	0.039	0.027	0.023
Sonora	27	0.015	0.034	0.088
Jalisco	25	0.018	0.027	0.029
Tamaulipas	25	0.035	0.013	0.181
Aguascalientes	25	0.015	0.014	0.046
Intermediate states				
Federal District	22	0.055	0.058	0.000
Coahuila	22	0.011	0.014	0.077
Yucatan	21	0.005	0.023	0.031
Puebla	19	0.009	0.015	0.015
Baja California Star	19	0.032	0.011	0.008
San Luis Potosi	18	0.028	0.011	0.013
Guanajuato	18	0.009	0.014	0.008
Sinaloa	17	0.005	0.027	0.001
Tlaxcala	17	0.019	0.010	0.020
Queretaro	16	0.013	0.011	0.011
Durango	16	0.001	0.012	0.035
Tabasco	16	0.010	0.017	0.000
Morelos	15	0.024	0.010	0.005
Mexico	15	0.031	0.008	0.004
Michoacan	15	0.000	0.016	0.000
Low exposure to globalization				
Zacatecas	15	0.003	0.013	0.008
Quintana Roo	12	0.006	0.011	0.000
Nayarit	10	0.006	0.011	0.000
Colima	9	0.002	0.014	0.000
Guerrero	9	0.004	0.007	0.002
Veracruz	8	−0.004	0.012	0.000
Chiapas	6	0.000	0.011	0.000
Campeche	5	0.001	0.008	0.000
Hildalgo	4	0.000	0.007	0.000
Oaxaca	2	0.000	0.005	0.000

Note: Shares of state GDP (foreign direct investment, imports, maquiladora value added) are averages over the period 1993–99.

exposure to globalization, but it is clearly not the whole story. Other states have become more integrated into the global economy by virtue of having more skilled workers, better transportation infrastructure, or larger markets. These features, while present before globalization took hold in Mexico, are not exogenous. They reflect the ability of these states to develop economically, which may in turn reflect the quality of their legal or political institutions or other historical factors. This suggests that my measure

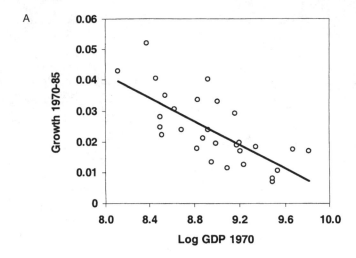

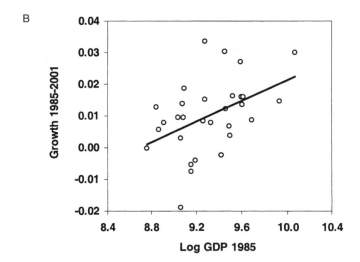

Fig. 10.6   Growth in log GDP across Mexican states, 1970–2001: *A*, annual growth 1970–85 versus initial GDP; *B*, annual growth 1985–2001 versus initial GDP

of exposure to globalization may proxy for institutional quality or other regional characteristics. Identifying the factors that determine regional variation in exposure to global markets, while beyond the scope of this paper, is important. Without this mapping, one cannot make policy recommendations. My findings will suggest that in Mexico regions more exposed to

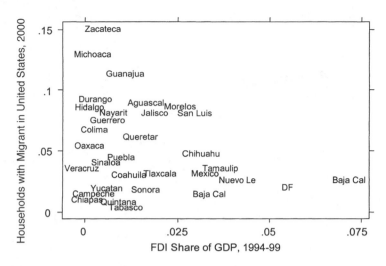

Fig. 10.7   International migration and FDI in Mexico

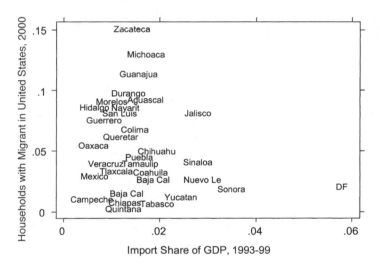

Fig. 10.8   International migration and imports in Mexico

globalization have done better in terms of income growth. But the policy implications of this result are unclear, as I leave unanswered the question of how one goes about increasing regional exposure.

10.3   Empirical Methodology

The empirical analysis involves comparing changes in income distribution during Mexico's globalization decade between two groups of states:

states with high exposure to globalization and states with low exposure to globalization. In this section, I describe nonparametric and parametric approaches for making these comparisons.

10.3.1 Estimating Counterfactual Income Densities

Let $f(w \mid x, i, t)$ be the density of labor income, w, conditional on a set of observed characteristics, x, in region i and time t. Define $h(x \mid i, t)$ as the density of observed characteristics among income earners in region i and time t. For regions, $i = H$ indicates high exposure to globalization and $i = L$ indicates low exposure to globalization; for time periods, $t = 00$ indicates the year 2000 and $t = 90$ indicates the year 1990. The observed density of labor income for individuals in i at t is

(1) $$g(w \mid i, t) = \int f(w \mid x, i, t)h(x \mid i, t)dx.$$

Differences in $f(w \mid x, H, t)$ and $f(w \mid x, L, t)$ capture differences in returns to observable characteristics in regions with high versus low exposure to globalization; differences in $h(x \mid H, t)$ and $h(x \mid L, t)$ capture differences in the distribution of observed characteristics in high- versus low-exposure regions.

To evaluate the change in income distributions across time and across regions, I would like to compare changes in $f(w \mid x, H, t)$ and $f(w \mid x, L, t)$, while holding the distribution of x constant. However, in the data I do not observe these conditional densities, but the only marginal densities, $g(w \mid x, H, t)$ and $g(w \mid x, L, t)$. To evaluate these densities, I apply techniques from DiNardo, Fortin, and Lemieux (1996). First, consider the cross-time change in income distribution in the high-exposure region that is due to changes in returns to observable characteristics, which can be written as

(2) $$\int f(w \mid x, H, 00)h(x \mid H, 90)dx - \int f(w \mid x, H, 90)h(x \mid H, 90)dx.$$

Equation (2) evaluates the change in income distribution in high-exposure regions between 1990 and 2000, fixing the marginal density of observables to be that in high-exposure regions in 1990. Rewrite equation (2) as

(3) $$\int (\theta^{H,90 \to H,00} - 1)f(w \mid x, H, 90)h(x \mid H, 90)dx,$$

where

(4) $$\theta^{H,90 \to H,00} = \frac{f(w \mid x, H, 00)}{f(w \mid x, H, 90)}.$$

Equation (3) is simply the observed marginal income density in high-exposure regions in 1990, adjusted by a weighting function. Given an estimate of the weighting function in equation (4), it would be straightforward to apply a standard kernel density estimator to equation (3). The key, then, to estimating the change in income distribution that is due to changes in returns to observables is estimating the weighting function in equation (4).

Before turning to the weighting functions, consider the analog to equation (2) for regions with low exposure to globalization. The change in income distribution in low-exposure regions that is due to changes in returns to observables is

(5) $\int f(w \mid x, L, 00)h(x \mid H, 90)dx - \int f(w \mid x, L, 90)h(x \mid H, 90)dx.$

Equation (5) evaluates the change in income distribution in regions with low exposure to globalization between 1990 and 2000, again fixing the marginal density of observables to be that in high-exposure regions in 1990. To rewrite equation (5) in terms of the marginal density of income in high-exposure regions in 1990, apply the weights

(6) $\theta^{H,90 \to L,00} = \dfrac{f(w \mid x, L, 00)}{f(w \mid x, H, 90)}$ and $\theta^{H,90 \to L,90} = \dfrac{f(w \mid x, L, 90)}{f(w \mid x, H, 90)},$

which yields

(7) $\int [\theta^{H,90 \to L,00} - \theta^{H,90 \to L,90}] f(w \mid x, H, 90)h(x \mid H, 90)dx.$

As in estimating equation (3), estimating equation (7) comes down to applying the appropriate weighting function to a standard kernel density estimator.

The changes in conditional income densities in equations (2) and (5) reflect in part the impact of globalization and in part the impact of other aggregate shocks to the Mexican economy. The *difference* between these changes amounts to a difference-in-difference estimator, which evaluates the change in returns to observables in regions with high exposure to globalization relative to the change in returns observables in regions with low exposure to globalization. Putting equations (3) and (7) together, we get the following:

(8) $\left[\int f(w \mid x, H, 00)h(x \mid H, 90)dx - \int f(w \mid x, H, 90)h(x \mid H, 90)dx \right]$

$- \left[\int f(w \mid x, L, 00)h(x \mid H, 90)dx - \int f(w \mid x, L, 90)h(x \mid H, 90)dx \right]$

$= \int [(\theta^{H,90 \to H,00} - 1) - (\theta^{H,90 \to L,90} - \theta^{H,90 \to L,90})] f(w \mid x, H, 90)$

$\cdot h(x \mid H, 90)dx$

Equation (8) shows the 1990-to-2000 change in income distribution in high-exposure regions relative to low-exposure regions, holding the distribution of observables constant. I use equation (8) to evaluate the impact of globalization on income distribution in Mexico. The choice of the high-exposure region in 1990 as the base case is purely arbitrary and should not affect the density difference. To check the robustness of the results, I will discuss estimates using other base cases.

To estimate the weighting functions in equations (4) and (6), I use Leibbrandt, Levinsohn, and McCrary's (2005) extension of the DiNardo, Fortin, and Lemieux (1996) paper. Applying the Bayes axiom to the weighting equations yields

(9) $\theta^{H,90 \to H,00} = \dfrac{f(w \mid x, H, 00)}{f(w \mid x, H, 90)} = \dfrac{\Pr(t = 00, i = H) \mid w, x)}{1 - \Pr(t = 00, i = H) \mid w, x)}$

$\cdot \dfrac{1 - \Pr(t = 00, i = H) \mid x)}{\Pr(t = 00, i = H) \mid x)}$

$\theta^{H,90 \to L,00} = \dfrac{f(w \mid x, L, 00)}{f(w \mid x, H, 90)} = \dfrac{\Pr(t = 00, i = L) \mid w, x)}{1 - \Pr(t = 00, i = L) \mid w, x)}$

$\cdot \dfrac{1 - \Pr(t = 00, i = L) \mid x)}{\Pr(t = 00, i = L) \mid x)}$

$\theta^{H,90 \to L,90} = \dfrac{f(w \mid x, L, 90)}{f(w \mid x, H, 90)} = \dfrac{\Pr(t = 90, i = L) \mid w, x)}{1 - \Pr(t = 90, i = L) \mid w, x)}$

$\cdot \dfrac{1 - \Pr(t = 90, i = L) \mid x)}{\Pr(t = 90, i = L) \mid x)}$

Each weighting function is the product of odds ratios. Consider the first weight. The first ratio is the odds an individual is from a high-exposure region in 2000 (based on a sample of individuals from high-exposure regions in 1990 and 2000), conditional on observables, x, and labor income, w. The second ratio is the (inverse) odds that an individual is from a high-exposure region in 2000 (again, based on a sample of individuals from high-exposure regions in 1990 and 2000), conditional just on x. I can estimate the odds ratios by estimating two logit models. In each case, the dependent variable is a 0–1 variable on the outcome $i = H$ and $t = 00$ (based on a sample of $i = H$ and $t = 90$ or 00). For the first logit model, the regressors are x and w; for the second, the regressor is x, alone. The other weights can be estimated analogously.

After estimating the weights, I apply them to a standard kernel density estimator to obtain estimates for the densities described by equations (3), (7), and (9). These estimates are for the *difference* in income densities, in the case of equations (3) and (7), and for the *double difference* in income densities, in the case of equation (9).

10.3.2   A Parametric Analog

The advantage of the approach described in subsection 10.3.1 is that it characterizes the difference in income across time periods and/or regions at all points in the distribution. The disadvantage is that there are no standard errors for these density differences. To examine the statistical significance of the results, I estimate a parametric analog to equation (8), which is simply a difference-in-difference wage equation.

I pool data on working age men in 1990 and 2000 from states with either

high exposure or low exposure to globalization and then estimate the following regression,

(10) $\ln w_{hst} = \alpha_s + \mathbf{X}_{hst}(\beta_1 + \beta_2 Y2000_{ht} + \beta_3 \text{High}_{hs})$

$+ \phi \cdot Y2000_{ht} \cdot \text{High}_{hs} + \varepsilon_{hst},$

where w is labor market earnings, $\mathbf{X}$ is a vector of observed characteristics, Y2000 is a dummy variable for the year 2000, and High is a dummy variable for high-exposure states. The regression includes controls for state fixed effects and allows returns to observable characteristics to vary across regions and across time. The coefficient, ϕ, captures the differential change in earnings from 1990 to 2000 between states with high exposure and low exposure to globalization.

Equation (10) is a standard difference-in-difference specification, which implies that I estimate the mean differential in wage growth between low-exposure and high-exposure states. This approach ignores the possibility that the wage effect of being in a state with high exposure to globalization may not be uniform throughout the wage distribution. The results presented in the next section will provide evidence consistent with this possibility. A more elegant approach would be to estimate the regional differential in wage changes nonparametrically, as in the framework derived by Athey and Imbens (2003).

10.3.3   Estimation Issues

Several estimation issues merit attention. First, individuals self-select into regions. Individuals who have chosen to live in a state with high exposure to globalization may have relatively high drive or ambition and may have moved to the state to take advantage of the opportunities globalization offers. Similarly, individuals who have chosen not to leave states with low exposure to globalization may have relatively low drive or ambition. Given this pattern of selection, unobserved components of labor income would tend to be positive for individuals in high-exposure states and negative for individuals in low-exposure states. The estimation exercises in equations (9) and (10) would then be polluted by systematic differences in unobserved characteristics between regions. To avoid this problem, I categorize individuals by birth state and not by state of residence. In this way, I pick up earnings differences in where people live based on where they were born—a factor out of their control—and not on where they have chosen to reside—a factor in their control. Consistent with expectations, in 1990 83 percent of those born in high-exposure states still lived in those states, compared to only 73 percent of those born in low-exposure states. In 2000, the figures were 82 percent and 70 percent.

A second estimation issue is that individuals self-select into the labor force. This is partly due to age. Over time, young workers enter the labor

force and older workers exit. To control for these movements, I limit the sample to the cohort of men who were twenty-five to fifty-five years old in 1990 (and thirty-five to sixty-five years old in 2000). Relatedly, if over the 1990s labor market conditions improved by more in high-exposure states than in low-exposure states, high-exposure states may have registered a larger increase in the fraction of low-ability individuals participating in the labor force. Given this pattern of selection, unobserved components of labor income may have increased by less in high-exposure states than in low-exposure states.[10] To control for selection into the labor force, I follow Lee (2004) and trim low-wage earners across the four samples (i.e., for $i = H, L$ and $t = 90,00$) such that the fraction included in the estimation is the same for each group.

A third estimation issue is that shocks other than globalization may have had differential impacts on regions with high versus low exposure to globalization. One such shock is the peso crisis of 1995. After a bungled devaluation of the peso in 1994, Mexico chose to float its currency, which proceeded to plummet in value relative to the dollar. The ensuing increase in the peso value of dollar-denominated liabilities contributed to a banking collapse and a severe macroeconomic contraction. It is hard to gauge whether the peso crisis would have hurt states with high exposure to globalization more or less than states with low exposure. On the one hand, high-exposure states are more specialized in the production of exports, and the devaluation of the peso would have increased demand for their output. On the other hand, high-exposure states are better integrated into Mexico's financial markets and the banking collapse may have hurt them more. Other important shocks in the 1990s included a reform of Mexico's land tenure system in 1992, the ongoing privatization of state-owned enterprises and deregulation of industries, and the ruling party's loss of majority control in Mexico's congress in 1997. Again, it is hard to say whether these shocks would have helped or hurt high-exposure states more. The existence of these other shocks leaves the results subject to the caveat that factors other than globalization may have accounted for any differential change in income distribution across regions of the country. I return to this issue in section 10.5.

10.4 Empirical Results

The sample for the analysis is men aged twenty-five to fifty-five in 1990 or thirty-five to sixty-five in 2000 who were born in one of the seven Mexican states with high exposure to globalization or in one of the ten Mexican states with low exposure to globalization. The dependent variable is log av-

---

10. This suggests that selection into the labor force would work against selection into regions, in terms of the impact on unobserved components of earnings.

Table 10.4   Summary statistics

	High exposure to globalization		Low exposure to globalization	
	Mean	Standard deviation	Mean	Standard deviation
	High grade of schooling completed, 1990			
Age	33.6	5.9	33.9	5.9
0	0.055	0.229	0.132	0.338
1 to 5	0.185	0.388	0.285	0.452
6 to 8	0.273	0.445	0.255	0.436
9 to 11	0.208	0.406	0.141	0.348
12 to 15	0.139	0.346	0.100	0.300
16+	0.140	0.347	0.087	0.282
Wage	2.590	2.610	1.781	2.073
No. of observations	13,771		19,351	
	High grade of schooling completed, 2000			
Age	43.0	5.7	43.2	5.8
0	0.036	0.187	0.093	0.290
1 to 5	0.178	0.383	0.255	0.436
6 to 8	0.259	0.438	0.259	0.438
9 to 11	0.207	0.405	0.157	0.364
12 to 15	0.142	0.349	0.109	0.312
16+	0.177	0.382	0.128	0.334
Wage	2.656	2.798	1.674	1.965
No. of observations	11,807		17,967	

Notes: Sample is men with positive labor earnings aged twenty-five to fifty-five in 1990 or thirty-five to sixty-five in 2000 born in states with either high exposure to globalization or low exposure to globalization. Wages are average hourly levels in 2000 U.S. dollars.

erage hourly labor earnings.[11] I also discuss results using log total labor income as the dependent variable. Summary statistics are in table 10.4.

10.4.1   Raw Income Distributions

To provide a starting point for the analysis, consider the raw distributions of labor income in states with either high exposure or low exposure to globalization. Figure 10.9 shows kernel density estimates for hourly labor earnings in 1990 and 2000. In both years, the density for high-exposure states is shifted to the right compared to low-exposure states. Between 1990 and 2000, the difference between the wage densities in the two groups of

11. For Mexico, average hourly wages are calculated as monthly labor income ÷ (4.5 × hours worked last week); for the United States, average hourly wages are calculated as annual labor income ÷ (weeks worked last year × usual hours worked per week). Assuming individuals work all weeks of a month could bias wage estimates downward. To avoid measurement error associated with implausibly low wage values or with top coding of earnings, I restrict the sample to be individuals with hourly wages between $0.05 and $20 (in 2000 dollars). This restriction is nearly identical to dropping the largest and smallest 0.5 percent of wage values.

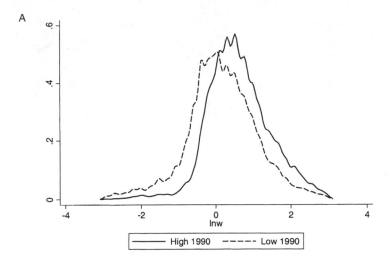

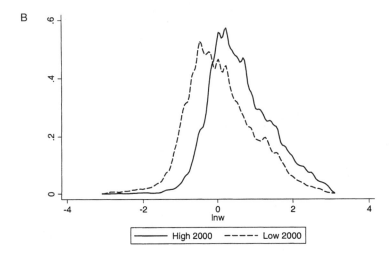

Fig. 10.9   Density of hourly labor income in states with high exposure and low exposure to globalization: *A,* **1990;** *B,* **2000**

states appears to widen. Higher wages in high-exposure states reflect in part thc fact these states have a more highly educated labor force, as indicated by table 10.4. Higher wages in high-exposure states may also reflect differences in the returns to observable characteristics across states in Mexico.

To see what these distributional differences imply about differences in the incidence of poverty between regions, figure 10.10 shows the cumulative distribution for wages in high-exposure and low-exposure states in the two years. The vertical line in each graph shows the hourly wage needed to

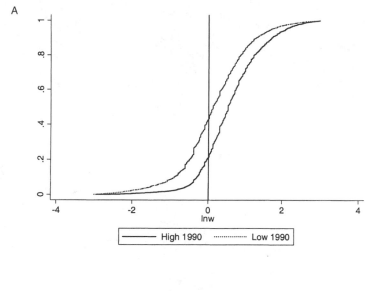

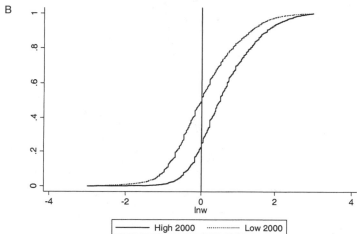

Fig. 10.10   Cumulative distribution of hourly labor income in states with high exposure and low exposure to globalization: *A*, 1990; *B*, 2000

provide the minimum caloric intake for a family of four with one wage earner working the mean number of annual labor hours in that year.[12] The

---

12. In 1990, the implied poverty cutoff for the hourly wage was $1.16 in low-exposure regions and $1.25 in high-exposure regions (in 2000 U.S. dollars), and in 2000, it was $1.13 in low-exposure regions and $1.22 in high-exposure regions. The poverty wage is lower in low-exposure regions because rural areas have lower prices for goods and because a higher fraction of the population in low-exposure regions lives in rural areas. The line shown in figure 10.9 is that for the log poverty wage in low-exposure regions (in log terms the poverty wage in high-exposure and low-exposure regions is nearly the same).

peso value for the minimum caloric intake is from Cortés et al. (2003). The poverty wage line in figure 10.10 is not meant to provide an accurate indicator of the fraction of individuals living in poverty. By focusing on labor income, I ignore other sources of household earnings. Government transfers, rental income, loans, in-kind receipts, and remittances also supplement family income, suggesting that the implied poverty wage threshold in figure 10.10 is set too high—some families below this threshold will receive enough income from other sources to allow them to afford a consumption level that is above the poverty cutoff. Still, the poverty wage is a useful benchmark for gauging the potential for a worker to sustain a family at above-poverty consumption levels on labor income alone (which is two-thirds of total income in Mexico).

In 1990, the fraction of workers earning less than the poverty cutoff wage in low-exposure regions (0.42) was twice that in high-exposure regions (0.21). In 2000, the difference was even larger, with the fraction of workers below the poverty wage at 0.49 in low-exposure regions and 0.22 in high-exposure regions. While it appears that poverty increased more rapidly in low-exposure regions, the results in figure 10.10 are inconclusive. Since both the price of labor and the composition of labor are changing across regions and over time, we do not know whether the apparent increase in the relative incidence of poverty in low-exposure regions is due to a deterioration in the returns to observable characteristics or to change in the relative composition of the labor force. To separate these effects, I construct counterfactual income densities.

10.4.2   Counterfactual Income Distributions

To control for regional differences in the distribution of observable characteristics, I apply the weights in equation (9) to the kernel density for high-exposure states in 1990. This produces the two sets of densities in figure 10.11. Panel A shows the actual income density in 1990 for high-exposure states and a counterfactual density that would obtain were workers in high-exposure states in 1990 paid according to the returns to observable characteristics in low-exposure states in 1990, or

$$\int f(w \mid x, L, 90)h(x \mid H, 90)dx = \int \theta^{H,90 \to L,90} f(w \mid x, H, 90)h(x \mid H, 90)dx.$$

Since the distribution of observable characteristics is the same in the actual and counterfactual densities, comparing the two makes it possible to isolate the regional differences in income densities that are attributable to regional differences in returns to characteristics. In figure 10.11, the density for high-exposure states in 1990 is again right-shifted relative to low-exposure states, although the regional difference in incomes is smaller than in figure 10.9. Thus, even before Mexico's globalization decade, incomes were higher across the distribution in high-exposure states. These income differences may be due to high-exposure states historically having better infrastructure, being more specialized in the high-wage manufacturing sec-

A

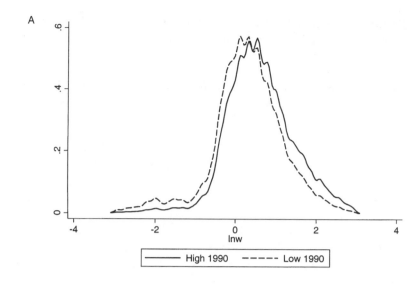

B

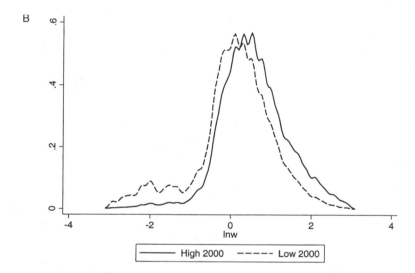

Fig. 10.11   Counterfactual income densities, high- and low-exposure states:
A, **1990;** *B,* **2000**

tor, or being less specialized in the low-wage agricultural sector, among other factors (see Chiquiar 2003 for a more complete discussion). This highlights the importance of controlling for initial income differences between states when examining changes in income distributions over time.

Panel B of figure 10.11 shows income densities in 2000, evaluated based on the distribution of observable characteristics in high-exposure states in

1990. For high-exposure states, the resulting counterfactual density is what workers in high-exposure states in 2000 would earn were they to have the observable characteristics of workers in high-exposure states in 1990, or

$$\int f(w \mid x, H, 00)h(x \mid H, 90)dx = \int \theta^{H,90 \to H,00} f(w \mid x, H, 90)h(x \mid H, 90)dx.$$

For low-exposure states, the counterfactual is what workers in low-exposure states in 2000 would earn had they the characteristics of high-exposure states in 1990, or

$$\int f(w \mid x, L, 00)h(x \mid H, 90)dx = \int \theta^{H,90 \to L,00} f(w \mid x, H, 90)h(x \mid H, 90)dx.$$

Comparing these counterfactuals isolates regional differences in income densities that are due to differences in returns to characteristics rather than to the distribution of observables. As in 1990, the density for high-exposure states in 2000 is right-shifted relative to low-exposure states. Comparing the two years, it appears that differences in income densities between high-exposure and low-exposure states have increased over time, suggesting that relative incomes have risen in the former.

To relate the counterfactual wage densities to poverty, figure 10.12 shows the cumulative distribution analogs to the counterfactual wage kernels in figure 10.11. Panel A of figure 10.12 thus shows the cumulative density for wages in high-exposure and low-exposure states in 1990, based on the characteristics of workers in high-exposure regions in 1990. Comparing this graph to panel A of figure 10.10, we again see that the fraction of workers below the poverty wage is higher in low-exposure states (0.32) than in high-exposure states (0.21). However, the difference in the incidence of wage poverty between the two groups of states in figure 10.12 (0.32 − 0.21 = 0.11) is considerably lower than in figure 10.10 (0.42 − 0.21 = 0.21). Holding constant the distribution of observable characteristics leaves the difference in cumulative distributions due to differences in returns to observables. Again, the apparent higher initial incidence of poverty in low-exposure states highlights the importance of controlling for initial conditions when comparing changes in income distributions.

Panel B of figure 10.12 shows the cumulative density for wages in high-exposure and low-exposure states in 2000, based on the characteristics of workers in high-exposure regions in 1990. The fraction of workers earning less than the poverty wage is 0.40 in low-exposure states and 0.22 in high-exposure states, which again is a smaller difference (0.40 − 0.22 = 0.18) than that for the actual wage distributions in figure 10.10 (0.49 − 0.22 = 0.27). Putting the 1990-to-2000 change in the incidence of wage poverty for low-exposure versus high-exposure states together yields a difference-in-difference estimate of (0.40 − 0.32) − (0.22 − 0.21) = 0.07. During Mexico's globalization decade of the 1990s, the incidence of wage poverty in low-exposure states appeared to increase relative to that in high-exposure states by approximately 7 percent.

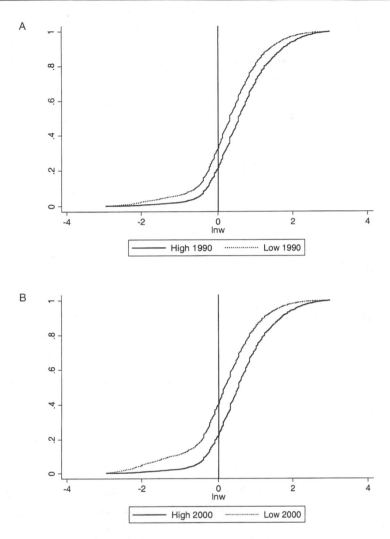

Fig. 10.12   Counterfactual cumulative income distributions, high- and low-exposure states: *A,* **1990;** *B,* **2000**

To explore these distributional changes in more detail, figure 10.13 shows estimates of equation (2)—the 1990-to-2000 change in income densities in high-exposure states—and of equation (5)—the 1990-to-2000 change in income densities in low-exposure states—where all densities are evaluated based on the distribution of observables in high-exposure states in 1990 (as shown in equations [3] and [7]). In low-exposure states, there was a pronounced shift in mass from the upper half of the distribution to the lower half of the distribution. In high-exposure states, there was a mod-

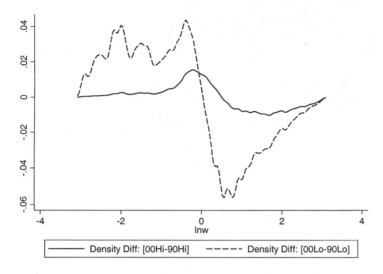

Fig. 10.13   **Estimated change in labor income densities, 1990 to 2000**

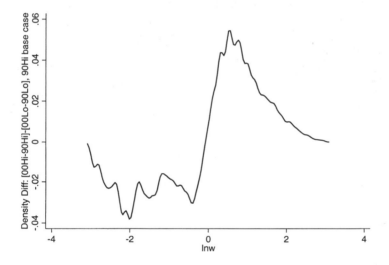

Fig. 10.14   **Double difference in labor income densities**

est shift in mass from the upper part of the distribution to the middle of the distribution. While labor incomes in the 1990s deteriorated in both regions, caused in part by Mexico's peso crisis in 1995, the deterioration was much less severe in states with high exposure to globalization.

The change in regional relative incomes is seen more clearly in figure 10.14, which shows an estimate of equation (8), the change in income density in high-exposure states relative to the change in income density in low-

exposure states (evaluated for the distribution of observable characteristics in high-exposure states in 1990). It is clear that the income of high-exposure states has increased relative to the income of low-exposure states. This appears as shift in mass in the double density difference from the lower half of the distribution to the upper half of the distribution. During Mexico's globalization decade, individuals born in states with high exposure to globalization appear to have done much better than individuals born in states with low exposure to globalization. These results appear to be robust to changing the sample of states with either high exposure or low exposure to globalization. In unreported results, I experimented with dropping high-exposure states one at a time from the sample and reestimating the income densities and with dropping low-exposure states one at a time and reestimating the densities. Both sets of results are very similar to those reported.

10.4.3   Additional Results

Throughout the analysis, we have evaluated labor income densities fixing the distribution of observable characteristics to be those in states with high exposure to globalization in 1990. This choice of the base case is arbitrary and should not affect the results. To examine the robustness of the findings, figure 10.15 reestimates the double difference in income densities in equation (8), evaluating all densities based on the distribution of observables in low-exposure states in 1990. Figure 10.15 is very similar to figure 10.14, confirming that the choice of base case does not matter for the results.

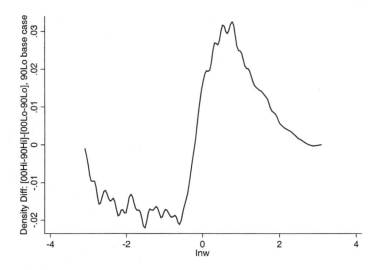

Fig. 10.15   Double difference in labor income densities (alternative base case)

The income densities shown so far are for average hourly labor earnings. If changes in wages affect individual labor supply, changes in hourly labor earnings may understate changes in total labor income. To see if this might be the case, figure 10.16 estimates the double density difference in equation (8), evaluated in terms of total labor income rather than average hourly labor income. Figure 10.16 is similar to figure 10.14, suggesting that regional changes in the distribution of total labor income mirror regional changes in the distribution of hourly labor income.

In the results so far, I have included the full sample of workers from low-exposure and high-exposure states in 1990 and 2000. One concern is that the nature of self-selection into work varies across states or across time. If labor force participation differs between low-exposure and high-exposure states, then cross-section comparisons in wage distributions may be contaminated by sample selection. If these differences are stable over time, they may not pose a problem for comparing changes in wage distributions. However, if labor force participation changes differentially over time between low-exposure and high-exposure states, then sample selection may also contaminate the difference-in-difference analysis. For males with nine or more years of education, labor force participation rates are very similar in low-exposure and high-exposure states. For low-education males, labor force participation rates are higher in high-exposure states, and these differences appear to increase over time. This suggests the data are missing more low-wage workers in low-exposure states than in high-exposure states, which would tend to compress the estimated difference in wage distributions for the two groups of states. Further, since the relative fraction

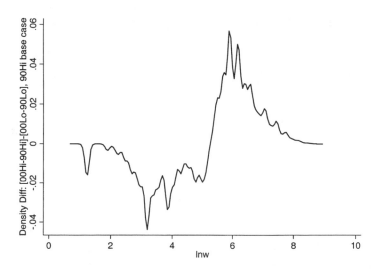

Fig. 10.16   Double difference in total labor income densities

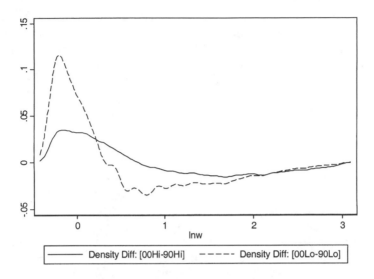

Fig. 10.17   Estimated change in labor income densities, 1990 to 2000, with observations trimmed to account for selection into work

of missing low-wage workers in low-exposure states rises over time, my estimates would tend to understate the full extent of the change in relative wages between the two groups of states over time.

To deal with sample selection associated with labor force participation, I apply Lee's (2005) technique for trimming observations to make them comparable across samples (which may vary by region, time, or some other dimension). The idea is that if both wages and labor force participation are monotonically increasing in the unobserved component of wages, then it is possible to make two samples comparable in terms of the distribution of unobservables by trimming low-wage observations in the group that has higher labor force participation. We cannot add low-wage workers who do not work into the sample in the low-labor-force-participation group, but we can drop from the sample low-wage workers in the high-labor-force-participation group (who presumably would not work if they were to be placed in the other group). I trim low-wage workers from the high-labor-force-participation group until I obtain two samples that are identical in terms of the fraction of wage earners included. Figures 10.17 and 10.18 redo figures 10.13 and 10.14 applying Lee's trimming procedure. It remains the case that wages deteriorate by more in low-exposure states. Income in high-exposure states increases relative to income in low-exposure states, which appears as a shift in mass in the double density difference from the lower half of the distribution to the upper half of the distribution. This is further evidence that during Mexico's globalization decade individuals

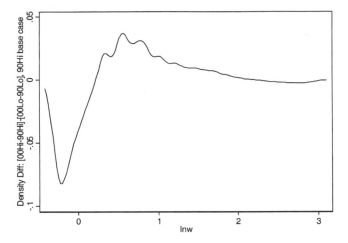

Fig. 10.18   Double difference in labor income densities, with observations trimmed to account for selection into work

born in states with high exposure to globalization did relatively well in terms of their labor earnings.

10.4.4   Parametric Results

While the nonparametric results show a strong increase in relative incomes in states with high exposure to globalization, they give no sense of the statistical precision of these estimates. As a check on the statistical significance of the results, table 10.5 shows estimation results for equation (10). The dependent variable is log average hourly labor earnings. The regressors are dummy variables for educational attainment, a quadratic in age, a dummy variable for the year 2000 and its interaction with the age and education variables, a dummy variable for having been born in a state with high exposure to globalization and its interaction with the age and education variables, dummy variables for the state, and the interaction of the year 2000 and high-exposure-to-globalization dummy variables. This last variable captures the differential change in wage growth in high-exposure states relative to low-exposure states. Standard errors are adjusted for correlation across observations within the same state.

Panel A of table 10.5 shows that during the 1990s the cohort of individuals born in states with high exposure to globalization enjoyed labor earnings growth that was 7.9 to 9.2 log points higher than earnings growth for individuals born in low-exposure states. These coefficients are precisely estimated. This is consistent with the counterfactual density estimates and again suggests that individuals in high-exposure states enjoyed higher growth in labor income that individuals in low-exposure states. The second

Table 10.5   **Regression results**

	All workers (1)	Workers with 20- to 80-hour work week (2)	All workers (3)	Workers with 20- to 80-hour work week (4)
	A. Full sample of workers			
Year 2000 · high exposure	0.092	0.079	0.115	0.116
	(0.039)	(0.033)	(0.053)	(0.050)
Year 2000 · high exposure · secondary education			−0.050	−0.079
			(0.042)	(0.046)
R^2	0.337	0.373	0.337	0.373
No. of observations	45,012	42,298	45,012	42,298
	B. Trimmed sample to account for sample selection			
Year 2000 · high exposure	0.109	0.090	0.159	0.153
	(0.029)	(0.025)	(0.040)	(0.039)
Year 2000 · high exposure · secondary education			−0.106	−0.130
			(0.031)	(0.034)
R^2	0.380	0.417	0.380	0.418
No. of observations	42,711	40,224	42,711	40,224

Notes: The dependent variable is log average hourly labor earnings. In columns (1) and (3), the sample is non-self-employed males born in states with high exposure to globalization or states with low exposure to globalization; in columns (2) and (4), the sample includes only the non-self-employed who report working twenty to eighty hours a week. Other regressors (quadratic in age, dummies for year of education, and their interactions with year 2000 dummy and with high exposure dummy; year 2000 dummy variable; state dummy variables) are not shown. Standard errors are in parentheses and are adjusted for correlation across observations within birth states. In panel A, the sample is working males in all states and time periods; in panel B, I trim low-wage workers in high-labor-force-participation state/year groups until the fraction of wage earners is the same in low-exposure and high-exposure states and in the two years.

two columns of table 10.5 show results where the year 2000/high-exposure interaction is interacted with a dummy variable for an individual having completed a secondary education. This term allows relative earnings growth to be larger for more-educated workers. The interaction term is negative, but imprecisely estimated.

Panel B of table 10.5 redoes the estimation, trimming observations across the samples to account for possible self-selection into work. Estimated relative wage growth for high-exposure states is higher using this estimation method, with individuals born in high-exposure states enjoying labor earnings growth 9.0 to 10.9 log points higher than that of individuals born in low-exposure states. In the second two columns, the interaction between the year 2000/high-exposure interaction and the dummy variable for secondary education is negative, precisely estimated, and similar in absolute value to the main effect (the year 2000/high-exposure interaction). This suggests that on average most of the relative wage growth for individuals born in high-exposure states went to individuals with low levels of

schooling. The income gains in moving from low-exposure to high-exposure states appear to be largest for low-wage workers.

10.5 Conclusion

In this paper, I examine the change in the distribution of labor income across regions of Mexico during the country's decade of globalization, the 1990s. I focus the analysis on men born either in states with high exposure to globalization or in states with low exposure to globalization, as measured by the share of FDI, imports, and export assembly in state GDP during the 1990s. Mexican states with high exposure to globalization are located along the U.S. border and in the relatively skill-abundant center-west region of the country; states with low exposure to globalization are primarily located in more rural southern Mexico. I exclude from the analysis individuals born in states with intermediate exposure to globalization.

Controlling for regional differences in the distribution of observable characteristics and for initial differences in regional incomes, the distribution of labor income in high-exposure states shifted to the right relative to the distribution of income in low-exposure states. This change in regional relative incomes was the result of a shift in mass in the income distribution of low-exposure states from upper-middle income earners to lower income earners. Labor income in low-exposure states fell relative to high-exposure states by 8–12 percent, and the incidence of wage poverty (the fraction of wage earners whose labor income would not sustain a family of four at above-poverty consumption levels) increased in low-exposure states relative to high-exposure states by 7 percent.

There are several possible interpretations of these results. One is that trade and investment liberalization raised incomes in states with high exposure to the global economy relative to states with low exposure to the global economy. However, trade and investment reforms were by no means the only shocks to the Mexican economy during the 1990s. The Mexican peso crisis in 1995 was another important event. The results are also consistent with the greater ability of states that were more integrated into the global markets to weather the large devaluation of the peso, the banking crisis, and the contraction in economic activity that occurred in Mexico during the mid-1990s. High-exposure states are relatively specialized in export production and would potentially benefit from a depreciation of the currency.

Other policy changes, such as the privatization and deregulation of Mexican industry or the reform of Mexico's land-tenure system, may also have had differential regional impacts in Mexico. Privatization and deregulation appeared to weaken Mexico's unions and lower wage premiums enjoyed by workers in these sectors (Fairris 2003). Since more heavily unionized in-

dustries are concentrated in Mexico's north and center, and relatively absent in Mexico's south (Chiquiar 2003), we might expect a loss in union power to lower relative incomes in states with higher exposure to globalization, contrary to what we observe in the data. The reform of Mexico's land-tenure system allowed individuals to sell agricultural land previously held in cooperative ownership. In principle we might expect this opportunity to raise relative incomes in rural southern Mexico, where agriculture accounts for a relatively high share of employment and output. Again, this is contrary to what we observe in the data.

Another possibility is that income growth in high-exposure states merely reflects continuing trends unrelated to globalization. This also does not appear to be the case. As seen in figure 10.6, poorer states, which include seven of the ten states with low exposure to globalization, had faster growth in per capita income than richer states, which include six of the seven high-exposure states. The process of income convergence in Mexico came to a halt in 1985, coinciding with the onset of trade liberalization. Since 1985, regional incomes have diverged in the country. The pattern of income growth I uncover does not appear to have been evident in the early 1980s or before.

A brief review of Mexico's other policy reforms during the 1990s does not suggest any obvious reason why they should account for the observed increase in relative incomes in states with high exposure to globalization. Still, it is important to be cautious about ascribing shifts in regional relative incomes to specific policy changes. In the end, we can only say that I find suggestive evidence that globalization has increased relative incomes in Mexican states that are more exposed to global markets.

References

Ariola, Jim, and Chinhui Juhn. 2003. Wage inequality in post-reform Mexico. University of Houston. Unpublished Manuscript.

Athey, Susan, and Guido Imbens. 2003. Identification and inference in nonlinear difference-in-differences models. NBER Technical Working Paper no. 0280. Cambridge, MA: National Bureau of Economic Research.

Attanasio, Orazio, Pinelopi Goldberg, and Nina Pavcnik. 2004. Trade reforms and wage inequality in Colombia. *Journal of Development Economics* 74:331–66.

Behrman, Jere, Nancy Birdsall, and Miguel Szekely. 2003. Economic policy and wage differentials in Latin America. PIER Working Paper no. 01-048. Philadelphia: Penn Institute for Economic Research.

Chiquiar, Daniel. 2003. Essays on the regional implications of globalization: The case of Mexico. PhD diss., University of California, San Diego.

———. 2005. Why Mexico's regional income convergence broke down. *Journal of Development Economics* 77 (1): 257–75.

Cortés, Fernando, Daniel Hernandez, Enrique Hernandez Laos, Miguel Szekely,

and Hadid Vera Llamas. 2003. Evolucion y caracteristicas de la pobreza en Mexico en la ultima decada del siglo XX. *Economia Mexicana* 12 (2): 295–328.

Cragg, Michael I., and Mario Epelbaum. 1996. The premium for skills in LDCs: Evidence from Mexico. *Journal of Development Economics* 51 (1): 99–116.

Currie, Janet, and Ann Harrison. 1997. Trade reform and labor market adjustment in Morocco. *Journal of Labor Economics* 15:S44–S71.

Deaton, Angus, and John Muellbauer. 1980. *Economics and consumer behavior.* Cambridge: Cambridge University Press.

DiNardo, John, Nicole M. Fortin, and Thomas Lemieux. 1996. Labor market institutions and the distribution of wages, 1973–1992: A semiparametric approach. *Econometrica* 64 (5): 1001–44.

Durand, Jorge, Douglas S. Massey, and Rene M. Zenteno. 2001. Mexican immigration in the United States. *Latin American Research Review* 36 (1): 107–27.

Fairris, David H. 2003. Unions and wage inequality in Mexico. *Industrial and Labor Relations Review* 56 (3): 481–97.

Feenstra, Robert C. 1998. Integration of trade and disintegration of production in the global economy. *Journal of Economic Perspectives* 12:31–50.

Feenstra, Robert C., and Gordon H. Hanson. 1997. Foreign direct investment and relative wages: Evidence from Mexico's maquiladoras. *Journal of International Economics* 42 (3–4): 371–94.

———. 1999. Productivity measurement and the impact of trade and technology on wages: Estimates for the U.S., 1972–1990. *Quarterly Journal of Economics* 114 (August): 907–40.

———. 2003. Global production and inequality: A survey of trade and wages. In *Handbook of international trade,* ed. James Harrigan, 146–85. Malden, MA: Basil Blackwell.

Feliciano, Zadia. 2001. Workers and trade liberalization: The impact of trade reforms in Mexico on wages and employment. *Industrial and Labor Relations Review* 55 (1): 95–115.

Freeman, Richard B. 1995. Are your wages set in Beijing? *Journal of Economic Perspectives* 9:15–32.

———. 2003. Trade wars: The exaggerated impact of trade in economic debate. NBER Working Paper no. 10000. Cambridge, MA: National Bureau of Economic Research.

Goldberg, Pinelopi, and Nina Pavcnik. 2004. Trade, inequality, and poverty: What do we know? Evidence from recent trade liberalization episodes in developing countries. NBER Working Paper no. 10593. Cambridge, MA: National Bureau of Economic Research.

Hansen, Niles. 1981. *The border economy: Regional development in the Southwest.* Austin: University of Texas Press.

Hanson, Gordon. 2004. What has happened to wages in Mexico since NAFTA? In *FTAA and beyond: Prospects for integration in the Americas,* ed. Toni Estevadeordal, Dani Rodrik, Alan Taylor, and Andres Velasco, 505–38. Cambridge, MA: Harvard University Press.

Hanson, Gordon, and Ann E. Harrison. 1999. Trade, technology, and wage inequality in Mexico. *Industrial and Labor Relations Review* 52 (2): 271–88.

Hsieh, Chang-Tai, and Keong Woo. 2005. The impact of outsourcing to China on Hong Kong's labor market. *American Economic Review* 95 (5): 1673–87.

Katz, Lawrence F., and David Autor. 1999. Changes in the wage structure and earnings inequality. In *Handbook of labor economics,* Vol. 3A, ed. Orley Ashenfelter and David Card, 1463–1555. Amsterdam: Elsevier Science.

Lee, David S. 2005. Training, wages, and sample selection: Estimating sharp

bounds on treatment effects. NBER Working Paper no. 11721. Cambridge, MA: National Bureau of Economic Research.

Leibbrandt, Murray, James Levinsohn, and Justin McCrary. 2005. Incomes in South Africa since the fall of apartheid. NBER Working Paper no. 11385. Cambridge, MA: National Bureau of Economic Research.

Nicita, Alessandro. 2004. Who benefited from trade liberalization in Mexico? Measuring the effects on household welfare. World Bank Policy Research Working Paper no. 3265. Washington, DC: World Bank.

Pavcnik, Nina. 2003. What explains skill upgrading in less developed countries? *Journal of Development Economics* 71:311–28.

Porto, Guido. 2003. Trade reforms, market access and poverty in Argentina. World Bank Policy Research Working Paper no. 3135. Washington, DC: World Bank.

Revenga, Anna L. 1997. Employment and wage effects of trade liberalization: The case of Mexican manufacturing. *Journal of Labor Economics* 15 (3): S20–S43.

Richardson, J. David. 1995. Income inequality and trade: How to think, what to conclude. *Journal of Economic Perspectives* 9:33–56.

Robertson, Raymond. 2000. Wage shocks and North American labor market integration. *American Economic Review* 90 (4): 742–64.

Robertson, Raymond. 2004. Relative prices and wage inequality: Evidence from Mexico. *Journal of International Economics* 64 (2): 387–409.

Winters, L. Alan, Neil McCulloch, and Andrew McKay. 2004. Trade liberalization and poverty: The evidence so far. *Journal of Economic Literature* 42:72–115.

Comment   Esther Duflo

Relative to the abundant number of papers on the impact of globalization on inequality, only a few papers (several of them in this volume) try to investigate its effects on poverty. This is unfortunate, since the effects on poverty are at the heart of the debate between proglobalization and antiglobalization camps, with each employing theoretical reasoning and anecdotal evidence to argue that globalization is good (or bad) for the poor.

The present paper is part of a most welcome change in this state of affairs. Hanson examines the impact of globalization on the shape of wage distribution in Mexico and, in particular, on the number of people whose wages would place them below the poverty line if they were to subsist on these wages. While this is not the whole story on poverty (some of the poor may be unemployed or self-employed, for example), this is clearly an essential ingredient. Moreover, data on wages are available from a large sample and are representative at the regional level, which is not the case for consumption data. In future work, it may be possible to use these data to attempt to say something about poverty, using the strategy developed by

Esther Duflo is the Abdul Latif Jameel Professor of Poverty Alleviation and Development Economics at the Massachusetts Institute of Technology, and a research associate of the National Bureau of Economic Research.

Elbers, Lanjouw, and Lanjouw (2003), for instance. Their strategy involves using a smaller data set containing both wages and consumption information to predict the relationship between poverty, wages, and other variables observed in the larger data set. Using this strategy as a foundation, one could construct an estimate of poverty at the regional level using the representative data set, and then use this as the dependent variable in the analysis.

Hanson's approach is to compare the evolution of wage distribution during the "decade of globalization" (1990–2000) in regions that were most exposed to globalization to that of regions that were less exposed to globalization. (Globalization is defined as a composite index, reflecting exposure to FDI and foreign trades.) He shows that the distribution of wages shifted to the right in exposed states between 1990 and 2000, relative to the distribution in unexposed states. The states with higher exposure were already richer in 1990, but they were even richer by 2000. In particular, the number of wage-poor in states with high exposure declined by 10 percent relative to the number in unexposed states. Globalization appears to have benefited more the states that were exposed to it most.

Hanson takes great care to ensure the robustness of these findings: he defines a person's region as his state of birth, in order to ensure that he is not picking up the effect of migration by high-ability migrants to the regions with more opportunities. He shows that before 1990, there tended to be a convergence between Mexican states, so that the effect found between 1990 and 2000 is not *prima facie* likely to be due to the continuation of a divergence trend. Some uncertainty is bound to remain: the convergence trend is established over a long period, and so is the result found in this paper. It is possible that the richer states would have started to diverge anyway, and that this is what is reflected in these results. Several serious shocks affected Mexico during this decade, and they could have had differential effects on different regions, varying systematically with their exposure to foreign investment and trade. It is difficult to assess in which direction these effects would have gone. The results are therefore far from definitive, but they should certainly affect our priors that the globalization in Mexico reduced poverty more (or increased poverty less) in regions that were more exposed to foreign investment and foreign trade.

One must be cautious in interpreting the results as saying that globalization was good for Mexico's poor, however. The strategy involves a comparison between regions and would not pick up any macroeconomic effect affecting Mexico as a whole. Mexico is an integrated economy, and the regions share a number of characteristics. These effects could go in either direction. For example, some may argue that the peso crisis was a consequence of globalization. If it made everyone poorer, this would not be picked up by the approach. This strategy can only tell us whether some regions pick up more of the benefits (or less of the burden) of globalization

than others, and whether this is related to how much more they were exposed to trade. This is an important question, and it has the advantage over the more general question (what was the impact of globalization on poverty in Mexico) in that it can be answered.

It is important to note that if the Mexican labor market was fully integrated, migration would operate to equalize factor prices, and there would be no differential impact of globalization on different regions. Hanson's paper therefore tells us that labor is relatively immobile across regions. In contrast, within regions, it seems to be mobile across sectors (employment in the maquiladoras, for example). A comparison between this paper and two other contributions in this volume (chap. 7, by Topalova, on India, and chap. 6, by Goldberg and Pavcnik, on Colombia) suggests that the extent of labor mobility may be at the heart of the impact of globalization on poverty, within and across regions. The chapters by Topalova and by Goldberg and Pavcnik both show that trade liberalization increased poverty in the regions (Topalova) and sectors (Goldberg and Pavcnik) it directly affected, relative to those that were less affected.[1] In both cases, in contrast to what Hanson finds in this paper, the mobility of labor seems to have been very limited, both across sectors and across regions. In turn, the mobility of labor may have been hindered by the absence of reallocation of capital across sectors.

These papers taken together seem to suggest that factor mobility may be at the heart of the impact of trade on poverty. A generation of new models (notably Banerjee and Newman 2004) focuses on developing the theory of trade with imperfect factor mobility. We can hope that these models will be followed by a new wave of empirical work explicitly testing some of these hypotheses.

References

Banerjee, Abhijit, and Andrew Newman. 2004. Capital market imperfection, export promotion and industry growth. Massachusetts Institute of Technology. Unpublished Manuscript.
Elbers, Chris, Jean O. Lanjouw, and Peter Lanjouw. 2003. Micro-level estimation of poverty and inequality. *Econometrica* 71 (1): 355–64.

1. All three papers use the same type of difference-in-differences strategies, which allow them to make only comparative statements.

III

Capital Flows and
Poverty Outcomes

Financial Globalization, Growth, and Volatility in Developing Countries

Eswar S. Prasad, Kenneth Rogoff, Shang-Jin Wei, and M. Ayhan Kose

11.1 Introduction and Overview

The wave of financial globalization since the mid-1980s has been marked by a surge in capital flows among industrial countries and, more notably, between industrial and developing countries. While these capital flows have been associated with high growth rates in some developing countries, a number of countries have experienced episodic collapses in growth rates and significant financial crises over the same period, crises that have exacted a serious toll in macroeconomic and social costs. As a result, an intense debate has emerged in both academic and policy circles about the effects of financial integration on developing economies. But much of the debate has been based on only casual and limited empirical evidence.

The objective of this paper is to provide an assessment of empirical evidence on the effects of financial globalization for developing economies. The paper will focus on a couple of related questions: (a) does financial

Eswar S. Prasad is currently the Chief of the Financial Studies division of the research department in the International Monetary Fund. Kenneth Rogoff is the Thomas D. Cabot Professor of Public Policy at Harvard University and a research associate of the National Bureau of Economic Research. Shang-Jin Wei is assistant director and chief of the Trade and Investment division of the research department at the International Monetary Fund and a research associate and director of the National Bureau of Economic Research's Working Group on the Chinese Economy. M. Ayhan Kose is an economist in the Financial Studies division of the research department of the International Monetary Fund.

We would like to thank Ann Harrison, Susan Collins, and the conference participants for their helpful suggestions. This paper is based on our earlier paper (Prasad et al. 2003). The views expressed in this paper are those of the authors and do not necessarily reflect the views of the IMF or IMF policy.

globalization promote economic growth in developing countries, and (b) what is its impact on macroeconomic volatility in these countries?

While this paper does not deal directly with poverty issues, its main subject—the effects of financial globalization on economic growth and volatility—has important indirect effects. First, as documented by several empirical studies, economic growth has been the most reliable source of poverty reduction. Moreover, in theory, there are several channels through which increased financial flows could help reduce poverty. As discussed later in the chapter, some of these channels are related to the growth-enhancing effects of increased financial flows. For example, augmentation of domestic savings, reduction in the cost of capital, increase in productivity through transfer of technological know-how, and stimulation of domestic financial-sector development could all provide direct growth benefits, which in turn should help reduce poverty.

Second, an increase in macroeconomic volatility tends to reduce the well-being of poor households. Recent empirical research finds that volatility has a significantly negative and causal impact on poverty (Laursen and Mahajan 2005). Why does macroeconomic volatility appear to be especially harmful for the poor? First, the poor have the least access to financial markets, making it difficult for them to diversify the risk associated with their income, which is often based on a narrow set of sources, including mainly labor earnings and government transfers. Second, since the poor rely heavily on various public services, including education and health, they are directly affected by changes in government spending. Given that fiscal policy is procyclical in most developing countries, this magnifies the negative impact of volatility on poverty, especially during financial crises. Moreover, the poor often lack necessary education and skill levels, which limits their ability to move across sectors in order to adjust to changes in economic conditions. As we discuss later in the chapter, in theory, increased trade and financial flows could help reduce macroeconomic volatility, which also could have beneficial effects for the poor (Aizenman and Pinto 2005).

The principal conclusions that emerge from our analysis of the macroeconomic effects of financial globalization are sobering but in many ways informative from a policy perspective. It is true that many developing economies with a high degree of financial integration have experienced higher growth rates. It is also true that, in theory, there are many channels by which financial openness could enhance growth. However, a systematic examination of the evidence suggests that it is difficult to establish a robust causal relationship between the degree of financial integration and output growth performance. Furthermore, from the perspective of macroeconomic stability, consumption is regarded as a better measure of well-being than output; fluctuations in consumption are therefore regarded as having a negative impact on economic welfare. There is little evidence that finan-

cial integration has helped developing countries to better stabilize fluctuations in consumption growth, notwithstanding the theoretically large benefits that could accrue to developing countries in this respect. In fact, new evidence presented in this paper suggests that low to moderate levels of financial integration may have made some countries subject to even greater volatility of consumption relative to that of output. Thus, while there is no proof in the data that financial globalization has benefited growth, there is evidence that some developing countries may have experienced greater consumption volatility as a result.

One must be careful, however, not to draw the inference from these results that financial globalization is inherently too risky and that developing countries should retreat into stronger forms of capital controls. First, as we discuss in an earlier, extended version of this paper (Prasad et al. 2003), empirical evidence supports the view that countries are considerably more likely to benefit from financial globalization when they take simultaneous steps—sometimes even modest ones—to improve governance, transparency, and financial-sector regulation. Second, it is almost surely the case that excessive reliance on fixed exchange rate regimes has been a major contributory factor to financial crises in emerging-market countries over the past fifteen years. Moving to more flexible exchange rate regimes is therefore likely to considerably alleviate some of the risks countries must endure as they become more financially globalized (for countries that are not financially globalized, fixed exchange rate regimes may be a perfectly good choice, as the empirical results in Rogoff et al. 2004 suggest). Third, countries that consistently face problems associated with government debt (referred to as "serial defaulters" by Reinhart and Rogoff 2004), are more likely to benefit from financial globalization if their governments simultaneously take measures to avoid an excessive buildup of debt.

It is also important to note that much of the analysis in this paper focuses on de facto rather than de jure financial globalization. This makes sense in an empirical paper since capital controls come in so many flavors, and enforcement varies so widely across countries, that cross-country empirical comparisons based on measures of de jure capital controls are extremely difficult to interpret. By contrast, de facto financial integration is not a variable that a country's government can easily regulate. Although many countries have tight capital controls on paper, their degree of de facto financial globalization is nevertheless high because these controls can be easily evaded in practice. This problem is almost surely exacerbated by the kind of domestic financial liberalizations that many countries have chosen to undergo over the past two decades in an effort to channel savings more efficiently and thereby spur growth. At the same time, some poor countries have few impediments to capital flows, but their level of de facto financial globalization is still very low, even when measured relative to national income.

As noted earlier, this paper does not look directly at how financial globalization affects absolute or relative measures of poverty. Based on the results from our analysis, the effects could easily go in opposite directions.[1] On the one hand, sustained high growth is the most consistently successful policy for alleviating absolute poverty, as China and India have succeeded in doing over the past two decades. On the other hand, periods of high growth are often associated with higher income inequality, and, therefore, relative measures of poverty may easily rise. Increased macroeconomic volatility, however, probably increases both absolute and relative measures of poverty, particularly in the case of financial crises that lead to sharp rises in unemployment. The evidence presented in this paper suggests that a detailed study of the link between financial globalization and poverty is likely to yield ambiguous results for emerging-market countries, albeit with the same caveats: countries that work simultaneously to improve institutions, and ones that avoid overly fixed exchange rate regimes, have a much better chance of seeing financial globalization lead to poverty reduction, at least by absolute measures.

The remainder of this section provides an overview of the structure of the paper. In brief, section 11.2 begins with documentation of some salient features of global financial integration from the perspective of developing countries. Sections 11.3 and 11.4 analyze the evidence on the effects of financial globalization on growth and volatility, respectively, in developing countries. Section 11.5 concludes.

11.1.1 Definitions and Basic Stylized Facts

Financial globalization and financial integration are, in principle, different concepts. Financial globalization is an aggregate concept that refers to rising global linkages through cross-border financial flows. Financial integration refers to an individual country's linkages to international capital markets. Clearly, these concepts are closely related. For instance, increasing financial globalization is perforce associated with rising financial integration on average. In this paper, the two terms are used interchangeably.

Of more relevance for the purposes of this paper is the distinction between de jure financial integration, which is associated with policies on capital account liberalization, and actual capital flows. For example, indicator measures of the extent of government restrictions on capital flows across national borders have been used extensively in the literature. By this

---

1. Since it is difficult to measure poverty and to isolate the impact of globalization on poverty from various other factors, recent studies do not reach an unambiguous conclusion on this issue. While Easterly (chap. 3 in this volume) documents that neither financial nor trade flows have any significant impact on poverty, Harrison (introduction to this volume) notes that "there is certainly no evidence in the aggregate data that trade reforms are bad for the poor." Winters, McCulloch, and McKay (2004) also argue that the empirical evidence often suggests that trade liberalization helps reduce poverty in the long run and note that "it lends no support to the position that trade liberalization generally has an adverse impact."

measure, many countries in Latin America would be considered closed to financial flows. On the other hand, the volume of capital actually crossing the borders of these countries has been large relative to the average volume of flows across all developing countries. Therefore, on a de facto basis, these countries are quite open to global financial flows. By contrast, some countries in Africa have few formal restrictions on capital account transactions but have not experienced significant capital flows. The analysis in this paper will focus largely on de facto measures of financial integration, as it is virtually impossible to compare the efficacy of various complex restrictions across countries. In the end, what matters most is the actual degree of openness. However, the paper will also consider the relationship between de jure and de facto measures.

As will be discussed in section 11.2, a few salient features of global capital flows are relevant for the central themes of the paper. First, the volume of cross-border capital flows has risen substantially in the last decade. Not only has there been a much greater volume of flows among industrial countries, but there has also been a surge in flows between industrial and developing countries. Second, this surge in international capital flows to developing countries is the outcome of both "pull" and "push" factors. Pull factors arise from changes in policies and other aspects of opening up by developing countries. These include liberalization of capital accounts and domestic stock markets, and large-scale privatization programs. Push factors include business cycle conditions and macroeconomic policy changes in industrial countries. From a longer-term perspective, this latter set of factors includes the rise in the importance of institutional investors in industrial countries and demographic changes (e.g., relative aging of the population in industrial countries). The importance of these factors suggests that, notwithstanding temporary interruptions in crisis periods or during global business cycle downturns, the past twenty years have been characterized by secular pressures for rising global capital flows to the developing world.

Another important feature of international capital flows is that the components of these flows differ markedly in terms of volatility. In particular, bank borrowing and portfolio flows are substantially more volatile than foreign direct investment. In spite of a caveat that accurate classification of capital flows is not easy, evidence suggests that the composition of capital flows can have a significant influence on a country's vulnerability to financial crises.

11.1.2   Does Financial Globalization Promote Growth in Developing Countries?

Section 11.3 will summarize the theoretical benefits of financial globalization for economic growth and then review the empirical evidence. Financial globalization could, in principle, help to raise the growth rate in de-

veloping countries through a number of channels. Some of these directly affect the determinants of economic growth (augmentation of domestic savings, reduction in the cost of capital, transfer of technology from advanced to developing countries, and development of domestic financial sectors). Indirect channels, which in some cases could be even more important than the direct ones, include increased production specialization due to better risk management, and improvements in both macroeconomic policies and institutions induced by the competitive pressures or the "discipline effect" of globalization.

How many of the advertised benefits for economic growth have actually materialized in the developing world? As documented in this paper, the average income per capita for the group of more financially open (developing) economies does grow at a more favorable rate than that of the group of less financially open economies. However, whether this actually reflects a causal relationship and whether this correlation is robust to controlling for other factors remain unresolved questions. The literature on this subject, voluminous as it is, does not present a conclusive picture. A few papers find a positive effect of financial integration on growth. However, the majority find no effect or at best a mixed effect. Thus, an objective reading of the vast research effort to date suggests that there is no strong, robust, and uniform support for the theoretical argument that financial globalization per se delivers a higher rate of economic growth.

Perhaps this is not surprising. As noted by several authors, most of the cross-country differences in per capita incomes stem not from differences in the capital-labor ratio but from differences in total factor productivity, which could be explained by "soft" factors like governance and rule of law. In this case, although embracing financial globalization may result in higher capital inflows, it is unlikely to cause faster growth by itself. In addition, some of the countries with capital account liberalization have experienced output collapses related to costly banking or currency crises. This is elaborated below. An alternative possibility, as noted earlier, is that financial globalization fosters better institutions and domestic policies but that these indirect channels cannot be captured in standard regression frameworks.

In short, while financial globalization can, in theory, help to promote economic growth through various channels, there is as yet no robust empirical evidence that this causal relationship is quantitatively very important. This points to an interesting contrast between financial openness and trade openness, since an overwhelming majority of research papers have found a positive effect of the latter on economic growth.

11.1.3 What Is the Impact of Financial Globalization on Macroeconomic Volatility?

In theory, financial globalization can help developing countries to better manage output and consumption volatility. Indeed, a variety of theories

implies that the volatility of consumption relative to that of output should go down as the degree of financial integration increases; the essence of global financial diversification is that a country is able to offload some of its income risk in world markets. Since most developing countries are rather specialized in their output and factor endowment structures, they can, in theory, obtain even bigger gains than developed countries through international consumption risk sharing—that is, by effectively selling off a stake in their domestic output in return for a stake in global output.

How much of the potential benefit in terms of better management of consumption volatility has actually been realized? This question is particularly relevant in terms of understanding whether, despite the output volatility experienced by developing countries that have undergone financial crises, financial integration has protected them from consumption volatility. New research presented in section 11.4 paints a troubling picture. Specifically, while the volatility of output growth declined, on average, in the 1990s relative to the three earlier decades, the volatility of consumption growth relative to that of income growth *increased* on average for the emerging-market economies in the 1990s, which was precisely the period of a rapid increase in financial globalization. In other words, as argued in more detail later in the paper, procyclical access to international capital markets appears to have had a perverse effect on the relative volatility of consumption for financially integrated developing economies.

Interestingly, a more nuanced look at the data suggests the possible presence of a threshold effect. At low levels of financial integration, an increment in financial integration is associated with an increase in the relative volatility of consumption. However, once the level of financial integration crosses a threshold, the association becomes negative. In other words, for countries that are sufficiently open financially, relative consumption volatility starts to decline. This finding is potentially consistent with the view that international financial integration can help to promote domestic financial-sector development, which in turn can help to moderate domestic macroeconomic volatility. However, thus far these benefits of financial integration appear to have accrued primarily to industrial countries.

In this vein, the proliferation of financial and currency crises among developing economies is often viewed as a natural consequence of the growing pains associated with financial globalization. These can take various forms. First, international investors have a tendency to engage in momentum trading and herding, which can be destabilizing for developing economies. Second, international investors (together with domestic residents) may engage in speculative attacks on developing countries currencies, thereby causing instability that is not warranted based on the economic and policy fundamentals of these countries. Third, the risk of contagion presents a major threat to otherwise healthy countries since international investors could withdraw capital from these countries for reasons unre-

lated to domestic factors. Fourth, a government, even if democratically elected, may not give sufficient weight to the interests of future generations. This becomes a problem when the interests of future and current generations diverge, causing the government to incur excessive amounts of debt. Financial globalization, by making it easier for governments to incur debt, might aggravate this overborrowing problem. These four hypotheses are not necessarily independent, and can reinforce each other.

There is some empirical support for these hypothesized effects. For example, there is evidence that international investors do engage in herding and momentum trading in emerging markets, more so than in developed countries. Recent research also suggests the presence of contagion in international financial markets. In addition, some developing countries that open their capital markets do appear to accumulate unsustainably high levels of external debt.

To summarize, one of the theoretical benefits of financial globalization, other than to enhance growth, is to allow developing countries to better manage macroeconomic volatility, especially by reducing consumption volatility relative to output volatility. The evidence suggests that, instead, countries that are in the early stages of financial integration have been exposed to significant risks in terms of higher volatility of both output and consumption.

11.1.4 The Role of Institutions and Governance in the Effects of Globalization

While it is difficult to find a simple relationship between financial globalization and growth or consumption volatility, there is some evidence of nonlinearities or threshold effects in the relationship. That is, financial globalization, in combination with good macroeconomic policies and good domestic governance, appears to be conducive to growth (see Prasad et al. 2003). For example, countries with good human capital and governance tend to do better at attracting foreign direct investment (FDI), which is especially conducive to growth. More specifically, recent research shows that corruption has a strongly negative effect on FDI inflows. Similarly, transparency of government operations, which is another dimension of good governance, has a strong positive effect on investment inflows from international mutual funds.

The vulnerability of a developing country to the risk factors associated with financial globalization is also not independent from the quality of macroeconomic policies and domestic governance. For example, research has demonstrated that an overvalued exchange rate and an overextended domestic lending boom often precede a currency crisis. In addition, lack of transparency has been shown to be associated with more herding behavior by international investors that can destabilize a developing country's financial markets. Finally, evidence shows that a high degree of corruption

may affect the composition of a country's capital inflows in a manner that makes it more vulnerable to the risks of speculative attacks and contagion effects.

Thus, the ability of a developing country to derive benefits from financial globalization and its relative vulnerability to the volatility of international capital flows can be significantly affected by the quality of both its macroeconomic framework and its institutions.

11.1.5   Summary

The objective of the paper is not so much to derive new policy propositions as it is to inform the debate on the potential and actual benefit-risk trade-offs associated with financial globalization by reviewing the available empirical evidence and country experiences. The main conclusions are that, so far, it has proven difficult to find robust evidence in support of the proposition that financial integration helps developing countries to improve growth and to reduce macroeconomic volatility.

Of course, the absence of robust evidence on these dimensions does not necessarily mean that financial globalization has no benefits and carries only great risks. Indeed, most countries that have initiated financial integration have continued along this path, despite temporary setbacks. This observation is consistent with the notion that the indirect benefits of financial integration, which may be difficult to pick up in regression analysis, could be quite important. Also, the long-run gains, in some cases yet unrealized, may far offset the short-term costs. For instance, the European Monetary Union experienced severe and costly crises in the early 1990s as part of the transition to a single currency throughout much of Europe today.

Although it is difficult to distill new and innovative policy messages from the review of the evidence, there appears to be empirical support for some general propositions. Empirically, good institutions and quality of governance are important not only in their own right but also in helping developing countries derive the benefits of globalization. Similarly, macroeconomic stability appears to be an important prerequisite for ensuring that financial integration is beneficial for developing countries. These points may already be generally accepted; the contribution of this paper is to show that there is some systematic empirical evidence to support them. In addition, the analysis suggests that financial globalization should be approached cautiously and with good institutions and macroeconomic frameworks viewed as preconditions.

11.2   Basic Stylized Facts

De jure restrictions on capital flows and actual capital flows across national borders are two ways of measuring the extent of a country's finan-

cial integration with the global economy. The differences between these two measures are important for understanding the effects of financial integration. By either measure, developing countries' financial linkages with the global economy have risen in recent years.[2] However, a relatively small group of developing countries has garnered the lion's share of private capital flows from industrial to developing countries, which surged in the 1990s. Structural factors, including demographic shifts in industrial countries, are likely to provide an impetus to these North-South flows over the medium and long term.

11.2.1 Measuring Financial Integration

Capital account liberalization is typically considered an important precursor to financial integration. Most formal empirical work analyzing the effects of capital account liberalization has used a measure based on the official restrictions on capital flows as reported to the International Monetary Fund (IMF) by national authorities. However, this binary indicator directly measures capital controls but does not capture differences in the intensity of these controls.[3] A more direct measure of financial openness is based on the estimated gross stocks of foreign assets and liabilities as a share of gross domestic product (GDP). The stock data constitute a better indication of integration, for our purposes, than the underlying flows since they are less volatile from year to year and are less prone to measurement error (assuming that such errors are not correlated over time).[4]

Although these two measures of financial integration are related, they denote two distinct aspects. The capital account restrictions measure reflects the existence of de jure restrictions on capital flows, while the financial openness measure captures de facto financial integration in terms of realized capital flows. This distinction is of considerable importance for the analysis in this paper and implies a 2×2 set of combinations of these two aspects of integration. Many industrial countries have attained a high degree of financial integration in terms of both measures. Some developing countries with capital account restrictions have found these restrictions ineffective in controlling actual capital flows. Episodes of capital flight from

---

2. Bordo and Eichengreen (2002), Obstfeld and Taylor (2002), and Mauro, Sussman, and Yafeh (2002) examine historical roots of international financial integration.
3. The restriction measure is available until 1995, when a new and more refined measure—not backward compatible—was introduced. The earlier data were extended through 1998 by Mody and Murshid (2002).
4. These stock data were constructed by Lane and Milesi-Ferretti (2001). Operationally, this measure involves calculating the gross levels of FDI and portfolio assets and liabilities via the accumulation of the corresponding inflows and outflows, and making relevant valuation adjustments. A similar measure using the same underlying stock data has been considered by Chanda (2006) and O'Donnell (2001). Other measures of capital market integration include saving-investment correlations and various interest parity conditions (Frankel 1992). These measures are difficult to operationalize for the extended time period and large number of countries in the data sample for this paper.

some Latin American countries in the 1970s and 1980s are examples of such involuntary de facto financial integration in economies that are de jure closed to financial flows (i.e., integration without capital account liberalization). On the other hand, some countries in Africa have few capital account restrictions but have experienced only minimal levels of capital flows (i.e., liberalization without integration).[5] And, of course, it is not difficult to find examples of countries with closed capital accounts that are also effectively closed in terms of capital flows.

How has financial integration evolved over time for different groups of countries based on alternative measures?[6] By either measure, the difference in financial openness between industrial and developing countries is quite stark. Industrial economies have had an enormous increase in financial openness, particularly in the 1990s. While this measure also increased for developing economies in that decade, the level remains far below that of industrial economies.

For industrial countries, unweighted cross-country averages of the two measures are mirror images and jointly confirm that these countries have undergone rapid financial integration since the mid-1980s (fig. 11.1).[7] For developing countries, the average restriction measure indicates that, after a period of liberalization in the 1970s, the trend toward openness reversed in the 1980s. Liberalization resumed in the early 1990s but at a slow pace. On the other hand, the average financial openness measure for these countries, based on actual flows, shows a modest increase in the 1980s, followed by a sharp rise in the 1990s. The increase in the financial openness measure for developing economies reflects a more rapid de facto integration than is captured by the relatively crude measure of capital account restrictions.

However, the effects of financial integration in terms of increased capital flows have been spread very unevenly across developing countries.[8] To

---

5. An analogy from the literature on international trade may be relevant here. Some countries, due to their remoteness from major world markets or other unfavorable geographical attributes, have low trade flows despite having minimal barriers to trade even after controlling for various other factors. Similarly, certain countries, due to their remoteness from major financial centers in either physical distance or historical relationships, may experience limited capital flows despite having relatively open capital accounts (see Loungani, Mody, and Razin 2003).

6. The data set used in this paper consists of seventy-six industrial and developing countries (except where otherwise indicated) and covers the period 1960–99. Given the long sample period, several countries currently defined as industrial (e.g., Korea and Singapore) are included in the developing-country group. The following were excluded from the data set: most of the highly indebted poor countries (which mostly receive official flows), the transition economies of Eastern Europe and the former Soviet Union (due to lack of data), very small economies (population less than 1.5 million), and oil-exporting countries in the Middle East. See appendix for a list of countries and further details on the data set.

7. A particularly rapid decline in controls occurred during the 1980s, when the members of the European Community, now the European Union, liberalized capital controls. A surge in cross-border capital flows followed.

8. Ishii et al. (2002) examine in detail the experiences of a number of developing countries.

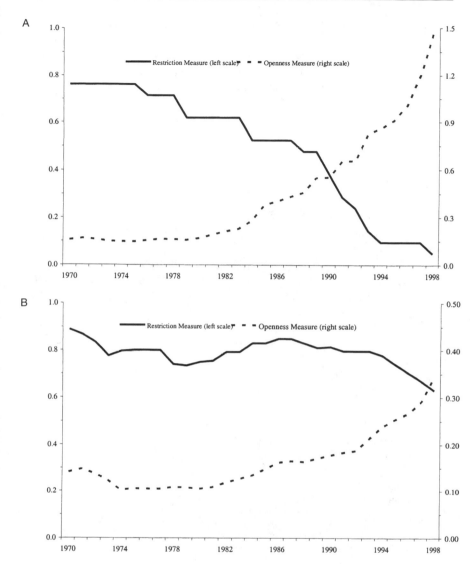

Fig. 11.1   Measures of financial integration: *A*, industrial countries; *B*, developing countries
Source: IMF *World Economic Outlook;* Lane and Milesi-Ferretti (2001)

examine the extent of these disparities, it is useful to begin with a very coarse classification of the developing countries in the sample into two groups based on a ranking according to the average of the financial openness measure over the last four decades (as well as an assessment of other indicators of financial integration).

The first group, which comprises twenty-two countries, is henceforth la-

beled as the set of more financially integrated (MFI) countries, and the second group, which includes thirty-three countries, as the less financially integrated (LFI) countries.[9] This distinction must be interpreted with some care at this stage. In particular, it is worth repeating that the criterion is a measure of de facto integration based on actual capital flows rather than a measure of the strength of policies designed to promote financial integration. Indeed, a few of the countries in the MFI group do have relatively closed capital accounts in a de jure sense. In general, as argued below, policy choices do determine the degree and nature of financial integration. Nevertheless, for the analysis in this paper, the degree of financial openness based on actual capital flows is a more relevant measure.

It should be noted that the main conclusions of this paper are not crucially dependent on the particulars of the classification of developing countries into the MFI and LFI groups. This classification is obviously a static one and does not account for differences across countries in the timing and degree of financial integration. It is used for some of the descriptive analysis presented below, but only in order to illustrate the conclusions from the more detailed econometric studies that are surveyed in the paper. The areas where this classification yields results different from those obtained from more formal econometric analysis will be clearly highlighted in the paper. The regression results reported in this paper are based on the gross capital flows measure described earlier, which does capture differences across countries and changes over time in the degree of financial integration.

Figure 11.2 shows that the vast majority of international private gross capital flows of developing countries, especially in the 1990s, are accounted for by the relatively small group of MFI economies.[10] By contrast, private capital flows to and from the LFI economies have remained very small over the last decade and, for certain types of flows, have even fallen relative to the late 1970s.

11.2.2 North-South Capital Flows

One of the key features of global financial integration over the last decade has been the dramatic increase in net private capital flows from industrial countries (the North) to developing countries (the South). Figure 11.3 breaks down the levels of these flows into the four main constituent categories. The main increase has been in terms of FDI and portfolio flows,

9. Not surprisingly, this classification results in a set of MFI economies that roughly corresponds to those included in the Morgan Stanley Country Index (MSCI) emerging-markets stock index. The main differences are that we drop the transition economies because of limited data availability and add Hong Kong Special Administrative Region (SAR) and Singapore.

10. Note that the scale of the graph in panel A is twice as big as that of the graph in panel B.

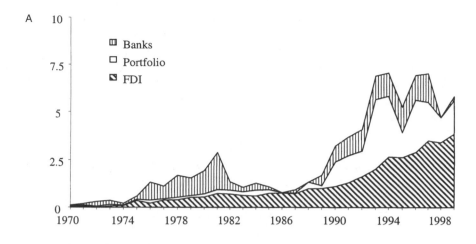

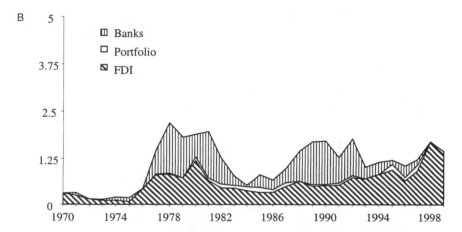

Fig. 11.2   Gross capital flows (percent of GDP): *A,* **MFI economies;**
B, **LFI economies**

Source: IMF *World Economic Outlook, International Financial Statistics*
Note: The reader should note that the left scales on the two panels are different.

while the relative importance of bank lending has declined somewhat. In
fact, net bank lending turned negative for a few years during the time of the
Asian crisis.

The bulk of the surge in net FDI flows from the advanced economies has
gone to MFI economies, with only a small fraction going to LFI economies
(figure 11.3, panels B and C). Net portfolio flows show a similar pattern, although both types of flows to MFI economies fell sharply following the

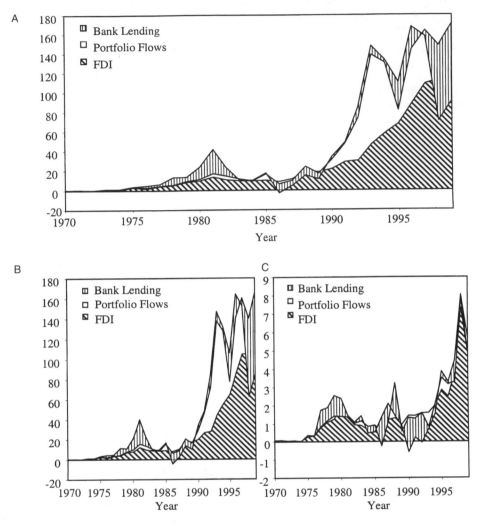

Fig. 11.3   Net private capital flows (billions of U.S. dollars): *A,* **all developing economies;** *B,* **MFI economies;** *C,* **LFI economies**

Source: IMF *World Economic Outlook*

Note: Bank lending to the MFI economies was negative between 1997 and 1999.

Asian crisis and have remained relatively flat since then. LFI economies have been much more dependent on bank lending (and, although not shown here, on official flows including loans and grants). There were surges in bank lending to this group of countries in the late 1970s and early 1990s.

Another important feature of these flows is that they differ substantially in volatility. Table 11.1 shows the volatility of FDI, portfolio flows, and bank lending to developing economies. Of the different categories of

Table 11.1   Volatility of different types of capital inflows

	FDI/GDP	Loan/GDP	Portfolio/GDP
Standard deviations (median for each group)			
MFI economies	0.007	0.032	0.009
LFI economies	0.010	0.036	0.002
Coefficients of variation (median for each group)			
MFI economies	0.696	1.245	1.751
LFI economies	1.276	1.177	2.494
Coefficients of variation for selected MFI economies			
Indonesia	0.820	0.717	1.722
Korea	0.591	2.039	1.338
Malaysia	0.490	4.397	3.544
Mexico	0.452	2.048	2.088
The Philippines	0.921	0.956	1.979
Thailand	0.571	0.629	1.137

Source: Wei (2001).

Notes: Computed over the period 1980–96. Only countries with at least eight nonmissing observations during the period for all three variables and with a population greater than or equal to one million in 1995 are kept in the sample. Total inward FDI flows, total bank loans, and total inward portfolio investments are from the IMF's *Balance of Payments Statistics*, various issues.

private capital flows to developing economies, FDI flows are the least volatile, which is not surprising given their long-term and relatively fixed nature. Portfolio flows tend to be far more volatile and prone to abrupt reversals than FDI. These patterns hold when the MFI and LFI economies are examined separately. Even in the case of LFIs, the volatility of FDI flows is much lower than that of other types of flows.[11] This difference in the relative volatility of different categories has important implications that will be examined in more detail later.

11.2.3   Factors Underlying the Rise in North-South Capital Flows

The surge in net private capital flows to MFIs, as well as the shifts in the composition of these flows, can be broken down into pull and push factors (Calvo, Leiderman, and Reinhart 1993). These are related to, respectively, (a) policies and other developments in the MFIs and (b) changes in global financial markets. The first category includes factors such as stock market

11. Consistent with these results, Taylor and Sarno (1999) find that FDI flows are more persistent than other types of flows. Hausmann and Fernandez-Arias (2000) find weaker confirmation of this result and also note that, although the volatility of FDI flows has been rising over time, it remains lower than that of other types of flows. In interpreting these results, there is a valid concern about potential misclassification of the different types of capital flows. Since most of the studies cited here use similar data sources, this is not a problem that can be easily resolved by examining the conclusions of multiple studies.

liberalizations and privatization of state-owned companies that have stimulated foreign inflows. The second category includes the growing importance of depositary receipts and cross-listings and the emergence of institutional investors as key players driving international capital flows to emerging markets.

The investment opportunities afforded by stock market liberalizations, which have typically included the provision of access to foreign investors, have enhanced capital flows to MFIs. How much have restrictions on foreign investors' access to local stock markets in MFIs changed over time? To answer this question, it is useful to examine a new measure of stock market liberalization that captures restrictions on foreign ownership of domestic equities. This measure, constructed by Edison and Warnock (2001), is obviously just one component of capital controls, but it is an appropriate one for modeling equity flows. Figure 11.4 shows that stock market liberalizations in MFI economies in different regions have proceeded rapidly, in terms of both intensity and speed.[12]

Mergers and acquisitions, especially those resulting from the privatization of state-owned companies, were an important factor underlying the increase in FDI flows to MFIs during the 1990s. The easing of restrictions on foreign participation in the financial sector in MFIs has also provided a strong impetus to this factor.[13]

Institutional investors in the industrial countries—including mutual funds, pension funds, hedge funds, and insurance companies—have assumed an important role in channeling capital flows from industrial to developing economies. They have helped individual investors overcome the information and transaction cost barriers that previously limited portfolio allocations to emerging markets. Mutual funds, in particular, have served as an important instrument for individuals to diversify their portfolios into

12. The stock market liberalization index is based on two indexes constructed by the International Finance Corporation (IFC) for each country—the Global Index (IFCG) and the Investable Index (IFCI). The IFCG represents the full market, while the IFCI represents the portion of the market available to foreign investors, where availability is determined by the IFC based on legal and liquidity criteria. Edison and Warnock (2001) propose using the ratio of the market capitalization of the IFCG to that of the IFCI as a measure of stock market liberalization. This ratio provides a quantitative measure of the degree of access that foreign investors have to a particular country's equity markets; one minus this ratio can be interpreted as a measure of the intensity of capital controls in this dimension.

13. The World Bank's (2001) *Global Development Finance* report notes that FDI in Latin America's financial sector has come about through the purchases of privately owned domestic banks, driving up the share of banking assets under foreign control from 8 percent in 1994 to 25 percent in 1999. In East Asia, foreign investors have purchased local banks in financial distress, leading to an increase in the share of banking assets under foreign control from 2 percent in 1994 to 6 percent in 1999.

14. The presence of mutual funds in MFIs grew substantially during the 1990s. For example, dedicated emerging-market equity funds held $21 billion in Latin American stocks by end 1995. By end 1997, their holdings had increased to $40 billion. While mutual funds' growth in Asia has been less pronounced, the presence of mutual funds is still important in many countries in that region. See Eichengreen, Mathieson, and Chadha (1998) for a detailed study on hedge funds.

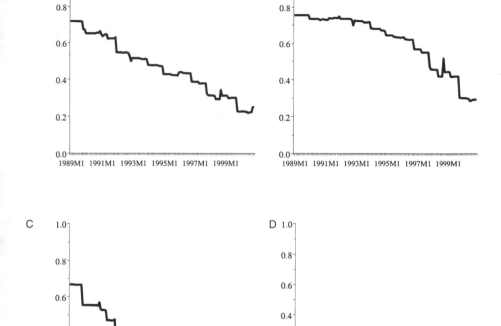

Fig. 11.4   Foreign ownership restrictions (MFI developing economies): *A,* **total;** *B,* **Asia;** *C,* **Western Hemisphere;** *D,* **Africa**
Source: Edison and Warnock (2001).
Note: This index measures the intensity of restrictions on the access that foreign investors have to a particular country's equity markets.

developing-country holdings.[14] Although international institutional investors devote only a small fraction of their portfolios to holdings in MFIs, they have an important presence in these economies, given the relatively small size of their capital markets. Funds dedicated to emerging markets alone hold on average 5–15 percent of the Asian, Latin American, and transition economies' market capitalization.

Notwithstanding the moderation of North-South capital flows following recent emerging-market crises, certain structural forces are likely to

lead to a revival of these flows over the medium and long term. Demographic shifts, in particular, constitute an important driving force for these flows. Projected increases in old-age dependency ratios reflect the major changes in demographic profiles that are underway in industrial countries. This trend is likely to intensify further in the coming decades, fueled by both advances in medical technology that have increased average life spans and the decline in fertility rates. Financing the postretirement consumption needs of a rapidly aging population will require increases in current saving rates, both national and private, in these economies. However, if such increases in saving rates do materialize, they are likely to result in a declining rate of return on capital in advanced economies, especially relative to that in the capital-poor countries of the South. This will lead to natural tendencies for capital to flow to countries where it has a potentially higher return.

All of these forces imply that, despite the recent sharp reversals in North-South capital flows, developing countries will eventually once again face the delicate balance of opportunities and risks afforded by financial globalization. Are the benefits derived from financial integration sufficient to offset the costs of increased exposure to the vagaries of international capital flows? The paper now turns to an examination of the evidence on this question.

11.3 Financial Integration and Economic Growth

Theoretical models have identified a number of channels through which international financial integration can help to promote economic growth in the developing world. However, it has proven difficult to empirically identify a strong and robust causal relationship between financial integration and growth.

11.3.1 Potential Benefits of Financial Globalization in Theory

In theory, there are a number of direct and indirect channels through which embracing financial globalization can help enhance growth in developing countries. Figure 11.5 provides a schematic summary of these possible channels. These channels are interrelated in some ways, but this delineation is useful for reviewing the empirical evidence on the quantitative importance of each channel.[15]

---

15. Some of these channels also come into play in transmitting the beneficial effects of globalization to the poor. For example, augmentation of domestic savings, reduction in the cost of capital, transfer of technological know-how, and stimulation of domestic financial-sector development could all provide direct growth benefits, which in turn help reduce poverty. Agénor (2003), Easterly (chap. 3 in this volume), and Goldberg and Pavcnik (2004) discuss various theoretical channels through which globalization affects poverty.

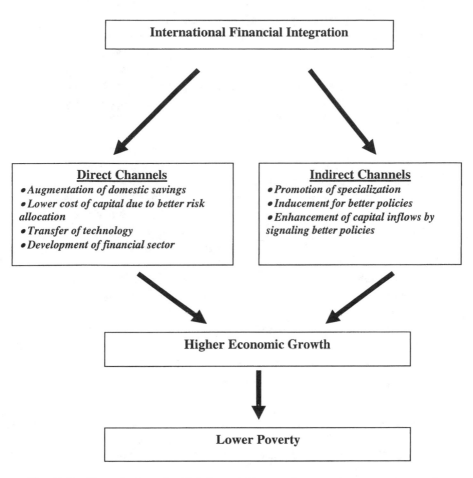

Fig. 11.5   Channels through which financial integration can raise economic growth

Direct Channels

Augmentation of domestic savings. North-South capital flows in principle benefit both groups. They allow for increased investment in capital-poor countries while they provide a higher return on capital than is available in capital-rich countries. This effectively reduces the risk-free rate in the developing countries.

Reduction in the cost of capital through better global allocation of risk. International asset pricing models predict that stock market liberalization improves the allocation of risk (Henry 2000; Stulz 1999a, 1999b). First, increased risk-sharing opportunities between foreign and domestic investors might help to diversify risks. This ability to diversify in turn encourages

firms to take on more total investment, thereby enhancing growth. Third, as capital flows increase, the domestic stock market becomes more liquid, which could further reduce the equity risk premium, thereby lowering the cost of raising capital for investment.

Transfer of technological and managerial know-how. Financially integrated economies seem to attract a disproportionately large share of FDI inflows, which have the potential to generate technology spillovers and to serve as a conduit for passing on better management practices. These spillovers can raise aggregate productivity and, in turn, boost economic growth (Borensztein, De Gregorio, and Lee 1998; Grossman and Helpman 1991a, 1991b).

Stimulation of domestic financial-sector development. It has already been noted that international portfolio flows can increase the liquidity of domestic stock markets. Increased foreign ownership of domestic banks can also generate a variety of other benefits (Levine 1996; Caprio and Honohan 1999). First, foreign bank participation can facilitate access to international financial markets. Second, it can help improve the regulatory and supervisory framework of the domestic banking industry. Third, foreign banks often introduce a variety of new financial instruments and techniques and also foster technological improvements in domestic markets. The entry of foreign banks tends to increase competition, which, in turn, can improve the quality of domestic financial services as well as allocative efficiency.

Indirect Channels

Promotion of specialization. The notion that specialization in production may increase productivity and growth is intuitive. However, without any mechanism for risk management, a highly specialized production structure will produce high output volatility and, hence, high consumption volatility. Concerns about exposure to such increases in volatility may discourage countries from taking up growth-enhancing specialization activities; the higher volatility will also generally imply lower overall savings and investment rates. In principle, financial globalization could play a useful role by helping countries to engage in international risk sharing and thereby reduce consumption volatility. This point will be taken up again in the next section. Here, it should just be noted that risk sharing would indirectly encourage specialization, which in turn would raise the growth rate. This logic is explained by Brainard and Cooper (1968), Kemp and Liviatan (1973), Ruffin (1974), and Imbs and Wacziarg (2003). Among developed countries and across regions within given developed countries, there is indeed some evidence that better risk sharing is associated with higher specialization (Kalemli-Ozcan, Sørensen, and Yosha 2001).

Commitment to better economic policies. International financial integration could increase productivity in an economy through its impact on the government's ability to credibly commit to a future course of policies. More specifically, the disciplining role of financial integration could change the dynamics of domestic investment in an economy to the extent that it leads to a reallocation of capital toward more productive activities in response to changes in macroeconomic policies. National governments are occasionally tempted to institute predatory tax policies on physical capital. The prospect of such policies tends to discourage investment and reduce growth. Financial opening can be self-sustaining and constrains the government from engaging in such predatory policies in the future since the negative consequences of such actions are far more severe under financial integration. Gourinchas and Jeanne (2003) illustrate this point in a theoretical model.

Signaling. A country's willingness to undertake financial integration could be interpreted as a signal that it is going to practice more friendly policies toward foreign investment in the future. Bartolini and Drazen (1997) suggest that the removal of restrictions on capital outflows can, through its signaling role, lead to an increase in capital inflows. Many countries, including Colombia, Egypt, Italy, New Zealand, Mexico, Spain, Uruguay, and the United Kingdom, have received significant capital inflows after removing restrictions on capital outflows.[16]

11.3.2   Empirical Evidence

On the surface, there seems to be a positive association between embracing financial globalization and the level of economic development. Industrial countries in general are more financially integrated with the global economy than developing countries. So embracing globalization is apparently part of being economically advanced.

Within the developing world, it is also the case that MFI economies grew faster than LFI economies over the last three decades. From 1970 to 1999, average output per capita rose almost threefold in the group of MFI developing economies, almost six times greater than the corresponding increase for LFI economies. This pattern of higher growth for the former group applies over each of the three decades and also extends to consumption and investment growth.

However, there are two problems with deducing a positive effect of financial integration on growth from this data pattern. First, this pattern may be fragile upon closer scrutiny. Second, these observations only reflect an association between international financial integration and economic performance rather than necessarily a causal relationship. In other words, these observations do not rule out the possibility that there is reverse cau-

16. See Mathieson and Rojas-Suarez (1993) and Labán and Larrain (1997).

sation: countries that manage to enjoy robust growth may also choose to engage in financial integration even if financial globalization does not directly contribute to faster growth in a quantitatively significant way.

To provide an intuitive impression of the relationship between financial openness and growth, table 11.2 presents a list of the fastest-growing developing economies during 1980–2000 and a list of the slowest-growing (or fastest-declining) economies during the same period. Some countries have undergone financial integration during this period, especially in the latter half of the 1990s.[17] Therefore, any result based on total changes over this long period should be interpreted with caution. Nonetheless, several features of the table are noteworthy.

An obvious observation that can be made from the table is that financial integration is *not a necessary condition* for achieving a high growth rate. China and India have achieved high growth rates despite somewhat limited and selective capital account liberalization. For example, while China became substantially more open to FDI, it was not particularly open to most other types of cross-border capital flows. Mauritius and Botswana have managed to achieve very strong growth rates during the period, although they are relatively closed to financial flows.

The second observation that can be made is that financial integration is *not a sufficient condition* for a fast economic growth rate either. For example, Jordan and Peru had become relatively open to foreign capital flows during the period, yet their economies suffered a decline rather than enjoying positive growth during the period. On the other hand, table 11.2 also suggests that declining economies are more likely to be financially closed, although the direction of causality is not clear, as explained before.

This way of looking at country cases with extreme growth performance is only informative up to a point; it needs to be supplemented by a comprehensive examination of the experience of a broader set of countries using a more systematic approach to measuring financial openness. To illustrate this relationship more broadly, figure 11.6 presents a scatter plot of the growth rate of real per capita GDP against the increase in financial integration over 1982–97. There is essentially no association between these variables. Figure 11.7 presents a scatter plot of these two variables after taking into account the effects of a country's initial income, initial schooling, average investment-GDP ratio, political instability, and regional location. Again, the figure does not suggest a positive association between financial integration and economic growth. In fact, this finding is not unique to the particular choice of the time period or the country coverage, as reflected in a broad survey of other research papers on the subject.

---

17. Table 11.2 reports the growth rates of real per capita GDP in constant local currency units. The exact growth rates and country rankings may change if different measures are used, such as per capita GDP in dollar terms or on a PPP basis.

Table 11.2   Fastest- and slowest-growing economies during 1980–2000 and their status of financial openness

	Fastest-growing economies	Total % change in per capita GDP	More financially integrated?	Slowest-growing economies	Total % change in per capita GDP	More financially integrated?
1	China	391.6	Yes/no	Haiti	−39.5	No
2	Korea	234.0	Yes	Niger	−37.8	No
3	Singapore	155.5	Yes	Nicaragua	−30.6	No
4	Thailand	151.1	Yes	Togo	−30.0	No
5	Mauritius	145.8	No	Côte d'Ivoire	−29.0	No
6	Botswana	135.4	No	Burundi	−20.2	No
7	Hong Kong SAR	114.5	Yes	Venezuela	−17.3	Yes/no
8	Malaysia	108.8	Yes	South Africa	−13.7	Yes
9	India	103.2	Yes/no	Jordan	−10.9	Yes
10	Chile	100.9	Yes	Paraguay	−9.5	No
11	Indonesia	97.6	Yes	Ecuador	−7.9	No
12	Sri Lanka	90.8	No	Peru	−7.8	Yes

Source: These calculations are based on the World Bank's World Development Indicators database.

Note: Growth rate of real per capita GDP, in constant local currency units.

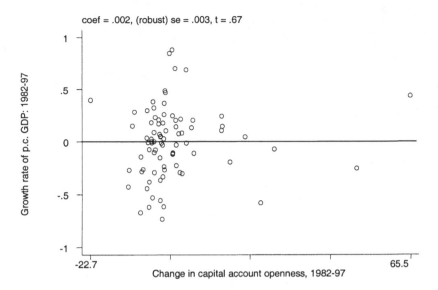

Fig. 11.6   Increase in financial openness and growth of real per capita GDP: Simple correlation, 1982–97

Source: Wei and Wu (2006).

Note: Capital account openness is measured as (gross private capital inflows + gross private capital outflows)/GDP.

A number of empirical studies have tried to systematically examine whether financial integration contributes to growth using various approaches to the difficult problem of proving causation. Table 11.3 summarizes the fourteen most recent studies on this subject.[18] Three out of the fourteen papers report a positive effect of financial integration on growth. However, the majority of the papers tend to find no effect or a mixed effect for developing countries. This suggests that, if financial integration has a positive effect on growth, it is probably not strong or robust.[19]

Of the papers summarized in table 11.3, the one by Edison, Levine, et al. (2002) is perhaps the most thorough and comprehensive in measures of financial integration and in empirical specifications. These authors measure a country's degree of financial integration both by the government's re-

18. This extends the survey in the October 2001 *World Economic Outlook* (IMF 2001) and Edison, Klein, et al. (2002).

19. As discussed in Prasad et al. (2004), there is some evidence that different types of capital flows may have different effects on growth (see appendix I in their paper for details). Recent research suggests that FDI flows are positively associated with domestic investment and output growth in a relatively consistent manner. For example, Bosworth and Collins (1999) find that although the impact of portfolio flows on investment growth is quite minor, there is a strong positive relationship between FDI flows and investment growth. In particular, their findings suggest that there exists an almost one-for-one relationship between FDI flows and domestic investment.

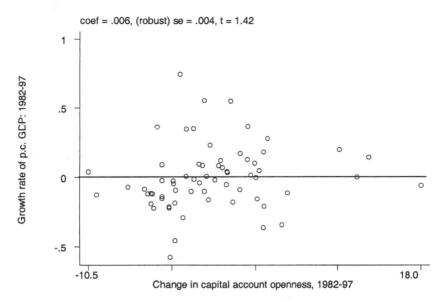

Fig. 11.7   Increase in financial openness and growth of real per capita GDP: Conditional relationship, 1982–97

Source: Wei and Wu (2006).

Notes: Increase is conditioning on initial income, initial schooling, average investment/GDP, political instability (revolution and coup), and regional dummies, 1982–97. Capital account openness is measured as (gross private capital flows + gross private capital outflows)/GDP.

Table 11.3   Summary of recent research on financial integration and economic growth

Study	Number of countries	Years covered	Effect on growth found
Alesina, Grilli, and Milesi-Ferretti (1994)	20	1950–89	No effect
Grilli and Milesi-Ferretti (1995)	61	1966–89	No effect
Quinn (1997)	58	1975–89	Positive
Kraay (1998)	117	1985–97	No effect/mixed
Rodrik (1998)	95	1975–89	No effect
Klein and Olivei (2000)	Up to 92	1986–95	Positive
Chanda (2001)	116	1976–95	Mixed
Arteta, Eichengreen, and Wyplosz (2001)	51–59	1973–92	Mixed
Bekaert, Harvey, and Lundblad (2001)	30	1981–97	Positive
Edwards (2001)	62	1980s	No effect for poor countries
O'Donnell (2001)	94	1971–94	No effect, or at best mixed
Reisen and Soto (2001)	44	1986–97	Mixed
Edison, Klein, et al. (2002)	Up to 89	1973–95	Mixed
Edison, Levine, et al. (2002)	57	1980–2000	No effect

strictions on capital account transactions as recorded in the IMF's Annual Report on Exchange Rate Arrangements and Exchange Restrictions (AREAER) and by the observed size of capital flows crossing the border, normalized by the size of the economy. The data set in that paper goes through 2000, the latest year analyzed in any existing study on this subject. Furthermore, the authors also employ a statistical methodology that allows them to deal with possible reverse causality—that is, the possibility that any observed association between financial integration and growth could result from the mechanism that faster-growing economies are also more likely to choose to liberalize their capital accounts. After a battery of statistical analyses, that paper concludes that, overall, there is no robustly significant effect of financial integration on economic growth.

11.3.3   Synthesis

Why is it so difficult to find a strong and robust effect of financial integration on economic growth for developing countries, when the theoretical basis for this result is apparently so strong? Perhaps there is some logic to this outcome after all. A number of researchers have now concluded that most of the differences in income per capita across countries stem not from differences in capital-labor ratios but from differences in total factor productivity, which, in turn, could be explained by soft factors or social infrastructure like governance, rule of law, and respect for property rights.[20] In this case, although financial integration may open the door for additional capital to come in from abroad, it is unlikely to offer a major boost to growth by itself. In fact, if domestic governance is sufficiently weak, financial integration could cause an exodus of domestic capital and, hence, lower the growth rate of an economy.

This logic can be illustrated using the results reported in Senhadji (2000). Over the period 1960 to 1994, the average growth rate of per capita output for the group of countries in sub-Saharan Africa was the lowest among regional groupings of developing countries. The difference in physical and human capital accumulation is only part of the story of why growth rates

---

20. See Hall and Jones (1999), Senhadji (2000), Acemoglu, Johnson, and Robinson (2001), Easterly and Levine (2001), and Rogoff (2002) on the role of productivity differences in explaining cross-country differences in income. Gourinchas and Jeanne's (2003) study is the only paper that has made a direct comparison between gains from international financial integration and those from a rise in productivity. In a calibrated model, they show that the welfare gain from perfect financial integration is roughly equivalent to a 1 percent permanent increase in consumption for the typical non-OECD economy. By contrast, a productivity increase of the order of magnitude experienced in postwar Korea yields a welfare benefit that is more than 100 times larger. The low gains from international financial integration come from the fact that less developed countries are on average not very far from their potential level of capital. Non-OECD countries are less developed not primarily because they are capital scarce but because productivity is constrained by quality of institutions, economic policies, and other factors.

differ across countries. The gap in total factor productivity is the major element in explaining the difference in the growth rates.

Another possible explanation for why it is difficult to detect a causal effect of financial integration on growth is the costly banking crises that some developing countries have experienced in the process of financial integration. The results in Kaminsky and Reinhart (1999) suggest that a flawed sequencing of domestic financial liberalization, when accompanied by capital account liberalization, increases the chance of domestic banking crises and/or exchange rate crises. These crises are often accompanied by output collapses. As a result, the benefits from financial integration may not be evident in the data.[21]

It is interesting to contrast the empirical literature on the effects of financial integration with that on the effects of trade integration. There is a large literature suggesting that openness to trade has a positive impact on growth (e.g., Sachs and Warner 1995; Frankel and Romer 1999; Dollar and Kraay 2002; and Wacziarg and Welch 2003), although some of the findings in this literature have been challenged by Rodriguez and Rodrik (2000), who raise questions about the measures of trade openness and the econometric methods employed in these studies. Nevertheless, an overwhelming majority of empirical papers employing various techniques, including country case studies as well as cross-country regressions, find that trade openness helps to promote economic growth. In a recent paper that surveys all the prominent empirical research on the subject, Berg and Krueger (2003) conclude that "varied evidence supports the view that trade openness contributes greatly to growth." Furthermore, "cross-country regressions of the level of income on various determinants generally show that openness is the most important policy variable."[22]

The differential effects between trade and financial integration are echoed in recent empirical research. As an alternative to examining the effect on economic growth or level of income, Wei and Wu (2006) examine the effects of trade and financial openness on a society's health status. In particular, they analyze the following questions: Do trade and financial openness help to raise life expectancy and reduce infant mortality in developing countries? Are their effects different?

There are three motivations for studying these questions. First, as life ex-

---

21. See Ishii et al. (2002) for country cases in this regard.

22. Baldwin (2003), Winters (2004), and Harrison and Tang (2006) also provide surveys of the literature on trade liberalization and economic growth. Winters (2004) concludes that "while there are serious methodological challenges and disagreements about the strength of the evidence, the most plausible conclusion is that liberalization generally induces a temporary (but possibly long-lived) increase in growth." Harrison and Tang (2006) argue that "while trade integration can strengthen an effective growth strategy, it cannot ensure its effectiveness. Other elements are needed, such as sound macroeconomic management, building trade-related infrastructure, and trade-related institutions, economy-wide investments in human capital and infrastructure, or building strong institutions."

pectancy and infant mortality are important dimensions of a society's well-being, they are interesting objects to look at in their own right. Second, data on income level or growth come from national accounts, so all studies on economic growth have to make use of variations of the similar data sources. In comparison, vital statistics come from an entirely different data source (i.e., birth and death records) and are typically collected by different government agencies. Therefore, they offer an independent and complementary check on the effect of openness on the livelihood of people. Third, to compare income levels or growth rates across countries, it is necessary to make certain purchasing power parity (PPP) adjustments to nominal income. However, existing PPP adjustments may not be reliable (Deaton 2001). In contrast, the definitions of life and death are consistent across countries, so there is a higher degree of comparability than in the data on poverty, income, or income distribution.

Wei and Wu (2006) examine data on seventy-nine developing countries over the period 1962–97. Their data set covers all developing countries for which the relevant data exist and for which changes in infant mortality and life expectancy are not dominated by large-scale wars, genocides, famines, or major outbursts of AIDS epidemics. They employ panel regressions with country fixed effects as well as dynamic panel regressions to account for other factors that may affect health and to account for possible endogeneity of the openness variables.

Their results suggest that the effects of trade and financial openness are different. There is no positive and robust association across developing countries between faster increase in financial integration and faster improvement in a society's health. By comparison, there are several pieces of evidence suggesting that higher trade integration is associated with a faster increase in life expectancy and a faster reduction in infant mortality. For example, an 11 percentage point reduction in the average statutory tariff rate—approximately equal to 1 standard deviation of the change in the statutory tariff rate over the 1962–97 period—is associated with between three and six fewer infants dying per thousand live births, even after controlling for the effects of changes in per capita income, average female education, and other factors. These findings suggest that, in the health dimension, as in the growth literature, it is harder to find a beneficial role for financial integration compared to trade integration for developing countries.[23]

In related research, Kose, Prasad, and Terrones (2006) analyze how trade and financial integration affect the relationship between growth and volatility. Running various regression models, first Ramey and Ramey

---

23. The contrast between financial and trade openness may have important lessons for policies. While there appear to be relatively few prerequisites for deriving benefits from trade openness, obtaining benefits from financial integration requires several conditions to be in place (this is discussed in more detail in Prasad et al. 2003, chap. 5).

(1995), then several other researchers (Martin and Rogers 2000; Fatas 2002; and Hnatkovska and Loayza 2005), document that volatility and growth are negatively correlated. The results by Kose, Prasad, and Terrones (2006) suggest that trade and financial integration weaken the negative growth-volatility relationship. Specifically, in regressions of growth on volatility and other control variables, they find that the estimated coefficients on interactions between volatility and trade integration are significantly positive. In other words, countries that are more open to trade appear to face a less severe trade-off between growth and volatility. The authors report a similar, although slightly less robust, result for the interaction of financial integration with volatility.

It is useful to note that there may be a complementary relationship between trade and financial openness.[24] For example, if a country has severe trade barriers protecting some inefficient domestic industries, then capital inflows may end up being directed to those industries, thereby exacerbating the existing misallocation of resources. Thus, there is a concrete channel through which financial openness without trade openness could *lower* a country's level of efficiency.

Of course, the lack of a strong and robust effect of financial integration on economic growth does not necessarily imply that theories that make this connection are wrong. One could argue that the theories are about the long-run effects, and most theories abstract from the nitty-gritty of institutional building, governance improvement, and other soft factors that are necessary ingredients for the hypothesized channels to take effect. Indeed, developing countries may have little choice but to strengthen their financial linkages eventually in order to improve their growth potential in the long run. The problem is how to manage the short-run risks apparently associated with financial globalization. Financial integration without a proper set of preconditions might lead to few growth benefits and more output and consumption volatility in the short run, a subject that is taken up in the next section.

Since growth and poverty reduction are intimately related, then the question of how financial globalization affects growth is closely linked to the question of how financial globalization affects poverty. The fact that the evidence on growth is indecisive almost surely implies that evidence on poverty reduction is as well. Recent research confirms this conclusion. For example, Easterly (chap. 3 in this volume) documents that neither financial nor trade flows have any significant impact on poverty. On the other hand, research by Dollar and Kraay (2002, 2004) suggests that increased trade flows could lead to higher economic growth, which in turn could reduce poverty. Kraay (2004) provides strong evidence for the importance of economic growth in poverty reduction, as his analysis shows that most of the

---

24. This point is stressed in the September 2002 *World Economic Outlook* (IMF 2002).

variation in changes in poverty during the 1980s and 1990s is explained by growth in average income in developing countries. Agénor (2003) finds that there is a nonlinear relationship between globalization and poverty. His empirical results indicate that although globalization could reduce poverty in countries with a higher degree of economic integration, it could have an adverse impact on the income levels of the poor in countries with a lower degree of integration.[25] This nonlinearity stems from the fact that globalization has a sizable impact on the quality of institutions only beyond a certain level of trade and financial integration, and institutions (including an efficient social safety net) play a major role in channeling the beneficial effects of globalization to the poor and shielding them from its costs.

Although there has been an intensive debate about the potentially adverse impact of globalization on income inequality, there is no clear empirical evidence that globalization has fostered a sharp rise in worldwide inequality. Several recent studies focus on the impact of globalization on income inequality across countries, but these studies have yet to provide a conclusive answer. For example, globalization could accentuate the already substantial inequality of national incomes and, in particular, lead to stagnation of incomes and living standards in countries that do not participate in this process. Consistent with this view, Quah (1997) has documented that there is evidence in cross-country data of a "twin peaks" phenomenon whereby per capita incomes converge within each of two groups of countries (advanced countries and globalizers) while average incomes continue to diverge across these two groups of countries. In other words, advanced countries and globalizers converge in terms of per capita incomes, and so do nonglobalizers, but these two groups diverge from each other in terms of their average incomes. Sala-i-Martin (2002), on the other hand, argues that a more careful analysis, using individuals rather than countries as the units of analysis, shows that global inequality has declined during the recent wave of globalization.

By the same token, if the institutional preconditions for financial globalization to benefit growth are in place, then it is likely that financial globalization will help to alleviate poverty as well.

11.4 Financial Globalization and Macroeconomic Volatility

International financial integration should, in principle, help countries to reduce macroeconomic volatility. The survey presented in this section, including some new evidence, suggests that developing countries, in particular, have not attained this potential benefit. The process of capital account liberalization has often been accompanied by increased vulnerability to crises.

---

25. Agénor (2003) uses a weighted average of trade and financial openness indicators as a measure of economic integration.

Globalization has heightened these risks, because financial linkages have the potential of amplifying the effects of both real and financial shocks.

Holding growth constant, higher macroeconomic volatility would normally be associated with an increase in inequality of income, and therefore measures of poverty based on inequality. If the growth benefits are large—as indeed they may well be, although the evidence is clearly very mixed—then of course increased financial integration may increase relative poverty measures in the short run while reducing absolute (but not necessarily relative) poverty measures in the longer run.[26]

11.4.1   Macroeconomic Volatility

One of the potential benefits of globalization is that it should provide better opportunities for reducing volatility by diversifying risks.[27] Indeed, these benefits are presumably even greater for developing countries, which are intrinsically subject to higher volatility because they are less diversified than industrial economies in their production structures. However, recent crises in some MFIs suggest that financial integration may in fact have increased volatility.

What is the overall evidence of the effect of globalization on macroeconomic volatility? In addressing this question, it is important to make a distinction between output and consumption volatility. In theoretical models, the direct effects of global integration on output volatility are ambiguous. Financial integration provides access to capital that can help capital-poor developing countries to diversify their production base. On the other hand, rising financial integration could also lead to increasing specialization of production based on comparative-advantage considerations, thereby making economies more vulnerable to shocks that are specific to industries (Razin and Rose 1994).

Irrespective of the effects on output volatility, theory suggests that financial integration should reduce consumption volatility. The ability to reduce fluctuations in consumption is regarded as an important determinant of economic welfare. Access to international financial markets provides better opportunities for countries to share macroeconomic risk and, thereby, smooth consumption. The basic idea here is that, since output fluctuations are not perfectly correlated across countries, trade in financial assets can be used to delink national consumption levels from the country-specific components of these output fluctuations (see Obstfeld and Rogoff 1998, chap. 5). In an earlier paper (Prasad et al. 2004) we provide a detailed analytical examination of this issue and show that the gains from consumption smoothing are potentially very large for developing economies (see appendix IV in that paper).

---

26. Mechanically, a rise in the volatility of consumption could lead to a decrease in the poverty head count. However, the increase in the volatility of consumption adversely affects the poor households' welfare.

27. This subsection draws heavily on Kose, Prasad, and Terrones (2003a).

Unlike the rich empirical literature focusing on the impact of financial openness on economic growth, there are only a limited number of studies analyzing the links between openness and macroeconomic volatility. Moreover, existing studies have generally been unable to document a clear empirical link between openness and macroeconomic volatility. Razin and Rose (1994) study the impact of trade and financial openness on the volatility of output, consumption, and investment for a sample of 138 countries over the period 1950–88. They find no significant empirical link between openness and the volatility of these variables.

Easterly, Islam, and Stiglitz (2001) explore the sources of output volatility using data for a sample of seventy-four countries over the period 1960–97. They find that a higher level of development of the domestic financial sector is associated with lower volatility. On the other hand, an increase in the degree of trade openness leads to an increase in the volatility of output, especially in developing countries. Their results indicate that neither financial openness nor the volatility of capital flows has a significant impact on output volatility.

Buch, Döpke, and Pierdzioch (2002) use data for twenty-five Organization for Economic Cooperation and Development (OECD) countries to examine the link between financial openness and output volatility. They report that there is no consistent empirical relationship between financial openness and the volatility of output. Gavin and Hausmann (1996) study the sources of output volatility in developing countries over the period 1970–92. They find that there is a significant positive association between the volatility of capital flows and output volatility. O'Donnell (2001) examines the effect of financial integration on the volatility of output growth over the period 1971–94 using data for ninety-three countries. He finds that a higher degree of financial integration is associated with lower (higher) output volatility in OECD (non-OECD) countries. His results also suggest that countries with more developed financial sectors are able to reduce output volatility through financial integration.

Bekaert, Harvey, and Lundblad (2006) examine the impact of equity market liberalization on the volatility of output and consumption during 1980–2000. They find that, following equity market liberalizations, there is a significant decline in both output and consumption volatility. Capital account openness reduces the volatility of output and consumption, but its impact is smaller than that of equity market liberalization. However, they also report that capital account openness increases the volatility of output and consumption in emerging market countries. The September 2002 *World Economic Outlook* (IMF 2002) provides some evidence indicating that financial openness is associated with lower output volatility in developing countries.

Since the existing literature has been quite limited and provided mostly inconclusive evidence, this paper now presents some new evidence about the impact of financial integration on macroeconomic volatility. Table 11.4 examines changes in volatility for different macroeconomic aggregates over the last four decades. Consistent with evidence presented in the

Table 11.4   Volatility of annual growth rates of selected variables (percentage standard deviations, medians for each group of countries)

	Full sample (1960–99)	1960s	1970s	1980s	1990s
A. Output (Y)					
Industrial countries	2.18	1.91	2.46	2.03	1.61
	(0.23)	(0.26)	(0.28)	(0.30)	(0.14)
MFI economies	3.84	3.31	3.22	4.05	3.59
	(0.20)	(0.42)	(0.37)	(0.44)	(0.62)
LFI economies	4.67	3.36	4.88	4.53	2.70
	(0.35)	(0.61)	(1.01)	(0.69)	(0.38)
B. Income (Q)					
Industrial countries	2.73	2.18	2.99	2.54	1.91
	(0.34)	(0.33)	(0.40)	(0.29)	(0.30)
MFI economies	5.44	3.60	5.43	5.45	4.78
	(0.50)	(0.47)	(0.45)	(0.65)	(0.72)
LFI economies	7.25	4.42	9.64	7.56	4.59
	(0.84)	(0.53)	(1.24)	(1.23)	(0.54)
C. Consumption (C)					
Industrial countries	2.37	1.47	2.16	1.98	1.72
	(0.30)	(0.27)	(0.25)	(0.28)	(0.20)
MFI economies	5.18	4.57	4.52	4.09	4.66
	(0.51)	(0.49)	(1.04)	(0.94)	(0.46)
LFI economies	6.61	5.36	7.07	7.25	5.72
	(0.78)	(0.58)	(0.11)	(0.81)	(0.78)
D. Total consumption (C + G)					
Industrial countries	1.86	1.38	1.84	1.58	1.38
	(0.23)	(0.28)	(0.18)	(0.19)	(0.20)
MFI economies	4.34	3.95	4.19	3.43	4.10
	(0.47)	(0.51)	(0.54)	(0.84)	(0.53)
LFI economies	6.40	4.85	6.50	6.34	4.79
	(0.56)	(0.55)	(0.93)	(0.91)	(0.82)
E. Ratio of total consumption (C + G) to income (Q)					
Industrial countries	0.67	0.75	0.56	0.61	0.58
	(0.02)	(0.09)	(0.03)	(0.06)	(0.06)
MFI economies	0.81	0.92	0.74	0.76	0.92
	(0.07)	(0.13)	(0.12)	(0.11)	(0.04)
LFI economies	0.80	0.95	0.68	0.82	0.84
	(0.08)	(0.06)	(0.10)	(0.51)	(0.14)

Notes: In panel E, the ratio of total consumption growth volatility to that of income growth volatility is first computed separately for each country. The reported numbers are the within-group medians of those ratios. (Note that this is not the same as the ratio of the median of consumption growth volatility to the median of income growth volatility.) Standard errors are reported in parentheses.

September 2002 *World Economic Outlook* (IMF 2002), MFI economies on average have lower output volatility than LFI economies. Interestingly, there is a significant decline in average output volatility in the 1990s for both industrial and LFI economies but a far more modest decline for MFI economies. The picture is similar for a broader measure of income that includes factor income flows and terms-of-trade effects, which are particularly important for developing countries. Figure 11.8 (panel A), which shows the evolution of the average volatility of income growth for different groups of countries, confirms these results and shows that they are not sensitive to the decade-wise breakdown of the data, although there is a pickup in volatility for MFIs toward the end of the sample.[28]

Panel C of table 11.4 shows that average consumption volatility in the 1990s has declined in line with output volatility for both industrial economies and LFI economies. By contrast, for MFI economies, the volatility of private consumption has in fact risen in the 1990s relative to the 1980s for MFI economies. It is possible that looking at the volatility of private consumption is misleading, because public consumption could be playing an important smoothing role, especially in developing economies. It is true, as shown in panel D of table 11.4, that total consumption is generally less volatile than private consumption. However, these results confirm the pattern that, on average, consumption volatility for industrial and LFI economies declined in the 1990s. By contrast, it increases for MFI economies over the same period. Figure 11.8 (panel B), which shows the evolution of the average volatility of total consumption growth over a ten-year rolling window, yields a similar picture. Could this simply be a consequence of higher income volatility for MFI economies?

Strikingly, for the group of MFI countries, the volatility of total consumption relative to that of income has actually increased in the 1990s relative to earlier periods. Panel E of table 11.4 shows the median ratio of the volatility of total consumption growth to that of income growth for each group of countries. For MFI economies, this ratio increases from 0.76 in the 1980s to 0.92 in the 1990s, while it remains essentially unchanged for the other two groups of countries. Thus, the increase in the 1990s in the volatility of consumption relative to that of income for the MFI economies suggests that financial integration has not provided better consumption-smoothing opportunities for these economies.[29]

More formal econometric evidence is presented by Kose, Prasad, and Terrones (2003a), who use measures of capital account restrictions as well

---

28. The figure shows the median standard deviation of income growth for each country group, based on standard deviations calculated for each country over a ten-year rolling window.

29. It should be noted that, despite the increase in the 1990s, the volatility of both private and total consumption for the MFI economies is, on average, still lower than for LFI economies.

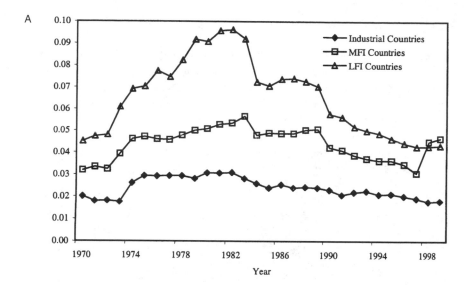

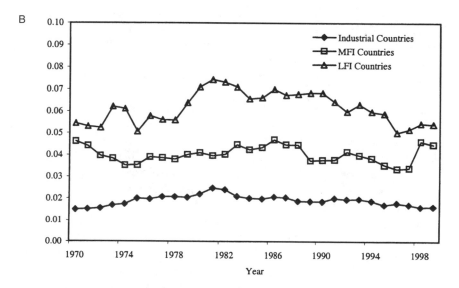

Fig. 11.8   Volatility of income and consumption growth (ten-year rolling standard deviations; medians for each group of countries); *A*, income; *B*, total consumption
Source: Kose, Prasad, and Terrones (2003a).

as gross financial flows to capture different aspects of financial integration, as well as differences in the degree of integration across countries and over time. This analysis confirms the increase in the relative volatility of consumption for countries that have larger financial flows, even after controlling for macroeconomic variables as well as country characteristics such as trade openness and industrial structure. However, these authors also identify an important threshold effect—beyond a particular level, financial integration significantly reduces volatility. Most developing economies, including MFI economies, are unfortunately well below this threshold.[30]

Why has the relative volatility of consumption increased precisely in those developing countries that are more open to financial flows? One explanation is that positive productivity and output growth shocks during the late 1980s and early 1990s in these countries led to consumption booms that were willingly financed by international investors. These consumption booms were accentuated by the fact that many of these countries undertook domestic financial liberalization at the same time that they opened up to international financial flows, thereby loosening liquidity constraints at both the individual and the national level. When negative shocks hit these economies, however, they rapidly lost access to international capital markets. For the financial integration measure used in this paper, the threshold occurs at a ratio of about 50 percent of GDP. The countries in the sample that have a degree of financial integration above this threshold are all industrial countries.

Consistent with this explanation, a growing literature suggests that the procyclical nature of capital flows appears to have had an adverse impact on consumption volatility in developing economies.[31] One manifestation of this procyclicality is the phenomenon of "sudden stops" of capital inflows (see Calvo and Reinhart 1999). More generally, access to international capital markets has a procyclical element, which tends to generate higher output volatility as well as excess consumption volatility (relative to that of income). Reinhart (2002), for instance, finds that sovereign bond ratings are procyclical. Since the spreads on bonds of developing economies are strongly influenced by these ratings, this implies that the costs of borrowing on international markets are procyclical as well. Kaminsky and Reinhart (2002) present more direct evidence on the procyclical behavior of capital inflows.[32]

30. For the financial integration measure used in this paper, the threshold occurs at a ratio of about 50 percent of GDP. The countries in the sample that have a degree of financial integration above this threshold are all industrial countries.

31. The notion of procyclicality here is that capital inflows are positively correlated with domestic business cycle conditions in these countries.

32. The World Bank's (2001) *Global Development Finance* report also finds some evidence of such procyclicality and notes that the response of capital inflows is typically twice as large when a developing country faces an adverse shock to GDP growth as when it faces a favorable shock. This is attributed to the fact that credit ratings are downgraded more rapidly during adverse shocks than they are upgraded during favorable ones.

11.4.2   Crises as Special Cases of Volatility

Crises can be regarded as particularly dramatic episodes of volatility. In fact, the proliferation of financial crises is often viewed as one of the defining aspects of the intensification of financial globalization over the last two decades. Furthermore, the fact that recent crises have affected mainly MFI economies has led to these phenomena being regarded as hallmarks of the unequal distribution of globalization's benefits and risks. This raises a challenging set of questions about whether the nature of crises has changed over time, what factors increase vulnerability to crises, and whether such crises are an inevitable concomitant of globalization.

Some aspects of financial crises have indeed changed over time, while in other respects it is often déjà vu all over again. Calvo (1998) has referred to such episodes in the latter half of the 1980s and 1990s as capital account crises, while earlier ones are referred to as current account crises. Although this suggests differences in the mechanics of crises, it does not necessarily imply differences in some of their fundamental causes. Kaminsky and Reinhart (1999) discuss the phenomenon of "twin crises," which involve balance-of-payments and banking crises. These authors also make the important point that, in the episodes that they analyze, banking-sector problems typically precede a currency crisis, which then deepens the banking crisis, activating a vicious spiral. In this vein, Krueger and Yoo (2002) conclude that imprudent lending by the Korean banks in the early and mid-1990s, especially to the chaebols, played a significant role in the 1997 Korean currency crisis. Opening up to capital markets can thus exacerbate such existing domestic distortions and lead to catastrophic consequences (Aizenman 2002).

One key difference in the evolution of crises is that, while the 1970s and 1980s featured crises that affected both industrial and developing economies, these have become almost exclusively the preserve of developing economies since the mid-1990s.[33] This suggests either that advanced economies have been able to better protect themselves through improved policies or that the fundamental causes of crises have changed over time, thereby increasing the relative vulnerability of developing economies. In this context, it should be noted that, while capital flows from advanced economies to MFI economies have increased sharply, these flows among industrial economies have jumped even more sharply in recent years, as noted earlier. Thus, at least in terms of volume of capital flows, it is not obvious that changes in financial integration can by themselves be blamed for crises in MFI economies.

Is it reasonable to accept crises as a natural feature of globalization,

---

33. In fact, in the 1990s, the exchange rate mechanism (ERM) crisis is the only significant one among industrial countries. The prolonged Japanese recession is in some sense a crisis, although the protracted nature of Japan's decline, which has not featured any sudden falls in output, would not fit the standard definition of a crisis.

much as business cycles are viewed as a natural occurrence in market economies? One key difference between these phenomena is that the overall macroeconomic costs of financial crises are typically very large and far more persistent. Calvo and Reinhart (2000, 2002) document that emerging-market currency crises, which are typically accompanied by sudden stops or reversals of external capital inflows, are associated with significant negative output effects.[34] Such recessions following devaluations (or large depreciations) are also found to be much deeper in emerging markets than in developed economies. In addition, the absence of well-functioning safety nets can greatly exacerbate the social costs of crises, which typically have large distributional consequences (see, e.g., Baldacci, de Mello, and Inchauste 2002).[35]

What is the impact on poverty of macroeconomic volatility associated with greater openness to trade and financial flows? Mechanically, an increase in the volatility of consumption could lead to a decrease in the poverty head count. However, the increase in the volatility of consumption adversely affects the poor households' welfare. Recent research examines various implications of macroeconomic volatility and financial crises on the dynamics of consumption and poverty in developing countries. For example, Duygan (2004) documents that household expenditure decreased by 5 percent on average during financial crises in sixteen developing countries. Some recent studies focus on the permanent impact of temporary negative income shocks on poverty. For example, Lustig (2000) concludes that crises in Latin America adversely affected the human capital of the poor and have had a permanent impact on poverty and inequality by diminishing the potential of the poor to escape poverty. Agénor (2002a) studies the asymmetric effects of macroeconomic fluctuations and crises on poverty. He finds that while the effects of shocks to income on poverty are quite small during periods of crisis, these shocks could decrease poverty during expansions.[36]

---

34. Currency crises can also affect firms directly and, by exacerbating the problems of the banking sector, can lead to a broader credit crunch, even for productive and solvent firms. Mishkin (1999) argues that the credit crunch resulting from sharp contractions in domestic bank credit following financial crises has been instrumental in aggravating these crises and reducing investment and economic activity. Rodrik and Velasco (2000) note that difficulties in rolling over short-term debt during crisis episodes rapidly squeeze the availability of liquidity, with immediate effects on investment and output.

35. Work by Wei and Wu (2001) using Chinese regional data shows that increases in trade openness are negatively associated with changes in inequality. However, the process of financial and trade liberalization can sometimes have negative distributional consequences within a country, especially in the short run. Attempts to address these issues using ad hoc redistributive measures can often result in distortions that adversely affect long-term growth. Nevertheless, given the vital need to maintain sociopolitical stability while undertaking significant reforms and liberalization, there is a need for judicious design and use of social safety nets to protect the economically vulnerable segments of the population.

36. Recent research also studies the adverse impact of macroeconomic volatility on food security and hunger (see Barrett and Sahn 2001).

11.4.3   Has Financial Globalization Intensified
the Transmission of Volatility?

What factors have led to the rising vulnerability of developing economies to financial crises? The risk of sudden stops or reversals of global capital flows to developing countries has increased in importance as many developing countries now rely heavily on borrowing from foreign banks or portfolio investment by foreign investors. These capital flows are sensitive not just to domestic conditions in the recipient countries but also to macroeconomic conditions in industrial countries. For instance, Mody and Taylor (2002), using an explicit disequilibrium econometric framework, detect instances of "international capital crunch"—where capital flows to developing countries are curtailed by supply-side rationing that reflects industrial-country conditions.[37] These North-South financial linkages, in addition to the real linkages described in earlier sections, represent an additional channel through which business cycles and other shocks that hit industrial countries can affect developing countries.

The effects of industrial-country macroeconomic conditions, including the stage of the business cycle and interest rates, have different effects on various types of capital flows to emerging markets. Reinhart and Reinhart (2001) document that net FDI flows to emerging-market economies are strongly positively correlated with U.S. business cycles. On the other hand, bank lending to these economies is negatively correlated with U.S. cycles. Edison and Warnock (2001) find that portfolio equity flows from the United States to major emerging-market countries are negatively correlated with both U.S. interest rates and U.S. output growth. This result is particularly strong for flows to Latin America and less so for flows to Asia. Thus, the sources of capital inflow for a particular MFI can greatly affect the nature of its vulnerability to the volatility of capital flows arising from industrial-country disturbances.[38]

The increase in cross-country financial market correlations also indicates a risk that emerging markets will be caught up in financial market bubbles. The rise in comovement across emerging- and industrial-country stock markets, especially during the stock market bubble period of the late 1990s, points to the relevance of this concern. This is a particular risk for the relatively shallow and undiversified stock markets of some emerging economies. For instance, as noted earlier, the strong correlations between emerging and industrial stock markets during the bubble period reflects the

37. This paper examines bond, equity, and syndicated loan flows to Brazil, Mexico, Korea, and Thailand over the period 1990–2000.

38. However, notwithstanding the differences in the types of sensitivities to industrial-country business cycle conditions, the fact still remains that FDI flows are generally less volatile and less sensitive to the factors discussed here than either portfolio flows or bank lending.

preponderance of technology and telecommunication-sector stocks in the former set of markets. It is, of course, difficult to say conclusively whether this phenomenon would have occurred even in the absence of financial globalization, since stock market liberalizations in these countries often went hand in hand with their opening up to capital flows.

The increasing depth of stock markets in emerging economies could alleviate some of these risks but, at the same time, could heighten the real effects of such financial shocks. In this vein, Dellas and Hess (2002) find that a higher degree of financial development makes emerging stock markets more susceptible to external influences (both financial and macroeconomic) and that this effect remains important after controlling for capital controls and trade linkages.[39] Consequently, the effects of external shocks could be transmitted to domestic real activity through the stock market channel.

Even the effects of real shocks are often transmitted faster and amplified through financial channels. There is a large literature showing how productivity, terms-of-trade, fiscal, and other real shocks are transmitted through trade channels.[40] Cross-country investment flows, in particular, have traditionally responded quite strongly to country-specific shocks.[41] Financial channels constitute an additional avenue through which the effects of such real shocks can be transmitted. Furthermore, since transmission through financial channels is much quicker than through real channels, both the speed and the magnitude of international spillovers of real shocks are considerably heightened by financial linkages.[42]

Rising financial linkages have also resulted in contagion effects. Potential contagion effects are likely to become more important over time as financial linkages increase and investors in search of higher returns and better diversification opportunities increase their share of international holdings and, due to declines in information and transaction costs, have access to a broader array of cross-country investment opportunities.[43]

There are two broad types of contagion identified in the literature—

39. These authors use standard measures of financial-sector development that are based on the competitive structure and the size of the financial intermediation sector in each country.

40. See Kouparitsas (1996); Blankenau, Kose, and Yi (2001); Kose and Riezman (2001); and Kose (2002).

41. See Glick and Rogoff (1995) for an empirical analysis of how country-specific productivity shocks affect national investment and the current account. These authors show how the responses to such shocks depend crucially on the persistence of the shocks. Kose, Otrok, and Whiteman (2003) examine the impact of world and country-specific factors in driving fluctuations in output, consumption, and investment.

42. For instance, a shock to GDP growth in one country may be transmitted gradually through trade channels but could far more quickly have an impact on economic activity in another country via correlations in stock market fluctuations. If the two countries were perfectly integrated through trade and financial linkages this outcome could, of course, simply reflect an optimal risk-sharing arrangement.

43. Contagion effects aside, Kose, Prasad, and Terrones (2003b) find that increasing financial linkages have only a small effect on cross-country output and consumption correlations.

fundamentals-based contagion and pure contagion. The former refers to the transmission of shocks across national borders through real or financial linkages. In other words, while an economy may have weak fundamentals, it could get tipped over into a financial crisis as a consequence of investors' reassessing the riskiness of investments in that country or attempting to rebalance their portfolios following a crisis in another country. Similarly, bank lending can lead to such contagion effects when a crisis in one country to which a bank has significant exposure forces it to rebalance its portfolio by readjusting its lending to other countries. This bank transmission channel, documented in van Rijckeghem and Weder (2000) and Kaminsky and Reinhart (2001), can be particularly potent since a large fraction of bank lending to emerging markets is in the form of short-maturity loans. While fundamentals-based contagion was once prevalent mainly at the regional level, the Russian crisis demonstrated its much broader international reach (Kaminsky and Reinhart 2002).[44]

Pure contagion, on the other hand, represents a different kind of risk since it can not easily be influenced by domestic policies, at least in the short run. There is a good deal of evidence of sharp swings in international capital flows that are not obviously related to changes in fundamentals. Investor behavior during these episodes, which is sometimes categorized as herding or momentum trading, is difficult to explain in the context of optimizing models with full and common information. Informational asymmetries, which are particularly rife in the context of emerging markets, appear to play an important role in this phenomenon. A related literature suggests that pure contagion may reflect investors' shifting appetite for risk, but it is no doubt difficult to disentangle such changes in risk appetite from shifts in underlying risks themselves (Kumar and Persaud 2001). Thus, in addition to pure contagion, financial integration exposes developing economies to the risks associated with destabilizing investor behavior that is not related to fundamentals.[45]

11.4.4 Some Factors That Increase Vulnerability to the Risks of Globalization

Empirical research indicates that the composition of capital inflows and the maturity structure of external debt appear to be associated with higher vulnerability to the risks of financial globalization. The relative impor-

---

44. Kim, Kose, and Plummer (2001) examine the roles of fundamentals-based contagion and pure contagion during the Asian crisis.

45. The paper by Claessens and Forbes (2001) contains a compilation of essays on the different dimensions of contagion effects. Boyer, Gibson, and Loretan (1999) and Forbes and Rigobon (2001) argue that the evidence for pure contagion against the alternative of fundamentals-based contagion is very weak. Corsetti, Pericoli, and Sbracia (2002) argue that, under more general assumptions, there is greater evidence of the former type of contagion. Bayoumi and others (2003) find evidence of "positive" contagion related with herding behavior of capital inflows to emerging markets.

tance of different sources of financing for domestic investment, as proxied by the following three variables, has been shown to be positively associated with the incidence and the severity of currency and financial crises: the ratio of bank borrowing or other debt to FDI, the shortness of the term structure of external debt, and the share of external debt denominated in foreign currencies.[46] Detragiache and Spilimbergo (2002) find strong evidence that debt crises are more likely to occur in countries where external debt has a short maturity.[47] However, the maturity structure may not entirely be a matter of choice since, as argued by these authors, countries with weaker macroeconomic fundamentals are often forced to borrow at shorter maturities since they do not have access to longer-maturity loans.

In addition to basic macroeconomic policies, other policy choices of a systemic nature can also affect the vulnerability of MFIs. Recent currency crises have highlighted one of the main risks in this context. Developing countries that attempt to maintain a relatively inflexible exchange rate system often face the risk of attacks on their currencies. While various forms of fully or partially fixed exchange rate regimes can have some advantages, the absence of supportive domestic policies can often result in an abrupt unraveling of these regimes when adverse shocks hit the economy.

Financial integration can also aggravate the risks associated with imprudent fiscal policies. Access to world capital markets could lead to excessive borrowing that is channeled into unproductive government spending. The existence of large amounts of short-term debt denominated in hard currencies then makes countries vulnerable to external shocks or changes in investor sentiment. The experience of a number of MFI countries that have suffered the consequences of such external debt accumulation points to the heightened risks of undisciplined fiscal policies when the capital account is open.

Premature opening of the capital account also poses serious risks when financial regulation and supervision are inadequate.[48] In the presence of weakly regulated banking systems and other distortions in domestic capital markets, inflows of foreign capital could exacerbate the existing inefficiencies in these economies. For example, if domestic financial institutions tend to channel capital to firms with excessive risks or weak fundamentals, financial integration could simply lead to an intensification of such flows.[49]

---

46. See, for example, Frankel and Rose (1996), Radelet and Sachs (1998), and Rodrik and Velasco (2000).

47. Some authors have found that the currency composition of external debt also matters. Carlson and Hernandez (2002) note that, during the Asian crisis, countries with more yen-denominated debt fared significantly worse. These authors attribute this to the misalignment between the countries' de facto currency pegs and the denomination of their debt.

48. See Ishii et al. (2002) and Bakker and Chapple (2002).

49. Krueger and Yoo (2002) discuss the interactions of crony capitalism and capital account liberalization in setting the stage for the currency-financial crisis in Korea. See also Mody (2002).

In turn, the effects of premature capital inflows on the balance sheets of the government and corporate sectors could have negative repercussions on the health of financial institutions in the event of adverse macroeconomic shocks.

11.5 Conclusions

The empirical evidence has not established definitive proof that financial integration has enhanced growth for developing countries. Furthermore, it may be associated with higher consumption volatility. Therefore, it may be valuable for developing countries to experiment with different paces and strategies in pursuing financial integration. Empirical evidence does suggest that improving governance, in addition to sound macroeconomic frameworks and the development of domestic financial markets, should be an important element of such strategies. This conclusion does not necessarily imply that a country must develop a full set of sound institutions matching the best practices in the world before embarking on financial integration. As we emphasized in Prasad et al. (2003, chap. 5), as a country makes progress in transparency, control of corruption, rule of law, and financial supervisory capacity, it will be in an increasingly better position to benefit from financial globalization.

Equally important is to avoid some of the recurrent traps that countries have fallen into as they have moved to liberalize domestic financial markets and engineer increased financial globalization. If, as appears to be the case, overly fixed exchange rates are a leading determinant of financial crises in emerging markets, then moving to more flexible exchange rate regimes should greatly improve a country's chances of being a winner from financial globalization even in the short term. Likewise, assuming a large external debt burden, especially if it is of a relatively short maturity structure, can be a damaging way to undertake financial integration.

It is also important to stress that financial integration is not necessarily a variable that can be tightly controlled by policy. Capital controls, aside from coming in myriads of forms with effects that are difficult to manage, are often ineffective. Even in countries where they are relatively more effective, such controls tend to become less so over time as the rising sophistication of international capital markets and investors, along with the global expansion of trade, increases the opportunities for evading capital controls. Some of the most consistently financially integrated countries based on our de facto measure—including, for example, many Latin American countries—have often been ones where capital controls are quite stringent, at least on paper. On the other hand, many countries in Africa offer unimpeded capital market access but have not yet succeeded in achieving a significant degree of integration.

Given that we have not been able to draw strong conclusions about the empirical links between financial globalization, growth, and macroeconomic volatility, one must conclude that there will almost surely be similar ambiguity in an investigation of the links between financial globalization and poverty, although we have not directly examined those links in this paper. Of course, in such an exercise one would ideally like to look at a broader range of human development indicators and measures of poverty than just income (for example, even in some countries such as Brazil that have experienced relatively slow income growth over the past fifteen years, educational attainment levels have continued to rise).[50]

In addition, to provide a comprehensive analysis of the complex relationship between globalization and poverty, one has to acknowledge that poverty is fundamentally a relative measure, which will probably gain an entirely different meaning as the world economy becomes more integrated (Rogoff 2004). For example, if global growth continues at a rapid pace during the next century, it is possible that by the end of the century emerging-market economies, including China and India, could attain income levels exceeding those of Americans today. This implies that Malthusian notions of poverty are likely to become a distant memory in most parts of the world as global income inexorably expands over the next century, and issues of inequality, rather than subsistence, will increasingly take center stage in the poverty debate.

However, our findings support the importance of employing various complementary policies to increase the benefits of globalization for the poor, as discussed in several other chapters of this volume. In particular, policies encouraging labor mobility, improving access to credit and technical know-how, and establishing social safety nets seem to increase the benefits of increased financial and trade integration for the poor. As discussed in other chapters of this volume, these policies are well defined in the case of trade liberalization. For example, trade liberalization could lead to contraction in some previously protected industries. Policies that could help workers move from such sectors to expanding ones could diminish the adverse effects on the poor in the short run while also contributing to poverty reduction in the long run.

The results that we have highlighted in this paper provide a framework to examine the different channels through which the forces of financial globalization could affect poverty and inequality outcomes. A great deal of additional work is clearly called for to gain a better understanding of these dimensions of the effects of financial globalization.

---

50. Ravallion (2003) argues that differences in the concept and definitions of poverty could lead to different conclusions about the impact of globalization on poverty and inequality.

Appendix

Data Sources

Unless indicated otherwise, the primary sources for the data used in this paper are the IMF's *International Financial Statistics* and the World Bank's World Development Indicators database. The basic data sample comprises seventy-six countries: twenty-one industrial and fifty-five developing.[51]

Industrial countries

Australia (AUS), Austria (AUT), Belgium (BEL), Canada (CAN), Denmark (DNK), Finland (FIN), France (FRA), Germany (DEU), Greece (GRC), Ireland (IRL), Italy (ITA), Japan (JPN), the Netherlands (NLD), New Zealand (NZL), Norway (NOR), Portugal (PRT), Spain (ESP), Sweden (SWE), Switzerland (CHE), the United Kingdom (GBR), and the United States (USA).

Developing countries

These are grouped into MFI countries (numbering twenty-two) and LFI countries (thirty-three) countries.

MFIs

Argentina (ARG), Brazil (BRA), Chile (CHL), China (CHN), Colombia (COL), Egypt (EGY), Hong Kong (HKG), India (IND), Indonesia (IDN), Israel (ISR), Korea (KOR), Malaysia (MYS), Mexico (MEX), Morocco (MAR), Pakistan (PAK), Peru (PER), the Philippines (PHL), Singapore (SGP), South Africa (ZAF), Thailand (THA), Turkey (TUR), and Venezuela (VEN).

LFIs

Algeria (DZA), Bangladesh (BGD), Benin (GEN), Bolivia (BOL), Botswana (BWA), Burkina Faso (BFA), Burundi (BDI), Cameroon (CMR), Costa Rica (CRI), Côte d'Ivoire (CIV), the Dominican Republic (DOM), Ecuador (ECU), El Salvador (SLV), Gabon (GAB), Ghana (GHA), Guatemala (GTM), Haiti (HTI), Honduras (HND), Jamaica (JAM), Kenya (KEN), Mauritius (MUS), Nicaragua (NIC), Niger (NER), Nigeria (NGA), Panama (PAN), Papua New Guinea (PNG), Paraguay

---

51. The following were excluded from the analysis: small countries (those with population below 1 million), transition economies, some oil producers, and other countries with incomplete or clearly unreliable data.

(PRY), Senegal (SEN), Sri Lanka (LKA), Syrian Arab Republic (SYR), Togo (TGO), Tunisia (TUN), and Uruguay (URY).

References

Acemoglu, Daron, Simon Johnson, and James A. Robinson. 2001. Reversal of fortune: Geography and institutions in the making of the modern world income distribution. MIT Working Paper no. 01/38. Cambridge, MA: MIT, Department of Economics.

Agénor, Pierre-Richard. 2002a. Business cycles, economic crises, and the poor: Testing for asymmetric effects. *Journal of Policy Reform* 5:145–60.

———. 2002b. Macroeconomic adjustment and the poor: Analytical issues and cross-country evidence. World Bank Working Paper no. 2788. Washington, DC: World Bank.

———. 2003. Does globalization hurt the poor? World Bank Working Paper. Washington, DC: World Bank.

Aizenman, Joshua. 2002. Volatility, employment, and the patterns of FDI in emerging markets. NBER Working Paper no. 9397. Cambridge, MA: National Bureau of Economic Research, December.

Aizenman, Joshua, and Brian Pinto. 2005. *Managing economic volatility and crises: A practitioner's guide.* New York: Cambridge University Press.

Alesina, Alberto, Vittorio Grilli, and Gian Maria Milesi-Ferretti. 1994. The political economy of capital controls. In *Capital mobility: The impact on consumption, investment, and growth,* ed. Leonardo Leiderman and Assaf Razin, 289–321. Cambridge: Cambridge University Press.

Arteta, Carlos, Barry Eichengreen, and Charles Wyplosz. 2001. On the growth effects of capital account liberalization. University of California, Berkeley, Department of Economics. Working Paper.

Bakker, Bas, and Bryan Chapple. 2002. Advanced country experiences with capital account liberalization. IMF Occasional Paper no. 214. Washington, DC: International Monetary Fund.

Baldacci, Emanuele, Luiz de Mello, and Gabriela Inchauste. 2002. Financial crises, poverty, and income distribution. *Finance and Development* 39 (2): 24–27.

Baldwin, Richard. 2003. Openness and growth: What is the empirical relationship? NBER Working Paper no. 9578. Cambridge, MA: National Bureau of Economic Research.

Barrett, Christopher B., and David E. Sahn. 2001. Food policy in crisis management. Cornell University, Department of Economics. Working Paper.

Bartolini, Leonardo, and Allan Drazen. 1997. Capital-account liberalization as a signal. *American Economic Review* 87 (1): 138–54.

Bayoumi, Tamim, Giorgio Fazio, Manmohan Kumar, and Ronald MacDonald. 2003. Fatal attraction: Using distance to measure contagion in good times as well as bad. IMF Working Paper. Washington, DC: International Monetary Fund.

Bekaert, Geert, Campbell R. Harvey, and Christian Lundblad. 2001. Does financial liberalization spur growth? NBER Working Paper no. 8245. Cambridge, MA: National Bureau of Economic Research.

———. 2006. Growth volatility and equity market liberalization. *Journal of International Money and Finance,* forthcoming.

Berg, Andrew, and Anne O. Krueger. 2003. Trade, growth, and poverty: A selective

survey. IMF Working Paper no. 03/30. Washington, DC: International Monetary Fund.

Blankenau, William, M. Ayhan Kose, and Kei-Mu Yi. 2001. Can world real interest rates explain business cycles in a small open economy? *Journal of Economic Dynamics and Control* 25:867–89.

Bordo, Michael, and Barry Eichengreen. 2002. Crises now and then: What lessons from the last era of financial globalization. NBER Working Paper no. 8716. Cambridge, MA: National Bureau of Economic Research.

Borensztein, Eduardo, José De Gregorio, and Jong-Wha Lee. 1998. How does foreign direct investment affect growth? *Journal of International Economics* 45 (June): 115–35.

Bosworth, Barry, and Susan Collins. 1999. Capital flows to developing economies: Implications for saving and investment. *Brookings Papers on Economic Activity,* Issue no. 1:143–69.

Boyer, Brian H., Michael S. Gibson, and Mico Loretan. 1999. Pitfalls in tests for changes in correlations. International Finance Discussion Paper no. 597R. Washington, DC: Federal Reserve Board.

Brainard, William C., and Richard N. Cooper. 1968. Uncertainty and diversification of international trade. *Food Research Institute Studies in Agricultural Economics, Trade, and Development* 8:257–85.

Buch, Claudia M., Jörg Döpke, and Christian Pierdzioch. 2002. Financial openness and business cycle volatility. Kiel, Germany: Kiel Institute for World Economics. Working Paper.

Calvo, Guillermo. 1998. Varieties of capital-market crises. In *The debt burden and its consequences for monetary policy,* ed. G. Calvo and M. King, 181–202. London: Macmillan.

Calvo, Guillermo, Leonardo Leiderman, and Carmen Reinhart. 1993. Capital inflows and real exchange rate appreciation in Latin America: The role of external factors. *IMF Staff Papers* 40 (March): 108–51.

Calvo, Guillermo, and Carmen M. Reinhart. 1999. Capital flow reversals, the exchange rate debate, and dollarization. *Finance and Development* 36 (September): 13–15.

———. 2000. When capital inflows come to a sudden stop: Consequences and policy options. In *Reforming the international monetary and financial system,* ed. P. Kenen and A. Swoboda, 175–201. Washington, DC: International Monetary Fund.

———. 2002. Fear of floating. *Quarterly Journal of Economics* 117 (2): 379–408.

Caprio, Gerard, and Patrick Honohan. 1999. Restoring banking stability: Beyond supervised capital requirements. *Journal of Economic Perspectives* 13 (4): 43–64.

Carlson, Mark A., and Leonardo Hernandez. 2002. Determinants and repercussions of the composition of capital inflows. IMF Working Paper no. 02/86. Washington, DC: International Monetary Fund.

Chanda, Areendam. 2006. The influence of capital controls on long run growth. *Journal of Development Economics,* forthcoming.

Claessens, Stijn, and Kristin Forbes. 2001. *International financial contagion.* Boston: Kluwer Academic.

Corsetti, Giancarlo, Marcello Pericoli, and Massimo Sbracia. 2002. Some contagion, some interdependence: More pitfalls in tests of financial contagion. CEPR Discussion Paper no. 3310. London: Centre for Economic Policy Research, April.

Deaton, Angus. 2001. Counting the world's poor: Problems and possible solutions. *World Bank Research Observer* 16 (2): 125–47.

Dellas, Harris, and Martin K. Hess. 2002. Financial development and the sensitivity of stock markets to external influences. *Review of International Economics* 10 (3): 525–38.

Detragiache, Enrica, and Spilimbergo, Antonio. 2002. Crisis and liquidity: Evidence and interpretation. IMF Working Paper no. 01/2. Washington, DC: International Monetary Fund.

Dollar, David, and Aart Kraay. 2002. Institutions, trade, and growth. *Journal of Monetary Economics* 50:133–62.

———. 2004. Trade, growth, and poverty. *Economic Journal* 114 (493): 22–49.

Duygan, Burcu. 2004. Consumption patterns during financial crises: An international comparison. Florence, Italy: European University Institute. Working Paper.

Easterly, William, Roumeen Islam, and Joseph E. Stiglitz. 2001. Shaken and stirred: Explaining growth volatility. In *Annual World Bank Conference on Development Economics 2000,* ed. B. Pleskovic and N. Stern, 191–212. Washington, DC: World Bank.

Easterly, William, and Ross Levine. 2001. It's not factor accumulation: Stylized facts and growth models. *World Bank Economic Review* 15:177–219.

Edison, Hali, Michael Klein, Luca Ricci, and Torsten Sløk. 2002. Capital account liberalization and economic performance: A review of the literature. IMF Working Paper no. 02/120. Washington, DC: International Monetary Fund, July.

Edison, Hali, Ross Levine, Luca Ricci, and Torsten Sløk. 2002. International financial integration and economic growth. *Journal of International Money and Finance* 21:749–76.

Edison, Hali, and Frank Warnock. 2001. A simple measure of the intensity of capital controls. International Finance Discussion Paper no. 705. Washington, DC: Federal Reserve Board, August.

Edwards, Sebastian. 2001. Capital mobility and economic performance: Are emerging economies different? NBER Working Paper no. 8076. Cambridge, MA: National Bureau of Economic Research.

Eichengreen, Barry J., Donald J. Mathieson, and Bankim Chadha. 1998. Hedge funds and financial market dynamics. IMF Occasional Paper no. 166. Washington, DC: International Monetary Fund.

Fatás, Antonio. 2002. The effects of business cycles on growth. In *Economic growth: Sources, trends, and cycles,* ed. N. Loayza and R. Soto, 191–219. Santiago, Chile: Central Bank of Chile.

Forbes, Kristin, and Robert Rigobon. 2001. Measuring contagion: Conceptual and empirical issues. In *International financial contagion,* ed. S. Claessens and Kristin Forbes, 43–66. Boston: Kluwer Academic.

Frankel, Jeffrey A. 1992. Measuring international capital mobility: A review. *American Economic Review* 82 (May): 197–202.

Frankel, Jeffrey A., and David Romer. 1999. Does trade cause growth? *American Economic Review* 89 (3): 379–99.

Frankel, Jeffrey A., and Andrew K. Rose. 1996. Currency crashes in emerging markets: An empirical treatment. *Journal of International Economics* 41 (3–4): 351–66.

Gavin, Michael, and Ricardo Hausmann. 1996. Sources of macroeconomic volatility in developing economies. IADB Working Paper. Washington, DC: Inter-American Development Bank.

Glick, Reuven, and Kenneth Rogoff. 1995. Global versus country-specific productivity shocks and the current account. *Journal of Monetary Economics* 35 (February): 159–92.

Goldberg, Pinelopi K., and Nina Pavcnik. 2004. Trade, inequality, and poverty: What do we know? Evidence from recent trade liberalization episodes in developing countries. In *Brookings trade forum 2004*, ed. Susan Collins and Carol Graham, 223–69. Washington, DC: Brookings Institution Press.

Gourinchas, Pierre-Olivier, and Olivier Jeanne. 2003. The elusive gains from international financial integration. NBER Working Paper no. 9684. Cambridge, MA: National Bureau of Economic Research.

Grilli, Vittorio, and Gian Maria Milesi-Ferretti. 1995. Economic effects and structural determinants of capital controls. *IMF Staff Papers* 42 (September): 517–51.

Grossman, Gene M., and Elhanan Helpman. 1991a. *Innovation and growth in the global economy.* Cambridge, MA: MIT Press.

———. 1991b. Trade, knowledge spillovers, and growth. *European Economic Review* 35 (2–3): 517–26.

Hall, Robert E., and Charles I. Jones. 1999. Why do some countries produce so much more output per worker than others? *Quarterly Journal of Economics* 114 (1): 83–116.

Harrison, Ann, and H. Tang. 2006. Liberalization of trade: Why so much controversy? In *The growth experience: Lessons from the 1990s,* ed. N. Roberto Zagha. Washington, DC: World Bank, forthcoming.

Hausmann, Ricardo, and Eduardo Fernandez-Arias. 2000. Foreign direct investment: Good cholesterol? IADB Working Paper no. 417. Washington, DC: Inter-American Development Bank.

Henry, Peter. 2000. Stock market liberalization, economic reform, and emerging market equity prices. *Journal of Finance* 55 (April): 529–64.

Hnatkovska, Viktoria, and Norman Loayza. 2005. Volatility and growth. In *Managing economic volatility and crises: A practitioner's guide,* ed. Joshua Aizenman and Brian Pinto, 65–100. Cambridge: Cambridge University Press.

Imbs, Jean, and Romain Wacziarg. 2003. Stages of diversification. *American Economic Review* 93 (1): 63–86.

International Monetary Fund (IMF). 2001. *World economic outlook.* Washington, DC: IMF, October.

———. 2002. *World economic outlook.* Washington, DC: IMF, September.

Ishii, Shogo, Karl Habermeier, Bernard Laurens, John Leimone, Judit Vadasz, and Jorge Ivan Canales-Kriljenko. 2002. Capital account liberalization and financial sector stability. IMF Occasional Paper no. 211. Washington, DC: International Monetary Fund.

Kalemli-Ozcan, Sebnem, Bent E. Sørensen, and Oved Yosha. 2001. Risk sharing and industrial specialization: Regional and international evidence. University of Houston, Department of Economics. Working Paper.

Kaminsky, Graciela, and Carmen M. Reinhart. 1999. The twin crises: The causes of banking and balance-of-payments problems. *American Economic Review* 89 (3): 473–500.

———. 2001. Bank lending and contagion: Evidence from the Asian crisis. In *Regional and global capital flows: Macroeconomic causes and consequences,* ed. Takatoshi Ito and Anne O. Krueger, 73–99. Chicago: University of Chicago Press.

———. 2002. The center and periphery: The globalization of financial turmoil. NBER Working Paper no. W9479. Cambridge, MA: National Bureau of Economic Research.

Kemp, Murray, and Nissan Liviatan. 1973. Production and trade patterns under uncertainty. *Economic Record* 49:215–27.

Kim, Sunghyun Henry, M. Ayhan Kose, and Michael Plummer. 2001. Understanding the Asian contagion. *Asian Economic Journal* 15 (2): 111–38.

Klein, Michael, and Giovanni Olivei. 2000. Capital account liberalization, financial depth, and economic growth. Tufts University, Fletcher School. Working Paper.

Kouparitsas, Michael A. 1996. North-South business cycles. Working Paper no. 96–9. Chicago: Federal Reserve Bank of Chicago.

Kose, M. Ayhan. 2002. Explaining business cycles in small open economies: How much do world prices matter? *Journal of International Economics* 56:299–327.

Kose, M. Ayhan, Christopher Otrok, and Charles Whiteman. 2003. International business cycles: World, region, and country specific factors. *American Economic Review* 93:1216–39.

Kose, M. Ayhan, Eswar S. Prasad, and Marco E. Terrones. 2003a. Financial integration and macroeconomic volatility. *IMF Staff Papers* 50:119–42.

———. 2003b. How does globalization affect the synchronization of business cycles? *American Economic Review* 93:57–62.

———. 2006. How do trade and financial integration affect the relationship between growth and volatility? *Journal of International Economics,* forthcoming.

Kose, M. Ayhan, and Raymond Riezman. 2001. Trade shocks and macroeconomic fluctuations in Africa. *Journal of Development Economics* 65:55–80.

Kraay, Aart. 1998. In search of the macroeconomic effect of capital account liberalization. Washington, DC: World Bank. Unpublished manuscript.

———. 2004. When is growth pro-poor? Cross-country evidence. IMF Working Paper no. 04/47. Washington, DC: International Monetary Fund.

Krueger, Anne O., and Jungho Yoo. 2002. Chaebol capitalism and the currency-financial crisis in Korea. In *Preventing currency crises in emerging markets,* ed. Sebastian Edwards and Jeffrey Frankel, 461–501. Chicago: University of Chicago Press.

Kumar, Manmohan S., and Avinash Persaud. 2001. Pure contagion and investors' shifting risk appetite: Analytical issues and empirical evidence. IMF Working Paper no. 01/134. Washington, DC: International Monetary Fund.

Labán, Raul M., and Felipe B. Larrain. 1997. What determines capital inflows? An empirical analysis for Chile. Discussion Paper no. 590. Cambridge, MA: Harvard Institute for International Development, June.

Lane, Philip R., and Giani Maria Milesi-Ferretti. 2001. The external wealth of nations: Measures of foreign assets and liabilities for industrial and developing nations. *Journal of International Economics* 55:263–94.

Laursen, Thomas, and Sandeep Mahajan. 2005. Volatility, income distribution and poverty. In *Managing economic volatility and crises: A practitioner's guide,* ed. Joshua Aizenman and Brian Pinto, 101–36. Cambridge: Cambridge University Press.

Levine, Ross. 1996. Foreign banks, financial development, and economic growth. In *International financial markets: Harmonization versus competition,* ed. Claude E. Barfield, 224–54. Washington, DC: American Enterprise Institute Press.

Loungani, Prakash, Ashoka Mody, and Assaf Razin. 2003. The global disconnect: The role of transactional distance and scale economies in gravity equations. IMF Working Paper. Washington, DC: International Monetary Fund.

Lustig, Nora. 2000. Crises and the poor: Socially responsible macroeconomics. IADB Sustainable Development Department Technical Papers Series. Washington, DC: Inter-American Development Bank.

Martin, Philippe, and C. A. Rogers. 2000. Long-term growth and short-term economic instability. *European Economic Review* 44:359–81.

Mathieson, Donald J., and Liliana Rojas-Suarez. 1993. Liberalization of the capital account: Experiences and issues. IMF Occasional Paper no. 103. Washington, DC: International Monetary Fund.

Mauro, Paolo, Nathan Sussman, and Yishay Yafeh. 2002. Emerging market spreads: Then versus now. *Quarterly Journal of Economics* 117 (2): 695–733.

Mishkin, Frederic S. 1999. Lessons from the Asian crisis. NBER Working Paper no. 7102. Cambridge, MA: National Bureau of Economic Research, April.

Mody, Ashoka. 2002. Is FDI integrating the world economy? Washington, DC: International Monetary Fund. Unpublished manuscript.

Mody, Ashoka, and Antu Panini Murshid. 2002. Growing up with capital flows. IMF Working Paper no. 02/75. Washington, DC: International Monetary Fund.

Mody, Ashoka, and Mark P. Taylor. 2002. International capital crunches: The time varying role of informational asymmetries. IMF Working Paper no. 02/34. Washington, DC: International Monetary Fund.

Obstfeld, Maurice, and Kenneth Rogoff. 1998. Foundations of international macroeconomics. Cambridge, MA: MIT Press.

O'Donnell, Barry. 2001. Financial openness and economic performance. Trinity College, Dublin, Department of Economics. Working Paper.

Prasad, Eswar, Kenneth Rogoff, Shang-Jin Wei, and M. Ayhan Kose. 2003. The effects of financial globalization on developing countries: Some empirical evidence. IMF Occasional Paper no. 220. Washington, DC: International Monetary Fund.

———. 2004. Financial globalization, growth and volatility in developing countries. NBER Working Paper no. 10942. Cambridge, MA: National Bureau of Economic Research.

Quah, Danny. 1997. Empirics for growth and distribution: Stratification, polarization, and convergence clubs. *Journal of Economic Growth* 2 (1): 27–59.

Quinn, Dennis P. 1997. The correlates of change in international financial regulation. *American Political Science Review* 91 (September): 531–51.

Radelet, Steven, and Jeffrey Sachs. 1998. The East Asian financial crisis: Diagnosis, remedies, prospects. *Brookings Papers on Economic Activity,* Issue no. 1:1–74.

Ramey, Gary, and Valerie Ramey. 1995. Cross-country evidence on the link between volatility and growth. *American Economic Review* 85 (5): 1138–51.

Ravallion, Martin. 2003. The debate on globalization, poverty and inequality: Why measurement matters. World Bank Policy Research Working Paper no. 3038. Washington, DC: World Bank.

Razin, Assaf, and Andrew K. Rose. 1994. Business-cycle volatility and openness: An exploratory cross-sectional analysis. In *Capital mobility: The impact on consumption, investment, and growth,* ed. Leonardo Leiderman and Assaf Razin, 48–76. Cambridge: Cambridge University Press.

Reinhart, Carmen M. 2002. Credit ratings, default and financial crises: Evidence from emerging markets. *World Bank Economic Review* 16 (2): 151–70.

Reinhart, Carmen M., and Vincent R. Reinhart. 2001. What hurts most? G-3 exchange rate or interest rate volatility. NBER Working Paper no. 8535. Cambridge, MA: National Bureau of Economic Research, October.

Reinhart, Carmen M., and Kenneth Rogoff. 2004. Serial default and the "paradox" of rich to poor capital flows. *American Economic Review* 94 (2): 52–58.

Reisen, Helmut, and Marcelo Soto. 2001. Which types of capital inflows foster developing-country growth? *International Finance* 4 (1): 1–14.

Rodriguez, Francisco, and Dani Rodrik. 2000. Trade policy and economic growth: A skeptic's guide to the cross-national evidence. In *NBER macroeconomics an-*

nual 2000, ed. Ben S. Bernanke and Kenneth Rogoff, 261–325. Cambridge, MA: MIT Press.

Rodrik, Dani. 1998. *Who needs capital-account convertibility?* Essays in International Finance no. 207. Princeton, NJ: Princeton University.

Rodrik, Dani, and Andres Velasco. 2000. Short-term capital flows. In *Annual World Bank Conference on Development Economics, 1999*, 59–90. Washington, DC: World Bank.

Rogoff, Kenneth. 2002. Rethinking capital controls: When should we keep an open mind? *Finance and Development* 39 (4): 55–56.

———. 2004. Some speculation on growth and poverty over the twenty-first century. In *Brookings trade forum 2004*, ed. Susan Collins and Carol Graham, 305–11.

Rogoff, Kenneth, Aasim M. Husain, Ashoka Mody, Robin J. Brooks, and Nienke Oomes. 2004. Evolution and performance of exchange rates regimes. IMF Occasional Paper no. 229. Washington, DC: International Monetary Fund.

Ruffin, Roy J. 1974. Comparative advantage under uncertainty. *Journal of International Economics* 4 (3): 261–73.

Sachs, Jeffrey, and Andrew Warner. 1995. Economic reform and the process of global integration. *Brookings Papers on Economic Activity*, Issue no. 2:523–64.

Sala-i-Martin, Xavier. 2002. The disturbing "rise" of world income inequality. NBER Working Paper no. 8904. Cambridge, MA: National Bureau of Economic Research.

Senhadji, Abdelhak. 2000. Sources of economic growth: An extensive growth accounting exercise. *IMF Staff Papers* 47 (1): 129–57.

Stulz, Rene. 1999a. Globalization of equity markets and the cost of capital. NBER Working Paper no. 7021. Cambridge, MA: National Bureau of Economic Research, March.

———. 1999b. International portfolio flows and security markets. In *International capital flows*, 257–93. Chicago: University of Chicago Press.

Taylor, Mark P., and Lucio Sarno. 1999. The persistence of capital inflows and the behaviour of stock prices in East Asia emerging markets: Some empirical evidence. CEPR Discussion Paper no. 2150. London: Centre for Economic Policy Research, May.

van Rijckeghem, Caroline, and Beatrice Weder. 2000. Spillover through banking centers: A panel data analysis. IMF Working Paper no. 00/88. Washington, DC: International Monetary Fund.

Wacziarg, Romain, and Karen Horn Welch. 2003. Trade liberalization and growth: New evidence. NBER Working Paper no. 10152. Cambridge, MA: National Bureau of Economic Research.

Wei, Shang-Jin. 2001. Domestic crony capitalism and international fickle capital: Is there a connection? *International Finance* 4 (Spring): 15–46.

Wei, Shang-Jin, and Yi Wu. 2001. Globalization and inequality: Evidence from within China. NBER Working Paper no. 8611. Cambridge, MA: National Bureau of Economic Research, November.

———. 2006. The life-and-death implications of globalization. IMF Working Paper. Washington, DC: International Monetary Fund, forthcoming.

Winters, L. Alan. 2004. Trade liberalization and economic performance: An overview. *Economic Journal* 114:4–21.

Winters, L. Alan, Neil McCulloch, and Andrew McKay. 2004. Trade liberalization and poverty: The evidence so far. *Journal of Economic Literature* 42 (1): 72–115.

World Bank. 2001. *Global development finance*. Washington, DC: World Bank.

Comment   Susan M. Collins

This paper promises a comprehensive assessment of empirical evidence about the impact of financial integration on growth and on volatility in developing countries. Given that this complex topic is the focus of a large and growing academic literature, not to mention perhaps an even larger and more heated nonacademic one, the goal is ambitious. The authors cover a lot of ground—carefully defining terms, establishing basic stylized facts, reviewing relevant economic theory, summarizing available empirical evidence, and presenting findings of new empirical analysis. In my view, the result is a thoughtful, informative, balanced, and well-written assessment—most of which I agree with. There is a lot in this very useful paper. Thus, my comments will necessarily be selective. I will begin by briefly summarizing the main conclusions. Then, taking my job as a discussant seriously, I will devote most of my comments to the two areas in which I see things somewhat differently: the implications of financial integration and of increased capital for economic growth. Both of these are areas in which the way that key concepts are measured affects interpretation.

The authors reach two main conclusions. First, they argue that a systematic examination of available evidence suggests that it is difficult to establish a robust causal relationship between the extent to which a country is integrated with global financial markets and its output growth. This is one area in which I think the evidence suggests a more nuanced view, as explained below.

Second, largely on the basis of their new analysis, they argue that there is little evidence that financial integration has helped developing countries to stabilize fluctuations in consumption. Indeed, they find that things may get worse at low to moderate levels of financial integration. They also argue that the problem may arise from the procyclicality of capital flows to developing countries. I see this section, and its focus on consumption instead of output volatility, as a convincing and important contribution of the paper. I also agree with the authors that more work is needed to better understand when and why integration may raise volatility.

Thus, the authors conclude that "it may be valuable for developing countries to experiment with different paces and strategies in pursuing financial integration." I fully agree. While this resulting cautionary take on financial integration may be in accord with today's conventional wisdom, it is a notable shift from the considerably more positive view of financial integration

Susan M. Collins is a professor of economics at Georgetown University, a senior fellow at the Brookings Institution, and a research associate of the National Bureau of Economic Research.

associated with the IMF until quite recently. Further, the paper's focus on backing up claims with empirical evidence is refreshing in a subject area rife with undocumented assertions.

Let me turn now to the two areas on which I have a somewhat different take. The first has to do with what we mean by financial integration. The paper quite appropriately makes a clear distinction between de jure and de facto measures. However, this distinction is not made explicit in the review of existing empirical studies on which the authors base their main conclusions in the section on financial integration and growth. (This discussion draws from Collins 2004.)

De jure measures are intended to capture the existence (and degree) of capital controls—in other words a measure of each country's official policy toward capital flows. The most widely used indicator is one constructed by the IMF, which takes the value of 1 when controls exist and 0 otherwise. An alternative, constructed by Dennis Quinn, attempts to measure the degree of capital account openness, ranging from 0 (closed) to 4 (fully open).[1] In contrast, de facto measures are intended to capture the actual amount of financial integration. Some studies use indicators based on realized capital flows, while others focus on accumulated stocks.[2]

As the authors here point out, de jure and de facto indicators of changes in financial integration show much lower correlation for developing countries than they do for industrial countries. Is one concept better than the other? I would argue that both are relevant. We are interested in whether policy stance and changes in policy matter, as well as in the effects of whatever capital flows actually materialize. I agree with the authors of this paper that actual controls and how they are enforced vary considerably across countries. Available indicators of policy (the de jure measures) seem quite rough, may not be very informative, and are difficult to interpret. From this perspective, it makes sense to focus, as they claim to, on de facto indicators. But as they recognize, the de facto measures, particularly the capital flow indicators, are clearly endogenous in a growth regression, making the causality difficult to pin down conclusively.

My main point about this section of the paper, however, is that which concept or indicator is used in empirical analyses appears to make a considerable difference. Thus, distinguishing between them is very important. The summary of existing studies presented here does not do this consis-

1. The IMF indicator is available annually for a large sample of countries during 1966–95. Unfortunately, the IMF replaced this single yes/no measure with a more informative, but not directly comparable, set of indicators for particular restrictions on capital inflows and outflows. The Quinn measure is available for a smaller set of countries and for selective years.

2. It is important to note that this paper (like the relevant literature) is not making a distinction between de jure as policy on the books versus de facto as the true effect of that policy. Instead, the distinction is between de jure (policy on the books) versus de facto (the outcome).

Table 11C.1   Recent research on financial integration and growth

	Type of indicators	
Total no. of studies	De jure	De facto
A. Studies in PRWK table 11.3		
13	12	4

	Positive effect on growth?		
Indicator	Yes	Mixed	No
B. Recent research using de jure indicators[a]			
IMF (12)	1	3	8
Quinn (5)	1	2	2
C. Recent research using de facto indicators			
Total capital flow or stock[b]	2 (OLS)	1 (OECD)	3 (LDC, IV)
FDI flows[c]	7	1	1

Source: Collins (2004) and author's calculations.
Notes: PRWK = Prasad et al.'s chapter in this volume; OLS = ordinary least squares; LDC = less developed countries; IV = instrumental variables.
[a]Includes a total of thirteen studies, one of which is not in PRWK.
[b]Includes three studies, all in PRWK.
[c]Includes eight studies, one in PRWK.

tently—and indeed, most of the studies listed in table 11.3 of the paper actually use de jure measures, not the de facto ones that are the focus of the text discussion.

The point can be made most clearly by regrouping the papers summarized in table 11.3 of the paper. In doing this, I exclude the one paper that studies effects of stock market liberalizations—which I would classify as a separate dimension of financial integration. As shown in panel A of table 11C.1, this leaves a total of thirteen studies. Of these, twelve report results using one or more de jure indicators, while only four report results based on de facto indicators.[3] Clearly, the conclusions in the paper are dominated by results based on de jure indicators. Panel B focuses on the results using de jure indicators. One study that was not reviewed in the authors' paper has been added to the twelve. As shown, only one of twelve studies using the IMF indicator finds clear evidence that financial liberalization positively affects growth. The evidence is somewhat more mixed using the Quinn indicator, suggesting that the difficulty in finding a relationship may be due, in part, to the coarseness of these measures. But like the IMF mea-

---

3. Three of the studies report both.

sure available since 1996, the Quinn indicator provides a limited picture of the differences in policy stance across countries and over time.

Panel C of table 11C.1 focuses on results based on de facto indicators. Here eight studies have been added to the three reviewed in table 11.3 of the paper. The top line shows results in which total capital flows or stocks (usually relative to each country's GDP) are used to proxy financial integration. An interesting picture emerges. Studies that use simple ordinary least squares (OLS) find a positive, and often quite strong, link to growth. However, it is unclear whether this reflects causality or simply a positive correlation. Those that use instrumental variables in an attempt to deal with the endogeneity of capital flows fail to find a significant effect. The causality may run mainly from faster growth to increased capital inflow. But in at least some of these cases, the first stage of the regression is quite weak, and the second-stage result may simply reflect difficulties in finding strong instruments. Finally, the last line in the table adds results in which de facto financial integration is measured using FDI flows only. Seven out of nine of these studies do find a strong positive effect on growth, including some that attempt to address endogeneity. The authors of the current paper are clearly aware of these results and seem to find them convincing. However, their discussion of these findings is relegated to a footnote (note 19), allowing the results based on de jure indicators to take central stage in the text discussion.

In sum, a statement such as "if financial integration has a positive effect on growth, it is probably not strong or robust" seems to me to be an overly stark and potentially misleading summary of what the evidence shows. Instead, my reading of the existing literature is as follows: There is little evidence relating available indicators of de jure financial integration to growth, which may reflect relatively uninformative indicators. Countries that are able to attract capital inflows tend to grow faster, but evidence does not suggest that this is a causal relationship. However, somewhat more support exists for a positive causal link between FDI and growth.

The second issue I would like to raise concerns the role of increased physical capital for economic growth. There is a well-known debate on this topic, with some claiming that capital accumulation explains most of the cross-country variation in output growth (or levels of output per capita) and others that it is total factor productivity (TFP), not capital, that really matters. Authors on both sides present empirical evidence to back up their claims. And in the recent development literature, those who come down on the side of TFP seem to be emerging on the top. The authors of this paper seem to agree. For example, they assert that "most of the cross-country differences in per capita incomes stem not from differences in the capital-labor ratio but from differences in total factor productivity." However, as I have argued with Barry Bosworth, much of the difference between whether one finds

that capital accumulation is important or that it matters very little is related to issues of measurement, which are typically ignored. My point in the remainder of these remarks is not to minimize the role of TFP, which is clearly critical to growth. Instead, it is to caution against interpretations of available evidence that suggest little or no role for capital accumulation. (This discussion draws from Bosworth and Collins 2003. Readers are referred to that paper for a fuller treatment and additional references.)

Consider first the way that capital accumulation is incorporated into growth regressions. Many of those that find a relatively weak role for capital accumulation use each country's average investment rate to proxy accumulation. The change in each country's capital stock over the relevant time period is clearly the more direct measure. We have looked at both, using data for eighty-four countries over the period from 1960 to 2000. Perhaps surprisingly, we find that there is a relatively low cross-country correlation between average investment and change in capital stock. (Countries with similar investment rates will have low capital accumulation if they grow slowly, but high accumulation if they grow rapidly.) And in a regression, investment rates exhibit a much smaller and less statistically significant correlation with output growth than changes in the capital stock. This is illustrated in table 11C.2. (We note that the point is robust to the inclusion of additional right-hand-side variables.)

A number of studies use growth (or levels) accounting to relate increases in capital to output across countries. The traditional approach puts change in output per worker on the left-hand side and uses change in capital per worker to measure capital input (deepening). This results in the growth decomposition in equation (1). More recently, it has become popular to measure capital's contribution to growth in terms of increases in the capital-

Table 11C.2   **Comparative performance: Investment and the change in the capital stock (eighty-four countries; dependent variable: growth in output per worker)**

	1960–2000		1960–80		1980–2000	
	(1)	(2)	(3)	(4)	(5)	(6)
Growth in physical capital per worker	0.56		0.38		0.70	
	(13.0)		(8.9)		(13.5)	
Investment share per worker		0.13		0.05		0.21
		(5.3)		(2.5)		(7.7)
Adjusted R^2	0.67	0.25	0.48	0.06	0.69	0.41
Standard error	0.82	1.24	1.08	1.46	1.04	1.42

Source: Bosworth and Collins (2003).

Notes: t-statistics are reported in parentheses; constant term is included but not reported. Growth in capital per worker is measured as mean of annual log changes ($\times 100$); investment per worker is measured as a share of GDP in constant national prices.

output ratio. The decomposition in equation (2) shows such a decomposition.

$$(1) \qquad \Delta \ln\left(\frac{Y}{L}\right) = \alpha\left[\Delta \ln\left(\frac{K}{L}\right)\right] + (1 - \alpha)\, \Delta \ln H + \Delta \ln A$$

$$(2) \qquad \Delta \ln\left(\frac{Y}{L}\right) = \frac{\alpha}{1 - \alpha} \cdot \left[\Delta \ln\left(\frac{K}{Y}\right)\right] + \Delta \ln H + \frac{1}{1 - \alpha} \Delta \ln A$$

(Y, L, K, L, and A are GDP, labor force, physical capital, human capital, and TFP, respectively, and α is capital's share.)

The rationale for the second decomposition is that using capital per worker ignores the endogeneity of capital accumulation, and that a portion of any change in capital is likely to have been induced by increases in TFP. However, as we discuss in Bosworth and Collins (2003), the assumption that countries' capital stocks adjust proportionately to all deviations in output growth induced by TFP seems to us extreme. Furthermore, one can recognize that changes in a country's capital stock are partially induced by changes in TFP without concluding that this induced portion should be excluded from measures of capital's contribution to growth. In any case, changing the definition of how to measure capital's contribution from that in equation (1) to that in equation (2) hardly seems the appropriate way to resolve the underlying conceptual dispute. And the formulation in equation (2) clearly increases the role for TFP by scaling it upward by a factor of $[1/(1 - \alpha)]$ equal to 1.54 in our analysis.

Table 11C.3 reports a variance decomposition of growth in output per worker using both formulations. As shown, the two definitions do suggest very different roles for capital accumulation. Measuring capital's contribution using changes in capital per worker implies that 34 percent of the variation in growth across countries can be related to capital, compared with 54 percent for TFP. However, measuring capital's contribution only by changes in the capital output ratio relates just 12 per-

Table 11C.3   **Variance/covariance analysis of income per worker, 1960–2000**

	Contribution to Y/L		
Equation	Physical capital	Education	Factor productivity
(1) K/L	0.43	0.03	0.54
(2) K/Y	0.12	0.05	0.83

Source: Bosworth and Collins (2003).

Notes: For row (1) the contribution of each factor to the growth in output per worker is defined as in equation (1) of the text. For row (2) contributions are defined as in equation (2).

cent of the output variation to capital, compared with 83 percent to TFP.

References

Bosworth, Barry, and Susan M. Collins. 2003. The empirics of growth, an update. *Brookings Papers on Economic Activity,* Issue no. 2: 113–206.
Collins, Susan M. 2004. International financial integration and growth in developing countries: Issues and implications for Africa. *Journal of African Economies* 13 (2): ii55–ii94.

Household Responses to the Financial Crisis in Indonesia
Longitudinal Evidence on Poverty, Resources, and Well-Being

Duncan Thomas and Elizabeth Frankenberg

12.1 Introduction

After almost three decades of sustained economic growth, Indonesia experienced a major economic and financial crisis in the late 1990s. Between 1970 and 1997, on average per capita gross domestic product (GDP) increased by almost 5 percent each year. In 1998, per capita GDP fell by about 15 percent, bringing the economy back to its level in 1994. The financial crisis was accompanied by dramatic shifts in the economic and political landscape in the country. (See, for example, Ahuja et al. 1997 and Cameron 1999 for descriptions.)

As indicated in figure 12.1, the Indonesian rupiah came under pressure in the last half of 1997 when the exchange rate began showing signs of weakness. It fell from around Rp2,400 per U.S. dollar to about Rp4,800 per U.S. dollar by December 1997. In January 1998, the rupiah collapsed. Over the course of a few days, the exchange rate lost over two-thirds of its value and fell to Rp15,000 per U.S. dollar. Although it soon recovered, by the middle of the year the rupiah had slumped back to the lows of January 1998. After June 1998, the rupiah strengthened, so that by the end of 1998 it stood at around Rp8,000 to the U.S. dollar and remained in the Rp8,000–

Duncan Thomas is a professor of economics and director of the California Center for Population Research, University of California, Los Angeles. Elizabeth Frankenberg is an assistant professor of sociology and research associate of the California Center for Population Research, University of California, Los Angeles.

Support for this research from the National Institute of Child Health and Human Development (HD40245 and HD28372) is gratefully acknowledged. We have benefited from discussions with Kathleen Beegle, Ann Harrison, Bondan Sikoki, James P. Smith, and Wayan Suriastini.

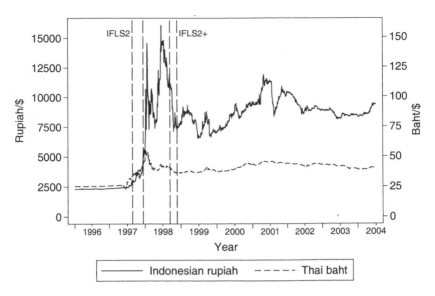

Fig. 12.1   Indonesian rupiah and Thai baht: 1996–2004 with timing of IFLS2 and IFLS2+

Rp10,000 range for the next five years. This is about one-quarter of its value prior to the onset of the crisis.

The East Asian financial crisis was presaged by the collapse of the Thai baht, which is also displayed relative to the U.S. dollar in figure 12.1. Two points are immediate. First, the collapse of the Indonesian rupiah was far greater than that of the baht. By the time the baht stabilized, it was worth about two-thirds of its precrisis level. Second, the baht did not display anything close to the same level of volatility as the rupiah. Declines in other currencies in the region were more muted than that of the baht. Even in the context of the East Asian crisis, the collapse of the Indonesian rupiah was very large and 1998 stands out as a year of extraordinary volatility and, therefore, tremendous uncertainty in the financial markets in Indonesia.

Interest rates in Indonesia behaved much like the exchange rate: they spiked in August 1997—when they quadrupled—and they remained extremely volatile for the remainder of the year. Chaos reigned in the banking sector. Several major banks were taken over by the Indonesian Bank Restructuring Agency. All of this turmoil wreaked havoc with both the confidence of investors and the availability of credit.

Prices of many commodities spiraled upward during the first three quarters of 1998. Annual inflation was estimated by the Central Statistical Bureau to be about 80 percent for 1998. Subsidies were removed on several goods—most notably rice, oil, and fuel. Food prices, especially staples, rose by about 20 percent more than the general price index, suggesting that

(net) food consumers were likely to be severely impacted by the crisis whereas food producers had some protection.

Simultaneously, Indonesia experienced dramatic transformation in the political sector. After over three decades as president, Suharto resigned in May 1998. Within days, the incoming president, Habibie, declared multiparty elections for the middle of 1999 and pledged reforms that were intended to revive political activity in the country.

Few Indonesians were untouched by the upheavals of 1998. For some, the turmoil was devastating. For others, it brought new opportunities. Exporters, export producers, and food producers probably fared far better than those engaged in the production of services and nontradables or those on fixed incomes. The crisis in Indonesia encompassed many dimensions, and individuals and families responded to it in a variety of ways. Precisely because of this complexity, empirical evidence is essential for untangling the combined impact of all facets of the crisis on the well-being of the population and also for deciphering how these impacts vary across socioeconomic and demographic groups. Research reported below provides some of that evidence.

Roubini and Setser (2004) discuss recent financial crises in emerging economies from a macroeconomic perspective. Prasad, Rogoff, Wei, and Kose (chap. 11 in this volume) discuss the relationship between financial globalization and growth. The macroeconomic research highlights the role of strong institutions, transparency, and good governance in harnessing the benefits of globalization. With these factors largely absent, the crisis in Indonesia was both large and relatively long lived. An examination of the impact of the Indonesian crisis thus provides insights into the effects of a major financial collapse on the well-being of the population.

Fallon and Lucas (2002) provide an excellent summary of the evidence on the effect of economic shocks on household poverty and well-being from a microeconomic perspective. Frankenberg, Thomas, and Beegle (1999) describe early evidence on the Indonesian crisis; those and other results are summarized in Poppele, Sudarno, and Pritchett (1999). Levinsohn, Berry, and Friedman (2003) explore the likely effects of the crisis using household budget data collected prior to the crisis. A discussion of some of the longer-term effects of the Indonesian crisis is contained in Strauss et al. (2004). Bresciani et al. (2002) contrast the impact of the crisis on farm households in Thailand and Indonesia. For other micro-level research about the impact of economic and financial crises on the well-being of households, see, inter alia, Maloney, Cunningham, and Bosch (2004), who discuss the Mexican crisis; Datt and Hoogeveen (2003) on the crisis in the Philippines; and Lokshin and Yemtsov (2004) on the Russian crisis.

This research uses longitudinal household survey data collected from the same households prior to the full brunt of the crisis unfolding in late

1997 and again a year later in 1998. The focus is on attempting to measure the magnitude of the crisis, identifying those demographic groups that were most severely affected by the crisis in the short run, and drawing out the implications for well-being in the longer term. An important contribution of this work is that a broad array of indicators of individual and household well-being are systematically examined. This provides a richer characterization of the impact of the crisis than is possible with a single indicator such as poverty or inequality. It also provides important insights into the ways in which individuals and households coped with the upheavals around the time of the crisis.

Data are drawn from the Indonesia Family Life Survey (IFLS), an ongoing broad-purpose longitudinal survey of individuals, households, and communities in Indonesia. Most of the results presented here rely on two waves of the survey: IFLS2, which was conducted in late 1997, and IFLS2+, which was conducted in late 1998. The latter survey was specially designed for this purpose. The well-being of individuals and households interviewed in 1998 is compared with their well-being from interviews conducted about a year earlier in 1997. Additional evidence is drawn from the 2000 wave of the IFLS.

The crisis affected the poorest, the middle-income households, and households in the upper part of the income distribution in Indonesia. While the precise magnitude of the crisis is subject to controversy, the crisis had a far-reaching effect on the purchasing power of the Indonesian population, and there were substantial increases in levels of poverty as the crisis unfolded.

It is very difficult to measure the impact of the crisis on expenditure-based indicators of poverty, for several reasons. First, measurement of the change in the value of real resources is not straightforward since the crisis was accompanied by high levels of inflation that varied substantially over time and space. Second, expenditures are measured at the household level and so are typically deflated by household size or some function of size and composition. One of the many ways in which individuals responded to the crisis was by households joining forces. This substantially complicates interpretation of expenditure-based poverty estimates.

In an effort to sidestep some of these issues, we turn to an examination of the household budget. The share of the budget spent on food, and especially staples, increased significantly, and these increases were largest for the poorest. To make room for these expenditures, purchases of semi-durables were delayed. To the extent that these delays were temporary, their welfare consequences are not clear. Expenditure-based poverty indicators are also complicated if households choose to delay expenditures so that current spending falls without a comparable decline in welfare.

Between 1997 and 1998, there were significant declines in the share of the budget spent on education, especially among the poorest, and in the share

spent on health. These declines in spending are reflected in reduced investments in human capital as indicated by lower levels of health care utilization, particularly for preventive care, and lower rates of school enrollment, particularly among young children in the poorest households. The evidence on health status suggests that overall general health and psychosocial health declined as the crisis unfolded while adults sought to protect the nutritional status of very young children by drawing down their own weight. By 2000, most of the reductions in human capital investments had been reversed, and so the longer-term consequences of these temporary reductions remain to be determined. It is possible that the longer-term welfare costs will be small.

Wages collapsed while labor supply increased slightly as households sought to shore up income. Since household income declined by substantially more than household expenditure, households must have depleted their assets. We discuss asset markets around the time of the crisis and identify gold as playing a key role in mitigating the impact of the crisis on spending.

The next section provides a description of the data and the IFLS sample. It is followed by the empirical evidence on the impact of the crisis. We begin with a discussion of the magnitude of the crisis as measured by changes in household expenditure. We describe the correlates of changes in levels of resources in order to provide a robust assessment of the characteristics of those population groups that were most deleteriously affected by the crisis. Several issues that complicate interpretation of changes in the level of household consumption are discussed. This leads to a discussion of the allocation of the budget to different commodities and the relationship between changes in those allocations and household characteristics. Special attention is paid to spending on health and education. These results are complemented with information on school enrollments and nutrition and health status to provide a fuller assessment of the impact of the crisis. We end with a discussion of the crisis on earnings and assets. The final section concludes.

12.2   Data

The IFLS is a large-scale integrated socioeconomic and health survey that collects extensive information on the lives of individuals, their households, their families, and the communities in which they live. The sample is representative of about 83 percent of the Indonesian population and contains over 30,000 individuals living in thirteen of the twenty-seven provinces in the country (as of 1993).

The IFLS is an ongoing longitudinal survey. The first wave was conducted in 1993–94 (IFLS1), with a follow-up in 1997–98 (IFLS2) and a special follow-up, designed for this project, in late 1998 (IFLS2+). This spe-

cial follow-up sampled 25 percent of the fuller IFLS sample and contains information on almost 10,000 individuals living in around 2,000 households. A full re-survey was conducted in 2000 (IFLS3), and the next wave is scheduled for 2007 (IFLS4). In this study, we draw primarily on interviews with the households surveyed in 1997 and 1998 in order to provide insights into the magnitude and distribution of the immediate impact of the economic and political turmoil in Indonesia.

A broad-purpose survey, IFLS contains a wealth of information about each household including consumption, assets, income, and family businesses. In addition, individual members are interviewed to obtain information on, inter alia, use of health care and health status; fertility, contraception, and marriage; education, migration, and labor market behavior; participation in community activities; interactions with non-coresident family members; and their role in household decision making. The IFLS also contains an integrated series of community surveys that are linked to the household survey; they include interviews with the community leader and head of the village women's group, as well as interviews with knowledgeable informants at multiple schools and multiple public and private health care providers in each IFLS community.

12.2.1   The IFLS Sample

The IFLS sampling scheme was designed to balance the costs of surveying the more remote and sparsely populated regions of Indonesia against the benefits of capturing the ethnic and socioeconomic diversity of the country. The scheme stratified on provinces, then randomly sampled within enumeration areas (EAs) in each of the thirteen selected provinces.[1] A total of 321 EAs were selected from a nationally representative sample frame used in the 1993 SUSENAS (a survey of about 60,000 households). Within each EA, households were randomly selected using the 1993 SUSENAS listings obtained from regional offices of the *Badan Pusat Statistik* (BPS). Urban EAs and EAs in smaller provinces were oversampled to facilitate urban-rural and Javanese–non-Javanese comparisons. A total of 7,730 households were included in the original listing for the first wave; 7,224 households (93 percent) were interviewed.[2]

The second wave of IFLS (IFLS2) was fielded four years later, between

1. The provinces include four on Sumatra (North Sumatra, West Sumatra, South Sumatra, and Lampung), all of Java, and four provinces from the remaining islands (Bali, West Nusa Tenggara, South Kalimantan, and South Sulawesi).
2. The IFLS1 exceeded the goal of a final sample size of 7,000 completed households. The assumed nonparticipation rate of about 10 percent was based on BPS experience. Approximately 2 percent of households refused and 5 percent were not found. In about two-thirds of those not found, no interview was obtained because either the building was vacated (14 percent), the household refused (25 percent), or no one was at home (29 percent). Other households were not interviewed due to a demolished building, illness, or an inability to locate the building.

August 1997 and early January 1998 (vertical dashed lines in figure 12.1). The goal was to recontact all 7,224 households interviewed in IFLS1. If during the course of the fieldwork we discovered that any household member had moved, we obtained information about their new location and followed them as long as they resided in any of the thirteen IFLS provinces. This means that, by design, we lose households that have moved abroad or to a non-IFLS province; they account for a very small proportion of our households (<1 percent) and are excluded because the costs of finding them are prohibitive.

Large-scale longitudinal household surveys remain rare in developing countries, and there is considerable skepticism that they can be fielded without suffering from high attrition because of the distances that need to be traveled and the lack of communication infrastructure. A respondent is typically not a phone call away. By the standard of most longitudinal surveys, the four-year hiatus between IFLS1 and IFLS2 is long, which probably compounds this difficulty.

Results from IFLS2 suggest that high attrition is not inevitable: 93.3 percent of the IFLS1 households were recontacted and successfully reinterviewed. Excluding those households in which everyone has died (usually single-person households), the success rate is 94 percent.[3]

Given this success, and the timing, IFLS2 was uniquely well positioned to serve as a baseline for another interview with the IFLS respondents to provide some early indicators of how they were affected by and responded to the economic crisis. Between August and December 1998, we fielded IFLS2+.

In a study of this nature, time is of the essence. It took two years to plan and test IFLS2. We did not have two years for IFLS2+. Nor could we raise the resources necessary to mount a survey of the same magnitude as IFLS2. Funding availability and human resources dictated that we field a scaled-down survey.

By design, IFLS2+ readministers many of the IFLS1 and IFLS2 questions so that comparisons across rounds can be made for characteristics of households and individuals (although some submodules were cut to reduce costs). The key dimension in which the survey was scaled down is sample size. Using all of the original 321 IFLS EAs as our sampling frame, we drew the IFLS2+ sample in two stages. First, to keep costs down, we decided to revisit seven of the thirteen IFLS provinces: North Sumatra, South Sumatra, Jakarta, West Java, Central Java, West Nusa Tenggara, and South Kalimantan. These provinces were picked so that they spanned the full spectrum of socioeconomic status and economic activity in the

---

3. Few of the respondents refused to participate (1 percent), so the vast majority of those households that were not reinterviewed were not found. About 15 percent of these are known to have moved to destinations outside Indonesia or in a non-IFLS province; they were, therefore, not followed. The rest are households that have moved but that we were unable to relocate.

fuller IFLS sample. Second, within those provinces, we randomly drew 80 EAs (25 percent of the full IFLS sample) with weighted probabilities in order to match the IFLS sample as closely as possible. These weights were based on the marginal distributions of sector of residence (urban or rural), household size, education level of the household head, and quartiles of per capita expenditure (measured in 1993). The IFLS2+ sample is representative of the entire IFLS sample, and our purposive sampling has, in fact, achieved a very high level of overall efficiency—74 percent relative to a simple random sample. This is very good given that the sample size is only 25 percent of the original sample.

Counting all the original households in IFLS1 (whether or not they were interviewed in IFLS2) as well as the split-offs in IFLS2, there are 2,066 households in the IFLS2+ target sample. The turmoil in Indonesia during 1998 made relocating and interviewing these households particularly tricky. Fortunately, the combination of outstanding field-workers, the experience of IFLS2, and the willingness of our respondents to participate meant that we achieved an even higher success rate than in IFLS2. As is shown in the first row of panel A of table 12.1, over 95 percent of the target households were reinterviewed; excluding those households that are known to have died by 1998, the household completion rate increases to over 96 percent.

12.2.2   Attrition in IFLS2+

From a scientific point of view, it is important to retain all the original respondents in our target sample, even if they were not interviewed in IFLS2. Our target sample therefore includes the (approximately) 6 percent of households in the IFLS2+ EAs that were not interviewed in 1997. In 1998, we successfully contacted over 60 percent of those households. However, for the purposes of this study, the households of central interest are those that were interviewed in both 1997 and 1998, since only for these households can we contrast their lives now with their lives a year ago. These are the households that form the analytic sample used in the rest of this study. Restricting ourselves to these 1,934 households, as shown in the second row of panel A of table 12.1, over 98 percent of the households were reinterviewed. The remainder of panel A of table 12.1 provides reinterview rates by province of residence prior to the crisis. The completion rate exceeds 95 percent in every province, and in one province, West Nusa Tenggara, we reinterviewed every IFLS2 household.[4]

---

4. It is useful to put these numbers into perspective by contrasting them with other longitudinal surveys. The Panel Study of Income Dynamics began as an annual survey in 1968 in the United States. In it, 88 percent of respondents were reinterviewed in the second round and 85 percent in the third wave. The Health and Retirement Survey has a two-year hiatus between each wave; 91 percent of respondents were reinterviewed in the second wave and 92 percent in the third wave. The China Health and Nutrition Survey interviewed 3,795 households in eight provinces in China in 1989 and reinterviewed 95 percent of those in 1991 and then 91 percent in 1993. The comparable reinterview rates in the IFLS are 94 percent, 95 percent, and 95 percent after four, five, and seven years, respectively.

Table 12.1   **IFLS2+: Household attrition**

Sample	Target no. of households	No. of households interviewed	% households interviewed All	Alive
A. Household completion rates				
All IFLS households	2,066	1,972	95.5	96.3
All IFLS2 households	1,934	1,903	98.4	98.5
By province				
North Sumatra	213	208	97.7	97.7
South Sumatra	289	283	98.0	99.0
Jakarta	181	178	98.3	98.3
West Java	318	312	98.1	98.1
Central Java	452	445	98.5	98.9
West Nusa Tenggara	295	295	100.0	100.0
South Kalimantan	186	182	97.9	97.9

	All households (1)	Alive in 1998 (2)	Interviewed in 1998 All (3)	In origin (4)	New location (5)
B. Characteristics of all households and reinterviewed households					
Per capita expenditure	78.69	78.69	75.26	72.67	111.59
(Rp000)	(2.99)	(3.02)	(2.69)	(2.68)	(12.8)
Food share	53.76	53.63	53.62	53.53	55.40
	(0.38)	(0.38)	(0.38)	(0.38)	(1.62)
Household size	4.51	4.54	4.57	4.62	3.82
	(0.05)	(0.05)	(0.05)	(0.05)	(0.19)
Age of household head	45.95	45.75	45.81	46.07	41.76
	(0.33)	(0.33)	(0.33)	(0.33)	(1.44)

Notes: Means and standard errors (in parentheses) based on data collected in 1993 for households that were living in the IFLS2+ EAs at that time. Columns based on all households in IFLS1, all households known to be alive in 1998, and all households interviewed in 1998. Among those households, those found in the original EA in 1998 are distinguished from those who were tracked to a new location by 1998.

While we succeeded in keeping attrition low in the survey, it is important to recognize that the households that were not recontacted are not likely to be random. To provide some sense of the magnitude of the problem, we can compare the observed characteristics (measured in 1993) of the households that were recontacted with the target sample of all IFLS households. Results for some key household characteristics are reported in panel B of table 12.1. The differences between the full sample of IFLS households in the EAs included in IFLS2+ (column [1]), households in which at least one 1993 member was still alive (column [2]), and the households that were reinterviewed in 1997 and again in 1998 (column [3]) is, in all cases, small and not significant. Households that were not reinterviewed tend to have

slightly higher levels of per capita expenditure (PCE), lower food shares, and fewer members than the full sample. We know a little more about households that have been lost to attrition. Recall that in 1998 we found 60 percent of the households that were originally living in IFLS2+ EAs but were not found in 1997. In terms of their characteristics in 1993 and 1998, these households are not significantly different from the sample of households that were interviewed in all three waves. We conclude, therefore, that attrition bias is not likely to be of overwhelming importance in the analyses discussed below.

The majority of longitudinal household surveys in developing countries have not attempted to follow households that move out of the community in which they were interviewed in the baseline. In the IFLS, we did attempt to follow movers. Had we followed the strategy of simply interviewing people who still live in their original housing structure, we would have reinterviewed approximately 83 percent of the IFLS1 households in IFLS2 and only 77 percent of the target households in IFLS2+ rather than the 96 percent that we did achieve. Thus, movers contribute about 20 percent to the total IFLS2+ sample, and they are extremely important in terms of their contribution to the information content of the sample. This is apparent in the last two columns of panel B of table 12.1, which present the characteristics (measured in 1993) of households that were found in the original location in 1997 and 1998 (column [4]) and movers (column [5]). Mover households are smaller and younger, and they had higher expenditures in 1993.[5] Given that our goal is to examine the impact of the crisis on expenditures of households, the fact that movers have expenditures that are 50 percent higher than stayers indicates the critical importance of following movers in order to interpret the evidence. Had we not attempted to follow movers, we would have started out with a substantially biased sample. (For a fuller discussion of attrition in IFLS along with a discussion of the costs and benefits of tracking movers in longitudinal surveys, see Thomas, Smith, and Frankenberg 2001.)

12.3 Results

We turn now to a description of the changes between 1997 and 1998 experienced by the households that were interviewed in IFLS2 and IFLS2+; attention is restricted to households for which we have complete information on expenditure, household composition, and location.[6] Drawing on household expenditures, we describe the magnitude of the crisis and present some evidence on the characteristics of the households and communi-

5. These differences are all significant; the relevant t-statistics are 4.1, 3.4, and 3.8, respectively.
6. The expenditure module was not completed in either IFLS2 or IFLS2+ by twenty households (1 percent of the sample).

ties that have been most affected by the crisis. This is followed by an analysis of changes in the allocation of the household budget among goods, placing particular emphasis on the relationship with household demographic composition prior to the crisis. Spending on education and health is highlighted, and so we turn next to evidence on school enrollments and nutrition and health status. We end with a discussion of the impact of the crisis on wages, household income, and asset depletion.

12.3.1 Household Expenditure

To put the magnitude of the crisis in perspective, we begin with household expenditure patterns.[7] Mean total monthly household expenditure in 1997 is reported in the first column of table 12.2: it is close to Rp1 million. Inflation for 1998 is estimated to be around 80 percent. It is thus important to deflate expenditures in 1998 so that they are comparable with 1997; we use a province-specific index based on urban price data from BPS.[8] Real monthly expenditure for the same households is reported in the second column of the table. The mean of the difference in expenditure (1998–1997) is reported in the third column. On average, total household expenditure has declined by about 10 percent. A similar comparison is drawn for changes in monthly PCE: it has declined, on average, by about 25 percent, which is both very large and significant. Looking at median expenditure, the story is strikingly different. It has remained stable during this period.

Essentially all the changes in the distribution of PCE have occurred in the bottom and top quartiles of the distribution, as is shown in the box-and-whisker plots in figure 12.2. The PCE of households in the top of the

7. Household expenditure in IFLS is based on respondents' recall of outlays for a series of different goods (or categories of goods); for each item, the respondent is asked first about money expenditures and then about the imputed value of consumption out of own production, consumption that is provided in kind, gifts, and transfers. The reference period for the recall varies depending on the good. The respondent is asked about food expenditures over the previous week for thirty-seven food items or groups of items (such as rice; cassava, tapioca, dried cassava; tofu, tempe, etc.; oil; and so on). For those people who produce their own food, the respondent is asked to value the amount consumed in the previous week. There are nineteen nonfood items; for some we use a reference period of the previous month (electricity, water, fuel; recurrent transport expenses; domestic services), and for others the reference period is a year (clothing, medical costs, education). It is difficult to get good measures of housing expenses in these sorts of surveys. We record rental costs (for those who are renting) and ask the respondent for an estimated rental equivalent (for those who are owner-occupiers or live rent free). All expenditures are cumulated and converted to a monthly equivalent. The analytical sample for expenditure-related analyses is restricted to those households that completed the expenditure module in both IFLS2 and IFLS2+.

8. To this end, 1998 expenditures in urban areas are deflated using a province-specific price deflator based on the BPS price indexes reported for forty-five cities in Indonesia matched to the provinces included in the sample. (The simple average of the price index is used for provinces with more than one city.) Price indexes for August, September, October, and November 1998 are used, deflating all 1998 expenditures to December 1997. The inflation rates are increased by an additional 5 percent in rural areas based on IFLS estimates of the difference in the increase in prices in the sectors. The urban inflation rates are given in appendix table 12A.1.

Table 12.2 IFLS households expenditure: 1997, 1998, and changes (all households and households stratified by sector of residence)

	Total household expenditure			Per capita expenditure			Poverty rate	
	1997 (1)	1998 (2)	Δ (3)	1997 (4)	1998 (5)	Δ (6)	1997 (7)	1998 (8)
			A. BPS forty-five city price index					
All Indonesia								
Mean	921	823	–98	246	186	–60	11.0	13.8
Standard error	(79)	(22)	(77)	(18)	(5)	(17)	(1.5)	(1.8)
Median	544	557	18	131	129	–4		
Standard IQR	(15)	(16)	(13)	(4)	(4)	(3)		
Sector of residence								
Urban								
Mean	1,227	944	–283	319	211	–108	9.2	12.0
Standard error	(184)	(41)	(181)	(41)	(10)	(40)	(2.3)	(2.6)
Median	620	593	–12	141	134	–8		
Standard IQR	(26)	(28)	(21)	(7)	(6)	(5)		
Rural								
Mean	705	703	–2	194	160	–34	12.4	16.2
Standard error	(33)	(24)	(27)	(8)	(5)	(7)	(2.1)	(2.5)
Median	481	503	14	127	120	–5		
Standard IQR	(19)	(19)	(16)	(5)	(4)	(4)		
			B. BPS-adjusted estimates of inflation using IFLS prices					
All Indonesia								
Mean	921	668	–253	246	151	–95	11.0	19.9
Standard error	(79)	(19)	(77)	(18)	(4)	(17)	(1.5)	(2.1)
Median	544	446	–69	131	104	–23		
Standard IQR	(15)	(13)	(12)	(4)	(3)	(3)		
Sector of residence								
Urban								
Mean	1,227	822	–405	319	184	–135	9.2	15.8
Standard error	(184)	(35)	(181)	(41)	(9)	(40)	(2.3)	(3.0)
Median	620	519	–81	141	116	–21		
Standard IQR	(26)	(25)	(20)	(7)	(5)	(5)		
Rural								
Mean	705	560	–146	194	128	–66	12.4	23.0
Standard error	(33)	(19)	(27)	(8)	(4)	(7)	(2.1)	(2.8)
Median	481	399	–66	127	95	–24		
Standard IQR	(19)	(15)	(15)	(5)	(4)	(4)		

Notes: There are 1,883 households, of which 797 are urban and 1,096 are rural. All expenditure estimates are converted to annual equivalents in thousands of rupiahs. 1998 estimates are expressed in terms of December 1997 prices. Columns (1)–(3) use province-specific price indexes based on the forty-five city price indexes published by BPS. Rural estimates assume inflation in rural areas is 5 percent higher than in urban areas as suggested by the IFLS community-level data. Columns (4)–(6) use a combination of BPS and IFLS prices. IFLS estimates of inflation for all IFLS2+ provinces are about 15 percent higher than BPS estimates; the IFLS also estimates that rural inflation is about 5 percent higher than urban inflation. The BPS forty-five city price indexes have been converted to province-specific price indexes, which have been inflated by an additional 14 percent in urban areas and 16 percent in rural areas to generate the IFLS estimates of inflation. Poverty rates are for the population. IQR = interquartile range.

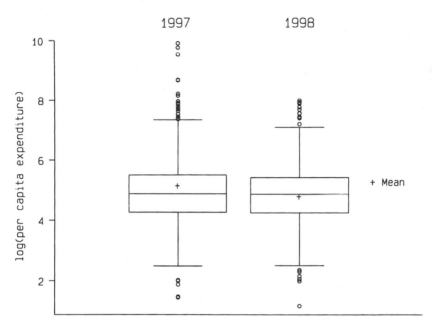

Fig. 12.2   Distribution of lnPCE, box-and-whisker plot

distribution is substantially lower in 1998, relative to 1997; the bottom tail has moved much less in absolute terms, although there is a suggestion that PCE among the very poorest is lower in 1998, relative to 1997. This is reflected in panel A of table 12.2, which indicates that the poverty rate has increased from 11 percent to about 14 percent.[9]

Figure 12.2 suggests that inequality as measured by PCE has declined during the period. This is confirmed by estimates of the standard deviation of the logarithm of PCE (which has fallen from 0.94 to 0.86) and is depicted in the Lorenz curves in figure 12.3. They indicate that the decline in inequality can be attributed to two factors: the reduction in PCE at the top of the distribution and the reduction in the mean of PCE.

We conclude that there has been a substantial shift in the structure of the distribution of expenditure, with the center of the distribution remaining relatively stable, the right tail being substantially truncated between 1997 and 1998, and the left tail becoming fatter. These facts are illustrated in panel A of figure 12.4, which is a nonparametric estimate of the density of

9. The appropriate definition of the poverty line is controversial. Province- and sector-specific poverty lines have been chosen in terms of PCE so that estimated poverty rates in IFLS2 correspond with the BPS province- and sector-specific poverty rates for 1996. Thus, the 11 percent poverty rate is constructed to match the official rate.

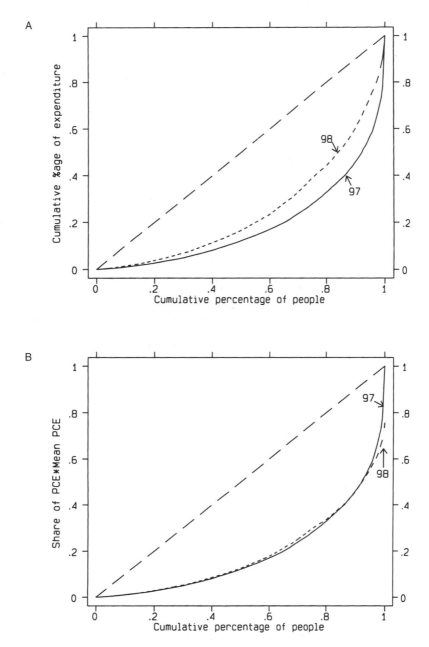

Fig. 12.3   Distribution of PCE: *A*, **PCE Lorenz curves, 1997 and 1998;** *B*, **PCE generalized Lorenz curves, 1997 and 1998**

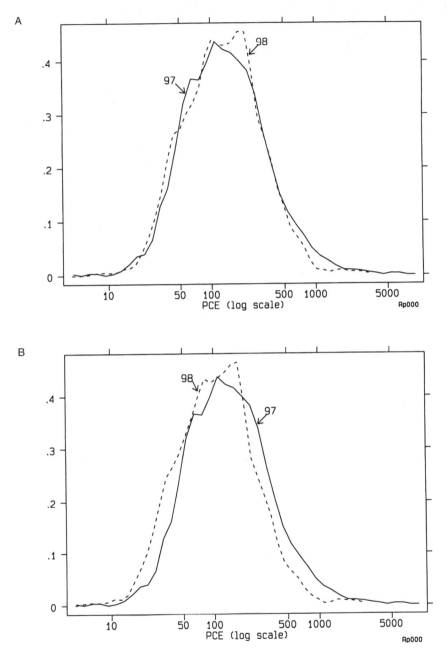

Fig. 12.4   Per capita expenditure distribution, 1997 and 1998: *A*, **BPS inflation rate;** *B,* **BPS-adjusted inflation rate**

PCE. It indicates that the poor, the middle class, and the better-off have all been affected by this crisis.[10]

12.3.2   Urban and Rural Differences in Expenditure

The second part of panel A of table 12.2 distinguishes those households that were living in an urban area in 1997 from those living in a rural area prior to the crisis. Description of the within-sector distribution of resources in 1998 requires taking into account migration across sectors. The goal here is to highlight the differential impact of the crisis on households depending on their location prior to the crisis. Recall that net food producers and producers of exported goods were insulated from bearing the brunt of the collapse of the rupiah. Net food producers and producers of agricultural goods for export are more likely to have been rural.

The data are consistent with this prediction. Relative to rural households, expenditures of households living in urban areas in 1997 were more seriously affected by the crisis. On average, total household expenditure fell by nearly 25 percent, PCE declined by 34 percent, and the poverty rate increased by 30 percent. In contrast, among households in rural areas, total household expenditure did not decline on average; PCE is estimated to have declined by 18 percent, although the impact on the poorest was about the same as among urban households since the poverty rate also rose by 30 percent in rural areas.

12.3.3   Changes in Living Arrangements

Since, on average, total household expenditure declined less than PCE, the size of the average household increased between 1997 and 1998. One response to the crisis was adjustment in living arrangements, as family members moved in together to exploit economies of scale of consumption. The increase in household size was greater among households in rural areas, which reflects both the effect of households joining together within the rural sector and the migration of individuals from urban areas to join households in rural areas. Specifically, individuals from the poorest urban households migrated to join households in rural areas where the cost of living was lower and where there were more opportunities to earn income. Frankenberg, Smith, and Thomas (2003) show that urban households at the bottom of the precrisis PCE distribution tended to lose household members, that household size tended to increase across the entire PCE distribution in rural areas, and that the increase in household size tended to rise with precrisis PCE in both rural and urban areas.

Thus, changes in PCE between 1997 and 1998 can be attributed to two factors: a decline in levels of resources and a change in household size. In

---

10. The nonparametric estimate of the density of PCE is based on an Epanechikov kernel with a 10 percent bandwidth.

the literature, changes in PCE have been interpreted as indicative of changes in well-being. Putting aside the impact of changes in household composition on changes in the distribution of resources within households and among members of different demographic groups, equating changes in PCE with changes in well-being is fraught with potential difficulties. Specifically, if household size and composition change in response to shocks and if these changes are correlated with the changes in expenditure, then changes in PCE will not in general be good indicators of changes in well-being. For example, part of the decline in PCE at the top of the distribution can be attributed to an increase in household size among these households. In addition, recall that poverty rates are estimated to have increased by around 30 percent in both the rural and urban areas. Part of the increase in poverty in rural areas is due to the increase in household size, whereas the estimated rise in urban poverty is smaller than it would have been without the loss of household members. Conclusions in the literature about the impact of shocks on poverty and well-being that fail to take into account the fact that both resources and living arrangements might change together are potentially seriously misleading. These results highlight the importance of treating economic resources and demographic composition of households as jointly determined.

12.3.4   Sensitivity to Estimates of Inflation Rate

Interpretation of evidence based on expenditures is further complicated in the presence of inflation. The price indexes available from BPS are based only on urban markets, and so it is implicitly assumed that inflation in the urban and rural sectors are the same. We can test that assumption using data reported in the IFLS community surveys. Those surveys collect information on ten prices of standardized commodities from up to three local stores and markets in each community; in addition, prices for thirty-nine items are asked of the Ibu PKK (leader of the local women's group) and knowledgeable informants at up to three *posyandus* (health posts) in each community. Using those prices, in combination with the household-level expenditure data, we have calculated EA-specific (Laspeyres) price indexes for the IFLS communities for 1997 and 1998. We estimate that in our EAs rural inflation is about 5 percent higher than urban inflation, and estimates reported for rural households in panel A of table 12.2 take this into account.

In an environment of rapidly changing prices, estimation of the inflation rate is not easy. In the BPS estimates, there is substantial heterogeneity in inflation across the forty-five cities that are included in the calculation of the national rate, ranging between 50 percent and 90 percent. See Levinsohn, Berry, and Friedman (2003) for a discussion. With this in mind, we have attempted to estimate the inflation rate that would be implied by the price data reported in IFLS for the EAs included in IFLS2+. Because we

do not have a complete set of prices in IFLS, we have matched the IFLS prices with subaggregates reported by BPS and compared the implied inflation rates for this subset of commodities. Using the IFLS data, we estimate inflation between the rounds of the survey to be about 15 percent higher than the BPS rate. While it is important to emphasize that IFLS is not designed to collect the detailed data necessary to calculate price indexes, this difference gives us pause. It might arise if our EAs are drawn from relatively high inflation areas, or it may reflect bias in either the BPS or IFLS estimates of inflation (or both). The difference, however, is large and suggests that it would be prudent to provide some assessment of likely bounds for the impact of the crisis by contrasting estimates of expenditure-based indicators using the BPS forty-five city inflation estimates and IFLS estimates of inflation.

To this end, we have explored the implications of the difference in the estimates of inflation both for the magnitude of the crisis and for the identification of who has been most seriously impacted by the crisis. Maintaining the 5 percent gap between rural and urban inflation implied by the IFLS, we have adjusted the BPS province-specific price indexes to match the IFLS inflation rate; specifically, we have inflated urban prices by an additional 14 percent and rural prices by an additional 16 percent. We refer to these as BPS-adjusted prices. Clearly, the higher inflation rates shift the entire real PCE distribution to the left. (See panel B of figure 12.4.) As shown in panel B of table 12.2, not only is there a decline in mean PCE of around 40 percent, but also the median declines by around 20 percent. There is a very substantial increase of around 80 percent in the fraction of the population below the poverty line, which rises to nearly 20 percent for the country as a whole.

In our judgment, it is likely that reality lies between these two extremes.[11] In a world of very high and variable inflation, estimates of well-being based exclusively on PCE (or income) may be seriously misleading if inflation estimates are available for only a small number of geographic units. Moreover, there are some conceptual concerns that are extremely difficult to address even with very good price data. The inflation rate that is relevant for a particular household will depend on its consumption patterns, which may not be the same as those of the average household, which is what is used in the construction of indexes. Specifically, poorer households typically spend a greater fraction of their budget on food; since the rate of in-

---

11. It is extremely difficult to estimate inflation when prices change as rapidly as they have in Indonesia in 1998. Based on other evidence in the IFLS, we conjecture that the IFLS-based estimates of inflation are biased upward. We do not have enough information in the market-based surveys to use those data alone, so we have combined them with information obtained from the PKK and *posyandu* informants, who appear to have overstated price increases. However, we have no reason to suppose that this overstatement is greater for rural than for urban households, and so in the absence of a better source for rural prices, we are inclined to rely on the IFLS estimate that rural inflation is slightly higher than urban inflation.

crease in food prices is about 20 percent higher than the overall inflation rate, price changes for the poor are likely to be higher than price changes for middle-income households. People are likely to substitute away from commodities that become relatively expensive, in which case inflation rates based on a fixed bundle of goods will tend to overstate actual inflation. If the poorest households have less scope for substitution than other households (say, because most of their budget is spent on staples), they are likely to be more severely affected by price increases than households that are better off.

While the magnitude of the impact of the crisis on expenditure-based measures is very sensitive to assumptions about inflation, the evolution of poverty after the crisis is not. By 2000, the level of poverty (as measured by the fraction below a fixed real poverty line) was below the level in 1997, and this inference is robust to the choice of poverty line. Moreover, over half the population that was judged poor in 1997 was no longer in poverty by 2000, and, by the same token, half the poor in 2000 were not deemed to be poor in 1997 (Strauss et al. 2004). There is not only substantial mobility into and out of poverty but also considerable variation in the decline and growth of resources across the entire distribution of PCE. We turn next to an assessment of the socioeconomic and demographic characteristics associated with changes in PCE around the time of the crisis.

12.3.5   Correlates of Changes in lnPCE

As a first step in putting the issue of measuring inflation into the background, we turn to an examination of the covariates that are associated with changes in lnPCE between 1997 and 1998 in a multivariate context. To the extent that these covariates are not related to price changes, we can interpret the regression coefficients as providing descriptive information about the types of households and communities that have been most seriously impacted by the crisis. Results are summarized in table 12.3. A negative coefficient indicates that lnPCE in 1998 is lower than lnPCE in 1997. Estimates of standard errors are robust to arbitrary forms of heteroskedasticity and permit within-cluster correlations in unobservables.

Estimates are presented separately for households in the urban and rural sectors. For each sector, regressions reported in the first two columns are based on the BPS inflation rates, the third column repeats the second regression using estimates of changes in lnPCE based on the adjusted inflation rate, and the fourth column includes a community-level fixed effect that sweeps out all fixed (and additive) community-level heterogeneity, including prices. The results in this column should, therefore, be robust to different estimates of the rate of inflation.

The first set of covariates is measured at the community level. They indicate that communities in which the main activity is agriculture (in rural areas) and those that have a higher fraction of households operating farm

Table 12.3   Changes in ln(per capita expenditure) between 1997 and 1998: Correlates associated with Δln(PCE)

	Urban				Rural			
	Official inflation (1)	Official inflation (2)	Adjusted inflation (3)	Community fixed effects (4)	Official inflation (5)	Official inflation (6)	Adjusted inflation (7)	Community fixed effects (8)
Community characteristics								
Mean lnPCE	—	-0.177 [1.79]	-0.143 [1.41]	—	—	-0.149 [0.90]	-0.095 [0.60]	—
Standard deviation lnPCE	—	-0.308 [2.05]	-0.307 [1.79]	—	—	0.274 [1.34]	0.295 [1.48]	—
Main activity = agriculture (1)	—	—	—	—	—	—	—	—
Trading	0.061 [0.73]	0.128 [1.46]	0.079 [0.82]	—	0.311	0.312	0.290	—
Services	-0.387 [2.59]	-0.289 [2.51]	-0.176 [1.64]	—	0.408 [2.08]	0.44 [2.13]	0.438 [2.22]	—
Construction	0.054 [0.58]	0.069 [0.92]	0.101 [1.28]	—	0.029 [0.5]	0.025 [0.42]	0.070 [1.23]	—
Military camp	0.105 [0.65]	0.168 [1.14]	0.071 [0.45]	—	-0.114 [1.13]	-0.102 [1.06]	-0.064 [0.65]	—
Fraction of households owning								
Nonfarm business	-0.289 [1.15]	-0.362 [1.63]	-0.23 [0.96]	—	-0.278 [1.37]	-0.295 [1.38]	-0.301 [1.31]	—
Farm business	0.525 [2.36]	0.464 [2.11]	0.459 [2.09]	—	0.152 [1.15]	0.126 [0.97]	0.126 [1.00]	—
Accessible by road all year (1)	0.238 [1.7]	0.22 [1.61]	0.222 [1.59]	—	-0.482 [4.00]	-0.515 [4.02]	-0.496 [4.34]	—
Kecamatan capital (1)	-0.053 [0.55]	-0.083 [0.97]	-0.055 [0.57]	—	-0.201 [2.81]	-0.242 [2.7]	-0.240 [2.9]	—
Province								
North Sumatra (1)	0.237 [1.73]	0.067 [0.43]	-0.007 [0.04]	—	-0.419 [3.68]	-0.370 [3.26]	-0.405 [3.78]	—
South Sumatra (1)	0.281 [1.61]	0.194 [1.36]	0.225 [1.41]	—	0.226 [2.02]	0.173 [1.35]	0.247 [1.97]	—

	(1)	(2)	(3)	(4)	(5)	(6)	(7)	(8)
Jakarta (1)	0.216 [1.56]	0.134 [1.02]	0.095 [0.61]	—	0.182 [0.7]	0.257 [0.97]	0.308 [1.17]	—
Central Java (1)	0.251 [1.68]	0.148 [1.15]	0.139 [0.91]	—	-0.103 [0.87]	-0.075 [0.68]	-0.082 [0.75]	—
West Nusa Tenggara (1)	0.175 [1.06]	0.065 [0.41]	-0.010 [0.05]	—	-0.150 [1.23]	-0.140 [1.09]	-0.059 [0.44]	—
South Kalimantan	0.121 [0.85]	0.034 [0.27]	0.005 [0.03]	—	-0.232 [1.73]	-0.161 [0.95]	-0.160 [1.09]	—
Household composition: number of each gender and age years								
Males 0–4	0.046 [0.67]	0.032 [0.48]	0.003 [0.04]	0.078 [1.03]	0.108 [1.58]	0.106 [1.55]	0.118 [1.67]	0.106 [1.54]
Females 0–4	0.139 [1.92]	0.119 [1.60]	0.158 [2.11]	0.129 [1.69]	0.062 [0.79]	0.059 [0.76]	-0.001 [0.02]	-0.007 [0.10]
Males 5–9	0.026 [0.36]	0.023 [0.33]	0.009 [0.13]	0.019 [0.26]	0.137 [2.6]	0.135 [2.61]	0.124 [2.61]	0.122 [2.09]
Females 5–9	0.029 [0.35]	0.025 [0.32]	0.012 [0.15]	0.024 [0.33]	0.019 [0.31]	0.022 [0.34]	0.019 [0.28]	0.008 [0.13]
Males 10–14	-0.043 [0.55]	-0.05 [0.64]	-0.104 [1.35]	-0.025 [0.39]	0.002 [0.05]	-0.005 [0.12]	0.013 [0.28]	0.000 [0.00]
Females 10–14	-0.011 [0.17]	-0.019 [0.28]	-0.002 [0.03]	-0.021 [0.35]	0.053 [1.09]	0.049 [1.01]	0.044 [0.89]	0.021 [0.34]
Males 15–24	0.025 [0.45]	0.023 [0.43]	0.021 [0.42]	0.066 [1.63]	0.033 [1.01]	0.033 [1.03]	0.03 [0.89]	0.056 [1.17]
Females 15–24	0.152 [3.04]	0.146 [2.89]	0.118 [2.33]	0.147 [3.1]	0.098 [1.60]	0.098 [1.60]	0.113 [1.89]	0.072 [1.39]
Males 25–64	0.048 [0.89]	0.048 [0.93]	0.048 [0.82]	0.09 [1.35]	0.044 [0.49]	0.043 [0.48]	0.02 [0.23]	0.042 [0.54]
Females 25–64	0.183 [2.85]	0.172 [2.54]	0.158 [2.25]	0.136 [2.44]	0.204 [2.57]	0.202 [2.56]	0.226 [2.99]	0.251 [3.84]
Males ≥65	0.047 [0.33]	0.046 [0.32]	0.115 [0.77]	0.03 [0.21]	0.021 [0.16]	0.021 [0.16]	0.026 [0.20]	0.051 [0.40]
Females ≥65	0.073 [0.75]	0.072 [0.72]	0.206 [1.94]	0.033 [0.32]	0.102 [0.98]	0.099 [0.94]	0.086 [0.83]	0.065 [0.65]

(continued)

Table 12.3   (continued)

Household characteristics	Urban				Rural			
	Official inflation (1)	Official inflation (2)	Adjusted inflation (3)	Community fixed effects (4)	Official inflation (5)	Official inflation (6)	Adjusted inflation (7)	Community fixed effects (8)
Age of head	-0.001	0.001	-0.002	-0.002	0.001	0.001	0.001	0.001
	[0.12]	[0.15]	[0.42]	[0.52]	[0.38]	[0.42]	[0.38]	[0.35]
Head is male (1)	-0.015	-0.038	-0.037	-0.037	-0.059	-0.051	-0.053	-0.063
	[0.12]	[0.31]	[0.28]	[0.33]	[0.45]	[0.39]	[0.42]	[0.57]
Education of head	-0.01	-0.004	-0.006	-0.011	-0.008	-0.007	-0.01	-0.006
	[1.14]	[0.38]	[0.61]	[1.2]	[0.78]	[0.67]	[0.95]	[0.63]
Intercept	-0.824	0.394	0.19	-0.324	-0.151	0.369	-0.238	-0.418
	[2.61]	[0.78]	[0.37]	[1.57]	[0.59]	[0.5]	[0.34]	[2.36]
F (Community fixed effects)	—	—	—	1.761	—	—	—	1.818
				(0.00)				(0.00)
F (all covariates)	7.33	11.98	6.09	2.21	12.43	12.24	19.67	2.35
	(0.00)	(0.00)	(0.00)	(0.01)	(0.00)	(0.00)	(0.00)	(0.00)
R^2	0.081	0.093	0.082	0.058	0.074	0.077	0.085	0.022
R^2 within community	—	—	—	0.043	—	—	—	0.034
R^2 between community	—	—	—	0.373	—	—	—	0.091
No. of observations	797				1,096			

Notes: Dependent variable is lnPCE – lnPCE97. t-statistics, in brackets under regression estimates, and p values, in parentheses below test statistics, are robust to heteroskedasticity and within EA correlations. West Java is the excluded province. (1) represents indicator variable that takes the value of 1 if condition is true and zero otherwise.

businesses (in urban areas) have, relative to other communities, had a positive income innovation over the last year. This suggests these communities are net food producers and that, on average, they have benefited from the increase in the relative price of foods over the last year. Rural communities that are primarily trading have also received a positive income innovation, although this is more than offset if the community is accessible by road throughout the year. Innovations have been especially negative in rural areas that serve as the kecamatan capital;[12] these areas have concentrations of civil servants, and the nominal incomes of most government workers have increased only slightly over the last year, so their real incomes have declined dramatically. Rural communities in North Sumatra have fared especially poorly, whereas those in South Sumatra appear to be doing slightly better than West Java, the excluded province.[13]

Among rural households, apparently those living in remote, agricultural communities have been most protected from the deleterious impact of the crisis. This is plausible given that the crisis is to a large extent financial and these communities are likely to have the least interaction with monetized sectors of the economy.

In the urban sector, communities that produce services (which are typically nontradable) have seen their incomes decline more than those in other areas. There is also a suggestion that poorer communities and communities with greater inequality have experienced relatively large negative income innovations. This suggests that poor urban communities—and the poorest households within them—may be worthy of special attention. These inferences, however, should be tempered by the fact that the significance of the effects of the services indicator and the community-level measures of PCE is, at best, marginal when we use the adjusted inflation rates. Getting inflation right is a substantive and serious concern.

The second part of table 12.3 reports the relationship between changes in lnPCE and household characteristics prior to the crisis. The estimates are remarkably robust to assumptions about the inflation rate, including the community fixed effects model in columns (4) and (8), which permits an arbitrary rate of change of the price level in each community.

The age of the household head, education of the head, and whether the head is male are not correlated with the impact of the crisis. This is, perhaps, surprising given that these characteristics are likely to be associated with higher levels of assets and, therefore, would be expected to be related to smoothing of consumption over time. The value of most assets collapsed

---

12. By way of comparison, a kecamatan is smaller than a country but larger than a zip code in the United States.

13. We observed a very substantial increase in migration rates out of North Sumatra between 1997 and 1998, with a large fraction of the movers relocating in neighboring Riau, which, relatively speaking, had been a boom area during the crisis because of oil, fishing, and lumber production for export.

with the economy. There were two exceptions: land and, most notably, gold, the price of which is set in world terms, so its value increased over threefold. Most gold is owned by women, and its ownership is not strongly associated with age or education. In contrast with characteristics of the head, household size in 1997 is associated with protection from the impact of the crisis: PCE has declined least in households that were larger in 1997. Not all household members are equal. In both the rural and the urban sector, households that contain more prime-age women (twenty-five to sixty-four years old) have seen the smallest declines in PCE; in the urban sector, the presence of more younger women (fifteen to twenty-five years old) in the household is also correlated with smaller declines in PCE. This is likely to be a reflection of an increase between 1997 and 1998 in the labor supply of these women.

This inference can be tested directly. In each wave of the IFLS, adult individuals are asked about their time allocation. Among prime-age adults, almost all men (99 percent) were working in both years, but among women there was a substantial increase in the fraction who reported themselves as working (from 70 percent to 83 percent), and this difference (or change) is significant (t-statistic $= 8.9$). The difference-in-difference (the gap in the change in participation rates between men and women) is both large (12 percent) and significant (t-statistic $= 7.4$). Many people in Indonesia work in family enterprises, and those enterprises have absorbed all the new entrants or reentrants into the labor force. Between 1997 and 1998, there has been a decline in the probability that a prime-age man is working for pay (from 91 percent to 87 percent) and no change in the probability a prime-age woman is working for pay (42 percent). This difference-in-difference (4 percent) is also significant (t-statistic $= 2.1$). We conclude that there has been a significant shift in the allocation of time, with prime-age women playing a bigger role in both family enterprises and in paid work. This is true in both the rural and the urban sector.

Among younger adults (fifteen to twenty-four) the story is quite different. Both males and females are more likely to be working and to be working for pay in 1998, relative to 1997. This is to be expected for life-course reasons alone. There are no significant differences in the rate of take-up of work between males and females except for one instance: among urban households, fifteen- to twenty-year-old males are 4 percent less likely to have taken on work that pays between 1997 and 1998, relative to a fifteen-to twenty-year-old female (and this effect is marginally significant: t-statistic $= 1.8$). See Smith et al. (1999) for a more detailed discussion of labor market responses during the crisis, along with other evidence that corroborates these interpretations.

Per capita expenditure appears to have been protected in those urban households with more young girls (zero to four years old) and in rural households with more young boys (zero to nine years old, particularly five

to nine years old). It is unlikely that these children are going out to work; rather, the estimates suggest that women with young children have attempted to keep household income from falling, presumably because they would like to protect their children from the deleterious impact of real income declines. While the gender differences between urban and rural households are intriguing, they are not significant, and so we do not want to make too much of them.

12.3.6   Household Budget Shares

We have noted above that the financial crisis was accompanied by large changes both in the absolute price level and in relative prices. We have also noted that interpretation of changes in (real) lnPCE is complicated by the uncertainty revolving around the changes in prices that households face. The analyses presented above are silent about the effects on household well-being of changes in relative prices. To address this issue, we turn to the allocation of the household budget to goods.

Table 12.4 reports the mean share of the household budget spent on fifteen commodity groups in 1997 and 1998 along with the change in the share (columns [3] and [7] for urban and rural households, respectively) and the change as a percentage of the 1997 share (columns [4] and [8] for urban and rural households, respectively). The BPS inflation rates are used throughout this section. Clearly changes in budget shares capture the impact of both changes in purchasing power and changes in relative prices.

Estimates of ordinary least squares (OLS) regressions that describe the relationship between changes in budget shares and household characteristics are reported in table 12.5. In order to put inflation into the background, the regressions include a community-level fixed effect. The covariates in the regressions, which are all measured in 1997, fall into three groups: income (which is entered as a spline in lnPCE with a knot at median PCE), household composition, and the demographic characteristics of the household head. In this section, we focus on changes in budget shares and their association with household income. A discussion of the links between budget shares and household composition is deferred to the next subsection.

Food accounts for more than half the budget of the average household in Indonesia, and the food share increased significantly (by about 5 percentage points) between 1997 and 1998. According to Engel's law (which says that household welfare is inversely related to the food share), the average Indonesian household is substantially worse off in 1998 than prior to the onset of the crisis. In 1988, urban households spent 60 percent of their budget on food, and rural households spent 80 percent of their budget on food.

To a large extent the increase in the food share reflects an increase in the allocation of expenditure to staples (primarily rice). Among urban house-

Table 12.4   IFLS expenditure shares: Urban and rural sectors

	Urban households				Rural households			
	1997 (1)	1998 (2)	Change (3)	%Δ (4)	1997 (5)	1998 (6)	Change (7)	%Δ (8)
Food	58.96	63.95	4.99 (0.86)	8	76.17	80.84	4.68 (0.62)	6
Staples	12.99	20.61	7.62 (0.77)	59	30.58	39.39	8.81 (0.90)	29
Meat	12.69	10.40	−2.29 (0.58)	−18	12.46	9.74	−2.72 (0.58)	−22
Dairy	3.66	3.74	0.08 (0.32)	2	2.67	2.64	−0.02 (0.22)	−1
Oil	1.93	2.89	0.96 (0.14)	50	2.70	2.48	−0.22 (0.20)	−8
Vegetables	8.91	8.51	−0.39 (0.45)	−4	11.47	12.94	1.48 (0.52)	13
Alcohol/tobacco	4.08	5.74	1.66 (0.80)	41	4.43	4.04	−0.39 (0.30)	−9
Household goods	8.17	6.80	−1.37 (0.31)	−17	3.59	3.17	−0.41 (0.16)	−12
Transport	3.15	3.20	0.40 (0.28)	1	1.80	1.51	−0.29 (0.18)	−16
Clothing	2.94	2.48	−0.46 (0.11)	−16	2.20	1.50	−0.69 (0.09)	−32
Housing	10.77	9.14	−1.63 (0.59)	−15	6.14	4.82	−1.32 (0.36)	−21
Recreation	2.58	2.05	−0.53 (0.22)	−21	1.83	1.70	−0.12 (0.16)	−7
Health	1.73	1.49	−0.24 (0.20)	−14	1.16	0.69	−0.47 (0.12)	−40
Education	4.91	4.51	−0.40 (0.27)	−8	2.38	1.81	−0.56 (0.13)	−24
No. of observations		797				1096		

Notes: Change is share in 1998 – share in 1997. Standard errors (in parentheses) are below change. %Δ is change as percentage of 1997 share.

holds, the staple share has increased by over 50 percent (to account for one-fifth of the total budget), and in rural households it has increased by 30 percent (to account for two-fifths of the total budget). These are very large increases. They are partially offset by a significant reduction (of about 20 percent) in the share of the budget spent on meat. Taken together, the results indicate a decline in the quality of the diet of the average Indonesian.

The estimates of income effects at the top of table 12.5 provide insights into how these changes are distributed across households. In both the urban and the rural sector, food shares have increased the most for the poorest. For households below median PCE in 1997, the increase in the food

Table 12.5   **Changes in budget shares**

| | Food | | | Nonfood | | | |
	Food (1)	Staples (2)	Meat (3)	Alcohol and tobacco (4)	Clothing (5)	Health (6)	Education (7)
			A. Urban households				
ln(PCE) (spline)							
Below median	−5.512	0.782	−4.278	2.643	1.038	−0.51	−0.483
	[2.24]	[0.36]	[2.6]	[1.37]	[3.13]	[0.9]	[0.62]
Above median	−0.075	−3.728	3.533	0.062	0.579	−0.353	1
	[0.05]	[2.68]	[3.4]	[0.05]	[2.76]	[0.99]	[2.02]
Household composition: number of each gender and age (years)							
Males 0–4	−1.429	−0.692	−0.809	−1.33	0.069	−0.766	0.907
	[0.71]	[0.39]	[0.6]	[0.85]	[0.26]	[1.67]	[1.42]
Females 0–4	3.419	1.061	0.859	0.015	−0.184	−0.624	0.393
	[1.68]	[0.58]	[0.63]	[0.01]	[0.67]	[1.34]	[0.61]
Males 5–9	1.772	−2.503	0.026	0.332	0.092	−0.237	−0.28
	[0.91]	[1.44]	[0.02]	[0.22]	[0.35]	[0.53]	[0.45]
Females 5–9	1.04	1.091	−1.262	−1.265	0.161	0.356	0.259
	[0.53]	[0.62]	[0.95]	[0.82]	[0.6]	[0.79]	[0.41]
Males 10–14	−2.054	−1.359	−1.518	0.673	0.555	0.672	−0.317
	[1.22]	[0.9]	[1.35]	[0.51]	[2.44]	[1.74]	[0.59]
Females 10–14	1.601	0.21	0.151	−0.742	−0.37	0.042	−1.049
	[1.02]	[0.15]	[0.14]	[0.6]	[1.75]	[0.12]	[2.11]
Males 15–19	−0.738	−0.616	0.784	−0.358	0.15	−0.332	2.466
	[0.56]	[0.53]	[0.89]	[0.35]	[0.85]	[1.11]	[5.91]
Females 15–19	0.173	0.372	0.645	−0.686	0.627	−0.192	−0.773
	[0.11]	[0.27]	[0.62]	[0.56]	[2.97]	[0.54]	[1.55]
Males 20–24	−1.481	1.927	−2.868	−0.394	−0.107	0.018	−0.398
	[0.73]	[1.06]	[2.11]	[0.25]	[0.39]	[0.04]	[0.62]
Females 20–24	0.79	−3.238	1.826	−1.116	0.53	0.102	−0.803
	[0.39]	[1.79]	[1.35]	[0.71]	[1.95]	[0.22]	[1.25]
Males 25–39	−2.008	−1.729	−2.292	−1.737	0.233	0.134	−0.492
	[1.19]	[1.15]	[2.03]	[1.31]	[1.02]	[0.35]	[0.92]
Females 25–39	−0.826	0.107	1.322	−0.539	−0.173	0.139	−0.111
	[0.48]	[0.07]	[1.14]	[0.4]	[0.74]	[0.35]	[0.2]
Males 40–54	1.058	0.751	−0.111	1.092	−0.107	0.175	−0.611
	[0.42]	[0.33]	[0.07]	[0.55]	[0.31]	[0.3]	[0.76]
Females 40–54	0.155	−1.394	0.68	−3.385	0.166	0.188	−0.639
	[0.07]	[0.71]	[0.46]	[1.97]	[0.56]	[0.37]	[0.92]
Males 55–64	−3.916	−0.091	−0.342	1.103	−0.599	1.121	−0.802
	[1.06]	[0.03]	[0.14]	[0.38]	[1.21]	[1.33]	[0.69]
Females 55–64	1.605	0.576	−0.423	−0.929	0.067	0.275	−0.249
	[0.57]	[0.23]	[0.23]	[0.42]	[0.18]	[0.43]	[0.28]
Males ≥65	1.398	0.66	−1.714	−3.506	−0.181	−0.322	1.071
	[0.34]	[0.18]	[0.63]	[1.1]	[0.33]	[0.34]	[0.83]
Females ≥65	−4.119	−0.464	0.447	−1.149	0.207	0.53	0.667
	[1.55]	[0.2]	[0.25]	[0.55]	[0.58]	[0.87]	[0.79]

(*continued*)

Table 12.5　　　　　(continued)

		Food		Nonfood			
				Alcohol and			
	Food (1)	Staples (2)	Meat (3)	tobacco (4)	Clothing (5)	Health (6)	Education (7)
Age of head	0.103	−0.065	0.005	0.061	−0.002	−0.048	−0.046
	[0.99]	[0.70]	[0.07]	[0.75]	[0.11]	[2.03]	[1.40]
Head is male (1)	−1.786	−1.544	2.889	0.023	0.834	−0.646	−0.603
	[0.58]	[0.56]	[1.40]	[0.01]	[2.00]	[0.91]	[0.61]
Education of head	0.347	0.424	−0.252	0.011	−0.059	−0.006	0.000
	[1.49]	[2.04]	[1.62]	[0.06]	[1.89]	[0.11]	[0.00]
Intercept	26.881	7.998	15.196	−10.543	−6.088	4.631	4.303
	[2.17]	[0.72]	[1.84]	[1.09]	[3.65]	[1.63]	[1.09]
Joint tests							
F (Community fixed effects)	1.826	1.794	0.928	0.881	1.058	0.512	1.961
	(0.00)	(0.00)	(0.63)	(0.73)	(0.36)	(1.00)	(0.00)
F (all covariates)	1.12	0.92	1.48	0.78	2.38	0.98	2.71
	(0.32)	(0.57)	(0.07)	(0.76)	(0.00)	(0.49)	(0.00)
F (equal effects across gender)							
0-to-4-year-olds	3.15	0.52	0.84	0.40	0.48	0.05	0.35
	(0.08)	(0.47)	(0.36)	(0.53)	(0.49)	(0.82)	(0.55)
5-to-9-year-olds	0.07	2.15	0.49	0.55	0.04	0.89	0.38
	(0.79)	(0.14)	(0.48)	(0.46)	(0.85)	(0.35)	(0.54)
10-to-14-year-olds	2.74	0.63	1.28	0.67	9.67	1.56	1.09
	(0.10)	(0.43)	(0.26)	(0.41)	(0.00)	(0.21)	(0.30)
15-to-19-year-olds	0.21	0.32	0.01	0.05	3.25	0.10	26.91
	(0.64)	(0.57)	(0.92)	(0.83)	(0.07)	(0.76)	(0.00)
20-to-24-year-olds	0.56	3.63	5.35	0.09	2.43	0.01	0.18
	(0.45)	(0.06)	(0.02)	(0.76)	(0.12)	(0.90)	(0.67)
R^2	0.019	0.028	0.04	0.019	0.066	0.03	0.069
R^2 within community	0.035	0.029	0.046	0.025	0.071	0.031	0.081
R^2 between community	0.022	0.131	0.002	0.006	0.123	0.00	0.267
			B. Rural households				
ln(PCE) (spline)							
Below median	−7.266	−9.695	−3.233	3.452	1.178	0.769	1.546
	[5.49]	[4.92]	[2.52]	[5.50]	[6.90]	[2.90]	[5.90]
Above median	−1.802	−2.299	0.025	0.927	0.765	−0.232	0.627
	[1.26]	[1.08]	[0.02]	[1.36]	[4.14]	[0.81]	[2.21]
Household composition: number of each gender and age (years)							
Males 0–4	−1.095	−1.974	−0.479	1.186	−0.03	0.07	0.233
	[0.76]	[0.92]	[0.35]	[1.74]	[0.16]	[0.24]	[0.82]
Females 0–4	−3.281	−1.673	−1.791	0.895	0.197	0.161	0.327
	[2.25]	[0.77]	[1.27]	[1.29]	[1.05]	[0.55]	[1.13]
Males 5–9	0.225	0.748	−1.536	0.873	0.096	0.077	−0.070
	[0.19]	[0.43]	[1.34]	[1.56]	[0.63]	[0.32]	[0.30]
Females 5–9	−1.121	0.159	−1.939	−0.386	0.127	−0.106	0.305
	[0.88]	[0.08]	[1.57]	[0.64]	[0.77]	[0.41]	[1.21]

Table 12.5 (continued)

	Food			Nonfood			
	Food (1)	Staples (2)	Meat (3)	Alcohol and tobacco (4)	Clothing (5)	Health (6)	Education (7)
Males 10–14	0.19	−0.739	1.203	0.758	−0.097	0.189	−0.400
	[0.16]	[0.41]	[1.03]	[1.32]	[0.62]	[0.78]	[1.67]
Females 10–14	0.124	−0.28	0.894	0.888	0.183	−0.073	−0.056
	[0.1]	[0.15]	[0.76]	[1.53]	[1.16]	[0.3]	[0.23]
Males 15–19	0.413	−0.147	1.665	0.723	0.171	0.281	−0.615
	[0.32]	[0.08]	[1.35]	[1.19]	[1.04]	[1.10]	[2.43]
Females 15–19	0.585	−0.935	0.103	−0.216	0.129	0.157	−0.175
	[0.48]	[0.51]	[0.09]	[0.37]	[0.81]	[0.64]	[0.72]
Males 20–24	−1.236	−0.3	−2.472	−0.397	−0.473	−0.585	−0.076
	[0.73]	[0.12]	[1.50]	[0.49]	[2.16]	[1.72]	[0.23]
Females 20–24	−1.98	−1.127	0.48	0.998	0.273	0.205	0.118
	[1.14]	[0.43]	[0.28]	[1.21]	[1.21]	[0.59]	[0.34]
Males 25–39	−0.759	−1.063	−0.658	−0.472	−0.124	−0.008	0.169
	[0.43]	[0.4]	[0.38]	[0.56]	[0.54]	[0.02]	[0.48]
Females 25–39	−1.483	−2.656	0.904	0.03	−0.145	−0.053	−0.318
	[0.9]	[1.08]	[0.56]	[0.04]	[0.68]	[0.16]	[0.97]
Males 40–54	2.203	1.731	1.006	−1.126	−0.325	−0.449	−0.406
	[0.97]	[0.51]	[0.46]	[1.05]	[1.11]	[0.99]	[0.90
Females 40–54	−2.574	−2.007	1.547	0.615	0.221	0.287	0.135
	[1.43]	[0.75]	[0.89]	[0.72]	[0.95]	[0.80]	[0.38]
Males 55–64	1.884	3.124	−2.253	−0.628	−0.062	−0.568	−0.410
	[0.66]	[0.73]	[0.81]	[0.46]	[0.17]	[0.98]	[0.72]
Females 55–64	0.917	−3.746	2.682	−0.770	−0.160	0.249	0.562
	[0.43]	[1.17]	[1.29]	[0.76]	[0.58]	[0.58]	[1.32]
Males ≥65	−0.253	3.888	−1.13	0.333	0.159	−0.301	0.551
	[0.08]	[0.84]	[0.38]	[0.23]	[0.40]	[0.48]	[0.90]
Females ≥65	−5.909	−6.045	−1.275	−0.137	0.571	−0.213	0.631
	[2.71]	[1.86]	[0.6]	[0.13]	[2.03]	[0.49]	[1.46]
Age head	0.012	−0.043	0.005	0.003	−0.009	0.003	−0.002
	[0.16]	[0.4]	[0.06]	[0.1]	[0.93]	[0.21]	[0.16]
Head is male (1)	−2.226	−6.531	1.455	−0.967	0.365	0.514	0.224
	[0.88]	[1.72]	[0.59]	[0.8]	[1.11]	[1.01]	[0.44]
Education of head	0.458	0.706	0.076	−0.117	−0.049	−0.044	−0.018
	[2.35]	[2.43]	[0.40]	[1.26]	[1.94]	[1.12]	[0.46]
Intercept	40.797	60.338	9.85	−15.921	−6.097	−4.189	−7.751
	[5.74]	[5.7]	[1.43]	[4.72]	[6.65]	[2.94]	[5.51]
Joint tests							
F (Community fixed effects)	1.431	1.88	1.565	1.047	1.256	0.605	1.78
	(0.03)	(0.00)	(0.01)	(0.39)	(0.11)	(0.99)	(0.00)
F (all covariates)	2.98	2.02	1.09	2.67	5.87	0.79	4.45
	(0.00)	(0.00)	(0.35)	(0.00)	(0.00)	(0.74)	(0.00)
F (equal effects across gender)							
0-to-4-year-olds	1.35	0.01	0.52	0.11	0.88	0.06	0.06
	(0.24)	(0.91)	(0.47)	(0.74)	(0.35)	(0.81)	(0.8)

(*continued*)

Table 12.5   (continued)

| | Food | | | Nonfood | | |
| | | | Alcohol and | | | |
Food (1)	Staples (2)	Meat (3)	tobacco (4)	Clothing (5)	Health (6)	Education (7)
5-to-9-year-olds	0.72	0.06	0.07	2.80	0.02	0.33	1.42
	(0.4)	(0.8)	(0.79)	(0.09)	(0.88)	(0.57)	(0.23)
10-to-14-year-olds	0.00	0.04	0.04	0.03	1.80	0.65	1.16
	(0.97)	(0.85)	(0.84)	(0.87)	(0.18)	(0.42)	(0.28)
15-to-19-year-olds	0.01	0.08	0.76	1.14	0.03	0.11	1.43
	(0.93)	(0.78)	(0.38)	(0.29)	(0.86)	(0.74)	(0.23)
20-to-24-year-olds	0.09	0.05	1.47	1.37	5.29	2.45	0.15
	(0.77)	(0.83)	(0.23)	(0.24)	(0.02)	(0.12)	(0.70)
R^2	0.058	0.028	0.019	0.052	0.115	0.016	0.083
R^2 within community	0.063	0.044	0.024	0.057	0.117	0.018	0.091
R^2 between community	0.004	0.141	0.014	0.099	0.103	0.009	0.175

Notes: Dependent variable-share$_{98}$ – share$_{97}$. t-statistics, in brackets under regression estimates, p-values, in parentheses below test statistics, are robust to heteroskedasticity and within EA correlations. West Java is excluded province.

share declines as PCE increases; above median PCE, there is no link between the change in the food share and PCE. A similar pattern emerges for staples in rural areas. In urban areas, the staple share has increased by the same amount for all households below median PCE, and only among those households with PCE above median does the increase in the staple share decline as PCE increases. Thus, the increase in the price of rice has had its biggest impact on the shares of those who were poorest prior to the crisis.

It would be premature to conclude that the poorest are necessarily the worst off since some of these households are likely to be rice producers. Both their total expenditure and the share of the budget spent on rice, staples, and food will have increased, simply because of the increase in the price of rice, even if they neither buy nor sell any rice.

There is some evidence along these lines when we turn to meat shares, which have, on average, declined. The decline is greatest for the median household—in both the rural and the urban sector—with the poorest having protected their budgets allocated to meat. In the urban sector, the meat share rises with PCE among those households with PCE above the median. The results underscore the fact that the impact of the crisis on household well-being is both complex and nuanced.

Alcohol and tobacco account for about 5 percent of the budget of the average household. In urban areas, the share spent on these commodities has increased, and the increase is the same across the entire PCE distribution. Among rural households, the poorest have cut back on the allocation to these goods, which account for proportionately more of the budget in 1998, relative to 1997, among those at the top of the PCE distribution.

Since food shares have increased, nonfood shares must have declined. The share of the budget spent on household goods (such as furniture and kitchen equipment), clothing, housing, and recreation have decreased in both the urban and the rural sector. The declines are greatest for the poorest; this is demonstrated for clothing in table 12.5. These might all be thought of as expenditures that can be delayed without serious immediate consequences and so may serve as a natural mechanism for smoothing consumption in the face of a negative income innovation.

This evidence provides a third reason for being cautious about interpreting changes in PCE as indicative of changes in welfare. Depending on expectations regarding the longevity of the crisis, it may be optimal for households to defer spending on some goods and thus reduce PCE in the current period. This realignment of the budget over the short term may not have a large impact on welfare. Of course, interpretation of this behavior is quite different if the spending cuts are permanent.

12.3.7   Investments in Human Capital

We turn next to investments in two important dimensions of human capital—health and education. Evidence from household budget data discussed here will be complemented below with additional individual-specific information on schooling, health status, and health care use. Between 1997 and 1998, there were substantial reductions in the share of the budget spent on health and education services. Health expenditures include the cost of preventive and curative visits to private or public health facilities as well as the costs of drugs and medications. Education expenditures include the costs of tuition and fees at schools, uniforms and transport for schools, and the costs of materials required at school.

In the urban sector, the decline in the health share is evenly distributed across the PCE distribution, but the education share has been cut most by those in the bottom half of the distribution. For example, among households in the bottom quartile of PCE, the education share has been cut by 20 percent (and this cut is significant).

In the rural sector, the share of the budget spent on health has declined by 40 percent; the share spent on education has declined by a quarter. These are both significant. Moreover, the declines are concentrated among the poorest. Households in the bottom quartile of PCE have cut the share of their budget spent on education by 50 percent, which is both very large and significant.

While neither health nor education accounts for a large fraction of the total budget, it is potentially troubling that the cuts tend to be concentrated among the poorest. Moreover, reductions in these expenditures may portend deleterious consequences for particular demographic subgroups. Cuts in education expenditures, for example, will probably affect those who are of school age and have little impact on adults or very young house-

hold members. Reducing the share of the budget spent on health is likely to have its biggest impact on young children, pregnant women, and the elderly. With this in mind, we turn next to examine the relationship between changes in budget shares and household composition and continue to focus on expenditures associated with investments in human capital.

12.3.8 Human Capital, Household Budget Shares, and Household Composition

The regressions in table 12.5 include controls for the number of household members in each of nine age groups, stratified by gender.[14] The key finding among urban households pertains to education expenditures. The shares are higher in households with more fifteen- to nineteen-year-old males, but this is not true for households that have more females in that age group. The difference between the male and female effects is significant. Additional adolescent females (ten to fourteen years old) in the households are associated with significantly lower education shares. Thus, young men (aged fifteen to nineteen) stand out as the only group associated with increases in education shares.

While the regression estimates do not identify who benefits from higher shares, two interpretations suggest themselves. First, households that have more young working-age men may be able to maintain their income by having these men enter the labor force; the rest of the household benefits from this additional income by increasing shares of commodities that are income elastic. That interpretation does not have much appeal since there is no evidence that any other shares are correlated with the presence of males in this age group. If the males are bringing income to the household, one would expect that income to be distributed to more goods than only education services. Moreover, this explanation does not provide a reason to expect the presence of teenage females to be associated with lower education shares, as is observed.

An alternative explanation is that it is these young men who are benefiting from the higher education shares and their sisters are making room for them in the household budget by having less spent on their own schooling. Two pieces of evidence provide some evidence in support of this interpretation. As discussed above, there is evidence that in the urban sector more young women have entered the labor market than young men between 1997 and 1998. Fifteen- to nineteen-year-old women are associated with higher shares spent on clothing—possibly in order to find or keep employment.

The issue is explored further in table 12.6, which is based on the same

---

14. The models include the number of members in each demographic group. We have experimented with including total household size and the number of members (excluding one group) to separate the effects of size from composition. The substantive results are essentially identical, so we report these estimates, which are slightly more directly interpreted.

Table 12.6   Changes in education shares: Interactions between household composition and lnPCE

Household composition: number of each gender and age	Urban		Rural	
	Direct effect (1)	Interaction with lnPCE (2)	Direct effect (3)	Interaction with lnPCE (4)
Males 0–4	−1.439	1.205	−0.347	0.177
	[0.75]	[1.39]	[0.31]	[0.50]
Females 0–4	−0.143	0.307	0.53	−0.06
	[0.09]	[0.42]	[0.47]	[0.17]
Males 5–9	−1.909	0.63	−1.059	0.345
	[1.03]	[0.80]	[1.16]	[1.20]
Females 5–9	−0.681	0.617	0.83	−0.126
	[0.41]	[0.86]	[0.79]	[0.39]
Males 10–14	−4.824	2.036	−2.903	0.807
	[3.12]	[3.18]	[3.19]	[2.96]
Females 10–14	−3.894	1.387	−2.302	0.672
	[2.97]	[2.56]	[2.46]	[2.52]
Males 15–19	7.747	−2.376	−2.36	0.540
	[5.74]	[3.96]	[2.15]	[1.68]
Females 15–19	2.529	−1.551	−0.545	0.116
	[1.65]	[2.40]	[0.51]	[0.37]
Males 20–24	−2.887	1.059	0.16	−0.076
	[1.55]	[1.40]	[0.12]	[0.19]
Females 20–24	−4.157	1.446	0.66	−0.177
	[1.95]	[1.61]	[0.49]	[0.45]
Males 25–39	0.038	−0.05	0.373	−0.105
	[0.03]	[0.10]	[0.31]	[0.29]
Females 25–39	−0.952	0.331	−1.591	0.384
	[0.62]	[0.56]	[1.26]	[1.05]
Males 40–54	−0.643	0.24	−0.437	−0.027
	[0.33]	[0.31]	[0.33]	[0.07]
Females 40–54	−5.017	1.749	0.404	−0.084
	[2.77]	[2.54]	[0.30]	[0.22]
Males 55–64	0.628	−0.413	0.894	−0.388
	[0.25]	[0.43]	[0.58]	[0.90]
Females 55–64	−1.21	0.324	1.268	−0.222
	[0.62]	[0.43]	[0.86]	[0.53]
Males ≥65	1.075	0.097	1.233	−0.233
	[0.40]	[0.11]	[0.81]	[0.55]
Females ≥65	0.589	−0.145	1.767	−0.343
	[0.26]	[0.16]	[1.25]	[0.85]

Notes: Dependent variable is share on education$_{98}$ − share on education$_{97}$. t statistics (in brackets) robust to heteroskedasticity and within EA correlations. Direct effect is measured for household at bottom of PCE distribution. Mean(lnPCE) − min(lnPCE) = 2.5 in urban sector, 3.4 in rural sector; max(lnPCE) − mean(lnPCE) = 5 in urban sector, 3.8 in rural sector.

education share regression expanded to include an interaction between lnPCE and each of the household composition covariates. The estimates are standardized so that the direct effect (in columns [1] and [3]) is the effect of more members in each demographic group on education shares for the poorest household.

Among the poorest, education shares are significantly higher if there are more males aged fifteen to nineteen, and this effect declines with expenditure. In poor households, additional females in this age group are associated with higher education shares, although the effect is much smaller than it is for males, and it is not significant. (The difference between the male and female estimated effect is significant.) Thus, the poor are not choosing to spend more on the schooling of the young men in the household while cutting education expenses for their sisters in the same age group: they are spending more on males while maintaining resources for both males and females to remain in school. Rather, the evidence indicates that among the poorest households, it is younger males *and* females (ten to fourteen years old) who are making room for the education expenses of their older siblings. Low-income households with more children in this age group have lower education shares. These (negative) effects are large and significant at the bottom of the PCE distribution, but they disappear as PCE increases, indicating that the poorest children are probably paying a very large price in terms of forgone education opportunities.

The interaction between lnPCE and the number of females aged fifteen to nineteen in table 12.6 is negative and significant. This indicates that the lower education shares associated with additional fifteen- to nineteen-year-old females in the household (in table 12.5) is important among higher-PCE households. It is apparently young women in these households who are less likely to be in school and, as noted above, more likely to be joining the labor force.

The links between household consumption and household composition are markedly different in the rural sector. Food shares (and staple shares) are lower in households with more older women and female infants. This suggests that older women are either cutting their own consumption or searching out ways to cut the fraction of the budget spent on food (say, by preparing less expensive foods or preparing more food at home). Whereas education shares are higher among urban households with more males aged fifteen to nineteen, in the rural sector, additional males in this age group are associated with lower education shares. Additional females in this age group have no impact on education shares.

Turning to the interactive model in table 12.6, we see the same pattern for younger children that is observed in the urban sector: education shares are substantially and significantly reduced in low-PCE households that have more ten- to fourteen-year-old children. The cuts are the same for male and female children, and the magnitude of the cut declines as PCE in-

creases. Furthermore, in rural households, there is a suggestion that education shares are lower if there are more young boys (five to nine years old) in the household.

Summarizing these results, there have been substantial reductions in the share of the household budget allocated to schooling between 1997 and 1998. The reductions are concentrated among the poorest households. The regression results suggest that poor households in both urban and rural areas are investing less in the schooling of their young children (ten to fourteen years old), and urban households are allocating resources to protect the schooling of adolescent males.

12.3.9   School Enrollment and the Crisis

We turn next to individual-level information on human capital in an effort to address some of the difficulties associated with interpreting changes in household-level expenditure to infer the impact of the crisis—specifically, the confounding impact of inflation and changes in household size and composition.

Thomas et al. (2004) examine school enrollment rates for school-age children in both IFLS and SUSENAS and report that the pattern of changes in enrollments between 1997 and 1998 are consistent with the inferences discussed above based on expenditure patterns. School enrollment declined most for young children and those from the poorest households. Among young urban children, those in the poorest households were less likely to be enrolled in 1998 if they had older siblings living in the household. The converse holds as well—older children in low-resource households were more likely to be in school if they had younger siblings. The evidence indicates that poor households have sought to protect their investments in the schooling of older children at the expense of the education of their younger children. In contrast, enrollment rates did not change significantly among children in households that are better off.

Why would poor households protect the education of older children at the expense of younger siblings? There are at least two potential reasons. First, in Indonesia, returns to primary schooling are low, whereas returns to secondary schooling are much higher. Keeping those children who were already in secondary school at the time of the crisis enrolled in school is likely to yield a bigger payoff than keeping a child in primary school. Second, if an older child leaves school, it is unlikely that that child will return to school later in life. In contrast, delaying the start of school for younger children by a year—or even disrupting their schooling for a year—is unlikely to preclude their enrollment in school in the future. Many Indonesian children start school at age seven or eight, and there is considerable movement in and out of school among young children.

Thus, if poor households who have faced a large, negative income shock did not have the resources to keep all children at school and if these house-

holds anticipated that the crisis would be short-lived—or that financial assistance for primary school education would be forthcoming in the future—it would make good sense to allocate resources toward maintaining the education of older children, even at the cost of the schooling of younger children. In addition to liquidity constraints, the discussion suggests the influence on behavioral responses to the crisis of expectations regarding its longevity, expectations regarding the future availability of support for schooling (or other forms of support). Clearly, if in the longer term young children did not enroll in school or performed poorly in school because of the disruptions to their education, these children will probably pay the price of the crisis throughout their lives.

The evidence on the long-term impact on school enrollments is unambiguous. By 2000, enrollment rates at all ages were higher than in 1997, especially among young children. The increase in enrollments is greatest for young children from poor households. This is, at least in part, a reflection of the social safety net that sought to reduce the costs of attending school by providing resources directly to publicly funded schools in lieu of their collecting school fees and providing scholarships for poor children to attend school. The jury is still out on whether there was any long-term impact of the disruption on learning and performance in the labor market.

12.3.10   Use of Health Care, Health Status, and the Crisis

The share of the budget allocated to health declined in both urban and rural areas, and especially deep cuts were recorded among the poorest rural households. This may reflect delaying—or forgoing—health care visits, which, if they are preventive, may not have a deleterious impact on the health of the average Indonesian in the longer term. It may also reflect switching from private care to subsidized public health care. In fact, there was considerable concern in Indonesia that public health services would be overwhelmed by increased demand for their services at a time when resources were very constrained because public health budgets had been determined in nominal terms prior to the crisis, and with very high inflation, real budgets had been decimated.

Evidence from IFLS suggests that lower spending is primarily due to reduced use of health care, which declined by around 30 percent between 1997 and 1998. Overall, these declines were largely in the public sector, where declines in service quality were substantial, as indicated by, for example, reduced drug availability. Part of the decline among young children can be attributed to a reduction in preventive care visits, particularly among children in poor households, which is potentially very troubling.

Putting aside preventive care visits, it is possible that the reduction in health care visits indicates that respondents felt their health status had improved. We turn next to exploit the richness of information on health contained in the IFLS, which includes biomarker assessments along with mul-

tiple self-reported indicators. We focus on three domains of health: nutrition, psychosocial health, and general health.

Nutritional status is a commonly used yardstick for measuring general health status. Among young children, height for age is a longer-run indicator of health, and weight for height a more short-run indicator. They are not only correlated with a broad array of health status indicators, but height is predictive of future health and also socioeconomic status as an adult. Among adults, weight or body mass index (BMI, which is weight divided by height squared in kg/m^2) has been shown to be predictive of mortality and morbidity (Strauss and Thomas, 1998).

There is little evidence that either height for age or weight for height of young children worsened significantly between 1997 and 1998. However, sample sizes are small among the youngest and arguably most vulnerable children, and there is a suggestion that, while not significant, weight for height among very young children is lower after the crisis. Height for age, on the other hand, is remarkably robust to the crisis for all young children.

Moreover, changes in the nutritional status of young children are trivial relative to changes in the weight of adults. Specifically, on average, BMI declined by around 2 percent for adults aged twenty-five and older, with the declines being greatest among older adults, females, and the poorest. For example, among women aged forty-five and older who had no education, BMI declined by nearly 4 percent.[15] Whereas in 1997 BMI was below 18.5 for 19 percent of these women, by 1998 the fraction had increased by nearly 50 percent to 27 percent of older women with no education. The decline in weight likely reflects the combination of two factors: increased energy output associated with greater work output and reduced energy intake due to the relative increase in the price of food. These results, in combination with the evidence on child nutrition, suggest that adults literally tightened their belts to protect the nutritional status of the next generation.

Why might adults have done that? Height is thought to be especially vulnerable during the first three years of life, and reduced growth during that period has been shown to affect attained height as an adult. In turn, greater height as an adult has been associated with improved health and greater economic and social prosperity. In contrast, the welfare effects of declines in adult weight, particularly temporary declines in adult weight, are more ambiguous except for those whose BMI was low in 1997. On average, by 2000, adult weight and BMI were no different from their levels in 1997. However, among older women with no education, the decline in BMI was not temporary and persisted to at least 2000. We conclude that families

15. Since height is fixed for prime-age adults, these estimates can be interpreted as indicative of weight declines among prime-age respondents. We use BMI rather than weight because BMI conditions on the stature of the respondent. Very low levels (below 18.5) have been shown to be associated with elevated risk of morbidity and mortality.

borrowed against the nutritional status of older adults in an effort to protect the health and nutrition of the next generation.

Hemoglobin status is measured in the home with blood from a pin prick. It is an indicator of iron status, which is associated with fatigue, work capacity, and susceptibility to disease. Hemoglobin levels improved between 1997 and 1998, particularly among those who were iron deficient in 1997. This probably reflects the impact of a change in diet, since rice consumption retards the absorption of iron in other goods, and, as noted above, people substituted away from rice because of the increase in its relative price.

Questions about psychosocial health were asked of adults. These markers were significantly worse around the time of the onset of the crisis in 1998, relative to before the crisis, and the effect persisted through 2000. For example, in 1993, around 17 percent of adults aged twenty-five and older reported themselves as being prone to bouts of sadness.[16] This fraction was 35 percent in 1998 and essentially the same in 2000. The fraction of adults who reported suffering from anxiety more than doubled from 7 percent in 1993 to 19 percent in 1998 and rose to 21 percent in 2000. These declines in psychosocial health are evident for males and females, the poorest and the better off, and for rural and urban dwellers.

All adult respondents also provided an assessment of their own overall general health status on a four-point scale. In contrast with nutritional status and psychosocial well-being, this indicator of health did not change between 1997 and 1998. It is not entirely clear how to interpret the indicator. It may indicate that respondents' perceptions of their own health did not change. Or it may reflect changes in what a respondent deems to be "good" or "poor" health, possibly as the health of the respondent's reference group changes.

With this concern in mind, IFLS incorporated a protocol that has not been widely adopted in socioeconomic surveys: after completing a battery of physical health assessments on each respondent, the health worker provided his or her own evaluation of each respondent's overall general health on a nine-point scale. The health worker, a trained nurse or doctor, measured anthropometry, hemoglobin from blood, blood pressure, lung capacity, and mobility and communicated with the respondents about their health but did not participate in the interviews that asked respondents to evaluate their own health. It is important to note that health worker evaluations are likely to be influenced by many more factors than health alone, including, perhaps, socioeconomic status.

According to the health workers, among respondents who were living in rural areas prior to the crisis, the health of both children and adults was significantly worse after the onset of the crisis in 1998, relative to their

---

16. Psychosocial questions were not asked in the 1997 wave of the survey.

health prior to the crisis in 1997. By 2000, the health workers judged the health of these respondents to be significantly improved relative to their health prior to the crisis. The health of urban respondents was no worse in 1998 than it was prior to the crisis, and by 2000 their health status was significantly improved relative to 1997.

The evidence of the impact of the crisis on health status highlights two important methodological issues. First, health is multidimensional, and the crisis did not have the same impact on all dimensions of health. Second, health measurement is not straightforward, and reliance on a single indicator may be seriously misleading. Moreover, biomarkers provide an important set of information that complements self-reported health status.

Overall, the evidence on human capital investments indicates that as the crisis unfolded, several dimensions of education and health were deleteriously affected, with the poorest and most vulnerable paying the biggest price in several important dimensions of human capital. However, permanent declines in physical health and education are difficult to detect, suggesting that households, families, and possibly communities adopted strategies that successfully mitigated longer-term negative consequences of the crisis on these indicators of well-being.

12.3.11   Earnings and the Crisis

We turn next to explicitly discuss two potentially important dimensions in which individuals and households likely respond to offset the impact of an economic shock on spending. We first summarize evidence on earnings and then turn to the depletion of assets.

Although Indonesia's economic crisis was accompanied by dire predictions of massive unemployment, the evidence is to the contrary (Smith et al. 2002). Between 1997 and 1998, there was a small decline in the fraction of the population working in the market wage sector (about 2 percent), which was more than offset by an increase in self-employed work. As noted above, the increase in labor force participation is, to a large extent, explained by a rise in the fraction of prime-age women who worked in family businesses.

The drama of the crisis is instead reflected in the collapse of real hourly earnings, which set the country back at least ten years in terms of wage levels. Between 1997 and 1998, real hourly earnings fell by around 40 percent for urban workers. This breathtaking decline is recorded for males and females, for market-sector workers, and for the self-employed. Declines of a similar magnitude are recorded for females who were working in the rural sector and for males working for a wage in rural areas. In stark contrast, real hourly earnings of self-employed males in rural areas remained essentially stable. This reflects the combination of two factors: increases in the price of agricultural output (particularly rice) and an increase in unpaid family labor on farm businesses (Smith et al. 2002; Thomas, Beegle, and Frankenberg 2003).

The combination of substantially lower wages and slight increases in labor supply suggest that individuals and households were doing everything they could to shore up income. Nonetheless, many households experienced very large declines in earnings. In urban areas, household income declined by around 40 percent on average. In rural areas, the decline was around 20 percent on average.

12.3.12   Wealth and the Crisis

Since household spending declined less than income, households must have depleted assets to mitigate the impact of the crisis on consumption. The IFLS pays considerable attention to the measurement of wealth, and only a very small fraction of households reported that they owned no assets in 1997. Much of the wealth of households was in farm and nonfarm businesses, housing, and land, which are not very liquid; with the collapse of the banking sector, markets for these assets were substantially curtailed. Liquid assets like cash and stock market investments are not likely to have been good buffers since their values plummeted as the crisis unfolded, the stock market collapsed, inflation soared, and bank deposits were frozen. There is, however, one asset that stands out as being critically important: gold.

Gold is more widely held than financial assets, and in 1997 well over half the households owned at least some gold. Gold is held by rural and urban households as well as by households across the entire distribution of PCE. Gold is widely and readily traded—the average distance to a gold trader in rural areas is less than the average distance to a bank. Key for the Indonesian crisis is that the price of gold is set in world terms, and so as the rupiah collapsed, the value of gold in terms of rupiah rose. Gold owned prior to the crisis was an important source of resources to buffer the impact of the crisis. Almost one-half of households who owned gold in 1997 had sold all of it by 1998—and it was the poorest who were most likely to sell gold. Regression evidence indicates that the gold was used to protect spending on health and education (Frankenberg, Smith, and Thomas 2003).

Depleting assets leaves these households vulnerable if they do not replenish these resources and if there are future shocks. In fact, there have been several major shocks since the financial crisis. These include the 2002 Bali bombing, which resulted in a collapse of tourism to that island, and the 2004 Indian Ocean tsunami, which devastated the coastal areas of Aceh and North Sumatra.

12.4   Conclusions

In the mid-nineties, Indonesia was often cited as a remarkable success, as it had emerged from being one of the poorest nations three decades be-

fore to being on the cusp of joining the middle-income countries. In early 1998, the tables were turned and Indonesia was in the midst of a serious economic and political crisis.

When the government was negotiating for assistance from the International Monetary Fund and international donors, there were dire predictions that the poverty rate in Indonesia would increase fivefold, turning back three decades of progress. Although the crisis in Indonesia was large and far-reaching, those predictions were simply wrong. Poverty did increase by perhaps 50 percent, although precise measurement of the magnitude of the impact is far from straightforward for at least three important reasons.

First, poverty is typically measured in terms of PCE levels. If household size and composition change in response to the crisis, then it is difficult to interpret changes in PCE as indicative of changes in well-being. It has been suggested that expenditure should be adjusted with equivalence scales. Putting aside important theoretical issues that arise with defining equivalence scales, the specification of the scales is not trivial. They need to take into account not only differences in need across demographic groups but also economies of scale associated with different household sizes and compositions. There is no consensus in the literature on how to define such scales.

Second, expenditure is the outcome of choices by individuals and households. In the face of a major shock to resources, it may be optimal to delay spending on semidurables. This will reduce expenditure—and potentially increase poverty—without necessarily having a substantial impact on well-being. This suggests examining the allocation of the budget across goods.

Third, financial crises are often accompanied by high and volatile inflation. Estimating inflation in these contexts is both difficult and very demanding of data. Without good estimates of location- and group-specific inflation, it is very difficult to estimate changes in poverty with any confidence.

This research has highlighted the practical importance of each of these issues in the context of the Indonesian crisis. In so doing, it has exploited the richness of the longitudinal data in the IFLS to examine the impact of the crisis on a broad array of indicators of well-being. The analyses provide insights into the coping mechanisms that individuals and households have adopted to mitigate the deleterious impact of the crisis.

The empirical evidence in the IFLS suggests that the crisis resulted in a dramatic decline in the standard of living, as indicated by reduced levels of consumption, increases in the share of the budget spent on food, cuts in investments in human capital, lower levels of income, and the spending down of assets. Although the effects of the crisis were felt by individuals and

households across the entire income distribution—the poorest, the middle-income groups, and those who were better off—the impacts on each indicator also varied substantially across the income distribution. In some cases, such as wages, the crisis was an equal-opportunity destroyer. In other cases, such as school enrollment of young children, the poorest paid the heaviest price. The effects also varied across space. Households living in communities that were net food producers were protected from the brunt of the crisis, benefiting from the increase in the relative price of food, particularly rice. Similarly, exporters and those who produced for the export market benefited from the collapse of the rupiah.

Several safety-net programs were implemented in response to the crisis, and some appear to have been successful. Subsidized food was distributed to many communities. Scholarships and free public schooling were implemented about a year after the crisis began, and there were subsequently substantial increases in school enrollments, particularly among the poorest. Similar subsidies for preventive health care visits and basic drugs might have arrested the decline in use of health care.

There is evidence that the safety nets were not especially well targeted—particularly the subsidized food program (Frankenberg, Thomas, and Beegle 1999). Moreover, many of the safety-net mechanisms were implemented well after the crisis began. Developing the information infrastructure to enable rapid implementation of well-targeted safety nets would probably be a profitable investment.

The evidence from the IFLS has also highlighted the manifold ways in which individuals, households, communities, and public policies responded to the crisis to mitigate its deleterious impact in the longer term. Households combined to exploit economies of scale of consumption and budgets were reallocated to provide for immediate needs. Individuals moved from urban to rural areas, where there were more employment opportunities and prices were lower; workers moved to the production of food and goods for export. Older adults tightened their belts to protect the nutritional status of young children; young children did not go to school while their older siblings stayed in school. Assets, especially gold, were sold off to smooth the impact of the crisis, particularly on human capital investments. A picture emerges of remarkable resilience of individuals and households in the face of a major economic and political crisis that carried with it tremendous uncertainty.

Appendix

Table 12A.1   Inflation rate (relative to December 1997)

Province	August	September	October	November
North Sumatra	68.2	78.2	76.7	77.9
West Sumatra	74.6	85.1	81.7	85.1
South Sumatra	76.4	87.7	85.4	85.0
Lampung	79.6	86.9	86.2	86.2
Jakarta	68.6	74.1	72.9	71.7
West Java	61.5	67.4	68.1	67.0
Central Java	61.4	67.6	67.3	68.1
East Java	69.2	76.7	76.4	76.0
Yogyakarta	78.8	83.4	83.6	85.0
Bali	62.7	70.5	71.3	73.8
West Nusa Tenggara	73.5	82.9	85.1	89.0
South Kalimantan	63.2	74.0	74.1	72.7
South Sulawesi	70.0	77.1	77.0	78.3

References

Ahuja, Vinod, Benu Bidani, Francisco Ferreira, and Michael Walton. 1997. *Everyone's miracle: Revisiting poverty and inequality in East Asia.* Washington, DC: World Bank.

Bresciani, Fabrizio, Gershon Feder, Daniel O. Gilligan, Hanan G. Jacoby, Tongroj Onchan, and Jaime Quizon. 2002. Weathering the storm: The impact of the East Asian crisis on farm households in Indonesia and Thailand. *World Bank Research Observer* 17 (1): 1–20.

Cameron, Lisa. 1999. Indonesia: A quarterly review. *Bulletin of Indonesian Economics Studies* 35 (1): 3–41.

Datt, Guarav, and Hans Hoogeveen. 2003. El Niño or el peso? Crisis, poverty and income distribution in the Philippines. *World Development* 31 (7): 1103–24.

Fallon, Peter R., and Robert E. B. Lucas. 2002. The impact of financial crises on labor markets, household incomes, and poverty: A review of evidence. *World Bank Research Observer* 17 (1): 21–45.

Frankenberg, Elizabeth, James P. Smith, and Duncan Thomas. 2003. Economic shocks, wealth and welfare. *Journal of Human Resources* 38 (2): 280–321.

Frankenberg, Elizabeth, Duncan Thomas, and Kathleen Beegle. 1999. The real costs of Indonesia's economic crisis: Preliminary findings from the Indonesia Family Life Surveys. Working paper no. DRU-2064-NIA/NICHD. Santa Monica, CA: RAND.

Levinsohn, James, Steven Berry, and Jed Friedman. 2003. Impacts of the Indonesian economic crisis: Price changes and the poor. In *Managing currency crises in emerging markets,* ed. Michael Dooley and Jeffrey Frankel, 393–424. Chicago: University of Chicago Press.

Lokshin, Michael, and Ruslan Yemtsov. 2004. Household strategies of coping with shocks in post-crisis Russia. *Review of Development Economics* 8 (1): 15–32.

Maloney, William F., Wendy Cunningham, and Mariano Bosch. 2004. The distribution of income shocks during crises: An application of quantile analysis to Mexico, 1992–95. *World Bank Economic Review* 18 (2): 253–87.

Poppele, Jessica, Sumarto Sudarno, and Lant Pritchett. 1999. Social impacts of the Indonesian crisis: New data and policy implications. World Bank SMERU Report. Jakarta, Indonesia: Social Monitoring and Early Response Unit.

Roubini, Nouriel, and Brad Setser. 2004. *Bailouts or bail-ins? Responding to financial crises in emerging economies.* Washington, DC: Institute of International Economics.

Smith, James P., Duncan Thomas, Elizabeth Frankenberg, Kathleen Beegle, and Graciela Teruel. 2002. Wages, employment, and economic shocks: Evidence from Indonesia. *Journal of Population Economics* 15:161–93.

Strauss, John, Kathleen Beegle, Agus Dwiyanto, Yulia Herawati, Daan Pattinasaramy, Elan Satriawan, Bondan Sikoki, Sukamdi, and Firman Witolear. 2004. *Indonesian living standards before and after the financial crisis.* Singapore: Institute of Southeast Asian Studies.

Strauss, John, and Duncan Thomas. 1998. Health, nutrition and economic development. *Journal of Economic Literature* 36:737–82.

Thomas, Duncan, Kathleen Beegle, and Elizabeth Frankenberg. 2003. Labor market transitions of men and women during an economic crisis: Evidence from Indonesia. In *Women in the labour market in changing economies: Demographic issues,* ed. B. Garcia, R. Anker, and A. Pinnelli, 37–58. Oxford: Oxford University Press.

Thomas, Duncan, Kathleen Beegle, Elizabeth Frankenberg, John Strauss, Bondan Sikoki, and Graciela Teruel. 2004. Education in a crisis. *Journal of Development Economics* 74:53–85.

Thomas, Duncan, James P. Smith, and Elizabeth Frankenberg. 2001. Lost but not forgotten: Attrition in the Indonesia Family Life Survey. *Journal of Human Resources* 36 (3): 556–92.

13

Does Food Aid Harm the Poor?
Household Evidence from Ethiopia

James Levinsohn and Margaret McMillan

In developing countries, food aid undermines local agriculture and creates dependence on imports. Many of the U.S.'s biggest markets—from Egypt to Colombia and Nigeria—once received large amounts of food aid. The arrival of U.S. surpluses effectively drove down local prices, undermined investment in farming and created this dependence on imports.
—Kevin Watkins, head of research, Oxfam (*The Independent,* October 18, 2003)

Food aid is a unique resource for addressing hunger and nutrition problems, addressing emergency food needs, supporting development programs, and directly feeding vulnerable groups. The United States is continuing its efforts to better target and increase the effectiveness of its food aid programs, while continuing their fundamental humanitarian nature.
—Ann M. Veneman, U.S. secretary of agriculture (*Economic Perspectives,* March 2002)

13.1 Introduction

Food aid is supposed to provide relief for the poor. Yet, by increasing the supply of food, food aid may actually reduce prices and farmers' incomes

James Levinsohn is the J. Ira and Nicki Harris Family Professor of Public Policy, a professor of economics, and associate dean of the Gerald R. Ford School of Public Policy, University of Michigan, and a research associate of the National Bureau of Economic Research (NBER). Margaret McMillan is an associate professor of economics at Tufts University, and a research associate of the NBER.

We thank Nzinga Broussard for excellent research assistance and participants in the NBER conference on Globalization and Poverty, and especially Rohini Pande, for helpful comments.

and ultimately discourage domestic production.[1] In developing countries, since the poor tend to be farmers and concentrated in rural areas, most people assume that the negative impact of food aid will be felt disproportionately by the poor. However, most food aid is a by-product of policies designed to aid farmers in *rich* countries, by disposing of surplus agricultural commodities. Thus, far from being created to help the poor, these policies are actually part of the overall agricultural policies of the rich countries. Such policies have been severely criticized during the most recent round of World Trade Organization (WTO) negotiations, and many researchers claim that food aid policies are responsible for keeping the poor, poor.

However, as Panagariya (2002) notes, the claim that these interventions in agriculture in the Organization for Economic Cooperation and Development (OECD) countries are hurting poor countries is not grounded in facts. Forty-eight of the world's sixty-three poorest countries were actually net food importers during the period 1995–97 (Valdes and McCalla 1999); thus, the removal of wealthy countries' subsidies on food products would lead to welfare losses for most of the world's poorest countries. This still leaves unanswered the question of what happens to the poorest members of the poor countries. Within any country, households that are net buyers of cereals would be hurt by a price increase, while households that are net sellers of cereals would see their welfare increase with cereal prices. Thus, the effect of a change in price on the poor depends on whether poor households are net buyers or net sellers of cereals. Therefore, one way to study the impact of these policies on the poor is to use the household as the unit of analysis.

Broadly speaking, the existing research on food aid can be divided into two areas—research on the disincentive effects of food aid and research on the efficacy with which food aid has been targeted. The work on the disincentive effects of food aid typically uses aggregate data to estimate country-level supply-and-demand equations. These estimates are then used to derive multipliers for determining the cumulative impact of food aid on domestic production and trade via the impact of food aid on the domestic price (see, for example, Bezuneh, Deaton, and Zuhair 2003).[2] Less work

---

1. Although food aid can take several different forms, some part of all types of food aid (including emergency relief) is sold on local markets and therefore either competes against domestic production or reduces the demand for commercial imports (Abbott and Young 2003). The idea that food aid could harm the poor was raised as a theoretical possibility by Nobel laureate Theodore Schultz (1960). In the United States, the potential disincentive effects of food aid were officially recognized by the Bellmon Amendment to Public Law 480[3], which sets out the following criteria for approving a food aid program: "1. The distribution of commodities in the recipient country will not result in a substantial disincentive or interference with domestic production or marketing in that country; and 2. Adequate storage facilities are available in the recipient country at the time of exportation of the commodity to prevent the spoilage or waste of the commodity" (Amendment to Section 401(b) of U.S. Public Law 480, 1977).

2. A body of work similar to this, although using less sophisticated econometric techniques, is reviewed by Maxwell and Singer (1970), who conclude that price disincentives can be avoided by an appropriate mix of policy.

has been done on the issue of targeting, at least in part because household data on the receipt of food transfers are usually unavailable (Jayne et al. 2002). The work that has been done typically uses household data and asks who is getting food aid and why. Our work is most closely related to recent work by Jayne et al. (2002), who study the targeting of food aid in rural Ethiopia. These authors use nationally representative rural household data from Ethiopia collected in 1996 to study the extent to which food aid is targeted to poor households and communities. They find that food aid does not tend to go to the poorest households and that there tends to be inertia in the distribution of food aid.

We ask a slightly different question: does food aid have the potential to help the poor in Ethiopia? In other words, who are the poor, and are they selling the items distributed by food aid programs? In theory, food aid could still hurt the poor if it lowered prices for poor net sellers of food *and* markets were sufficiently segmented that it didn't lower prices for poor net buyers of food. This theoretical possibility seems practically implausible for at least two reasons. First, according to Harrison (2002), there is a high degree of serial and spatial correlation between producer and consumer prices of grain.[3] And second, although Jayne et al. (2002) and Dercon and Krishnan (2003) find evidence of imperfect targeting, they do find that poorer households are significantly more likely to receive food aid. They also find that women, children, and the elderly are more likely to receive food aid.

In addition, we use more recent data (1999–2000) and a sample that includes not just rural households but also urban households. Including urban households is particularly important for our study because one of the criticisms of food aid is that it is used to feed the relatively better-off urban residents at the expense of poor rural farmers. Finally, we obtain empirical estimates of the likely impact of food aid on cereals prices using a standard supply and demand framework.

We choose to focus on Ethiopia for several reasons. Ethiopia receives more food aid than almost any other country in the world. Food aid reached 15 percent of annual cereal production in 2003 and typically represents between 5 and 15 percent of total annual cereal production (Jayne et al. 2002). At the same time, it is widely recognized that raising the productivity and profitability of smallholder agriculture is essential for poverty reduction in Ethiopia. In 1992, the Ethiopian government launched its poverty reduction strategy of Agricultural Development-Led Industrial-

---

3. One drawback of the analyses by Harrison (2002) and others is that they are based on prices between major wholesale centers. According to a personal communication from Eleni Gabre-Madhin, an economist and specialist on Ethiopia then based at the International Food Policy Research Institute, there is some evidence that markets in remote areas are not as well integrated. In future work, we plan to test this hypothesis using HICES data on unit values appropriately adjusted for quality.

ization (ADLI). The centerpiece of this strategy has been a massive extension program aimed at diffusing agricultural technology, the Participatory Demonstration and Training Extension System, dubbed PADETES. Recent work by the Ethiopian Economic Association (EEA; 2000, 2001) suggests that the results of ADLI have been somewhat disappointing. For most crops, average yields have remained stagnant, in spite of increased imports of agricultural inputs. Average farm size has declined and prices have fallen, leaving many farmers worse off than they were when ADLI began (Hamory and McMillan 2003). Although it is unlikely that food aid alone is responsible for the failure of PADETES, it is conceivable that food aid has contributed to the decline in prices.

Interestingly, in the June 2004 meetings of the EEA, in a presentation titled "The Impact of Globalization: Its Promises and Perils to the Ethiopian Economy," author Amdetsion GebreMichael claimed that

> One major problem facing farmers has been the absence of appropriate policy instruments to stabilize farm gate price and to safeguard the income of small farmers. In the case of cereal prices, the absence of such a policy combined with uncoordinated food aid flows, has led to depressed cereal farm gate prices—often to levels below costs of production.

GebreMichael goes on to argue that the downward pressure on cereal prices owing in part to the uncoordinated delivery of food aid has undoubtedly reduced farmers' incentives to enhance productivity and increase output. The author provides no evidence for this statement but does cite a report by a consultant to the World Bank that makes the same claim (Harrison 2002).

We take the household as our basic unit of analysis, and we ask whether households are net buyers or sellers of the basic foodstuffs typically distributed in the form of food aid. The first-order approximation of the welfare effect of food aid is net production of the commodity multiplied by the change in the price of the commodity caused by food aid (see Deaton 1989 and 1997 for a more detailed discussion). Thus, if a household buys more wheat than it sells, we call that household a net buyer of wheat. Since food aid is expected to depress food prices, food aid will benefit net food buyers and harm net food sellers. To determine the poverty impact of food aid, we then classify households according to expenditure per capita on an adult equivalency basis and ask whether the households classified as poor are net buyers or net sellers of food.[4]

Finally, we obtain some rough estimates of the magnitude of the price

---

4. This analysis ignores the cross-price effects of a reduction in the price of wheat. A reduction in the price of wheat could depress the prices of other crops for which the poor are net sellers, such as teff or maize. However, an analysis not included in this version of the paper suggests that the poor are net sellers of all crops (teff, maize, sorghum, and barley) that are close substitutes for wheat.

change caused by food aid and hence the magnitude of the first-order welfare effects of an increase in the price of food. To do this, we use supply and demand elasticities for cereals, combined with information on total cereal production and cereal food aid, to identify the equilibrium price and quantity of cereals in the absence of food aid. Using the equilibrium price and quantity in the absence of food aid and the observed prices and quantities, we obtain an estimate of the aggregate welfare effects of the price change associated with eliminating food aid.[5] In future work we hope to refine this analysis by using the household data to compute regional elasticity estimates and by using regional data on food aid and food production to compute welfare effects by region.

Our household data come from two surveys conducted by the Central Statistical Authority (CSA) of the Government of Ethiopia. The Household Consumption and Expenditure Survey 1999–2000 is a nationally representative survey that covers 17,332 households. The Welfare Monitoring Survey is also nationally representative and covers 25,917 households. Our food aid data come from Ethiopia's Disaster Prevention and Preparedness Committee and the WFP. Our data on national cereal production come from the CSA.

Our results indicate that (a) net buyers of wheat are poorer than net sellers of wheat, (b) there are more net buyers of wheat than net sellers of wheat at all levels of income, (c) the proportion of net sellers is increasing in living standards, and (d) net benefit ratios are higher for poorer households, indicating that poorer households benefit proportionately more from a drop in the price of wheat. In light of this evidence, it appears that households at all levels of income benefit from food aid and that—somewhat surprisingly—the benefits go disproportionately to the poorest households. Several caveats must be kept in mind, however. First, even the nonparametric regressions are averages by income category and so could mask underlying trends. The extent to which these averages reflect the true effects of price changes on poverty depend on whether these averages truly represent the typical household, or whether there is a significant amount of variation *among* poor households even at the poorest income levels. Second, it is important to note that we do not attempt to quantify the possible dynamic effect of higher food prices. It is possible that higher food prices, by increasing the incentives to invest in agriculture, could eventually lead to lower food prices.

---

5. The Ethiopian government has no official restrictions on commercial imports of wheat or other grains. However, Ethiopia imports virtually no grains on a commercial basis. In 1999, commercial imports of wheat amounted to only 6 percent of all wheat imports; these were imported by four large food processing companies based in Addis Ababa. Ethiopia does not import wheat or any other grain on a commercial basis because transport costs are prohibitive. Thus, "dumping" of food aid will depress market prices. This hypothesis has been tested and confirmed in a recent review of grain marketing in Ethiopia (Harrison 2002).

In interpreting our results, it is also important to note that we are considering only the effects of food aid that is imported into the country and not food aid that is purchased from local farmers and redistributed. An increasing amount of food aid is purchased locally. However, most donors do not purchase any food aid locally but rather purchase the food from their own farmers for distribution in Ethiopia. It may be that local purchase is a preferable alternative for Ethiopians; however, at least so far, it has not been deemed a politically feasible option for the majority of the donating countries.

Recently, the United States has been heavily criticized for refusing to purchase food aid locally. However, it is important to note that importing food aid appears to be a widespread practice not limited to the United States. In 1999, for example, 663,000 tonnes (t) of wheat food aid were imported into Ethiopia, while only 30,000 t of wheat food aid were purchased locally. Of the 663,000 t that were imported, only 21 percent came directly from the United States; 31 percent came from the WFP, and 32 percent from the European Community. In 2000, the numbers look similar: 1,074,000 t of wheat food aid were imported, and only 59,000 t were purchased locally.[6]

The remainder of the paper is organized as follows: section 13.2 describes our methodology. Section 13.3 describes our data and presents descriptive statistics. Section 13.4 presents our results. Section 13.5 considers the impact of food aid on cereal prices, and section 13.6 synthesizes our conclusions.

13.2   Methodology

The approach we use follows Deaton (1989) and considers the impact of changes in cereal prices on the distribution of income. In general, households that are net sellers of cereals will gain from higher prices, while net buyers will lose. Changes in these prices will affect the distribution of real income between urban and rural areas as well as the distribution within sectors, depending on the relationship between living standards and the net consumption and production of cereals.

Many rural households are both producers and consumers of these products, and the empirical strategy takes this into account. Following Deaton (1989), we model the effects of price changes using an indirect utility function in which the household's utility is written as a function of its income and prices. These effects can be summarized in the following way:

(1) $$\frac{\partial W}{\partial \ln p_{\text{cereal}}} = \sum_h \theta_h(x_h, z_h) p_{h,\text{cereal}} (y_{h,\text{cereal}} - c_{h,\text{cereal}}) / x_h,$$

6. See table 13.3 for details and sources.

where W is the social welfare function, θ captures the social marginal utility of money, h is household, x is the household's total consumption, z is household characteristics, y is household production of the food crop, and c is household consumption of the food crop. The general approach is to calculate net benefit ratios for each household and to examine the distribution of these ratios in relation to living standards and region.[7] As noted by Deaton, higher food prices are likely to redistribute real income from the urban to rural sectors. What is less obvious is how price changes redistribute real income between the rich and poor within the rural sector.

Note that these are only the first-order effects of price changes and ignore both the partial equilibrium effects of food price changes on quantities demanded and supplied as well as the general equilibrium effects on employment patterns, wages, the price of other factors, and technological innovation.

Our approach is best thought of as a good approximation to what would happen in the short run (see Panagariya 2002; Barrett 1998). We focus on these short-run changes for several reasons. First and most important, using short-run changes seems to be most appropriate for studying the impact of price changes on the poor, who, as Barrett and Dorosh (1996) say, are "likely to be teetering on the brink of survival" and less able to take advantage of supply-side effects of price changes. We are also limited by our data. To the extent that food aid drives prices down, food aid may act as a disincentive to food production over the long run. We do not have time series data and so are unable to directly test this hypothesis. However, for all five cereals produced in Ethiopia, there is an upward trend in production over the period 1980–2000 (Hamory and McMillan 2003).

As we mentioned earlier, it is important to disaggregate the analysis. Although the agricultural sector might benefit as a whole from higher food prices, aggregation could disguise a highly concentrated intrasectoral distribution of the benefits and costs of food price changes. Following standard procedure, we use per capita consumption as a conditioning variable. In future work, we intend to condition on land holdings and per capita income.

Our approach is to study the way in which the net benefit ratio varies according to living standards. The ratio is unitless and measures the elasticity of real income with respect to a price change. The manner in which the net benefit ratio varies across the income distribution tells us something about how the price change affects households across the distribution of income. For this reason, we estimate the net benefit ratio relative to measures of per capita expenditure or the conditional expectation of the net benefit ratio given a household's expenditure.

---

7. For a complete discussion of this type of analysis and its limitations, see Deaton (1997).

Note that we could simply run a linear regression with the net benefit ratio as the dependent variable and per capita expenditure as the explanatory variable. However, to avoid the problems associated with specifying a functional form, we choose instead to analyze the net benefit ratios using the nonparametric techniques introduced by Deaton (1989). The advantage of using nonparametric techniques is that they let the data do the talking. Readers are directed elsewhere for a comprehensive treatment of the nonparametric techniques employed here.

We also estimate density functions of the per capita expenditure (adult equivalent) according to whether individuals are net buyers or sellers of cereals. In the univariate case, the best way to conceptualize what we are doing is to imagine first creating a histogram where the heights of the bars represent the proportion of the population falling within a given band. The problem with the histogram is the arbitrariness of the choice of the number of bands and their width. Kernel estimates of the density function allow us to smooth the histogram and place confidence intervals around the distribution. In the univariate case, the kernel estimate of the density function of per capita expenditure, x, is given by

$$(2) \qquad \hat{f}(x) = \frac{1}{nh} \sum_{i=1}^{n} K\left[\frac{x - x_i}{h}\right],$$

where n is the number of households, h is the bandwidth, and K is the kernel. The kernel function K and the bandwidth h are chosen with the efficiency bias trade-off in mind. A larger bandwidth will generate a smoother estimate and reduce the variance but increase the bias.

To determine whether an increase in the price of food would be regressive or progressive, we use a nonparametric regression. This regression is the conditional expectation corresponding to the joint densities computed for expenditure and net benefit ratios and hence contains no new information. However, the regression does provide the answer to the question of by how much the people at each level of per capita expenditure would lose from the increase in the price of food. Since the net benefit ratio expresses the net benefit as a fraction of total household expenditure, a flat line would indicate that all rural households benefit proportionately, an upward sloping line that richer households benefit proportionately more and a downward sloping line that poor households benefit disproportionately. The kernel regression estimator can be written as follows:

$$(3) \qquad \hat{\beta}(x) = \frac{\sum_{i=1}^{n} y_i K\left[\dfrac{x - x_i}{h}\right]}{\sum_{i=1}^{n} K\left[\dfrac{x - x_i}{h}\right]}$$

13.3   Data

Our household data are taken from two nationally representative surveys administered by Ethiopia's CSA during the period 1999–2000, the Welfare Monitoring Survey (WMS) and the Household Income, Consumption, and Expenditure Survey (HICES). The WMS was introduced in 1994 with the explicit purpose of monitoring poverty in Ethiopia and is conducted every two years. The WMS 2000 covered 25,917 households and 123,735 individuals. The HICES, also introduced in 1994, covers a subset of the households surveyed in the WMS and collects more detailed information on consumption and expenditure by product by household than the WMS. One of the primary purposes of the HICES is to provide a basis for computing national accounts statistics. The HICES covered 17,332 households in 1999–2000.

Table 13.1 describes the size and structure of the two data sets employed to study whether households are net buyers or sellers of various crops. Both data sets employ standard clustered samples, derived from a two-stage sampling procedure. The first stage of sampling selected a random sample of small geographic units called enumeration areas (EAs), or neighborhoods of around 200 (100) households in urban (rural) areas. In the second stage, random samples of 12 to 35 households were selected from within each EA, as described in the table. The sample frame for both of these data sets excludes the nonsedentary populations concentrated in the regions of Afar and Somali. For details on sample design and data collection, see CSA (2001a, 2001b).

Ethiopia's sedentary population is about 14 percent urban and 86 percent rural (CSA 2001a). According to the CSA, the urban category includes the capitals of regions, zones, and weredas, any locality that is within an Urban Dweller's Association (or kebele), any locality with 2,000 or more residents, and any locality with 1,000 or more residents whose residents are "primarily engaged in nonagricultural activities." Our merged data set includes 8,212 urban and 8,308 rural households. Ethiopia is administratively divided into eleven regions, called killils. Certain killils correspond with urban areas, such as Addis Ababa, Harari, and Dire Dawa. The other killils contain a combination of urban and rural areas.

Our measures of total expenditure are taken from the HICES. Because the version of the HICES that provides information on prices and quantities of crops purchased and sold is not yet available to the public, we use information from the WMS on total income and total expenditure by crop to compute net buyer status. The WMS includes two measures each for income and expenditure: for each cereal, it records the income in the past month, income in the past six months, expenditure in the past week, and expenditure in the past month. We use income in the past six months supplemented by income in the past month times 6 when income in the past six

Table 13.1   **Data structure**

Regional states	Welfare Monitoring Survey 2000 Sample EAs	Welfare Monitoring Survey 2000 Sample households	1999–2000 HICES Sample EAs	1999–2000 HICES Sample households
Tigray				
Rural	100	1,196		
Urban	43	687		
Total	143	1,883	90	1,252
Afar				
Rural	59	699		
Urban	25	400		
Total	84	1,099	58	792
Amhara				
Rural	283	3,393		
Urban	100	1,593		
Total	383	4,986	245	3,340
Oromia				
Rural	360	4,318		
Urban	119	1,903		
Total	479	6,221	271	3,728
Somalia				
Rural	56	672		
Urban	30	480		
Total	86	1,152	61	852
Benishangul-Gumuz				
Rural	75	900		
Urban	25	400		
Total	100	1,300	68	916
SNNPR				
Rural	394	4,727		
Urban	48	768		
Total	442	5,495	204	2,640
Gambela				
Rural	30	360		
Urban	24	283		
Total	54	743	54	744
Harari				
Rural	30	360		
Urban	23	368		
Total	53	728	53	728
Addis Ababa				
Rural	25	300		
Urban	75	1,181		
Total	100	1,481	100	1,500
Dire Dawa Adm council				
Rural	30	360		
Urban	30	480		
Total	60	840	60	840
Rural total	1,442	17,285	722	8,660
Urban total	542	8,643	542	8,672
Grant total	1,984	25,928	1,264	17,332

Note: SNNPR = Southern Nations, Nationalities, and Peoples Region.

months is missing, and expenditure in the past month times 6 supplemented by expenditure in the past week times 24 when expenditure in the past month is missing to measure net expenditure. Because the WMS covers only a subset of the HICES, we end up with a sample of 16,520 households after merging the two data sets.

To obtain measures of income and expenditure that can be meaningfully compared across households, we adjust for variations in regional prices and household composition. First, we deflate nominal values of income and expenditure by a regional price index computed by the CSA and reported in the "Poverty Profile of Ethiopia" (Welfare Monitoring Unit 2002). Next, it is useful to recognize that the same total household expenditure may feed more (fewer) members of a family with relatively more (fewer) children (adults) and relatively more (fewer) women. Thus, we convert our measure of real household expenditure to a measure of real per capita expenditure on an adult equivalency basis using the East African adult equivalency scale developed by Dercon.[8]

The WMS 2000 was conducted from January to February 2000. Therefore, the variable for six-month income covers the main harvesting season, which is September to December. Thus, the six-month income variable that we use to calculate net expenditure measures income from the latter half of the year and so includes the harvest months as well as the months immediately preceding the harvest, when cereals are least plentiful. Therefore, it is likely to be representative of annual cereal consumption. However, because the period of data collection immediately follows the harvest, the weekly and monthly expenditure variables may overstate average cereal consumption. However, since prices of cereals are likely to be lower during this period, this bias is likely to be minimal.

The HICES was conducted to capture the seasonality aspect of agriculture in Ethiopia. Each household was visited eight times: four times (once a week over the period of a month) during the rainy or lean season when stocks are low (June 11, 1999, to August 7, 1999) and then four times during the harvest period when stocks are plentiful (January 3, 2000, to February 26, 2000).[9] Monthly totals for the two periods are then averaged to obtain monthly annual average household consumption expenditure and income.

Table 13.2 presents means of the main variables of interest. We use total real household expenditure per adult equivalent (rexpae) as our primary measure of household living standards. It is measured as total consumption expenditure per adult equivalent per year adjusted for regional varia-

---

8. Thanks are due to Julie Schaffner for providing the adult equivalency scale and regional index programs for Stata. The adult equivalency scale is for East Africa and is based on a program provided by Stefan Dercon.

9. There are two rainy seasons in Ethiopia. The main rainy season, *meher,* falls between May and September. The secondary rainy season, *belg,* falls between February and May.

Table 13.2 Means of variables used in analysis

	All	Urban	Rural	Tigray	Afar	Amhara	Oromia	Somali	Benishangul-Gumuz	SNNPR	Gambela	Harari	Addis Ababa	Dire Dawa
A. Household characteristics														
Family size	4.87	4.54	4.92	4.69	4.44	4.52	5.07	5.08	4.61	5.05	4.45	4.39	5.05	4.59
Head's age	43.76	43.74	43.76	48.02	40.93	44.52	43.28	42.23	41.76	42.29	39.67	44.58	45.36	43.15
Total expenditure	5,713.02	7,336.59	5,443.09	4,472.35	5,835.32	5,533.80	5,922.37	7,089.05	4,909.17	5,379.48	4,833.55	6,909.33	9,078.13	6,814.38
Expenditure per capita	1,303.63	1,859.12	1,211.27	1,059.23	1,578.70	1,352.40	1,300.83	1,718.06	1,194.74	1,174.44	1,288.95	1,755.70	1,985.57	1,737.75
Expenditure per adult equiv	1,576.31	2,146.85	1,481.46	1,309.74	1,819.47	1,632.22	1,585.12	2,028.09	1,453.95	1,427.88	1,514.82	2,081.07	2,231.76	2,042.74
B. Production value income														
Teff	121.07	60.89	131.07	102.13	232.15	131.98	162.81	22.28	27.42	58.33	1.06	0.17	98.95	0.96
Mean income from positive income	543.16	1730.58	515.82	319.45	1236.49	422.24	774.15	1507.87	280.62	365.77	425.55	102.88	7328.94	452.47
% reporting positive income	11.24	1.89	20.49	17.19	5.44	17.56	12.19	2.65	8.05	15.26	0.31	0.14	9.20	0.37
Wheat	73.94	58.53	76.51	45.46	0.00	30.54	140.60	58.80	4.47	45.94	0.00	0.00	8.97	2.52
Mean income from positive income	603.63	1928.84	555.12	263.33	0.00	277.86	978.89	952.62	343.04	371.80	0.00	0.00	1101.92	2352.28
% reporting positive income	6.65	1.45	11.78	11.21	0.00	6.68	8.94	5.69	1.03	9.86	0.00	0.00	8.43	0.24
Barley	24.53	16.32	25.89	37.85	0.17	28.18	22.51	74.97	3.50	23.34	0.88	0.00	0.29	0.64
Mean income from positive income	234.88	1567.23	215.66	258.40	323.95	188.20	320.61	1247.97	299.21	190.72	594.47	0.00	317.45	188.40
% reporting positive income	5.17	0.61	9.68	9.47	0.27	9.10	4.46	3.92	1.15	9.51	0.16	0.00	0.21	0.49
Maize	97.56	28.03	109.12	45.92	202.08	44.23	98.26	104.13	90.94	198.73	188.99	4.19	0.04	1.63
Mean income from positive income	427.86	1169.62	416.57	280.73	1039.92	263.90	402.67	622.75	202.65	594.62	465.25	296.37	369.07	314.53
% reporting positive income	12.99	2.46	23.40	9.14	22.58	8.91	13.95	8.47	26.55	22.86	27.74	1.28	0.14	0.98
Sorghum	28.63	45.09	25.89	51.19	23.20	32.20	34.61	94.04	67.69	6.17	24.89	7.25	0.16	19.02
Mean income from positive income	358.29	2882.77	285.78	407.94	340.27	363.16	390.43	633.79	221.78	168.77	197.43	416.85	191.51	541.22
% reporting positive income	5.95	1.23	10.62	7.56	2.26	5.29	4.84	7.21	25.63	5.63	7.99	1.71	0.07	5.61
Coffee	87.20	23.67	97.77	0.35	27.91	1.53	78.27	0.00	84.56	265.16	141.50	1.16	0.00	10.09
Mean income from positive income	659.33	2226.45	641.16	20240.80	143.12	611.91	0.00	1256.08	699.64	831.54	151.93	4.79	475.34	
% reporting positive income	6.57	0.78	12.29	0.33	0.40	0.90	7.90	0.00	4.60	24.50	8.93	0.86	0.07	3.41

C. Expenditures

Teff	542.44	774.89	503.79	1065.33	673.40	959.39	370.24	167.73	161.98	104.65	167.79	362.21	966.74	377.82
Mean expenditure from positive expenditure	1231.02	1014.60	1302.05	2075.05	1152.23	1529.50	879.72	1240.76	561.05	624.58	953.42	811.33	1167.74	852.15
% reporting positive expenditure	54.56	76.36	33.02	61.96	51.00	73.76	59.82	25.54	42.07	33.85	40.96	39.09	85.02	35.24
Wheat	206.47	173.24	211.99	292.28	38.13	232.35	237.98	329.55	16.04	119.09	40.96	271.30	112.77	78.21
Mean expenditure from positive expenditure	624.13	405.70	673.40	660.99	384.26	718.05	625.73	645.66	300.09	481.52	416.77	598.27	427.46	398.07
% reporting positive expenditure	35.65	39.10	32.25	49.09	13.15	30.15	46.70	52.72	14.02	36.10	12.70	48.50	34.56	22.32
Barley	123.82	44.34	137.04	217.58	27.01	189.64	110.11	46.25	9.57	67.17	7.30	19.32	13.23	19.75
Mean expenditure from positive expenditure	512.60	295.45	533.71	638.18	319.20	648.28	461.37	323.45	244.48	320.75	391.90	196.91	338.28	212.27
% reporting positive expenditure	17.72	13.92	21.47	24.09	7.44	19.75	25.07	15.68	4.37	27.21	2.04	9.27	4.11	7.07
Maize	289.11	116.70	317.78	233.82	481.52	171.05	352.61	562.67	299.04	380.07	522.29	163.58	25.34	87.22
Mean expenditure from positive expenditure	565.45	380.37	582.77	641.17	890.64	515.37	608.15	776.36	428.20	518.90	759.88	518.17	309.56	691.78
% reporting positive expenditure	42.26	27.83	56.54	24.92	61.75	22.50	52.23	45.13	56.78	70.26	65.67	37.09	9.48	17.80
Sorghum	189.24	70.91	208.92	262.55	210.08	234.85	211.03	231.55	286.35	78.70	184.85	492.89	4.91	510.12
Mean expenditure from positive expenditure	609.07	341.83	637.21	698.62	695.64	778.62	557.35	705.92	469.54	391.48	499.48	768.37	165.09	890.60
% reporting positive expenditure	30.79	21.51	39.97	28.41	13.94	22.79	30.65	30.34	71.61	26.71	31.50	68.05	2.79	67.20
Coffee	144.58	152.45	143.28	117.44	150.66	111.67	146.36	154.00	144.07	195.78	104.10	93.00	139.40	105.65
Mean expenditure from positive expenditure	168.48	169.27	168.34	148.73	191.73	127.63	173.75	170.59	164.99	222.15	178.50	131.10	152.49	131.60
% reporting positive expenditure	85.40	90.12	80.73	83.64	80.35	87.28	89.19	90.77	91.38	85.33	63.64	67.76	92.96	76.22

D. Budget shares

Teff	0.10	0.12	0.10	0.28	0.15	0.18	0.06	0.02	0.03	0.02	0.03	0.06	0.14	0.06
Mean expenditure from positive expenditure	0.24	0.16	0.26	0.54	0.26	0.29	0.15	0.15	0.09	0.11	0.16	0.13	0.17	0.13
Wheat	0.04	0.03	0.04	0.07	0.01	0.05	0.04	0.05	0.00	0.02	0.01	0.04	0.02	0.01
Mean expenditure from positive expenditure	0.12	0.07	0.13	0.17	0.09	0.15	0.11	0.10	0.04	0.09	0.09	0.08	0.06	0.07
Barley	0.03	0.01	0.03	0.06	0.01	0.04	0.02	0.01	0.00	0.01	0.00	0.00	0.00	0.00
Mean expenditure from positive expenditure	0.11	0.05	0.12	0.17	0.08	0.14	0.10	0.06	0.03	0.07	0.09	0.03	0.04	0.03
Maize	0.06	0.03	0.07	0.06	0.12	0.04	0.07	0.10	0.08	0.08	0.12	0.03	0.01	0.01
Mean expenditure from positive expenditure	0.12	0.08	0.12	0.16	0.22	0.12	0.12	0.13	0.11	0.11	0.18	0.08	0.08	0.12
Sorghum	0.04	0.02	0.04	0.07	0.06	0.05	0.04	0.05	0.07	0.02	0.04	0.08	0.00	0.09
Mean expenditure from positive expenditure	0.13	0.08	0.13	0.19	0.20	0.16	0.11	0.14	0.12	0.10	0.12	0.12	0.03	0.15
Coffee	0.03	0.03	0.03	0.03	0.03	0.02	0.03	0.02	0.03	0.04	0.02	0.02	0.02	0.02
Mean expenditure from positive expenditure	0.03	0.03	0.04	0.04	0.04	0.03	0.03	0.03	0.04	0.05	0.04	0.02	0.03	0.02

tions in prices. Not surprisingly, judging by this standard, urban households enjoy a higher standard of living than rural households. In addition, there are marked variations across regions, with Addis Ababa recording the highest rexpae, 2,232 birr (Br), and Tigray recording the lowest rexpae, Br1,310. Using the 1999 average nominal dollar-birr exchange rate of 8.23, these translate into US$271 and US$159, respectively. The poorest regions in Ethiopia (Amhara; Oromia; Southern Nations, Nationalities, and Peoples Region [SNNPR]; and Tigray) also produce the majority of the nation's cereals. However, these regions are vast, and agroecological conditions—and hence poverty—vary widely within the regions. Note also that the poorer regions tend to have larger households and that there appears to be no systematic variation in the age of household heads.

Panels B and C of table 13.2 show the regional distribution of total real annual income and expenditure from the various cereals and coffee. We include coffee as a point of interest since it is widely consumed in Ethiopia and is Ethiopia's largest source of export earnings. For each crop, three items are reported: the mean across all households, the mean across only households who report receiving income from that crop, and the percent of households reporting positive income from this crop. Based on these data, it appears that households tend to earn income from only one or two cereals, probably based on agroecological conditions. Looking at panel B, we see that rural households rely much more heavily on income from cereals than do urban households, with 21 percent of rural households reporting positive income from teff, 12 percent from wheat, 10 percent from barley, 24 percent from maize, 11 percent from sorghum, and 12 percent from coffee. For urban households, these figures are 2 percent, 1 percent, 0.6 percent, 3 percent, 1 percent, and 0.8 percent respectively.

Panel C presents information on total real expenditure per household. On average, expenditures exceed income for all crops, and a much larger share of the population reports positive expenditures on the various crops, with more than half reporting that they spent some money on teff, for example. There is a marked difference between urban and rural expenditures, with a much larger percentage of the urban population (76 percent) reporting expenditure on the most expensive cereal, teff, than the rural population (33 percent). The most widely consumed cereals in the rural sector are maize (57 percent), sorghum (40 percent), teff (33 percent), wheat (32 percent), and barley (22 percent). The most widely consumed cereals in the urban sector are teff (76 percent), wheat (39 percent), maize (28 percent), sorghum (22 percent), and barley (14 percent).

Panel D presents data on budget shares for all households and then only for those households that report spending anything on that particular item. These figures indicate that households spend a large fraction of their annual income on cereals, ranging from 26 percent to 12 percent for rural households and 16 percent to 5 percent for urban households. Thus,

changes in cereal prices can have substantial welfare effects, and reduction in cereal prices is likely to transfer real income from urban households to rural households. Only 12 percent of rural households in the survey received any income from wheat, the only cereal imported in the form of food aid, and it is these households that stand to gain from an increase in the price of wheat.

The fact that mean expenditures on cereals exceed mean income from cereals naturally leads to the following question: what are the other sources of income in Ethiopia? Also using these data, Peacemaker-Arrand (2004) reports that rural respondents predominantly describe themselves as subsistence farmers, with 87 percent reporting that the household's main source of income is subsistence farming. Interestingly, she finds that the most widespread source of income among these rural households is livestock. Only 4.1 percent of rural households support themselves with formal employment, while 2.4 percent rely on "casual labor." Moreover, the picture is very different in urban areas, where the majority of households report main income source as formal employment, while an additional 10 percent rely on casual labor. Interestingly, Peacemaker-Arrand also finds that urban residents rely more on pensions, rent, and family remittances than rural households.

Our data on food aid come from the WFP and Ethiopia's Disaster Preparedness and Prevention Centre (DPPC). Table 13.3 presents cereal production and cereal food aid from 1995 to 2001. Several facts are worth noting. First, virtually all imported cereal food aid comes in the form of wheat. Second, although the United States provides a substantial share of the wheat food aid (42.5 percent in 1999), the *majority* of the imported wheat comes from a variety of other donors, mostly European. This is notable because of the Europeans' tendency to blame these phenomena on the United States. Third, although some food aid is purchased locally, the majority of food aid is imported, and the majority of food aid is wheat. Over the period 1995–2001, an average of 20 percent of cereal food aid was purchased locally. Locally purchased food aid consists primarily of wheat, maize, and sorghum and accounts for a tiny fraction of the total production of each of these commodities. By contrast, 663,000 t of wheat food aid were imported in 1999, while only 1,114 t were produced locally. Thus, wheat food aid accounted for more than a third of the total supply of wheat and potentially had a significant effect on the price of wheat.

13.4   Who Benefits from Food Aid?

Since all imported cereal food aid is wheat, we now restrict our attention to the impact of an increase in the price of wheat that would probably result if there were no food aid. The averages reported in table 13.2 do not tell us anything about production and consumption patterns of wheat accord-

Table 13.3   Cereal production and food aid (in thousands of tonnes)

	1995	1996	1997	1998	1999	2000	2001
Imported cereal food aid (wheat)	643	320	369	579	663	1074	574
Food aid imported from the United States	151	64	114	85	144	251	155
Food aid imported from Other[a]	492	256	255	494	493	813	419
Commercial imports	0	0	0	78	26	10	10
Locally procured cereal food aid	34	109	111	58	111	213	235
Total cereal food aid	677	429	480	637	774	1287	809
Imported as % of total	94.98	74.59	76.88	90.89	85.66	83.45	70.95
Locally procured as % of total	5.02	25.41	23.13	9.11	14.34	16.55	29.05
Total cereal production	6,740	9,379	9,473	7,197	8,013	8,310	9,209
Total wheat production	1,024	1,076	1,002	1,107	1,114	1,213	1,571
Imported wheat food aid as % of wheat production	62.79	29.74	36.83	52.30	59.52	88.54	36.54
Total maize production	1,673	2,539	2,532	1,929	2,417	2,526	3,139
Total teff production	1,298	1,752	2,002	1,307	1,642	1,718	1,737
Total sorghum production	1,122	1,723	2,007	1,070	1,321	1,181	1,538

Source: World Food Programme (1995 2000).

Notes: Cereals include barley, maize, millet, sorghum, teff, and wheat. For the years 1999–2001, all imported cereals are in the form of wheat and all locally procured cereals are in the form of maize.

[a]In 1999, other includes 206,000t from the World Food Programme, 166,000t from the European Commission, and roughly 10,000t each from Denmark, Italy, France, and the Netherlands. In 2000, other includes: 464,799t from the World Food Programme, roughly 20,000t each from Canada, Italy, Great Britain, the EC and DFID, 12,572t from Germany, and 6,000t from France.

ing to income level. We are specifically interested in the impact of changes in the price of wheat on the poor; thus, we need to know whether the poor earn more or less income from wheat than rich households. We would also like to know whether they spend more or less on wheat than rich households. In what follows, we examine the living standards of buyers and sellers of wheat. We also examine who is most likely to benefit in proportional terms from a reduction in wheat prices.

Figures 13.1–13.3 show estimates of the distribution of real per-adult-equivalent expenditure across households that are net buyers of wheat and across households that are net sellers of wheat. Since the distribution for the entire population is almost identical to the distribution of net buyers, we do not overlay this density function on figures 13.1–13.3. Rather, the densities for the entire population are presented in appendix figure 13A.1. Figure 13.1 is the distribution for the entire population, figure 13.2 is the distribution for the rural population, and figure 13.3 is the distribution for the urban population. All three graphs show the estimated density functions of the logarithm of household per-adult-equivalent expenditure by whether a household is classified as a net seller or buyer of wheat. The log transformation is chosen because the distribution of expenditure per

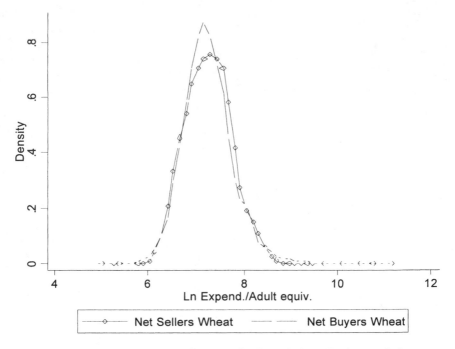

Fig. 13.1   Living standard of net buyers and sellers of wheat: Entire population

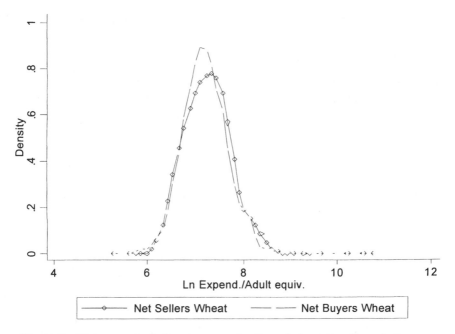

Fig. 13.2   Living standard of net buyers and sellers of wheat: Rural population

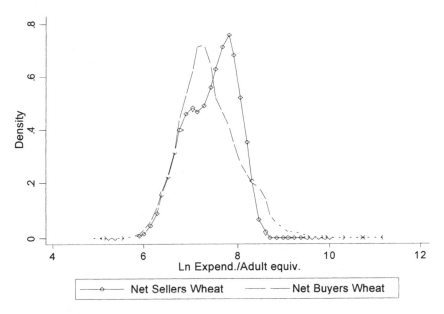

Fig. 13.3   Living standard of net buyers and sellers of wheat: Urban population

capita is strongly positively skewed and taking logs introduces something closer to symmetry.

The most striking feature of figure 13.1 is the similarity of the two distributions. The modal net seller is only slightly wealthier than the modal net buyer: modal expenditure per capita per adult equivalent of the net buyer is Br1,096 ($134), compared to Br1,211 ($148) for net sellers.[10] Although the patterns are similar, the differences are slightly more pronounced once the sample is split into urban and rural households. Figure 13.2 shows that for rural households, modal expenditure per capita per adult equivalent of the net buyer is Br1,096 ($134), compared to Br1,339 ($163) for net sellers. Figure 13.3 shows that the differences are most pronounced for urban households, where the modal expenditure per capita per adult equivalent of the net buyer is Br1,212 ($148), compared to Br2,981 ($364) for net sellers. Figures 13.2 and 13.3 confirm the fact that urban households tend to enjoy a higher standard of living and that there is more diversity among the urban population.

Figures 13.4–13.11 show results of nonparametric regressions of buyers and sellers of wheat by expenditure category. Each graph contains two lines. The line that is connected by squares shows the proportion of households out of all households that report spending any money on wheat. The

10. All dollar figures are obtained using the nominal average exchange rate of Br8.2 per U.S. dollar in 1999.

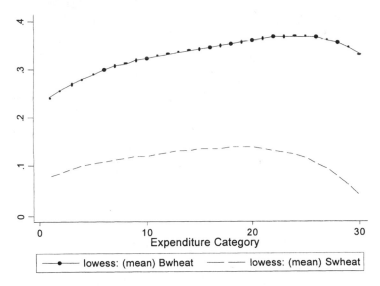

Fig. 13.4   Buyers and sellers of wheat by expenditure category: Entire country (with fitted values based on nonparametric regression)

line that is connected by diamonds shows the proportion of households out of all households that report earning any income from selling wheat. These are the results of two separate nonparametric regressions where the dependent variable takes a value of 1 if the household reports purchasing (selling) any wheat and 0 otherwise and the explanatory variable is expenditure per adult equivalent divided into thirty quantiles. The bottom third of the expenditure per adult equivalent distribution ranges between Br1,113 ($136) and Br2,302 ($281). The middle third of the distribution ranges between Br2,417 ($295) and Br3,718 ($453). The top third of the distribution ranges between Br3,933 ($480) and Br10,762 ($1,312). For each quantile, these graphs tell us the proportion of households that report spending any money on wheat and the proportion of households that report purchasing any wheat. The graphs provide more detail on the structure of our data. In figure 13.4, we report this information for the entire country. We then present results for rural and urban populations and for several regions separately.

Figures 13.4–13.11 all show that at all levels of income there are more buyers than sellers of wheat. This is important because it means that at all levels of living standards, more households will benefit from food aid (a reduction in wheat prices) than will be hurt. This is consistent with the fact that Ethiopia is a net importer of food. However, even though Ethiopia is a net food importer, it is not the case that among the poor the majority of

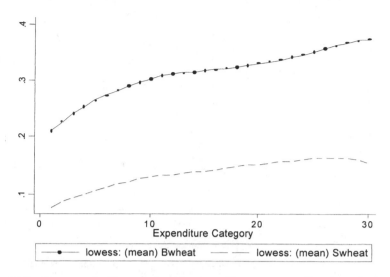

Fig. 13.5 Buyers and sellers of wheat by expenditure category: Rural population (with fitted values based on nonparametric regression)

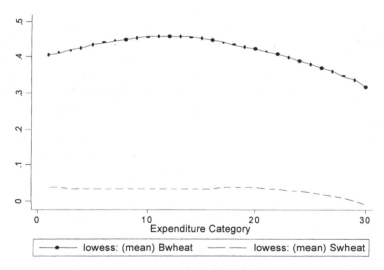

Fig. 13.6 Buyers and sellers of wheat by expenditure category: Urban population (with fitted values based on nonparametric regression)

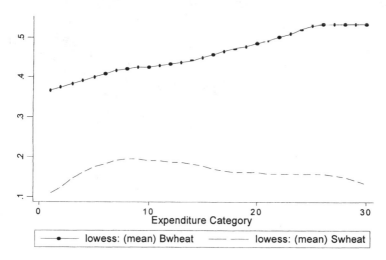

Fig. 13.7   Buyers and sellers of wheat by expenditure category: Tigray (with fitted values based on nonparametric regression)

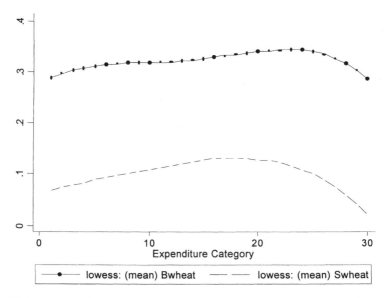

Fig. 13.8   Buyers and sellers of wheat by expenditure category: Amhara (with fitted values based on nonparametric regression)

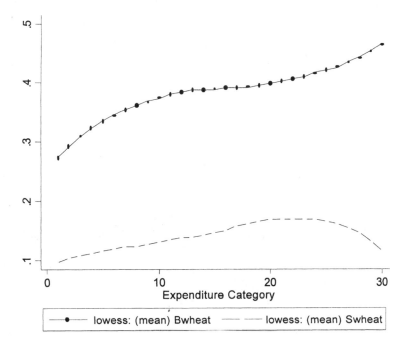

Fig. 13.9   Buyers and sellers of wheat by expenditure category: Entire Oromiya (with fitted values based on nonparametric regression)

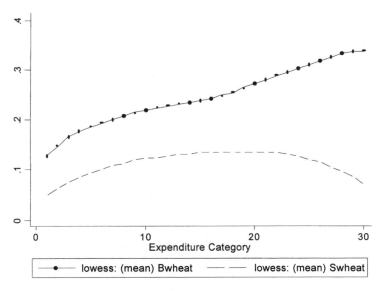

Fig. 13.10   Buyers and sellers of wheat by expenditure category: SNNPR (with fitted values based on nonparametric regression)

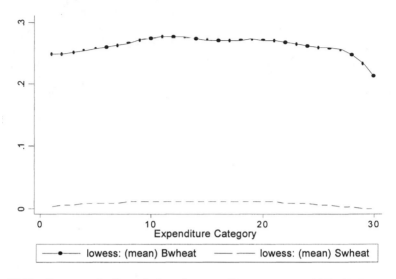

Fig. 13.11   Buyers and sellers of wheat by expenditure category: Addis Ababa (with fitted values based on nonparametric regression)

households are net sellers of food. Thus, it is not the case that food imports benefit only the relatively better-off urban population.

For the population as a whole, the proportion of households that sells wheat hovers around 10 percent until it drops sharply at the very highest levels of income. The proportion of households that purchase wheat tends to increase with income starting at around 25 percent and tapering off at around 35 percent until it too falls—though less sharply—at the very highest levels of income.

Figure 13.5 shows that among the rural population, the proportion of households that sell wheat is increasing in income. The proportion of households that buy wheat is also increasing in income and goes from around 20 percent for the poorest households to almost 40 percent for the wealthiest households. Figure 13.6 shows that among urban households there is no significant relationship between living standards and the proportion of buyers and sellers of wheat—except at the very highest levels of income, where both taper off. A comparison between figures 13.5 and 13.6 yields some interesting insights. There is much more diversity among rural households, and—at all levels of income—more rural households are engaged in selling wheat than are urban households.

Figures 13.7 through 13.11 confirm that the importance of wheat also varies by region. Figure 13.7 confirms the statistics in table 13.2 that suggest that wheat is most important in Tigray, where more than 11 percent of

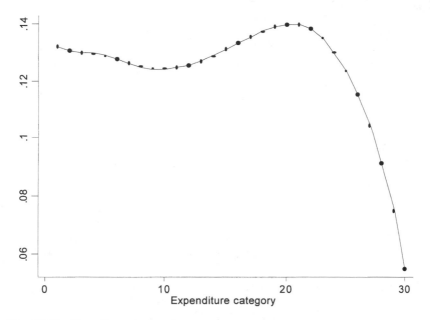

Fig. 13.12   Net sellers of wheat by expenditure category: Entire country

households report earning income from wheat and 49 percent of households report spending any money on wheat. Interestingly, Tigray is also the poorest region and the region from which most of the current government originates. The pattern of income in Tigray appears to be slightly different from the pattern for the rest of the country. The proportion of households reporting income from wheat increases with income and then begins to taper off after the tenth quantile, suggesting that more poorer households in Tigray rely on wheat as a source of income than do richer households—though the differences are not large (20 percent versus 15 percent). On the income side, the pattern is similar, with one interesting difference: even among the very poorest households, roughly 40 percent spend money on wheat. This compares with between 10 and 30 percent for the remaining regions and 20 percent for the country as a whole. Thus, Tigray is the region most likely to be affected by changes in wheat prices.

The next step is to combine the information on income and expenditure of wheat and to examine net sellers of wheat by expenditure category. Net sellers of wheat are the households that would be hurt by the reduction in wheat prices associated with food aid. Figure 13.12 presents these results for the entire population, while figure 13.13 presents results for the rural population and figure 13.14 for the urban population. These figures are results of a nonparametric regression where the dependent variable takes a value of 1 if the household is a net seller and 0 otherwise and the explana-

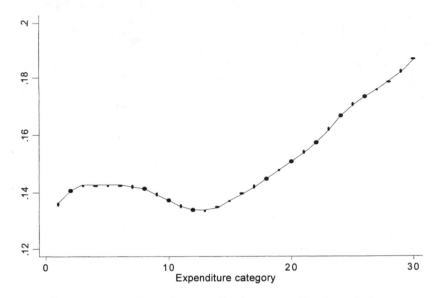

Fig. 13.13   Net sellers of wheat by expenditure category: Rural population

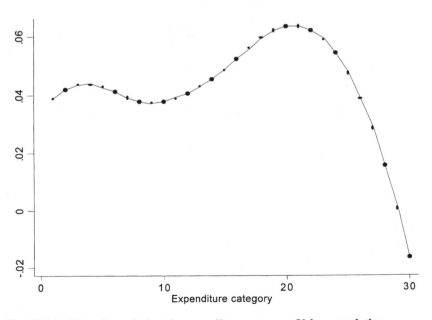

Fig. 13.14   Net sellers of wheat by expenditure category: Urban population

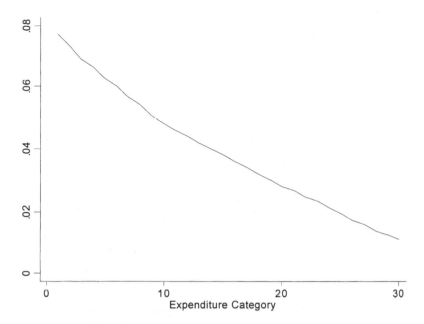

Fig. 13.15   Net benefit ratio by expenditure category: Entire country

tory variable is expenditure quantiles. The shape of the line in figure 13.12 is clearly driven by the households in the upper tail of the expenditure categories, so we turn immediately to figures 13.13 and 13.14, which are easier to interpret. Figure 13.13 shows that there is a positive relationship between whether a household is a net seller of wheat and living standards. Among the rural population, contrary to popular wisdom, there are more net sellers of wheat among the richer households, and the relationship is close to linear. Figure 13.13 also makes it clear that roughly 85 percent of the poorest households are net buyers of wheat. Figure 13.14 shows that net seller status among urban households is also increasing in income for the first two terciles of the distribution. Among the wealthiest urban households net sellers of wheat drop off quickly. Not surprisingly, a comparison of figures 13.13 and 13.14 shows that at all levels of income there are proportionately more net sellers among the rural population.

Figures 13.15–13.17 show results of regressions of the net benefit ratio on quantiles of per-adult-equivalent expenditure.[11] The net benefit ratio is defined as total household expenditure on wheat per year less total household income from wheat per year divided by total household expenditure per year. Thus, a ratio greater than zero indicates that the household is a

---

11. Note that these figures exclude households that report both zero income from wheat and zero expenditure on wheat.

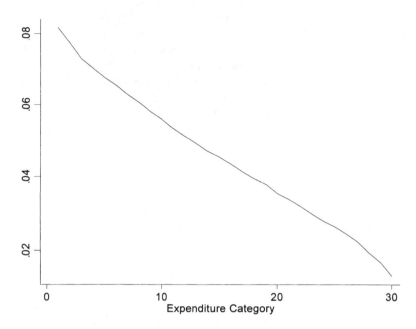

Fig. 13.16   Net benefit ratio by expenditure category: Rural population

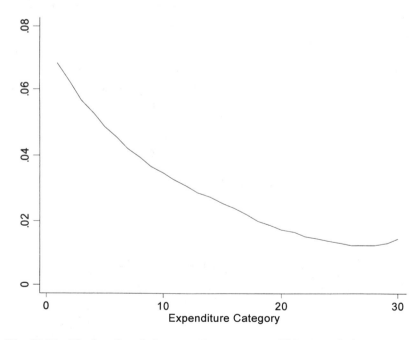

Fig. 13.17   Net benefit ratio by expenditure category: Urban population

net buyer of wheat and expresses the household's deficit as a fraction of total household expenditure. These figures show by how much Ethiopians at
each level of living would benefit from a reduction in the price of wheat.
Since the ratio expresses the net benefit as fraction of total household consumption, a flat line would show that all rural households benefit proportionately; thus, the change is neither regressive nor progressive. Our data
show that a reduction in the price of wheat would benefit poor households
disproportionately and hence be progressive. This is true for the population as a whole (figure 13.15), for the rural population (figure 13.16), and
for the urban population (figure 13.17). These figures also suggest that the
magnitude of the deficit as a share of total expenditure is fairly large for the
poorest households (slightly higher than 8 percent) and close to insignificant for the richest households (between 1 and 2 percent).

In summary, our analysis indicates that (a) net buyers of wheat are
poorer than net sellers of wheat, (b) there are more buyers of wheat than
sellers of wheat at all levels of income, (c) the proportion of net sellers is increasing in living standards, and (d) net benefit ratios are higher for poorer
households, indicating that poorer households benefit proportionately
more from a drop in the price of wheat. In light of this evidence, it appears
that the *average* household at all levels of income benefits from food aid
and that—somewhat surprisingly—the benefits go disproportionately to
the poorest households. Several caveats must be kept in mind. First, even
the nonparametric regressions are averages by income category and so
could mask underlying trends. The extent to which these averages reflect
the true effects of price changes on poverty depend on whether these averages truly represent the typical household, or whether there is a significant
amount of variation *among* poor households even at the poorest income
levels. Second, we have not considered dynamic effects. It is possible that
higher wheat prices could increase the incentive to invest in agriculture and
eventually lead to lower wheat prices.

We have established that food aid is likely to help the poor disproportionately. We have also established that for the poorest households the
deficit is large at around 8 percent, and so the overall impact of food aid on
household welfare can have a substantial impact on the poorest households. What we still do not know is whether food aid has a significant impact on prices. We turn now to this issue.

13.5   Does Food Aid Depress Wheat Prices?

To answer this question, we use the supply-and-demand framework presented in figure 13.18. For simplicity, we assume constant-elasticity demand and supply functions,

$$D = k_0 P^{-\varepsilon} \text{ and } S = k_1 P^{\nu},$$

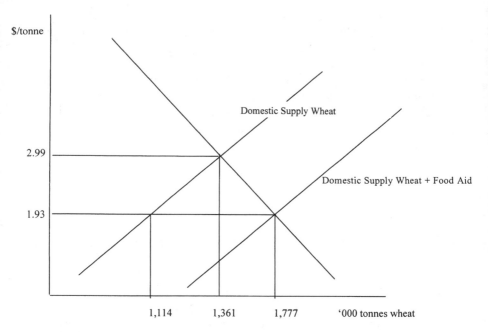

Fig. 13.18   Price effects of food aid

Notes: $1.93 is the production weighted (by region) average of producer prices for wheat received in Ethiopia in 1999 converted at the average nominal exchange rate of 8.23 birr per dollar. 1,114 is total thousands of tonnes of wheat produced in Ethiopia in 1999. 1,777 is total thousands of tonnes of wheat consumed in Ethiopia in 1999 or 1,114 plus food aid equal to 663 thousand tonnes of wheat. $2.99 is the price that would prevail in the market if food aid wheat were not imported. It is obtained assuming constant elasticity of supply and demand functions, an elasticity of supply of wheat equal to .45, and an elasticity of demand for wheat equal to −.6.

where k_0 and k_1 are parameters, P is the market price of wheat, and ε and v are demand and supply elasticities, respectively. Our estimate of P is a production weighted regional average of wheat producer prices for 1999. Our estimate of the elasticity of supply is 0.45 and is based on Soledad Bos (2003). Our estimate of the elasticity of demand is based on Regmi et al. (2001), who found that low-income countries have own-price elasticities of demand for cereals of about −.6. Using these estimates and the observed quantities of wheat produced and consumed in Ethiopia, we are able to calibrate the model. The resulting supply and demand for wheat in Ethiopia are given by

$$D = 41{,}325P^{-.6} \text{ and } S = 104P^{.45}.$$

Using these estimates of the supply and demand functions, we find that the price of wheat would be $295 per tonne in the absence of food aid compared with an average observed price of $193 per tonne in 1999. We also

find that the price increase would lead to an increase in producer surplus of around US$125 million and a reduction in consumer surplus of around US$159 million. Overall, the increase in the price of wheat leads to a net welfare loss of approximately US$34 million. There were roughly 12 million households in Ethiopia in 1999, of which 4.3 million reported spending money on wheat and 0.8 million reported earning income from wheat. Therefore, *on average,* the loss in consumer surplus works out to roughly US$37 per household per year for households that consume wheat, and the gain in producer surplus works out to roughly US$157 per household per year for households that sell wheat. In Ethiopia, where the poverty line is roughly Br1,057 ($132), these effects are quite large.

13.6   Conclusions

The argument against developed countries' agricultural subsidies is largely motivated by a desire to improve the living standards of the world's rural poor. Yet, for countries like Ethiopia that are net food importers, a rise in food prices leads to a *net* welfare loss. This might be acceptable if, in the process, real income were being transferred from the relatively better-off urban population to the rural poor. However, our analysis suggests that this is not the case. Although households at all levels of living standards benefit from a reduction in food prices, the benefits are proportionately larger for the poorest households. Rough estimates suggest that the welfare impacts of the price changes associated with food aid are substantial.

Because of the magnitude of the average welfare effects per household, we believe that this issue warrants further attention. In particular, it will be important in future work to confirm that prices in remote areas follow the same pattern as prices in major retail centers. To better understand where the price effects of food aid are being felt and how the magnitude of these effects varies across locations, it will also be important to compare food aid deliveries to local production by region or wereda. A somewhat more difficult issue has to do with the timing of food aid deliveries. If food aid is not delivered in a timely manner, it could aggravate the cyclicality of prices associated with the harvesting and lean seasons due to inadequate storage. The most difficult issue has to do with the disincentive effects of food aid. Again, given the magnitude of the price changes associated with food aid and the associated per-household welfare implications, this seems like an issue worth exploring.

Appendix

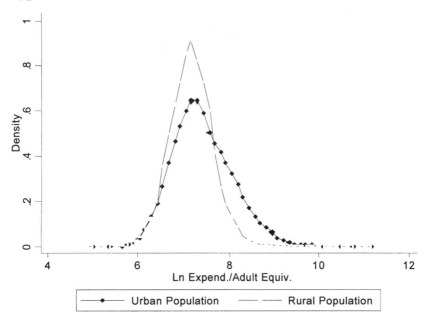

Fig. 13A.1   Living standard of entire population by urban/rural

References

Abbott, P. C., and L. M. Young. 2003. Export competition issues in the Doha round. Paper presented at the conference Agricultural Policy Reform and the WTO: Where Are We Heading? 23–26 June, Capri, Italy.

Barrett, C. B. 1998. Food aid: Is it development assistance, trade promotion, both or neither? *American Journal of Agricultural Economics* 80:566–71.

Barrett, C. B., and Dorosh, P. A. 1996. Nonparametric evidence from rice in Madagascar. *American Journal of Agricultural Economics* 78 (August): 656–69.

Bezuneh, M., B. Deaton, and S. Zuhair. 2003. Food aid disincentives: The Tunisian experience. *Review of Development Economics* 7 (4): 609–21.

Central Statistical Authority (CSA), Federal Democratic Republic of Ethiopia. 2001a. *Report on the 1999/2000 Household Income, Consumption, and Expenditure Survey.* Addis Ababa: Federal Democratic Republic of Ethiopia, March.

———. 2001b. *Report on the 1999/2000 Welfare Monitoring Survey.* Vols. I and II. Addis Ababa: Federal Democratic Republic of Ethiopia.

Deaton, A. 1989. Rice prices and income distribution in Thailand: A nonparametric analysis. *Economic Journal* 99 (395, suppl.): 1–37.

———. 1997. *The analysis of household surveys: A microeconometric approach to development policy.* Baltimore, MD: Johns Hopkins University Press.

Dercon, S., and P. Krishnan. 2003. Food aid and informal insurance. CSAE Work-

ing Paper no. WPS/2003-01. Oxford, UK: Centre for the Study of African Economies, January.

Ethiopian Economics Association (EEA). 2000. Annual report on the Ethiopian economy: Vol. I, 1999–2000. Addis Ababa, Ethiopia: Ethiopian Economics Association.

———. 2001. Annual report on the Ethiopian economy: Vol. II, 2000–1. Addis Ababa, Ethiopia: Ethiopian Economics Association.

GebreMichael, A. 2003. The impact of globalization: Its promises and perils to the Ethiopian economy. Paper presented at the Conference on Successes in African Agriculture. December, Pretoria, South Africa.

Hamory, J., and M. McMillan. 2003. What will it take to raise rural incomes in Ethiopia? Tufts University, Department of Economics. Working Paper, February.

Harrison, P. 2002. Ethiopia: Grain marketing; Review of recent trends. Washington, DC: World Bank. Unpublished Report, August.

Jayne, T. S., J. Strauss, T. Yamano, and D. Molla. 2002. Targeting of food aid in rural Ethiopia: Chronic need or inertia? *Journal of Development Economics* 68 (2): 247–88.

Maxwell, S. J., and H. W. Singer. 1970. Food aid to developing countries: A survey. *World Development* 7:225–47.

Panagariya, A. 2002. Trade and food security: Conceptualizing the linkages. Paper presented at the Conference on Trade, Agricultural Development, and Food Security: The Impact of Recent Economic and Trade Policy Reform. 11–12 July, Rome, Italy.

Peacemaker-Arrand, B. 2004. The impact of a new WTO agricultural agreement on cereals markets in sub-Saharan Africa. Senior honors thesis, Tufts University.

Regmi, A., M. S. Deepak, J. L. Seale, Jr., and J. Bernstein. 2001. Cross country analysis of food consumption patterns. In *The changing structure of global food consumption and trade.* Working Paper no. WRS-01-1. Washington, DC: U.S. Department of Agriculture, Economic Research Service.

Schultz, T. W. 1960. Value of U.S. farm surpluses to underdeveloped countries. *Journal of Farm Economics* 42:1019–30.

Soledad Bos, M. 2003. The impact of maize subsidies on sub-Saharan Africa. Master's thesis, University of California, Berkeley.

Valdez, A., and A. F. McCalla. 1999. Issues, interests, and options of developing countries. Washington, DC: World Bank.

Welfare Monitoring Unit, Central Statistical Agency. 2002. *Poverty profile of Ethiopia.* Addis Ababa: Federal Democratic Republic of Ethiopia.

World Food Programme (WFP). 1995–2001. Shipping bulletins. Addis Ababa, Ethiopia: World Food Programme.

Comment   Rohini Pande

Food donations or sales substantially below market price by a country with an exportable surplus of food to a country in need are defined as food aid.

Rohini Pande is an associate professor of economics at Yale University.

Supporters of this form of aid have argued that it is an effective means of reducing hunger; that, used for food for work programs, it may stimulate development; and that by reducing the need for food imports it prevents large cumulative deficits for poor countries, and so provides a platform for growth. Opponents argue that food aid increases the dependence of developing countries on food imports. The dumping of the surplus production for free or nearly no cost to poorer nations means that the farmers from such countries either cannot produce at competitive prices or lose the incentive to produce entirely (leading, over time, to the deterioration of the infrastructure of production). They also argue that food aid is inefficient—it often doesn't reach the most needy, and has high administrative costs.

Credible empirical evidence on the role of food aid in combating poverty is, however, very limited. Levinsohn and McMillan's study is an important first step. They use household-level nonparametric regressions, based on two Ethiopian household surveys (1999–2000), to identify the relationship between household income and the household's selling or buying wheat (a cereal typically distributed by food aid programs). Their main results are as follows:

1. Net buyers of wheat are poorer than net sellers.
2. At all income levels there are more buyers of wheat than sellers. Only 12 percent of Ethiopian households sell wheat.
3. The net benefit ratios are higher for poorer households, indicating that poorer households benefit proportionately more from a drop in the price of wheat.

Levinsohn and McMillan also undertake a welfare analysis of food aid in Ethiopia. They treat the Ethiopian wheat market as a partial equilibrium in a closed country, which received extra wheat via food aid. They observe the actual price (with the wheat aid), and then calculate a counterfactual wheat price that they believe would have held, given some posited elasticity of demand, absent food aid. Finally, they calculate the distributional effect under the counterfactual price and conclude that the poor were typically better off with the low (with food aid) price rather than the high (without food aid) price.

Based on these findings, they conclude that Ethiopian households at all levels of income potentially benefit from food aid, and that the benefits go disproportionately to the poorest households.

Discussion

While focused on food aid, this paper is an important contribution to the broader program evaluation literature, which examines the poverty impact of different public policy interventions. The paper provides valuable evidence on the potential impact of food aid on households at different points in the income distribution. However, the exclusive focus on household ben-

efit ratios at a single point in time limits the lessons to be learned regarding the overall worth of food aid. In order to conclude whether food aid is a beneficial policy intervention one would need a more comprehensive analysis of the history of food aid in Ethiopia, and an analysis of the way that aid is targeted. I will address these issues in turn.

History and Context

Levinsohn and McMillan consider households' wheat trading status as of 1999–2000 and show that food aid today can benefit the poor. However, food aid has been important in Ethiopia since the early 1980s (see figure 1 in Jayne et al. 2002). This history implies that to evaluate more effectively the worth of food aid as a public policy one must also ask whether the observed short-run beneficial effect of food aid is a result of a history of food aid. That is, in the long run can food aid change production patterns and thereby worsen poverty? This is particularly important because most critics of food aid point to the long-run disincentive effects of food aid for domestic production.

Ideally, therefore, one would like to augment this study with an analysis of net benefit ratios along the Ethiopian income distribution pre- and post–food aid. This would tell us whether the provision of food aid was associated with households' changing from being net producers of wheat to becoming net consumers of wheat. In the absence of longitudinal or repeated cross-sectional data that allow for such a direct assessment of the dynamics of food production, indirect evidence could be used to examine the dynamics of food aid.

One possibility would be to use aggregate data to examine the evolution of annual wheat production, amount of food aid, and wheat prices between 1980 and 2000.[1] Such an analysis, while unlikely to be informative about the causal impact of food aid, can provide evidence on whether changes in food aid provision were correlated with long-term changes in production patterns in Ethiopia.

It may also be possible to exploit the fact that food aid programs do not cover all crops to provide further indirect evidence on the long-term effects of food aid. It would be interesting to see whether the net benefit ratios along the income distribution look similar for another important crop that is not covered by food aid programs. This analysis could be made more rigorous by undertaking a difference-in-difference analysis that exploits, in addition to differential crop coverage by food aid, cross-regional differences in food aid flows.

Turning to the welfare analysis undertaken by the authors, it would have been good to have more information on the relevance of the assumed de-

1. Figure 1 in Jayne et al. (2002) suggests that the responsiveness of food aid to domestic food production is relatively limited.

mand and supply elasticities in the welfare analysis for Ethiopia. For, despite food aid, Ethiopia remains a net importer of wheat. Hence, if Ethiopia is a small player in the world wheat market, then the relevant wheat price for Ethiopia would be the world wheat price, and food aid need not depress food prices.[2]

Targeting

Levinsohn and McMillan's study examines the potential of food aid to help the poor. However, if this analysis is to be relevant for policy design it is important to ask who, in reality, benefits from food aid programs. Two recent papers, Jayne et al. (2002) and Clay, Molla, and Habtewold (1999), specifically examine who received food aid in Ethiopia during 1995–96. Both papers found evidence of imperfect targeting—the very poor are more likely to get food aid, but so are the very rich. They also report evidence of inertia in both the regional and household-level allocation of food aid over time. That is, the best predictor of a household or region's current food aid recipient status is its previous recipient status. In contrast, the food aid need of a region or household does vary over time. They therefore hypothesize that the rigidity in food aid targeting is probably due to high fixed program costs, rigidities in the governmental process of determining food aid allocations to local administrative units, and political income-transfer objectives.

Per se, these findings do not affect any of Levinsohn and McMillan's analysis. They do, however, suggest that any welfare calculation of the impact of food aid should take into account the partial targeting of such schemes.

Conclusion

If there are domestic markets for food, then an alternative to food aid is cash transfers. Clearly, all the welfare effects of cash transfers to the poor would be positive if they led to poor consumers buying up poor farmers' wheat. More generally, Coate (1989) shows that whether food aid is preferable to cash transfers depends on whether the relief agency distributing food aid is more efficient at transferring food to the poor than traders.

Food aid began in the 1950s as a means for rich countries to dispose of agricultural surplus. If the domestic imperatives of rich countries are such that some fraction of aid from rich to poor countries will always take the form of food aid, then Levinsohn and McMillan's results are reassuring (at least for the short run). However, if the form of aid to developing countries can be altered and food aid replaced with other forms of aid, such as cash transfers, then it remains unclear whether food aid is a preferred public policy intervention in situations other than emergencies.

2. I am grateful to Don Davis for this observation.

References

Clay, D., D. Molla, and D. Habtewold. 1999. Food aid targeting in Ethiopia: A study of who needs it and who gets it. *Food Policy* 24:391–409.

Coate, S. 1989. Cash versus direct food relief. *Journal of Development Economics* 30 (2): 199–224.

Jayne, T. S., J. Strauss, T. Yamano, and D. Molla. 2002. Targeting of food aid in rural Ethiopia: Chronic need or inertia? *Journal of Development Economics* 68 (2): 247–88.

IV

Other Outcomes Associated with Globalization (Risk, Returns to Speaking English)

14

Risk and the Evolution of Inequality in China in an Era of Globalization

Ethan Ligon

14.1 Introduction

Changes in poverty rates within a country, whether due to globalization or some other source, can be usefully thought of as reflecting either changes in aggregate resources (growth) for the country as a whole, or changes in the within-country distribution of these resources (inequality). Over the last twenty years China has experienced huge rates of economic growth, reducing poverty. Although at the same time China has experienced substantial increases in rural-urban and interregional inequality, the increase in the size of the Chinese economic pie has much more than offset any increase in inequality for the vast majority of China's households. Ravallion and Chen (2004) report that although 17.6 percent of Chinese households were poor in 1985, the poverty rate had fallen by more than half by 2001.

Faced with evidence of high rates of aggregate growth and relatively modest increases in inequality, and with evidence that poor households have shared in the aggregate windfall, one might be tempted to conclude that China's recent experience has had clear net benefits for almost all households. Yet this conclusion (while possibly correct) isn't justified by the kinds of evidence given above. The kinds of changes described above are likely to involve a large increase in the *risk* faced by Chinese households. Would a typical household in China in the early eighties, given a choice between their "iron rice bowl" and the risky promises of economic reform, have willingly chosen the latter? We can't know without some way

Ethan Ligon is an associate professor of agricultural and resource economics at the University of California, Berkeley.

of measuring the welfare costs of the increased risks actually borne by these households.

The welfare loss due to risk faced by households at a point in time is intimately related to changes in inequality in expenditures. In particular, risk-averse households with time-separable preferences will tend to prefer to smooth shocks to income over time, so that even entirely transitory shocks to income will tend to have a permanent effect on future consumption expenditures. Thus, the same shocks to income that make next period's consumption uncertain will also determine the household's position in next period's distribution of expenditures.

In this paper we exploit this link by using data on the evolution of expenditure inequality to estimate both household risk preferences and the welfare loss due to risk actually borne by urban Chinese households over the period 1985–2001, an era during which China's economy has undergone dramatic reforms and experienced remarkable growth. Others have noted that increases in inequality imply that the rising tide of the aggregate Chinese economy has not lifted all boats equally (Kahn and Riskin 2001). Here we note that because households may change their position in the wealth (and expenditure) distribution, merely looking at changes in inequality will understate the displacement and (ex ante) welfare loss experienced by risk-averse households facing dramatic economic change.

Although the chief contribution of this paper is the application of a method to infer household-level idiosyncratic risk from aggregate data on the cross-sectional distribution of consumption, it also has something to say about changes in inequality in the absence of this risk. In particular, we see that although there has been a notable increase in inequality among urban households, this increase is dwarfed by the increase in inequality between rural and urban households. We are also interested in documenting any relationship between globalization (as measured by changes in trade volume across sectors) and changes in urban inequality. In section 14.3 we show that after controlling for any effects that globalization may have on aggregate urban consumption the trade shocks we measure can't account for any of the observed changes in inequality observed within the urban population.

Models having complete markets à la Arrow-Debreu yield fully Pareto efficient outcomes; in such a model any changes in inequality must be preferred by all market participants, and so they yield little in terms of interesting policy implications. Complete market models that feature Gorman aggregable preferences (Wilson 1968) yield the very strong prediction that the distribution of consumption across households is invariant (see subsection 14.2.1 for an illustration and appendix A for a general treatment). More interesting are models in which some friction prevents allocations from being fully Pareto optimal, and that have enough dynamic structure to yield interesting predictions regarding the evolution of the distribution of consumption.

To estimate the importance of idiosyncratic risk we assume that all households have similar preferences, and that these preferences exhibit constant relative risk aversion (Arrow 1964). We further assume that all households have access to credit markets on equal terms, and that households exploit these credit markets to smooth their consumption over time, à la the permanent income hypothesis.[1] Beyond this, we make no notably restrictive assumptions. We allow quite arbitrary forms of technology and shocks, and avoid the problem of measuring asset returns. Although this framework is quite general in several dimensions, we will show that conditional on the distribution of production shocks the model yields rather sharp predictions regarding the evolution of the distribution of resources across households. In particular, the model gives us the law of motion governing the inverse Lorenz curves that describe inequality in the economy; the idiosyncratic risk borne by households can be shown to depend entirely on the distribution of "relative surprises" experienced by the household.

The law of motion for inverse Lorenz curves allows us to make predictions about the sequence of Lorenz curves we would expect to observe, conditional on household risk preferences, on rates of aggregate economic growth, and on the distribution of unforecastable shocks facing households in different years, at different wealth levels, and in different occupations. By comparing realized and predicted Lorenz curves, we can estimate these preferences and distributions. This same procedure yields a Markov transition function mapping shares of consumption today into a probability distribution over possible shares tomorrow, and we use this object to calculate the risk borne by differently situated urban Chinese households in different years and to relate this risk to measures of globalization during this period.

The key to the empirical strategy of this paper involves exploiting the restrictions placed on data by Euler equations to make statements about the evolution of inequality. Related literature includes Deaton and Paxson (1994), who derive a martingale property from the consumption Euler equation and use several long panels of household-level expenditure data to argue that within-cohort inequality in industrialized countries is increasing over time, and Storesletten, Telmer, and Yaron (2004), who use household panel data on expenditures from the United States and a more completely specified general equilibrium model to estimate a law of motion for the distribution of consumption. The central idea of those papers is to exploit intertemporal restrictions to estimate the law of motion for individual households' consumption growth, and then in effect to integrate over households to infer what the law of motion is for the distribution of

---

1. For the reader who regards this assumption as unreasonable, we note that if some households are constrained so as to not have equal access to credit markets, then our estimates of risk for these households are likely to be underestimates.

consumption *across* households. The present paper reverses these last two steps—we derive equations that impose intertemporal restrictions on individual households' consumption growth, but then integrate over these equations to obtain restrictions on the law of motion for the distribution of consumption across households before taking these restrictions to the data. The cost of the procedure followed in this paper is that one can't exploit all the information that would be available from the trajectories of consumption for many different individual households. The (closely related) benefit is that we can get by without panel data, using instead only a relatively limited set of data obtainable from repeated cross-sectional surveys of household expenditures, of the sort that many countries conduct in order, for example, to compute consumer price indexes.

14.2   An Example of Risk and Inequality

The central idea of this paper is to use evidence on changes in the cross-sectional distribution of consumption to draw inferences about the welfare of households. In this section we'll construct a simple example, meant to illustrate the connection between the evolution of inequality and household welfare, while appendix A provides a more general treatment. As will be seen, the connection between household welfare and changes in inequality can be more complicated and interesting than one might suppose.

To set the stage for our example, consider an environment with many households, but only two types (each type comprising one-half of the population), indexed by $i = 1, 2$. There are two periods, indexed by $t = 1, 2$. Households of both types derive momentary utility from consumption according to a logarithmic utility function:

$$(1) \qquad\qquad u(c_{it}) = \log(c_{it}).$$

Both types of households also discount future utility using a common discount factor, $\beta \in (0, 1)$.

Critical to the example is that there be some source of underlying uncertainty that may affect the second-period distribution of consumption. Let $\omega \in \Omega$ denote the realized state of the economy in this second period. Assuming Ω is finite, let $\Pr(\omega)$ denote the probability of state ω being realized.

Per capita consumption in period t is some exogenously determined (but possibly random) quantity $\bar{c}_t$; we choose a normalization for consumption so that $\bar{c}_1 = 1$. The characteristic that distinguishes the two different types of households is that each type begins with different shares of aggregate consumption. In particular, let the consumption of type 1 households in period 1 be $c_{11} = 0.4$, so that consumption of the second type is $c_{21} = 0.6$.

We now consider three different market structures and ask how these influence the evolution of inequality.

14.2.1 Complete Markets

When there are complete markets, we can exploit the second welfare theorem to compute changes in inequality for our example economy. Accordingly, consider the planning problem of allocating consumption across representative households of each type,

$$\max_{\{c_{i1},\{c_{i2}(\omega)\}_{\omega\in\Omega}\}_i} \sigma u(c_{11}) + (1 - \sigma)u(c_{21})$$

$$+ \beta \sum_{\omega\in\Omega} \Pr(\omega)\{\sigma u[c_{11}(\omega)] + (1 - \sigma)u[c_{22}(\omega)]\},$$

subject to resource constraints in each period,

$$c_{11} + c_{21} \leq \overline{c}_1,$$

and

$$c_{12}(\omega) + c_{22}(\omega) \leq \overline{c}_2(\omega).$$

Here the parameter σ is a "planning weight" that determines the weight of type one households relative to type two in the planner's problem. With the form of utility function assumed above, it follows immediately from the first-order conditions that

$$c_{11} = \sigma\overline{c}_1$$

and

$$c_{12} = \sigma\overline{c}_2(\omega).$$

Note from this that the parameter σ corresponds to the share of aggregate consumption for type 1 households, and that this parameter doesn't vary across either dates or states. As a consequence, any Pareto efficient outcome in this example will assign 40 percent (the share of type one households in the initial period) of aggregate consumption to households of type one in both periods, regardless of the realized value of ω.

This point generalizes. When households have identical utility functions featuring constant elasticities of substitution (of which logarithmic utility is a special case) and when markets are complete, then we should expect the distribution of consumption to be unchanging. Conversely, if the distribution of consumption is observed to change over time, then this is evidence that either our assumptions regarding household preferences are mistaken or markets are incomplete (Lucas 1992).

14.2.2 Segmented Markets

Taking our cue from subsection 14.2.1, we next imagine a particular sort of simple market incompleteness that can give rise to nontrivial changes in

consumption inequality. In particular, suppose that although households of type i can engage in exchange with other households of the same type, circumstances contrive to make it impossible for households of type 1 to make exchanges with households of type 2. Thus, a social planner must keep track of aggregate resources available to households of each type. Within the set of type i households there will be perfect insurance, so we can write $c_{i2}(\omega) = \bar{c}_{i2}(\omega)$, where $\bar{c}_{i2}(\omega)$ is the per capita consumption available to households of type i in state ω.

To be concrete, suppose that the share of type 1 households happens to fall from 0.4 in the first period to 0.3 in the second, but that total consumption across both groups remains constant. Then the ex post welfare outcome for each household type relative to the complete markets case is the same in the first period, but in the second the difference is given by

(2) $\log(0.3) - \log(0.4) \approx -0.288$

(3) $\log(0.7) - \log(0.6) \approx 0.154.$

Though very contrived, this accounting seems to capture the usual idea behind analyses of changes in inequality—in this case, poor households (type 1) are hurt by an increase in inequality, while wealthy households (type 2) fare better. The chief point missed by this idea is that in the face of uninsured shocks individual households are likely to change their position in the consumption distribution.

14.2.3   Credit Markets

We next eliminate the supposition of segmented markets and suppose that households of both types can exchange debt in competitive credit markets. However, for whatever reason, we also suppose that households can't perfectly insure their future consumption, as they did in subsection 14.2.1. We then derive intertemporal restrictions on the evolution of each household's share of aggregate consumption. The key assumptions we exploit here (and later in our empirical work) are that households all have similar preferences featuring constant relative risk aversion, and that all households have access to credit on the same terms. Note that this latter assumption is weaker than assuming that credit markets are perfect—in particular, it may be the case that at the interest rates faced by households for some reason credit markets fail to clear.

At date 1, households of each type can exchange claims to consumption at date 2 with other households at a price β, solving the problem

(4) $\max_{b_i} u(c_{i1} - b_i\beta) + \beta Eu(c_{i2} + b_i),$

where E denotes the expectations operator conditional on information available at time 1, b_i denotes the debt issued by a household of type i in the first period, and c_{it} denotes the household's time t consumption expenditures.

We modify our notation slightly to let the index i refer to individual

households $i = 1, \ldots, n$, while maintaining our assumption that all of these households are of one of two distinct types. The modification is necessary because we want to consider the possibility that households of the same type may face different shocks, even though the distribution of these shocks will be the same for all households of the same type ex ante.

The first-order conditions associated with the household's problem of debt issuance indicate that the household will consume c_{it} at t if the usual Euler equation

(5) $$u'(c_{it}) = Eu'(c_{it+1})$$

is satisfied.

Exploiting our assumption of logarithmic utility, equation (5) implies that

$$1 = E\left(\frac{c_{i1}}{c_{i2}}\right)$$

for $i = 1, 2, \ldots, n$.

Let

(6) $$\varepsilon_i = \left(\frac{c_{i1}}{c_{i2}}\right) - 1$$

denote household i's time 1 forecast error. Note from the properties of equation (6) that $E\varepsilon_i = 0$, as is usual when evaluating forecast errors from Euler equations. Note also from equation (5) and Jensen's inequality we have $c_{i1}/Ec_{i2} \leq 1$, so that

$$Ec_{i2} \geq c_{i1};$$

that is, expected consumption is increasing for both types of households.

Risk

The risk facing any individual household with consumption c_{it} at time t that may reduce its utility at time $t + 1$ depends on the distribution on the forecast error ε_i.

Let σ_{it} denote household i's consumption share at date t. Define the idiosyncratic risk borne by the household at time 1 to be the ex ante loss in expected utility due solely to variation in the purely idiosyncratic shock ε_i, or

(7) $$R_i \equiv u(\overline{c}_2 \sigma_{i1}) - E[u_i(c_{i2})].$$

Here the first term is the utility the household would obtain in period 2 if the household's share of expenditures was unchanged (as would be the case if no household faced any idiosyncratic risk) and if the household knew in advance what aggregate consumption would be in period 2. The second term is the expected utility of the household given that it remained ignorant of the idiosyncratic shocks it would experience.

As demonstrated above, in a world with complete markets and the assumed logarithmic preferences we work with here, it's easy to establish that each household's share of aggregate consumption will remain constant, eliminating all idiosyncratic risk. Thus, we can interpret the first term of equation (7) as the utility the household would obtain if no households bore any idiosyncratic risk less the expected utility of consumption when the household does bear this risk. It's trivial to establish that this *cardinal* measure of risk is uniquely consistent (up to a linear transformation of u) with the notion of increasing risk defined by Rothschild and Stiglitz (1970). Because our measure of idiosyncratic risk is denominated in utils, it is straightforward to construct a variety of useful measures of the welfare loss associated with this risk.

Again, for the sake of concreteness, let us assume that $\log(1 + \varepsilon_i)$ is distributed $N(-v_i^2/2, v_i)$, with the consequence that $E\varepsilon_i = 0$, as is required by our definition of the forecast error above, with v_i a parameter equal to the standard deviation of $\log(1 + \varepsilon_i)$ for household i. With this assumption it follows that household i's idiosyncratic risk (that is, holding aggregate consumption constant) is given by

$$R_i = \frac{v_i^2}{2}.$$

Thus the ex ante welfare loss due to the uninsurability of idiosyncratic shocks is simply equal to one-half the variance of $\log(1 + \varepsilon_i)$.

Distribution

Now, how is this risk related to the evolution of inequality? Let $\Psi(\sigma_{i2} \,|\, \sigma_{i1})$ denote the Markov transition function for the household's share σ between periods 1 and 2. Then the expression for household i's time t idiosyncratic risk, as defined above, may be written

$$R_i = u(\bar{c}_2 \sigma_{i1}) - \int u(\bar{c}_2 \sigma')d\Psi(\sigma' \,|\, \sigma_{i1}).$$

We've already seen that we can compute risk R_i from knowledge of the distribution of i's forecast errors ε_i, so this equation allows us to relate the transition function Ψ to the parameters of this distribution.

The Markov transition function Ψ, which is critical for calculating average risk in the population, is also critical for understanding how the distribution of resources changes over time. In particular, the distribution of consumption shares (inverse Lorenz curves) $\{\Gamma_t\}$ will satisfy a law of motion

(8) $$\Gamma_2(\hat{\sigma}) = \int_{\{\sigma' < \hat{\sigma}\}} d\Psi(\sigma' \,|\, \sigma)d\Gamma_1(\sigma).$$

Accordingly, knowledge of the transition function Ψ suffices to characterize both average risk and the evolution of inequality in the population.

Let us now discuss how knowledge of the cross-sectional distribution of

consumption can be used to draw inferences about household-level risk. Recall that an individual household's risk depends only on forecast errors ε_i. In particular, we can use equation (6) to express Ψ in terms of the distribution of forecast errors in the population. Let ε_i have the cumulative probability distribution $F(\varepsilon \mid \sigma_i)$. Then equation (6) implies

(9) $$c_{i2} = c_{i1}(1 + \varepsilon_{it+1})^{-1},$$

so that, conditioning on consumption growth $g = \bar{c}_2/\bar{c}_1$,

(10) $$\Psi(\sigma' \mid \sigma) = \int_{\{\varepsilon > [(\sigma/\sigma')-1]/g\}} dF(\varepsilon \mid \sigma).$$

Now, let us suppose that the change in the distribution of consumption is as above in subsection 14.2.2. In particular, the share of the bottom 50 percent of households falls from 40 percent in the first period to 30 percent in the second. We maintain our assumption that (one plus) forecast errors are distributed log normal and that these forecast errors have mean zero. We also maintain our assumption that the two different types of households are ex ante identical, and use the change in the distribution of consumption to infer the parameters v_i that govern the distribution of forecast errors and risk borne by the households.

Using equations (8) and (10) it is straightforward to compute (see appendix B) the values of v_i implied by this change in distribution. In particular, households of type 1 will have v_i 0.267, while households of type 2 will have v_i of 0.55. As an immediate consequence the risk borne by poor households will be equal to 0.0385, while the risk borne by wealthy households will be equal to 0.1540 (bear in mind that these risk figures are denominated in utils).

The quite surprising result is that the apparent increase in wealthy households' share of consumption from 60 to 70 percent on average *hurts* the households that were wealthy ex ante. The cross-sectional distribution of consumption can't change unless at least some households face some idiosyncratic risk, and the only way to get the share of ex post wealthy households to increase is to expose all ex ante wealthy (type 2) households to a great deal of risk. As a consequence, even though *expected* consumption is increasing for all households, for type 2 households the probability of having a big drop in consumption offsets the expected consumption increase. Figure 14.1 shows the distribution of period 2 log consumption for each of the two household types. Note that although the mean of the type 2 distribution is still greater than the mean of the type 1 distribution, the much greater variance in outcomes for the initially wealthier households means that some of these households will be at the very bottom of the consumption distribution in period 2.

This apparently perverse result depends less on the details of our quite special example than one might suppose. As long as preferences exhibit decreasing absolute risk aversion, it will be the initially wealthy households

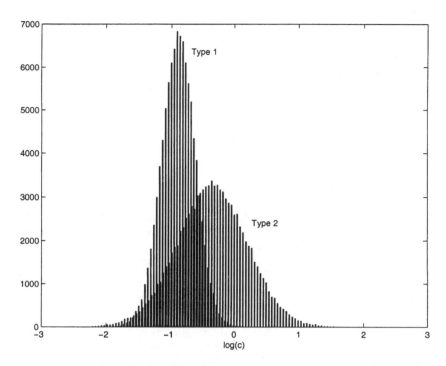

Fig. 14.1 **Distribution of log consumption for different household types implied by shift in Lorenz curve**

that will choose to take larger risks. Thus, big falls in the share of the bottom consumption quantile are likely to be due to some previously wealthy households having very bad luck, while a larger share of previously poor households will move into higher quantiles. In the example just presented, the matrix governing the transition between the bottom 50 percent and the top 50 percent turns out to be

$$\begin{pmatrix} 0.88 & 0.12 \\ 0.06 & 0.94 \end{pmatrix}.$$

Accordingly, we can see that 12 percent of type 1 households move up into the top quantile, while 6 percent of type 2 households fall down into the bottom quantile. The basic flavor of the result seems to depend only on decreasing absolute risk aversion and common access to credit markets. With these two ingredients apparent increases in inequality may actually imply that ex ante wealthy households are bearing large amounts of risk that often cast them far down the consumption distribution.

14.3   The Data

We next turn to an application of some of the ideas developed in the preceding example and make an effort to draw inferences regarding the risk borne by households in China from data from the sequence of Lorenz curves describing the evolution of consumption inequality in China over the period 1985–2001.

In this section we document a few basic facts about Chinese inequality and then assume a structure similar to that of subsection 14.2.2, so that households *within* a population quantile stay within that quantile, sharing the variable consumption that accrues to the quantile. In a later section we instead assume equal access to credit markets and then use variation in Lorenz curves to draw inferences about idiosyncratic risk.

14.3.1   Chinese Inequality

Numerous authors have documented notable increases in inequality within China over the last two decades, although over the same period there has been a dramatic increase in aggregate consumption.

There are two observations about changes in Chinese inequality that seem to qualify as stylized facts. The first is that there have been large increases in the difference between rural and urban incomes over the last twenty years, while the second is that there has been increasing inequality in income across regions (especially between the coastal and interior areas).

In support of the first observation, Kahn and Riskin (2001) document notable increases in income inequality between rural and urban households over the period 1988–95. Ravallion (2004) and Chen and Ravallion (2004) explain part of this increase in urban-rural inequality by computing the effects of World Trade Organization (WTO) accession on rural and urban poverty, finding that on average rural households tend to lose due to decreases in the price of their mostly agricultural output, while urban consumers gain.

In support of the second observation, a number of authors have documented notable increases in regional inequality. Yang (1997) documents large shifts in the resources transferred between coastal and interior regions, and argues that such shifts entail increased regional inequality as a consequence. While using data on outcomes, Yao and Zhang (2001) document increases in interprovincial inequality, and posit the existence of "clubs" of provinces with incomes diverging from the incomes of other clubs.

Of course, even if both these observations are true, it may be the case that one observation is a consequence of the other. In particular, since there is wide variation in the proportion of rural households across provinces, it

may well be the case that the observed increase in inequality across regions is simply a consequence of increased rural-urban inequality. Bhalla, Yao, and Zhang (2003) and Kanbur and Zhang (2005) use data on province-level incomes to argue that most inequality is due to rural-urban differences rather than to provincial-level differences; however, both papers still find a large role for provincial differences even after accounting for differences in rural-urban composition.

The general connection between trade and inequality (or poverty) discussed by Chen and Ravallion (2004) can also be found using much more aggregate provincial-level data. Kanbur and Zhang (2005) find that increases in interprovincial income inequality over time are associated with differences in openness, while Zhang and Zhang (2003) decompose a Theil measure of inequality and find that 20 percent of differences in per capita gross domestic product (GDP) across provinces in 1995 can be attributed to measures of trade (Milanovic 2005 shows that it is critical to weight provinces by population to obtain this result). However, as Ravallion (2004) cautions, this kind of association between two endogenous aggregates (inequality and trade) doesn't allow us to draw any inference about cause.

In an important reminder that inequality isn't mostly about aggregates, Benjamin, Brandt, and Giles (2005) examine a large panel of rural Chinese households and find evidence of larger increases in inequality within small geographical regions than across them.

14.3.2   Urban Inequality

Against this background of rapid increases in overall Chinese inequality, how should we assess changes in urban inequality? The way in which inequality changes over time matters greatly for evaluating household welfare. If all the increase in inequality is due to increases in equality *between* different groups, then the idiosyncratic risk due to this increasing inequality will be small. For example, one of the key features of Chinese reform has to do with the fact that reform began in the countryside, with the establishment of the household responsibility system in the late 1970s and the corresponding introduction of market prices (at the margin) for agricultural goods. These reforms ushered in a decade of rapid rural economic growth. The nineties brought an important change. A decade of rural growth was followed by an extended period of urban growth and relative rural stagnation. Yang (1997) argues convincingly that this shift was due to quite conscious and quite visible policy choices made by the central government, which exploited its control of nonagricultural prices to implicitly tax the interior of the country and to use the proceeds of these implicit taxes to finance investment in coastal urban areas. To the extent that one could predict that urban households would benefit from these policies at the expense of rural households, neither urban nor rural households would

face any risk subsequent to this policy shift, but simply different expected growth trajectories.

Since the focus of this paper is on urban households, let us henceforth set aside changes in overall inequality due to the well-documented divergence in the consumption expenditures of rural and urban China. Instead, let us ask what our data can tell us about the evolution of inequality among urban Chinese households.

At the beginning of the period for which we have data, inequality in China was remarkably low. Although one still does not observe gross inequities in the distribution of consumption in China, over the course of 1985–2001 one *does* observe an increase in urban inequality. This point is made most clearly by figure 14.2. This figure shows the *change* in Lorenz curves for urban consumption over the period 1985–2001. Individual changes are shown year by year. It is apparent from these that inequality is not always increasing—from year to year one sees increases in equality with almost the same frequency as decreases. However, the average decrease in equality is larger than the average increase, with the consequence that when we aggregate all these changes, we see that the total change in Lorenz curves is considerable, with the bottom 60 percent of the distribu-

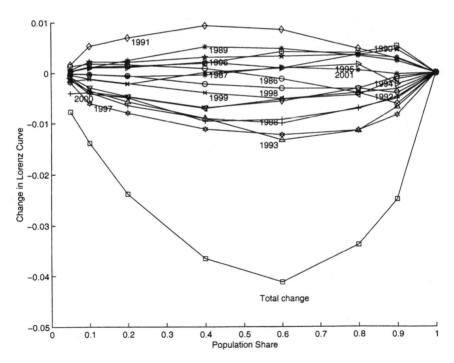

Fig. 14.2   Changes in consumption Lorenz curves for registered urban households

Table 14.1   **Increasing inequality?**

Quartile	5%	10%	20%	40%	60%	80%	90%	100%
Growth rate	0.123	0.117	0.112	0.117	0.110	0.128	0.133	0.113
t-statistic	5.064	4.786	4.593	4.816	4.531	5.272	5.440	4.629
5%	0.000	0.197	0.333	0.176	0.377	−0.146	−0.266	0.308
10%	−0.197	0.000	0.136	−0.021	0.180	−0.344	−0.463	0.111
20%	−0.333	−0.136	0.000	−0.157	0.044	0.480	−0.599	−0.025
40%	−0.176	0.021	0.157	0.000	0.201	−0.322	−0.442	0.132
60%	−0.377	−0.180	−0.044	−0.201	0.000	−0.523	−0.643	−0.069
80%	0.146	0.344	0.480	0.322	0.523	0.000	−0.119	0.454
90%	0.266	0.463	0.599	0.442	0.643	0.119	0.000	0.574
100%	−0.308	−0.111	0.025	−0.132	0.069	−0.454	−0.574	0.000

Notes: Average growth rates of consumption expenditures for different quantiles of the consumption distribution appear in the first row of the table, with *t*-statistics for these point estimates immediately below. The remaining rows of the table present *t*-tests of differences among the growth rates of different quantiles.

tion seeing a fall in its aggregate share of consumption of about 4 percent. The bottom 10 percent of the distribution sees a much larger (proportional) drop, with its share falling from about 8 percent in 1985 to about 6.5 percent in 2001, or a nearly 20 percent fall. Of course, as we see in table 14.1, this same bottom 10 percent has seen large increases in total consumption, so this fall in share has been much more than offset by increases in aggregate consumption.

We tackle the measurement of changes in urban inequality in two stages. First, we use aggregate data on the distribution of consumption expenditures to characterize changes in welfare and inequality *across* consumption quartiles. Subsequently we turn our attention to the problem of inferring the distribution of possible consumption outcomes for individual households at different points in the cross-sectional consumption distribution. We will use the inferences so drawn to quantify the idiosyncratic risk borne by these households.

We begin by trying to understand consumption growth by population quantile. Table 14.1 reports the average rate of consumption growth for each of eight quantiles over the period 1986–2001. The results of this exercise show that, when averaged over this entire period, there is remarkably little difference in the average rate of consumption growth for different quantiles. All of the eight quantiles have consumption growth that averages about 12 percent per year, and no quantile has a rate of growth significantly greater than that of any other quantile.

Of course, the fact that different quantiles all have roughly the same rate of consumption growth over a long period doesn't imply that there aren't differences over shorter periods. Accordingly, we next ask about how much of the variation in individual quantiles' consumption can be explained by

Table 14.2   **Analysis of variance of consumption growth**

Variables	Individual contribution (R^2)	Cumulative contribution (R^2)	p-value
Quantile	0.008	0.008	0.998
Country shocks	0.893	0.901	0.000
Import shocks	0.496	0.963	0.998

Table 14.3   **Decomposition of risk across quantiles**

	Sources of risk		
Risk	Country	Trade	Quantile risk
5%	0.249	0.323	1.664
10%	0.003	0.196	2.703
20%	0.139	0.101	1.894
40%	0.117	−0.070	1.969
60%	0.002	−0.030	2.372
80%	0.171	−0.062	1.548
90%	0.069	−0.111	2.080
100%	0.057	−0.182	1.779

Note: These figures do *not* include estimates of the risk due to idiosyncratic shocks.

country-level shocks. We begin by asking what proportion of quantiles' consumption growth is attributable to aggregate growth. These results are reported in the first row of table 14.2. We see from this that nearly 90 percent of variation in quantile consumption is due entirely to aggregate variation.

Finally, table 14.3 displays estimates of the welfare loss for households due to aggregate sources of risk (risk shared by all households in the country, quantile-level risk related to trade shocks, and residual quantile-level risk). All measures are denominated in utils and are computed in a manner analogous to the approach taken by Ligon and Schechter (2003). Note, however, that these measures of risk completely neglect idiosyncratic factors. Inferring this idiosyncratic component is the chief task of the remainder of this paper.

14.4   Idiosyncratic Risk

In this section we use the logic developed in the example of section 14.2 to draw inferences about the level of idiosyncratic risk from a sequence of Lorenz curves. We relax many of the most restrictive assumptions of the example, developing a more general framework for inference in appendix A and appendix B. One useful generalization involves giving a parametric form for the variance (or scale) that governs risk, permitting this variance

to depend on a variety of observable variables. The general form for this scale parameter is given by equation (21).

14.4.1   Error Components Structure

We begin (adapting some language from Amemiya 1984) with a simple "error components" structure, permitting the log of the variance of the relative forecast error to depend on the sum of a year-specific constant and a quantile-specific constant, so that

$$\log v_{it} = \alpha_i + v_t.$$

Here v_{it} is the standard error of the relative forecast shock for a household in the ith quantile of the consumption share distribution in year y; in practice we divide this distribution into seventeen different quantiles, but for the sake of identifying these parameters we constrain the top quantile to have $\alpha_{17} = 0$.

Table 14.4 presents the fitted parameters given this error-components variance structure. Columns (1) and (2) of the table show parameters that vary across years. Estimates of the normalizing constants $\{\eta_t\}$ appear in the first column of this panel, while the "year effects" part of the variance structure, $\{v_t\}$, appears in the second column. Recall from our earlier discussion the interpretation of η_t as a measure of the aggregate uncertainty at time t—this specification gives us a simple way to check the model, since

Table 14.4   **Parameter estimates assuming log-normal relative forecast errors and error-components variance specification**

Year	η_t (1)	v_t (2)	Quantile (3)	α_i (4)
1986	1.0635	−1.2862	0.0139	−3.5888
1987	1.1295	−1.1886	0.0278	0.0009
1988	1.2037	−1.1411	0.0539	−0.0004
1989	1.0884	−1.2590	0.0800	3.8415
1990	1.0463	−1.1884	0.1142	−0.6764
1991	1.1009	−1.2512	0.1485	−0.5182
1992	1.1228	−1.1603	0.2280	−0.0510
1993	1.2187	−1.1499	0.3075	−0.2359
1994	1.2660	−1.1199	0.4008	1.5517
1995	1.2004	−1.2411	0.4940	0.0261
1996	1.0926	−1.2052	0.6030	0.3490
1997	1.0868	−1.1026	0.7120	−0.0000
1998	1.0682	−1.2444	0.7756	0.0001
1999	1.1003	−1.2407	0.8393	−0.1229
2000	1.1205	−1.1694	0.9197	0.7127
2001	1.1064	−1.3337		
γ		0.7229		
R^2		0.4723		

v_t provides a direct measure of aggregate uncertainty. In this case, the correlation between the two measures is 0.47, consistent with our expectations.

The primary virtue of this error-components specification of the structure of the variance of relative forecast errors has to do with the simplicity of interpreting estimates of α_i and v_t. In particular, for years in which v_t is relatively large, the entire population faces greater risk than usual. At the same time the specification allows for variation in uncertainty by wealth (consumption share); the average household in a quantile for which α_i is negative faces less uncertainty in an average year than do the very wealthiest households, while the average household in a quantile with α_i greater than zero faces more.

Turning our attention to differences in the uncertainty faced by households across the distribution, consider columns (3) and (4) of table 14.4. Here we see that the households in the bottom quantile that collectively consume 1.4 percent of the aggregate face the least uncertainty, with a quantile fixed effect of –3.59. However, households in the 5–8 percent quantile face the most, with an estimated quantile fixed effect of 3.84. Eight of the consumption share quantiles bear more uncertainty than does the topmost quantile, while seven bear less.

At this point let us pause a moment to be careful about what is meant by "uncertainty" above. Differences in the parameters $\{v_t\}$ across time or $\{\alpha_i\}$ across quantiles are really just related to the standard deviation of the relative forecast errors ε_{it}. These relative forecast errors have numerous desirable properties, but they do not have a straightforward interpretation either in terms of the welfare costs of uncertainty or in terms of variation in quantities that might be observable. In particular, the distribution of ε_{it} depends both on households' risk preferences (here γ) and on the distribution of consumption growth, making it critical to estimate γ and the variance structure of the forecast errors simultaneously. In the present case, the estimated value of the coefficient of relative risk aversion is 0.723. This is on the low end of the range of estimates of this parameter in the microeconometric literature, but it does not seem obviously wrong.

To get a sense of the magnitude of the risk facing individual households, we use the parameters reported in table 14.4 to estimate the risk facing the average household at selected consumption-share quantiles in figure 14.3. To construct this figure we have started with estimates of the measure of risk given by equation (16), but rather than reporting the welfare loss due to uncertainty in utils (which may be difficult to interpret), we have computed the growth rate of aggregate consumption expenditures that would be just enough to compensate households for the risk they bear.

In the present case, because we assume constant elasticity of substitution (CES) utility functions future aggregate consumption $\bar{c}_{t+1}$ cancels out of this calculation. Substituting in our estimates of the parameters $\{\eta_t\}$ and

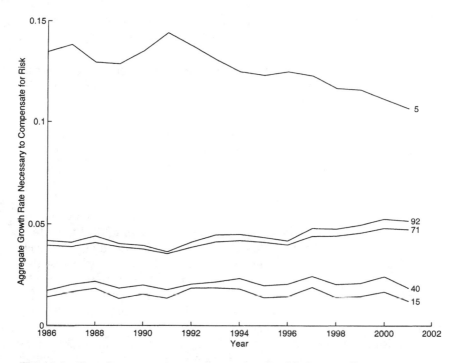

Fig. 14.3   Growth rate necessary to compensate for risk, by quantiles

Notes: Each line indicates the minimum rate of growth necessary to compensate for the risk faced by the average household at the consumption share quantile indicated at the far right. For example, the line labeled "5" gives the rate of growth in each year necessary to compensate the average household ex ante at the 5 percent quantile for the risk borne by that household.

of the marginal Markov transition function makes it possible to use a simple line-search algorithm to find the compensating growth rates.

These compensating growth rates are shown for selected consumption-share quantiles in figure 14.3. Note first that the growth we refer to is the rate of growth in aggregate consumption expenditures for urban households; this quantity grew at an average annual rate of 12 percent over the period 1985–2001. Using the quantity $g_t(\sigma)$ as our measure of the welfare loss of uncertainty, the poorest (displayed) quantile of households is much the worst off—from 1985 to 1986 these households would have needed urban expenditures to have grown by nearly 14 percent before they would have preferred the status quo to stagnation and an iron rice bowl. Setting the poorest households aside, risk does increase in a monotone way, with households at the 92 percent quantile requiring compensation that never exceeds 5 percent. Thus, were we to graph it, this measure of risk would display a U pattern, with the poorest households bearing a great deal of risk, low-income households bearing the least, and risk gradually increasing with consumption shares throughout the rest of the distribution.

We now turn our attention from risk to incquality. Recall that we're now able to construct estimates of the Markov transition functions. If these functions were invariant across time, it would be a trivial matter to calculate the future evolution of the distribution of consumption for as many periods as we choose, simply by using an estimate of some initial distribution Γ_0, and then applying equation (17) iteratively to trace out future distributions.

Of course, matters are not quite so simple. Instead, we have estimates of the transition function for sixteen different values of t, from 1985–2001, and while it's a simple matter to trace out the predicted trajectory over the course of this sample period, this tells us little about future inequality. We adopt the following simple strategy. Given our collection of 16 different estimated transition functions, we simply assume that these functions are representative of the kinds of transition functions which may be realized in the future. Thus, to estimate the evolution of the distribution of consumption over τ periods we simply make τ random draws (with replacement) from the collection of transition functions $\{\hat{\Psi}_t\}$. Starting with the actual distribution of consumption shares in 2001, we substitute these draws sequentially into (17); inverting the resulting function Γ_t yields an estimate of the Lorenz curve L_t. Then we use these τ equations to calculate one possible sample trajectory of the Lorenz curves, which we denote by $\{\hat{L}_t^i\}_{t=1}^{\tau}$. We repeat this procedure many times, so that we have a bootstrapped sample of m possible trajectories for the Lorenz curve over time, or $\mathcal{L} = \{\{\hat{L}_t^i\}_{t=1}^{\tau}\}_{i=1}^{m}$.

Now, for any population quantile x we can compute a mean trajectory by computing

$$\overline{L}_t(x) = \frac{1}{m} \sum_{i=1}^{m} L_t^i(x),$$

or characterize the distribution of possible trajectories by simply working with the bootstrap sample $\mathcal{L}$.

Figure 14.4 shows values of $\overline{L}_t(x)$ for selected values of x (the solid lines),[2] along with 80 percent confidence intervals, for predicted trajectories beginning in 2001 and running through 2025. The figure has several notable features. First, note that the confidence intervals are very tight, relative to the variation across population quantiles. This is a reflection of a fact already noted above—differences across households are much more pronounced than differences across time. The very small variation in our estimated "time effects" $\{v_t\}$ and normalizing constants $\{\eta_t\}$ mean that in fact our estimated transition functions don't change very much over time at all; as a consequence it doesn't matter very much what actual sequence of transition functions we draw in our bootstrap exercise.

2. These values are those available in the China Statistical Yearbooks, and are equal to $(0.05, 0.1, 0.2, 0.4, 0.6, 0.80, 0.9)$.

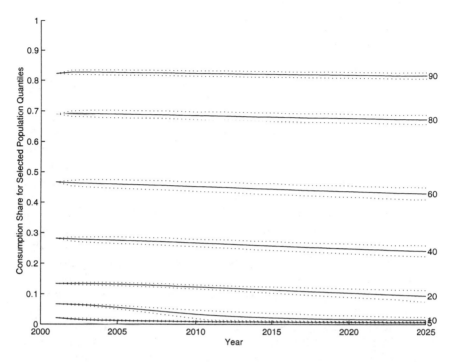

Fig. 14.4   Predicted evolution of consumption shares $L(x)$ for selected population quantiles x

Thus emboldened, we henceforth refer to the evolution of $\overline{L}_t$. Our estimated model predicts that inequality will continue to increase in China through 2025, but at a relatively slow rate. However, the bottom ten percent of the population will, by then, consume a much smaller share in 2025 (2 percent) than at present (6.5 percent). Neglecting the welfare costs of risk discussed above, to keep the *level* of consumption constant for this poorest 10 percent of the population, aggregate urban consumption must grow at an average rate of about five percent to compensate this part of the population whose share is sharply declining. To compensate for risk, of course, much higher growth rates would have to be sustained.

14.5   Conclusion

China's economy has changed dramatically over the last two decades, but household level data to understand the effects of China's growth and opening to the outside world are very difficult to come by—data from China's National Bureau of Statistics either have very limited coverage or are very aggregated.

In this paper we make a silk purse of a sow's ear by using aggregate data

on the distribution of consumption expenditures across (registered) urban households to construct a sequence of Lorenz curves, and then use intertemporal restrictions on individual households' consumption expenditures implied by optimizing behavior by risk-averse households to derive the restrictions on the evolution of these Lorenz curves implied by theory. The evolution of the Lorenz curve turns out to depend on just two kinds of objects: household utility functions, and the distribution of "relative forecast errors" for intertemporally optimizing households.

To pin down household utility, we assume that household preferences exhibit constant relative risk aversion. To pin down the distribution of relative forecast errors we choose a three-parameter log-normal specification, based on an examination of data from a small subset of urban households for which we construct the empirical probability distribution for these relative forecast errors.

For any estimate of the coefficient of relative risk aversion and parameters governing the distribution of relative forecast errors, we are able to predict a sequence of future Lorenz distributions. We compare this predicted trajectory with the actual sequence of distributions realized between 1986 and 2001, choosing our preference and distributional parameters so as to minimize a measure of the distance between these sequences of Lorenz curves.

We present two major empirical findings. First, the risk (ex ante welfare loss due to variation in future consumption) borne by households depends much more on households' resources than it does on the year—even though there are enormous changes in China's aggregate economy over this period, idiosyncratic risk is much more important than any aggregate shock in determining household welfare and in determining evolution of inequality over time.

Second, our estimates of the law of motion governing the Lorenz curves for urban China allow us to make predictions about future consumption inequality. Looking at the entire distribution, we predict that most of the increase in inequality between 1985 and 2025 has already occurred; however, we also predict that the share of consumption accruing to the poorest decile of these households will continue to fall at a relatively rapid rate, lowering the share of consumption for these households from 6.5 percent in 2001 to only 2 percent in 2025.

Appendix A

A Model with Idiosyncratic Risk

In this section we describe a model in which households can exchange debt in competitive credit markets, and derive restrictions on the evolution of

each household's share of aggregate consumption. The key assumptions we exploit are that households all have similar preferences featuring constant relative risk aversion and that all households have access to credit on the same terms. Note that this latter assumption is weaker than assuming that credit markets are perfect—in particular, it may be the case that at the interest rates faced by households for some reason credit markets fail to clear.

Consider, then, an environment with n infinitely lived households. We index these households by $i = 1, 2, \ldots, n$. Time is discrete and is indexed by t. Household i derives momentary utility from consumption according to some function $u_i \colon \mathbb{R} \to \mathbb{R}$, and discounts future utility at a common rate $\beta \in (0, 1)$.

Intertemporal Restrictions

At any date t, household i can exchange claims to consumption at $t + 1$ with other households at a price $1/\rho_t$, solving the problem

$$(11) \qquad \max_{b_{it}} u_i\left(c_{it} - \frac{b_{it}}{\rho_t}\right) + \beta E_t\left[u_i(c_{it+1} + b_{it}) + \sum_{j=2}^{\infty} \beta^{j-1} u_i(c_{it+j})\right],$$

where E_t denotes the expectations operator conditional on information available at time t, b_{it} denotes the debt issued by the household at time t, and c_{it} denotes the household's time t consumption expenditures.

The first-order conditions associated with the household's problem of debt issuance at time t indicate that the household will consume c_{it} at t if the usual Euler equation

$$(12) \qquad u_i'(c_{it}) = \beta \rho_t E_t u_i'(c_{it+1})$$

is satisfied.

It is convenient to restrict our attention to the case in which utility functions exhibit constant relative risk aversion, so that

$$(13) \qquad u_i(c_{it}) = \frac{c_{it}^{1-\gamma} - 1}{1 - \gamma},$$

where γ is the coefficient of relative risk aversion. In this case, equation (12) implies that

$$[\beta \rho_t]^{-1} = E_t\left(\frac{c_{it+1}}{c_{it}}\right)^{-\gamma}$$

for all $i = 1, \ldots, n$ and all t. As a consequence, we have

$$(14) \qquad E_t\left(\frac{c_{it+1}}{c_{it}}\right)^{-\gamma} = \frac{1}{n}\sum_{j=1}^{n} E_t\left(\frac{c_{jt+1}}{c_{jt}}\right)^{-\gamma}.$$

We can interpret this as a prediction that with the ability to freely exchange debt all households will have the same expected growth in their marginal utilities of consumption.

Because we want to understand the links between intertemporal restrictions on consumption such as equation (14) and the evolution of inequality, we'll translate equation (14) into a statement about shares of consumption expenditures. Let $\bar{c}_t = \Sigma_{i=1}^n c_{it}$ denote aggregate consumption expenditures at t, and $\sigma_{it} = c_{it}/\bar{c}_t$ denote i's share of expenditures at t. Then

$$\mathrm{E}_t\left\{\left[\left(\frac{\sigma_{it+1}}{\sigma_{it}}\right)^{-\gamma} - \frac{1}{n}\sum_{j=1}^n\left(\frac{\sigma_{jt+1}}{\sigma_{jt}}\right)^{-\gamma}\right]\left(\frac{\bar{c}_{t+1}}{\bar{c}_t}\right)^{-\gamma}\right\} = 0.$$

Let

(15)
$$\varepsilon_{it+1} \equiv \left[\left(\frac{\sigma_{it+1}}{\sigma_{it}}\right)^{-\gamma} - \frac{1}{n}\sum_{j=1}^n\left(\frac{\sigma_{jt+1}}{\sigma_{jt}}\right)^{-\gamma}\right]\left(\frac{\bar{c}_{t+1}}{\bar{c}_t}\right)^{-\gamma}$$

denote household i's time t forecast error relative to the average forecast error. Note from the properties of equation (15) that $\mathrm{E}_t\varepsilon_{it+1} = 0$, as is usual when evaluating forecast errors from Euler equations. However, as Chamberlain (1984) points out, in the usual analysis there may be an aggregate shock that induces correlation across households' forecast errors in the cross section, so that there is no guarantee that realized forecast errors at $t + 1$ will in fact average to zero. We've avoided this problem here by eliminating ρ_t; for us $1/n \sum_{j=1}^n \varepsilon_{jt} = 0$ by construction.

Risk

The uncertainty facing any individual household with consumption share σ_{it} at time t that may reduce its utility at time $t + 1$, then, can be summarized by three random variables. The first of these just has to do with variation in the growth of aggregate consumption, $g_{t+1} \equiv \bar{c}_{t+1}/\bar{c}_t$. The second represents household-specific surprises that may change the household's share of aggregate expenditures, ϵ_{it}. Third and finally, the aggregate of surprises facing all other households may change the distribution of resources, $\eta_{t+1} \equiv 1/n \sum_{j=1}^n[(\sigma_{jt+1}/\sigma_{jt}]$.

Define the idiosyncratic risk borne by the household at time t to be the ex ante loss in expected utility at $t + 1$ due solely to variation in the purely idiosyncratic shock ε_{it+1}, or

(16)
$$R_{it} \equiv u_i(\bar{c}_{t+1}\sigma_{it}) - \mathrm{E}[u_i(c_{it+1})\,|\,I_t, \eta_{t+1}, g_{t+1}],$$

where I_t denotes the information set at time t. Here the first term is the utility the household would obtain at $t + 1$ if the household's share of expenditures was unchanged (as would be the case if no household faced any idiosyncratic risk) and the household knew in advance what aggregate consumption would be in $t + 1$. The second term is the utility the household would *expect* if it somehow knew in advance what the realization of all the relevant aggregate random variables would be, so that it remained ignorant only of the idiosyncratic shocks it would experience in the first period.

In a world with complete markets and the assumed CES preferences we

work with here, it's easy to establish that each household's share of aggregate consumption will remain constant, eliminating all idiosyncratic risk. Thus, we can interpret the first term of equation (16) as the utility the household would obtain if no households bore any idiosyncratic risk less the expected utility of consumption when the household does bear this idiosyncratic component of risk. It is trivial to establish that this *cardinal* measure of risk is uniquely consistent (up to a linear transformation of u_i) with the notion of increasing risk defined by Rothschild and Stiglitz (1970). Because our measure of idiosyncratic risk is denominated in utils, it is straightforward to construct a variety of useful measures of the welfare loss associated with this risk.

Let $\Psi_t(\sigma_{it+1} \mid \sigma_{it}, x_{it}, g_{t+1}, \eta_{t+1})$ denote the time t Markov transition function for the household's share σ given household characteristics x_{it} and knowledge of the aggregate quantities g_{t+1} and η_{t+1}. Then the expression for household i's time t idiosyncratic risk, as defined above, may be written

$$R_{it} = u_i(\overline{c}_{t+1}\sigma_{it}) - \int u_i(\overline{c}_{t+1}\sigma')d\Psi_t(\sigma' \mid \sigma_{it}, x_{it}, g_{t+1}, \eta_{t+1}).$$

Note that idiosyncratic risk can depend on both household characteristics x_{it} and on the household's current position in the consumption distribution, σ_{it}. Let the distribution of characteristics x of households having a share σ of aggregate consumption time t be given by $G_t(x \mid \sigma)$. Then to calculate *average* idiosyncratic risk of households with share σ we integrate out the characteristics x, obtaining the marginal Markov transition function $\tilde{\Psi}_t(\sigma' \mid \sigma, g_{t+1}, \eta_{t+1}) = \int(\int \sigma' d\Psi_t)dG_t(x \mid \sigma)$.

Let the distribution of σ at t be given by $\Gamma_t(\sigma)$; this is the inverse of the Lorenz curve. Average idiosyncratic risk is then given by

$$R_t = \int u_i(\overline{c}_{t+1}\sigma)d\Gamma_t(\sigma) - \int u_i(\overline{c}_{t+1}\sigma')d\tilde{\Psi}_t(\sigma' \mid \sigma, g_{t+1}, \eta_{t+1})d\Gamma_t(\sigma).$$

Distribution

The Markov transition function $\tilde{\Psi}_t$, which is critical for calculating average risk in the population, is also critical for understanding how the distribution of resources changes over time. In particular, the inverse Lorenz curves $\{\Gamma_t\}$ satisfy a law of motion

(17) $$\Gamma_{t+1}(\hat{\sigma}) = \int_{\{\sigma' < \hat{\sigma}\}} d\tilde{\Psi}_t(\sigma' \mid \sigma, g_{t+1}, \eta_{t+1})d\Gamma_t(\sigma).$$

Accordingly, knowledge of the transition functions $\tilde{\Psi}_t$ suffices to characterize both average risk and the evolution of inequality in the population.

Forecast Errors and Markov Transitions

Recall that an individual household's uncertainty depends only on relative forecast errors ε_{it+1}, η_{t+1}, and on g_{t+1}. In particular, we can use equation (15) to express $\tilde{\Psi}_t$ in terms of the distribution of relative forecast errors in

the population. Let ε_{it+1} have the cumulative probability distribution $F_t(\varepsilon \mid \sigma_{it}, x_{it})$. Then note from equation (15) that we have

$$(18) \qquad \sigma_{it+1} = \sigma_{it}(g_{t+1}^{\gamma}\varepsilon_{it+1} + \eta_{t+1})^{-1/\gamma},$$

so that

$$(19) \quad \check{\Psi}_t(\sigma' \mid \sigma, g_{t+1}, \eta_{t+1}) = \iint_{\{\varepsilon > [(\sigma/\sigma')^{\gamma} - \eta_{t+1}]/g_{t+1}^{\gamma}\}} d\tilde{F}_t(\varepsilon \mid \sigma, x) dG_t(x \mid \sigma).$$

Let $\tilde{F}_t(\varepsilon \mid \sigma) = \int dF_t(\varepsilon \mid \sigma, x) dG_t(x \mid \sigma)$ denote the marginal distribution of relative forecast errors ε for households having consumption share σ. Then, because time $t + 1$ shares must integrate to 1, we have the adding-up restriction

$$(20) \qquad \int \sigma(\eta_{t+1} + \varepsilon g_{t+1}^{\gamma})^{-1/\gamma} d\tilde{F}_t(\varepsilon \mid \sigma) d\Gamma_t(\sigma) = 1,$$

which pins down the value of the $\{\eta_t\}$ in terms of the remaining objects in equation (20). Accordingly, given knowledge of the distributions $\{(F_t, G_t)\}$, the sequence of realized aggregate consumptions to pin down $\{g_t\}$, and the risk aversion parameter γ, we can completely describe the evolution of inequality and the distribution of risk in the population.

Appendix B

Estimating Idiosyncratic Risk

How can we go about using data on the evolution of Lorenz curves to estimate the risk borne by differently situated households? Given our maintained assumption of equal access to credit markets and some initial distribution of consumption shares Γ_0, equation (17) allows us to trace out changes in the distribution over time given knowledge of the Markov transition functions $\{\check{\Psi}_t\}$ and of the sequence $\{g_t, \eta_t\}$. However, each $\{\Psi_t\}$ must be consistent with the law of motion for shares in equation (18), while the unknown sequence $\{\eta_t\}$ is determined by the adding-up restriction in equation (20). As a consequence, the extent of our ignorance regarding $\{\check{\Psi}_t\}$ amounts to ignorance regarding the risk-aversion parameter γ and the marginal distributions of relative forecast errors in each period, $\{\tilde{F}_t\}$.

Although we don't begin with knowledge of the distributions of errors $\{\tilde{F}_t\}$, the first moment of each $\tilde{F}_t$ must be equal to zero by equation (12), while the support of the distribution at t must be a subset of $[\eta_{t+1}/g_{t+1}^{\gamma}, \infty)$. After examining the empirical distribution of estimated relative forecast errors for a small panel of urban Chinese households, it appears that this empirical distribution at t is adequately represented by what Johnson and

Kotz (1970) call the "three-parameter log-normal distribution," with log(ε + θ_{t+1}) distributed $N(\mu_t(\sigma), v_t^2(\sigma))$. Of the three parameters (θ_t, $\mu_t(\sigma)$, $v_t(\sigma)$) only two are free, with $\theta_t = \eta_t/g_t^\gamma$—since shares must all lie in the (0, 1) interval—and $\mu_t = \log(\theta_t) - v_t^2(\sigma)/2$ (since the expected value of ε must be zero).

With these restrictions on the distribution of relative forecast errors, the only things that remain for us to infer from data are the coefficient of relative risk aversion γ and the scale parameters $\{v_t(\sigma)\}$. In practice we only work with a finite number (say n) of share values, and have only a finite number of periods (T) of data on the distribution of consumption. We impose a log-linear structure on these scale parameters, assuming that for every year $t = 1, \ldots, T$ and share $\sigma \in \{\sigma_1, \ldots, \sigma_n\}$ there exists an ℓ-vector of observable variables x_{it} that determines the scale parameters via

$$(21) \qquad \log v_t(\sigma_i) = \delta' x_{it}$$

for some ℓ-vector δ. This assumption allows us to estimate a set of ℓ parameters that may be presumed to be smaller than Tn, and guarantees that estimated values of $v_t(\sigma)$ will be positive, as they must be to be interpretable as the standard deviation of a normally distributed variable.

As a consequence of the foregoing, we're left with the problem of estimating $\ell + 1$ parameters $b_0 = (\gamma, \delta')$. We have data on the share of consumption expenditures for population quantiles ($x_1, x_2, \ldots, x_m$) for each of $T + 1$ years. We use these data on consumption expenditures to approximate the Lorenz curves $\{L_t(x)\}_{t=1}^T$ of expenditure shares. We fix an initial guess of our parameters b. Noting that $L_t = \Gamma_t^{-1}$, conditional on this guess we use the law of motion in equation (17) (along with the adding-up restriction in equation [20], and equation [21]) to predict a sequence of Lorenz curves $\{\hat{L}_t(x \mid b)\}_{t=1}^T$. We compute a simple measure of distance between the predicted and actual Lorenz curves

$$(22) \qquad d(b) = \sum_{t=1}^{T} \sum_{i=1}^{m} (L_t(x_i) - \hat{L}_t(x_i \mid b))^2,$$

and then use a simplex minimization routine to find the value $\hat{b} = \mathrm{argmin}_b d(b)$.

References

Amemiya, T. 1984. Tobit models: A survey. *Journal of Econometrics* 24 (1–2): 3–61.

Arrow, K. J. 1964. The role of securities in the optimal allocation of risk bearing. *Review of Economic Studies* 31:91–96.

Benjamin, D., L. Brandt, and J. Giles. 2005. The evolution of income inequality in rural China. *Economic Development and Cultural Change* 53 (4): 769–824.

Bhalla, A. S., S. Yao, and Z. Zhang. 2003. Causes of inequalities in China. *Journal of International Development* 15:939–55.

Chamberlain, G. 1984. Panel data. In *Handbook of econometrics,* ed. Z. Griliches and M. D. Intriligator, 1247–1318. Amsterdam: North-Holland.

Chen, S., and M. Ravallion. 2004. Household welfare impacts of WTO accession in China. *World Bank Economic Review* 18 (1): 29–58.

Deaton, A., and C. Paxson. 1994. Intertemporal choice and inequality. *Journal of Political Economy* 102 (3): 437–67.

Johnson, N. L., and S. Kotz. 1970. *Continuous univariate distributions—1.* New York: Wiley.

Kahn, A. R., and C. Riskin. 2001. *Inequality and poverty in China in the age of globalization.* Oxford, UK: Oxford University Press.

Kanbur, R., and X. Zhang. 2005. Fifty years of regional inequality in China: A journey through central planning, reform, and openness. *China Economic Review* 16:189–204.

Ligon, E., and L. Schechter. 2003. Measuring vulnerability. *Economic Journal* 113 (486): C95–C102.

Lucas, R. E., Jr. 1992. On efficiency and distribution. *Economic Journal* 102:233–47.

Milanovic, B. 2005. Can we discern the effect of globalization on income distribution? Evidence from household surveys. *World Bank Economic Review* 19 (1): 21–44.

Ravallion, M. 2004. Looking beyond averages in the trade and poverty debate. World Bank Policy Research Paper no. 3461. Washington, DC: World Bank.

Ravallion, M., and S. Chen. 2004. China's (uneven) progress against poverty. World Bank Policy Research Working Paper no. 3408. Washington, DC: World Bank, September.

Rothschild, M., and J. E. Stiglitz. 1970. Increasing risk, I: A definition. *Journal of Economic Theory* 2:225–43.

Storesletten, K., C. I. Telmer, and A. Yaron. 2004. Consumption and risk sharing over the life cycle. *Journal of Monetary Economics* 51 (3): 609–33.

Wilson, R. 1968. The theory of syndicates. *Econometrica* 36 (January): 119–32.

Yang, D. L. 1997. *Beyond Beijing: Liberalization and the regions in China.* New York: Routledge.

Yao, S., and Z. Zhang. 2001. On regional inequality and diverging clubs: A case study of contemporary China. *Journal of Comparative Economics* 29:466–84.

Zhang, X., and K. H. Zhang. 2003. How does globalization affect regional inequality within a developing country? Evidence from China. *Journal of Development Studies* 30 (4): 47–67.

Comment   Shang-Jin Wei

This is a sophisticated paper. An important contribution of the paper is methodological in nature. Deaton and Paxson (1994) and other papers in the literature on income inequality have provided theoretical justification for an empirical specification on household panel data. However, a com-

Shang-Jin Wei is assistant director and chief of the trade and investment division at the International Monetary Fund, a senior fellow at the Brookings Institution, and director of the National Bureau of Economic Research's working group on the Chinese Economy.

mon data constraint that empirical researchers face is that only repeated cross sections are available, rather than a true panel. This is the case for the data on Chinese urban income that Ethan Ligon is working with. In this paper, Ligon provides a methodology that can be applied to such data sets. Specifically, by integrating the intertemporal restrictions on individual household consumption, he derives a law of motion for the *distribution* of consumption across households at a given point in time. While such a specification cannot exploit all the information from a panel household data set if one exists, it allows researchers to work with more commonly available (and less demanding) data sets on repeated cross sections of households.

As to possible areas for improvement, I would propose two. First, it seems possible that some of the key inferences may be driven by noise rather than information. More robustness checks may be helpful. Second, conceptually, the paper does not quite address the key question in the theme of the conference, namely, the impact of globalization on inequality or poverty. Indeed, it does not quite address the question implied in the title of the paper—the impact of globalization on China's inequality. Let me discuss these two comments in turn.

The first comment has to do with noise versus information in the empirical inferences in the paper. The estimates are presented in table 14.1. As an example, one can look at the estimates of the alphas—the estimated excess uncertainty an average household in a given quantile faces relative to the very wealthiest households in the sample. (The author divides the households into seventeen bins by their income levels.) Which households face the greatest uncertainty? According to table 14.1, the top five are those in the 4th, 9th, 15th, 11th, and 10th quantiles. Which households face the least uncertainty? Table 14.1 says that the top five are those in the 1st, 5th, 6th, 8th, and 14th quantile. Why do we observe so much fluctuation in the ranks? Since the number of bins into which one classifies households is somewhat arbitrary, how robust is the inference to alternative classifications? Another set of key parameters is the etas. They are within the range of [1.04, 1.26]. Can we reject the null that they are all the same? We don't know. To summarize the comments so far, before we can conclude which inferences are robust and which are fragile, it would be useful to perform more perturbations of the basic specification and more statistical tests.

A potentially more serious shortcoming with working with repeated cross sections is what I call a "shifting base" problem that could render the resulting inferences invalid and misleading. Recall that the paper makes inferences on the relative rank of risks that urban households face as a function of their income in the distribution. An important assumption is that the underlying distribution of the households stays the same even though in any different year a different cross section of households gets surveyed. However, over the period of the sample (1986–97), there may have been systematic migration from the relatively poor rural areas to relatively well-off urban areas. In addition, administrative units that were previously clas-

sified as rural counties have been gradually reclassified as cities (and the households residing there reclassified as urban households). These facts imply that the true characters of the households in any given income bin may change from year to year in the sample. Inferences based on an assumption of a fixed household character may be misleading (especially when the risk ranks jump around in table 14.1).

My second comment has to do with the theme of the conference—the impact of globalization on income inequality or poverty, which Ligon's paper alludes to in the title but does not directly address. Which part of change in the Chinese household income over the recent past can be attributed to China's greater exposure to international trade (and other dimensions of globalization)? The answer cannot be inferred from the statistical table and figures in the current paper.

To start with, let me note the temptation to conclude that globalization has increased the inequality: China's exposure to trade and FDI openness has increased greatly (from a trade-GDP ratio of 5 percent in 1980 to about 35 percent now). At the same time, income inequality as measured by the Gini coefficient has risen dramatically. This has led some observers to draw the conclusion that globalization has increased the inequality.

Of course, association does not imply causation. Moreover, inequality is a function of many factors. If one could isolate the effect of trade globalization, what is its effect on China's household income inequality? This is the question that Yi Wu and I have looked at. Working with a combination of household data sets and a data set of urban and rural average incomes, we decompose the question into three parts: the impact of trade openness on the within-rural income inequality, the within-urban inequality, and the inequality between urban and rural areas. We find evidence that trade globalization reduces within-rural inequality, raises the within-urban inequality (by a moderate amount), and reduces the rural-urban inequality (by a significant amount). Combining the three findings, we find that greater trade openness has led to a moderate decline (rather than an increase) in household income. If one is interested in reducing income inequality in China, the right approach would not be to reduce the degree of openness of the already open areas but to speed up the opening-up of currently less open regions.

I learned much from Ligon's paper. If the author could work with a true panel data set and offer more statistical tests, readers' confidence in the inference could be enhanced.

Reference

Deaton, A., and C. Paxson. 1994. Intertemporal choice and inequality. *Journal of Political Economy* 102 (3): 437–67.
Wei, S.-J., and Y. Wu. 2004. "Trade openness and income equality: the case of China," working paper, IMF.

Globalization and the Returns to Speaking English in South Africa

James Levinsohn

15.1 Introduction

The literature on globalization and wages is, by the standards of economics, huge. It is a literature that compensates for its volume by offering precious little in the way of convincing results. This is not (usually) the fault of the researchers. Rather, it is just very difficult to identify the role of international trade and/or investment on wages relative to the multitude of other factors that influence wages (and which frequently occur simultaneously with globalization). This has led researchers to debate, for example, whether trade explains a growing wage gap between high-wage and low-wage earners or whether the real determinant of increasing wage disparity is coincident skill-biased technical change. Yet others (correctly) claim that even this dichotomy is a false one since international trade and investment and skill-biased technical change are themselves codetermined.

With this cacophony as background, this paper steps back and experiments with a very different approach to investigating the impact of globalization on wages. Noting the special circumstances around South Africa's emergence from the apartheid era (and the relatively closed economy that accompanied the apartheid era), this paper asks whether the return to speaking English (measured in a narrow way) increased as the South

James Levinsohn is the J. Ira and Nicki Harris Family Professor of Public Policy, a professor of economics and associate dean of the Gerald R. Ford School of Public Policy, University of Michigan, and a research associate of the National Bureau of Economic Research (NBER).

I would like to thank without implicating Raquel Fernandez, Ann Harrison, Mark Rosenzweig, and Duncan Thomas as well as participants at the NBER conference on globalization and poverty. Thanks to Nzinga Broussard for research assistance.

African economy embarked upon its integration with the rest of the industrialized world.

There is a certain logic to trying to measure the impact of globalization on wages in this manner. Following the advent of democracy in South Africa in 1994, there were several huge changes in the economy, many of which might be expected to change wages. One, but only one, of these changes was South Africa's reintegration with the global economy. Others included legislated changes in the labor market (with an emphasis on affirmative action) and the outbreak of the HIV/AIDS pandemic. Decomposing the changes in South African wages into those fractions due to increased disease, the dismantling of apartheid and ensuring affirmative action, changes in technology during the 1990s, and increased integration into the global economy is a Herculean (or outright impossible) task. Measuring changes in the return to speaking English is a simple task, and I argue below that it is one that at least stands a chance of shedding light on the impact of globalization on wages in South Africa.

The underlying idea is that as South Africa reintegrated with the rest of the world, the return to speaking an international language of commerce might plausibly increase. In South Africa, English is that language. (The other widely spoken languages, such as Zulu and Afrikaans, are not used much in international commerce.) It is less obvious why some of the other changes concurrent with the fall of apartheid should change the return to speaking English. It is, for example, unclear why AIDS should have much of an impact on the returns to speaking English (although it almost surely impacts wages).[1] Nor is it clear why the sort of skill-biased technological change that occurred worldwide in the 1990s ought to impact returns to speaking English. Skill-biased technical change probably changes the returns to different levels of education, but, conditional on education, it is hard to see why this sort of technical change would elevate the returns to speaking English. It is easier to suspect that affirmative action might impact the return to speaking English. This is a confounding influence that is explicitly discussed when presenting econometric specification and when interpreting results.

When substantial parts of the world did not openly trade with or invest in South Africa, there was still a return to speaking English. South Africa, after all, was not Albania. There remained some international trade, the mining industry produced traded goods, and there was some, albeit minimal, international investment in South Africa. Each of these areas might support a return to speaking English. Furthermore, speaking English was probably coincident with other factors that impacted wages given South

---

1. One can of course concoct stories, some of them plausible, but few involve as direct a link between global integration and wages as that associated with the returns to speaking English.

Africa's history (see the Boer War). For these reasons, this paper focuses on whether the return to speaking English *changed.* Of course, if there is no return to speaking English in the first place, searching for changes in that return is not especially informative.

This approach to investigating the impact of globalization on wages is intended as a complement to the way economists usually address this question. My aims are pretty modest. This approach will not offer the definitive word on the impact of globalization on wages in postapartheid South Africa. Put another way, it is hard to imagine evidence on language as being dispositive. Nonetheless, when the cultural situation is appropriate, this approach might usefully add to the trade and wages debate (a.k.a. "cacophony"). Furthermore, this approach uses the sort of survey data that have for the most part been ignored in the trade and wages literature.

That is what this paper is about. It is also important to note what this paper is not about. This paper does not directly speak to the issue of poverty. While it is indirectly related, since wages and incomes are of course related to poverty, this paper does not focus on poverty. The evidence from other sources suggests that the overall distribution of real individual incomes have shifted to the left in the period covered by this paper. This is shown in figure 15.1. That figure shows an almost 40 percent decline in real incomes throughout much of the income distribution from 1995 to 2000. Further examination reveals that Blacks have become relatively worse off since the fall of Apartheid. See Leibbrandt, Levinsohn, and McCrary (2005) for details. Finally, yet other evidence points to increased poverty for Blacks over the period covered by the language data in this paper. See Hoogeveen and Ozler (2004) for further information. To the extent that the return to English has increased, and English is spoken mostly by non-Blacks, the evidence on language and the evidence on incomes and poverty are consistent with one another. It would be wrong, though, to infer any causality.

This paper is not the first to examine the economic implications of speaking English. One paper even does so in the context of considering globalization. Munshi and Rosenzweig (2003) use Indian data to show that lower-caste families are increasingly sending their female children to English schools and that this has encouraging implications for occupational outcomes. Most of the literature on the returns to speaking English uses U.S. data and focuses on the role of language on immigrant earnings. See, for example, Bleakley and Chin (2004a, 2004b) and the literature cited therein. A paper in this vein using U.K. data is Shields and Price (2002).

The paper proceeds in section 15.2 by first describing some of the changes in openness in South Africa since the fall of apartheid. Section 15.3 introduces the data that are used and provides some descriptive statistics. Section 15.4 estimates changes in the return to speaking English, while section 15.5 concludes.

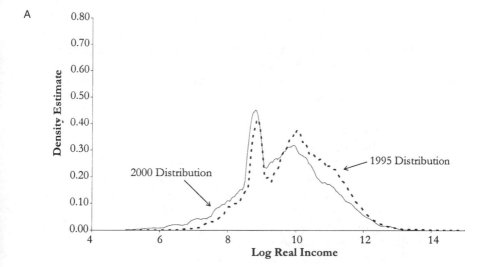

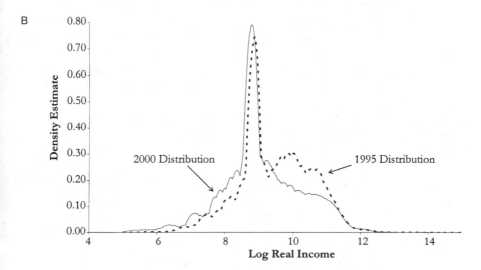

**Fig. 15.1   Distribution of real incomes in South Africa, 1995 and 2000: *A*, men;
B, women**

Notes: Figure gives weighted kernel density estimates of log real total income (2000 rand) for
men (panel A) and women (panel B) in 1995 and 2000. All four density estimates use an
Epanechnikov kernel and a bandwidth selector three-quarters the size of the Silverman (1986)
rule of thumb (cf. Silverman's equation [3.31]). Sample sizes for 1995 and 2000 are 21,882 and
16,893 for men, respectively, and 18,868 and 17,776 for women, respectively.

15.2   Background

In 1993, the first year of my data, South Africa was preparing for its first nationally representative election in decades. It was clear to all that a new government would be taking power in 1994. There was, though, considerable uncertainty regarding just what economic policies would be pursued by President Nelson Mandela. There were competing pressures to assure the international financial community of continued stability on the one hand, and to dramatically improve the lot of those who had for decades been excluded under the policies of the previous governments (and who were principally responsible for electing the new government) on the other hand.

South Africa quickly implemented a policy of macroeconomic stabilization to reassure the international financial community. Called GEAR for Growth, Employment, and Redistribution, the policy seemed to contribute to stabilization of key macroindicators such as inflation, real interest rates, and the budget deficit. It is less obvious that the policy enhanced growth, employment, and redistribution, but this of course depends on the counterfactual. Each component of the GEAR moniker might have been that much worse in the absence of the policy.

Encouraged by the sober fiscal policies of GEAR, companies from around the world that had hesitated before investing substantially in South Africa began to get off the sidelines. Foreign direct investment skyrocketed. Table 15.1 presents data for foreign direct investment (FDI) in millions of rand (R). The data in table 15.1 show that annual FDI inflows went from only R33 million to over R1.3 billion as soon as the new government was ensconced and proceeded to increase to over R6 billion by 2000. The

Table 15.1   Foreign direct investment (FDI) in South Africa

Year	FDI
1993	33
1994	1,348
1995	4,502
1996	3,515
1997	17,587
1998	3,104
1999	9,184
2000	6,083
2001[a]	53,000

Source: OECD Global Forum on International Investment.
Note: All figures are nominal millions of rand.
[a]Data are only for the first half of 2001.

huge inflow for the first half of 2001 is not typical and represents the one-off purchase of De Beers by the London-listed Anglo American Corporation. Even excluding that transaction, 2001 showed continued healthy increases in FDI inflows. According to the South African Reserve Bank, FDI was split pretty evenly between mining, manufacturing, and the financial sector.

South Africa also joined the World Trade Organization (WTO) on January 1, 1995. Tariffs, never that high anyway, fell into the single-digit range. The largest barrier to trade during the Apartheid era, though, was never tariffs. Rather, it was the willingness of the rest of the world to trade with South Africa. Under the new government, South Africa entered into regional free trading agreements with the European Union and with the Southern African Development Community. Trade, as a percentage of GDP, increased substantially. Table 15.2 presents these figures. From 1991 to 1993, a period during which it became pretty clear that apartheid was going to be replaced with a representative democracy, the ratio of trade to GDP was pretty flat. It was with the new government in 1994 that trade as a fraction of GDP started to really increase. By 2000, the last year of my survey data, the trade-GDP ratio had risen almost 50 percent from .424 to .611. The ratio continued to rise and was .704 in 2002. By almost any standard, these are meteoric increases. Considering that they were mirrored by the even greater increases in FDI, there is little doubt that the South African economy "globalized." South Africa clearly became more integrated with the global economy after 1993. I turn now to the question of whether the return to speaking English increased over the course of this period.

Table 15.2   **Trade/GDP in South Africa**

Year	Trade/GDP
1991	.440
1992	.423
1993	.424
1994	.452
1995	.48
1996	.514
1997	.520
1998	.550
1999	.541
2000	.611
2001	.656
2002	.704

Source: South African Reserve Bank web site (http://www.resbank.co.za).
Notes: Data are for imports and exports of goods and services and annual GDP.

15.3 Data

This study uses data drawn from three South African household surveys—one from 1993 and two from 2000. The 1993 data are from the Living Standards Measurement Study (LSMS), a household survey conducted by the World Bank. This survey included about 44,000 individuals comprising just over 8,800 households.[2] The version of the data often used by researchers contains about 300 variables.[3] Information on language and income are key variables for the study at hand. The data on language are not ideal due to the way that the survey instrument was worded. In particular, language is a household-level variable, and the head of the household was asked to identify the "main language spoken at home." The fact that language is a household-level variable is not of particular concern, since the language spoken at home typically does not vary within the household. The fact that there is no information on whether a person could speak English instead of whether it was the main language spoken at home is a cause for concern, and the results presented below must be considered in light of this. One would of course like to know whether respondents could speak English and how well, not whether it was spoken at home.

This is an example of one-sided measurement error. Some of those who are reported as not speaking English (as measured by the language spoken at home) can in fact speak English quite fluently. On the other hand, few or none of those who stated that English was their first language were in fact unable to speak English. This is because the answer to the language question was asked at the outset and determined the language in which the survey was administered. For example, if someone who spoke only Zulu stated that English was their language, that individual would then have to complete a multihour survey in English. It would not be hard to detect the misstatement of language in this instance.

The 1993 data on income are pretty good. The measure I use in this paper is an individual's total monthly income and is a constructed variable composed mostly of wage income. It is common in developing countries to highlight the importance of accounting for self-production of food to properly compute income, but this is not an issue in South Africa. Own production is negligible.

For the 2000 data, I combine two surveys, the September 2000 Labour Force Survey (LFS) and the 2000 Income and Expenditure Survey

2. A cleaned and ready-to-use version of the data set, along with a primer for analyzing household survey data in Stata and the survey instruments, is available at the South Africa Distance Learning Project web site, http://saproject.psc.isr.umich.edu/.

3. The original data set includes over 2,000 variables, although many of these are essentially individual-level variables that are easily aggregated. Researchers who have used these data include Case and Deaton (1998), Thomas (1996), and Duflo (2000).

(IES).[4] Although the surveys are not explicitly linked, it turns out that the same households were included in both. The merged surveys result in a data set with about 101,000 individuals comprising about 26,000 households. The language question is in the 2000 LFS, while income comes from the 2000 IES. The wording of the language question is the same as in 1993: it again asks about the language spoken most often at home. The 2000 individual income data are used to compute total individual income in a manner most comparable with the 1993 definition. This amounts to subtracting various grants and pensions from individual income.

Table 15.3 presents frequency counts of language by race for each year of the sample. The sample is taken only among those reporting positive income and between the ages of twenty and sixty. The lower bound is intended to exclude students, and results are robust to a lower bound of twenty-five years instead of the somewhat arbitrary twenty. The advantage of using age twenty instead of twenty-five is that the sample size increases substantially. The upper bound is intended to exclude those receiving old-age pensions, since those clearly do not depend on language spoken. Also, old-age pensions are not going to be impacted by globalization as wage income might be. Some women begin to collect these pensions at age sixty, hence the upper bound. There are three key messages from table 15.3. First, very few Blacks list English as their primary language.[5] This is especially true in 1993, and it suggests that the return to speaking English within Blacks is going to be identified off of precious few observations. Second, Coloreds and Whites have a substantial numbers of English speakers. For each, Afrikaans is the majority language, and for each there are substantial shifts in the fraction of the population group reporting English as their primary language. That fraction declines for Coloreds and increases for Whites. Third, English is essentially colinear with Indian, so that it will not be possible to separately identify the impact of English from the impact of being Indian on wages.

Whereas table 15.3 indicated the racial composition of English speakers, table 15.4 illustrates in which sectors of the economy these English speakers work. Tabulating only individuals between the ages of twenty and sixty, table 15.4 shows what fraction of workers in each of eleven sectors list English as their first language. That fraction is highest in business services (composed mostly of the financial sector) at 35.75 percent in 1993 and 32.2 percent in 2000. Other sectors with large fractions of English speakers (or,

4. There was also an IES in 1995 and a linkable household survey (the October Household Survey, or OHS). The 1995 IES and OHS are an attractive data source since questions are asked in the same way and one can be comfortable that income is measured consistently across the 1995 and 2000 surveys. Alas, the 1995 survey "forgot" to include the standard question on language.

5. I use the term "Blacks" since this seems to be preferred by most South Africans to the term "Africans," which is used in the survey instrument. For data purposes, the two terms are interchangeable. I use the term "Colored" to refer to the well-defined racial group used in South African government statistics.

Table 15.3   **Primary language among wage earners twenty to sixty years old**

Language	Black	Colored	Indian	White	Total
		A. 1993			
English	6	160	232	202	600
Afrikaans	11	411	0	522	944
Xhosa	421	0	0	0	421
Zulu	624	0	0	0	624
Tswana	493	0	0	0	493
N. Sotho	285	0	0	0	285
S. Sotho	91	0	0	0	91
Venda	79	0	0	0	79
Tsonga	209	0	0	0	209
Swazi	173	0	0	0	173
Ndebele	69	0	0	0	69
Other	7	0	3	6	16
Total	2,468	571	235	730	4,004
		B. 2000			
English	118	534	626	783	2,075
Afrikaana	230	3,032	6	1,540	4,838
Ndebele	435	0	0	0	435
Xhosa	3,789	17	0	0	3,806
Zulu	5,487	3	0	0	5,490
N. Sotho	2,238	1	0	0	2,239
S. Sotho	2,681	6	0	1	2,688
Tswana	2,601	17	0	0	2,618
Swazi	871	4	0	0	876
Venda	577	0	0	0	577
Tsonga	1,109	0	0	0	1,109
Other	72	2	22	19	120
Missing	14	0	0	0	14
Total	20,222	3,616	654	2,343	26,885

Note: 2000 row totals do not sum properly due to the exclusion of nonresponses to the race question.

more accurately, English "listers") include manufacturing, electricity, wholesale and retail trade, and community services (which includes doctors, teachers, and lawyers). In all sectors, the fraction listing English declined from 1993 to 2000, usually modestly. There are in principle two ways that the economy might adapt to an increased demand for English: the supply could increase, or the return could increase (or both). Table 15.4 suggests that the supply did not increase. I turn next to examining whether the return to speaking English increased.

15.4   The Return to Speaking English

The question at hand is whether the return to speaking English (as imperfectly measured) increased as South Africa opened up to the interna-

Table 15.4   Share of industry employment by language

Sector	1993		2000	
	Other	English	Other	English
Agriculture	98.09	1.91	98.36	1.64
Mining	95.45	4.55	97.25	2.75
Manufactures	75.26	24.74	82.70	17.30
Electric	83.30	16.70	83.77	16.23
Construction	83.25	16.75	90.54	9.46
Wholesale and retail	81.35	18.65	85.61	14.39
Transport	82.78	17.22	84.47	15.53
Business services	64.25	35.75	67.76	32.24
Community services	81.67	18.33	84.56	15.44
Private households	99.11	0.89	97.58	2.42
Other	79.42	20.58	82.46	17.54
Total	84.87	15.13	86.95	13.05

Notes: Cell entries give the share of employment in a given industry that lists English as the first language. The 1993 and 2000 data sets had different industry categories, and the categories in this table reflect a concordance to the 2000 industry definitions. In particular, the 1993 categories of wholesale and retail trade and restaurant and hotel services were combined. Also, the 1993 categories of education, medical, and legal services were combined to form "community services." Industry names are from the Statistics South Africa Labour Force Survey 2000 report, page vii.

tional economy from 1993 to 2000. The return to speaking English is not directly observable and so needs to be inferred from econometric evidence. The approach adopted here is to estimate Mincer-like wage regressions and include as an explanatory variable whether the wage-earner listed English as his or her primary language. While this is simple in principle, several issues arise in practice.

First, it is necessary even in the cross section to include as explanatory variables key determinants of wages.[6] Omission of an explanatory variable that itself might be correlated with speaking English will bias the estimate on the return to speaking English. Second, the many changes in South Africa from 1993 to 2000 probably impacted many of the determinants of wages. It is widely believed, for example, that the return to education and the wage differentials apparently due to race changed over this period. Holding them constant and only allowing the return to English to change will yield biased estimates of the true change in the return to speaking English. (On the other hand, such an approach pretty much guarantees find-

6. A difference-in-differences approach is not advised because of concurrent changes in many other variables that impact wages. That is, although one could measure the difference in wages between those who list English as their first language and those who do not, and one could then examine the difference over time in this difference, the result would be hard to interpret. This is because many other variables changed over this period, and some of those changes are not orthogonal to an observed return to speaking English.

ing a pretty big change in the return to speaking English.) Third, the fact that about 40 percent of English speakers are Indian and there is virtually no language variation within this population group poses a challenge. The most flexible approach to estimating the returns to speaking English examines the change in that return within population group, yet this approach is going to be noninformative for Indians.

The simplest specification regresses log individual income (y_i) on indicator variables for each value of j years of education (ED), experience (EX), experience squared, an indicator variable for whether the worker is male (M), indicator variables for population group (CO for Colored, IN for Indian, and WH for White, with Blacks as the excluded group), and an indicator for whether English is the language spoken at home (ENG). Experience is defined as age minus 20. Hence,

$$(1) \quad \ln y_i = \beta_0 + \sum_{j=2}^{j=13} \beta_{1,j} ED_j + \beta_2 EX + \beta_3 EX^2 + \beta_4 M + \beta_5 CO + \beta_6 IN$$
$$+ \beta_7 WH + \beta_8 ENG + \varepsilon_i.$$

Equation (1) is estimated separately for each year of the sample using ordinary least squares (OLS) with the appropriate sample weights. Estimating the regression separately for each year is necessary to capture the changes in returns to education between 1993 and 2000 as well as changes in the return to being male and/or of a particular population group. Use of indicator variables for each level of education permits returns to vary nonlinearly with years. The coefficient on English, β_8, is interpreted as the percentage wage differential attributable to speaking English conditional on the other included regressors. The results from this specification applied to the 1993 and 2000 data are presented in table 15.5.

The results from 1993 are discussed first to fix ideas. The first twelve rows show the usual returns to education. For example, someone with twelve years of education, all else being equal, earns about 168 percent more than those with one year or less of education conditional on the other covariates. The wage premium for being a member of a race other than Black ranges from 32 percent for Colored to 98 percent for White. Males earn 46 percent more than similar females. The coefficient of interest for this study, though, is that on "English." Conditional on education, experience, gender, and race, people who list English as their primary language earn about 18 percent more than those who list another language. This differential is quite precisely estimated.

Equation (1) is estimated using the 2000 data, and the results are shown in the second column of table 15.5. While there are several interesting comparisons between 1993 and 2000 to be made (the changing pattern of the return to education, for instance), the focus here is on the impact of speaking English. The "English premium" jumps from .183 in 1993 to .252 in

Table 15.5   **The returns to speaking English among those twenty to sixty years old**

	1993	2000
ED2	−.093	.092
	(.071)	(.035)
ED3	.219	.233
	(.067)	(.038)
ED4	.299	.224
	(.065)	(.036)
ED5	.449	.295
	(.060)	(.034)
ED6	.472	.380
	(.052)	(.031)
ED7	.733	.549
	(.051)	(.030)
ED8	.622	.646
	(.060)	(.032)
ED9	.948	.820
	(.050)	(.030)
ED10	.993	.908
	(.063)	(.031)
ED11	1.274	1.240
	(.047)	(.027)
ED12	1.688	1.796
	(.054)	(.031)
ED13	1.788	2.126
	(.075)	(.036)
EX	.062	.099
	(.004)	(.002)
EX2	−.001	−.001
	(.000)	(.000)
Colored	.326	.360
	(.037)	(.020)
Indian	.394	.421
	(.071)	(.041)
White	.984	.921
	(.037)	(.021)
English	.183	.252
	(.043)	(.024)
Male	.463	.501
	(.024)	(.012)
Constant	5.041	7.183
	(.050)	(.030)
R^2	.58	0.46
No. of observations	3,979	26,616

Note: Standard errors in parentheses.

Table 15.6   **The returns to speaking English: Within-group results**

	1993	2000
All	0.183	0.252
	(0.043)	(.024)
Black	0.592	0.380
	(0.290)	(.084)
Colored	0.521	0.410
	(0.0765)	(.042)
White	−0.017	0.145
	(.050)	(.036)

Note: Standard errors in parentheses.

2000. The 2000 premium is precisely estimated, and the change between the two years is significantly different from zero. Allowing the entire pattern of returns to years of schooling to vary from 1993 to 2000, and allowing for differing returns to race, gender, and experience, it is still the case that the return to speaking English increased substantially. This change in the English premium, as well as its level, is of an economically large magnitude. By 2000, English speakers were earning about 25 percent more after conditioning on other observables, and the premium had increased by 7 percentage points since 1993.

The specification reported in table 15.5 imposes that the returns to education, experience, and gender are identical across racial groups. A convincing body of research suggests that this is too strong an assumption. I proceed by looking for the English premium within each of the racial groups. Doing so allows the returns on all the other observables to vary by racial group. This flexibility is clearly a good thing, for it lets the data speak more freely. The flexibility, though, will carry a price. Of the sample that listed English as the language spoken at home, 30 to 40 percent are Indian, and virtually all Indians list English as the primary language. There is, then, no within-group language variation for Indians. Hence, it is not feasible to estimate a return to speaking English for Indians since that return is not identifiably different from the return to simply being Indian.[7]

Table 15.6 reports results from the within-group regressions for Blacks, Coloreds, and Whites. In the interest of parsimony, only the coefficient on speaking English is reported.[8] This approach is pretty flexible. It allows

7. It is possible to estimate a return to speaking English among Indians, but the effect is identified off of three individuals who listed "Other" in 1993 and about six Afrikaans-speaking Indians in 2000. The English premium, when separate regressions are run for Indians, is never significantly different from zero.

8. Were it the case that the returns on the other observables (not reported in this table) did not vary significantly across racial groups, it would be efficient to pool groups. Alas, coefficients vary across groups, and one can readily reject the hypothesis that the returns to observables other than the English premium are the same across groups.

the returns on all observables to vary both over time and across racial groups.

As is usually the case with a more flexible specification, the messages are more mixed than those reported in table 15.5. The first row of table 15.6 reports the English premium from table 15.5 for comparison's sake. The next three rows report the English premium for the other racial groups (except Indian, for reasons discussed above). For Blacks, the English premium stayed constant from 1993 to 2000. It was huge (about 60 percent) but did not increase over time, although the precision of the estimate did increase. One should recall, though, that this premium is being identified off of very few individuals: 6 out of 2,468 in 1993 and 118 out of 20,222 in 2000. For Coloreds, the return to speaking English fell about 11 percentage points. The decline, while not large, is statistically significantly different from zero. The largest change from 1993 to 2000 in the English premium impacted Whites. The return went from being basically nonexistent in 1993 to a precisely estimated 14.5 percent. Another way to interpret this result is that the "penalty" to speaking Afrikaans among Whites skyrocketed.

The general pattern reported in table 15.6 is robust to many alternative specifications. For example, the inclusion of indicator variables for the province in which a household lives, using a single variable for years of education instead of the more flexible set of indicator variables, the exclusion of the variable for male, using age twenty-five as a lower age bound, using sixty-five as an upper age bound, and interacting the return to English with education all yield basically the same message when it comes to the English premium. Namely, that premium became much larger for Whites and fell slightly for Coloreds and for Blacks.[9] These results, though, exclude a large number of those with positive income for whom English is the first language—Indians.

15.5   Concluding Remarks

Did globalization really cause the return to speaking English to increase in South Africa? The evidence in this paper is, in some cases, corroborating, but hardly conclusive. The strongest and most robust result is that the return to speaking English increased for Whites over the period during which South Africa reintegrated with the world economy. This result is strong because it results from the flexible within-group estimates, and it is robust because it arises in all the investigated specifications. When Indians are included and a (necessarily) less flexible estimation strategy is adopted, I again find that the return to English increased and that the increase is precisely estimated. These are the results in table 15.5. If one thinks of these

9. For some specification, the premium rises slightly for Blacks.

results as indicating an average effect of speaking English, that effect is positive. There is less evidence, though, that the return to speaking English increased among Blacks and Coloreds.

One explanation for the lack of an increase in the return to speaking English among Blacks is the following. In 1993, there were few Blacks who spoke English, and they earned a premium for their language skills. With the advent of affirmative action, the premium for speaking English fell as more Blacks were promoted into higher-paying jobs. In this case, it was no longer just the few English-speaking Blacks earning the relatively higher wages. This scenario illustrates one of the difficulties of disentangling the impact of globalization (which might actually increase the return to speaking English) with the impact of affirmative action for Blacks (which was concurrent with globalization and which might actually decrease the extra return to speaking English).

There was no affirmative action for Whites, and among this group the return to speaking English clearly rose. Put another way, the penalty for speaking Afrikaans rose for Whites. This is consistent with capturing an impact of globalization. Afrikaans is much less useful than English in international commerce. Those Whites whose first language was English benefited conditional on education, gender, and experience. This is, as noted above, corroborating but not conclusive evidence.

The finding that the return to speaking English did not increase for Coloreds muddies the waters. Coloreds did not benefit from affirmative action as did Blacks under the new government. Still, the return to speaking English did not rise; in fact, it fell. If globalization is what moves the return to speaking English, one should have found an increase to speaking English among Coloreds, and this was not the case.

The evidence in the end is mixed. On the whole, the return to speaking English increased, but within racial groups the pattern is not consistent.[10] The approach adopted in this paper is perhaps a novel way to revisit the wages and globalization issue. It is an approach that is especially well suited to developing countries, many of which have a rich variety of languages spoken, as they integrate with the global economy. In other contexts (India, for example), or with better data (industry of employment data, for example), the approach adopted here may prove more conclusive. Or not. Even if language is an accurate way to isolate an impact of globalization on wages, it may simply be that globalization has differing impacts on differing segments of a population. This appears to be the case in South Africa.

10. It should be noted that precious few of the English speakers are among the very poor. In 1993, virtually none are, while in 2000 only a handful are. Hence, this approach does not speak to the role of globalization on the incomes of the very poor.

References

Bleakley, H., and A. Chin. 2004a. Language skills and earnings: Evidence from childhood immigrants. *Review of Economics and Statistics* 86 (2): 481–96.
———. 2004b. What holds back the second generation? The intergenerational transmission of language human capital among immigrants. Working Paper no. 104. University of California, San Diego, Center for Comparative Immigration Studies, October.
Case, A., and A. Deaton. 1998. Large cash transfers to the elderly in South Africa. *Economic Journal* 108:1330–61.
Duflo, E. 2000. Grandmothers and granddaughters: Old age pensions and intra-household allocation in South Africa. Massachusetts Institute of Technology, Department of Economics. Working Paper.
Hoogeveen, J., and B. Ozler. 2004. Not separate, not equal: Poverty and inequality in postapartheid South Africa. Washington, DC: World Bank. Unpublished Manuscript.
Leibbrandt, M., J. Levinsohn, and J. McCrary. 2005. Incomes in South Africa since the fall of apartheid. NBER Working Paper no. 11384. Cambridge, MA: National Bureau of Economic Research.
Munshi, K., and M. Rosenzweig. 2003. Traditional institutions meet the modern world: Caste, gender and schooling choice in a globalizing economy. Working Paper 03-23. Massachusetts Institute of Technology, Department of Economics.
Shields, M., and S. W. Price. 2002. The English language fluency and occupational success of ethnic minority immigrant men living in English metropolitan areas. *Journal of Population Economics* 15:137–60.
Silverman, B. W. 1986. *Density estimation for statistics and data analysis.* Monographs on Statistics and Applied Probability no. 26. London: Chapman and Hall.
Thomas, D. 1996. Education across the generations in South Africa. *American Economic Review* 86 (2): 330–34.

Comment   Raquel Fernández

This paper by James Levinsohn seeks to add to the large literature on globalization, trade, and wages by examining the change in the returns to speaking English in South Africa. This strategy has the potential to avoid the usual problem that plagues this literature—that of distinguishing the effects of globalization from other concurrent changes—if, as the author argues, the change in the returns to speaking English is independent of other sources of changes in the economy.

The period examined is from 1993 to 2000. This was a time of important changes in South Africa. The end of apartheid was followed by the first nationally representative election, and the country joined the WTO and var-

Raquel Fernández is a professor of economics at New York University and a research associate of the National Bureau of Economic Research.

ious regional free trade agreements. Trade and foreign direct investment as a percentage of GDP increased dramatically over this period as South Africa integrated with rest of the world.

Using household data sets from 1993 and 2000, Levinsohn finds that the returns to speaking English (where the latter is really "the main language spoken at home") changes over this time period. He finds that, constraining the returns to speaking English to be the same across population groups (Whites, Blacks, Coloreds, and Indians), and running a standard Mincer wage regression that controls for age, education, experience, gender, and population group, the returns to speaking English increase by 7 percentage points.

Acknowledging that the returns to education or to any of the other explanatory variables are likely to differ across groups, Levinsohn runs the same wage regression for each racial group separately. In this case, however, the results look disturbingly different. The return to speaking English dropped by 21 percentage points for Blacks and by 11 points for Coloreds. It increased only for Whites, by 13 percentage points.

I found the results difficult to interpret. Levinsohn argues that an explanation for the decrease for Blacks may be due to affirmative action's ending the premium for speaking English as more Blacks were promoted to high-wage jobs. Maybe. It is very hard to make sense of a result that, in any case, relies on only six observations of Blacks who declare English as the primary language spoken in the household in 1993. This hypothesis does not, in any case, help explain the decrease in the return to speaking English for Coloreds, as this group probably did not benefit from affirmative action. Furthermore, although the author interprets the increase in the return to English for Whites (or the decrease in the return to speaking Afrikaans) as resulting from globalization, another possibility is again the end of apartheid. Presumably this would hurt primarily those Whites who were most associated with the apartheid regime—those Whites of Dutch heritage—rather than all Whites. Hence, it is not at all clear what is driving these results.

Another possible explanation for the results is the traditional one of skill-biased technological change. The author's argument for discarding this possibility is that skill-biased technological change should show up in the returns to education. A plausible counterargument, however, is that the quality of education is higher precisely in those schools attended by students who primarily speak English at home. This would also explain why the returns only went up for Whites if only this group attends high-quality schools. Is this so? It is hard to answer this question without knowing more about who attends which type of school in South Africa.

In general this paper would have benefited from presenting the socioeconomic and political-economic history and present of South Africa in greater detail. As it stands, it is very hard to evaluate the validity of alter-

native hypotheses. For example, to what extent were Afrikaans-speaking Whites at a greater disadvantage than other Whites in the new South Africa? What was and what happened to the position of individuals of mixed race?

I also had some questions about the data. Neither the racial proportions in the data sets nor the languages spoken seem very comparable across years. Whites, for example, constitute a bit over 18 percent of population in 1993 and under 9 percent in 2000. Is this due to Whites leaving the country? In general, the percentage of Blacks increased significantly relative to all other races. Similarly, how are we to interpret the large increase in the proportion of Coloreds that declare Afrikaans to be their primary language? Since it is doubtful that the primary language spoken at home changed during this seven-year period, it renders the results for this group questionable at best.

In conclusion, I think that the author has explored an interesting hypothesis that could fruitfully be applied to other countries. It would be very interesting to examine whether increased integration changed the returns to speaking English in India or Argentina, for example. For the present study, the analysis unfortunately suffers from an important data limitation (in particular the inability to identify whether individuals can speak English) and, more easily transcended, from not placing individuals and their race, education, and language abilities in a socioeconomic context.

Contributors

Emma Aisbett
Department of Agricultural and
  Resource Economics
306 Giannini Hall, #3310
University of California, Berkeley
Berkeley, CA 94720-3310

Nava Ashraf
Harvard Business School
Soldiers Field
Boston, MA 02163

Jorge F. Balat
The World Bank
1818 H Street, NW
Washington, DC 20433

Irene Brambilla
Department of Economics
Yale University
PO Box 208264
New Haven, CT 06520-8264

Robin Burgess
R524, Department of Economics
  and STICERD
LSE Research Laboratory
London School of Economics
Houghton Street
London WC2A 2AE
England

Susan M. Collins
The Brookings Institution
1775 Massachusetts Avenue, NW
Washington, DC 20036

Mitali Das
Department of Economics
Columbia University
1028A International Affairs Building,
  MC 3308
420 West 118th Street
New York, NY 10027

Don Davis
Department of Economics
Columbia University
1014 International Affairs Building,
  MC 3308
420 West 118th Street
New York, NY 10027

Esther Duflo
Department of Economics
Massachusetts Institute of Technology
50 Memorial Drive, E52-252G
Cambridge, MA 02142

William Easterly
Department of Economics
New York University
269 Mercer Street
New York, NY 10003

Raquel Fernández
Department of Economics
New York University
269 Mercer Street
New York, NY 10003

Elizabeth Frankenberg
Department of Sociology
University of California, Los Angeles
264 Haines Hall, Box 951551
Los Angeles, CA 90095-1551

Chor-ching Goh
The World Bank
1818 H Street, NW
Washington, DC 20433

Pinelopi Koujianou Goldberg
Department of Economics
Yale University
PO Box 208264
New Haven, CT 06520-8264

Gordon H. Hanson
IR/PS 0519
University of California, San Diego
9500 Gilman Drive
La Jolla, CA 92093-0519

Ann Harrison
University of California, Berkeley
329 Giannini Hall
Berkeley, CA 94720

Chang-Tai Hsieh
Department of Economics
University of California, Berkeley
549 Evans Hall, #3880
Berkeley, CA 94720-3880

Douglas A. Irwin
Department of Economics
Dartmouth College
Hanover, NH 03755

Beata S. Javorcik
Development Economics Research
    Group
The World Bank
1818 H Street, NW
Washington, DC 20433

M. Ayhan Kose
Financial Studies Division
International Monetary Fund
700 19th Street, NW
Washington, DC 20431

Aart Kraay
Mail Stop MC3-301
The World Bank
1818 H Street, NW
Washington, DC 20433

James Levinsohn
Department of Economics and Ford
    School of Public Policy
University of Michigan
Ann Arbor, MI 48109-1220

Ethan Ligon
Department of Agricultural and
    Resource Economics
331 Giannini, 3-5411
University of California, Berkeley
Berkeley, CA 94720-3310

Margaret McMillan
Department of Economics
304 Braker Hall
Tufts University
8 Upper Campus Road
Medford, MA 02155-6722

Branko Milanovic
Development Research
The World Bank
Room MC3-581
1818 H Street, NW
Washington, DC 20433

Prachi Mishra
Fiscal Affairs Department
International Monetary Fund
700 19th Street, NW
Washington, DC 20431

Rohini Pande
Department of Economics
Yale University
Box 208269
New Haven, CT 06520-8269

Nina Pavcnik
Department of Economics
6106 Rockefeller Center
Dartmouth College
Hanover, NH 03755

Guido G. Porto
Development Research Group
The World Bank
MC3-335
1818 H Street, NW
Washington, DC 20433

Eswar S. Prasad
International Monetary Fund
700 19th Street, NW
Washington, DC 20431

Kenneth Rogoff
Economics Department
Littauer Center 232
Harvard University
Cambridge, MA 02138

Xavier Sala-i-Martin
Department of Economics
Columbia University
420 West 118th Street, 1005
New York, NY 10027

Matthew J. Slaughter
Tuck School of Business
Dartmouth College
100 Tuck Hall
Hanover, NH 03755

Lyn Squire
Global Development Network
2nd floor, West Wing, ISID Complex
Plot No. 4
Vasant Kunj Institutional Area
New Delhi 110070
India

Duncan Thomas
Department of Economics
Bunche Hall, Box 951477
University of California, Los Angeles
Los Angeles, CA 90095-1477

Petia Topalova
Economic Growth Center
Yale University
PO Box 208269
New Haven, CT 06520-8269

Shang-Jin Wei
International Monetary Fund
Room 10-700
700 19th Street, NW
Washington, DC 20431

Alix Peterson Zwane
Department of Agricultural and
    Resource Economics
207 Giannini Hall
University of California, Berkeley
Berkeley, CA 94720

Author Index

Abbott, P. C., 562n1
Acemoglu, Daron, 185n4, 483n20
Ades, A., 64
Agénor, Pierre-Richard, 13n11, 40, 475n15, 487n25, 495
Aghion, Philippe, 105
Ahluwalia, Montek, 323
Aisbett, Emma, 22n15, 23–24
Aizenman, Joshua, 458, 494
Akmal, M., 47n9, 47n11, 48, 49
Alcala, Francisco, 139, 140
Alesina, Alberto, 129n7
Amiti, Mary, 359
Anderson, Simon P., 101
Andrews, E. L., 184
Aragrande, M., 65n43
Arbache, Jorge Saba, 146
Argenti, O., 65n43
Ariola, Jim, 418n2
Arrow, Kenneth J., 601
Artecona, Rachel, 156
Ashraf, Nava, 9, 18–19
Atkinson, Anthony B., 125
Attanasio, O., 244n3, 248, 273, 294, 417
Autor, David, 417, 418

Bajpai, Nirupam, 323
Bakker, Bas, 499n48
Balat, Jorge F., 18, 19
Baldacci, Emanuele, 495
Baldwin, Richard, 38n6, 39n7, 102n4, 484n22

Bandyopadhyay, Sanghamitra, 323
Banerjee, Abhijit, 292n1, 453
Baqir, Reza, 129n7
Barceinas Paredes, F., 207
Bardhan, Pranab, 1n3, 33, 37, 41, 55n25, 64, 64n39, 64n41, 65
Baron, J., 57
Barrett, Christopher B., 495n36, 567
Barrientos, S., 53
Barro, Robert J., 116, 129, 145, 146, 149
Bartolini, Leonardo, 478
Baumol, William J., 95
Bayoumi, Tamim, 498n45
Beegle, Kathleen, 519, 555
Beghin, J., 186, 186n7
Behrman, Jere, 147, 418n2
Bekaert, Geert, 489
Berg, A., 38n6, 39n7, 64, 484
Berry, Steven, 519
Besley, Timothy, 13, 13n9, 323, 323n27
Beyer, Harald, 146
Bezuneh, M., 562
Bhagwati, Jagdish, 1n3, 7, 33, 37n4, 38n6, 39n7, 40n8, 41, 55, 61, 65, 306
Bhalla, S., 45
Bigman, D., 38n6, 39n7
Birdsall, Nancy, 60, 147, 418n2
Blankenau, William, 497n40
Blom, Andreas, 98
Boeri, Tito, 349
Bolaky, B., 39n7, 64
Bordo, Michael, 466n2

Borensztein, Eduardo, 477
Borjas, George J., 120, 130
Bosch, Mariano, 519
Bosworth, Barry, 481n19, 514
Bouillon, César, 131
Bourguignon, F., 38n6, 39n7
Bowen, Harry P., 95
Boyer, Brian H., 498n45
Brainard, William C., 477
Brandolini, Andrea, 125
Bresciani, Fabrizio, 519
Bronars, Stephen G., 120
Brown, Drussila K., 346
Brunner, A. D., 198
Buch, Claudia M., 489
Burgess, Robin, 13, 13n9, 321n26, 323, 323n27
Burtless, G., 36

Calvo, Guillermo, 472, 493, 494, 495
Caprio, Gerard, 477
Carlson, Mark A., 499n47
Carrington, William J., 120, 120n1
Case, A., 635n3
Cavanagh, John, 109
Cerra, Valerie, 295
Chanda, Areendam, 466n4
Chapple, Bryan, 499n48
Chen, Shaohua, 2n4, 43, 53, 243, 248, 248n10, 599
Chiquiar, Daniel, 418n2, 427
Ciccone, Antonio, 128n5, 139, 140
Claessens, Stijn, 498n45
Clay, D., 596
Coate, S., 595
Collier, Paul, 121
Collins, Susan, 481n19, 511, 514
Cooper, Richard N., 477
Corsetti, Giancarlo, 498n45
Cortés, Fernando, 420
Cox, David, 346
Coyle, W., 207, 209n23
Cragg, Michael I., 294, 418n2
Crook, C., 47n10
Cunat, Alejandro, 292n1
Cunningham, Wendy, 519
Currie, Janet, 294, 309n12, 418

Damian, A., 215n28
Danaher, Kevin, 62
Dasgupta, P., 51
Datt, Gaurav, 323

Davis, Donald R., 7–8, 95–96, 97, 99, 100, 102n4, 104, 292n1
Deardorff, Alan, 64n39, 65n42, 346
Deaton, Angus, 10, 41, 42, 45, 46, 53n21, 54, 249, 300, 309n13, 383, 418, 420, 485, 564, 566, 568, 601, 635n3
Deaton, B., 562
De Gregorio, José, 477
Dehejia, R., 388, 391
Deichmann, Uwe, 340
de Janvry, A., 204, 204n19, 207
Dellas, Harris, 497
de Mello, Luiz, 495
De Palma, Andre, 101
Dercon, S., 563
Detragiache, Enrica, 120, 120n1, 499
Devarajan, Shanta, 123
Devooght, K., 59
Dickerson, Andy, 146
DiNardo, John, 420
Di Tella, R., 64
Djankov, Simeon, 339
Dollar, David, 10, 13n11, 61n33, 81, 81n3, 95, 127, 138, 145, 149, 292n2, 484, 486
Döpke, Jörg, 489
Dornbusch, Rudiger, 99
Dowrick, S., 46, 47n10, 47n11, 48, 49, 49n15
Drazen, Allan, 478
Duflo, E., 635n3
Durand, Jorge, 427
Duygan, Burcu, 495

Easterly, William, 8, 22, 123, 128, 129n7, 185n4, 483n20, 489
Edison, Hali, 473, 473n12, 481n18, 496
Edwards, Sebastian, 145, 148, 247, 267n18, 292n2
Eichengreen, Barry, 466n2
Elbehri, A., 186n7
Elbers, Chris, 453
Emmott, B., 40
Epelbaum, Mario, 294, 418n2

Fairris, David H., 418n2
Fallon, Peter R., 519
Fatas, Antonio, 486
Feder, Gershon, 127
Feenstra, Robert C., 99, 100, 143, 292n1, 417
Fehr, E., 58
Feliciano, Zadia, 98, 294, 369, 418n2

Fernandes, Ana, 346
Fernandez-Arias, Eduardo, 472n11
Fies, N., 213n26
Fischer, Stanley, 34, 47n10, 54, 55, 99
Fitoussi, Jean-Paul, 110
Fo, Dario, 109
Forbes, Kristin, 498n45
Fortin, Nicole M., 420
Frankel, Jeffrey, 127, 139, 185n4, 466n4, 484, 499n46
Frankenberg, Elizabeth, 21, 519, 526, 555, 556
Freeman, Richard B., 145, 148, 151, 417
Freund, C., 39n7, 64
Friedman, Jed, 519
Fujita, Masahisa, 102n4

Galbraith, James K., 47n10, 152
Gang, Ira, 309
Gardawski, J. B., 349
Garibaldi, Pietro, 349
Gaston, Noel, 338, 357, 369, 371
GebreMichael, Amdetsion, 564
Ghadar, F., 65, 66
Ghemawat, P., 65, 66
Gibson, Michael S., 498n45
Giddens, Anthony, 110
Glick, Reuven, 497n41
Goh, Chor-ching, 18
Goldar, Bishwanath, 296
Goldberg, Pinelopi, 2, 2n4, 38n6, 39, 39n7, 242n2, 243, 244n3, 248, 267, 267n19, 273, 294, 309n12, 315, 338, 369, 371, 417, 418n1, 475n15
Gordillo de Anda, G., 204, 204n19, 207, 221
Gourinchas, Pierre-Olivier, 478, 483n20
Graaf, J. de V., 51
Graham, C., 54, 61
Green, Francis, 146
Greider, William, 109
Grossman, Gene M., 105, 304, 477
Grubel, Herbert G., 120

Habtewold, D., 595
Hall, Robert E., 128n5, 483n20
Hallak, J. C., 243
Hamory, J., 567
Hansen, Niles, 423
Hanson, Gordon H., 99, 100, 102n4, 143, 146, 149, 155, 292n1, 294, 303, 309n12, 417, 418n2, 427
Harris, Richard, 346, 418

Harrison, Ann, 1n2, 27, 35, 39n7, 146, 149, 155, 294, 309n12, 418n2, 484n22
Harrison, P., 463, 463n3, 565, 565n5
Harvey, Campbell R., 489
Hasan, Rana, 305, 323, 323n27
Hausmann, Ricardo, 472n11
Hay, Donald A., 346
Heckman, J., 388, 391
Helpman, Elhanan, 105, 304, 477
Henderson, Vernon, 340
Henry, Peter, 476
Hernandez, Leonardo, 499n47
Hertel, Thomas W., 1, 2n4, 186n7
Hess, Martin K., 497
Heston, A., 48n13
Hnatkovska, Viktoria, 486
Hoeffler, Anke, 121
Hoekman, B., 186n7
Honohan, Patrick, 477
Horstman, Ignatius, 345
Howitt, Peter, 105
Hsieh, Chang-Tai, 417

Ichimura, H., 388, 391
Imbs, Jean, 477
Inchauste, Gabriela, 495
Ishii, Shogo, 467n5, 484n21, 499n48
Islam, Roumeen, 489

Javorcik, Beata S., 18
Jayne, T. S., 563, 594n1, 595
Jeanne, Oliver, 478, 483n20
Johnson, Simon, 185n4, 483n20
Jones, Charles I., 483n20
Jospin, Lionel, 110
Juhn, Chinhui, 418n2

Kahn, A. R., 600
Kalemli-Ozcan, Sebnem, 477
Kaminsky, Graciela, 484, 493, 494, 498
Kanbur, Ravi, 24, 37n4, 42, 51, 52, 53, 55, 56, 59, 64
Kanji, N., 53
Katz, Lawrence F., 417, 418
Kedir, A. M., 38n6, 39n7
Kemp, Murray, 477
Keynes, John Maynard, 61
Kim, Euysung, 346
Kim, Sunghyun, 498n44
Klamer, Arjo, 75
Klein, Michael, 481n18
Klein, Naomi, 63

Konings, Jozef, 359
Korten, D., 37n5, 62, 63
Kose, M. Ayhan, 6, 485, 486, 488n27, 491, 497nn40–41, 497n43, 498n44
Kouparitsas, Michael A., 497n40
Kraay, Aart, 9, 10, 13n11, 61n33, 81, 81n3, 127, 135, 137, 138, 145, 149, 292n2, 484, 486
Kremer, Michael, 292n1
Krishna, Pravin, 346
Krishnan, P., 563
Krueger, Anne, 7, 38n6, 39n7, 40n8, 64, 484, 494, 499n49
Krugman, Paul, 102n4
Kugler, A., 267n18
Kuhl, Karol, 338
Kum, Hyunsub, 152
Kumar, Manmohan S., 498
Kumar, Utsav, 101

Labán, Raul M., 478n16
Lane, Philip R., 466n4
Lanjouw, Jean O., 453
Lanjouw, Peter, 453
Larrain, Felipe B., 478
Laursen, Thomas, 458
Leamer, Edward E., 95
Lederman, D., 213n26
Lee, Ha Yan, 10n8, 138
Lee, Jong-Wha, 477
Legovini, Arianna, 131
Leibbrandt, Murray, 420
Leidermman, Leonardo, 472
Lemieux, Thomas, 420
Levine, Ross, 123, 128, 185n4, 477, 483n20
Levinsohn, James, 19, 22, 243, 420, 519
Levy, David, 109
Levy, S., 204n19, 221, 223
Litchfield, J. A., 59
Little, I. M. D., 40n8
Liviatan, Nissan, 477
Loayza, Norman, 486
Londono, Juan Luis, 145, 146
Loretan, Mico, 498n45
Loungani, P., 47n10, 54, 467n5
Lucas, Robert E., Jr., 104, 120, 135
Lundberg, Mattias, 146, 148, 149, 292n2
Lundblad, Chrstian, 489
Lustig, Nora, 131, 495

Maffezzoli, Marco, 292n1
Mahajan, Sandeep, 458

Maloney, W., 247n9, 271n23
Maloney, William F., 519
Mander, Jerry, 109
Mankiw, N. Gregory, 116, 117
Markusen, James, 345
Martin, Philippe, 486
Maskin, Eric, 292n1
Massey, Douglas S., 427
Masters, W. A., 186n7, 196n13
Mathieson, Donald J., 478n16
Mauro, Paolo, 466n2
Maxwell, S. J., 562n2
Mayda, Anna Maria, 180
McCalla, A. F., 10, 184, 187n8, 562
McCrary, Justin, 420
McCulloch, Neil, 2, 2n4, 38n6, 39n7, 41, 55, 56, 242n2, 243, 383–84, 418n1, 460n1
McKay, Andrew, 2, 2n4, 38n6, 39n7, 41, 55, 56, 242n2, 243, 383–84, 418n1, 460n1
McMillan, Margaret, 9, 10, 18–19, 567
McMurtry, J., 62
Melitz, Marc J., 99, 101
Micklethwait, J., 55, 110
Milanovic, Branko, 9, 22, 22n15, 47n10, 48, 75n1, 83n5, 146, 149, 292n2
Milesi-Ferretti, Giani Maria, 466n4
Mishkin, Frederic S., 495n34
Mishra, Prachi, 7–8, 101
Mitra, Devashish, 305, 323, 323n27, 346
Mody, Ashoka, 466n3, 467n5, 496, 499n49
Molla, D., 595
Mookherjee, D., 55n25, 64n41
Morriset, J., 121
Muellbauer, John, 418, 420
Muendler, Marc-Andreas, 346
Murshid, Antu Panini, 466n3

Narayan, D., 54
Newman, Andrew, 292n1, 453
Ng, F., 186n7
Nicita, Alessandro, 418, 419, 420
Nunez, J., 247n9, 271n23

Obstfeld, Maurice, 466n2, 488
O'Donnell, Barry, 466n4
Olarreaga, M., 186n7
Oostendorp, R. H., 148, 151
Otrok, Christopher, 497n41

Panagariya, A., 10, 184, 184n3, 186, 187n8, 562, 567
Pandey, Mihir, 309, 321n26

Patillo, Catherine, 121
Pavcnik, Nina, 2, 2n4, 38n6, 39, 39n7,
    242n2, 243, 244n3, 248, 267, 267n19,
    273, 294, 309n12, 315, 338, 346, 369,
    371, 417, 418n1, 475n15
Paxson, C., 249, 601
Peart, Sandra, 109
Pericoli, Marcello, 498n45
Persaud, Avinash, 498
Pierdzioch, Christian, 489
Pinto, Brian, 458
Plummer, Michael, 498n44
Pogge, T. W., 43, 45, 46
Poppele, Jessica, 519
Porto, Guido G., 18, 19, 243, 251n12, 294,
    384n6, 418, 420, 567
Prasad, Eswar S., 6, 9, 20, 22, 35, 38n6,
    39n7, 55, 459, 481n19, 485, 485n23,
    486, 488, 488n27, 491, 497n43
Pritchett, Lant, 113, 519
Przybyla, Marcin, 340
Psacharopolous, George, 123
Puga, Diego, 102
Putnam, H., 51

Quah, Danny, 487

Radelet, Steven, 499n46
Ram, Rati, 127
Rama, Martin, 156, 292n2
Ramaswamy, K. V., 305, 323, 323n27
Ramey, Gary, 485–86
Ramey, Valerie, 485–86
Ramiath, Ananthi, 323
Ravallion, Martin, 2, 2n4, 13n11, 23, 37n4,
    41, 42, 43, 47n10, 52, 53, 53n21, 56n26,
    59, 61n33, 79, 131, 146, 243, 248,
    248n10, 323, 501n50, 599
Razin, Assaf, 467n5, 488
Redding, Stephen, 102n4
Reddy, S. J., 43, 45, 46
Regmi, A., 589
Reimer, J. J., 38, 38n6, 39n7
Reinhart, Carmen M., 459, 472, 484n, 493,
    494, 495, 496, 498
Reinhart, Vincent R., 496
Renner, M., 64n40
Revenga, Anna L., 294, 418n2
Ricci, Antonio, 10n8, 138
Richardson, David J., 145, 417
Riezman, Raymond, 497n40
Rigobon, Roberto, 10n8, 138, 140, 498n45

Riskin, C., 600
Robbins, L., 51
Robertson, Raymond, 100, 146, 155, 418n2
Robinson, James A., 51, 185n4, 483n20
Roberts, Mark, 346
Rodriguez, Francisco, 138, 484
Rodrik, Dani, 138, 140, 180, 185n4, 484,
    495n34, 499n46
Rogers, C. A., 486
Rogoff, Kenneth, 6, 58, 58n27, 459, 483n20,
    488, 497n41, 501
Rojas, Patricio, 146
Rojas-Suarez, Liliana, 478n16
Roland-Holst, D., 186, 186n7
Romer, David, 127, 139, 185n4, 484
Romer, Paul M., 105, 117
Rose, Andrew K., 488, 499n46
Rosenbaum, P., 388
Roubini, Nouriel, 519
Rubin, D., 388
Ruffin, Roy J., 477
Rutkowski, Jan, 340

Sachs, Jeffrey, 127, 139, 323, 484, 499n46
Sadoulet, E., 204, 204n19, 207
Sahn, David E., 495n36
Salai-i-Martin, Xavier, 9, 22n15, 47n10, 48,
    49, 52, 79n2, 116, 129
Salas, J. M., 215n28
Samuelson, P. A., 51, 99
Sarel, M., 185n5
Sarno, Luico, 472n11
Saxena, Sweta, 295
Sbracia, Masimo, 498n45
Schmidt, K., 58
Schott, Peter K., 96
Schultz, Theodore, 562n1
Scitovksy, T., 40n8
Scorse, Jason, 27
Scott, Anthony, 120
Scott, M., 40n8
Sen, A., 37n4
Senhadji, Abdelhak, 483
Sethi, S. P., 65n42
Setser, Brad, 519
Shapouri, S., 186
Shiva, V., 65n43
Singer, H. W., 562n2
Singh, I., 384n6
Smith, James P., 526, 555, 556
Soledad Bos, M., 589
Sørensen, Bent E., 477

Spilimbergo, Antonio, 146, 499
Squire, Lyn, 9, 22, 22n15, 146, 148, 149, 292n2, 384n6
Srinivasan, T. N., 7, 38n6, 39n7, 40n8, 41
Stern, Robert, 346
Stiglitz, Joseph E., 103, 105, 292n1, 489
Storesletten, K., 601
Strauss, John, 384n6, 519, 535
Subramanian, A., 185n4
Sudarno, Sumarto, 519
Summers, R., 48n13
Sussman, Nathan, 466n2
Sutcliffe, B., 47n9, 59n30, 60n31, 61n33
Svedberg, P., 47n9, 59n30, 60n31
Sveikauskas, Leo, 95
Szekely, Miguel, 146, 147, 418n2

Tang, Helena, 1n2, 484n22
Tarozzi, Alessandro, 309n13
Taylor, Mark P., 472n11, 496
Telmer, C. I., 601
Tenenbaum, J., 61
Terrones, Marco E., 485, 486, 488n27, 491, 497n43
Thisse, Jacques-François, 101
Thomas, Duncan, 21, 519, 526, 551, 555, 556, 635n3
Thorbecke, E., 53
Todd, P., 388, 391
Topalova, Petia, 16–17, 22, 100, 306, 325
Topinska, Irena, 338
Trebbi, F., 185n4
Trefler, Daniel, 338, 357, 369, 371
Trejo, Stephen J., 120
Trueblood, M., 186n7
Tybout, James, 346

Valdes, A., 10, 184, 187n8, 562
van der Mensbrugghe, D., 186, 186n7
van Rijckeghem, Caroline, 498
van Wijnbergen, S., 204n19, 221, 223
Varshney, Ashutosh, 305
Velasco, Andres, 495n34, 499n46

Venables, Anthony J., 102, 102n4
Vergara, Rodrigo, 146
Verhoogen, Eric, 101

Wacziarg, Romain, 138, 139, 477, 484
Wade, R., 43, 45, 46, 47n10, 53nn21–22, 58, 60, 82
Wahba, S., 388, 391
Warner, Andrew, 127, 139, 484
Warnock, Frank, 473, 473n12, 496
Weder, Beatrice, 498
Wei, Shang-Jin, 6, 23, 54, 180, 484, 485, 495n35
Weinstein, David E., 95–96, 99, 102n4
Welch, Karen Horn, 138, 139, 484
Whiteman, Charles, 497n41
Wilson, R., 600
Winters, L. Alan, 1n3, 2, 2n4, 38n6, 39n7, 40, 41, 55, 56, 242n2, 243, 383–84, 418n1, 460n1, 484n22
Wise, T. A., 196, 206
Wodon, Quentin, 131
Wolff, Edward M., 95
Woo, Keong, 417
Wooldridge, A., 55, 110
Wu, Yi, 54, 180, 484, 485, 495n35

Xiang, Chong, 102n4
Xu, Bin, 99

Yafeh, Yishay, 466n2
Yaron, A., 601
Yi, Kei-Mu, 497n40
Yoo, Jungho, 494, 499n49
Yosha, Oved, 477
Young, Alwyn, 104
Young, L. M., 562n1
Yunez-Naude, A., 207

Zahniser, S., 207, 209n23
Zenteno, Rene M., 427
Zuhair, S., 462
Zwane, Alix Peterson, 9, 18–19

Subject Index

Page numbers followed by f or t refer to figures or tables respectively.

Abundant factor, 7

Agriculture, OECD subsidies for: introduction to, 183–87; poor countries and, 187–94; poorest people in poor countries and, 194–203

Antiglobalization, 36–37. *See also* Financial globalization; Globalization

Benefits, of financial globalization, 475–83

Big business, role of, 62–64

Budget shares, of Indonesian households, 541–47, 543–46t

Capital: human, 116–18; physical, 116–18

Capital flight, 121, 121t

Capital flows, 116–18, 120–22; North-South, 469–75; poverty and, 19–21

China: data for inequality in, 609–13; globalization and household welfare in, 22–23; idiosyncratic risk in, 613–18, 619–27; introduction to risk and inequality in, 599–602; market structures and inequality in, 602–8

Colombia, 3–4; cross-country studies of, 16–17; description of poor, 251–60; evolution of aggregate poverty rate in, 260–63; National Households Survey data of, 246–47; poverty head count ratios for, 250–51, 250t; poverty measurements for, 247–51; poverty rates in, 242; trade liberalization in, 244–46; trade policy and compliance with minimum wage legislation, 271–73; trade policy and informality in, 267–71; trade policy and poverty in, 273–75; trade policy and unemployment in, 263–67; trade reform and inequality in, 22

CONASUPO (Mexico), 207, 207n21

Contagion effects, 497–98

Corn: consumption of, in Zambia, 401–7, 406t; determinants of Mexican producer price of, 208–14; subsidies for, 185–86, 203–28

Corporate greed, 109–10

Corporate political power, 64

Crises. *See* Financial crises

Cross-country studies, 3, 18, 41; of Colombia, 16–17; evidence of, 9–15; limitations of, 40–41; of Poland, 16; review of, 15–19

Democracy, globalization and, 55

Domain, 145–49; defined, 144

Domestic policies, importance of, 185

Economic geography, 102–3, 102n4

Elites, global, 62–63

Elteto, Koves, Szulc (EKS) method, 46, 49, 49n15

Ethiopia, 4; beneficiaries of food aid in, 575–88; data for study of food aid in, 569–75; food aid in, 563–64; food aid and wheat prices in, 588–90; household as unit of analysis for study of, 564–65; linkages of agricultural prices in, 18–19; methodology for study of food aid in, 566–68. *See also* Food aid

European Community (EC), Poland and, 364–66

Export growth, effect of, on poverty, 4

Factor movements, poverty and, 111–13

50-and-2 rule, 128

Financial crises: poor and, 4; as special cases of volatility, 494–95

Financial globalization: defined, 460; empirical evidence of benefits of, 478–83; factors that increase vulnerability to risks of, 498–500; growth in developing countries and, 461–62; impact of, on macroeconomic volatility, 462–64; macroeconomic volatility and, 487–500; overview of, 457–60; role of institutions and governance in effects of, 464–65; theoretical potential benefits of, 475–78. *See also* Globalization

Financial integration, 460; difficulty of relating economic growth for developing countries and, 483–87; economic growth and, 475–87; measuring, 466–69; North-South capital flows, 469–75

Food aid: existing research on, 562–63; farmers' incomes and, 562–63; wheat prices and, in Ethiopia, 588–90. *See also* Ethiopia

Foreign investment, effect of, on poverty, 4

Geary-Khamis (GK) method, 46, 49, 49n15

General Agreement on Trade in Services (GATS), 55

Geography, economic, 102–3, 102n4

GK method. *See* Geary-Khamis (GK) method

Global elite, 62–63

Globalization: approaches for measuring extent of, 35–36; big business and, 62–64; causation of, 37–42; concentration of poverty and, 129–31; cutbacks in government services to poor and, 55–56; defined, 35, 111; empirical evidence on trade and factor flows across coun-

tries and, 118–22; empirical methods used in research on, 38–39; factor returns within countries and, 123; household welfare and, 22–23; impact on poor of, 2; inequality and, 21–22, 57–61; labor markets and, 417–18; literature on impacts of, 40–42; measuring, 5–7; migration, income, and population density within countries and, 128–29; poor and, 4–5; poverty and, 1–2; predictions of theoretical models of, 119t; productivity growth and, 126–27; reasons for criticisms of, 23–24; spread of democracy and, 55; standard models of channels of, for affecting poverty, 111–18; summary of disagreements over, 40, 68–70; theoretical linkages between poverty and, 7–9; time horizon and, 56; trade and domestic inequality and, 123–26; unanswered research questions for, 24–26; vulnerability to shocks and, 55–56. *See also* Antiglobalization; Financial globalization

Greed, corporate, 109–10

Growth: financial integration and, 475–87; poverty reduction and, 138–41; trade and, 126–27, 138–41

Health care, expenditures on, Indonesian financial crisis and, 552–55

Heckscher-Ohlin (HO) framework, 3, 8

Household survey data, 45

Household welfare, globalization and, 22–23

Human capital: immobile, 116–18; investments in, in Indonesia, 547–48

Idiosyncratic risk: in China, 613–18; estimating, 623–27; model of, 619–23

ILO. *See* International Labour Organization (ILO) data

Import liberalization, review of measures of, 154–56

Import substitution industrialization strategy, of Mexico, 422–23

Incomes: concentration of, within countries, globalization and, 128–29; farmers, food aid and, 562–63; methods of estimating, 45

India, 3–4; cross-country studies of, 16–18; data sources for study of, 300–303; effect of liberalization in, 100; empirical strategy for study of, 303–13; intro-

duction to, 291–95; labor mobility in, 326; measuring poverty and inequality in, 309–13; migration estimates for, 323–25, 324t; results of effects of trade liberalization in, 313–22; tariff changes in, 306–9; trade liberalization and, 295–300; trade policy as endogenous outcome in, 304–6; trade reform and inequality in, 22; wages and tariff changes in, 325

Individual-country studies, 3

Indonesia, 4; changes in living arrangements in, 532–33; correlates of changes in per capita expenditure in, 535–41; depletion of assets and financial crisis in, 556; earnings and financial crisis in, 555–56; health care expenditures and financial crisis in, 552–55; household budget shares in, 541–47; household composition and household expenditures, 548–51; household expenditure results of study for, 527–532; household survey data used for study of, 521–26; investments in human capital in, 547–48; overview of financial crisis of 1990s in, 517–21; school enrollment and financial crisis in, 551–52; sensitivity to estimates of inflation rate in, 533–35; urban and rural differences in household expenditures in, 532

Indonesia Family Life Survey (IFLS), 21, 520, 521–26

Inequality: in China, 609–13; in Colombia, 22; globalization and, 21–22, 57–61, 123–26; in India, 22, 309–13; interindustrial wage, and trade liberalization, 164–69; measuring, 42–43, 47–50, 148; occupational wage, and trade liberalization, 156–64; top-driven, 60–61; trade and, 123–26; trade flows and, 113–15; trade reforms and, 22; University of Texas Inequality Project, 152–53, 172–75; world, 47–50, 49t, 50f

Institutions, supranational, 64

Integration. See Financial integration

Interindustrial wage inequality, trade liberalization and, 164–69

International Labour Organization (ILO) data, 151

Investment: effect of foreign, on poverty, 4; foreign direct, in Mexico, 425–26, 426f; in human capital, in Indonesia, 547–48

Labor, migration of, 118–20

Labor Force Survey (LFS) (Poland), 346–47

Labor markets, globalization and, 417–18

Land, effect of, on poverty, 115–16

Liberalization. See Tariff liberalization; Trade liberalization

Macroeconomic volatility: financial globalization and, 487–500; intensification of, financial globalization and, 496–98

Maize consumption, in Zambia, 401–7, 406t. See also Corn

Maquiladoras, 422–24, 423f

Market concentration, 64–65

Mexico, 4; cross-country studies of, 16–18; data sources for, 421; drop in producer prices and poor corn farmers in, 214–27; empirical methodology for income distribution and globalization in, 430–35; empirical results for income distribution and globalization in, 435–49; foreign direct investment in, 425–26, 426f; importance of domestic policies and, 185; import substitution industrialization strategy of, 422–23; linkages of agricultural prices in, 18–19; literature on trade liberalization and poverty in, 418–19; maquiladoras in, 422–24, 423f; opening of economy to globalization in, 421–24; policy environment in, 206–8; regional exposure to globalization in, 424–30; U.S. corn subsides and poor corn farmers in, 203–28

Migration: within countries, globalization and, 128–29; of labor, 118–20

Minimum wage legislation, 217–73

NAC. See Nominal assistance coefficient (NAC)

NAFTA. See North American Free Trade Agreement (NAFTA)

Neoclassical growth, factor endowment model of, 111

Nominal assistance coefficient (NAC), 196

Nominal protection coefficient (NPC), 196

North American Free Trade Agreement (NAFTA), 418; U.S.-Mexican corn trade and, 206–14

North-South capital flows, 469–72; factors underlying rise in, 472–75

NPC. See Nominal protection coefficient (NPC)

Occupational wage inequality, trade liberalization and, 156–64
Occupational Wages around the World (OWW) data, 150–51; summary of data from, 170–71t
OECD. *See* Organization for Economic Cooperation and Development (OECD)
Organization for Economic Cooperation and Development (OECD), 183–84
Organization for Economic Cooperation and Development (OECD) subsidies, for agriculture: introduction to, 183–87; poor countries and, 187–94; poorest people in poor countries and, 194–203

Physical capital, 116–18
Poland, 4; Association Agreement between European Community and, 364–66; cross-country studies of, 16, 18; data and methodology for study of tariffs and wages in, 346–48; descriptive statistics for, 348–52; distribution of male employment by industries and regions, 362–63t; empirical results for study of tariffs and wages in, 352–61; firm productivity and trade liberalization in, 366–67; overview of trade liberalization in, 337–42; poverty in, 338–39, 339t, 340f; related literature on, 345–46; rigidity of labor market in, 339–40, 341f; tariff reductions and wages in, 342; tariff reductions in, 340–41; trade liberalization in, 343–45
Poor countries: agricultural trade positions of, 191–93t; OECD agricultural subsidies and, 187–94; Stolper-Samuelson theorem and, 95–97
Poor people: in Colombia, 251–60; financial crises and, 4; globalization and, 4–5; themes of chapters about, 3–4
Population densities, incomes and, 128–29
Poverty: capital flows and, 19–21; concentration of, globalization and, 129–31; concept of, 51–57; defined, 1; effect of export growth on, 4; effect of incoming foreign investment on, 4; effect of land on, 115–16; factor movements and, 111–13; globalization and, 1–2; maintaining consistency across countries for measuring, 45–46; maintaining consistency across time for, 46; measuring, 5–

7, 42–46; monetary *versus* multidimensional measures of, 53–56; numbers *versus* incidence for conceptualizing, 52–53; reduction in, growth and, 138–41; standard models of channels by which globalization affects, 111–18; theoretical linkages between globalization and, 7–9; trade flows and, 113–15; trade theory and, 7; urban (*see* Colombia)
Poverty lines, 43–45
Poverty rates, 1; in Colombia, 242
Power, corporate political, 64
PROCAMPO program (Mexico), 207–8
PRODUCE program (Mexico), 208
Producer support estimate (PSE), 195–96
Productivity growth, trade and, 126–27
PSE. *See* Producer support estimate (PSE)
Purchasing power parity (PPP), 43; consumption basket for calculating, 45–46

Risk. *See* Idiosyncratic risk
Roles, of institutions and government, financial globalization and, 464–65

School enrollment, Indonesian financial crisis and, 551–52
South Africa: data sources for study of, 635–37; impact of globalization in, 22, 629–32; returns for speaking English in, 637–42; review of economic policies in, 633–34
Specification, 149–50; defined, 144
Specific-factors model, 345
Specific-sector framework, 8
Stolper-Samuelson (SS) theorem, 7, 88–89; complex world and, 97–102; economic geography and, 102–3; issues of, 89–95; problem of aggregation and, 95–96; production of same goods by rich and poor countries and, 95–97; trade and growth and, 103–5
Supranational institutions, 64

Tariff liberalization: description of data for, 150–56; empirical literature on, 144–50
Tariff rates, summary of unweighted average, 175–77
Top-driven inequality, 60–61
Trade: domestic inequality and, 123–26; productivity growth and, 126–27
Trade flows, poverty and, 113–15

Trade liberalization, 102; case study of
Mexican corn farmers and, 185; in
Colombia, 244–46; effect of, on wages,
337–38; interindustrial wage inequality
and, 164–69; measuring, 148; in Mexico, 418–19; occupational wage inequality and, 156–64; in Poland, 337–
42, 343–45, 366–67; results of, in India,
295–300, 313–22
Trade reforms, 241–43; inequality and, 22;
poor and, 8
Trade-Related Aspects of Intellectual Property Rights (TRIPS), 39, 55
Trade theory, poverty and, 7
TRIPs agreement, 64

United Nations Industrial Development
Organization (UNIDO) statistics, 152
United States: corn subsidies in, 186; corn
subsidies in, and poor Mexican corn
farmers, 203–28
University of Texas Inequality Project
(UTIP), 152–53; summary of data
from, 172–75t
Urban poverty. *See* Colombia

Volatility. *See* Macroeconomic volatility

Wage inequality: interindustrial, and trade
liberalization, 164–69; occupational,
trade liberalization and, 156–64. *See
also* Inequality
Wages: effect of trade liberalization on,
337–38
Wheat prices, food aid and, in Ethiopia,
588–90
World inequality, 49t, 50f; defined, 48; measuring, 47–50. *See also* Inequality
World Trade Organization (WTO), 64

Zambia, 4; consumption effects of price
reforms in, 407–10; effects of trade on
household income in, 382–400; exports
of, 380–82, 381t; household expenditures in, 400–401, 401t; impact of globalization on poverty in, 18; income
sources in, 382–83; linkages of agricultural prices in, 18–19; maize consumption in, 401–10, 406t; major reforms in,
377–80, 379t; overview of economic reforms in, 373–74; poverty in, 375–77;
trading partners of, 380

A National Bureau
of Economic Research
Conference Report

Globalization and Poverty